T0141809

Lecture Notes in Computer Science 1057

Springer
Berlin
Heidelberg
New York
Barcelona
Budapest
Hong Kong
London
Milan
Paris
Santa Clara
Singapore
Tokyo

P. Apers   M. Bouzeghoub   G. Gardarin (Eds.)

Advances in Database Technology – EDBT '96

5th International Conference
on Extending Database Technology
Avignon, France, March 25-29, 1996
Proceedings

 Springer

Series Editors

Gerhard Goos, Karlsruhe University, Germany

Juris Hartmanis, Cornell University, NY, USA

Jan van Leeuwen, Utrecht University, The Netherlands

Volume Editors

Peter Apers
University of Twente, Computer Science Department
P.O. Box 217, 7500 AE Enschede, The Netherlands

Mokrane Bouzeghoub
Georges Gardarin
University of Versailles, PRiSM Laboratory
45 avenue des Etats-Unis, F-78000 Versailles, France

Cataloging-in-Publication data applied for

Die Deutsche Bibliothek - CIP-Einheitsaufnahme

Advances in database technology : proceedings / EDBT '96, 5th
International Conference on Extending Database Technology,
Avignon, March 1996. P. Apers ... (ed.). - Berlin ; Heidelberg ;
New York ; Barcelona ; Budapest ; Hong Kong ; London ;
Milan ; Paris ; Santa Clara ; Singapore ; Tokyo : Springer, 1996
  (Lecture notes in computer science ; Vol. 1057)
  ISBN 3-540-61057-X
NE: Apers, Peter [Hrsg.]; EDBT <5, 1996, Avignon>; GT

CR Subject Classification (1991): H.2, H.3.3, E.2, D.3.3,F.4.1, H.5.1, H.4.3,
I.2.1, E.5

ISBN 3-540-61057-X Springer-Verlag Berlin Heidelberg New York

© Springer-Verlag Berlin Heidelberg 1996
Printed in Germany

Typesetting: Camera-ready by author
SPIN 10512805   06/3142 - 5 4 3 2 1 0   Printed on acid-free paper

Foreword

The fifth international conference on Extending Data Base Technology (EDBT 96) was held in Avignon, France, March 25-29, 1996. Strategically, Avignon is ideally situated, and it is also a town of great historical and cultural value. At the end of the 19th and the first half of the 20th century a lot of outstanding painters lived in this area, among them Picasso. The picture "Les Demoiselles d'Avignon", which illustrated the poster and the program of EDBT'96, marked the start of the cubism style, and is one of the major works of Picasso.

This conference is the fifth in a row of successful international database conferences held in Europe, starting in 1988. This shows that there is a strong and active database research community in Europe with an emphasis on advancing technology and supporting new types of applications.

The program consists of a scientific track, of which the papers appear in these proceedings, and an industrial track. For the scientific track the program committee selected 31 papers out of 178, from 25 different countries. The quality of the papers submitted was high, which unfortunately meant that many good papers had to be rejected. For the industrial track, industries participating in ESPRIT projects were also invited to present their results.

To enrich the program, three keynote speakers and six tutorial speakers were invited. Keynote speeches were given on data warehousing, information retrieval in artificial reality, and object databases by Jennifer Widom, Keith van Rijsbergen, and Francois Bancilhon respectively. The tutorial program consisted of contributions by Tamer Ozsu on distributed object management, Jean-Francois Abramatic on WWW and databases, Christos Faloutsos on multimedia, C. Mohan on workflow management, Stefano Ceri on active database systems, and Arno Siebes on data mining.

Many people contributed to the success of EDBT 96. Thanks to all of them for their effort and time. Special thanks to the program committee members, especially those who attended the program committee meeting in Zurich, and to Maurice van Keulen and Jacek Skowronek for their technical support. Special thanks also to the organization committee members and the sponsors.

March 1996   Peter Apers, Mokrane Bouzeghoub, Georges Gardarin

Sponsorship

Promoted by EDBT Foundation

Sponsored by   ADB/MATISSE, AFUU, CEPIS, CINCOM, CNRS-PRC/BD3,
EDS France, European Union, France Telecom/CNET, IDOMENEUS,
INFORMIX, INFORSID, INRIA, MICROSOFT, ORACLE, UNILOG,
Université de Versailles St-Quentin.

Organization

Conference Chairman: Georges Gardarin (PRiSM Lab. France)
Program Committee Chairman: Peter Apers (Univ. Twente, The Netherlands)

Organising Committee

Mokrane Bouzeghoub (PRiSM & AFCET, France, Chairman

Claude Chrisment (IRIT, Toulouse)	Marie-France Kalogera (AFCET)
Anne Doucet (Laforia, Univ. Paris VI)	Elisabeth Métais (PRiSM, Versailles)
Béatrice Finance (PRiSM, Versailles)	Eric Simon (INRIA, Rocquencourt)
Danièle Gardy (PRiSM, Versailles)	

Regional Co-ordinators

Janis Bubenko	(Sweden)	Rosana Lanzelotte	(Brazil)
Alex Buchman	(Germany)	Peri Loucopoulos	(UK)
Lois Delcambre	(USA)	Timos Sellis	(Greece)
Oscar Diaz	(Spain)	Arne Solvberg	(Norway)
Abdelhamid El-Iraki	(Morroco)	Stefano Spaccapietra	(Switzerland)
Robert Goldstein	(Canada)	Hermann Stephen	(Urugway)
Remigijus Gustas	(Lithuania)	A Min Tjoa	(Austria)
Jean-Luc Hainaut	(Belgium)	Kam-Fai Wong	(Hong Kong)
Ramamohanarao Kotagiri	(Australia)		

Tutorials Co-ordinator

Martin Kersten   (The Netherlands)

EDBT Foundation Representatives

Stefano Ceri	(Milano, Italy)	Michel Missikoff	(Rome, Italy)
Joachim Schmidt	(Hamburg, Germany)	Keith Jeffery	(London, UK)

Program Committee

Serge Abiteboul	(France)	Rosana Lanzelotte	(Brazil)
Michel Adiba	(France)	Withold Litwin	(France
Maristella Agosti	(Italy)	Florian Matthes	(Germany)
Elisa Bertino	(Italy)	Dennis McLeod	(USA)
Jorge Bocca	(Chili/UK)	Guido Moerkotte	(Germany)
Mike Brodie	(USA)	Ken Moody	(UK)
Janis Bubenko	(Sweden)	Shojiro Nishio	(Japan)
Alex Buchmann	(Germany)	Antoni Olive	(Spain)
Sharma Chakravarthy	(USA)	Tamer Ozsu	(Canada)
Claude Chrisment	(France)	Mike Papazoglou	(Australia)
Stavros Christodoulakis	(Greece)	Stefano Paraboschi	(Italy)
Wesley Chu	(USA)	Alain Pirotte	(Belgium)
Wolfgang Effelsberg	(Germany)	Andreas Reuter	(Germany)
Andre Flory	(France)	Keith van Rijsbergen	(UK)
Mike Freeston	(Germany)	Felix Saltor	(Spain)
Hans-Peter Frei	(Switzerland)	Peter Scheuermann	(USA)
Hector Garcia-Molina	(USA)	Marc Scholl	(Germany)
Jane Grimson	(Ireland)	Amit Sheth	(USA)
Bill Grosky	(USA)	Letizia Tanca	(Italy)
Theo Haerder	(Germany)	Patrick Valduriez	(France)
Yannis Ioanniddis	(USA)	Jan Van den Bussche	(Belgium)
Keith Jeffery	(UK)	Yannis Vassiliou	(Greece)
Christian Jensen	(Denmark)	Gerhard Weikum	(Germany)
Masaru Kitsuregawa	(Japan)	Kyu-Young Whang	(South Korea)
Wolfgang Klas	(Germany)	Jennifer Widom	(USA)

Additional Referees

Aiken A.	Fraternali P.	Mose F.	Shoens K.
Amghar Y.	Frecon L.	Muth P.	Sidell J.
Andonoff E.	Garcia-Solaco M.	Nah Y.	Siebert R.
Aslan G.	Gross R.	Nakano M.	Simcox L.
Ayache M.	Grust T.	Nemoto T.	Simon E.
Baralis E.	Guerrini G.	Nink U.	Sinnwell M.
Becker W.	Gustas R.	Nolte D.	Sistac J.
Berndtsson M.	Hammer J.	Ohmori T.	Souza dos Santos C.
Boehm K.	Harada L.	Orci T.	Tamura T.
Bratvold T.	Hasan W.	Paredaens J.	Tari Z.
Byeon K. J.	Hsu C-C.	Pernici B.	Tesch T.
Castellanos M.	Jean-Robert G.	Pollak R.	Theodoratos D.
Catania B.	Jen C.	Psaila G.	Thiel U.
Cervantes O.	Johannesson P.	Quass D.	Thimm H.
Chawathe S. S.	Kahng J.	Radeke E.	Thomas J.
Chen Q.	Kersten M.	Ramakrishnan R.	Tomasic A.
Costa P.	Kim K-G.	Dr. Riedel	Ullman J.
Davis S.	Kim W-S.	Reinert J.	Urpi T.
Dechamboux P.	Klingemann J.	Rezende F.	Voruganti K.
Delis A.	Kutschera P.	Ribeiro C. R.	WaeschJ.
Du W.	Laasch C.	Ritter N.	Wei Song W.
Dyreson C. E.	Li Z	Roncancio C.	Weissenfels J.
Ehlert A.	Liao K.	Samos J.	Wilschut A. N.
Ekenberg L.	Lifschitz S.	Sancho M-R.	Wodtke D.
Esculier C.	Liu L.	Schmidt D.	Yokota H.
Eum D-H.	Loehr M.	Schneider K.	Yoon C.
Fadia R.	Martin C.	Scholl P.C.	Ziane M.
Fauvet M.C.	Martin H.	Schuetzle A.	Zimanyi E.
Ferber R.	Mena E.	Schwenkreis F.	Zink L.
Florescu D.	Montesi D.	Shinji	Zurfluh G.

Table of Contents

Data Mining

Mining Sequential Patterns: Generalizations and Performance Improvements

Ramakrishnan Srikant* and Rakesh Agrawal

{srikant, ragrawal}@almaden.ibm.com
IBM Almaden Research Center
650 Harry Road, San Jose, CA 95120

Abstract. The problem of mining sequential patterns was recently introduced in [3]. We are given a database of sequences, where each sequence is a list of transactions ordered by transaction-time, and each transaction is a set of items. The problem is to discover all sequential patterns with a user-specified minimum support, where the support of a pattern is the number of data-sequences that contain the pattern. An example of a sequential pattern is "5% of customers bought 'Foundation' and 'Ringworld' in one transaction, followed by 'Second Foundation' in a later transaction". We generalize the problem as follows. First, we add time constraints that specify a minimum and/or maximum time period between adjacent elements in a pattern. Second, we relax the restriction that the items in an element of a sequential pattern must come from the same transaction, instead allowing the items to be present in a set of transactions whose transaction-times are within a user-specified time window. Third, given a user-defined taxonomy (*is-a* hierarchy) on items, we allow sequential patterns to include items across all levels of the taxonomy.
We present GSP, a new algorithm that discovers these generalized sequential patterns. Empirical evaluation using synthetic and real-life data indicates that GSP is much faster than the AprioriAll algorithm presented in [3]. GSP scales linearly with the number of data-sequences, and has very good scale-up properties with respect to the average data-sequence size.

1 Introduction

Data mining, also known as knowledge discovery in databases, has been recognized as a promising new area for database research. This area can be defined as efficiently discovering interesting rules from large databases.

A new data mining problem, *discovering sequential patterns*, was introduced in [3]. The input data is a set of sequences, called *data-sequences*. Each data-sequence is a list of *transactions*, where each transaction is a sets of literals, called *items*. Typically there is a transaction-time associated with each transaction. A *sequential pattern* also consists of a list of sets of items. The problem is to find all

---

* Also, Department of Computer Science, University of Wisconsin, Madison.

sequential patterns with a user-specified minimum *support*, where the support of a sequential pattern is the percentage of data-sequences that contain the pattern.

For example, in the database of a book-club, each data-sequence may correspond to all book selections of a customer, and each transaction to the books selected by the customer in one order. A sequential pattern might be "5% of customers bought 'Foundation', then 'Foundation and Empire', and then 'Second Foundation'". The data-sequence corresponding to a customer who bought some other books in between these books still contains this sequential pattern; the data-sequence may also have other books in the same transaction as one of the books in the pattern. Elements of a sequential pattern can be sets of items, for example, "'Foundation' and 'Ringworld', followed by 'Foundation and Empire' and 'Ringworld Engineers', followed by 'Second Foundation'". However, all the items in an element of a sequential pattern must be present in a single transaction for the data-sequence to support the pattern.

This problem was motivated by applications in the retailing industry, including attached mailing, add-on sales, and customer satisfaction. But the results apply to many scientific and business domains. For instance, in the medical domain, a data-sequence may correspond to the symptoms or diseases of a patient, with a transaction corresponding to the symptoms exhibited or diseases diagnosed during a visit to the doctor. The patterns discovered using this data could be used in disease research to help identify symptoms/diseases that precede certain diseases.

However, the above problem definition as introduced in [3] has the following limitations:

1. **Absence of time constraints.** Users often want to specify maximum and/or minimum time gaps between adjacent elements of the sequential pattern. For example, a book club probably does not care if someone bought "Foundation", followed by "Foundation and Empire" three years later; they may want to specify that a customer should support a sequential pattern only if adjacent elements occur within a specified time interval, say three months. (So for a customer to support this pattern, the customer should have bought "Foundation and Empire" within three months of buying "Foundation".)

2. **Rigid definition of a transaction.** For many applications, it does not matter if items in an element of a sequential pattern were present in two different transactions, as long as the transaction-times of those transactions are within some small time window. That is, each element of the pattern can be contained in the union of the items bought in a set of transactions, as long as the difference between the maximum and minimum transaction-times is less than the size of a *sliding time window*. For example, if the book-club specifies a time window of a week, a customer who ordered the "Foundation" on Monday, "Ringworld" on Saturday, and then "Foundation and Empire" and "Ringworld Engineers" in a single order a few weeks later would still support the pattern "'Foundation' and 'Ringworld', followed by 'Foundation and Empire' and 'Ringworld Engineers'".

3. **Absence of taxonomies.** Many datasets have a user-defined taxonomy

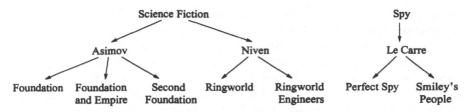

Fig. 1. Example of a Taxonomy

(*is-a* hierarchy) over the items in the data, and users want to find patterns that include items across different levels of the taxonomy. An example of a taxonomy is given in Figure 1. With this taxonomy, a customer who bought "Foundation" followed by "Perfect Spy" would support the patterns "'Foundation' followed by 'Perfect Spy'", "'Asimov' followed by 'Perfect Spy'", "'Science Fiction' followed by 'Le Carre'", etc.

In this paper, we generalize the problem definition given in [3] to incorporate time constraints, sliding time windows, and taxonomies in sequential patterns. We present GSP (Generalized Sequential Patterns), a new algorithm that discovers all such sequential patterns. Empirical evaluation shows that GSP scales linearly with the number of data-sequences, and has very good scale-up properties with respect to the number of transactions per data-sequence and number of items per transaction.

1.1   Related Work

In addition to introducing the problem of sequential patterns, [3] presented three algorithms for solving this problem, but these algorithms do not handle time constraints, sliding windows, or taxonomies. Two of these algorithms were designed to find only maximal sequential patterns; however, many applications require all patterns and their supports. The third algorithm, AprioriAll, finds all patterns; its performance was better than or comparable to the other two algorithms. Briefly, AprioriAll is a three-phase algorithm. It first finds all itemsets with minimum support (frequent itemsets), transforms the database so that each transaction is replaced by the set of all frequent itemsets contained in the transaction, and then finds sequential patterns. There are two problems with this approach. First, it is computationally expensive to do the data transformation on-the-fly during each pass while finding sequential patterns. The alternative, to transform the database once and store the transformed database, will be infeasible or unrealistic for many applications since it nearly doubles the disk space requirement which could be prohibitive for large databases. Second, while it is possible to extend this algorithm to handle time constraints and taxonomies, it does not appear feasible to incorporate sliding windows. For the cases that the extended AprioriAll can handle, our empirical evaluation shows that GSP is upto 20 times faster.

Somewhat related to our work is the problem of mining association rules [1]. Association rules are rules about what items are bought together within a transaction, and are thus intra-transaction patterns, unlike inter-transaction sequential patterns. The problem of finding association rules when there is a user-defined taxonomy on items has been addressed in [6] [4].

The problem of discovering similarities in a database of genetic sequences, presented in [8], is relevant. However, the patterns they wish to discover are sub-sequences made up of consecutive characters separated by a variable number of noise characters. A sequence in our problem consists of list of sets of characters (items), rather than being simply a list of characters. In addition, we are interested in finding *all* sequences with minimum support rather than some frequent patterns.

A problem of discovering frequent episodes in a sequence of events was presented in [5]. Their patterns are arbitrary DAG (directed acyclic graphs), where each vertex corresponds to a single event (or item) and an edge from event A to event B denotes that A occurred before B. They move a time window across the input sequence, and find all patterns that occur in some user-specified percentage of windows. Their algorithm is designed for counting the number of occurrences of a pattern when moving a window across a single sequence, while we are interested in finding patterns that occur in many different data-sequences.

1.2 Organization of the Paper

We give a formal description of the problem of mining generalized sequential patterns in Section 2. In Section 3, we describe GSP, an algorithm for finding such patterns. We empirically compared the performance of GSP with the AprioriAll algorithm [3], studied the scale-up properties of GSP, and examined the performance impact of time constraints and sliding windows. Due to space limitations, we could not include the details of these experiments which are reported in [7]. However, we include the gist of the main results in Section 4. We conclude with a summary in Section 5.

2 Problem Statement

Definitions Let $\mathcal{I} = \{i_1, i_2, \ldots, i_m\}$ be a set of literals, called *items*. Let $\mathcal{T}$ be a directed acyclic graph on the literals. An edge in $\mathcal{T}$ represents an *is-a* relationship, and $\mathcal{T}$ represents a set of taxonomies. If there is an edge in $\mathcal{T}$ from p to c, we call p a *parent* of c and c a *child* of p. (p represents a generalization of c.) We model the taxonomy as a DAG rather than a tree to allow for multiple taxonomies. We call $\hat{x}$ an *ancestor* of x (and x a *descendant* of $\hat{x}$) if there is an edge from $\hat{x}$ to x in transitive-closure($\mathcal{T}$).

An *itemset* is a non-empty set of items. A *sequence* is an ordered list of itemsets. We denote a sequence s by $\langle s_1 s_2 \ldots s_n \rangle$, where s_j is an itemset. We also call s_j an *element* of the sequence. We denote an element of a sequence by $(x_1, x_2, \ldots, x_m)$, where x_j is an item. An item can occur only once in an element of a sequence, but can occur multiple times in different elements. An itemset is considered to be a sequence with a single element. We assume without loss of generality that items in an element of a sequence are in lexicographic order.

A sequence $\langle a_1 a_2 ... a_n \rangle$ is a *subsequence* of another sequence $\langle b_1 b_2 ... b_m \rangle$ if there exist integers $i_1 < i_2 < ... < i_n$ such that $a_1 \subseteq b_{i_1}$, $a_2 \subseteq b_{i_2}$, ..., $a_n \subseteq b_{i_n}$. For example, the sequence $\langle (3) (4 \; 5) (8) \rangle$ is a subsequence of $\langle (7) (3, 8) (9) (4, 5, 6) (8) \rangle$, since $(3) \subseteq (3, 8)$, $(4, 5) \subseteq (4, 5, 6)$ and $(8) \subseteq (8)$. However, the sequence $\langle (3) (5) \rangle$ is not a subsequence of $\langle (3, 5) \rangle$ (and vice versa).

Input We are given a database $\mathcal{D}$ of sequences called *data-sequences*. Each data-sequence is a list of transactions, ordered by increasing transaction-time. A transaction has the following fields: sequence-id, transaction-id, transaction-time, and the items present in the transaction. While we expect the items in a transaction to be leaves in $\mathcal{T}$, we do not require this.

For simplicity, we assume that no data-sequence has more than one transaction with the same transaction-time, and use the transaction-time as the transaction-identifier. We do not consider quantities of items in a transaction.

Support The *support count* (or simply *support*) for a sequence is defined as the fraction of total data-sequences that "contain" this sequence. (Although the word "contains" is not strictly accurate once we incorporate taxonomies, it captures the spirit of when a data-sequence contributes to the support of a sequential pattern.) We now define when a data-sequence *contains* a sequence, starting with the definition as in [3], and then adding taxonomies, sliding windows, and time constraints :

- **as in [3]:** In the absence of taxonomies, sliding windows and time constraints, a data-sequence contains a sequence s if s is a subsequence of the data-sequence.

- **plus taxonomies:** We say that a transaction T *contains* an item $x \in \mathcal{I}$ if x is in T or x is an ancestor of some item in T. We say that a transaction T *contains* an itemset $y \subseteq \mathcal{I}$ if T contains every item in y. A data-sequence $d = \langle d_1 ... d_m \rangle$ contains a sequence $s = \langle s_1 ... s_n \rangle$ if there exist integers $i_1 < i_2 < ... < i_n$ such that s_1 is contained in d_{i_1}, s_2 is contained in d_{i_2}, ..., s_n is contained in d_{i_n}. If there is no taxonomy, this degenerates into a simple subsequence test.

- **plus sliding windows:** The sliding window generalization relaxes the definition of when a data-sequence contributes to the support of a sequence by allowing a set of transactions to contain an element of a sequence, as long as the difference in transaction-times between the transactions in the set is less than the user-specified window-size. Formally, a data-sequence $d = \langle d_1 ... d_m \rangle$ contains a sequence $s = \langle s_1 ... s_n \rangle$ if there exist integers $l_1 \leq u_1 < l_2 \leq u_2 < ... < l_n \leq u_n$ such that

    1. s_i is contained in $\cup_{k=l_i}^{u_i} d_k$, $1 \leq i \leq n$, and
    2. transaction-time(d_{u_i}) − transaction-time$(d_{l_i}) \leq$ window-size, $1 \leq i \leq n$.

- **plus time constraints:** Time constraints restrict the time gap between sets of transactions that contain consecutive elements of the sequence. Given user-specified window-size, max-gap and min-gap, a data-sequence $d = \langle d_1 ... d_m \rangle$ contains a sequence $s = \langle s_1 ... s_n \rangle$ if there exist integers $l_1 \leq u_1 < l_2 \leq u_2 < ... < l_n \leq u_n$ such that

  1. s_i is contained in $\cup_{k=l_i}^{u_i} d_k$, $1 \leq i \leq n$,
  2. transaction-time(d_{u_i}) − transaction-time$(d_{l_i}) \leq$ window-size, $1 \leq i \leq n$,
  3. transaction-time(d_{l_i}) − transaction-time$(d_{u_{i-1}}) >$ min-gap, $2 \leq i \leq n$, and
  4. transaction-time(d_{u_i}) − transaction-time$(d_{l_{i-1}}) \leq$ max-gap, $2 \leq i \leq n$.

The first two conditions are the same as in the earlier definition of when a data-sequence contains a pattern. The third condition specifies the minimum time-gap constraint, and the last the maximum time-gap constraint.

We will refer to transaction-time(d_{l_i}) as *start-time*(s_i), and transaction-time(d_{u_i}) as *end-time*(s_i). In other-words, start-time(s_i) and end-time(s_i) correspond to the first and last transaction-times of the set of transactions that contain s_i.

Note that if there is no taxonomy, min-gap $= 0$, max-gap $= \infty$ and window-size $= 0$ we get the notion of sequential patterns as introduced in [3], where there are no time constraints and items in an element come from a single transaction.

2.1 Problem Definition

Given a database $\mathcal{D}$ of data-sequences, a taxonomy $\mathcal{T}$, user-specified min-gap and max-gap time constraints, and a user-specified sliding-window size, the problem of mining sequential patterns is to find all sequences whose support is greater than the user-specified minimum support. Each such sequence represents a *sequential pattern*, also called a *frequent* sequence.

Given a frequent sequence $s = \langle s_1 ... s_n \rangle$, it is often useful to know the "support relationship" between the elements of the sequence. That is, what fraction of the data-sequences that support $\langle s_1 ... s_i \rangle$ support the entire sequence s. Since $\langle s_1 ... s_i \rangle$ must also be a frequent sequence, this relationship can easily be computed.

2.2 Example

Consider the data-sequences shown in Figure 2. For simplicity, we have assumed that the transaction-times are integers; they could represent, for instance, the number of days after January 1, 1995. We have used an abbreviated version of the taxonomy given in Figure 1. Assume that the minimum support has been set to 2 data-sequences.

With the [3] problem definition, the only 2-element sequential patterns is:

$\langle$ (Ringworld) (Ringworld Engineers) $\rangle$

Database $\mathcal{D}$

Sequence-Id	Transaction Time	Items
C1	1	Ringworld
C1	2	Foundation
C1	15	Ringworld Engineers, Second Foundation
C2	1	Foundation, Ringworld
C2	20	Foundation and Empire
C2	50	Ringworld Engineers

Taxonomy $\mathcal{T}$

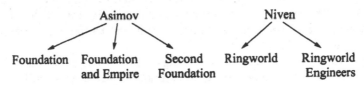

Fig. 2. Example

Setting a sliding-window of 7 days adds the pattern

$\langle$ (Foundation, Ringworld) (Ringworld Engineers) $\rangle$

since C1 now supports this pattern. ("Foundation" and "Ringworld" are present within a period of 7 days in data-sequence C1.)

Further setting a max-gap of 30 days results in both the patterns being dropped, since they are no longer supported by customer C2.

If we only add the taxonomy, but no sliding-window or time constraints, one of the patterns added is:

$\langle$ (Foundation) (Asimov) $\rangle$

Observe that this pattern is not simply a replacement of an item with its ancestor in an existing pattern.

3 Algorithm "GSP"

The basic structure of the GSP algorithm for finding sequential patterns is as follows. The algorithm makes multiple passes over the data. The first pass determines the support of each item, that is, the number of data-sequences that include the item. At the end of the first pass, the algorithm knows which items are frequent, that is, have minimum support. Each such item yields a 1-element frequent sequence consisting of that item. Each subsequent pass starts with a seed set: the frequent sequences found in the previous pass. The seed set is used to generate new potentially frequent sequences, called *candidate* sequences. Each candidate sequence has one more item than a seed sequence; so all the candidate sequences in a pass will have the same number of items. The support for these candidate sequences is found during the pass over the data. At the end of the pass, the algorithm determines which of the candidate sequences are actually frequent. These frequent candidates become the seed for the next pass. The algorithm terminates when there are no frequent sequences at the end of a pass, or when there are no candidate sequences generated.

We need to specify two key details:

1. *Candidate generation:* how candidates sequences are generated before the pass begins. We want to generate as few candidates as possible while maintaining completeness.

2. *Counting candidates:* how the support count for the candidate sequences is determined.

Candidate generation is discussed in Section 3.1, and candidate counting in Section 3.2. We incorporate time constraints and sliding windows in this discussion, but do not consider taxonomies. Extensions required to handle taxonomies are described in Section 3.3.

Our algorithm is not a main-memory algorithm. If the candidates do not fit in memory, the algorithm generates only as many candidates as will fit in memory and the data is scanned to count the support of these candidates. Frequent sequences resulting from these candidates are written to disk, while those candidates without minimum support are deleted. This procedure is repeated until all the candidates have been counted. Further details about memory management can be found in [7].

3.1 Candidate Generation

We refer to a sequence with k items as a k-sequence. (If an item occurs multiple times in different elements of a sequence, each occurrence contributes to the value of k.) Let L_k denote the set of all frequent k-sequences, and C_k the set of candidate k-sequences.

Given L_{k-1}, the set of all frequent $(k-1)$-sequences, we want to generate a superset of the set of all frequent k-sequences. We first define the notion of a contiguous subsequence.

Definition Given a sequence $s = \langle s_1 s_2 ... s_n \rangle$ and a subsequence c, c is a *contiguous* subsequence of s if any of the following conditions hold:

1. c is derived from s by dropping an item from either s_1 or s_n.

2. c is derived from s by dropping an item from an element s_i which has at least 2 items.

3. c is a contiguous subsequence of c', and c' is a contiguous subsequence of s.

For example, consider the sequence $s = \langle (1, 2) (3, 4) (5) (6) \rangle$. The sequences $\langle (2) (3, 4) (5) \rangle$, $\langle (1, 2) (3) (5) (6) \rangle$ and $\langle (3) (5) \rangle$ are some of the contiguous subsequences of s. However, $\langle (1, 2) (3, 4) (6) \rangle$ and $\langle (1) (5) (6) \rangle$ are not.

We show in [7] that any data-sequence that contains a sequence s will also contain any contiguous subsequence of s. If there is no max-gap constraint, the data-sequence will contain all subsequences of s (including non-contiguous

Frequent	Candidate 4-Sequences	
3-Sequences	after join	after pruning
$\langle (1, 2) (3) \rangle$	$\langle (1, 2) (3, 4) \rangle$	$\langle (1, 2) (3, 4) \rangle$
$\langle (1, 2) (4) \rangle$	$\langle (1, 2) (3) (5) \rangle$	
$\langle (1) (3, 4) \rangle$		
$\langle (1, 3) (5) \rangle$		
$\langle (2) (3, 4) \rangle$		
$\langle (2) (3) (5) \rangle$		

Fig. 3. Candidate Generation: Example

subsequences). This property provides the basis for the candidate generation procedure.

Candidates are generated in two steps:

1. **Join Phase.** We generate candidate sequences by joining L_{k-1} with L_{k-1}. A sequence s_1 joins with s_2 if the subsequence obtained by dropping the first item of s_1 is the same as the subsequence obtained by dropping the last item of s_2. The candidate sequence generated by joining s_1 with s_2 is the sequence s_1 extended with the last item in s_2. The added item becomes a separate element if it was a separate element in s_2, and part of the last element of s_1 otherwise. When joining L_1 with L_1, we need to add the item in s_2 both as part of an itemset and as a separate element, since both $\langle (x) (y) \rangle$ and $\langle (x\ y) \rangle$ give the same sequence $\langle (y) \rangle$ upon deleting the first item. (Observe that s_1 and s_2 are contiguous subsequences of the new candidate sequence.)

2. **Prune Phase.** We delete candidate sequences that have a contiguous $(k-1)$-subsequence whose support count is less than the minimum support. If there is no max-gap constraint, we also delete candidate sequences that have any subsequence without minimum support.

The above procedure is reminiscent of the candidate generation procedure for finding association rules [2]; however details are quite different. A proof of correctness of this procedure is given in [7].

Example Figure 3 shows L_3, and C_4 after the join and prune phases. In the join phase, the sequence $\langle (1, 2) (3) \rangle$ joins with $\langle (2) (3, 4) \rangle$ to generate $\langle (1, 2) (3, 4) \rangle$ and with $\langle (2) (3) (5) \rangle$ to generate $\langle (1, 2) (3) (5) \rangle$. The remaining sequences do not join with any sequence in L_3. For instance, $\langle (1, 2) (4) \rangle$ does not join with any sequence since there is no sequence of the form $\langle (2) (4\ x) \rangle$ or $\langle (2) (4) (x) \rangle$. In the prune phase, $\langle (1, 2) (3) (5) \rangle$ is dropped since its contiguous subsequence $\langle (1) (3) (5) \rangle$ is not in L_3.

3.2 Counting Candidates

While making a pass, we read one data-sequence at a time and increment the support count of candidates contained in the data-sequence. Thus, given a set of candidate sequences C and a data-sequence d, we need to find all sequences in C that are contained in d. We use two techniques to solve this problem:

1. We use a *hash-tree* data structure to reduce the number of candidates in C that are checked for a data-sequence.

2. We transform the representation of the data-sequence d so that we can efficiently find whether a specific candidate is a subsequence of d.

3.2.1 Reducing the number of candidates that need to be checked

We adapt the hash-tree data structure of [2] for this purpose. A node of the hash-tree either contains a list of sequences (a *leaf* node) or a hash table (an *interior* node). In an interior node, each non-empty bucket of the hash table points to another node. The root of the hash-tree is defined to be at depth 1. An interior node at depth p points to nodes at depth $p+1$.

Adding candidate sequences to the hash-tree. When we add a sequence s, we start from the root and go down the tree until we reach a leaf. At an interior node at depth p, we decide which branch to follow by applying a hash function to the pth item of the sequence. Note that we apply the hash function to the pth item, not the pth element. All nodes are initially created as leaf nodes. When the number of sequences in a leaf node exceeds a threshold, the leaf node is converted to an interior node.

Finding the candidates contained in a data-sequence. Starting from the root node, we find all the candidates contained in a data-sequence d. We apply the following procedure, based on the type of node we are at:

- *Interior node, if it is the root*: We apply the hash function to each item in d, and recursively apply this procedure to the node in the corresponding bucket. For any sequence s contained in the data-sequence d, the first item of s must be in d. By hashing on every item in d, we ensure that we only ignore sequences that start with an item not in d.

- *Interior node, if it is not the root*: Assume we reached this node by hashing on an item x whose transaction-time is t. We apply the hash function to each item in d whose transaction-time is in $[t - \text{window-size}, t + \max(\text{window-size}, \text{max-gap})]$ and recursively apply this procedure to the node in the corresponding bucket.
  To see why this returns the desired set of candidates, consider a candidate sequence s with two consecutive items x and y. Let x be contained in a transaction in d whose transaction-time is t. For d to contain s, the transaction-time corresponding to y must be in $[t - \text{window-size}, t + \text{window-size}]$ if y is part of the same element as x, or in the interval $(t, t + \text{max-gap}]$ if y is part of the next element. Hence if we reached this node by hashing on an item x with transaction-time t, y must be contained in a transaction whose transaction-time is in the interval $[t - \text{window-size}, t + \max(\text{window-size}, \text{max-gap})]$ for the data-sequence to support the sequence. Thus we only need to apply the hash function to the items in d whose transaction-times are in the above interval, and check the corresponding nodes.

- *Leaf node*: For each sequence s in the leaf, we check whether d contains s, and add s to the answer set if necessary. (We will discuss below exactly how to find whether d contains a specific candidate sequence.) Since we check each sequence contained in this node, we don't miss any sequences.

3.2.2 Checking whether a data-sequence contains a specific sequence

Let d be a data-sequence, and let $s = \langle s_1 ... s_n \rangle$ be a candidate sequence. We first describe the algorithm for checking if d contains s, assuming existence of a procedure that finds the first occurrence of an element of s in d after a given time, and then describe this procedure.

Contains test: The algorithm for checking if the data-sequence d contains a candidate sequence s alternates between two phases. The algorithm starts in the forward phase from the first element.

- **Forward phase:** The algorithm finds successive elements of s in d as long as the difference between the end-time of the element just found and the start-time of the previous element is less than max-gap. (Recall that for an element s_i, start-time(s_i) and end-time(s_i) correspond to the first and last transaction-times of the set of transactions that contain s_i.) If the difference is more than max-gap, the algorithm switches to the backward phase. If an element is not found, the data-sequence does not contain s.

- **Backward phase:** The algorithm backtracks and "pulls up" previous elements. If s_i is the current element and end-time(s_i) = t, the algorithm finds the first set of transactions containing s_{i-1} whose transaction-times are after $t -$ max-gap. The start-time for s_{i-1} (after s_{i-1} is pulled up) could be after the end-time for s_i. Pulling up s_{i-1} may necessitate pulling up s_{i-2} because the max-gap constraint between s_{i-1} and s_{i-2} may no longer be satisfied. The algorithm moves backwards until either the max-gap constraint between the element just pulled up and the previous element is satisfied, or the first element has been pulled up. The algorithm then switches to the forward phase, finding elements of s in d starting from the element after the last element pulled up. If any element cannot be pulled up (that is, there is no subsequent set of transactions which contain the element), the data-sequence does not contain s.

This procedure is repeated, switching between the backward and forward phases, until all the elements are found. Though the algorithm moves back and forth among the elements of s, it terminates because for any element s_i, the algorithm always checks whether a later set of transactions contains s_i; thus the transaction-times for an element always increase.

Example Consider the data-sequence shown in Figure 4. Consider the case when max-gap is 30, min-gap is 5, and window-size is 0. For the candidate-sequence $\langle (1, 2) (3) (4) \rangle$, we would first find $(1, 2)$ at transaction-time 10, and then find (3) at time 45. Since the gap between these two elements (35 days)

14

Transaction-Time	Items
10	1, 2
25	4, 6
45	3
50	1, 2
65	3
90	2, 4
95	6

Item	Times
1	→ 10 → 50 → NULL
2	→ 10 → 50 → 90 → NULL
3	→ 45 → 65 → NULL
4	→ 25 → 90 → NULL
5	→ NULL
6	→ 25 → 95 → NULL
7	→ NULL

Fig. 4. Example Data-Sequence

Fig. 5. Alternate Representation

is more than max-gap, we "pull up" (1, 2). We search for the first occurrence of (1, 2) after time 15, because end-time((3)) = 45 and max-gap is 30, and so even if (1, 2) occurs at some time before 15, it still will not satisfy the max-gap constraint. We find (1, 2) at time 50. Since this is the first element, we do not have to check to see if the max-gap constraint between (1, 2) and the element before that is satisfied. We now move forward. Since (3) no longer occurs more than 5 days after (1, 2), we search for the next occurrence of (3) after time 55. We find (3) at time 65. Since the max-gap constraint between (3) and (1, 2) is satisfied, we continue to move forward and find (4) at time 90. The max-gap constraint between (4) and (3) is satisfied; so we are done.

Finding a single element: To describe the procedure for finding the first occurrence of an element in a data sequence, we first discuss how to efficiently find a single item. A straightforward approach would be to scan consecutive transactions of the data-sequence until we find the item. A faster alternative is to transform the representation of d as follows.

Create an array that has as many elements as the number of items in the database. For each item in the data-sequence d, store in this array a list of transaction-times of the transactions of d that contain the item. To find the first occurrence of an item after time t, the procedure simply traverses the list corresponding to the item till it finds a transaction-time greater than t. Assuming that the dataset has 7 items, Figure 5 shows the tranformed representation of the data-sequence in Figure 4. This transformation has a one-time overhead of O(total-number-of-items-in-dataset) over the whole execution (to allocate and initialize the array), plus an overhead of O(no-of-items-in-d) for each data-sequence.

Now, to find the first occurrence of an element after time t, the algorithm makes one pass through the items in the element and finds the first transaction-time greater than t for each item. If the difference between the start-time and end-time is less than or equal to the window-size, we are done. Otherwise, t is set to the end-time minus the window-size, and the procedure is repeated.[2]

---

[2] An alternate approach would be to "pull up" previous items as soon as we find that the transaction-time for an item is too high. Such a procedure would be similar to the algorithm that does the contains test for a sequence.

Example Consider the data-sequence shown in Figure 4. Assume window-size is set to 7 days, and we have to find the first occurrence of the element (2, 6) after time $t = 20$. We find 2 at time 50, and 6 at time 25. Since end-time((2,6)) − start-time((2,6)) > 7, we set t to 43 (= end-time((2,6)) − window-size) and try again. Item 2 remains at time 50, while item 6 is found at time 95. The time gap is still greater than the window-size, so we set t to 88, and repeat the procedure. We now find item 2 at time 90, while item 6 remains at time 95. Since the time gap between 90 and 95 is less than the window size, we are done.

3.3 Taxonomies

The ideas presented in [6] for discovering association rules with taxonomies carry over to the current problem. The basic approach is to replace each data-sequence d with an "extended-sequence" d', where each transaction d'_i of d' contains the items in the corresponding transaction d_i of d, as well as all the ancestors of each item in d_i. For example, with the taxonomy shown in Figure 1, a data-sequence ⟨ (Foundation, Ringworld) (Second Foundation) ⟩ would be replaced with the extended-sequence ⟨ (Foundation, Ringworld, Asimov, Niven, Science Fiction) (Second Foundation, Asimov, Science Fiction) ⟩. We now run GSP on these "extended-sequences".

There are two optimizations that improve performance considerably. The first is to pre-compute the ancestors of each item and drop ancestors which are not in any of the candidates being counted before making a pass over the data. For instance, if "Ringworld", "Second Foundation" and "Niven" are not in any of the candidates being counted in the current pass, we would replace the data-sequence ⟨ (Foundation, Ringworld) (Second Foundation) ⟩ with the extended-sequence ⟨ (Foundation, Asimov, Science Fiction) (Asimov, Science Fiction) ⟩ (instead of the extended-sequence ⟨ (Foundation, Ringworld, Asimov, Niven, Science Fiction) (Second Foundation, Asimov, Science Fiction) ⟩). The second optimization is to not count sequential patterns with an element that contains both an item x and its ancestor y, since the support for that will always be the same as the support for the sequential pattern without y. (Any transaction that contains x will also contain y.)

A related issue is that incorporating taxonomies can result in many redundant sequential patterns. For example, let the support of "Asimov" be 20%, the support of "Foundation" 10% and the support of the pattern ⟨ (Asimov) (Ringworld) ⟩ 15%. Given this information, we would "expect" the support of the pattern ⟨ (Foundation) (Ringworld) ⟩ to be 7.5%, since half the "Asimov"s are "Foundation"s. If the actual support of ⟨ (Foundation) (Ringworld) ⟩ is close to 7.5%, the pattern can be considered "redundant". The interest measure introduced in [6] also carries over and can be used to prune such redundant patterns. The essential idea is that given a user-specified interest-level I, we display patterns that have no ancestors, or patterns whose actual support is at least I times their expected support (based on the support of their ancestors).

4 Performance Evaluation

We compared the performance of GSP to the AprioriAll algorithm given in [3], using both synthetic and real-life datasets. Due to lack of space, we only summarize the main results in this section. Details of the experiments, including performance graphs and detailed explanations of the results, can be found in [7].

Comparison of GSP and AprioriAll. On the synthetic datasets, GSP was between 30% to 5 times faster than AprioriAll, with the performance gap often increasing at low levels of minimum support. The results were similar on the three customer datasets, with GSP running 2 to 20 times faster than AprioriAll. There are two main reasons why GSP does better than AprioriAll.

1. GSP counts fewer candidates than AprioriAll.

2. AprioriAll has to first find which frequent itemsets are present in each element of a data-sequence during the data transformation, and then find which candidate sequences are present in it. This is typically somewhat slower than directly finding the candidate sequences.

Scaleup. GSP scales linearly with the number of data-sequences. For a constant database size, the execution time of GSP increases with the number of items in the data-sequence, but only gradually.

Effects of Time Constraints and Sliding Windows. To see the effect of the sliding window and time constraints on performance, we ran GSP on the three customer datasets, with and without the min-gap, max-gap, sliding-window constraints. The sliding-window was set to 1 day, so that the effect on the number of sequential patterns would be small. Similarly, the max-gap was set to more than the total time-span of the transactions in the dataset, and the min-gap was set to 1 day. We found that the min-gap constraint comes for "free"; there was no performance degradation due to specifying a min-gap constraint. However, there was a performance penalty of 5% to 30% for using the max-gap constraint or sliding windows.

5 Summary

We are given a database of sequences, where each sequence is a list of transactions ordered by transaction-time, and each transaction is a set of items. The problem of mining sequential patterns introduced in [3] is to discover all sequential patterns with a user-specified minimum support, where the support of a pattern is the number of data-sequences that contain the pattern.

We addressed some critical limitations of the earlier work in order to make sequential patterns useful for real applications. In particular, we generalized the definition of sequential patterns to admit max-gap and min-gap time constraints between adjacent elements of a sequential pattern. We also relaxed the restriction that all the items in an element of a sequential pattern must come from the same transaction, and allowed a user-specified window-size within which the items can be present. Finally, if a user-defined taxonomy over the items in the database is available, the sequential patterns may include items across different levels of the taxonomy.

We presented GSP, a new algorithm that discovers these generalized sequential patterns. It is a complete algorithm in that it guarantees finding all rules that have a user-specified minimum support. Empirical evaluation using synthetic and real-life data indicates that GSP is much faster than the AprioriAll algorithm presented in [3]. GSP scales linearly with the number of data-sequences, and has very good scale-up properties with respect to the average data-sequence size.

The GSP algorithm has been implemented as part of the Quest data mining prototype at IBM Research, and is incorporated in the IBM data mining product. It runs on several platforms, including AIX and MVS flat files, DB2/CS and DB2/MVS. It has also been parallelized for the SP/2 shared-nothing multiprocessor.

References

1. R. Agrawal, T. Imielinski, and A. Swami. Mining association rules between sets of items in large databases. In *Proc. of the ACM SIGMOD Conference on Management of Data*, pages 207–216, Washington, D.C., May 1993.
2. R. Agrawal and R. Srikant. Fast Algorithms for Mining Association Rules. In *Proc. of the 20th Int'l Conference on Very Large Databases*, Santiago, Chile, September 1994.
3. R. Agrawal and R. Srikant. Mining Sequential Patterns. In *Proc. of the 11th Int'l Conference on Data Engineering*, Taipei, Taiwan, March 1995.
4. J. Han and Y. Fu. Discovery of multiple-level association rules from large databases. In *Proc. of the 21st Int'l Conference on Very Large Databases*, Zurich, Switzerland, September 1995.
5. H. Mannila, H. Toivonen, and A. I. Verkamo. Discovering frequent episodes in sequences. In *Proc. of the Int'l Conference on Knowledge Discovery in Databases and Data Mining (KDD-95)*, Montreal, Canada, August 1995.
6. R. Srikant and R. Agrawal. Mining Generalized Association Rules. In *Proc. of the 21st Int'l Conference on Very Large Databases*, Zurich, Switzerland, September 1995.
7. R. Srikant and R. Agrawal. Mining Sequential Patterns: Generalizations and Performance Improvements. Research Report RJ 9994, IBM Almaden Research Center, San Jose, California, December 1995.
8. J. T.-L. Wang, G.-W. Chirn, T. G. Marr, B. Shapiro, D. Shasha, and K. Zhang. Combinatorial pattern discovery for scientific data: Some preliminary results. In *Proc. of the ACM SIGMOD Conference on Management of Data*, Minneapolis, May 1994.

SLIQ: A Fast Scalable Classifier for Data Mining

Manish Mehta, Rakesh Agrawal and Jorma Rissanen

IBM Almaden Research Center
650 Harry Road, San Jose, CA 95120

Abstract. Classification is an important problem in the emerging field of data mining. Although classification has been studied extensively in the past, most of the classification algorithms are designed only for memory-resident data, thus limiting their suitability for data mining large data sets. This paper discusses issues in building a scalable classifier and presents the design of SLIQ[1], a new classifier. SLIQ is a decision tree classifier that can handle both numeric and categorical attributes. It uses a novel pre-sorting technique in the tree-growth phase. This sorting procedure is integrated with a breadth-first tree growing strategy to enable classification of disk-resident datasets. SLIQ also uses a new tree-pruning algorithm that is inexpensive, and results in compact and accurate trees. The combination of these techniques enables SLIQ to scale for large data sets and classify data sets irrespective of the number of classes, attributes, and examples (records), thus making it an attractive tool for data mining.

1 Introduction

The success of computerized data management has resulted in the accumulation of huge amounts of data in several organizations. There is a growing perception that analyses of these large data bases can turn this "passive data" into useful "actionable information". The recent emergence of Data Mining, or Knowledge Discovery in Databases, is a testimony to this trend. Data mining involves the development of tools that can extract patterns from large data bases.

Classification is an important data mining problem [1] and can be described as follows. The input data, also called the *training set*, consists of multiple examples (records), each having multiple attributes or *features*. Additionally, each example is tagged with a special *class* label. The objective of classification is to analyze the input data and to develop an accurate description or model for each class using the features present in the data. The class descriptions are used to classify future *test* data for which the class labels are unknown. They can also be used to develop a better understanding of each class in the data. Applications of classification include credit approval, target marketing, medical diagnosis, treatment effectiveness, store location, etc.

Classification has been studied extensively (see [13] for an excellent overview of various techniques). However, the existing classification algorithms have the

---

[1] SLIQ stands for *S*upervised *L*earning *I*n *Q*uest, where Quest is the Data Mining project at the IBM Almaden Research Center.

problem that they do not scale. Most of the current algorithms have the restriction that the training data should fit in memory. This is perhaps a result of the type of applications to which classification has been hitherto applied. In many applications, there were simply not many training examples available. As a matter of fact, the largest dataset in the Irvine Machine Learning repositary is only 700KB with 20000 examples. Even in [5], a classifier built with database considerations, the size of the training set was overlooked. Instead, the focus was on building a classifier that can use database indices to improve the retrieval efficiency while classifying test data.

In data mining applications, very large training sets with several million examples are common. Our primary motivation in this work is to design a classifier that scales well and can handle training data of this magnitude. The ability to classify larger training data can also improve the classification accuracy [2][3].

Given our goal of classifying large data sets, we focus mainly on decision tree classifiers [4][10]. Decision tree classifiers are relatively fast compared to other classification methods. Methods like neural networks can have extremely long training times even for small datasets. A decision tree can be converted into simple and easy to understand classification rules [10]. They can also be converted into SQL queries for accessing databases [5]. Finally, tree classifiers obtain similar and sometimes better accuracy when compared with other classification methods [7]. Figure 1 gives an example of a decision tree classifier for a toy dataset of six examples.

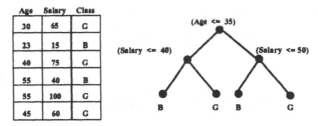

Fig. 1. Example of a decision tree

The idea of modifying tree classifiers to enable them to classify large datasets has been explored previously. Previous proposal include sampling of data at each decision tree node [2], and discretization of numeric attributes [2]. These methods decrease classification time significantly but also reduce the classification accuracy. Chan and Stolfo [3] have studied the method of partitioning the input data and then building a classifier for each partition. The outputs of the multiple classifiers are then combined to get the final classification. Their results show that classification using multiple classifiers never achieves the accuracy of a single classifier that can classify *all* of the data.

The decision-tree classifier we present, called SLIQ, uses novel techniques that improve learning time for the classifier without loss in accuracy. At the same time, these techniques allows classification to be performed on large disk-resident training data. Consequently, given training data that can be handled by other decision tree classifiers, SLIQ exhibits the same accuracy characteristics, but executes faster and produces small trees. However, SLIQ imposes no restrictions on the amount of training data or the number of attributes in the examples. Therefore, SLIQ can potentially obtain higher accuracies by classifying larger training datasets which cannot be handled by other classifiers.

The rest of the paper is organized as follows. Section 2 describes a generic decision tree classifier and Section 3 discusses scalability issues. Sections 4 and 5 present the design and a detailed performance analysis of SLIQ, respectively. Finally, Section 6 contains our conclusions.

2 Decision-Tree Classification

Most decision-tree classifiers (e.g. CART [4], C4.5 [10]) perform classification in two phases: *Tree Building* and *Tree Pruning*.

Tree Building An initial decision tree is grown in this phase by repeatedly partitioning the training data. The training set is split into two or more partitions using an attribute[2]. This process is repeated recursively until all the examples in each partition belong to one class. Figure 2 gives an overview of the process.

```
MakeTree(Training Data T)
    Partition(T);

Partition(Data S)
    if (all points in S are in the same class)) then return;
    Evaluate splits for each attribute A
    Use best split found to partition S into S₁ and S₂;
    Partition(S₁);
    Partition(S₂);
```

Fig. 2. Tree-Building Algorithm

Tree Pruning The tree built in the first phase completely classifies the training data set. This implies that branches are created in the tree even for spurious "noise" data and statistical fluctuations. These branches can lead to errors when classifying test data. Tree pruning is aimed at removing these branches from the decision tree by selecting the subtree with the least estimated error rate.

3 Scalability Issues

3.1 Tree Building

There are two main operations during tree building: i) evaluation of splits for each attribute and the selection of the best split and ii) creation of partitions using the best split. Having determined the overall best split, partitions can be created by a simple application of the splitting criterion to the data. The

---

[2] Multivariate splits based on values of multiple attributes have also been proposed[4].

complexity lies in determining the best split for each attribute. The choice of the splitting criterion depends on the domain of the attribute being numeric or categorical (attributes with a finite discrete set of possible values). But let us first specify how alternative splits for an attribute are compared.

3.1.1 Splitting Index A splitting index is used to evaluate the "goodness" of the alternative splits for an attribute. Several splitting indices have been proposed in the past[13]. We use the *gini* index, originally proposed in [4]. If a data set T contains examples from n classes, $gini(T)$ is defined as

$$gini(T) = 1 - \sum p_j^2$$

where p_j is the relative frequency of class j in T.

3.1.2 Splits for Numeric Attributes A binary split of the form $A \leq v$, where v is a real number, is used for numeric attributes. The first step in evaluating splits for numeric attributes is to *sort* the training examples based on the values of the attribute being considered for splitting. Let $v_1, v_2, \cdots, v_n$ be the sorted values of a numeric attribute A. Since any value between v_i and v_{i+1} will divide the set into the same two subsets, we need to examine only $n-1$ possible splits. Typically, the midpoint of each interval $v_i - v_{i+1}$ is chosen as the split point. The cost of evaluating splits for a numeric attribute is dominated by the cost of sorting the values. Therefore, an important scalability issue is the reduction of sorting costs for numeric attributes.

3.1.3 Splits for Categorical Attributes If $S(A)$ is the set of possible values of a categorical attribute A, then the split test is of the form $A \in S'$, where $S' \subset S$. Since the number of possible subsets for an attribute with n possible values is 2^n, the search for the best subset can be expensive. Therefore, a fast algorithm for subset selection for a categorical attribute is essential.

3.2 Tree Pruning

The tree pruning phase examines the initial tree grown using the training data and chooses the subtree with the least estimated error rate. There are two main approaches to estimating the error rate: one using the original training dataset and the other using an independent dataset for error estimation.

Cross-validation [4] belongs to the first category. Multiple samples are taken from the training data and a tree is grown for each sample. These multiple trees are then used to estimate the error rates of the subtrees of the original tree. Although this approach selects compact trees with high accuracies, it is inapplicable for large data sets, where building even one decision tree is expensive. Alternative approaches [10] that use only a single decision tree often lead to large decision trees.

The second class of methods divide the training data into two parts where one part is used to build the tree and the other for pruning the tree. The data used for pruning should be selected such that it captures the "true" data distribution, which brings up a potential problem with this method. How large should the test sample be and how should it be selected? Moreover, using portions of the data only for pruning, reduces the number of training examples available for the tree growing phase, which can lead to reduced accuracy.

The challenge for a scalable classifier in the pruning phase is to use an algorithm that is fast, and leads to compact *and* accurate decision trees.

4   SLIQ Classifier

We first give a brief overview of SLIQ and then give details about the techniques used in SLIQ to address the scalability issues identified in the previous section.

4.1   Overview

SLIQ is a decision tree classifier that can handle both numeric and categorical attributes. SLIQ uses a pre-sorting technique in the tree-growth phase to reduce the cost of evaluating numeric attributes. This sorting procedure is integrated with a breadth-first tree growing strategy to enable SLIQ to classify disk-resident datasets. In addition, SLIQ uses a fast subsetting algorithm for determining splits for categorical attributes. SLIQ also uses a new tree-pruning algorithm based on the Minimum Description Length principle [11]. This algorithm is inexpensive, and results in compact and accurate trees. The combination of these techniques enables SLIQ to scale for large data sets and classify data sets with a large number of classes, attributes, and examples.

4.2   Pre-Sorting and Breadth-First Growth

For numeric attributes, sorting time is the dominant factor when finding the best split at a decision tree node [2]. Therefore, the first technique used in SLIQ is to implement a scheme that eliminates the need to sort the data at each node of the decision tree. Instead, the training data are sorted just once for each numeric attribute at the beginning of the tree growth phase.

To achieve this pre-sorting, we use the following data structures. We create a separate list for each attribute of the training data. Additionally, a separate list, called *class list*, is created for the class labels attached to the examples. An entry in an attribute list has two fields: one contains an attribute value, the other an index into the class list. An entry of the class list also has two fields: one contains a class label, the other a reference to a leaf node of the decision tree. The ith entry of the class list corresponds to the ith example in the training data. Each leaf node of the decision tree represents a partition of the training data, the partition being defined by the conjunction of the predicates on the path from the node to the root. Thus, the class list can at any time identify the partition to which an example belongs. We assume that there is enough memory to keep the class list memory-resident. Attribute lists are written to disk if necessary.

Initially, the leaf reference fields of all the entries of the class list are set to point to the root of the decision tree. Then a pass is made over the training

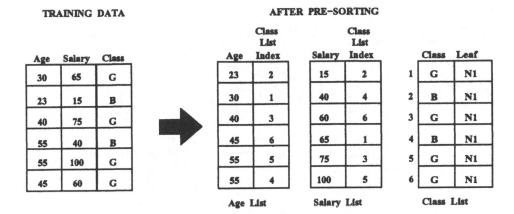

Fig. 3. Example of Pre-Sorting

```
EvaluateSplits()
    for each attribute A do
        traverse attribute list of A
        for each value v in the attribute list do
            find the corresponding entry in the class list, and
                hence the corresponding class and the leaf node (say l)
            update the class histogram in the leaf l
            if A is a numeric attribute then
                compute splitting index for test (A ≤ v) for leaf l
            if A is a categorical attribute then
                for each leaf of the tree do
                    find subset of A with best split
```

Fig. 4. Evaluating Splits

data, distributing values of the attributes for each example across all the lists. Each attribute value is also tagged with the corresponding class list index. The attribute lists for the numeric features are then sorted independently. Figure 3 illustrates the state of the data structures before and after pre-sorting.

4.2.1 Processing Node Splits Rather than using a depth-first strategy used in the earlier decision-tree classifiers, we grow trees breadth-first. Consequently, splits for all the leaves of the current tree are simultaneously evaluated in one pass over the data. Figure 4 gives a schematic of the evaluation process.

To compute the gini splitting-index (see Section 3.1) for an attribute at a node, we need the frequency distribution of class values in the data partition corresponding to the node. The distribution is accumulated in a class histogram attached with each leaf node. For a numeric attribute, the histogram is a list of pairs of the form <class, frequency>. For a categorical attribute, this histogram is a list of triples of the form <attribute value, class, frequency>.

Attribute lists are processed one at a time (recall that the attribute lists can be on disk). For each value v in the attribute list for the current attribute A, we

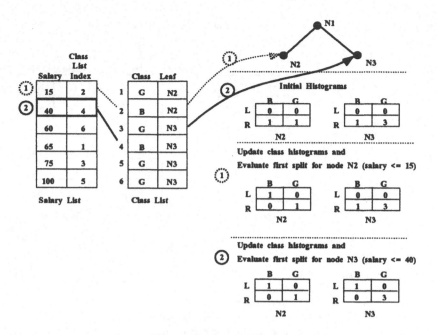

Fig. 5. Evaluating Splits: Example

find the the corresponding entry in the class list, which yields the corresponding class and the leaf node. We now update the histogram attached with this leaf node. If A is a numeric attribute, we compute at the same time the splitting-index for the test $A \leq v$ for this leaf. If A is a categorical attribute, we wait till the attribute list has been completely scanned and then find the subset of A with the best split. Thus, in one traversal of an attribute list, the best split using this attribute is known for *all* the leaf nodes. Similarly, with one traversal of all of the attribute lists, the best *overall* split for all of the leaf nodes is known. The best split test is saved with each of the leaf nodes.

Figure 5 illustrates the evaluation of splits on the salary attribute for the second level of the decision tree. The example assumes that the data has been initially split on the age attribute using the split $age \leq 35$. The class histograms reflect the distribution of the points at each leaf node as a result of the split. The L values represent the distributions for examples that satisfy the test and R values represent examples that do not satisfy the test. We show how the class histograms are updated as each split is evaluated. The first value in the salary list belongs to node $N2$. So the first split evaluated is ($salary \leq 15$) for $N2$. After this split, the corresponding example (salary 15, class index 2) which satisfies the predicate belongs to the left branch and the rest belong to the right branch. The class histogram of node $N2$ is updated to reflect this fact. Next, the split ($salary \leq 40$) is evaluated for node $N3$. After the split, the corresponding example (salary 40, class index 4) belongs to the left branch and the class histogram of node $N3$ is updated to reflect this fact.

4.2.2 Updating the Class List The next step is to create child nodes for each of the leaf nodes and update the class list. Figure 6 gives the update process.

```
UpdateLabels()
    for each attribute A used in a split do
        traverse attribute list of A
        for each value v in the attribute list do
            find the corresponding entry in the class list (say e)
            find the new class c to which v belongs by applying
                the splitting test at node referenced from e
            update the class label for e to c
            update node referenced in e to the child corresponding to the class c
```

Fig. 6. Updating Class List

As an illustration, Figure 7 shows the class list being updated after the nodes $N2$ and $N3$ have been split on the salary attribute. The salary attribute list is being traversed and the class list entry (entry 4) corresponding to the salary value of 40 is being updated. First, the leaf reference in the entry 4 of class list is used to find the node to which the example used to belong ($N3$ in this case). Then, the split selected at $N3$ is applied to find the new child to which the example belongs ($N6$ in this case). The leaf reference field of entry 4 in the class list is updated to reflect the new value.

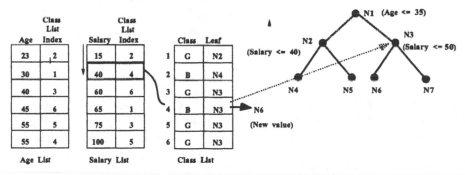

Fig. 7. Class List Update: Example

4.2.3 An Optimization While growing the tree, the above two steps of splitting nodes and updating labels are repeated until each leaf node becomes a pure node (i.e. it contains examples belonging to only one class) and no further splits are required. Note that some nodes may become pure earlier than others and it may be better to condense the attribute lists to discard entries corresponding to examples belonging to these pure nodes. This optimization can easily be implemented by rewriting condensed lists when the the savings from reading smaller lists outweigh the extra cost of writing condensed lists. The information required to make this decision is available from the previous pass over the data.

The important thing to note about pre-sorting and breadth-first growth is that these strategies allow SLIQ to scale for large data sets with *no* loss in accuracy. This is because the set of splits evaluated with and without pre-sorting is *identical*. Pre-sorting simply eliminates the task of resorting data at each node and removes the restriction that the training set be memory-resident.

4.3 Subsetting for Categorical Attributes

The splits for a categorical attribute A are of the form $A \in S'$, where $S' \subset S$ and S is the set of possible values of attribute A. The evaluation of all the subsets of S can be prohibitively expensive, especially if the cardinality of S is large.

SLIQ uses a hybrid approach to overcome this issue. If the cardinality of S is less than a threshold, MAXSETSIZE, then all of the subsets of S are evaluated [3]. Otherwise, a greedy algorithm (initially proposed for IND [8]) is used to obtain the desired subset. The greedy algorithm starts with an empty subset S' and adds that one element of S to S' which gives the best split. The process is repeated until there is no improvement in the splits. This hybrid approach finds the optimal subset if S is small and also performs well for larger subsets.

4.4 Tree Pruning

The pruning strategy used in SLIQ is based on the principle of Minimum Description Length (MDL) [11]. We first review briefly the MDL principle and then show its application in decision-tree pruning.

The MDL principle states that the best model for encoding data is the one that minimizes the sum of the cost of describing the data in terms of the model and the cost of describing the model. If M is a model that encodes the data D, the total cost of the encoding, $cost(M, D)$, is defined as:

$$cost(M, D) = cost(D \mid M) + cost(M)$$

where, $cost(D \mid M)$ is the cost, in number of bits, of encoding the data given a model M and $cost(M)$ is the cost of encoding the model M. In the context of the decision tree classifiers, the models are the set of trees obtained by pruning the initial decision tree T, and the data is the training set S. The objective of MDL pruning is to find the subtree of T that best describes the training set S.

Earlier applications of the MDL principle to tree pruning [9][12] showed that the resultant trees were "over-pruned", causing a decrease in the classification accuracy. In [6], an alternative application of MDL was presented that yielded small trees without sacrificing accuracy. However, the pruning algorithm in [6] was limited; it either pruned all or none of the children of a node in the decision tree. We present a new algorithm that is able to prune a subset of the children at each node and thus subsumes the previous algorithm.

There are two components of the pruning algorithm: the encoding scheme that determines the cost of encoding the data and the model, and the algorithm used to compare various subtrees of T.

---

[3] We use a default MAXSETSIZE of 10, since 2^{10} subsets can be evaluated fairly quickly.

4.4.1 Data Encoding The cost of encoding a training set S by a decision tree T is defined as the sum of all classification errors. A classification of an example is an error if the classification produced by T is not the same as the original class label of the example. This count of misclassification errors is collected during the tree building phase. So, the data encoding step is inexpensive.

4.4.2 Model Encoding The encoding scheme for the model has to provide for the cost of describing the tree and the costs of describing the tests used in the tree at each internal node.

- **Encoding the Tree:** Given a decision tree, a node in the decision tree can be an internal node with one or two children, or a leaf node. The number of bits required to encode the tree depends on the permissible tree structures. We explore three possible ways of encoding the tree:
  1. $Code_1$: A node is allowed either 0 or two children. Since there are only two possibilities, it takes only one bit to encode each node.
  2. $Code_2$: Each node can have no children, a left child, a right child, or both children. Therefore, 2 bits are needed to encode the four possible values of each node.
  3. $Code_3$: Only internal nodes are examined. So each node can have a left child, a right child, or both children. This requires $\log(3)$ bits
- **Encoding the Splits:** The cost of encoding the splits depends on the type of attribute tested for the split:
  1. *Numeric Attributes:* If the split is of the form $A \leq v$ where A is a numeric attribute and v is a real-valued number, the cost of encoding this test is simply the overhead of encoding v, say P. Although the value of P should optimally be determined independently for each such test in the decision tree, we assume a constant value of 1 throughout the tree. The value of 1 was empirically determined.
  2. *Categorical Attributes:* For tests of the form $A \in S$, where A is a categorical attribute and S is a subset of the possible values of A, the cost is calculated in a two-step process. First, we count the number of such tests used in the tree, n_{A_i}, for each categorical attribute A_i. Then the cost of the test is calculated as $\ln n_{A_i}$.

From now on, L_{test} denotes the cost of encoding any test at an internal node.

4.4.3 Pruning Algorithms The MDL pruning evaluates the code length at each decision tree node to determine whether to convert the node into a leaf, prune the left or the right child, or leave the node intact. For each of the above options, the code length $C(n)$ for a node n is calculated as follows:

$$
\begin{aligned}
C_{leaf}(t) &= \qquad\quad L(t) + \text{Errors}_t, & \text{if } t \text{ is a leaf (1)} \\
C_{both}(t) &= L(t) + L_{test} + C(t_1) + C(t_2), & \text{if } t \text{ has both children (2)} \\
C_{left}(t) &= L(t) + L_{test} + C(t_1) + C'(t_2), & \text{if } t \text{ has only } t_1 \text{ as a child (3)} \\
C_{right}(t) &= L(t) + L_{test} + C'(t_1) + C(t_2), & \text{if } t \text{ has only } t_2 \text{ as a child (4)}
\end{aligned}
$$

Except for $C'(t_i)$, all the other quantities are self-explanatory. In the case of partial pruning when either t_1 or t_2 is pruned, the examples that fall into the pruned branch are encoded using the statistics at the parent node. $C'(t_i)$ represents the cost of encoding the children's examples using the parent's statistics.

We consider three pruning strategies:

1. *Full:* This strategy, first presented in [6], considers only options (1) and (2). If $C_{leaf}(t)$ is smaller than $C_{both}(t)$ for a node t then both the children are pruned and the node is converted into a leaf. This approach codes the decision tree using only one bit (method Code$_1$).
2. *Partial:* The partial pruning strategy chooses amongst all four options. Each node is converted into the option with the shortest code length. This approach uses the second method for coding trees, Code$_2$, which requires 2 bits for each node.
3. *Hybrid:* The hybrid method prunes the tree in two phases. It first uses the Full method to get a smaller tree and then considers only options (2), (3) and (4) to further prune the tree.

5 Performance Results

This section presents a detailed performance evaluation of SLIQ. We first discuss the metrics used in the evaluation and then describe the experimental methodology. This is followed by a comparison of SLIQ with other tree classification methods and the result of experiments showing SLIQ's scalability.

5.1 Metrics

The primary metric for evaluating classifier performance is *classification accuracy* – the percentage of *test* samples that are correctly classified. We also present the *classification time*, and the *size* of the decision tree as secondary metrics. The ideal goal for a classifier is to produce compact, accurate trees in a short time.

5.2 Experimental Setup

The performance evaluation of SLIQ was divided into two parts. The first part compares SLIQ with the classifiers provided with the IND classifier package [8]. The IND package implements two of the most popular decision tree classifiers: CART [4] and C4 (a predecessor of C4.5 [10]). These implementations are henceforth referred to as IND-Cart and IND-C4. Since the IND classifiers handle only datasets that fit in memory, the comparison used datasets from the STATLOG classification benchmark [7]. Table 1 summarizes the important parameters of this benchmark.

The second part of the performance evaluation examines SLIQ's performance on disk-resident data. In the absence of a benchmark with large classification datasets, we used the evaluation methodology and synthetic databases proposed in [1]. Each tuple in these databases has nine attributes. Ten classification functions were used in [1] to produce data distributions of varying complexities. In

Dataset	Domain	#Attributes	#Classes	#Examples
Australian	Credit Analysis	14	2	690
Diabetes	Disease diagnosis	8	2	768
DNA	DNA Sequencing	180	3	3186
Letter	Handwriting Recognition	16	26	20000
Satimage	Landusage Images	36	6	6435
Segment	Image Segmentation	19	7	2310
Shuttle	Space Shuttle Radiation	9	7	57000
Vehicle	Vehicle Identification	18	4	846

Table 1. STATLOG Benchmark Datasets

this paper, we use the functions which were the hardest to characterize and led to the highest classification errors - functions 5 and 10. All experiments were performed on an IBM RS/6000 250 workstation with a buffer pool of 64 MB and executing the AIX 3.2.5 OS.

5.3 MDL Pruning

Section 4.4 presented the *partial* and *hybrid* MDL-based pruning algorithms that can remove a subset of the children at any decision tree node. The first experiment compares the performance of these algorithms to the *full* pruning algorithm. Table 2 shows the classification accuracy of the different algorithms while Table 3 shows the sizes of the final decision tree. The execution times of the three algorithms nearly the same and have therefore not been shown.

Dataset	full	partial	hybrid
Australian	84.9	85.1	84.9
Diabetes	75.8	74.9	75.4
DNA	92.1	91.9	92.1
Letter	84.6	81.7	84.6
Satimage	86.3	85.3	86.3
Segment	94.6	94.1	94.6
Shuttle	99.9	99.9	99.9
Vehicle	70.3	68.7	70.3

Table 2. Classification Accuracy

Dataset	full	partial	hybrid
Australian	14.6	9.6	10.6
Diabetes	35.2	11	21.2
DNA	55.0	45.0	45.0
Letter	1141.0	729.0	879.0
Satimage	159.0	91.0	133.0
Segment	18.6	15.2	16.2
Shuttle	29	27	27
Vehicle	68.3	42.6	49.4

Table 3. Decision Tree Size

The tables show that compared to full pruning, the partial pruning leads to much smaller trees but at the cost of lower classification accuracy. This implies that the partial MDL pruning is "over-aggressive". Hybrid pruning, on the other hand, achieves the same accuracy as full pruning, *and* leads to decision trees that are, on the average, 22% smaller. Hybrid pruning is therefore the preferred approach, and is used for the rest of the experiments in this paper.

5.4 Small Datasets

The next experiment compares the performance of SLIQ with IND-Cart and IND-C4. Table 4 shows the classification accuracy of each of the algorithm on the STATLOG benchmark. The results show that all the three classifiers achieve similar accuracy. The largest difference is only 5.3% (Diabetes). However, Table 5 shows that there is a significant difference in the sizes of the decision trees produced by the classifiers. IND-C4 produces the largest decision trees for all the datasets. The trees produced by IND-Cart are 2 (Segment) to 16.4 (Australian) times smaller. SLIQ also produces trees that are comparable in size to IND-Cart and 2.1 (Shuttle) to 8.5 (Diabetes) times smaller than IND-C4.

Dataset	IND-Cart	IND-C4	SLIQ
Australian	85.3	84.4	84.9
Diabetes	74.6	70.1	75.4
DNA	92.2	92.5	92.1
Letter	84.7	86.8	84.6
Satimage	85.3	85.2	86.3
Segment	94.9	95.9	94.6
Shuttle	99.9	99.9	99.9
Vehicle	68.8	71.1	70.3

Table 4. Classification Accuracy

Dataset	IND-Cart	IND-C4	SLIQ
Australian	5.2	85	10.6
Diabetes	11.5	179.7	21.2
DNA	35.0	171.0	45.0
Letter	1199.5	3241.3	879.0
Satimage	90.0	563.0	133.0
Segment	52.0	102.0	16.2
Shuttle	27	57	27
Vehicle	50.1	249.0	49.4

Table 5. Pruned-Tree Size

Dataset	IND-Cart	IND-C4	SLIQ
Australian	2.1	1.5	7.1
Diabetes	2.5	1.4	1.8
DNA	33.4	9.21	19.3
Letter	251.3	53.08	39.0
Satimage	224.7	37.06	16.5
Segment	30.2	9.7	5.2
Shuttle	460	80	33
Vehicle	7.62	2.7	1.8

Table 6. Execution Times

The final criterion for comparing the pruning algorithms is the execution times of the algorithms. Table 6 shows that IND-Cart, which uses cross-validation for pruning, has the largest execution time. The other two algorithms grow a single decision tree, and therefore are nearly an order of magnitude faster in comparison. SLIQ is faster than IND-C4, except for the Australian, Diabetes, and DNA data. The Australian and Diabetes data are very small and, therefore, the full potential of pre-sorting and breadth-first growth cannot be fully exploited by SLIQ. The DNA data consists only of categorical attributes, and hence there are no sorting costs that SLIQ can reduce.

In summary, this set of experiments has shown that IND-Cart achieves good accuracy and small trees. However, the algorithm is nearly an order of magnitude slower than the other algorithms. IND-C4 is also accurate and has fast execution times, but leads to large decision trees. SLIQ, on the other hand, does not suffer from any of these drawbacks. It produces accurate decision trees that are significantly smaller than the trees produced using IND-C4. At the same time, SLIQ executes nearly an order of magnitude faster than IND-Cart.

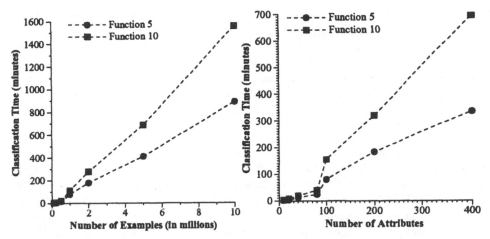

Fig. 8. SLIQ Scalability: #Examples   **Fig. 9.** SLIQ Scalability: #Attributes

5.5 Scalability

The last set of experiments showed that SLIQ achieves good performance on memory-resident data. This section examines the scalability of SLIQ along two dimensions: the number of training examples, and the number of attributes in the data. Synthetic databases (Section 5.2) were used for these experiments.

Scalability on number of training examples Figure 8 shows the performance of SLIQ as the number of training examples is increased from 100,000 to 10 million. This corresponds to an increase in total database size from 4MB to 400MB.

The results show that SLIQ achieves near-linear execution times on disk-resident data. This is because the total classification time is dominated by I/O costs. Recall that SLIQ makes at most two complete passes over the data for each level of the decision tree. Since I/O costs are directly proportional to the size of the data, the total classification time also becomes a near-linear function of data size. The two functions show different slopes because the size of the tree and hence the number of passes made over the data is function-dependent. Total linearity is not achieved because of two reasons. First, the pre-sorting time is non-linear in the size of the data. Second, classifying larger data sets sometimes leads to larger decision trees which requires extra passes over the data.

Scalability on number of attributes The next experiment studies the performance of SLIQ as the number of attributes increases. Since the original synthetic databases have only 9 attributes, extra attributes were created by adding randomly generated values to each example. Note that the addition of these attributes does not substantially change the final decision tree produced because the extra attributes are not used by SLIQ anyway. The additional attributes simply increase the classification time because of the need to examine additional attributes at each level of the decision tree. The number of training examples was fixed at 100,000 for this experiment. The number of attributes was increased from 9 to 400, which represents an increase in the database size from 4MB to 160MB. Figure 9 shows the performance for functions 5 and 10. There is a discontinuity at 100 attributes, when the database size is just over 40 MB and the attribute lists (80 MB) do not fit in memory. Recall that the buffer pool size was fixed at 64 MB of memory for all the experiments[4]. For disk-resident data, the classification time increases linearly, again due to the domination of I/O costs.

6 Conclusions

Classification is an important problem in data mining. Although classification has been studied extensively in the past, the various techniques proposed for classification do not scale well for large data sets. We presented a new decision-tree classifier, called SLIQ, which is designed specifically for scalability. SLIQ uses the novel techniques of pre-sorting, breadth first growth, and MDL-based pruning. An empirical performance evaluation shows that compared to other classifiers, SLIQ achieves comparable or better classification accuracy but produces small decision trees *and* and has small execution times. We also demonstrated that SLIQ achieves good scalability and performs well for datasets with a large number of examples and attributes.

References

1. R. Agrawal, T. Imielinski, and A. Swami. Database mining: A performance perspective. *IEEE Trans. on Knowledge and Data Engineering*, 5(6), Dec. 1993.
2. J. Catlett. *Megainduction: Machine Learning on Very Large Databases*. PhD thesis, University of Sydney, 1991.
3. P. K. Chan and S. J. Stolfo. Meta-learning for multistrategy and parallel learning. In *Proc. Second Intl. Workshop on Multistrategy Learning*, pages 150–165, 1993.
4. L. Breiman et. al. *Classification and Regression Trees*. Wadsworth, Belmont, 1984.
5. R. Agrawal et. al. An interval classifier for database mining applications. In *Proc. of the VLDB Conf.*, Vancouver, British Columbia, Canada, August 1992.
6. M. Mehta, J. Rissanen, and R. Agrawal. MDL-based decision tree pruning. In *Int'l Conf. on Knowledge Discovery in Databases and Data Mining (KDD-95)*, Montreal, Canada, Aug. 1995.
7. D. Michie, D. J. Spiegelhalter, and C. C. Taylor. *Machine Learning, Neural and Statistical Classification*. Ellis Horwood, 1994.
8. NASA Ames Res. Ctr. *Intro. to IND Version 2.1*, GA23-2475-02 edition, 1992.
9. J. R. Quinlan and R. L. Rivest. Inferring decision trees using minimum description length principle. *Information and Computation*, 1989.
10. J. Ross Quinlan. *C4.5: Programs for Machine Learning*. Morgan Kaufman, 1993.
11. J. Rissanen. *Stochastic Complexity in Statistical Inquiry*. World Scientific Publ. Co., 1989.
12. C. Wallace and J. Patrick. Coding decision trees. *Machine Learning*, 11:7–22, 1993.
13. S. M. Weiss and C. A. Kulikowski. *Computer Systems that Learn: Classification and Prediction Methods from Statistics, Neural Nets, Machine Learning, and Expert Systems*. Morgan Kaufman, 1991.

---

[4] A similar discontinuity also occurs in the previous experiment at 800K tuples.

Active Databases

The PARK Semantics for Active Rules

Georg Gottlob[1], Guido Moerkotte[2], V.S. Subrahmanian[3]

[1] Institut für Informationssysteme, Lehrstuhl für Informatik III, Technische Universität Wien, A-1040 Wien, Austria, gottlob@vexpert.dbai.tuwien.ac.at
[2] Lehrstuhl für Informatik III, RWTH-Aachen, 52056 Aachen, Germany, moer@gom.informatik.rwth-aachen.de
[3] Department of Computer Science, University of Maryland, College Park, MD 29742, USA, vs@cs.umd.edu

Abstract. Active databases are an important topic of current database research. However, the semantics of the underlying mechanism, event-condition-action rules (or ECA rules for short), is unclear so far. In order to define a clear semantics for sets of active rules, we first derive the requirements such a semantics must fulfill. Since currently no semantics fulfills these requirements, we continue with the definition of the PARK semantics adhering to all requirements. The PARK semantics is a smooth integration of inflationary fixpoint semantics [7] with conflict resolution. Through this approach, the PARK semantics is powerful enough to deal with recursive active rules. Furthermore, the actual conflict resolution strategy is a parameter of the PARK semantics. This guarantees a wide range of applicability.

1 Introduction

During the last few years, there has been increasing interest in active database systems. Independent of the underlying data model, event-condition-action rules [8] are at the core of all approaches. Since the introduction of ECA rules, many different languages for ECA rules have been proposed and quite a few prototype systems have been built. (For an overview see [2, 1].) Nevertheless, current research falls short of supplying a clean semantics for these systems. It is our intention to fill this gap.

When it comes to defining a semantics for active rule systems, several challenges have to be met. Besides recursion, the most striking challenge is inconsistency, i.e., the possibility of situations where two conflicting rules are firable. Whereas this situation can naturally occur in active databases, it does not occur in pure deductive rule systems. Hence, their semantics cannot directly be applied to active rule systems.

Nevertheless, research in semantics for deductive rule systems should not be neglected: if no two conflicting rules are ever firable, some fixpoint semantics maybe appropriate. It is only in the case of conflicts that deviations become necessary. These deviations, i.e., the special treatment necessary to deal with conflicts, are typically referred to as the conflict resolution strategy. Following these lines, our approach to define a semantics for active rule systems offers a smooth integration of an existing well-known semantics for deductive rule systems (the inflationary semantics [7]) with conflict resolution. Furthermore, since conflict resolution strategies are highly system and application dependent, any semantics should be parameterizable with a special conflict resolution strategy. This avoids the necessity to define a new semantics each time the conflict resolution strategy changes. The PARK semantics for active rule systems as defined in this paper provides this modularity.

Before one can study the semantics of active rule systems, the requirements and obstacles should be made clear. Section 3 gives a list of requirements a semantics for active rule systems should fulfill. Further, this section lists existing semantics for deductive and active rule systems together with the requirements they fail on. Keeping these requirements in mind, we discuss, by means of examples, the obstacles of active semantics (Sec. 4.1). Then, we are well prepared to introduce the PARK semantics of active rule systems in Section 4.2 for condition action rules. In a later step, the semantics is enhanced in order to capture full ECA rules (Sec. 4.3). Several more involved examples demonstrate the flexibility and naturalness of the PARK semantics (Sec. 5). Section 6 provides a discussion on the limitations of the PARK semantics. Further, it points out several possible extensions to turn the PARK semantics into a semantics for practical systems.

Before we start with the requirements, let us first introduce the basic concepts used throughout the paper.

2 Basic Concepts

An active rule is a rule of the form

$$l_1, l_2, \ldots, l_n \rightarrow \pm l_0$$

where the following holds:

- The body literals l_i for $1 \leq i \leq n$ may be positive or negated atoms. Negation $\neg a$ of an atom a is understood as negation by failure and not as classical negation.
- The head literal l_0 is positive and prefixed by a "+" or "−". The intuition is that it should be inserted into the database or deleted from the database, respectively.

So far, active rules do not allow the specification of events within their body. That is, the rules are restricted to a condition-action form. At the end of Section 4 we give a treatment for event specifications within rule bodies, thus yielding full event-condition-action rules.

As an example of a condition-action rule, consider the rules

$$emp(X), \neg active(X), payroll(X, SALARY) \rightarrow -payroll(X, SALARY)$$

which specifies that if a non-active employee has a record in the salary relation, then this record should be deleted.

As is common for datalog, we require active rules to fulfill the following safety conditions:

1. Each variable occurring in a rule head should also occur in the body of the same rule.
2. Each variable occurring in a negated literal in the rule body must also occur in some positive literal in the rule body.

A database instance, D, is a set of (positive) ground atoms. The semantics of a set of active rules w.r.t. a database instance D will be defined in Section 4, after discussing the requirements for a semantics of active rules in the next section.

3 Desired Properties of Active Rule Semantics

In this section we will discuss the desired properties of a good active rule semantics and conclude that none of the existing semantics has these properties:

Unambiguous Semantics. Since the evaluation of active rules implies updates to the database instance D, we do not want to end-up with two or more different database states. This is possible in logic programming (e.g. stable model semantics) or for query answering, but inconceivable in the case of active databases.

However, there might exist cases where some degree of indeterminism — so called don't care indeterminism — could be tollerated, although the authors don't necessarily agree with that.

Independence from Conflict Resolution Policies. In all known active database systems, conflicts may arise naturally. A conflict is a situation where two or more active rules are firable and one of these rules requires the insertion of some atom a while (at least) one of the others requires the deletion of a. A *conflict resolution policy* is a method of determining which of these conflicting actions is to be performed and which is to be suppressed. Each existing approach to active databases has a *fixed* conflict resolution policy which is an integral part of the semantics. We postulate that *given any conflict resolution policy* SELECT, *there must be a uniform method of defining a semantics of active databases based on that policy*. In other words, the overall semantics of active databases has two components: an *inference component* and a *conflict resolution component* that work together. The design of these two components should be largely independent. This will ensure that it is not necessary to redefine the semantics of active databases over and over again just because new conflict resolution policies are required in new domains. Instead, when designing the inference engine, the conflict resolution policy can be treated as a "black-box" or an "oracle."

Flexible Conflict Resolution. Consider a situation where two active rules are firable – one of these requires addition of a, while the other requires the deletion of a. As we shall demonstrate later in the paper (through an example), which of these two actions must be performed may depend critically upon the atom in question. Therefore, conflict resolution must be flexible and allow for the articulation of sophisticated policies that vary from atom to atom depending, perhaps, on other properties in the database and the program, or via interactive input from the user. This means that in the formal semantics for active databases, a conflict resolution policy may be viewed as a function, SELECT, which, given all the context information of the conflict yields for a ground atom either insert or delete. The context information includes the database instance D, the program P, the current state of the computation I, and a description of a conflict c. (The constituents I and c will be formalized later on.) Intuitively, $\text{SELECT}(D, P, I, c) = \text{insert}$ means that in the event of a conflict about whether to insert or delete a, a should be inserted. The actual implementation of the function can be logical, or procedural, depending upon the needs of the application.

Basic Inference Engine. In the absence of conflicts, the basic inference engine which computes the updates must be compatible with some well-understood semantics, e.g., for Datalog. Further, it must be powerful enough to deal with recursive active rules.

The semantics should preferably be explained by a fixed-point construction which can be directly implemented. We believe that a fixed point semantics combines the advantages of being both mathematically clean and directly implementable.

Summarizing, we can state the following:

ActiveDBSemantics = DeclarativeSemantics + ConflictResolutionPolicy.

Further, the semantics has to treat full event-condition-action rules.

Polynomial Tractability. The method should be tractable, i.e., the result database state should be computable in time polynomial in the size of the input database instance. This immediately implies that they should at least terminate.

All existing semantics fall short on at least one of the above requirements. Those developed for deductive rules do not have any conflict resolution strategy [7, 5]. Special semantics for active databases are not only rare but also fail on the requirements above. Some do not necessarily terminate [3, 14], are not polynomial [9], or do not always result in a unique state [3, 9].

A recent approach to define a semantics for active databases is taken by Picouet and Vianu [11]. They extend relational machines which are themselves based on Turing machines to define a semantics for active database systems. However, the major focus here is not to define an intuitive semantics but to investigate the expressive power of several proposals for active databases.

Lately, Fraternelli and Tanca proposed a very elaborate semantics for active rule systems [4]. It includes all the semantics subleties that can be found in existing implementations of active database systems. At the core is their EECA language capable of capturing these subleties explicitly. EECA rules are then translated into a core language with a formal semantics. The paper also provides a very good overview of the features incorporated into existing systems.

4 The PARK semantics

4.1 Introductory Examples

The major problem with the semantics of active rules is that the straightforward processing of rules may lead to *conflicting actions*, i.e. insertion and deletion of the same data item. In this subsection we use examples to illustrate how the inflationary semantics of Kolaitis and Papadimitriou [7] may be used in conjunction with appropriate conflict resolution policies to define a semantics for active databases.

In order to simplify discussion, in this section we will use a specific fixed conflict resolution policy called the *principle of inertia*. This principle ignores conflicting actions. For instance if actions $+a$ and $-a$ are both implied by some firable rules r_1 and r_2, respectively, then both actions are ignored as they are conflicting commands, and the status of a in the result remains the same as in the input database (hence the name *inertia*). A conflict c of the above kind is described by a triple $(a, \{r_1\}, \{r_2\})$ where a is the atom for which the conflict arizes and the second (third) component is the set of all ground rule instances with valid body that require the addition (deletion) of a. Here, the validity of the body of the rule depends on the validity of the literals with respect to a given state of computation I (see below for a formalization).

In other words, the principle of inertia corresponds to the case where the function SELECT is defined as follows: SELECT$(D, P, I, (a, ins, del)) = $ insert iff a was present in the original database instance D; SELECT$(D, P, I, (a, ins, del)) = $ delete otherwise.

It is important to note that the conflict resolution policy (whatever it may be) is enforced even if $+a$ and $-a$ are not computed in the same computation step. For example, consider the following rule-set P_1 operating on a database $D = \{p\}$:

1. $p \rightarrow + q$
2. $p \rightarrow - a$
3. $q \rightarrow + a$

During the computation, we will mark added facts with $+$ and deleted facts with $-$ while facts that were present in the original database remain unmarked in order to distinguish them later from computed actions.

If we envisage, as usual, a step by step computation which at each step applies all rules in parallel (producing *immediate consequences*), then, after the first step, we would get the intermediate result $\{p, +q, -a\}$ and after the second step the final fixed point $\{p, +q, -a, +a\}$. This includes a conflict which must be resolved using the conflict resolution policy (which in our case, happens to be the principle of inertia). This causes us to eliminate $+a, -a$ getting $\{p, +q\}$. Finally, we effectively *apply* the remaining non conflicting actions, in our case, the unique action $+q$, getting the result database state $\{p, q\}$. Note that by eliminating the conflicting pair $+a$, $-a$, the status of a remains the one of the original database (namely, "absent"), since no action whatsoever on a is executed.

So far so good. However, a slightly more complicated program may create considerable confusion. This confusion is due to the fact that some intermediately asserted (or deleted) facts which will later become obsolete entail some further deletions or insertions.

Consider, for instance, the same database $D = \{p\}$ and the program P_2

1. $p \rightarrow + q$
2. $p \rightarrow - a$
3. $q \rightarrow + a$
4. $\neg a \rightarrow + r$
5. $a \rightarrow + s$

If we stubbornly apply the immediate consequence operator, we get the following intermediate results after each step:

after step 1: $\{p, +q, -a, +r\}$
after step 2: $\{p, +q, -a, +r, +a\}$
after step 3: $\{p, +q, -a, +r, +a, +s\}$ = final fixed point.

Now, in this final fixed point, as before, we recognize that $-a$ and $+a$ are conflicting and eliminate these two marked atoms using the principle of inertia as the conflict resolution policy. We are thus left with $\{p, +q, +r, +s\}$. After effectively incorporating the updates, we get the result database state $\{p, q, r, s\}$.

But is this what we really want? Note that $+s$ was obtained by rule (5) based on the presence of $+a$. However, $+a$ was afterwards recognized to be conflicting and was eliminated. Since a was not present in the original database and is not present in the result, rule (5) should not fire. As a consequence, s should not stay in the final result.

In a similar manner, atom r is introduced based on rule (4) whose body depends on the conflicting atom a. However, in this case, since a is not present in the original nor in the final database, rule (4) may well fire and produce r. The desired result database state is thus $\{p, q, r\}$.

In summary, in order to get the correct result, we cannot just compute the fixed point of the immediate consequence operator and then eliminate conflicting marked literals. Whether a marked fact will stay in the result or not should depend on the reasons why it was asserted. Basically, if the reason for existence of such a literal is solely grounded on conflicting literals that are afterwards invalidated, then the literal should stay out. If, however, there are valid reasons for the literal, such as nondeleted atoms of the original database or nonconflicting marked literals, etc., then it should stay in.

Yet another problem is the problem of *false conflicts*.

Consider, for example, the following program P_3 on database instance $D = \{p\}$.

1. $p \rightarrow\!\!\!\!/ \, + q$
2. $p \rightarrow\!\!\!\!/ \, - q$
3. $q \rightarrow\!\!\!\!/ \, + a$
4. $q \rightarrow\!\!\!\!/ \, - a$
5. $p \rightarrow\!\!\!\!/ \, + a$

Applying the immediate consequence operator, we get the following intermediate results after each step:

after step 1: $\{p, +q, -q, +a\}$

after step 2: $\{p, +q, -q, +a, -a\}$ = final fixed point.

It would thus seem that a is ambiguous. However, the ambiguity of a is a false ambiguity! Since q, which is derived before a is ambiguous, and thus maintains its original status (=absent from the database according to the principle of inertia), we should not use q to derive $+a$ or $-a$. Therefore, $-a$ should not be derivable and thus a should not be an ambiguous literal. However, since we can derive $+a$ by rule (5), $+a$ should stay in the final fixed point. The correct result is therefore $\{p, +a\}$, or, after incorporating the updates, $\{p, a\}$.

The last example shows that it is very important to forbid that any consequences are drawn from ambiguous marked literals. But how are we to achieve this? The algorithm in the next subsection will show that this is effectively – and easily – possible.

4.2   The PARK fixed-point semantics

In this subsection we give a complete formal definition of the PARK semantics. The semantics is illustrated by means of two examples with different conflict resolution strategies in Section 5. Let us start with the definition of some relevant concepts. The *Herbrand base* $H(P, D)$ of a database instance D and a program P is defined as usual. It consists of all ground positive literals made from predicate and constant symbols found in P and D.

Extended Herbrand base. The *extended Herbrand base* $H^{\pm}(P, D)$ corresponding to a set of active rules P operating on a database instance D is defined by:

$$H^{\pm}(P, D) = \{a, +a, -a \,|\, a \in H(P, D)\}.$$

If P and D are understood, we just write $H^{\pm}$.

Intermediate interpretations. An *intermediate interpretation* (shortly i-interpretation) consists of a set of positive atoms plus a set of atoms marked by $+$ or $-$. We say that an i-interpretation is *consistent* if it does not contain a pair of literals $+a$, $-a$. If I is an i-interpretation, then I^{-} denotes all atoms in I marked by $-$, I^{+} denotes all atoms in I marked by $+$, and $I^{\perp}$ denotes all unmarked atoms in I. If P is a set of active rules and D a database, then an $i - interpretation$ of (P, D) is a subset of $H^{\pm}(P, D)$.

Literal validity. The *validity* of a ground literal a in an i-interpretation I is defined as follows. If a is positive, then a is valid in I iff $I \cap \{a, +a\} \neq \emptyset$, thus, iff at least one, a or $+a$ is contained in I. If $a = \neg b$ is a negative literal, then a is valid in I iff one of the following conditions applies: (1) $-b \in I$ or (2) $I \cap \{b, +b\} = \emptyset$, in words, iff either there exists a delete action on b or neither b nor $+b$ appear in I (and hence, $\neg b$ is true by negation as failure or the closed world assumption). If a literal a is valid in an i-interpretation I, we write $valid(a, I)$.

Conflicts. A tuple (r, σ) where r is a rule and σ is a ground substitution for r is called a *rule grounding*. Let P be a set of active rules and I an i-interpretation. Then $conflicts(P, I)$ is a set of maximal triples of the form (a, ins, del) such that a is a ground atom and ins and del are sets of rule groundings. For each such triple the following conditions must hold:

1. a is a ground atom and there exist
2. rules r and r' in P and ground substitutions σ and σ' such that
   - $valid(l_i\sigma, I)$ for all body literals l_i of r,
   - $valid(l'_i\sigma', I)$ for all body literals l'_i of r', and
   - for the heads $+l_0$ of r and $-l'_0$ of r', $l_0\sigma = l'_0\sigma' = a$ holds.
3. For all possible r, r' and σ, σ' fulfilling 2), $(r, \sigma) \in ins$ and $(r', \sigma') \in del$.

Each tuple $(a, ins, del) \in conflicts(P, I)$ is called a *conflict*.

Consider the program P containing the rules $r_1 : p(x) \rightarrow +q(x)$ and $r_2 : p(x) \rightarrow -q(x)$ together with the i-interpretation $I = \{p(a)\}$. Then

$$conflicts(P, I) = \{(q(a), \{(r_1, [x \leftarrow a])\}, \{(r_2, [x \leftarrow a])\})\}.$$

Note that *conflicts* looks one step into the future. That is, conflicts detected need not be present in I.

Conflict resolution policy. A conflict resolution policy is a map SELECT from

1. a database instance D,
2. a program P,
3. an i-interpretation I, and
4. a conflict c

to insert, delete. Intuitively, $\text{SELECT}(D, P, I, (a, ins, del)) = \text{delete}$ (resp. insert) means that for the current conflict, the action to take on atom a is deletion (resp. insertion).

The subsequent definition is motivated as follows. Whenever a conflict arises, its derivation must be hindered. In order to do so, we block rule instances from being fired.

Blocked Rule Instances. Let P be a set of active rules, SELECT be a conflict resolution policy, and I an i-interpretation. Suppose we set

$X = \{del \mid (a, ins, del) \in conflicts(P, I) \text{ and } SEL(D, P, I, (a, ins, del)) = insert\}$

$Y = \{ins \mid (a, ins, del) \in conflicts(P, I) \text{ and } SEL(D, P, I, (a, ins, del)) = delete\}.$

Then

$$blocked(D, P, I, \text{SELECT}) = \left(\bigcup_{del \in X} del \right) \cup \left(\bigcup_{ins \in Y} ins \right).$$

As an example, suppose $D = \{p(a)\}$ and P consists of the rules

$$r_1 : p(x) \rightarrow + q(x)$$
$$r_2 : p(x) \rightarrow - q(x)$$

and $I = \{p(a), +q(a), -q(a)\}$. Then

- conflicts(P,I) $= \{(q(a), \{(r_1, [x \leftarrow a])\}, \{(r_2, [x \leftarrow a])\})\}$

and for

$$\text{SELECT}(D, P, I, (q(a), \{(r_1, [x \leftarrow a])\}, \{(r_2, [x \leftarrow a])\})) = insert$$

we have

- blocked(D,P,I,SELECT) $= \{(r_2, [x \leftarrow a])\}$

The incorporate operator. The operator *incorp* transforms a consistent i-interpretation into a traditional (2-valued) Herbrand interpretation by incorporating the updates:

$$incorp(I) := (I^{\perp} \cup \{a \mid + a \in I^{+}\}) - \{a \mid - a \in I^{-}\}$$
$$= (I^{\perp} - \{a \mid - a \in I^{-}\}) \cup \{a \mid + a \in I^{+}\}).$$

Immediate consequence operator $\Gamma_{P,B}$. After these important definitions, we are ready to define the immediate consequence operator $\Gamma_{P,B}$ for a set P of active rules and a set of blocked rule instances B. For each i-interpretation I, $\Gamma_{P,B}(I)$ is the smallest set U satisfying the following conditions:

- $I \subseteq U$
- If $r = l_1, \ldots, l_n \rightarrow \pm l_0$ is a rule in P and σ a ground substitution for r such that
  - $(r, \sigma) \notin B$ and
  - $valid(l_i\sigma, I)$ for all body literals l_i of r
  then $\pm l_0\sigma \in U$.

So far, this is an almost traditional definition of the immediate consequence operator except that in the traditional definition

1. the first condition is omitted and

2. certain rule instances can not be blocked

in classical LP. However, as we have seen in the last section, we can *not* just compute its least fixed-point due to conflicts without paying attention to conflicting rules. So far, B captures part of the mechanism to cope with conflicts. As already indicated by the definition of Γ, it does not suffice to compute a fixpoint starting from some i-interpretation. Instead of i-interpretations, we have to work on bi-structures which we introduce next.

Bi-structures. A bi-structure $< B, I >$ consists of a set B of blocked rule instances and an i-interpretation I. Bi-structures are ordered according to the ordering $\prec$:

$$< B, I > \prec < B', I' > \quad \text{iff} \quad \begin{cases} B \subset B' & \text{or} \\ B = B' \text{ and } I \subset I'. \end{cases}$$

For two bi-structures $\mathcal{A}$ and $\mathcal{B}$, let us write $\mathcal{A} \preceq \mathcal{B}$ if either $\mathcal{A} = \mathcal{B}$ or $\mathcal{A} \prec \mathcal{B}$. Note that $\preceq$ is a partial ordering on bi-structures.

For a bi-structure $\mathcal{A} = (B, I)$ we write $int(\mathcal{A})$ to denote I.

The idea is now to operate on bi-structures instead of operating on i-interpretations. We therefore define a transition operator Δ from bi-structures to bi-structures as follows. Let $\mathcal{A} = (B, I)$ be a bi-structure and SELECT be a conflict resolution policy. Then we define $\Delta_P(\mathcal{A})$ by

$$\Delta_P(\mathcal{A}) = \begin{cases} < B, \Gamma_{P,B}(I) > & \text{if } \Gamma_{P,B}(I) \text{ is consistent} \\ < B \cup blocked(P, I, \text{SELECT}), I^\perp > & \text{otherwise.} \end{cases}$$

Strictly speaking, the operator Δ should be subscripted with SELECT – however, for the sake of simplicity, we will omit such subscripts whenever this is clear from context.

Note that as shown in the theorem below, the Δ operator is *growing*; this means that for each bi-structure $\mathcal{A}$, $\mathcal{A} \preceq \Delta(\mathcal{A})$. Let us denote the *repeated* applications of Δ as follows: $\Delta_P^0(\mathcal{A}) = \mathcal{A}$; $\Delta_P^{i+1}(\mathcal{A}) = \Delta_P(\Delta_P^i(\mathcal{A}))$; as there are only finitely many pairs (B, I), it follows that there must be a minimal integer k such that $\Delta_P^k(\mathcal{A}) = \Delta_P^{k+1}(\mathcal{A})$; instead of explicitly talking of this minimal integer k, we will usually denote $\Delta_P^k(\mathcal{A})$ by $\Delta_P^\omega(\mathcal{A})$. It follows immediately from the fact that Δ_P is growing that $\Delta_P^\omega(\mathcal{A})$ is a well-defined bi-structure and that $\Delta_P^\omega(\mathcal{A})$ is a fixed-point of Δ_P. Moreover, if $\Delta_P^\omega(\mathcal{A}) = (B, I)$, then $I = lfp(\Gamma_P)$.

Let us discuss the relationship of Δ with the inflationary fixpoint operator [7]. If no conflict arises Δ does not change the program P; only the i-interpretation of the bistructure is changed by Δ. This is done the following way. The Δ operator successively applies Γ to some i-interpretation and unions the result with the original i-interpretation. This strongly resembles the inflationary fixpoint [7]. On the other hand, as soon as a conflict arises, the Δ operator immediately stops its inflationary computation and performs instead a conflict resolution step. Thus, the PARK semantics — building on Δ — may be viewed as a smooth cycle integrating inflationary fixpoint computation and conflict resolution policies.

Theorem 4.1 Suppose P is a set of active rules, and $\mathcal{A} = (B, I)$ is a bi-structure. Then:

1. $\mathcal{A} \preceq \Delta_P(\mathcal{A})$, and
2. $\Delta_P^\omega(\mathcal{A})$ is a least fixed-point of Δ_P, and
3. if $\Delta_P^\omega(\mathcal{A}) = (B', I')$, then $I' = lfp(\Gamma_{P',B'})$.

Proof. (1) Let $\Delta_P(\mathcal{A}) = (B', I')$. If I' is a consistent i-interpretation, then $B' = B$ and $I' = \Gamma_{P,B}(I) \supseteq I$; hence, $(B, I) \preceq (B', I')$. On the other hand, if I' is an inconsistent i-interpretation, then B' is obtained from B by adding one or more blocked rule instances to B, i.e. $B \subset B'$; therefore, $(B, I) \preceq (B', I')$.

(2) Immediate consequence of (1) above.

(3) As $\Delta_P^\omega(\mathcal{A})$ is a fixed-point of Δ_P, $\Delta_P(B', I') = (B', I')$. As the B' component of the pair (B', I') remains unchanged upon application of the Δ operator, it follows that $I' = \Gamma_{P,B'}(I')$, by definition of the Δ operator. Thus, I' is a fixed-point of $\Gamma_{P,B'}$.

Suppose now that I' is not the least fixed-point of $\Gamma_{P,B'}$, i.e there is a $J \subset I'$ such that J is a fixed-point of $\Gamma_{P,B'}$. Since $\Gamma_{P,B'}$ is monotonic, $\Gamma_{P,B'}(J) \subseteq \Gamma_{P,B'}(I')$. Thus, $\Gamma_{P,B'}(J)$ is a consistent i-interpretation. Then

$$\Delta_P(B', J) = (B', \Gamma_{P,B'}(J)) = (B', J),$$

i.e. (B', J) is a fixed-point of Δ, contradicting the fact that (B', I') is the least fixed-point of Δ. $\qquad\square$

We are now ready for defining the PARK semantics. To a given set of active rules P, database instance D, and a conflict resolution policy SELECT, the result database instance $PARK(P, D)$ is defined as follows:

$$PARK(P, D) = incorp(int(\Delta_P^\omega((\emptyset, D)))).$$

Clearly, if P is a finite rule set and if D is a finite database, then Δ_P^ω is computable in polynomial time in the size of D when the conflict resolution policy SELECT is implementable in polynomial time. Notice that any conflict that arises during the PARK computation does so because of two atoms of the form $+A$ and $-A$ occurring in the fixpoint computation procedure. For any given atom A involved in such a conflict, the sets *ins* and *del* are bounded by the size of P. Thus, the total complexity of identifying all conflicts is bounded by the product of the sizes of D and P. It is now clear that when the conflict resolution policy is implementable in polynomial-time, the PARK semantics is implementable in polynomial time as well because the above iterative procedure is only executed at most $size(P)$ times where $size(P)$ is the number of rule instances of rules in P. Since $size(P)$ is polynomial in the size of the database, and after each conflict resolution, at least one rule instance from P is eliminated, the claim follows.

Informally, $PARK(P, D)$ is computed as follows: apply all rules in parallel (operator Γ) and repeat this process until some conflicting literals are computed. When these literals, say $+a$ and $-a$, are detected, the computation is interrupted. All blocked rule instances are collected. This means that in the course of the further computation these rule instances will not be allowed to derive any updates. The computation is then resumed with a larger set of blocked rule instances and the initial database instance $(D = I^{\perp})$. We must resort to the initial database instance because some facts depending on $-a$ or $+a$ may have been computed which are now obsolete. The process is repeated until the final fixed-point is reached. Again, note the similarity between inflationary fixpoint and PARK in the case that no conflict occurs. The PARK semantics is illustrated by the subsequent example. The next section contains two more examples illuminating the PARK semantics for two different select strategies.

Consider a database instance $D = \{p(a), p(b), p(c)\}$ together with the program P containing the rules

r_1: $p(x), p(y) \rightarrow +q(x, y)$

r_2: $q(x, x) \rightarrow -q(x, x)$

r_3: $q(x, y), q(x, z), q(z, y) \rightarrow -q(x, y)$

The intuition is that we want to build some irreflexive graph not containing any arc implied by transitivity of existing edges. The first application of $\Gamma_{P,\emptyset}$ to D results in I_1

$$I_1 = \{p(a), p(b), p(c), +q(a, a), +q(a, b), +q(a, c),$$
$$+q(b, a), +q(b, b), +q(b, c), +q(c, a), +q(c, b), +q(c, c)\}$$

Since

$$\Gamma_{P,\emptyset}(I_1) = \{p(a), p(b), p(c), +q(a, a), +q(a, b), +q(a, c),$$
$$+q(b, a), +q(b, b), +q(b, c), +q(c, a), +q(c, b), +q(c, c),$$
$$-q(a, a), -q(a, b), -q(a, c), -q(b, a), -q(b, b), -q(b, c),$$
$$-q(c, a), -q(c, b), -q(c, c)\}$$

is inconsistent, we have to follow the second case of Δ_P. We first compute $conflicts(P, I_1)$

which is

$$(q(a,a), \ \{ \ (r_1, [x \leftarrow a, y \leftarrow a])\},$$
$$\{ \ (r_2, [x \leftarrow a])$$
$$(r_3, [x \leftarrow a, y \leftarrow a, z \leftarrow a])$$
$$(r_3, [x \leftarrow a, y \leftarrow a, z \leftarrow b])$$
$$(r_3, [x \leftarrow a, y \leftarrow a, z \leftarrow c])\})$$
$$(q(b,b), \ \dots)$$
$$(q(c,c), \ \dots)$$
$$(q(a,b), \ \{ \ (r_1, [x \leftarrow a, y \leftarrow b])\},$$
$$\{ \ (r_3, [x \leftarrow a, y \leftarrow b, z \leftarrow a])$$
$$(r_3, [x \leftarrow a, y \leftarrow b, z \leftarrow b])$$
$$(r_3, [x \leftarrow a, y \leftarrow b, z \leftarrow c])\})$$
$$(q(a,c), \ \{ \ (r_1, [x \leftarrow a, y \leftarrow c])\},$$
$$\{ \ (r_3, [x \leftarrow a, y \leftarrow c, z \leftarrow a])$$
$$(r_3, [x \leftarrow a, y \leftarrow c, z \leftarrow b])$$
$$(r_3, [x \leftarrow a, y \leftarrow c, z \leftarrow c])\})$$

$\dots$

In order to get $blocked(D, P, I_1, \text{SELECT})$, we have to fix the conflict resolution strategy SELECT. We decide to block all instances of rule r_1 with $x = y$ and those connecting a and c. In all other cases, the instances of r_3 are blocked. This results in $B := blocked(D, P, I_1, \text{SELECT}) =$

$$(r_1, [x \leftarrow a, y \leftarrow a])$$
$$(r_1, [x \leftarrow b, y \leftarrow b])$$
$$(r_1, [x \leftarrow c, y \leftarrow c])$$
$$(r_1, [x \leftarrow a, y \leftarrow c])$$
$$(r_1, [x \leftarrow c, y \leftarrow a])$$
$$(r_3, [x \leftarrow a, y \leftarrow b, z \leftarrow a])$$
$$(r_3, [x \leftarrow a, y \leftarrow b, z \leftarrow b])$$
$$(r_3, [x \leftarrow a, y \leftarrow b, z \leftarrow c])$$

$\dots$

Then $I_2 := \Gamma_{B,P}(I_1^\perp) =$

$$\{p(a), p(b), p(c), +q(a,b), +q(b,a), +q(b,c), +q(c,b)\}.$$

Further, (B, I_2) is the final fixpoint of Δ_P and $PARK(P, D) =$

$$\{p(a), p(b), p(c), q(a,b), q(b,a), q(b,c), q(c,b)\}.$$

Note that we had to block the rule instances of rule r_3 unnecessarily, since they can no longer be involved in any conflict. This minor disadvantage of the PARK semantics can be overcome by allowing to include only (a non-empty) part of *conflicts* into *blocked*.

4.3 Full ECA-rules

Last in this section, we discuss the extensions necessary to capture full event-condition-action rules. We define an event as the occurrence of an update, i.e., the insertion or deletion of a literal. As before, updates for a literal l are denoted by $+l$ or $-l$. In order to allow an active rule to be triggered by an event and not just a condition, we allow update literals to occur within the rules body. In order to capture the semantics of full ECA-rules some extensions on the way to the PARK semantics are necessary.

We extend the PARK semantics for the case that during the user's transaction a set U of updates, i.e. of insertions $+l$ and deletions $-l$ for positive ground literals l, occurred. There exist several possibilities to capture these *initial* updates. One could argue that these cannot be overwritten by some rules but this unnecessarily constrains the semantics. But remembering the generality of the conflict resolution mechanism, it is easy to code the semantics where transaction updates cannot be overwritten into the conflict resolution policy. Hence, we allow a transaction's update to be overwritten. Nevertheless, some care has to be taken in case a conflict arises. There are two major points to consider:

1. In case of a conflict — witness the definition of Δ — we restart with $I^\perp$. This results in discarding not only conflicting updates but *all* the transaction's updates. This clearly is not what we want.
2. Conflicts may not only occur between rules but also between transaction updates and rules. This case is not covered by the definition of *conflicts*.

To solve these problems, we model the transaction updates U by a set of new rules $\rightarrow \pm a$ for all $\pm a \in U$. These rules then enhance the program P. More formally, we define for a given program P and a set of transaction updates U the modified program

$$P_U := P \cup \{\pm a | \pm a \in U\}.$$

The second extension necessary concerns the definition of validity of a literal. In order to allow an event to trigger a rule with $\pm l$ in its body, we must enhance the original definition of *valid* for events by two cases. For an i-interpretation and a positive ground literal a, we define

- $valid(+a, I)$ if and only if $+a \in I$ and
- $valid(-a, I)$ if and only if $-a \in I$.

Now, we can state the PARK semantics for a database instance D, a program P and a set of transaction updates U:

$$PARK(D, P, U) := incorp(int(\Delta_{P_U}^\omega((\emptyset, D))))$$

We illustrate the semantics for full event-condition-action rules by the following example. The database instance under consideration is $D = \{p(a), s(a), s(b)\}$ and the program P consists of the rules

r_1: $p(x) \rightarrow +q(x)$
r_2: $q(x) \rightarrow +r(x)$
r_3: $+r(x) \rightarrow -s(x)$

The transaction update is $U = \{+q(b)\}$. Then, P_U becomes

r_1: $p(x) \rightarrow +q(x)$
r_2: $q(x) \rightarrow +r(x)$
r_3: $+r(x) \rightarrow -s(x)$
r_4: $\rightarrow +q(b)$

and

$$I_1 := \Gamma_{\emptyset, P_U}(D) = \{p(a), +q(a), +q(b), s(a), s(b)\}$$
$$I_2 := \Gamma_{\emptyset, P_U}(I_1) = \{p(a), +q(a), +q(b), +r(a), +r(b), s(a), s(b)\}$$
$$I_3 := \Gamma_{\emptyset, P_U}(I_2) = \{p(a), +q(a), +q(b), +r(a), +r(b), s(a), s(b), -s(a), -s(b)\}$$

$(\emptyset, I_3)$ is the final fixpoint of Δ_{P_U} and after incorporating the updates, we obtain

$$PARK(D, P, U) = \{p(a), q(a), q(b), r(a), r(b)\}.$$

The preceding example does not contain any conflicts. Let us consider yet another example to see how conflicts are handled; for this example, we assume that rules derived from the updates of the transaction are of higher priority. If there is still ambiguity in how to resolve the conflict, the principle of inertia is applied.

Suppose $D = \{p(a, a), p(a, b), p(a, c)\}$ and program P has three rules:

r_1: $q(x, a) \rightarrow -p(x, a)$
r_2: $q(a, x) \rightarrow +r(a, x)$.
r_3: $+r(x, y) \rightarrow +p(x, y)$.

Suppose the transaction update is $\{+q(a, a)\}$. Then P_U becomes

r_1: $q(x, a) \rightarrow -p(x, a)$
r_2: $q(a, x) \rightarrow +r(a, x)$.
r_3: $+r(x, a) \rightarrow +p(x, a)$.
r_4: $\rightarrow +q(a, a)$.

The PARK-fixpoint construction procedure now works as follows:

$$I_1 := \Gamma_{\emptyset, P_U}(D) = \{p(a, a), p(a, b), p(a, c), +q(a, a)\}$$
$$I_2 := \Gamma_{\emptyset, P_U}(I_1) = \{p(a, a), p(a, b), p(a, c), +q(a, a), -p(a, a), +r(a, a)\}$$
$$I_3 := \Gamma_{\emptyset, P_U}(I_2) = \{p(a, a), p(a, b), p(a, c), +q(a, a), -p(a, a) + r(a, a), +p(a, a)\}$$

At this point, an inconsistency is detected involving rules r_1 and r_3 – so we re-start the computation with

$$I_4 := \Gamma_{\{r_1, r_3\}, P_U}(D) = \{p(a, a), p(a, b), p(a, c), +q(a, a)\}$$
$$I_5 := \Gamma_{\{r_1, r_3\}, P_U}(I_4) = \{p(a, a), p(a, b), p(a, c), +q(a, a), +r(a, a)\}.$$

This is the final fixpoint; after incorporating the updates, we get

$$PARK(D, P, U) = \{p(a, a), p(a, b), p(a, c), r(a, a)\}.$$

5   Examples of different conflict resolution strategies

A conflict resolution strategy is a means to resolve conflicts by making a choice between two sets of rule groundings — one voting for the insertion and one voting for the deletion of a ground atom. It is important to note that the conflict resolution strategy is orthogonal to the fixpoint computation. This point is illuminated by the two subsequent examples where the same database instances and programs are used. The same fixpoint procedure — as defined by the PARK semantics — is applied. Nevertheless, the outcome is different due to the different conflict resolution strategies is applied. This by itself is not surprising, but the major point here is that the fixpoint procedure is flexible enough to capture this.

In order to keep the discussion simple, we restrict ourselves to the propositional case of condition-action rules. Both examples are based on the same database instance D and program P. The only difference is the conflict resolution strategy.

The database instance is $D = \{p\}$ and P consists of the following rules:

r_1: $p \rightarrow +a$
r_2: $p \rightarrow +q$
r_3: $a \rightarrow +b$
r_4: $a \rightarrow -q$
r_5: $b \rightarrow +q$

The Principle of Inertia: The conflict resolution strategy in this paragraph is the already discussed principle of inertia.

The first application of Γ results in

(1) $\{p, +a, +q\}$

which is consistent. However, the next iteration yields

(2) $\{p, +a, +q, +b, -q\}$

which is inconsistent. Hence, the second case in the definition of Δ takes place. Since we deal with the propositional case only, we can neglect the substitutions for blocked rule instances. Instead, we can deal with rules directly. Since we apply the principle of inertia, we have

$blocked(D, P, \{p, +a, +q, +b, -q\}, SELECT) = \{r_2\}$

Now, the iteration starts over with $B = \{r_2\}$ and $I^\perp = \{p\}$. The next two applications of Γ yield

(3) $\{p, +a\}$
(4) $\{p, +a, +b, -q\}$

The next step again results in an inconsistent i-interpretation:

(5) $\{p, +a, +b, -q, +q\}$

The set B of blocked rule instances is supplemented by

$$blocked(D, P, \{p, +a, +b, -q, +q\}, SELECT) = \{r_5\}$$

The last iterations are

(6) $\{p, +a\}$
(7) $\{p, +a, -q, +b\}$.

At this state the final fixpoint

$$< \{r_2, r_5\}, \{p, +a, -q, +b\} >$$

is reached letting $\{p, a, b\}$ be the new database instance.

Consider yet another example, where the principle of inertia leads to counterintuitive results. Let the database instance D be $D = \{a\}$ and the program P contain the following rules:

r_1: $a \rightarrow +b$
r_2: $a \rightarrow +d$
r_3: $b \rightarrow +c$
r_4: $b \rightarrow -d$
r_5: $c \rightarrow -b$

Due to the conflict in the chain $a \rightarrow +b \rightarrow +c \rightarrow -b$ one would expect this chain to be withdrawn, and by the principle of inertia assume $\neg b$ within the final result. Further, any offspring of this contradictory chain should be neglected. In this case $-d$ should not be considered. However, this is not what happens under the principle of inertia: The first two applications of Γ result in $\{a, b, c, +d, -d\}$. A conflict concerning d arises and, by the principle of inertia is resolved by assuring $-d$ since d was not present within D. The rule $a \rightarrow +d$ is blocked. Resuming the computation the next conflict, now due to the contradictory chain shows up at $\{a, b, c, -d, -b\}$. The resolution is by blocking $a \rightarrow b$, since $b \notin D$. The final result is $\{a\}$ and differs from the expected — more intuitive — $\{a, +d\}$.

Rule Priority: The next conflict resolution strategy is based on rule priorities. Rule priorities can be found in several proposals for active rules processing. Among these are the proposals for the systems Ariel [6], Postgres [12], and Starburst [13]. For our example, we assume that rule r_i has priority i. Within the sets *ins* and *del* of the set of *conflicts*, the set containing the rule with the highest priority is chosen by SELECT.

As above, the first two applications of Γ result in

(1) $\{p, +a, +q\}$
(2) $\{p, +a, +q, +b, -q\}$

Since $+q$ is derived by a rule with priority 2 and $-q$ by a rule with priority 4,

$$blocked(D, P, \{p, +a, +q, +b, -q\}, SELECT) = \{r_2\}$$

We proceed as above with

(3) $\{p, +a\}$
(4) $\{p, +a, +b, -q\}$
(5) $\{p, +a, +b, -q, +q\}$

Since $-q$ has been derived by a rule with priority 4 and $+q$ has been derived by a rule with priority 5, we enhance the set of blocked rule instances B by

$$blocked(D, P, \{p, +a, +b, -q, +q\}, SELECT) = \{r_4\}$$

The computation resumes at $I^\perp$ and subsequent applications of Γ yield

(6) $\{p, +a\}$
(7) $\{p, +a, +b\}$
(8) $\{p, +a, +b, +q\}.$

resulting in the final database instance $\{p, a, b, q\}$.

In addition to the above conflict resolution strategies, it is possible to develop several others as well – we briefly describe four more strategies below – due to space restrictions, we are unable to give a comprehensive description in this paper.

Specificity-based Conflict Resolution: An old AI principle says that more "specific" rules (i.e., rules dealing with a more specific subset of facts) should be given priority over more general rules. For example $bird(X) \rightarrow +flies(X)$ is more general than $penguin(X) \rightarrow -flies(X)$, hence in the case of a penguin, even though both rules apply, the second should be preferred. This principle is not a complete conflict resolution strategy, since there may exist conflicting rules of equal or of incomparable specificity, but this principle may be combined with other conflict resolution strategies.

Interactive Conflict Resolution: In this scheme, as soon as a conflict is found, the user is queried and may resolve the conflict by choosing one among the conflicting rules.

Voting Scheme: In this scheme, it is assumed that a set of *critics* are available to the system. A critic is a program that takes as input, a conflict (as defined earlier), and returns the value insert or delete. When a conflict occurs, the PARK semantics invokes the set of critics and asks each of them for "its vote". The majority opinion of the critics is then adopted to resolve the conflict. An interesting aspect of critics is that each critic may use a different intuition in order to resolve a conflict. For instance, one critic may use background information it possesses on when various tuples were placed in the database (e.g. later information may be preferred by this critic). Another critic may use source-based approach (it may know that the two rules that are involved in the conflict came from two different sources, and that one of these sources is "more reliable" than the other). The Interactive conflict resolution scheme above is a special case of the voting scheme where there is one critic – viz. the human user.

Random Conflict-Resolution: In some cases it may be convenient that the system just randomly chooses one from the conflicting rules in order to resolve the conflict.

Which of the above strategies is picked for a particular application depends critically upon the declarative needs of the application as well as efficiency concerns.

Declarative Needs: For instance, in banking applications, the principle of inertia may be used by the system, delaying a transaction, until the human banker can be queried. In many cases where the preconditions of rules define classes and a clear object-class hierarchy exists, then the principle of specificity may be used. The voting scheme can be used when good critics are available for the application at hand. In databases that monitor critical systems (e.g. power plants, machine tools, etc.), the interactive conflict resolution scheme is perhaps the most appropriate strategy. Furthermore, in many applications, humans may prefer to adopt this strategy anyway.

Efficiency Needs: From the point of efficiency, the principles of inertia, rule priority, interactive conflict resolution and random conflict resolution are all easy to implement and can be viewed as constant time operations (i.e., operations that require a constant number of database accesses).

In contrast, the principle of specificity *may* be more intensive computationally, in particular, if specificity of rules is not determined a-priori, but is determined on the fly by computing and comparing the sets of ground factsd to which the rules apply. (There may be, however completely different and much simpler ways of defining and determining rule specificity).

Lastly, the voting scheme's computational properties are constant-time modulo the complexity of the critics themselves. If the critics take large amounts of time for their processing, then this scheme could be time-consuming.

6   Discussion

Over the last few years, there has been extensive work on active database systems. However, most of the formal treatments of active databases have been ad-hoc, and have failed to satisfy at least one of the following criteria that we consider critical to active databases – either they result in an update generate a multiplicity of database states, or they take non-polynomial (exponential) time to compute, or they are unable to resolve conflicts.

In this paper, we first outlined the requirements for a semantics of active rule systems. Subsequently, we defined the PARK semantics for active rules – this semantics satisfies the previously articulated criteria. The PARK semantics can be seen as a smooth integration of inflationary fixpoint semantics [7] and conflict resolution. It fulfills all our requirements including the treatment of recursive rules.

However, some issues are not discussed within this paper. First, one might argue that the semantics is very strict — it comes close to the datalog semantics. At the other end of the spectrum there exist very loose semantics in that they allow any conflict to occur and for example don't resolve them or resolve them indeterministically. However, we think that the semantics at the loose end is not very practical: active rules would resemble multiple concurrent gotos with complex label definitions.

Another point is the still restricted language we use. More complex events, other kinds of triggering, and queries (rules) over past database states have to be incorporated. The first two points do not bear new principle problems for the PARK semantics It would be interesting to investigate whether the internal event calculus [10] can be integrated with PARK semantics in order to solve the latter point.

Another point fairly neglected in the paper is the coupling mode of rules to updates and transactions. But we think that this is an orthogonal issue. PARK semantics could be applied to those rules with immediate coupling immediarly after the triggering update occurred or it could be applied to the deferred rules at the end of the transaction. Hence, we did not elaborate on this point.

An issue not touched in the paper is a semantics for choice rules, that is disjunction in the head of rules. We leave this issue for future research.

Acknowledgement. We gratefully acknowledge the stimulating critics provided by the anonymous referees.

V.S. Subrahmanian's research was supported by ARO grant DAAH-04-95-10174, AFOSR grant F49620-93-1-0065, ARPA/Rome Labs contract F30602-93-C-0241 (Order Nr. A716), and NSF grants IRI-9357756 and IRI-9314905.

References

1. A. Buchmann. Active object systems. In A. Dogac, M. Özsu, A. Biliris, and T. Sellis, editors, *Advances in Object-Oriented Database Systems*, pages 201–224, 1994.
2. U. Dayal, E. Hanson, and J. Widom. Active database systems. In W. Kim, editor, *Modern Database Systems*, pages 434–456. Addison Wesley, 1995.
3. P. Fraternelli and L. Tanca. A toolkit for the design of active database semantics. Rapporto Interno 93-078, Politecnico di Milano, Milano, Italy, 1993.
4. P. Fraternelli and L. Tanca. A structured approach for the definition of the semantics of active databases. Rapporto Interno 95-028, Politecnico di Milano, Milano, Italy, 1995. To appear in Trans. on Database Systems.
5. A. Van Gelder, K. Ross, and J. S. Schlipf. The well-founded semantics for general logic programs. *Journal of the ACM*, 38(3):620–650, July 1991.
6. E. Hanson. Rule condition testing and action execution in ariel. In *Proc. of the ACM SIGMOD Conf. on Management of Data*, pages 49–58, San Diego, CA, Jun. 1992.

7. P. Kolaitis and C. Papadimitriou. Why not negation by fixpoint? *Journal of Computer and System Sciences*, 43:125–144, 1991.

8. A.M. Kotz. *Trigger Mechanisms for Maintaining Design Data Consistency in Database Systems*. PhD thesis, Univ. of Karlsruhe, 1988.

9. W. Marek and M. Truszczyński. Revision Programming, Database Updates, and Integrity Constraints. In *Int. Conf. on Database Theory*, pages 368–382, Prague, Jan. 1995. Springer.

10. A. Olive. On the design and implementation of information systems from deductive databases. In *Proc. Int. Conf. on Very Large Data Bases*, pages 3–11, 1989.

11. Ph. Picouet, V. Vianu. Semantics and Expressiveness Issues in Active Databases. In *Proc. ACM Symposium on Principles of Database Systems*, pages 126-138, 1995.

12. M. Stonebraker, A. Jhingran, J. Goh, and S. Potamianos. On rules, procedures, caching and views in data base systems. In *Proc. ACM SIGMOD Int. Conf. on Management of Data*, pages 281–290, 1990.

13. J. Widom and S. Finkelstein. Set-oriented production rules in relational databases. In *Proc. of the ACM SIGMOD Conf. on Management of Data*, pages 259–270, 1990.

14. C. Zaniolo. On the unification of active databases and deductive databases. In *Rules in Database Systems*, (N. Paton, ed.), Springer Verlag, 1994.

Composite Events in Chimera

Rosa Meo[1]   Giuseppe Psaila[1]   Stefano Ceri[2]

[1] Politecnico di Torino, Dipartimento di Automatica e Informatica
Corso Duca degli Abruzzi, 24 - I-10129 Torino, Italy
[2] Politecnico di Milano, Dipartimento di Elettronica e Informazione
Piazza L. Da Vinci, 32 - I-20133 Milano, Italy
rosimeo@polito.it, psaila/ceri@elet.polimi.it

Abstract. In this paper, we extend event types supported by Chimera, an active object-oriented database system. Chimera rules currently support disjunctive expressions of set-oriented, elementary event types; our proposal introduces instance-oriented event types, arbitrary boolean expressions (including negation), and precedence operators. Thus, we introduce a new event calculus, whose distinguishing feature is to support a minimal set of orthogonal operators which can be arbitrarily composed. We use event calculus to determine when rules are triggered; this is a change of each rule's internal status which makes it suitable for being considered by the rule selection mechanism.

The proposed extensions do not affect the way in which rules are processed after their triggering; therefore, this proposal is continuously evolving the syntax and semantics of Chimera in the dimension of event composition, without compromising its other semantic features. For this reason, we believe that the proposed approach can be similarly applied for extending the event language of other active database systems currently supporting simple events or their disjunction.

1 Introduction

Active database systems provide tight integration of Event-Condition-Action (ECA) rules within a database system. Such a tight integration is normally achieved by reusing database system components for implementing conditions (database predicates or queries) and actions (database manipulations, often embedded within a procedural component). In general, when a rule is selected for execution (or triggered), then its condition is evaluated (or considered), and if the condition is satisfied, then the action is immediately executed [3]. Thus, the condition-action (CA) components of an active database have a simple and uniform behavior, which is common to most active databases.

Instead, event type specification, evaluation, and coupling to conditions and actions have to be designed and implemented specifically for each active database system. Thus, it is not surprising that the notions of elementary event type, of event type composition, and of binding between event occurrences and the CA

---

[3] An exception is HiPAC [9] which supports several coupling modes between conditions and actions.

components are quite different in each active database, and such differences are responsible for most of the diversity of active databases.

Most active databases recognize just data manipulation operations (such as insert, delete, and update) as event types. The proposed SQL3 standard, currently under development by ANSI and ISO, associates to each rule just one event type; this can be considered as the simple extreme of a spectrum of solutions [17]. Most relational database products supporting active rules (called triggers) associate each of them to a disjunction of event types whose instances are relative to the same table [23]; this solution is also used by Starburst [24], Postgres [21], and Chimera, an active object-oriented database prototype developed at Politecnico di Milano in the context of the IDEA Esprit Project [4, 5]. More complex event calculus are supported by active database prototypes (see Section 1.1). In these approaches, rules are associated to event expressions which normally include generic boolean expressions, precedence operations, and explicit time references.

In all active rule systems, event instances cause rules to change an internal state; the corresponding state transition is called *triggering* of the rule. Once a rule is triggered, active rule systems react in several ways. When multiple rules are triggered at the same time, a *rule selection mechanism* determines which of them should be considered first; this mechanism may be influenced by priorities which are statically associated to rules. In addition, the rule selection may occurr *immediately* after the triggering operation or be *deferred* to some later point in transaction execution (such as the commit time). With immediate execution, it is possible to further identify the cases of rules executing *before, after,* or *instead of* the operation generating the triggering event occurrence. Finally, the triggering and execution of rules can be repeated for each tuple or object affected by an operation (*row-level granularity* in [17]) or instead relate to the overall set of tuples or objects manipulated by means of the same operation (*statement-level granularity* in [17]).

Due to all these alternatives, active rule systems present themselves with a variety of possible behaviors (a thorough comparative analysis of semantics supported by active rule systems is presented in [10]). In order to control the introduction of complex events in Chimera, and therefore the increase of semantic complexity due to this extension, we have strictly followed some design principles:

- We have defined the event calculus by means of a minimal set of orthogonal operators.
- The semantics of the event calculus is given simply by defining the conditions upon which rules having as event type a complex event calculus expression become triggered; detriggering occurs when a rule is selected for consideration and execution. No other state transitions characterize the internal state of each rule.
- The event calculus extension does not affect the way in which rules are processed after their triggering; therefore, this proposal continuously evolves the syntax and semantics of Chimera in the dimension of event type composition, without compromising its other semantic features.

We believe that these design principles are general and should drive the design of event calculus for active databases; therefore, we also believe that the proposed approach extends naturally to active database systems currently supporting simple event types or their disjunction.

The paper is organized as follows: Section 2 reports the current fundamental Chimera features; Section 3 introduces the proposed extension, while Section 4 formally gives its semantics; Section 5 deals with implementation issues; finally, Section 6 draws the conclusions.

1.1 Related work

There exist several Active Database Systems that have been provided with a language for event type composition; these languages are presented in [13], [7], [11], [19], [22]. The way all these proposals deal with composite event types is quite different depending on the particular systems; in fact, though they have similar sets of operators, different semantics have been proposed. In the rest of the section, we briefly discuss the most important proposals.

Ode [13] has a rich event language based on a small set of primitive operators. These operators deal with event occurrences in a set-oriented way, using set operations like intersection and complement: they produce subsets of the primitive event occurrence history, considered as an ordered set based on the event occurrence time-stamps. For example, event conjunction is the set of event occurrences that satisfy both component event types (and it produces a not null result provided that the two event occurrence sets corresponding to the two operands have at least one common element); event negation is the complement with respect to the whole history; *relative* of an event type A with respect to type B is the set of occurrences of type B subsequent to the first occurrence of type A. Other operators, like event disjunction, temporal precedence (*prior*), strict sequence (*sequence*), etc., are derived from the primitive operators. The user is allowed to specify conditions on event properties directly in the composition expressions, i.e. in the event part of the rule. Since the expressive power is that of regular expressions, composite events are checked by means of a finite state automata.

HiPAC [8] makes available *data manipulations* events, *clock* events and *external* events. Clock events can be specified as *absolute, relative* and *periodic*. Composite event types are defined with the use of the following operands: *disjunction, sequence* (temporal precedence of event signals) and *closure* (event signals occurred one or more times).

Snoop [7] interprets an event E as a boolean function defined on the time domain that is true at time t if an event occurrence of that event type occurs at time t. Event conjunction and disjunction are obtained by the boolean algebra applied on their operands. Negation of an event E is defined as the absence of an occurrence of E in a closed interval determined by two events E_1 and E_2. While the *aperiodic* operator determines the presence of all the occurrences of an event E between two subsequent occorrences of E_1 and E_2, the *periodic* operator is equivalent to a periodic event generator: given a time period t_p, it is true at instants separated each other by t_p, starting from an occurrence of an event E_1 and stopping at the subsequent occurrence of an event E_2. The *cumulative* versions of these two last operators are defined as "accumulating" respectively occurrences of E and time instants. Depending on the application, it is possible to define different *contexts* in order to let a rule be triggered in correspondance of either all the possible combinations of primitive event occurrences matching the event expression or only some of them.

Samos [11] has a rather rich language as well, which provides the usual event disjunction, conjunction and *sequence* (ordered conjunction). A *Times* operator returns the point in time when the n-th occurrence of a specified event is observed in a given time interval. The negation is defined as the absence of any occurrence of an event type from a given time interval, and occurs at its end point. A star (*) operator returns the first occurrence of a given event type, regardless of the number of occurrences. Samos allows information passing from the event to the condition part of the rule by means of *parameters* like the identifier of the transaction in which a given event occurred (c_tid), or the point in time of the event occurrence (occ_point). Composite event parameters are derived: disjunction and star (*) receive the parameters of the component event occurrences, conjunction and *Times* their union. A keyword *same* specifies that the component events of a composition must have the same parameters.

The Reflex system [19] is an active database system designed for knowledge management applications. Its event algebra provides operators similar to those of Samos. These operators can be classified as logical (*and*, *or*, *xor* and *not*) or temporal (*precedes*, *succeeds*, *at*, *between*, *within* time-spec, *every* time-spec, etc..)

IFO_2 [22] is a conceptual model designed to capture both the structural and behavioural aspects of the modeled reality. The behavioural nodel is based on the notion of event, that represents either a fact of the modelled system which occurs in a spontaneous manner (in the case of external or temporal events) or is generated by the application. The event constructors are *composition* (conjunction), *sequence* (temporal precedence), *grouping* (collection of events of the same type) and *union* (disjunction). When a IFO_2 schema is defined, it is possible to translate it into a set of *ECA* rules by means of an ad hoc algorithm.

2 Introduction to Chimera

Chimera is a novel active, object-oriented and deductive database system; the main goal of its design was the definition of a clear semantics, especially for those aspects concerning active rules, such as rule execution, coupling modes, triggering.

Chimera active rules (also called *triggers*) follow the ECA (Event-Condition-Action) paradigm. Each trigger is defined on a set of *triggering events*, and it becomes active if *any* of its triggering events occurs. The Chimera event language was designed to consider only *internal events*, i.e. events generated by updates or queries on the database, like *create*, *modify*, *delete*, *generalize*, *specialize*, *select*, etc.. In particular, a rule is defined either as *targeted* or *untargeted*: if targeted to a class, only events regarding that class are considered for triggering, otherwise events regarding any class in the database can appear in the event part of the rule.

The condition part is a logical formula that may perform a query on the database; its evaluation is called *consideration*. Depending on the success of this evaluation, the action part is executed coupled with the condition part.

Chimera does not permit binding transfer from the event section to the condition section because of the set-oriented approach; nevertheless, it is important for conditions to obtain objects affected by occurred events. Thus, a condition may include *event formulas*, particular formulas that query the event base and create bindings to the objects affected by a specified set of event types. Two predicates are available to write event formulas: the *occurred* predicate and the *holds* predicate. The former one extracts all the objects affected by the specified event types; the latter considers event composition.

A rule is *triggered* as soon as one of the triggering events arises, and it is no longer taken into account for triggering, until it has been considered. The triggering mechanism checks for new triggered rules immediately after a non interruptable execution block (either a user instruction sequence, called *transaction line*, or a rule action).

Based on the Event-Condition (EC) *coupling mode* chosen by the user, the rule behaves differently: if the rule is defined as *immediate*, the consideration is performed as soon as possible after the termination of the non interruptable block that generated the triggering event occurrence; if the rule is *deferred*, it is suspended until the *commit* command is given.

After the triggering mechanism has checked for new triggered rules, it chooses a rule to be considered and possibly executed, if there is any triggered rule; the choice is made based on a partial order derived from rule priorities provided by the user. Notice that after the consideration and possibly the execution of the rule, it is detriggered and it can be triggered again only by new event occurrences, because events occurred before the consideration loose the capability of triggering the rule.

The user can influence the behaviour of the rule specifying the Event Consumption mode as either *consuming* or *preserving*: in the former case, only event occurrences more recent than the last consideration of the trigger are accessible to event formulas; in the latter, all the events occurred since the beginning of the transaction are available.

An example of rule is the following one, that reacts to the creation of stock items, to check whether the quantity exceeds the maximum quantity admitted for that item.

```
define immediate checkStockQty for stock
events: create
condition: stock(S),occurred(create, S),S.quantity>S.max_quantity
action: modify(stock.quantity, S, S.max_quantity)
end;
```

The rule, called *checkStockQty* is defined with *immediate* EC coupling mode and is targeted to the *stock* class. The event part indicates that the rule is triggered when a *create* event on class *stock* occurs. The condition is structured as follows: a variable S is defined on class *stock*; the *occurred* predicate binds the objects affected by the creation to that variable and finally the constraint is checked. If there is some object that violates the constraint, then the action changes its quantity setting it to the maximum quantity for that object. Note that the rule is executed in a set-oriented way, so all the objects created and not checked yet by the rule are processed together in a single rule execution.

3 Extending Chimera with Composite Events

Our extension of Chimera with composite event types moves from the currently available features in order to preserve the characterizing aspects of this system. In particular, the introduction of an event calculus language should change neither the triggering/detriggering semantics, nor the processing of triggered rules, in particular with respect to *EC compling modes* and *event consumption*.

A composite event is an event expression obtained from primitive event types by means of a set of operators, such as *conjunction, disjunction, negation* and temporal *precedence*. These operators are divided in set-oriented and instance-oriented operators: in the former case, we consider the occurrence of a combination of event types independently of the affected objects; in the latter, the specified combination must occur on the same object. They are reported in Figure 1, listed in decreasing priority order: set-oriented operators have lower priority than instance-oriented ones, and conjunction and precedence operators have the same priority. While designing the language, we moved on three orthogonal dimensions, as depicted in Figure 1: due to the *boolean dimension*, we introduced operators such as *conjunction, disjunction* and *negation*; due to the *granularity dimension*, these operators are divided in *instance-oriented* and *set-oriented*; due to the *temporal dimension* we introduced two *precedence* operators, one instance-oriented and the other set-oriented.

In the following two Sections, we introduce the set-oriented and instance-oriented operators. For each composite event built by means of these operators, we indicate whether the event has occurred (we say that the event is *active*) and we indicate the most recent time when the event has occurred (called its *activation time-stamp*). We make use of some sample event expressions based on classes *stock*, describing stock products, and *show*, indicating products on shelves in a sale-room.

3.1 Set-Oriented Operators

A *primitive event* occurs when an occurrence of that event type arises, independently of the object affected by it. For instance, let us imagine that two occurrences of the event create(stock) arise at time t_1 and t_2. At time $t < t_1$

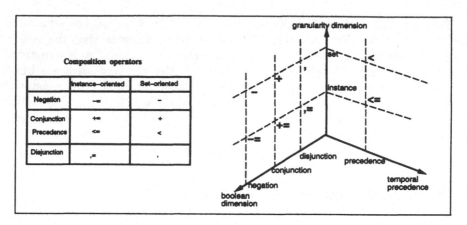

Fig. 1. Set of Event Operators and their dimensions

the event is not active; at time $t_1 \leq t < t_2$ the event is active and its activation time-stamp is t_1; finally, at time $t_2 \leq t$ the event is active and its activation time-stamp is t_2.

The first version of Chimera already provided the disjunction among primitive events, that was described by a list of primitive event types separated by commas. We keep the same notation, extending its application to generic event expressions. Intuitively the *disjunction* $\mathcal{E}_1, \mathcal{E}_2$ of two event expressions arises as soon as one of the component events becomes active. To be more precise, we say that at a certain time t the disjunction is active if at least one of the component events is active. If only one of the component events is active, its activation time-stamp becomes the activation time-stamp of the disjunction; if both the components events are active, the highest activation time-stamp of them is assumed to be the activation time-stamp of the disjunction.

As an example, let us consider the sample event expression
```
create(stock), modify(stock.quantity)
```
and two occurrences of the primitive event `create(stock)` at times t_1 and t_3, and one occurrence of the primitive event `modify(stock.quantity)` at time t_2, with $t_1 < t_2 < t_3$. At time $t < t_1$ the disjunction event is not active; at time $t_1 \leq t < t_2$ the disjunction is active and its activation time-stamp is t_1; at time $t_2 \leq t < t_3$, the disjunction is active and its activation time-stamp is now t_2; finally, at time $t \geq t_3$ the disjunction is active and its activation time-stamp is now t_3.

When we consider the *conjunction* $\mathcal{E}_1 + \mathcal{E}_2$ of two events, it is intuitive that it is active when both of the component events are active. If so, the activation time-stamp is the highest of the activation time-stamps of the component events.

As an example, let us consider the sample event expression
```
create(stock) + modify(stock.quantity)
```

and consider again two occurrences of the primitive event `create(stock)` at times t_1 and t_3, and an occurrence of the primitive event `modify(stock.quantity)` at time t_2, with $t_1 < t_2 < t_3$. At time $t < t_1$ the conjunction event is not active; at time $t_1 \leq t < t_2$ the conjunction is still not active; at time $t_2 \leq t < t_3$, the conjunction is active and its activation time-stamp is t_2; finally, at time $t \geq t_3$ the conjunction is active and the activation time-stamp is now t_3.

In complex applications it is often necessary to consider the absence of an event; a *negation* event $- \mathcal{E}$ is active when the *negated* event (also called component event) is not active; in particular, if there are no occurrences of the negated event at time t, the activation time-stamp is the current time. Normally, negated events are used in conjunction with positive events, thus yielding meaningful event expressions.

For instance, let us consider the first occurrence of the event `create(stock)` at time t_1 and its negation, `-create(stock)`. At time $t \geq t_1$, since the event `create(stock)` is active, the negation is not active; at time $t < t_1$, since `create(stock)` is not active, the negation is active and its activation time-stamp is t, because it is occurring at time t.

Similarly to the conjunction, the *precedence* $\mathcal{E}_1 < \mathcal{E}_2$ of two event expressions is active provided that both the component events are active; moreover, the first component event must become active earlier than the second one.

As an example let us consider the sample event expression

$$\texttt{create(stock)} < \texttt{modify(stock.quantity)}$$

and two occurrences of the primitive event `create(stock)` at times t_1 and t_3, and one occurrence of the primitive event `modify(stock.quantity)` at time t_2, with $t_1 < t_2 < t_3$. At time $t < t_1$ the precedence event is not active; at time $t_1 \leq t < t_2$ the precedence is still not active; at time $t_2 \leq t < t_3$, the precedence is active and its activation time-stamp is t_2; finally, at time $t \geq t_3$ the precedence is active and its activation time-stamp still remains at t_2, because the second creation has time-stamp greater than that of the last modification.

We are able to write any complex set-oriented event expression, e.g.

```
modify(show.quantity) +
   ( -( create(stockOrder) < modify(stockOrder.del_quantity)) ,
     ( modify(stock.min_quantity) < modify(stock.quantity) ) )
```

interpreted as follows: the composite event is active if there is a modification of the product quantity on a *shelf*, and there is not a creation of a *stock order* followed by a modification of the delivered quantity for a *stock order*, or there is a modification of the minimum quantity for a *stock* followed by a modification of the quantity for a *stock*.

3.2   Instance-Oriented Operators

Instance-Oriented operators are useful to catch the occurrence of composite events on the same object. For this reason, instance-oriented operators have higher priority than set-oriented ones, and they cannot be applied to event sub-expressions obtained by means of set-oriented operators.

In contrast, an event expression obtained using instance-oriented operators can appear as an operand of a set-oriented operator; in fact, it is very intuitive to pass from the instance-oriented to the set-oriented level, as we will show later.

A *primitive event* occurs on an object O when a new occurrence of that event type arises and affects O. As in the set-oriented case, at time t the following situations are possible: no event occurrences of that type have arisen yet on O, so the primitive event is *not active* for O; at least one occurrence of that type has arisen on O, then the primitive event is *active* for O and the *activation time-stamp* is that of the more recent occurrence. For instance, let us imagine that two occurrences of the event `create(stock)` arise at time t_1 and t_2 on the objects O_1 and O_2 respectively. At time $t < t_1$ the event is not active for both the objects; at time $t_1 \leq t < t_2$ the event is active only for O_1 and its activation time-stamp is t_1; finally, at time $t_2 \leq t$ the event is still active for O_1 with activation time-stamp t_1, but it becomes active for O_2 too and its activation time-stamp is t_2.

The *instance-oriented conjunction* $\mathcal{E}_1 \mathrel{+=} \mathcal{E}_2$ of two events on the same object O, is active when both the component events are active for O. The activation time-stamp for O is the highest of the activation time-stamps for the component events. For instance, `create(stock) += modify(stock.quantity)` is an instance-oriented conjunction that becomes active for a *stock* object O when O has been created and its quantity has been changed.

We give examples of instance-oriented disjunction in comparison with set-oriented disjunction. When used in a set-oriented expression, an instance-oriented conjunction is active if there is at least one object affected by the two component event expressions. For instance, consider the expression

`modify(show.quantity) + (create(stock) += modify(stock.quantity))`

which is active when a change of a shown product quantity occurs and at least a *stock* object has been created and its quantity modified.

The *instance-oriented disjunction* $\mathcal{E}_1 \mathrel{,=} \mathcal{E}_2$ of two event expressions on an object O intuitively arises as soon as one of the component events becomes active for O. Precisely, at a certain time t the disjunction is active for O if at least one of the component events is active for O. If only one of the component events is active for O, its activation time-stamp becomes the activation time-stamp of the disjunction; if both the components events are active for O, the highest activation time-stamp of them is assumed to be the activation time-stamp of the disjunction. Consider the expression `create(stock),= modify(stock.quantity)` as an example of instance-oriented disjunction, two occurrences of the primitive event `create(stock)` at times t_1 and t_3 on objects O_1 and O_3 respectively, and two occurrences of the event `modify(stock.quantity)` at time t_2 on objects O_1 and O_2 respectively, with $t_1 < t_2 < t_3$. At time $t < t_1$ the disjunction event is not active for all the three mentioned objects; at time $t_1 \leq t < t_2$ the disjunction is active for O_1 with activation time-stamp t_1 and still not active for O_2 and

O_3; at time $t_2 \leq t < t_3$, the disjunction is still active for O_1 with activation time-stamp t_1 but is now active for O_2 with activation time-stamp t_2; finally, at time $t \geq t_3$ the disjunction is now active also for O_3 with activation time-stamp t_3. When used in a set-oriented expression, an instance-oriented disjunction is active if there is at least one object affected by the disjunction of the component event expressions. For instance, consider the expressions:

1. `modify(show.quantity)+(create(stock),=modify(stock.quantity))`
2. `modify(show.quantity)+(create(stock),modify(stock.quantity))`
3. `modify(show.quantity)+(create(stock)+=modify(stock.quantity))`

The first one is active when a change of a shown product quantity occurs and either a *stock* object has been created or its quantity modified. Observe that the instance-oriented disjunction is not different from a set-oriented disjunction, as shown by the second expression, that is active when a change of a shown product quantity occurs and there are a creation of a *stock* object or a modification of the quantity for a *stock* object, the two objects being possibly different; in fact, the instance-oriented disjunction operator has been introduced for completeness of instance-oriented event expressions. The third expression clarifies this concept, because it is active when a change of a shown product quantity occurs and there is a creation of a *stock* object on which a modification of the quantity occur.

The *instance-oriented negation* $-=$ $\mathcal{E}$ expresses the absence of occurrences of an event type for an object O: it is active when the *negated* event is not active for O and the activation time-stamp is the current time. For instance, let us consider two occurrences of the event `create(stock)` at time t_1 and t_2 affecting O_1 and O_2 respectively, and the negation event $-=$`create(stock)`. At time $t < t_1$ the negation is active for both O_1 and O_2, with activation time-stamp t for both; at time $t_1 \leq t < t_2$, since the event `create(stock)` is active for O_1 but not for O_2, the negation is not active for O_1 but is still active for O_2 with activation time-stamp t. For instance, consider the expressions:

`modify(show.quantity) + -=(create(stock)+=modify(stock.quantity))`
`modify(show.quantity) + -(create(stock) + modify(stock.quantity))`

The first one is active when a change of a shown product quantity occurs and no *stock* object has been created and its quantity modified. Instead, the second one is active when a change of a shown product quantity occurs and there is neither a creation of a *stock* object nor a modification of the quantity for a *stock* object, the two objects being possibly different.

Similarly to the conjunction, the *instance-oriented precedence* $\mathcal{E}_1$`<=`$\mathcal{E}_2$ of two events is active when both the component events are active on the same object O, and the first one becomes active earlier than the second one. For instance, let us consider `modify( stock.min_quantity) <= modify( stock.quantity)`, two occurrences of the event `modify(stock.min_quantity)` at times t_1 and t_3 on the same object O_1, and one occurrence of the event `modify(stock.quantity)` at time t_2 again on the object O_1, with $t_1 < t_2 < t_3$. At time $t < t_1$ the precedence event for O_1 is not active; at time $t_1 \leq t < t_2$ the precedence is still not active for O_1; at time $t_2 \leq t < t_3$, the precedence is active for O_1 and its activation time-stamp is t_2; finally, at time $t \geq t_3$ the precedence is active for O_1

and its activation time-stamp is still t_2. When used in a set-oriented expression, an instance-oriented precedence is active if there is at least one object affected by the sequence of the two component event expressions. For instance, consider the expressions:

```
modify(show.quantity) + (create(stock) <= modify(stock.quantity))
modify(show.quantity) + (create(stock) < modify(stock.quantity))
```

The first one is active when a change of a shown product quantity occurs and at least a *stock* object has been created and later its quantity modified. Instead, the second one is active when a change of a shown product quantity occurs and there is a creation of a *stock* object followed by a modification of the quantity for a *stock* object, the two objects being possibly different.

3.3   Event Formulas

As introduced in Sections 3, event formulas (see Section 2) are extended in consequence of the introduction of the event language.

Event expressions. The *occurred* predicate now supports event expressions limited to *instance-oriented* operators. This is due to the semantics of the predicate: it returns all the objects affected by the specified event expression [4]. For example:

```
occurred( create(stock) <= modify(stock.quantity) , X )
```

binds all the objects created whose attribute quantity has been modified to variable X. Depending on the *consumption mode* selected for the rule, the above formula retrieves either all the objects affected by that particular combination of event types since the beginning of the transaction (*preserving* rule) or only those affected since the last consideration of the rule (*consuming* rule). Observe that this is exactly the same semantics of Chimera without composite events, reviewed in Section 2.

Occurrence time-stamp. This new predicate is similar to the *occurred* predicate but it provides the time-stamp of the specified composite event occurrences as well. For example:

```
at( create(stock) <= modify(stock.quantity) , X, T )
```

where T is a variable defined on type *time*.

Its semantics is defined as follows: given an object X, T assumes all the time-stamps, in the observed time interval, at which an occurrence of the specified

---

[4] Chimera supports also a predicate *holds* which composes event types. However, there is no need of such predicate in the new Chimera extended with event calculus, since event composition can be explicitily evaluated by the calculus. For instance, net effect for the creation operation in presence of sequences of modifications and deletions is given by the following event formula:

```
create(class) ≡
  (create(class) ,= (create(class) <= modify(class.attr))) +=
  -=(create(class) <= delete(class))
```

event expression arises for that object. In the above example, if the creation of a stock object is followed by two updates of its `quantity` attribute, the specified composite event occurs twice, exactly when the two updates occur.

The observed time interval depends on the consumption mode selected for the rule: it can range either from the beginning of the transaction to the current time (*preserving* rules), or from the last consideration of the rule to the current time (*consuming* rule).

4   Formal Semantics

This Section is organized as follows: at first, we describe our approach to the definition of event calculus; then we precisely define our model of *Event Base*, a basis for all subsequent definitions; then, we give the formal semantics for both *set-oriented* and *instance-oriented* operators; finally, triggering semantics is formulated in formal way.

Composite event semantics   The main goal of our work is to provide the event language with a semantics that preserves boolean properties, such as De Morgan rules, and at the same time gives a useful algorithm for testing whether a given composite event has occurred.

The main idea is the following: for each primitive event type we construct a function dependent on time t, called the *time-stamp of the more recent event occurrence*, indicated with ts. The ts function of an event type is constructed on the basis of the positive time-stamp of the last occurrence of the event type, if an event occurrence exists. Otherwise, ts calculated in t is set to a negative value, equal to $-t$.

From these basic ts functions, our event calculus algebraically derives ts functions for event expressions from ts functions associated to its primitive components. As already said, these expressions are obtained applaying arbitrarily boolean operators and precedence operator to primitive event types.

The sign of the ts function of an event type states whether an occurrence of that event type exists in the portion of EB relevant for rule triggering: if positive, an event type occurrence exists; if negative, otherwise. Consequently, it is sufficient to determine an instant t in which function ts is positive to solve rule triggering.

4.1   The Event Base

The Event Base (EB) is the log containing all the event occurrences since the beginning of the transaction. In this paper we model the EB as a table having the structure depicted in Figure 2.

Each row contains an event occurrence, characterized by its unique identifier (EID), the event type, the Object Identifier (OID) of the object affected by the event occurrence, and the time-stamp of the time instant the event occurred at. The event type is described by the name of the command that changed the object

EID	event-type	OID	time-stamp
e_1	$< create,\ stock >$	o_1	t_1
e_2	$< create,\ stock >$	o_2	t_2
e_3	$< create,\ order >$	o_3	t_3
e_4	$< modify,\ stock,\ quantity >$	o_1	t_4
e_5	$< modify,\ stock,\ quantity >$	o_2	t_4
e_6	$< delete,\ stock >$	o_1	t_5

Fig. 2. Example of EB.

$type:\ e_1 \rightarrow < create, stock >$	$obj\ :\ e_3 \rightarrow o_3$
$type:\ e_5 \rightarrow < modify, stock, quantity >$	$obj:\ e_4 \rightarrow o_1$
$type:\ e_6 \rightarrow < delete, stock >$	$obj:\ e_5 \rightarrow o_2$
$timestamp:\ e_2 \rightarrow t_2$	$eventonclass:\ e_1 \rightarrow stock$
$timestamp:\ e_3 \rightarrow t_3$	$eventonclass:\ e_5 \rightarrow stock$
$timestamp:\ e_4 \rightarrow t_4$	

Fig. 3. Examples of event attribute matches on events in EB.

state, possibly followed by the object class name and an attribute name. In the following, we refer to the EID of a generic event occurrence as e. Observe that the two event occurrences e_4 and e_5 have the same time-stamp: this is due to the set-oriented execution semantics of operations in Chimera (in this particular case, the modification of the state of the two objects o_1 and o_2 belonging to the same class *stock* is performed at the same time t_4).

Given an event occurrence e, we can define a set of useful functions returning properties of e stored in the EB. Figure 3 contains examples of the defined functions; derived from the EB state of Figure 2.

type $type:\ EID \rightarrow eventtype$
This function matches each event occurence to its event type.

obj $obj:\ EID \rightarrow OID$
This relation matches each event occurrence to the object whose state has been modified by that event.

timestamp $timestamp:\ EID \rightarrow time$
This function matches each event occurrence to its time-stamp.

eventonclass $eventonclass:\ EID \rightarrow classname$
This function matches each event occurrence to the class to which the object affected by the event occurrence belongs. Note that this piece of information is part of the *event-type* attribute.

4.2   Set-Oriented Case

The definition of ts of a primitive event type $\mathcal{E}$ at time t is:

$$ts(\mathcal{E}, t) \stackrel{def}{=} \begin{cases} -t & if \; \forall t' \; (t' \le t \wedge \nexists e \in R \; (\\ & \quad type(e) = \mathcal{E} \wedge timestamp(e) = t')) \\ t_E & otherwise, where \\ & \quad t_E = max\{t'(t' \le t \; \wedge \; \exists e \in R(type(e) = \mathcal{E} \\ & \quad \wedge \; timestamp(e) = t'))\} \end{cases}$$

where R is the set of event occurrences to which the event calculus applies.

We also introduce two useful functions in order to simplify the definitions that will follow.

$$u(t) \stackrel{def}{=} \begin{cases} 0 & if \; t < 0 \\ 1 & if \; t \ge 0 \end{cases} \qquad\qquad occ(\mathcal{E}, t) \stackrel{def}{=} \begin{cases} true & if \; u(\, ts(\mathcal{E}, t)) = 1 \\ false & otherwise \end{cases}$$

The above definitions are useful to indicate the presence of an event occurrence in R at time t: the boolean function $occ(\mathcal{E}, t)$ will be used in the logical formulation of the semantics, while the function $u(t)$ will be used in the algebraic formulation.

As already said informally, the function ts of *negation* is $ts(-\mathcal{E}, t) \stackrel{def}{=} -ts(\mathcal{E}, t)$.

Semantics of the other set-oriented operators is given in two steps: at first, we give a precise definition in logical style; second, that definition is translated into an algebraic equivalent expression that can be used for the evaluation of the ts function associated to the overall event expression.

Logical Style Semantics

1) $ts(\mathcal{A}+\mathcal{B}, t) \stackrel{def}{=} \begin{cases} min\{ts(\mathcal{A}, t), ts(\mathcal{B}, t)\} \; if \; \neg occ(\mathcal{A}, t) \vee \neg occ(\mathcal{B}, t) \\ max\{ts(\mathcal{A}, t), ts(\mathcal{B}, t)\} \; if \; occ(\mathcal{A}, t) \wedge occ(\mathcal{B}, t) \end{cases}$
2) $ts((\mathcal{A}, \mathcal{B}), t) \stackrel{def}{=} \begin{cases} min\{ts(\mathcal{A}, t), ts(\mathcal{B}, t)\} \; if \; \neg occ(\mathcal{A}, t) \wedge \neg occ(\neg\mathcal{B}, t) \\ max\{ts(\mathcal{A}, t), ts(\mathcal{B}, t)\} \; if \; occ(\mathcal{A}, t) \vee occ(\mathcal{B}, t) \end{cases}$
3) $ts((\mathcal{A}<\mathcal{B}), t) \stackrel{def}{=} \begin{cases} -t & if \; \neg occ(\mathcal{A}, t) \vee \neg occ(\mathcal{B}, t) \\ & \quad \vee \; occ(\mathcal{A}, t) \wedge occ(\mathcal{B}, t) \\ & \quad \wedge \; ts[\mathcal{A}, ts(\mathcal{B}, t)] < 0 \\ ts(\mathcal{B}, t) \; if \; occ(\mathcal{A}, t) \wedge occ(\mathcal{B}, t) \\ & \quad \wedge \; ts[\mathcal{A}, ts(\mathcal{B}, t)] \ge 0 \end{cases}$

Algebraic Semantics

1)	$ts(\mathcal{A}+\mathcal{B}, t) = min\{ts(A, t), ts(B, t)\} \, [1 - u(\, ts(A, t))\, u(\, ts(B, t))] + \\ \qquad max\{ts(A, t), ts(B, t)\} \, [u(\, ts(A, t))\, u(\, ts(B, t))]$
2)	$ts((\mathcal{A}, \mathcal{B}), t) = max\{ts(A, t), ts(B, t)\} \, [1 - u(-ts(A, t))\, u(-ts(B, t))] + \\ \qquad min\{ts(A, t), ts(B, t)\} \, [u(-ts(A, t))\, u(-ts(B, t))]$
3)	$ts((\mathcal{A}<\mathcal{B}), t) = -t[1 - u(\, ts(B, t))\, u(\, ts(A, ts(B, t)))] + \\ \qquad ts(B, t)[u(\, ts(B, t))\, u(\, ts(A, ts(B, t)))]$

It is possible to show that several properties holds, like the De Morgan property that $ts(-((-\mathcal{A})+(-\mathcal{B})), t)$ is equivalent to $ts((\mathcal{A}, \mathcal{B}), t)$.

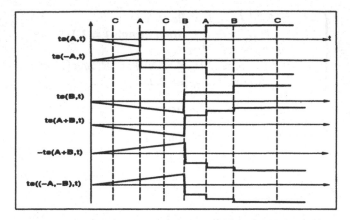

Fig. 4. Examples of *ts* functions with event expression

$$ts(-((-\mathcal{A})+(-\mathcal{B})),t) =$$
$$= -min\{ts(-\mathcal{A},t), ts(-\mathcal{B},t)\}\,[1 - u(\,ts(-\mathcal{A},t))\,u(\,ts(-\mathcal{B},t))]+$$
$$\quad max\{ts(-\mathcal{A},t), ts(-\mathcal{B},t)\}\,[u(ts(-\mathcal{A},t))\,u(\,ts(-\mathcal{B},t)))] =$$
$$= max\{ts(\mathcal{A},t), ts(\mathcal{B},t)\}\,[1 - u(-ts(\mathcal{A},t))\,u(-ts(\mathcal{B},t))]+$$
$$\quad min\{ts(\mathcal{A},t), ts(\mathcal{B},t)\}\,[u(-ts(\mathcal{A},t))\,u(-ts(\mathcal{B},t))] =$$
$$= ts((\mathcal{A},\mathcal{B}),t)$$
□

A graphical proof of this property is shown in Figure 4: for a set of event occurrences (of type A, B, and C, where event type C is not involved in the expression), it shows *ts* functions for both primitive and complex event expressions used in De Morgan proof.

The dual De Morgan property $ts((\mathcal{A}+\mathcal{B}),t) = ts(-(-\mathcal{A},-\mathcal{B}),t)$ and the following properties can be proved analogously.

$\mathcal{E}_1+\mathcal{E}_2 = \mathcal{E}_2+\mathcal{E}_1$	$(\mathcal{E}_1+\mathcal{E}_2)<\mathcal{E}_3 = (\mathcal{E}_1<\mathcal{E}_3)+(\mathcal{E}_2<\mathcal{E}_3)$
$\mathcal{E}_1,\mathcal{E}_2 = \mathcal{E}_2,\mathcal{E}_1$	$(\mathcal{E}_1,\mathcal{E}_2)<\mathcal{E}_3 = (\mathcal{E}_1<\mathcal{E}_3),(\mathcal{E}_2<\mathcal{E}_3)$
$(\mathcal{E}_1+\mathcal{E}_2)+\mathcal{E}_3 = \mathcal{E}_1+(\mathcal{E}_2+\mathcal{E}_3)$	$\mathcal{E}_1<(\mathcal{E}_2+\mathcal{E}_3) = (\mathcal{E}_1<\mathcal{E}_2),(\mathcal{E}_1<\mathcal{E}_3)$
$(\mathcal{E}_1,\mathcal{E}_2),\mathcal{E}_3 = \mathcal{E}_1,(\mathcal{E}_2,\mathcal{E}_3)$	$\mathcal{E}_1<(\mathcal{E}_2,\mathcal{E}_3) = (\mathcal{E}_1<\mathcal{E}_2)+(\mathcal{E}_1<\mathcal{E}_3)$
$\mathcal{E}_1+(\mathcal{E}_2,\mathcal{E}_3)) = \mathcal{E}_1+\mathcal{E}_2,\mathcal{E}_1+\mathcal{E}_3$	$\mathcal{E}_1<\mathcal{E}_2<\mathcal{E}_3 = (\mathcal{E}_1<\mathcal{E}_2)<\mathcal{E}_3$

4.3 Instance-Oriented Case

The definition of the semantics of instance-oriented operators follows a schema similar to that of Section 4.2: after the introduction of basic definitions and instance-oriented composition operators, we show how instance-oriented event expressions are evaluated inside set-oriented expressions.

In the *instance-oriented* case we make use of *ots* functions, which are very similar to *ts* functions, except for the fact that they refer to a single object.

$$ots(\mathcal{E},t,oid) \stackrel{\text{def}}{=} \begin{cases} -t & if\ \forall t'(t' \leq t \wedge \not\exists e \in R(type(e) = \mathcal{E} \\ & \wedge\ timestamp(e) = t' \wedge obj(e) = oid)) \\ t_E & otherwise,\ where \\ & t_E = max\{t'(t' \leq t\ \wedge \exists e \in R(type(e) = \mathcal{E} \\ & \wedge\ timestamp(e) = t' \wedge obj(e) = oid))\} \end{cases}$$

where R is the set of event occurrences to which the event calculus applies. As in the set-oriented case, we introduce an instance-oriented boolean function $oocc(\mathcal{E},t,oid)$, whose value is true when the event has occurred and false otherwise. Note that in the following we will make use again of the function $u(t)$ previously defined.

$$oocc(\mathcal{E},t,oid) \stackrel{\text{def}}{=} \begin{cases} true & if\ u(\ ots(\mathcal{E},t,oid)) = 1 \\ false & otherwise \end{cases}$$

Conjunction: Logical Style Semantics

$$ots(\mathcal{A}\mathbf{+=}\mathcal{B},t,oid) \stackrel{\text{def}}{=}$$
$$\begin{cases} min\{ots(\mathcal{A},t,oid), ots(\mathcal{B},t,oid)\}\ if\ \neg oocc(\mathcal{A},t,oid) \vee \neg oocc(\mathcal{B},t,oid) \\ max\{ots(\mathcal{A},t,oid), ots(\mathcal{B},t,oid)\}\ if\ oocc(\mathcal{A},t,oid) \wedge oocc(\mathcal{B},t,oid) \end{cases}$$

Conjunction: Algebraic Semantics

$$ots(\mathcal{A}\mathbf{+=}\mathcal{B},t,oid) =$$
$$min\{ots(A,t,oid), ots(B,t,oid)\}\ [1 - u(ots(A,t,oid))u(ots(B,t,oid))]+$$
$$max\{ots(A,t,oid), ots(B,t,oid)\}\ [u(ots(A,t,oid))u(ots(B,t,oid)))]$$

The disjunction, negation and precedence operators are similarily extended to the instance-oriented case, and expressed respectively with ",=", "-=" and "<=". So all the properties valid for the set-oriented operators, can be easily extended to the instance-oriented case.

We now show how ots functions are related to ts functions to be evaluated inside set-oriented expressions, and which properties can be proved.

ots to ts	$ts(\mathcal{A}\mathbf{+=}\mathcal{B},t) = min\{ots(\mathcal{A}\mathbf{+=}\mathcal{B},t,oid)\},\ \forall oid \in R$
	$ts(\mathcal{A}\mathbf{<=}\mathcal{B},t) = min\{ots(\mathcal{A}\mathbf{<=}\mathcal{B},t,oid)\},\ \forall oid \in R$
	$ts(\mathcal{A}\mathbf{,=}\mathcal{B},t) = min\{ots(\mathcal{A}\mathbf{+=}\mathcal{B},t,oid)\},\ \forall oid \in R$
	$ts(\mathbf{-=}\mathcal{A},t) = max\{ots(\mathbf{-=}\mathcal{A},t,oid)\},\ \forall oid \in R$
properties	$ots(\mathcal{A},t,oid) \leq ts(\mathcal{A},t)\ \forall oid$
	$ts(\mathcal{A}\mathbf{+=}\mathcal{B},t) \leq ts(\mathcal{A}\mathbf{+}\mathcal{B},t) \qquad ts(\mathcal{A}\mathbf{,=}\mathcal{B},t) \leq ts(\mathcal{A},\mathcal{B},t)$
	$ts(\mathcal{A}\mathbf{<=}\mathcal{B},t) \leq ts(\mathcal{A}\mathbf{<}\mathcal{B},t) \qquad ts(\mathbf{-=}\mathcal{A},t) \geq ts(\mathbf{-}\mathcal{A},t)$

4.4 Specification of rule triggering

The set $\mathcal{T}$ of triggered rules r at time t is defined by the following formula:

$$\mathcal{T} \stackrel{\text{def}}{=} \{r \mid\ R = \{e|e \in EB \wedge r.t_0 < timestamp(e) \leq t\} \wedge$$
$$R \neq \emptyset\ \wedge$$
$$\exists\ t'(r.t_0 < t' \leq t \wedge ts(r.\mathcal{E}, t') > 0)\ \}$$

where $r.t_0$ is the time-stamp of the last consideration of the rule, while $r.\mathcal{E}$ is the triggering event expression of the rule. A rule r belongs to the set of triggered rules $\mathcal{T}$ if the set R of events occurred from the last consideration of the rule is not empty and if there is an instant $t' > r.t_0$ such that the ts function associated to the triggering event expression of r ($r.\mathcal{E}$) is positive.

Observe that the formula defines the set R which the ts function must be computed on, since ts functions are defined for a generic R.

Note that this semantics implies that a rule can be triggered only if something happened ($R \neq \emptyset$); otherwise, the triggering mechanism ends because there is nothing which rules can react to. The reason of this choice is that a rule triggered by a negated event expression were not fired in absence of new event occurrences.

5   Implementation

The introduction of the event calculus language does not change the general architecture of the implementation of Chimera, described in [3], but affects only some specialized component, like the *Event Handler* and the *Trigger Support*: the former deals with event occurrences and stores them into the *Occurred Events* data structure; the latter maintains the current status of active rules (called *triggers* and chooses the trigger to be executed among those activated.

Chimera has a component, called *Block Executor*, which executes non interruptable execution blocks (user transaction lines or rule actions), finishes the execution of a block, it sends all the last generated event occurrences to the *Event Handler* in order to store them into the *Occurred Events* data structure. This data structure is mantaned as an event tree whose leaves are lists of event occurrences of the same type; furthermore, each leaves keeps the time-stamp of the more recent occurrence of the associated event type.

At this moment, the *Event Handler* calls the *Trigger Support* whose task is the determination of new activated rules. The *Trigger Support* maintains in the *Rule Table* the current status of all defined rules; this table is managed by means of a hash table, for fast access, but rules are also linked together by means of a queue on the basis of the priority order. To deal with composite events, each rule has two time-stamps associated to it: one, called *last-consideration*, stores the last consideration time-stamp; the other, called *last-consumption*, stores the time-stamp of the last event consumption, which is either the last consideration time if the rule is *consuming* or the initial time-stamp of the transaction if the rule is *preserving*. Another flag associated to a rule is the *triggered* flag, set to *true* if the rule is triggered or to *false* otherwise.

The *Trigger Support* checks for activated rules in the following way. It looks up into the *Rule Table* for all rules which are not triggered. When it finds one, it computes the ts value for the associated triggering event expression: if the computed value is positive, the rule is then triggered and the *triggered* flag is set to *true* (the rule will be detriggered once after its consideration).

Once new triggered rules are determined, the one to be executed is chosen by means of the rule queue, and passed to the *Block Executor*.

The evaluation of ts should take into account a certain number of things. At first, to determine the ts of a primitive event type is sufficient to query the *occurred events* table to get the last occurrence time-stamp of the desired event type E: if this time-stamp is not less than the value of *last-consideration*, this is the value of $ts(E,t)$, otherwise $ts(E,t)$ value is $-t$ (where t is the current time-stamp). Second, when dealing with instance-oriented operators, it is necessary to keep trace of all monitored events occurred on a single object: to do that, a sparse data structure can be associated to each rule and maintained until the consideration, then it is made empty; each item in this data structure stores the OID of an object affected by some event type since the last consideration and the list of event occurrences affecting that object since the last consideration.

5.1 Static Optimization

$\Delta^+(-\mathcal{E}) \to \Delta^-(\mathcal{E})$ $\Delta^-(-\mathcal{E}) \to \Delta^+(\mathcal{E})$ $\Delta^+(\mathcal{E}_1 < \mathcal{E}_2) \to \Delta^+(\mathcal{E}_2)$ $\Delta^-(\mathcal{E}_1 - \mathcal{E}_2) \to \Delta^-(\mathcal{E}_2)$ $\Delta^+(\mathcal{E}_1 \text{bin-op} \mathcal{E}_2) \to \Delta^+(\mathcal{E}_1), \Delta^+(\mathcal{E}_2)$ $\Delta^-(\mathcal{E}_1 \text{bin-op} \mathcal{E}_2) \to \Delta^-(\mathcal{E}_1), \Delta^-(\mathcal{E}_2)$	$\Delta^+(-=\mathcal{E}) \to \Delta_O^-(\mathcal{E})$ $\Delta^-(-=\mathcal{E}) \to \Delta_O^+(\mathcal{E})$ $\Delta_O^+(-=\mathcal{E}) \to \Delta_O^-(\mathcal{E})$ $\Delta_O^-(-=\mathcal{E}) \to \Delta_O^+(\mathcal{E})$ $\Delta^+(\mathcal{E}_1 <= \mathcal{E}_2) \to \Delta_O^+(\mathcal{E}_2)$ $\Delta_O^+(\mathcal{E}_1 <= \mathcal{E}_2) \to \Delta_O^+(\mathcal{E}_2)$ $\Delta^-(\mathcal{E}_1 <= \mathcal{E}_2) \to \Delta_O^-(\mathcal{E}_2)$ $\Delta_O^-(\mathcal{E}_1 <= \mathcal{E}_2) \to \Delta_O^-(\mathcal{E}_2)$ $\Delta^+(\mathcal{E}_1 \text{bin-op}= \mathcal{E}_2) \to \Delta_O^+(\mathcal{E}_1), \Delta_O^+(\mathcal{E}_2)$ $\Delta_O^+(\mathcal{E}_1 \text{bin-op}= \mathcal{E}_2) \to \Delta_O^+(\mathcal{E}_1), \Delta_O^+(\mathcal{E}_2)$ $\Delta^-(\mathcal{E}_1 \text{bin-op}= \mathcal{E}_2) \to \Delta_O^-(\mathcal{E}_1), \Delta_O^-(\mathcal{E}_2)$ $\Delta_O^-(\mathcal{E}_1 \text{bin-op}= \mathcal{E}_2) \to \Delta_O^-(\mathcal{E}_1), \Delta_O^-(\mathcal{E}_2)$

Fig. 5. Derivation Rules.

$\{\Delta_O^+(\mathcal{E}), \Delta_O^-(\mathcal{E})\} \to \{\Delta_O(\mathcal{E})\}$	$\{\Delta^-(\mathcal{E}), \Delta_O^+(\mathcal{E})\} \to \{\Delta(\mathcal{E})\}$
$\{\Delta_O(\mathcal{E}), \Delta_O^+(\mathcal{E})\} \to \{\Delta_O(\mathcal{E})\}$	$\{\Delta_O(\mathcal{E}), \Delta^+(\mathcal{E})\} \to \{\Delta(\mathcal{E})\}$
$\{\Delta_O(\mathcal{E}), \Delta_O^-(\mathcal{E})\} \to \{\Delta_O(\mathcal{E})\}$	$\{\Delta_O(\mathcal{E}), \Delta^-(\mathcal{E})\} \to \{\Delta(\mathcal{E})\}$
$\{\Delta^+(\mathcal{E}), \Delta_O^+(\mathcal{E})\} \to \{\Delta^+(\mathcal{E})\}$	$\{\Delta^+(\mathcal{E}), \Delta^-(\mathcal{E})\} \to \{\Delta(\mathcal{E})\}$
$\{\Delta^-(\mathcal{E}), \Delta_O^-(\mathcal{E})\} \to \{\Delta^-(\mathcal{E})\}$	$\{\Delta^+(\mathcal{E}), \Delta(\mathcal{E})\} \to \{\Delta(\mathcal{E})\}$
$\{\Delta^+(\mathcal{E}), \Delta_O^-(\mathcal{E})\} \to \{\Delta(\mathcal{E})\}$	$\{\Delta^-(\mathcal{E}), \Delta(\mathcal{E})\} \to \{\Delta(\mathcal{E})\}$

Fig. 6. Simplification Rules.

In general, the computation of the ts function for a given rule is an expensive task, especially if a large rule set has been defined. Our approach is to reduce the ts recomputation, by doing it only when it is highly probable that ts value becomes positive. The goal of the static optimization is to extract conditions on an event expression that guarantees, if not met, that the value of ts cannot become positive (recall rule triggering condition). This analysis should be performed when a rule is defined, and its results used to drive the *Trigger Support* in determining triggered rules.

The occurrence of composite event type $\mathcal{E}$, at time t, is indicated by the fact that the associated function ts assumes a new positive value at time t; thus, we need to check positive variations of ts, that we indicate as $\Delta^+(\mathcal{E})$. Depending on the composition operator, it may depend on positive or negative (indicated with $\Delta^-(\mathcal{E})$) variations of the component event expressions: the first case arises with conjunction, disjunction and precedence, the second one with negation.

This process can be recursively repeated until primitive event types are reached using a proper set of derivation rules (see Figure 5). In these rules for simplicity, we have used the symbol "bin-op" to indicate either the conjunction or the disjunction operator. These rules consider the instance-oriented operators as well; in order to deal with them, they use the symbols $\Delta_O^+(\mathcal{E})$, $\Delta_O^-(\mathcal{E})$ and $\Delta_O(\mathcal{E})$, which are analougous to the previous ones, but indicating *ots* variations for a single object. In the end, it leads to a set $V(\mathcal{E})$ of variations (positive or negative) for primitive event types describing whether or not the value of ts must be recomputed, because it might have changed, when new event occurrences arise; in practice, the conditions described by $V(\mathcal{E})$ are sufficient conditions ensuring that if new arising event occurrences do not match $V(\mathcal{E})$, no recomputation of ts is required.

Set $V(\mathcal{E})$ can be simplified using rules in Figure 6; in particular, with the symbol $\Delta(\mathcal{E})$ both a positive and negative variation is indicated. As an example, consider the following event expression $\mathcal{E}$.

$$\mathcal{E} \equiv (B,(C+(-A)))+(C<=(-=(B<=A)))$$

The $V(\mathcal{E})$ set is obtained applying at first the derivation rules, then the simplification rules, as shown below.

$$
\begin{aligned}
V(\mathcal{E}) = \Delta^+(\mathcal{E})\ &= \\
&= \{\Delta^+(B,(C+(-A))), \Delta^+(C<=(-=(B<=A)))\}\ = \\
&= \{\Delta^+(B), \Delta^+(C), \Delta^-(A), \Delta_O^+(C), \Delta_O^-(B<=A)\}\ = \\
&= \{\Delta^+(B), \Delta^+(C), \Delta^-(A), \Delta_O^+(C), \Delta_O^-(B), \Delta_O^-(A)\}\ = \\
&= \{\Delta^-(A), \Delta(B), \Delta^+(C)\}
\end{aligned}
$$

This particular example shows that we can avoid to monitor positive variations of the function ts associated to A and negative variations of the function ts associated to C.

6 Conclusions

This paper has proposed an extension of event calculus for Chimera, characterized by the following features:

- It requires a minimal set of orthogonal operators.

- It continuously evolves the semantics of Chimera by enabling more sophisticated rule triggering, while preserving the other semantic features of the rule system.
- It supports a formal and efficient evaluation of triggering caused by event expressions of arbitrary complexity, based on the use of a function ts which associates each event expression to an integer value; a rule is triggered when the corresponding ts expression is positive, and not triggered otherwise.
- The function ts is assigned in such a way that certain obvious properties of calculus hold, such as De Morgan's rules or distributivity, associativity, and factoring of precedence expressions. Although this requirement seems mandatory to us, indeed it is not explicitly demontrated by some other event calculus proposals in the literature; achieving this result has required to us a nonobvious "twisting" of the ts functions.
- As an optimization, the evaluation of the ts function is required when certain operations occur which have the potential of "changing the sign" of ts, and can be skipped otherwise.

Given the above features, we believe that the proposed event calculus applies not only to Chimera, but also to all other systems which currently support individual or disjunctive events (including all relational products which support triggers).

References

1. H. Branding, A. Buchmann, T. Kudrass, and J. Zimmermann. Rules in an open system: The reach rule system. In *Proc. of the 1st Int. Workshop on Rules in Database Systems*, pages 127–142, Edimburgh, August 1993.
2. H. Branding, A. Buchmann, T. Kudrass, and J. Zimmermann. Rules in an open system: The reach rule system. In *Proc. of the 1st Int. Workshop on Rules in Database Systems*, pages 111–125, Edimburgh, August 1993.
3. S. Castangia, G. Guerrini, D. Montesi, and G. Rodriguez. Design and implementation for the active rule language of chimera. In *DEXA-95 6th international Workshop and Conference on Database and Expert Systems Applications*, London, UK, September 1995.
4. S. Ceri, P. Fraternali, S. Paraboschi, and L. Tanca. Active rule management in chimera. In *[23]*.
5. S. Ceri and R. Manthey. Consolidated specification of chimera. Technical Report IDEA DE.2P.006.01, November 1993.
6. S. Chakravarthy, E. Anwar, L Maugis, and D. Mishra. Design of sentinel: an object-oriented dbms with event-based rules. *Information and Software Technology*, 36(9), 1994.
7. S. Chakravarthy, V. Krishnaprasad, E. Anwar, and S. K. Kim. Composite events for active databases: Semantics, context and detection. In *Proceedings of the 20th International Conference on Very Large Data Bases*, pages 606–617, Santiago, Chile, September 1994.
8. U. Dayal, A. P. Buchmann, and S. Chakravarthy. The hipac project. In *[23]*.

9. U. Dayal, A. P. Buchmann, and D. R. McCarthy. Rules are objects too: A knowledge model for an active object-oriented database system. In K. R. Dittrich, editor, *Proceedings of the 2nd International Workshop on Object-Oriented Databases*. Springer-Verlag, 1988. LNCS 334.

10. P. Fraternali and L. Tanca. A structured approach for the definition of the semantics of active databases. June 1995. To appear on ACM-TODS.

11. S. Gatziu and K. R. Dittrich. Events in an active object-oriented database system. In *Proc. of the 1st Int. Workshop on Rules in Database Systems*, pages 23–39, Edimburgh, August 1993.

12. N. H. Gehani and H. V. Jagadish. Ode as an active database: Constraints and triggers. In *Proceedings of the 17th International Conference on Very Large Data Bases*, pages 327–336, Barcelona, Spain, September 1991.

13. N. H. Gehani, H. V. Jagadish, and O. Shmueli. Composite event specification in active databases: Model and implementation. In *Proceedings of the 18th International Conference on Very Large Data Bases*, pages 327–338, Vancouver, Canada, 1992. British Columbia.

14. N. H. Gehani, H. V. Jagadish, and O. Shmueli. Event specification in an active object-oriented database. In *1992 ACM SIGMOD*, pages 81–90, San Diego, CA, USA, May 1992.

15. E. N. Hanson. Rule condition testing and action execution in ariel. In *Proceedings of the 17th International Conference on Very Large Data Bases*, pages 327–336, Barcelona, Spain, September 1991.

16. E. N. Hanson, M. Chaabouni, C-H. Kim, and Y-W. Wang. A predicate matching algorithm for database rule systems. *ACM Journal*, pages 271–280, May 1990.

17. ISO-OSI. *SQL3 Document X3H2-94-080 and SOU-003, ISO-ANSI Working Draft*, 1994.

18. R. Maiocchi and B. Pernici. Temporal data management systems: A comparative view. *IEEE Transactions on Knowledge and Data Engineerging*, 3(4):504–524, December 1991.

19. W. Naqvi and M. T. Ibrahim. Rule and knowledge management in an active database system. In *[23]*.

20. N. W. Paton, O. Diaz, M. H. Williams, J. Campin, A. Dinn, and A. Jaime. Dimensions of active behaviour. In *Proc. of the 1st Int. Workshop on Rules in Database Systems*, pages 40–57, Edimburgh, August 1993.

21. M. Stonebraker, A. Jhingran, J. Goh, and S. Potamios. On rules, procedures, chaching, and views in data base systems. In *Proc.ACM-SIGMOD Int. Conference*, pages 281–290, Atlantic City, June 1990.

22. M. Teisseire, P. Poncelet, and R. Cicchetti. Towards event-driven modelling for database design. In *Proceedings of the 20th International Conference on Very Large Data Bases*, pages 327–336, Santiago, Chile, September 1994.

23. J. Widom and S. Ceri. *Active Database Systems*. Morgan Kaufmann, San Matteo, California, August 1995.

24. J. Widom, R. J. Cohrane, and B. G. Lindsay. Implementing set-oriented production rules as an extension od starburst. In *Proceedings of the 17th International Conference on Very Large Data Bases*, pages 275–285, Barcelona, Spain, September 1991.

25. J. Widom and S. J. Finkelstein. Set-oriented production rules in relational database systems. In *Proc.ACM-SIGMOD Int. Conference*, pages 250–270, Atlantic City, June 1990.

Design Tools

Management of Multiple Models in an Extensible Database Design Tool*

Paolo Atzeni[1] and Riccardo Torlone[2]

[1] Terza Università di Roma, c/o DIS, Via Salaria 113, 00198 Roma, Italy
[2] Terza Università di Roma, c/o IASI–CNR, Viale Manzoni 30, 00185 Roma, Italy

Abstract. We describe the development of a tool, called **MDM**, for the management of multiple models and the translation of database schemes. This tool can be at the basis of an integrated CASE environment, supporting the analysis and design of information systems, that allows different representations for the same data schemes. We first present a graph-theoretic framework that allows us to formally investigate desirable properties of schema translations. The formalism is based on a classification of the constructs used in the known data model into a limited set of types. Then, on the basis of formal results, we develop general methodologies for deriving "good" translations between schemes and, more in general, between models. Finally, we define the architecture and the functionalities of a first prototype that implements the various features of the approach.

1 Introduction

During the past decade, the availability and use of automated tools for the analysis and development of information systems have rapidly increased. It has been observed however that, although these tools provide significant benefits to their users with productivity gains, current systems still present various limitations. Hence, a new generation of database design tools is currently under definition and development with the goal of extending functionalities and improving usability [6].

One important reason for the gap between user expectations and reality is the so-called *impedance mismatch* between methodologies and tools [6, Chapter 15], that is, the differences between the model for a given methodolgy and the model effectively supported by a specific CASE tool. A natural way for overcoming this problem is the design of *extensible* systems that support multiple data models and manage the translations of schemes from one model to another. The possibility of customizing the environment (with the definition of a model suitable for a given methodology) is a big step towards the solution of the impedance mismatch problem. Moreover, the availability of different, custom-defined models and their interaction is useful for a number of reasons: (i) to let each designer work with his/her favorite model, yet allowing the exchange, reuse

---

* This work was partially supported by Consiglio Nazionale delle Ricerche and by MURST.

and integration of their work, (ii) to tackle different subproblems with different models, suitable with the specific aspects of each, and (iii) to integrate the results of independent design activities (a need that may arise when companies merge or get involved in a federated project).

The goal of our research is the definition of an environment that allows the specification of conceptual data models by means of a suitable formalism called a *metamodel*. Then, for any two models M_1 and M_2 defined in this way, and for each scheme S_1 (the *source scheme*) of M_1 (the *source model*), it should be possible to obtain a scheme S_2 (the *target scheme*) that be the *translation* of S_1 into M_2 (the *target model*). The solution we have proposed in our preliminary study [3] is based on the following points:

- Since all the constructs used in most known models fall in a rather limited set of categories [11] (lexical type, abstract type, aggregation, generalization, function and a few others) a metamodel can be defined by means of a basic set of *metaconstructs*, corresponding to the above categories. Then, a model can be described by defining its constructs by means of the metaconstructs in the metamodel. It can be argued that this approach is not "complete", as it does not cover all possible models, but it is however easily extensible: should a model with a completely new construct be proposed, the corresponding type could be introduced in the metamodel.
- Since there is no clear notion of when a translation is correct (a lot of research has been conducted in the last decades on scheme equivalence with reference to the relational model [2, 10, 15] or to heterogeneous frameworks [1, 12, 13, 14], but there is no general, agreed definition) we follow a pragmatic approach. We assume that the constructs that correspond to the same metaconstruct have the same semantics, and then we define translations that operate on individual constructs (or simple combinations thereof) as follows: for each construct x of the source scheme such that there is no construct of the same type in a target model M, we try to replace x by other constructs which are instead allowed in M. This work is supported by the use of a predefined set of elementary transformations which implement the standard translations between constructs studied in the literature [6] (which we assume to be correct by definition)[3]. Thus, a complex translation can be obtained just as composition of elementary steps.

To the best of our knowledge, there is not much literature related to the problem we tackle and the goal we set. Some work exists on the idea of a metamodel for the representation of models [5, 12], but the goal is more on the integration of heterogeneous databases in a federated environment [16] than on the translation of schemes to generic target models.

The approach has been studied within a graph-theoretic framework that allows us to define in an uniform way schemes and models [4]. In this framework a model M is defined by means of a set of *patterns* $\mathcal{P}$, directed graphs whose

---

[3] The approach could be called "axiomatic": this is coherent with the difficulty in defining correct translations.

nodes have different types (corresponding to the basic metaconstructs we mentioned above, such as lexical, abstract, aggregation and function) and edges have *ranges* as labels. A partial order can be introduced on patterns, which, suitably extended, becomes a lattice on sets of patterns. Elementary transformations are described on the basis of the patterns they eliminate and the patterns they introduce: clearly, this is only part of their description (we say this is the *signature* of a basic translation, as opposed to its *implementation*), but it is sufficient for studying general properties of translations. Using this description we are able to define and characterize desirable properties of translations, and to develop general methodologies for the automatic generation of translations that satisfy such properties. The results are obtained in an elegant way by means of the lattice framework on patterns.

On the basis of these results, we have defined functionalities and architecture of a first prototype of the system which is currently under development at University of Rome "La Sapienza". On this system, we are testing the various features of the approach in an important case which involves the various versions of the Entity-Relationship model.

The paper is organized as follows. In Section 2 we informally describe our graph-theoretic framework (presented in [4]). In Section 3, we develop practical methods for deriving translations between models and between schemes of different models. In Section 4, we discuss operational issues and present the architecture of a first prototype of the system. In Section 5 we show a brief example of application of our methodology. Finally, in Section 6, we draw some conclusions.

2   A formal approach to the problem

2.1   Structures and Patterns

We have introduced a graph-theoretic formalism that allows us to define in an uniform way schemes and models [4]. In this framework, the components of the metamodel are represented by a fixed set of node types $\mathcal{N}$ and a fixed set of edge types $\mathcal{E}$. In the following, we will refer to a (simple) metamodel that consists of three types of nodes, corresponding to *abstracts* (denoted by the symbol $\triangle$), *aggregations* ($\otimes$), and *lexicals* ($\square$); and six types of edges, corresponding to *functions* (denoted by $\rightarrow$), *multivalued functions* ($\twoheadrightarrow$), *components of aggregation* ($\longrightarrow$), *keys of aggregation* ($\longrightarrow\!\!\!\triangleright$), *keys of abstract* ($\longrightarrow\!\!\bullet$) and *subset relations between abstracts* ($\Rightarrow$). We point out however that the approach can handle a variety of metamodels [4].

Two main notions have been introduced for describing schemes and models: the notion of a *structure*, a directed acyclic graph whose nodes and edges are elements of the metamodel, and the notion of a *pattern*, a tree whose nodes and edges are elements of the metamodel and where the edges have *ranges* as labels. Roughly speaking, a range denotes the number of times a certain edge can appear in a structure. Thus, a pattern describes a collection of structures that involve a specific composition of metaconstructs. A mapping between structures and sets of patterns can be easily defined, so that, given a set of patterns $\mathcal{P}$ and a structure S, we can verify whether S is an *instance* of (that is, can be described by) $\mathcal{P}$. The set of all instances of a set of patterns $\mathcal{P}$ is denoted by $Inst(\mathcal{P})$.

Figure 1 shows an example of a set of patterns and Figure 2 one of its instances (n is a parameter denoting a fixed integer). The instances of this set of patterns may be: (1) isolated abstracts with key combined with (monovalued or multivalued) functions from abstracts to lexicals (pattern P_1), and (2) (one-to-many or many-to-many) binary aggregations of abstracts combined as above (patterns P_2 and P_3).

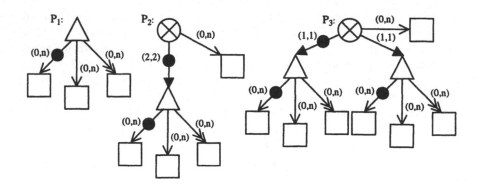

Fig. 1. A set of patterns describing a version of the E-R model.

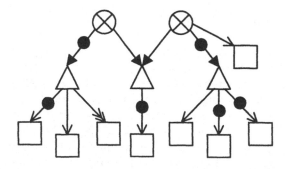

Fig. 2. A structure that is an instance of the set of patterns in Figure 1.

A natural partial order relationship $\preceq$ can be defined on sets of patterns, which yields a practical way to test whether a set of patterns $\mathcal{P}_1$ is *subsumed* by another set of patterns $\mathcal{P}_2$, that is, whether the set of all instances of $\mathcal{P}_1$ is contained in the set of all instances of $\mathcal{P}_2$ (in symbols $Inst(\mathcal{P}_1) \subseteq Inst(\mathcal{P}_2)$). For instance, the set of patterns in Figure 3 subsumes (and therefore describes at least all the structures described by) the set of patterns in Figure 1.

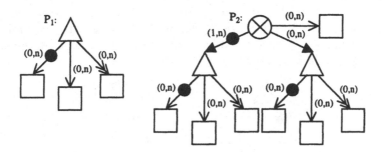

Fig. 3. A set of patterns that subsumes the set of patterns in Figure 1.

Finally, we have shown that the partial order relation $\preceq$ induces a *lattice* on the set of sets of patterns, that is, every finite collection **P** of sets of patterns has both a *greatest lower bound* and a *least upper bound*.

2.2 Models and Schemes

In the framework above, a *model* can be defined by a set of patterns $\mathcal{P}$ and by a labeling function γ that maps each element of $\mathcal{N} \cup \mathcal{E}$, occurring in $\mathcal{P}$, to a label. These labels corresponds to the names given to the constructs in a specific model.

Let us consider for instance the patterns in Figure 1. If we associate the label "Entity" to the node $\triangle$, the label "Relationship" to the node $\otimes$, the label "Domain" to the node $\square$, the label "simple attribute" to the edge $\rightarrow$ and the label "multivalued attribute" to the edge $\twoheadrightarrow$, we define a version of the Entity-Relationship model (E-R for short) involving binary relationships on entities which can have simple and/or multivalued attributes.

Similarly, a *scheme* is defined by a structure S and by a labeling function λ that maps each node and each edge of S to a label. The labels associated with the components of a scheme correspond to names of the various concepts represented in the scheme (e.g., *persons*, *books* and so on).

It is important to note that in our approach, the definition of scheme is completely independent of the notion of model. Clearly, it is possible to establish a correspondence between schemes and models: a scheme $\mathbf{S} = (S, \lambda)$ is *allowed* in a model $M = (\mathcal{P}, \gamma)$ if $S \in Inst(\mathcal{P})$. It is easy to see that, on the basis of the subsumption relationship, we can always verify whether a scheme $\mathbf{S}$ is allowed in a model M.

2.3 Schema translations

A *schema translation* τ is a function that operates on structures by replacing constructs with other constructs. The behavior of a translation can be effectively described in our framework by a pair of patterns $\sigma = (P_1, P_2)$ (we say this is the *signature* of a basic translation, as opposed to its implementation or *body*). Intuitively, a translation signature represents: (1) the constructs eliminated by τ and (2) the constructs introduced by τ, as effect of its execution. For instance, the following translation signature:

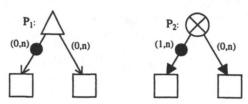

represents a translation that replaces abstracts and (optional) functions from abstracts to lexical (e.g., an entity of the E-R model with its attributes), with an aggregation on lexicals (e.g., a relation of the relational model). Note that, also in this case, a translation signature is independent of a specific model. A *translation rule* has the form $\sigma[\tau]$, where τ is a translation function and σ is a translation signature for τ.

A nice property of translation signatures is that they can be used to characterize translations in terms of sets of patterns, that is, we can compute the *effect* of σ on a set of patterns $\mathcal{P}$, denoted by $\sigma(\mathcal{P})$ (intuitively, $\sigma(\mathcal{P}) = \mathcal{P} - \{P_1\} \cup \{P_2\}$), such that, for each $S \in Inst(\mathcal{P})$, it is the case that: $\tau(S) \in Inst(\sigma(\mathcal{P}))$.

In our approach, a complex translation T can be obtained as a composition of a number of predefined *basic* translation rules: $T = \sigma_1[\tau_1], \ldots, \sigma_k[\tau_k]$. These basic translations implement the standard translations between the constructs present in the traditional data models (e.g., from an entity of the Entity-Relationship model to a relation of the relational model, or from a n-ary relation to a set of binary ones) [3]. The effect of the execution of a complex translation T on a set of patterns $\mathcal{P}$, denoted by $\sigma_T(\mathcal{P})$, can be easily computed as the composition of the effects of the components of T.

2.4 Formal properties of schema translations

Using the results described above, we can formally verify the *correctness* of a translation T from a model $M_s = (\mathcal{P}_s, \gamma_s)$ to a model $M_t = (\mathcal{P}_t, \gamma_t)$, that is, the fact that the application of T to any scheme of M_s always generates a scheme allowed in M_t. Indeed, T is a correct translation from M_s to M_t if and only if $\sigma_T(\mathcal{P}_s) \preceq \mathcal{P}_t$.

One of the major result in [4] is that, as a consequence of the lattice framework, given a *set* of models $\mathcal{M}$, there is no need to specify a translation for each pair of models in $\mathcal{M}$ since, for each model $M_t = (\mathcal{P}_t, \gamma_t) \in \mathcal{M}$, it is sufficient to look a translation from $\mathcal{P}_T$ (the least upper bound of the sets of patterns describing the models in $\mathcal{M}$) to $\mathcal{P}_t$: this translation will be correct from any model in $M_s \in \mathcal{M}$ to M_t. Thus, the number of required translations is linear in terms of the number of involved models, rather than quadratic. It could be said that the set of patterns $\mathcal{P}_T$ represents a *supermodel* containing all the possible combination of constructs used in the various models in $\mathcal{M}$.

Intuitively, a set of basic translation rules $\mathcal{R}$ is *complete* with respect to a set of models $\mathcal{M}$ if it is possible to find a correct translation T, using the rules in $\mathcal{R}$, from any pair of models in $\mathcal{M}$. Another important result in [4] is that we can test completeness by verifying the existence of translations from the supermodel (see above) to the *minimal models* (the models whose description is subsumed by the description of any other model).

We can also formally define a natural measure of the "quality" of a translation from one model to another. Given two different correct translations T_1 and T_2 from a source model $M_s = (\mathcal{P}_s, \gamma_s)$ to a target model $M_t = (\mathcal{P}_t, \gamma_t)$, T_1 *is preferable* than T_2 if $\sigma_{T_2}(\mathcal{P}_s) \preceq \sigma_{T_1}(\mathcal{P}_s) \preceq \mathcal{P}_t$. Intuitively, a translation is preferable than another if the effect of its execution is "closer" to the target model. For instance, a translation towards a version of the E-R model with n-ary relationships that is able to generate both binary and ternary relationships is preferable than another translation that generates only binary relationships.

Finally, two reasonable notions of "optimization" can be defined for translations. A correct translation T from a source model M_s to a target model M_t is *minimal* if there is no rule R in T such that $T - \{R\}$ is correct and preferable to T. A correct translation T from a source model M_s to a target model M_t is *optimal* if there is no other correct translation T' from M_s to M_t, such that T' is preferable to T.

3 Generating translations

On the basis of the formal results on translations, we present in this section a number of practical algorithms for deriving correct and (possibly) optimal translations between models. We will refer to a set of basic translations $\mathcal{R}_b$, which we assume to be predefined, but we will not assume that this set is complete. Then, the algorithm we propose can be also used to test for completeness as described in the previous section.

3.1 Preliminaries

We will start by proposing a method for deriving *reductions*, that is translation between models described by sets of patterns $\mathcal{P}_s$ and $\mathcal{P}_t$ such that $\mathcal{P}_t \preceq \mathcal{P}_s$.[4] Indeed, this is not a restrictive hypothesis since, by the results on the lattice framework, for any pair of models M_1 and M_2 which are not comparable, a translation from their least upper bound (which, by definition, subsumes both

---

[4] Actually, a reduction may contain steps introducing new patterns, but at the end, it always generates a set of patterns that is subsumed by the original set.

of them) to M_1 (M_2) is also a correct translation from M_2 to M_1 (from M_1 to M_2).

A very general method for generating a reduction from P_s to P_t consists in selecting rules that eliminate patterns of P_s which are not allowed in P_t. Unfortunately, this cannot be done naively since the order in which the rule are selected is crucial. In fact, it may happen that a rule that eliminates a certain pattern P is selected before a rule that eliminates another pattern but, as a side effect, introduces P again. A *monotonic* reduction is one in which if it is never the case that a pattern is eliminated in one step and introduced again in a subsequent step. It turns out that this property can be verified locally, by analyzing the set of rules at disposal. Given a set of rules R, the analysis needs the construction of a graph G_R, called *precedence graph* of R, such that the nodes represent the rules in T and there is an edge from a rule R_i to a rule R_j if R_i introduce a pattern which is deleted by R_j. If the graph G_R does not contain any cycle, the set R is *serializable*. Then, it is possible to show that a *serialization* of R (that is, a translation T based on an order of the rules in R that satisfies the partial order induced by G_R) is monotonic.

3.2 Reductions

The first algorithm we propose is based on the assumption that the set of rule of reference R_b is serializable. We will later relax this hypothesis by refining the algorithm. This assumption is indeed very useful since we have proved in [4] that if a set of rules R is serializable, then any serialization based on R produces the same effect and therefore, in this case, the order in which the rule are selected is immaterial. It follows that the basic algorithm is quite simple.

Algorithm REDUCTION-SET-1
Input: *A pair of models $M_s = (P_s, \gamma_s)$ and $M_t = (P_t, \gamma_t)$ such that $P_t \preceq P_s$*
        and a set of basic rules R_b.
Output: *A set of rules $R_{out} \subseteq R_b$.*
begin
{**Part 1: search for a correct translation**}
    $R_{out} := \emptyset; P := P_s;$
    for each $R \in R_b$ do
        if R *deletes patterns in P that are not in P_t*
        then $R_{out} := R_{out} \cup \{R\}; P := P \cup$ {*patterns introduced by R*} endif;
    until $P \preceq P_t$ *or all the rules in R_b have been selected;*
    if $P \npreceq P_t$ then return($\emptyset$) and exit;
{**Part 2: search for a minimal rule set**}
    for each *rule* $R \in R_{out}$ do
        $P' :=$ *the effect of $R_{out} - \{R\}$ on P_s;*
        if $P \preceq P' \preceq P_t$
        then $R_{out} := R_{out} - \{R\}; P := P'$ endif;
    endfor
end.

Given a pair of models $M_s = (\mathcal{P}_s, \gamma_t)$ and $M_t = (\mathcal{P}_t, \gamma_t)$, in the first step the above algorithm selects every rule of $\mathcal{R}_b$ whose effect deletes patterns in $\mathcal{P}_s$, which are not in $\mathcal{P}_t$. At each step, new patterns eventually introduced by selected rules are added to $\mathcal{P}_s$. At the end, if the effect of the selected rules on $\mathcal{P}_s$ (we can speak of effect of a *set* of rules for the property mentioned above) is a set of patterns subsumed by $\mathcal{P}_t$, then the set $\mathcal{R}_b$ is not complete, the algorithm interrupted and the empty set is returned. In the second step, a minimal translation is derived from the set of rules selected in the first step by deleting "redundant" rules (if any), that is, rules whose elimination produce a preferable translation.

Now, assume that the set of rule $\mathcal{R}_b$ is not necessarily serializable. The algorithm can be slightly modified by assuming, in searching for a correct translation, that the selected set of rules is serializable (and so the first two steps of the algorithm are not modified) and then verifying, a posteriori, the serialization of the obtained set of rules. If this set is not serializable, the algorithm is recursively executed over the set of rules $\mathcal{R}_b - \{R\}$, where R is one of the rules that causes the set to be non-serializable. This is summarized in the following general algorithm.

Algorithm REDUCTION-SET-2
Input: *A pair of models $M_s = (\mathcal{P}_s, \gamma_s)$ and $M_t = (\mathcal{P}_t, \gamma_t)$ such that $\mathcal{P}_t \preceq \mathcal{P}_s$*
   and a set of rules $\mathcal{R}_b$.
Output: *A set of rules $\mathcal{R}_{out} \subseteq \mathcal{R}_b$.*
begin
{**Part 1: search for a correct translation**}
{**Part 2: search for a minimal rule set**}
{**Part 3: search for a serializable rule set**}
   $\mathcal{R}_c := \{rules \ in \ \mathcal{R}_{out} \ involved \ in \ a \ cycle \ in \ G_P\}$;
   while $\mathcal{R}_{out}$ *is not serializable and* $\mathcal{R}_c \neq \emptyset$ **do**
      pick a rule R from $\mathcal{R}_c$;
      $\mathcal{R}'_{out} := $ REDUCTION-SET-2$(\mathcal{P}_s, \mathcal{P}_t, \mathcal{R}_c - \{R\})$;
      if $\mathcal{R}'_{out} \neq \emptyset$ **then** $\mathcal{R}_{out} := \mathcal{R}'_{out}$
   endwhile;
   if $\mathcal{R}_{out}$ *is not serializable* **then return**($\emptyset$) **and exit**;
end.

Finally, the algorithm can be further refined for achieving optimality. Similarly to the second algorithm, this can be done by applying the algorithm recursively to the set of rules $\mathcal{R}_b - \{R\}$, where R is a rule that deletes patterns which are indeed in the target model. The rationale under this choice is that there could be "finer" functions which are able to replace the work done by R and which do not require the deletion of patterns in the target model.

3.3   Model translations

According to the properties on translations between models described in Section 2, the general algorithm for deriving model translations is the following:

Algorithm MODEL-TRANSLATION
Input: *A pair of models* $M_s = (\mathcal{P}_s, \gamma_s)$ *and* $M_t = (\mathcal{P}_t, \gamma_t)$
   and a set of rules $\mathcal{R}_b$.
Output: *A correct translation from* M_s *to* M_t.
begin
   $\mathcal{P}_\mathsf{T} :=$ *the least upper bound of* $\mathcal{P}_s$ *and* $\mathcal{P}_t$;
   if $\mathcal{R}_b$ *is serializable*
   then $\mathcal{R}_{out} :=$ REDUCTION-SET-1$(\mathcal{P}_\mathsf{T}, \mathcal{P}_t, \mathcal{R}_b)$
   else $\mathcal{R}_{out} :=$ REDUCTION-SET-2$(\mathcal{P}_\mathsf{T}, \mathcal{P}_t, \mathcal{R}_b)$;
   if $\mathcal{R}_{out} \neq \emptyset$
   then $T_{out} :=$ *a serialization of* $\mathcal{R}_{out}$;
   return(T_{out}) **endif**;
end.

3.4 Schema translations

Let $\mathbf{S}$ be a scheme of a certain model M_s and assume we want to translate $\mathbf{S}$ in another model M_t. Also, let T be a correct and optimal translation from M_s to M_t. Actually, before applying T to $\mathbf{S}$, we can *refine* T adapting the translation to the scheme, by deleting basic steps of T_M that are "useless", that is, steps operating on constructs allowed in M_s, but not used in $\mathbf{S}$. This can be easily done by comparing the constructs of $\mathbf{S}$ and the signatures of the basic translations occurring in T (cf. Section 2). Then, we have the following general algorithm for translating schemes.

Algorithm SCHEMA-TRANSLATION
Input: *A scheme* $\mathbf{S} = (S, \lambda)$ *of a model* $M_s = (\mathcal{P}_s, \gamma_s)$
   and a model $M_t = (\mathcal{P}_t, \gamma_t)$;
Output: *A scheme* $\mathbf{S}_{out} = (S_{out}, \lambda)$ *allowed in* M_t.
begin
   $T :=$ MODEL-TRANSLATION$(M_s, M_t, \mathcal{R}_b)$;
   for each *rule* R *occurring in* T **do**
   if R *has a null effect on* S
   then $T := T - \{R\}$;
   $S_{out} := \tau_T(S)$;
   return$(\mathbf{S}_{out})$;
end.

Clearly, from a practical point of view, the translation between models are computed once for all, at definition time, as described in the next section.

4 Implementation issues

On the basis of the theoretical results and the practical algorithms described in the previous sections, we have designed a tool (whose architecture is reported in

Figure 4), called **MDM** (Multiple Data Models), for the management of multiple models and the translation of schemes. More specifically, the operations offered by this tool are the following:

1. *The definition of a model by means of a (menu-driven) "Model Definition Language".* This language has been designed according to a metamodel that involves (at the moment) the following metaconstructs: lexical types, abstract types, functions, binary and n-ary aggregations and generalizations between abstracts. The task of defining models should not be done by any user, but rather by a specialist that we call *model engineer.* His work is supported by a number of menus (for choosing the appropriate type of construct between the available metaconstructs) and forms. When a new model M is defined, the system automatically generates a *default translation* from the supermodel to M (see below).

2. *The specification of a scheme belonging to a model (previously defined) by means of a graphical "Schema Definition Language".* This language is automatically provided with the definition of a model. More specifically, there is a predefined graphical language for describing schemes that is expressive enough for any scheme allowed in the metamodel. Then, the SDL for a certain model M is obtained by tailoring this general language to the features of M. The work of defining schemes is supported by a flexible graphical interface.

3. *The request for an ad-hoc translation from a source model M_s to a target model M_t.* The translation is permanently stored and can be later applied to any scheme belonging to M_s.

4. *The request for a translation of a scheme into a specific target model.* The system satisfies the request by applying the default translation for the target model, or an ad-hoc translation previously computed if one exists.

The MDM tool consists of the following main components (see Figure 4).

- A **Graphical User Interface.** It allows the interaction with the system by means of a graphical (as well as textual) language. We have used for this component *Diagram Server* [8, 9], a tool developed at the University of Rome "La Sapienza" that allows the editing and the automatic layout of complex diagrams. With this tool, it is possible to customize edges and nodes. This is very useful in our context since, using this feature, the users can also specify their preferred diagram style. The GUI also transforms schemes and models from their *external representation* (diagrams) into an *internal representation* (and vice versa) whose structures have been designed according to the notions of *structure* and *pattern*, respectively.

- A **Model Manager.** It takes as input data model specifications done with respect to the metamodel, and store them in a **Model Dictionary.** The Model Dictionary contains all the data models defined by the model engineer together with a special model, called *supermodel* (SM), that subsumes each other model. The supermodel is automatically generated by the Model Manager by finding the least upper bound of the sets of patterns describing the

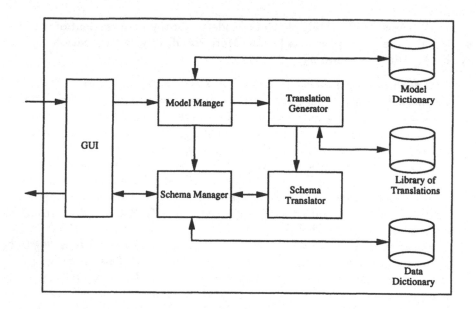

Fig. 4. The architecture of the MDM tool.

models in the Model Dictionary (cf. Section 2). According to the results in Section 3, this model is the model of reference for generating schema translations. The system is able to store, together with a model description, further informations like special constraints on the application of the constructs of the model that cannot be described with the notion of pattern.

- A Schema Manager. Similarly to the Model Manager, this component takes as input the specification of a new scheme **S** of a model M stored in the Model Dictionary, checks whether **S** belongs to the model M (according to the definition of Section 2) and, if so, stores **S** in a Schema Dictionary. The Schema Dictionary is the repository of schemes and can store different versions of the same scheme obtained after modifications and/or translations of the original scheme (this relationship between schemes is implemented by means of suitable *scheme identifiers*). Also in this case, a number of information can be stored together with a scheme like integrity constraints that cannot be expressed with the scheme itself.

- A Translation Generator. This module generates new translations between pairs of models, on the basis of a set of predefined basic translations $\mathcal{R}_b$ permanently stored in the Library of Translations. More specifically, it implements Algorithms REDUCTION-SET and MODEL-TRANSLATION described in Section 3. The computed translations can be modified by the model engineering. All the translations generated by this module can be stored (according to a request done by the Model Manager) in the Library of Translations (for later use).

– A Schema Translator. It actually executes translations of schemes, by applying the appropriate translation generated by the Translation Generator, to
a source scheme received by the Schema Manager. Thus, the module implements Algorithm SCHEMA-TRANSLATION described in Section 3. The output
scheme is returned to the Schema Manager to be stored in the Schema Dictionary or displayed through the GUI. Also in this case, the users can modify
the generated scheme.

The various components of MDM co-operate as follows.

1. When a new model M is defined, the Model Manager first checks whether
   SM subsumes M or not. In the former case, the Model Manager stores M
   in the Model Dictionary and sends a request to the Translation Generator
   for the generation of the *default translation* (a reduction in this case) from
   the SM to M which will be stored in the Library of Translations. In the
   latter case, the Model Manager stores M and generates a new supermodel
   SM' that replaces SM in the Model Dictionary. Then, a request is sent to
   the Translations Generator for translations from the new supermodel SM'
   to *each* other model stored in the Model Dictionary. Those new translations replace the old default translations in the Library of Translations. This
   is indeed a quite complex task that however should not be very frequent.
   Actually, this work can be avoided by permanently storing in the Model
   Dictionary a predefined supermodel that is the *most general model* we can
   define with the given metamodel. However, with this approach, the quality
   of translations is surely degraded (since they are generated with respect to
   a model that is, in many cases, too general).
2. When a new scheme S for a model M is defined, the Schema Manager checks
   whether S is allowed in M (cf. Section 2) by matching S with the definition
   of M, which is stored in the Model Manager. If the matching is successful,
   the scheme can be stored in the Data Dictionary. The schemes can also be
   modified (by saving the old versions if necessary) and deleted.
3. When a user submits a request for a translation of a scheme S to a model M,
   the Schema Translator loads from the Library of Translations, through the
   Translation Generator, either the default translation T_M for the model M
   or an ad-hoc translation (if any). Then, the translation is applied according
   to the algorithm described in Section 3.

During the various activities performed by the tool, some problems may
arise. First, it may happen that the metamodel is not enough expressive for
describing a new data model. However, metaconstructs and other features of the
metamodel are stored in special files accessible by the system only. This files
can be updated quite easily without modifying the code of the components of
the tool. Moreover, it can be the case that the basic translations used to build
more complex translations are not sufficient for a certain translation. This can
be solved by adding new basic translations in the Library of Translations, as
well as modifying the old once. It turns out that MDM is easily adaptable and

provides a very flexible framework for the development of more complex and general environments.

5 An example of application

In this section we briefly present a practical example of application of methodologies and tools described in the previous sections.

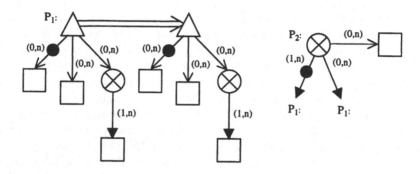

Fig. 5. A set of patterns describing M_s: a version of the E-R model.

We will consider two models M_s and M_t (both of them are indeed different versions of the E-R model) and derive a translation from M_s to M_t. Then, this translation will be applied to a specific schema of M_s. The model M_t is the one described by the set of patterns in Figure 1. We recall that this model is a version of the E-R model that involves binary relationships on entities which can have simple and/or multivalued attributes (that is, attributes whose instances are sets of values). The model M_s is instead described by the set of patterns reported in Figure 5. It is possible to see that this model is a version of the E-R model involving n-ary relationships on entities, which can have simple and/or composite attributes (that is, attributes whose instances are sets of tuples of values), and is-a relationships between entities. The translation from M_s to M_t requires the following basic steps:

- The translation of n-ary relationships in binary ones;
- The translation of is-a relations between entities in relationships on entities (actually, other translations could be applied here);
- The translation of composite attributes in new entities;
- The translations of functions between entities with relationships on entities (this function is needed to eliminate a side-effect produced by step 3 as described in the following).

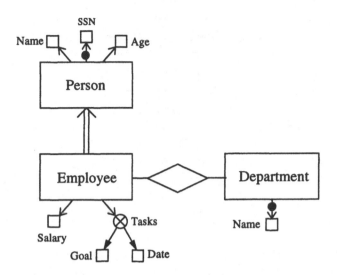

Fig. 6. A schema for the model M_s described by the patterns in Figure 5.

Now consider the scheme of the model M_s in Figure 6. Note that this scheme uses a notation that is slightly different from the notation used to describe the model (specifically, entities are represented by rectangles and relationships between entities are represented by rhombs) but this is coherent with the possibility, offered by the tool, of customizing the diagrammatic notation for the model constructs. The scheme represents persons and employees. The employees have a salary and work in departments having a name. Tasks with specific goals, to be executed within a certain date, are assigned to employees. This is represented by means of a composite attribute of the entity Employee.

By applying the translation described above, we obtain the scheme reported in Figure 7. Actually, the first step does not produce any effect on the scheme since the relationships in original scheme are already binary (this step can be indeed deleted before the execution of the translation as described in Section 3). The second step translates the is-a relation between the entities Person and Employee in a relationship on them. The third step translates the composite attribute Tasks of the entity Employee in a new entity. This step generates an undesired side-effect: a function from the entity Employee to the entity Tasks, which is a construct not allowed in the target model. This construct is eliminated in the last step by replacing it with a relationship between the involved entities.

6 Conclusions

In this paper we have presented theoretical and practical aspects of the development of MDM: a tool for the management of different data models and the

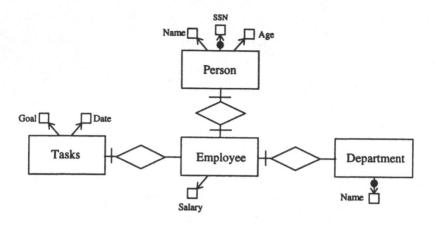

Fig. 7. The result of the application, to the scheme in Figure 6, of the translation from the model M_s (described by the patterns in Figure 5) to the model M_t (described by the patterns in Figure 1).

translations of schemes from one model to another. We have started by presenting a graph-theoretic framework for the description of models and schemes. This formal framework allows us to compare different data models and to define and characterize various interesting properties of schema translations. We have then derived general methodologies for deriving translations that satisfy those desirable properties. On the basis of these results, we have designed architecture and functionalities of a tool that supports the desired features, showing the feasibility of the approach and the practical impact of the formal results.

We believe that this research brings a contribution not only to the development of new generation database design tools, but also to several problems related to cooperative activities within heterogeneous database environments. The formal basis and the prototypical tool yield promising contexts for further theoretical and practical investigations, on these and related issues. For instance, it could be very interesting to extend the approach presented in this paper to behavioral models (e.g. DFD, SADT). Currently, from a theoretical point of view, we are working on extending the results to more general cases. From a practical point of view we are working on the development of a solid prototype of the system by testing its capabilities in complex cases.

References

1. S. Abiteboul and R. Hull. Restructuring hierarchical database objects. *Theoretical Computer Science*, 62(3):3–38, 1988.
2. P. Atzeni, G. Ausiello, C. Batini, and M. Moscarini. Inclusion and equivalence between relational database schemata. *Theoretical Computer Science*, 19(2):267–285, 1982.

3. P. Atzeni and R. Torlone. A metamodel approach for the management of multiple models and the translation of schemes. *Information Systems*, 18(6):349–362, 1993.

4. P. Atzeni, R. Torlone. Schema Translation between Heterogeneous Data Models in a Lattice Framework. In *Sixth IFIP TC-2 Working Conference on Data Semantics (DS-6), Atalanta*, pages 218–227, 1995.

5. T. Barsalou and D. Gangopadhyay. M(DM): An open framework for interoperation of multimodel multidatabase systems. In *International Conference on Data Engineering*, pages 218–227, Tempe, AZ, February 1992.

6. C. Batini, S. Ceri, and S.B. Navathe. *Conceptual Database Design, an Entity-Relationship Approach*. Benjamin and Cummings Publ. Co., Menlo Park, California, 1992.

7. P.P. Chen. The entity-relationship model: toward a unified view of data. *ACM Trans. on Database Syst.*, 1(1):9–36, March 1976.

8. G. Di Battista, G. Liotta, and S. Vargiu. Diagram Server. *Journal of Visual Languages and Computing*, 1995. To appear.

9. G. Di Battista et al. A tailorable and extensible automatic layout facility. *IEEE Workshop on Visual Languages*, pages 68–73, 1991.

10. R.B. Hull. Relative information capacity of simple relational schemata. *SIAM Journal on Computing*, 15(3):856–886, 1986.

11. R.B. Hull and R. King. Semantic database modelling: survey, applications and research issues. *ACM Computing Surveys*, 19(3):201–260, September 1987.

12. L.A. Kalinichenko. Methods and tools for equivalent data model mapping construction. In *EDBT'90 (Int. Conf. on Extending Database Technology), Venezia, Lecture Notes in Computer Science 416*, pages 92–119, Springer-Verlag, 1990.

13. Y.E. Lien. On the equivalence of database models. *Journal of the ACM*, 29(2):333–362, 1982.

14. R.J. Miller, Y.E. Ioannidis, and R. Ramakrishnan. The use of information capacity in schema integration and translation. In *Eighteenth International Conf. on Very Large Data Bases, Dublin*, 1993.

15. J. Rissanen. On equivalence of database schemes. In *ACM SIGACT SIGMOD Symp. on Principles of Database Systems*, pages 23–26, 1982.

16. A.P. Sheth and J.A. Larson. Federated database systems for managing distributed database systems for production and use. *ACM Computing Surveys*, 22(3):183–236, 1990.

17. D. Tsichritzis and F.H. Lochovski. *Data Models*. Prentice-Hall, Englewood Cliffs, New Jersey, 1982.

An Assessment of Non-Standard DBMSs for CASE Environments

Udo Kelter, Dirk Däberitz

Praktische Informatik, Fachbereich Elektrotechnik und Informatik
Universität Siegen, D-57068 Siegen, Germany
kelter, dirk@informatik.uni-siegen.de

Abstract. Many new non-standard database management systems (NDBMSs) and data models have been proposed with the promise to facilitate the construction of better engineering environments and tools and to solve integration problems in environments. However, there is hardly any evidence or experience to what extent these goals are actually met. This paper summarizes experience gained in several major experiments in which different classes of tools in CASE environments (graphical editors, consistency checkers, transformators) have been built using several design approaches and architectures. It turns out that, regrettably, most NDBMSs proposed so far have quite substantial weaknesses and that their overall value for tool designers is fairly modest. The paper first shows that advantages are only possible if the tool architecture is "redundancy-free" and if the tools operate directly on the database. Assuming this "DB-oriented" architecture, we examine typical features of an NDBMS (schema management, integrity controls, transactions etc.) with respect to their usefulness in tool implementation. We discuss the resulting requirements on the performance and on the design of the API and the runtime kernel of the NDBMS. We also point out useful new features which do not seem to exist in any NDBMS so far.

1 Introduction and Overview

Database systems for CASE environments have been the subject of intensive research for the last ten years. Many new *non-standard database management systems* (NDBMSs) and data models have been proposed, mostly based on the ER-approach or the object paradigm and including features like versioning, flexible schema management, support of distribution, new transaction models etc. These new data models and NDBMSs were supposed to:

1. make the construction of tools and integrated environments easier. This means that the amount of code needed to write tools should become less in comparison with conventional tools working on file-systems[1], and that this

---

[1] This should be seen in analogy to conventional applications, where fairly complex hand-written algorithms can be replaced by a simple query. Here, the total amount of code and the implementation effort are significantly reduced through the DBMS.

code should be more easily maintainable. This goal is mainly to be achieved by moving complex functionality from the tool into the NDBMS.

2. allow better tools to be built, i.e. to realize functionalities and features in tools which are too costly to implement with conventional file systems

3. make a higher degree of data integration between the tools of an environment possible

Ultimately, these goals deal with the engineering of tools and environments, i.e. these are software engineering goals applied to tool code. In this paper, we will very much take the attitude of a tool writer who asks himself *what real benefits can be gained by using an NDBMS to manage development data.*

In contrast to the rich literature about features of NDBMSs, there are only very few papers describing experience to what extent the goals mentioned above are actually met by NDBMSs ([5, 10] are some of the rare examples), why these goals are not met and how NDBMSs should be changed (in their interface or architecture) in order to remedy the situation. This paper tries to fill this gap.

In our group, we have investigated tools and environments built on top of different NDBMSs. We have ported existing CASE tools and implemented new tools, mainly graphical editors (for net-like languages such as ER-Diagrams, Petri-nets, state-transition diagrams etc.), but also consistency checkers, correction tools, transformators etc. [3, 4, 11, 14, 23, 25, 27] on top of the NDBMS H-PCTE. We have experimented with alternative designs for the same or similar CASE tools and have evaluated the effort needed to build these tools and assessed their maintainability and other qualities.

H-PCTE [13, 15], our own prototype NDBMS, implements the NDBMS defined in the international standard PCTE [22]. It falls into the class of systems based on the ER approach and offers extensive data modelling facilities, dynamic schema management, navigational access, non-standard transactions, transparent distribution, access controls with support of working groups etc. H-PCTE offers some additional features such as non-navigational access [8, 12] and extended transaction facilities. Most problems and experiences reported here apply, however, to virtually all NDBMSs which are either object-oriented or based on the ER approach[2].

A first important experience is that the first goal mentioned above is *not* met if the file system is just replaced by an NDBMS (without changing the design of a tool), most notably in the important class of editors. From a tool writer's point of view, parsers and unparsers (which convert the textual representation of a document stored in a file into a runtime data structure and vice versa) are just replaced by similar or even more complex software which scans the database and converts the database contents into a runtime data structure and

---

[2] However, our results are *not* applicable to CAD tools and other types of engineering tools which handle significantly larger amounts of data since, due to performance problems, the tool architecture proposed in section 2.2 is not usable here.

vice versa. Things even appear to get worse through the database since the tool writer – in addition to writing the "real tool" – now has to develop a database schema and to control (and to get familiar with) all sorts of complicated database mechanisms and features. These problems explain why many tool writers are extremely reluctant to use NDBMSs.

Section 2 explains the issues in more detail and shows that the real problem is the "redundant" implementation of the functionality of a tool within the DBMS and within the tool code. We conclude that an essential precondition for NDBMSs to be useful is a redundancy-free tool architecture. We will assume such an architecture, which is optimized for exploiting an underlying NDBMS, in the rest of the paper.

We then examine several areas of NDBMS services and their potential to facilitate certain parts of a tool's implementation. Examples of such areas and their potential benefit are:

– to automatically generate document-type specific menus in editors from the database schema

– to integrate different tools and to filter displayed data by means of views (or external schemata)[3]

– to propagate modifications between different windows using a notification mechanism

– to realize undo commands in editors using transactions

– to realize consistency tests using consistency constraints in the DB schema

Although the DB features mentioned above certainly have a potential to facilitate the implementation of tools, their usefulness is, according to our experience, often very limited because certain less obvious technical issues in the design of the NDBMS are not adequately solved. We will show that, for these features to be really useful, the NDBMS must fulfill certain conditions, notably with respect to performance and the design of the application program interface (API). We will also show that some of these requirements have a substantial impact on how the kernel of the NDBMS has to be implemented and optimized.

2   Issues in the Implementation of CASE Tools

In this section, we will assume that the reader is at least superficially familiar with one of the many (upper or lower) CASE environments on the market, e.g. ADW, Software through Pictures, ProMod, etc. etc. An environment typically comprises several graphical editors and browsers, checking functions (either as separate tools or embedded within editors), transformators, report generators etc.

---

[3] Since all OODBMSs we are aware of do not support views and since – as will be shown in this paper – views as extremely important, we will primarily discuss NDBMSs based on the ER model in this paper.

In the following, we will mostly refer to graphical editors for net-like modelling languages such as entity relationship diagrams, Petri nets, OOA/OOD diagrams or data flow diagrams. Although these graphical editors support different modelling languages, they basically appear quite similar, they only differ in the set of symbols for nodes and connections within a diagram, in the set of items in the menus for the manipulation of nodes and connections and their attributes, and in the consistency test or transformations offered for their modelling language. All tools offer basic editing commands for, e.g., creating and deleting nodes and connections in a diagram. Most tools offer in addition an undo command, cut and paste facilities, options for selectively displaying a diagram (e.g. an OOA diagram without attributes) and other more advanced features. We will discuss some of them in more detail later.

2.1 Conventional Tool Architectures

Editors are typically based on two underlying systems: a user interface management system (UIMS) and a data storage system, either a file system or an (N)DBMS. Virtually all tools based on file systems have the very coarse structure shown below (examples of detailed descriptions can be found in [7, 10, 30]):

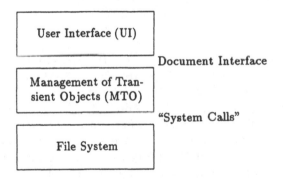

A diagram is typically stored in the contents of a file, which has to obey a certain syntax. The user commands cannot be directly executed in the contents of the file, therefore the module called "Management of Transient Objects" (MTO) is necessary. This module maintains copies of diagrams in the runtime system of the tool. When the user "opens" a document, the file is parsed and a transient copy of the document is produced. When the user "closes" or saves a document, the transient copy is unparsed into a file contents. The MTO module offers not only operations to load or store a document, but also to create an empty document, create or delete nodes or connections, to read or set attributes of nodes or connections, etc.; all the editing operations check the consistency constraints which apply for this particular document type.

The user interface identifies the command to be executed, asks the user for input parameters where necessary, and invokes typically one operation of the MTO module which "really" executes the command. Then it displays the results and modifies the contents of its window.

A number of details of both modules discussed above depend on the specific document type, e.g:

- the entries in the menus offered by the user interface
- the layout of symbols
- consistency tests (for intra-document and inter-document constraints)
- the attributes of nodes or connections
- specific editing commands

etc. Both modules must therefore be re-implemented for each document type. According to several major experiments we made, the MTO module alone has a typical size between 3,000 and 8,000 lines of code, depending on the complexity of the diagram type. The user interface module was typically smaller since we used a very powerful UI toolkit (ET++ [6]).

An environment typically comprises 5 to 10 graphical editors for different languages; thus the size of the code for all editors can easily reach 50,000 LOC; this is a major problem for the initial implementation and later maintenance.

The use of files for storing development data has a number of well-known disadvantages (low data independence of tools, low data integration, etc.). The question to be asked now is what can be gained if the file system is just replaced by an NDBMS with a suitable database schema in the above architecture. Instead of parsing file, data are checked out from the database and later checked in.

Of primary interest is the question whether the amount of code can be reduced significantly. In section 1 several services of an NDBMS and their potential exploitation in tools have been listed. Unfortunately, virtually no service of an NDBMS can be successfully exploited in the desired way. We illustrate this with consistency testing: Consistency criteria defined in a schema are checked only when a document is checked in into the database. However, this is too late, the basic consistency tests must be performed after each editing command of a user. Thus, although the tests are implemented in the NDBMS, they must be implemented again in the MTO module! This is what we call the *redundancy problem* of architectures based on the check-out / check-in paradigm: Data is stored redundantly in the database *and* in the MTO module (possibly in different type systems), services are implemented redundantly in the database *and* in the MTO module.

This redundancy is highly undesirable from the point of view of software engineering and causes all sorts of problems, particularly with respect to the maintenance of the tools[4]. Things are even made worse by the fact the User

---

[4] A good example of a less obvious, but hard problem arising in redundant architectures is the problem of versions of tools which may have (slightly) different associated schemata. Since different versions of the tool must operate in parallel, the type names in their associated database schemata must differ. On the other hand, different versions of the tool, which are typically forward compatible, should be able to operate on the same data as much as possible. Thus, one needs a mechanism which binds type names appearing in the tool code "very lately" to type names in the data base (e.g. as proposed in [1]).

Interface module also depends on the particular document type. According to our experience, editors implemented using the above redundant architecture are extremely difficult to maintain.

2.2 A Redundancy-Free Tool Architecture

There are two basic approaches to solve the redundancy problem: get rid of the DBMS or get rid of the MTO module. We chose the second approach and a "DB-oriented" architecture of tools which allows us to exploit database services. This architecture has the following basic features:

- User commands are *executed directly in the database*. No copies of the data are maintained in the tool (except in rare cases for performance optimization). The tool manages *references to objects* in the database rather than *copies* of the data.
- There is no encoding of relevant data structures in long fields. All the relevant *fine-grained structures* are modelled in the DB schema.
- Each graphical object has *one* corresponding object in the database.
- The UI module is "generic" in the sense that it dynamically interprets the external schema through which it accesses the database. It can be regarded as a browser which is dynamically configured by its current external schema.

More details of this architecture are described in [4].

General Performance Requirements. A first important consequence due to directly accessing objects in the database is

> **Requirement 1:** The NDBMS must have a very high average response time of around 1 millisecond per basic operation (reading or writing of attributes, creating or deleting of objects or relationships, etc.).

This performance cannot be achieved with conventional DBMS architectures in which the database can only be accessed through a separate server process, because the communication delays between application process and server process would be far too high. Consequently, application code, NDBMS code and buffers must be in the same process (*single process data access architecture*), all relevant data must be cached in main memory, and logging should be asynchronous (i.e. the write ahead log protocol should not be applied). An example of this architecture is the kernel of the H-PCTE system [13, 15].

Basic Requirements on Schema Management. Further consequences due to the interpretation of the database schema are:

> **Requirement 2:** The NDBMS must provide external schemata (or views) since the conceptual schema of an environment will contain other types which are not relevant for a single editor.

> **Requirement 3:** The NDBMS must offer an API through which the tool can *efficiently* retrieve all relevant information about the current external schema.

The queries about type information must be performed very efficiently. In self-referential NDBMSs, which represent schemata (i.e. type definitions) by objects, the queries must *not* be implemented by accessing the object base and by interpreting the objects which represent the schema. Instead of this, a cache containing all information about the types in the current external schema must be constructed.

In the following sections, we will assume a redundancy-free architecture and generic, interpretative editors, checking tools, correctors, or other tools built in the same way, and we will discuss in more detail whether and how individual DB features can be exploited.

3   Generation of Menus

An editor typically provides a user with a large set of commands which are offered in the form of pull-down menus, pop-up menus, separate windows with an icon for each command or in further forms. Figure 1 shows one of numerous possible layouts. The actual form and layout does not matter here, so we will simply speak about menus and items in menus.

The commands can be classified into two categories: firstly *"generic"* (i.e. not document-type-specific) commands which

- create an empty diagram
- display a specified diagram
- move nodes or intermediate points of connections
- undo and redo the last commands
- close the tool

and secondly *document-type-specific* commands which

- create nodes or connections of certain types in a diagram (s. menus labelled "Elements" and "Connections" in figure 1),
- edit attributes (s. menus labelled "Edit/Modify" and "Connections" in figure 1); the actual editing is performed in a further window which is opened after having chosen a menu item.

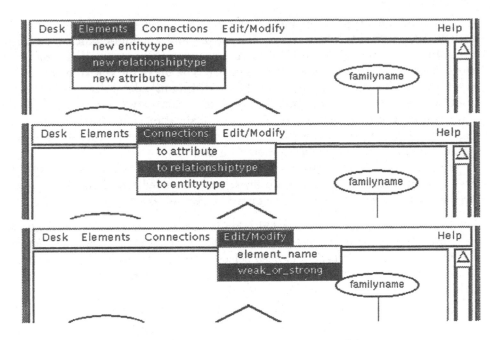

Fig. 1. Menus of an editor for ERA models

In this section, we are going to discuss only document-type-specific commands.

In redundant architectures, the document-type-specific menus and their items are typically hard-wired in the code of the UI module. Special care must be taken that the set of node types offered in the menu for creating nodes is consistent with the set of node types implemented in the MTO module and with the schema in the database. The same observation applies to the set of connection types and to the attributes of nodes and connections.

The obvious idea to avoid these problems is to generate these menus from the database schema. With this assumption we have to reinforce the requirement that the NDBMS must offer efficient facilities to dynamically query the external schema of an application.

The "Elements" menu can now be dynamically constructed as follows: The schema should have one object type called selectable_node and all object types which represent selectable node types (e.g. in a DFD: process, data store, external connector) should be subtypes of selectable_node. The UI module simply asks for the names of all subtypes of selectable_node and constructs the menu from this list of names.

The creation of connections is somewhat more complicated. There can be several admissible types of connection between two nodes. Assume for example an ER diagram containing several entity types and a symbol which represents the subtype relationship (half-circle)[5]. A connection between a half-circle and an entity type can either express that the entity type plays the role of a supertype or the role of a subtype. This should be distinguished by different types of connections (although their graphical representation may be the same). Some ER languages further distinguish between specializations and generalization and use differently shaped arrows for the associated subtype relationships. Here again, different connection types should be used.

The essential point here is that the UI must ask the user who wants to create a connection which type of connection is intended and should present the applicables choices in a menu. The question can be asked:

- after the origin object is selected (this is assumed in figure 1): then all the connection types which can go out from the selected object should be offered[6]. After a connection type has been selected, the destination object, which is selected later, may have the wrong type; in this case an error message must be produced (see section 7.2).

- after the origin object and the destination object are selected: then all the connection types which can connect the selected objects should be offered in a menu if there are 2 or more such connection types. If there is just one such type, this type is automatically chosen. If there is no such type, an error message is displayed.

In either case, we get the following requirement:

> **Requirement 4:** The NDBMS must enable a tool to retrieve the set of admissible relationship types which can go out from a given object type, and the set of admissible destination object types of a relationship type. The type system of the NDBMS must support all the involved notions.

Similar arguments as above apply to the "Edit/Modify" menu, which displays the editable attributes of a selected node or connection. We can derive

> **Requirement 5:** The NDBMS must enable a tool to retrieve the set of attributes of a given object type or relationship type.

The above requirements are *not* fulfilled by most NDBMSs, notably those which assume a fixed conceptual schema (often in C-notation). Self-referential NDBMSs which represent all the details of the schemata by objects basically allow to retrieve all necessary information, however without caching one runs into serious performance problems.

---

[5] For reasons which are beyond the scope of this discussion, these symbols have also to be modelled as objects in the data base. A similar example is the part-of relationship between classes in OOA diagrams.

[6] Unapplicable connection types should either be "greyed out" or not be included in the menu at all.

4 Selective Display

Another feature of many editors is their ability to selectively display a diagram. For example in an OOA diagram, a user may wish to see – as a survey – only the classes and their subtype structure, but not the names of the attributes and operations of the classes, the part-of structure and all the other structures between classes. One can image several degrees to selectively display a diagram; we call them *selective modes* of the tool. We assume that the selection is defined in terms of the *types* of nodes, connections and attributes which are not to be displayed. Important requirements on this feature are:

- It must be possible to switch at any time between different selective modes. The switching must be performed in the same speed as normal user commands.
- It must be possible to perform all sensible update operations in a selective mode, particularly to create and delete nodes and connections and to modify their attributes.
- The menus and all other aspects on the interaction with the user must be adapted to the current selective mode. For example, if attribute names of classes in an OOA diagram are not shown, then there should be no menu item to add, to delete or to rename attributes of a class (or these menu items should not be selectable).

The last requirement leads to a lot of special cases and causes a significant implementation effort (which can be seen as the reason why most CASE tools do not offer selective display).

If we assume again an underlying NDBMS and direct operation of the tool on the database, then the obvious idea is to realize selective modes through different external schemata. We have shown elsewhere that this idea works very well (in the tools described in [4]), but only if the underlying NDBMS meets certain requirements:

> **Requirement 6:** The external schema mechanism must at least be able to filter data based on their type, e.g. to make relationships of a certain type invisible (which corresponds to projections in relational DBMSs).

It appears to be less important to support selections.

> **Requirement 7:** All the external schemata must support updates.

This is, of course, partly a question of the design of the schema. However, systems which have materialized views or views based on non-closed query languages (which return complex values instead of references to objects) are not acceptable.

> **Requirement 8:** A running application must be able to change its external schema. The switching of external schemata must be performed in fractions of a second.

> **Requirement 9:** The schema query facilities must apply to the external schemata.

> **Requirement 10:** References to objects must remain valid after the modification of the external schema.

The last requirement is not due to the objects displayed in a diagram (these objects must be re-scanned anyway), but rather due to objects which represent the diagram as a whole or which serve for other auxiliary purposes.

> **Requirement 11:** It must not be necessary to stop the current transaction in order to modify the external schema. Locks on objects must be preserved (even for objects which have become invisible).

More details on transactions are discussed below.

4.1 Implementation Issues

The requirement to provide fast switching between different external schemata has a very significant impact on how the NDBMS has to be implemented.

Schema Caches. Firstly, we recall that due to the general performance requirements, all the data must be cached in the application process and that the NDBMS front end must use a *schema cache*, a special data structure which supports very efficient queries about the current schema. The construction of these caches can be fairly expensive[7]. Requirement 8 implies that the front end must manage *several* schema caches.

If a user session is partially undone using the rollback mechanism of the DBMS (s. 8) then changes of external schema should also be undone. This implies that the backward log should have corresponding types of records.

Two-Level Schema Mechanism. A second, more subtle problem has to do with security. Generally, external schemata are an important mechanism to protect data from unauthorized access. A user can be restricted to use only certain external schemata. In design environments, different developers may play different roles and may have different associated access rights.

In a secure DBMS implementation, all the parts of the database which reside in the buffers of the front end must therefore be filtered according to the rights implied by the current external schema. Different external schemata will require different filters; therefore after a switch of the external schema, the buffer might contain data which are not readable according to the new schema. The straightforward solution is to pass back all the buffers contents to the server, to clear

---

[7] In H-PCTE, this data structure is constructed by scanning the metabase (i.e. the objects which represent the type definitions), which typically reside on another server. The resulting execution time is around 2 – 10 seconds.

them, and to reconstruct them according to the new external schema. Obviously, this solution is far too inefficient and the overhead is not really required: an external schema which realizes a selective mode corresponds to a subset of the rights of a user. A better solution would be a "two-level" mechanism for external schemata:

- The "outer" level deals with the normal aspects of external schemata. The schema query facilities apply to this level.
- The "inner" level deals with the filtering of data which are passed from the DB server to the front end. The external schema on this level comprises the "complete" set of types of the application, i.e. the union of all types appearing in the different external schemata

An application must have means to set both schemata explicitly. The schema for the inner level would be set only once when the tool ist started.

5 Multiple Window Tools

Assume an editor for data flow models which has one window in which the hierarchy of DFDs is displayed and several other windows each displaying one DFD. If, for example, the name of a process or its refining DFD is changed then this change should be automatically propagated to all other windows which display the same information, no matter in which form. This problem leads to

> **Requirement 12:** The NDBMS should provide a notification mechanism which enables a tool to be informed about changes of data it displays.

Such a tool has to explicitly inform the DBMS about the objects and the type of changes it wants to be informed about.

A problem is now the amount of information delivered by the NDBMS in case of a notification. Many notification mechanisms provide the notified application only with the mere fact of a change ("an attribute of object X has been changed"; "a new node has been inserted in diagram Y"). The notified application must then retrieve the new data from the data base. However, without knowledge about the prior state of the diagram, it can be difficult to decide which parts of a displayed diagram need correction and, in many cases, the editor must read all the objects for whole diagram and construct the whole diagram from scratch. This is fairly inefficient. A far more efficient solution is to correct just the necessary parts of the window. This should be supported be the notification mechanism as follows:

> **Requirement 13:** The notification mechanism should deliver all relevant information about the event which has caused a notification. The tool should not have to issue further queries to get the information needed to correct a window.

For example, if several attributes of an object are modified then the notification message should contain a list of attribute names (or references) and for each attribute the new value.

6 Multiple View Environments

The data flow model tool mentioned above is just one example of an environment which comprises several tools (or tool fragments) which operate on the same data through different views. The usefulness of the Multiple View approach to build environments has been shown elsewhere [7, 18, 19, 24]. We emphasize once more the importance of a view mechanism in NDBMSs.

In section 2.3, we showed that our tool architecture requires the DBMS and the tool code to be in the same operating system process (*single process data access architecture*). If a running environment consists of several concurrently running tools (e.g. one for each window on the screen) then the code for all these tools must be bound into one executable program; this executable program is run as an operating system process and, herein, each tool must be executed as a *light weight process* (or thread). Thus we get

> **Requirement 14:** The NDBMS should enable a client process to start several light-weight processes (LWP). Each LWP must have its own external schema and must be able to replace it at any time (s. Requirement 8).

The LWPs within one operating system process must not be protected by locks against each other; concurrent access to the same data is dealt with by notification.

7 Checking of Consistency Constraints

7.1 Consistency Levels

Most NDBMSs allow users to define consistency constraints in a schema. Non-conventional applications have fairly complex data structures and related consistency constraints; this has triggered a lot of research into powerful languages for expressing consistency constraints, trigger mechanisms etc.

However, it turns out that the NDBMS features are not generally applicable for a simple reason: Users want to be able (1) to produce inconsistent initial or intermediate states of a document (e.g. ER diagrams where an entity type name appears twice, because a part of the diagram has been copied), and (2) to store these intermediate states at any time (e.g. after a message on the screen "shutdown in 20 seconds!! save your files!!"). This is an extremely strong requirement.

As a result of this, at least two, possibly more consistency levels (e.g. called "unchecked" / "partially checked" / "completely checked" etc.) have to be supported. The lowest level typically enforces only the most basic "syntactic" correctness, e.g. an attribute cannot be connected with another attribute in an ER diagram. Uniqueness of names, correct export/import relations between module descriptions and similar more complex constraints are typically not enforced at this level.

There has to be always a DB schema for the lowest level. In our experience, basic NDBMS features for integrity control are sufficient for this level. For example, we have never used cardinalities in our schemata although they are provided in PCTE.

7.2 Information about Error Conditions

There is another reason why it does not make much sense to define more than fairly trivial consistency constraints in a schema (in all NDBMSs we are aware of): the effect of these constraints is that a write operation which is issued by a tool and which would break any of the consistency constraints which are currently applicable just fails with a standard error code. Except for very simple cases, this error code does not provide the invoking tool with enough information to produce a useful error message for the user.

The user whose edit command has just failed wants to know more than that the command has failed, he wants to know *why* it has failed, i.e. *which particular constraint* would be broken, and expects the tool to give him useful information on *which part* of this or another document (there can be consistency constraints between several documents in integrated CASE environments) has caused the problem. The tool can only find this information if it *repeats* all the consistency tests which the NDBMS has just performed!! Thus, essential functionality of the NDBMS has to be re-implemented in the tool, no programming effort has been saved through the NDBMS and there is a danger that the consistency tests in the tool and the NDBMS are actually not quite the same.

In other words, consistency constraints in a schema are only useful if there are means for a tool to retrieve detailed information about the reasons why a write operation has failed. However, is it less than obvious how such a feature could look like.

7.3 Higher Consistency Levels

Now we get back to the question how the higher consistency levels should be supported. One idea is to express them in additional schemata. Generally, this is a bad idea since it requires copying the data to perform the check; this causes all sorts of problems (in addition to the problem of insufficient information about error conditions).

From a user's point of view, the optimal approach to support higher consistency levels are commands offered by an editor (or a corrector tool) which find all the parts of a document which are wrong or missing according to a given consistency level. These erroneous parts of the document should be immediately displayed. It turns out that the optimal NDBMS support for such commands is a non-navigational query language which allows the tool to easily retrieve references to objects involved in the violation of a constraint.

For example, the user wishes to know all the duplicate names in an ER diagram. The tool should issue a query against the DB which returns a list of names which appear more than once in the diagram, and for each name a list of object references to objects which represent entity types in the diagram which have this name. The tool can then display these parts of the document, highlight erroneous items etc. The useful information in case of violations depends a lot on the consistency constraints and the type of document; thus a powerful query language is needed here (in addition to the navigational access).

Our main conclusion is that the checking of more complex consistency constraints in tools can mainly be supported by a powerful query language, not by constraints defined in a schema.

A last point to note is that CASE environments are typically distributed and parts of the database may be inaccessible. As a consequence, the query language must be usable even if only a part of the database is accessible, which leads to vague results. An approach to deal with this problem is presented in [9].

8 Undo and Redo Commands

Most editors offer a button labelled "Undo" which undoes the last command or, if it was already undone, redoes it. Good editors allow users to undo arbitrarily many commands, up to the first command of a session. Internally, the tool has to maintain a log in which all commands are logged with full undo and redo information.

It is quite obvious that these operation logs in a tool duplicate much of the work which is done for recovery logging in the NDBMS. It suggests itself to use the recovery log instead of implementing almost the same log mechanism in the tool. In order to do this, conventional transaction concepts have been enhanced by savepoints. Before an editor executes a user command, it installs a savepoint. If the command is undone, the transaction is partially rolled back to the last savepoint[8].

After an editor has partially rolled back its current transaction, it has to correct the window. But how to find out which parts of the window have been changed (without a log in the editor)? The obvious solution is to use the notification mechanism mentioned in section 5. We get the additional

Requirement 15: The notification mechanism must also generate messages due to changes caused by (partial) rollback.

---
[8] This can make it necessary to store the window position and other transient, application-specific data in the NDBMS. This problem is discussed in more detail in [16].

With the above requirements, we have covered the undo of commands. The biggest problem, however, is that an undo command without redo is completely unacceptable for users of CASE tools, and that DB recovery logs do not normally support incremental redo within a transaction. Thus, *savepoints without redo facilities are worthless.*

DB recovery logging which supports incremental redo is somewhat complicated (we are not aware of any NDBMS supporting this), notably in the presence of LWPs. Due to lack of space, we cannot discuss the details here; one possible solution of the problem, which we are currently implementing for the next version of H-PCTE, is described in [17]. We summarize the problem by

> **Requirement 16:** The transaction concept of the NDBMS must support savepoints with redo between savepoints (also within light-weight processes). The management of locks and the switching between external schemata must be designed so as to allow as many redo steps as possible.

9 Conclusion

In this paper we have analyzed whether and how the construction of CASE tools can be made easier if the development data are managed in an NDBMS. The negative result is that virtually all NDBMSs proposed so far offer only very limited value because they lack one or several important features. The most prominent weaknesses of many NDBMSs (notably OODBMSs) are

- insufficient performance of data manipulation operations
- their lack of external schemata, fast switching between external schemata, and efficient query facilities for the external schema
- inappropriate features of transactions

The positive result of this paper are suggested strategies how to enhance NDBMSs in order for them to meet the requirements. Most of these strategies have been implemented in the H-PCTE system [13] and have been practically tested with the ToolFrame environment [4][9].

Another result of this paper is that the architecture of tools must be appropriately chosen if the services of an NDBMS are to be fully exploited. The architecture of tools written for file systems is generally inappropriate.

---

[9] The current version of H-PCTE satisfies all but the last two requirements. It offers external schemata, schema query facilities and consistency constraints as defined in [22] (in PCTE, an external schema can be dynamically composed of several modules called *schema definition sets*, which are groups of related type definitions). The navigational access defined in [22] is complemented by two query languages [8, 12]. Additional features are: savepoints in transactions, LWPs with own external schemata, and distributed notification of LWPs. Undo and redo for LWPs and related locking mechanisms are currently being developed.

112

Acknowledgements

The results reported in this paper summarise the work of many persons who contributed to the implementation the H-PCTE system, most notably Oliver Haase, Andreas Henrich, Dirk Platz, Michael Roschewski, Wolfgang Seelbach and Bernd Sonderkötter, and the work of many students which have implemented tools and environments on top of H-PCTE. Their contribution is gratefully acknowledged.

References

1. Cheesman, J.; Simmonds, I.: Managing the evolution of the data schemas of a PCTE-based software engineering environment; p.169-189 in: Proceedings of PCTE'93; 1993
2. Curtis, M.: ToolPark: An architecture for cooperating tools; p.205-216 in: [21]
3. Däberitz, D.; Kelter, U.: Port of PROMOD-PLUS onto H-PCTE; EUREKA Project EU710 OPERA, University of Siegen, FB12/PI; 1994
4. Däberitz, D.; Kelter, U.: Rapid prototyping of graphical editors in an open SDE; p.61-72 in: [28]
5. Emmerich, W.; Schäfer, W.; Welsh, J.: Databases for software engineering environments – *the goal has not yet been attained*; p.145-162 in: Sommerville, I.; Paul, M. (ed.): Proc. 4th European Software Engineering Conference, Garmisch-Partenkirchen, Sept. 1993 (ESEC 93); LNiCS 717, Springer-Verlag; 1993/09
6. Gamma, E.: Objektorientierte Softwareentwicklung am Beispiel von ET++; Springer-Verlag; 1992
7. Groth, B.; Herrmann, S.; Jähnichen, S.; Koch, W.: Project integrating reference object library (PIROL): an object-oriented multiple-view SEE; p.184-193 in: [28]
8. Haase, O.: NTT – a set-oriented algebraic query language for PCTE; Memo 95/5, FG Praktische Informatik, Univ. Siegen; 1995
9. Haase, O.; Henrich, A.: Error propagation in distributed databases; p.387-394 in: Proc. 4th Int. Conf. on Information and Knowledge Management (CIKM'95), Baltimore; 1995
10. Hallmann, M.; Müller, T.: Konzepte der Datenintegration in der Architektur von ProMod-PLUS - Ein Entwicklungs- und Erfahrungsbericht; p.87-94 in: Proc. GI-Fachtagung Softwaretechnik 93, Dortmund, 8.-10.11.1993; 1993
11. Heinrich, J.: Design and implementation of tools for analysis and administration of the persistent data of a prototyping environment; (in German); Diploma Thesis, University of Dortmund; 1995
12. Henrich, A.: P-OQL: an OQL-oriented query language for PCTE; p.48-60 in: [28]
13. Release note for H-PCTE Version 2.x; University of Siegen; (available on ftp.informatik.uni-siegen.de, file: /pub/pi/hpcte/readme-2.x)
14. Kappert, C.: Integration of persistency in a prototyping language and its realisation with a non-standard DBMS (in German); Diploma Thesis, University of Dortmund; 1995
15. Kelter, U.: H-PCTE – a high-performance object management system for system development environments; p.45-50 in: Proc. COMPSAC '92, Chicago, Illinois, September 23-25; 1992
16. Kelter, U.: Fine-grained data in PCTE: notions, issues and proposed solutions; p.41-57 in: Proceedings of the PCTE '94 Conference, San Francisco, 29.11.-1.12.1994; 1994/11

17. Kelter, U.; Platz, D.; Seelbach, W.: A process an transaction model for fine-grained tools (in German); Univ. of Siegen, FB12/PI, internal report; 1995/02
18. Long, F.; Leung, C.C.: Representing Ada program constructs in PCTE; p.262-283 in: [21]
19. Meyers, S.: Difficulties in integrating multiview editing environments; IEEE Software 8:1, p.49-57; 1991
20. Mulcahy, D.; O'Riordan, D.: H-PCTE Evaluation Report (ESPRIT Project ASSET, Doc. No. D3.3.7/5); SSE, Dublin; 1994
21. Proceedings of the PCTE '94 Conference, San Francisco, 29.11.-1.12.1994; 1994/11
22. Portable Common Tool Environment - Abstract Specification / C Bindings / Ada Bindings (Standards ECMA-149/-158/-165, 3rd edition, and ISO IS 13719-1/-2/-3); 1994
23. Design and Implementation of a graphical tool for analysis and design; Internal Report 94/6, FG PI, Dep. Electrical Engineering and Computer Science, University of Siegen; 1994
24. Reiss, S.P.: PECAN: Program development systems that support multiple views; IEEE ToSE SE-12, p.276-284; 1985/03
25. Scheffel, C.: Realisation of a graphical design tool as fine-grained application on top of H-PCTE (in German); Diploma Thesis, Universities of Hagen / Siegen; 1995
26. Schefström, D.; van den Broek, G.: Tool integration - environments and frameworks; Wiley; 1993
27. Seelig, A.: A design tool based on H-PCTE (in German); Diploma Thesis, University of Hagen; 1993
28. Proc. 7th Conf. on Software Engineering Environments (SEE'95), Noordwijkerhout, Netherlands, 5-7 April 1995; IEEE Computer Society Press; 1995
29. Wakeman, L.; Jowett, J.: PCTE the Standard for Open Repositories; Prentice Hall; 1993
30. Wasserman, A.I.: Tool integration in software engineering environments; p.137-149 in: Long, F. (ed.): Software Engineering Environments. Proc. Ada Europe International Workshop on Environments, Chinon, September 1989; LNiCS 467, Springer Verlag; 1990

Correct Schema Transformations*

Xiaolei Qian

Computer Science Laboratory, SRI International, CA 94025, USA

Abstract. We develop a formal basis of correct schema transformations. Schemas are formalized as abstract data types, and correct schema transformations are formalized as information-preserving signature interpretations. Our formalism captures transformations of all schema components, making it possible to transform uniformly constraints and queries along with structures. In addition, our formalism captures schema transformations between different data models as easily as those within the same data model. Compared with Hull's notion of relative information capacity, our notion of information preservation captures more schema transformations that are natural, and fewer schema transformations that are unnatural. Our work lays the foundation of a transformational framework of schema manipulations.

1 Introduction

Schema transformations, such as removing anomalies and redundancies, schema restructuring, and translating one schema to another (possibly in a different data model), constitute the major activities in schema integration [3]. Central to schema transformations is the need to compare the information content of schemas: in transforming one schema to another, the information content of the source schema should be preserved. A schema usually consists of three components [19]: (1) a set of structures, (2) a set of constraints on the structures, and (3) a set of operators on the structures. The constraints capture the invariant properties common to all instances of the schema, and the operators provide the vocabulary for formulating queries in the schema.

Most work on schema transformations has focused on the structure component of a schema (see [19, Chapter 14] for a summary of existing approaches). A classic example of schema transformations is the decomposition of a relation into various normal forms under functional and multivalued dependencies [20, Chapter 7]. When constraints are limited to functional dependencies in the relational model and schema transformations are expressed as conjunctive queries, Klug gave an algorithm for deriving constraints in the target schema from those in the source schema [13]. When constraints are limited to functional and inclusion dependencies in the relational model, optimization rules are given in [7, 8] to

---

* This work was supported in part by the U.S. Department of Defense Advanced Research Projects Agency and the U.S. Air Force Rome Laboratory under contracts F30602-92-C-0140 and F30602-94-C-0198, and in part by the National Science Foundation under grant ECS-94-22688.

remove redundant relations, attributes, and constraints in a schema. However, the problem of constraint and operator transformations remains open for general constraints and operators. Since constraints capture important information in a schema, schema transformations without the constraint component are incomplete at best. Without the operator component, it is impossible to transform queries in the source schema to those in the target schema, even if the structure component is transformed correctly.

Another major problem with existing work is that schema transformations are almost always limited to schemas within the same data model—in most cases the relational model or some dialect of the entity-relationship model. For example, most approaches to schema integration make the assumption that the schemas to be integrated are already formulated in some canonical data model (see [3] for a survey). As pointed out in [19], schema transformations between schemas in different data models are usually specified by ad hoc mapping rules, with no formalisms to guarantee correctness in terms of either information preservation or equivalence. In [14], correct translation is studied from entity-relationship schemas to relational schemas, using a notion of schema equivalence from [11]. However, only primitive forms of cardinality constraints are translated, and query translation is not considered.

It is customary to treat a schema as a logical theory and instances of the schema as models of the theory. What constitutes the information content of a schema? According to Bar-Hillel and Carnap [2], the (semantic) information carried by a logical theory (schema) can be characterized by the set of sentences (i.e., constraints) logically implied by the axioms of the theory relative to some language system (i.e., structures and operators). Thus, all three components of a schema contribute to its information content. In turn, the information content of the structure component of a schema can be characterized by the set of instances of the schema. In other words, a schema is capable of storing information not only in its instances but also in its structures, constraints, and operators.

Most work on schema transformations uses ad hoc and very limited measures in comparing the information content of schemas. In [6] for example, a schema contains less information than another if every instance of the first is an instance of the second. The first systematic study was done by Hull [11], where he introduced the notion of relative information capacity for comparing the information content of relational schemas. It has been widely used as the formal basis of schema containment and schema equivalence for object models [1, 12], and for entity-relationship models [15, 17]. In [21], Hull's notion is extended to take into account update semantics. However, the constraint and operator components of schemas are largely ignored in these studies, even though Hull observed that the structure component alone of a relational schema does not contain much information at all [11]. In fact, it is very difficult to generalize the notion of relative information capacity to deal with constraints and operators. For example, it is shown in [15] that the information capacity of a schema can be increased by reducing its capacity of storing constraints, which is counterintuitive.

Traditionally, schemas have been formalized using a structural approach, which describes the structure component of a schema using a (fixed) set of type constructors. However, the type constructors have been limited to simple ones that can be stored and manipulated directly, such as tuples and sets. Recently, Beeri [4, 5] has advocated a behavioral approach based on the theory of abstract data type (ADT) and algebraic specification (see [22] for a survey), which describes uniformly all components of a schema using a set of ADT specifications. The behavioral approach has the additional advantage of supporting more complex and extensible data models.

We adopt the behavioral approach to schema specification, and develop a formal basis of correct schema transformations that solves the problems discussed above. In particular, schemas are formalized as ADTs (Section 2), schema transformations are formalized as signature interpretations (Section 3), and correct schema transformations are formalized as information-preserving signature interpretations (Section 4). We compare our notion of information preservation with Hull's notion of relative information capacity (Section 5), and solve an open problem posed in [11]. Our formalism is used in Section 6 to demonstrate the correctness of some common schema transformations that have been proposed in the literature, such as redundancy removal, schema integration, and schema translation. Finally, Section 7 provides some concluding remarks.

2 Schemas

2.1 Basics

We borrow the definitions of order-sorted signatures and algebras from the standard abstract data type literature [10]. A *partially ordered set*, or *poset*, is a pair $(S, \leq)$, where S is a set and $\leq$ is a partial ordering on S. Let S^* be the set of finite sequences of members in S. The partial ordering $\leq$ can be extended to S^* such that $\langle s_1 \ldots s_n \rangle \leq \langle s'_1 \ldots s'_n \rangle$ if and only if $s_i \leq s'_i$ for $1 \leq i \leq n$.

An *order-sorted signature* Σ is a triple $(S, \leq, \Omega)$, where S is a set of *sort symbols*, $(S, \leq)$ is a poset, and Ω is a family of sets $\{\Omega_{v,s}\}_{v \in S^*, s \in S}$ of *function symbols* that satisfies the monotonicity condition

$$\Omega_{v,s} \cap \Omega_{v',s'} \neq \emptyset \text{ and } v \leq v' \text{ imply } s \leq s'.$$

We write $f: v \to s$ to denote $v \in S^*, s \in S$, and $f \in \Omega_{v,s}$. $\Omega_{\langle\rangle,s}$ is a set of *constant symbols* (i.e., 0-ary function symbols) of sort s. For example, we could have a signature BOOL containing one sort *bool* and two constant symbols *true* and *false*. The logical connectives $\lor, \land, \neg, \to, \leftrightarrow$ are considered as function symbols in BOOL. $\Omega_{v,bool}$ is a set of *predicate symbols* for $v \in S^*$. For every sort $s \in S$ we assume that there is an (infix) predicate symbol $=_s \in \Omega_{\langle s,s \rangle,bool}$. For BOOL, $=_{bool}$ is simply $\leftrightarrow$.

Given two signatures $\Sigma = (S, \leq, \Omega)$ and $\Sigma' = (S', \leq', \Omega')$, we say that $\Sigma \subseteq \Sigma'$ if

1. $S \subseteq S'$,

2. $s_1 \leq s_2$ implies $s_1 \leq' s_2$ for $s_1, s_2 \in S$, and
3. $\Omega_{v,s} \subseteq \Omega'_{v,s}$ for $v \in S^*, s \in S$.

We say that Σ and Σ' are *union-compatible* if

1. $\leq$ is identical to $\leq'$ on $S \cap S'$, and
2. $\Omega_{v,s} \cap \Omega'_{v',s'} \neq \emptyset$ implies $v = v'$ and $s = s'$.

For signature $\Sigma = (S, \leq, \Omega)$, the Σ-*terms* are defined inductively as the well-sorted composition of sorted variables, function symbols, and sorted quantifiers $\forall$ and $\exists$ in Ω. A Σ-*formula* is a Σ-term of sort *bool*. A Σ-*sentence* is a closed Σ-formula.

Let $\Sigma = (S, \leq, \Omega)$ be a signature. An *order-sorted* Σ-*algebra* A consists of an S-indexed family of *carrier sets* $\{A_s\}_{s \in S}$, and a function $f_A: A_v \to A_s$ for every $\Omega_{v,s}$ in Ω and $f \in \Omega_{v,s}$, where $v = \langle v_1, \ldots, v_n \rangle$ and $A_v = A_{v_1} \times \cdots \times A_{v_n}$, such that

1. $s \leq s'$ implies $A_s \subseteq A_{s'}$, and
2. $f \in \Omega_{v,s} \cap \Omega_{v',s'}$ and $v \leq v'$ imply $f_A: A_v \to A_s$ equals to $f_A: A_{v'} \to A_{s'}$ on A_v.

A *schema* Γ is a pair (Σ, Φ), where $\Sigma = (S, \leq, \Omega)$ is a signature and Φ is a set of Σ-sentences called *axioms*. For every sort $s \in S$ we assume that the equality axioms of reflexivity, symmetry, transitivity, and substitutivity are in Φ. A Γ-*instance* is a Σ-algebra that satisfies Φ. The semantics of Γ is given by the set of Γ-instances. A Σ-sentence p is a Γ-*constraint*, denoted as $\Gamma \models p$, if p is a logical consequence of the Γ-axioms. The set of Γ-constraints forms Γ-*theory*. A Γ-*query* is a Σ-formula.

2.2 Examples

For a schema $\Gamma = (\Sigma, \Phi)$, its signature Σ specifies the structure and operator components of Γ, while its axioms Φ specify the constraint component of Γ. A typical example is the specification of schema SET, which is parameterized by another schema ATOM with sort *atom*.

$$\text{SET}(\text{ATOM}) \stackrel{\text{def}}{=} (\textbf{sort} \quad set(atom)$$

$$\textbf{subsort} \quad atom \leq set(atom)$$

$$\textbf{function} \; \{\}: \to set$$

$$\_ \bullet \_: atom, set \to set$$

$$\ldots$$

$$\textbf{axiom} \quad \neg(x \bullet S = \{\})$$

$$x \bullet (y \bullet S) = y \bullet (x \bullet S)$$

$$x \bullet (x \bullet S) = x \bullet S$$

$$\ldots).$$

The subsort declaration states that every atom is a set (of size one). There is a constant $\{\}$ denoting the empty set, and an insertion function $\bullet$ for inserting an atom into a set. As a second example, LIBRARY1 is a schema specification in the object model.

$$\text{BOOK} \quad \overset{\text{def}}{=} \quad (\textbf{extend} \quad \text{STRING}$$

$$\textbf{sort} \quad book$$

$$\textbf{function} \quad title(\_): book \rightarrow string$$

$$isbn(\_): book \rightarrow string$$

$$\textbf{axiom} \quad isbn(x) = isbn(y) \rightarrow x = y)$$

$$\text{AUTHOR} \quad \overset{\text{def}}{=} \quad (\textbf{extend} \quad \text{STRING, INTEGER}$$

$$\textbf{sort} \quad author$$

$$\textbf{function} \quad name(\_): author \rightarrow string$$

$$year\text{-}of\text{-}birth(\_): author \rightarrow integer)$$

$$\text{LIBRARY1} \quad \overset{\text{def}}{=} \quad (\textbf{extend} \quad \text{BOOK, AUTHOR}).$$

The keyword **extend** introduces a list of imported schemas. There are two classes of objects: books and authors. Books have attributes title and isbn, and authors have attributes name and year-of-birth. In addition, books have unique isbn values. As a third example, LIBRARY2 is a more elaborate schema specification in the complex-object model.

$$\text{LIBRARY2} \quad \overset{\text{def}}{=} \quad (\textbf{extend} \quad \text{LIBRARY1, SET(BOOK)}$$

$$\textbf{function} \quad author\text{-}of(\_): author \rightarrow set(book)$$

$$\textbf{axiom} \quad \neg(author\text{-}of(x) = \{\})$$

$$(\exists x)(y \in author\text{-}of(x))).$$

Compared with LIBRARY1, authors in LIBRARY2 have an additional set-valued attribute denoting the set of books that they are an author of. The two additional axioms state that every author has at least one book, and every book has at least one author. As a fourth example, LIBRARY3 is an alternative schema specification in the entity-relationship model.

$$\text{LIBRARY3} \quad \overset{\text{def}}{=} \quad (\textbf{extend} \quad \text{LIBRARY1}$$

$$\textbf{function} \quad authorship(\_,\_): book, author \rightarrow bool$$

$$\textbf{axiom} \quad (\exists x)\, authorship(x, y)$$

$$(\exists y)\, authorship(x, y)).$$

Compared with LIBRARY1, LIBRARY3 has a many-to-many relationship relating books to their authors. The two additional axioms state cardinality constraints on the relationship: every author has at least one book and every book has at least one author.

3 Schema Transformation

Let $\Sigma = (S, \leq, \Omega)$ be a signature. We denote by $\Sigma_{v,s}(x)$ the set of Σ-terms of sort s whose list of free variables is x of sort v, where $v \in S^*$ and $s \in S$.

The following definition is based on the notion of theory interpretation in [9, Section 2.7]. Let $\Sigma' = (S', \leq', \Omega')$ be another signature. A *signature interpretation* $\sigma: \Sigma \rightarrow \Sigma'$ is a pair (δ, θ), where

1. $\delta: S \to S'$ is a map such that $s_1 \leq s_2$ implies $\delta(s_1) \leq' \delta(s_2)$, and
2. θ is a family of maps $\{\theta_{v,s}: \Omega_{v,s} \to \Sigma'_{\delta^*(v),\delta(s)}(x)\}_{v \in S^*, s \in S}$

where $\delta^*(\langle v_1, \ldots, v_n \rangle)$ denotes $\langle \delta(v_1), \ldots, \delta(v_n) \rangle$. We write $\sigma(s)$ for $\delta(s)$, $\sigma(v)$ for $\delta^*(v)$, and $\sigma(f)$ for $\theta_{v,s}(f)$. We can extend σ to Σ-formulas as follows. Given a Σ-formula p, $\sigma(p)$ denotes the Σ'-formula resulted from replacing every term $f(t)$ in p by $\theta_{v,s}(f)[\sigma(t)/x]$, where $f \in \Omega_{v,s}$ and $\theta_{v,s}: \Omega_{v,s} \to \Sigma'_{\delta^*(v),\delta(s)}(x)$.

It should be noticed that the notion of signature interpretation is more general than the notion of signature morphism commonly seen in the algebraic specification literature [22], in that a function symbol in the source signature can be mapped to an arbitrary term, not just a function symbol, in the target signature.[2]

Let $\Sigma = (S, \leq, \Omega)$ and $\Sigma' = (S', \leq', \Omega')$ be two signatures, and $\sigma: \Sigma \to \Sigma'$ be a signature interpretation. A map M_σ from Σ'-algebras to Σ-algebras can be induced from σ as follows. Given a Σ'-algebra A', we construct a Σ-algebra A by assigning the value of $\sigma(s)$ in A' to s for every sort symbol $s \in S$ and assigning the value of $\sigma(f)$ in A' to f for every function symbol $f \in \Omega$. Notice that a signature interpretation and its induced map are in opposite directions.

Let $\Gamma = (\Sigma, \Phi)$ and $\Gamma' = (\Sigma', \Phi')$ be two schemas. A *schema transformation* $\sigma: \Gamma \to \Gamma'$ is a signature interpretation $\sigma: \Sigma \to \Sigma'$. Since Γ-constraints and Γ-queries are Σ-formulas, σ transforms not only the structures and operators of Γ, but also the constraints and queries of Γ. By using the more general notion of signature interpretation, constructs in the source schema can be transformed to combinations of constructs in the target schema.

For example, a schema transformation from BOOK to AUTHOR could be

$$\{book \mapsto author, title \mapsto name(x), isbn \mapsto int\text{-}to\text{-}str(year\text{-}of\text{-}birth(x))\} \quad (1)$$

where *int-to-str* is a unary function symbol in schema STRING that converts an integer to a string. The BOOK-axiom is transformed to an AUTHOR-sentence

$$int\text{-}to\text{-}str(year\text{-}of\text{-}birth(x)) = int\text{-}to\text{-}str(year\text{-}of\text{-}birth(y)) \to x = y.$$

As we argued in Section 1, all components and instances of a schema contribute to its information content. A schema transformation preserves the structures and operators of the source schema. However, it is not sufficient to preserve either the constraints or the instances of the source schema. For example, the above schema transformation does not preserve the constraints of BOOK, since the BOOK-axiom is not mapped to an AUTHOR-constraint. The inverse of the above schema transformation

$$\{author \mapsto book, name \mapsto title(x), year\text{-}of\text{-}birth \mapsto str\text{-}to\text{-}int(isbn(x))\} \quad (2)$$

---

[2] For ease of presentation, our notion of signature interpretation is less general than the notion of theory interpretation in [9], in that a sort symbol in the source signature can only be mapped to a sort symbol in the target signature. It is not hard to generalize the notion of signature interpretation to allow a sort symbol to be mapped to an arbitrary sort expression.

where *str-to-int* is a unary function symbol in schema STRING that converts a string to an integer, does not preserve the instances of AUTHOR, since an AUTHOR-instance containing two authors with the same name but different years of birth does not correspond to any BOOK-instance.

4 Correct Schema Transformation

4.1 Constraint-Preserving Transformation

Let $\Gamma = (\Sigma, \Phi)$ and $\Gamma' = (\Sigma', \Phi')$ be two schemas, $\sigma: \Gamma \to \Gamma'$ be a schema transformation, and M_σ be the induced map from Σ'-algebras to Σ-algebras. We say that σ is *constraint-preserving* if, for every Γ-axiom p, $\sigma(p)$ is a Γ'-constraint.

A classic example of constraint-preserving schema transformation in the relational model is the dependency-preserving decomposition of a relation into the third normal form (3NF) [20, Section 7.8].

Constraint preservation is not sufficient to preserve the instances of the source schema. An example is schema transformation (2) in Section 3. The simplest form of constraint-preserving schema transformation is schema extension, where the schema transformation consists of identity maps, and every Γ-axiom is a Γ'-constraint.

For the examples in Section 2.2, LIBRARY1 can in fact be transformed to LIBRARY2 and LIBRARY3 by schema extension. As a more complicated example of constraint-preserving schema transformation, suppose that we extend LIBRARY3 to LIBRARY4:

LIBRARY4 $\stackrel{\text{def}}{=}$ (**extend** LIBRARY3, SET(BOOK)
               function *author-of'*(_): *author* $\to$ *set(book)*
               axiom *author-of'*$(x) = \{y \,|\, authorship(y, x)\}$).

The schema transformation from LIBRARY2 to LIBRARY4, which maps *author-of* to *author-of'* and everything else to itself, is constraint-preserving, because the two LIBRARY2-axioms are mapped to two LIBRARY4-constraints

$$\neg(author\text{-}of'(x) = \{\})$$
$$(\exists x)(y \in author\text{-}of'(x))$$

which follow from the axioms of LIBRARY3 and LIBRARY4.

4.2 Instance-Preserving Transformation

Let $\Gamma = (\Sigma, \Phi)$ and $\Gamma' = (\Sigma', \Phi')$ be two schemas, $\sigma: \Gamma \to \Gamma'$ be a schema transformation, and M_σ be the induced map from Σ'-algebras to Σ-algebras. We say that σ is *instance-preserving* if, for every Γ-instance I, there is a Γ'-instance I' such that $M_\sigma(I') = I$.

A classic example of instance-preserving schema transformation in the relational model is the lossless-join decomposition of a relation into the Boyce-Codd normal form (BCNF) [20, Section 7.7].

Instance preservation is not sufficient to preserve the constraints of the source schema. An example is schema transformation (1) in Section 3. The simplest form of instance-preserving schema transformation is schema reduction, where the schema transformation consists of identity maps, and every Γ'-axiom is a Γ-constraint.

For example, suppose that we define LIBRARY5 as follows:

LIBRARY5 $\overset{\text{def}}{=}$ (extend   LIBRARY3, SET(BOOK)
          function $author\text{-}of'(\_): author \to set(book)$
          axiom $authorship(y, x) \to y \in author\text{-}of'(x))$.

The schema transformation from LIBRARY4 of Section 4.1 to LIBRARY5, which consists of identity maps, is instance-preserving because LIBRARY5-theory is weaker than LIBRARY4-theory.

4.3 Information-Preserving Transformation

As we have argued in Section 1, a correct schema transformation should preserve all components and instances of the source schema. Since schema transformations preserve structures and operators, constraint-preserving schema transformations preserve constraints, and instance-preserving schema transformations preserve instances, we have the following definition for correct schema transformations.

Let $\Gamma = (\Sigma, \Phi)$ and $\Gamma' = (\Sigma', \Phi')$ be two schemas, and $\sigma\colon \Gamma \to \Gamma'$ be a schema transformation. We say that σ is *information-preserving* if it is both constraint-preserving and instance-preserving. If σ is information-preserving, then we say that Γ is *contained* in Γ', denoted by $\Gamma \sqsubseteq \Gamma'$. If $\Gamma \sqsubseteq \Gamma'$ and $\Gamma' \sqsubseteq \Gamma$, then we say that Γ and Γ' are *equivalent*, denoted by $\Gamma \equiv \Gamma'$.

A classic example of information-preserving schema transformation in the relational model is the dependency-preserving and lossless-join decomposition of a relation into 3NF [20, Section 7.8]. For another example, suppose that we define LIBRARY6 as follows:

LIBRARY6 $\overset{\text{def}}{=}$ (extend   LIBRARY1, SET(BOOK)
          function $authorship(\_, \_): book, author \to bool$
                   $author\text{-}of'(\_): author \to set(book)$
          axiom $authorship(y, x) \leftrightarrow y \in author\text{-}of'(x)$
                   $\neg(author\text{-}of'(x) = \{\})$
                   $(\exists x)(y \in author\text{-}of'(x)))$.

The schema transformations from LIBRARY4 of Section 4.1 to LIBRARY6 and back, which consist of identity maps, are both information-preserving, and hence LIBRARY4 $\equiv$ LIBRARY6.

The simplest forms of information-preserving schema transformation include instance-preserving schema extension and constraint-preserving schema reduction.

5   Relationship to Relative Information Capacity

In [11], Hull introduced four progressively more restrictive measures of the information content of schemas—relative information capacity. We first briefly define these measures, and then characterize their relationships to our notion of information preservation. Through this, we solve an open problem posed in [11].

A schema $\Gamma = (\Sigma, \Phi)$ is *relational* if every function symbol in Σ is either a constant or a predicate. A relational schema corresponds to a schema in the relational model. In particular, every predicate is a relation, every Σ-formula is an expression in (domain) relational calculus, and every Σ-sentence in Φ is an integrity constraint.

Since Hull's original notion of relative information capacity is introduced in the context of the relational model, we limit ourselves to relational schemas in the rest of this section.

5.1   Relative Information Capacity

Let $\Gamma = (\Sigma, \Phi)$ and $\Gamma' = (\Sigma', \Phi')$ be two schemas. The domain of a Γ-instance I, denoted as $\mathrm{dom}(I)$, is the union of its carrier sets. Let **DOM** be a set of values containing the domains of all Γ-instances and Γ'-instances, and $Z \subseteq \mathbf{DOM}$.

1. A Z-permutation of **DOM** is a bijective map on **DOM** that is identical on Z.
2. A map M from Γ-instances to Γ'-instances is Z-generic if it commutes with every Z-permutation of every Γ-instance.
3. A map M from Γ-instances to Γ'-instances is Z-internal if $\mathrm{dom}(M(I)) \subseteq \mathrm{dom}(I) \cup Z$ for every Γ-instance I.

Let $\Gamma = (\Sigma, \Phi)$ and $\Gamma' = (\Sigma', \Phi')$ be two schemas. Also let M be a map from Γ-instances to Γ'-instances, and M' be a map from Γ'-instances to Γ-instances. Γ' dominates Γ via (M, M') if $M' \circ M$ is the identity map on Γ-instances.

1. Γ' dominates Γ *absolutely*,[3] denoted as $\Gamma \preceq \Gamma'(\mathrm{abs})$, if Γ' dominates Γ via (M, M') for some M, M'.
2. Γ' dominates Γ *internally*, denoted as $\Gamma \preceq \Gamma'(\mathrm{int})$, if there is a finite $Z \subseteq \mathbf{DOM}$ such that Γ' dominates Γ via (M, M') for some Z-internal M, M'.
3. Γ' dominates Γ *generically*, denoted as $\Gamma \preceq \Gamma'(\mathrm{gen})$, if there is a finite $Z \subseteq \mathbf{DOM}$ such that Γ' dominates Γ via (M, M') for some Z-generic M, M'.
4. Γ' dominates Γ *calculously*, denoted as $\Gamma \preceq \Gamma'(\mathrm{calc})$, if there are two schema transformations $\sigma \colon \Gamma \to \Gamma'$ and $\tau \colon \Gamma' \to \Gamma$ with induced maps M_σ and M_τ respectively, such that Γ' dominates Γ via (M_τ, M_σ).

Hull has shown that calculus dominance implies generic dominance, which in turn implies internal dominance, which in turn implies absolute dominance.

---

[3] This definition is from [12], which is simpler and is not limited to relational schemas. The two definitions are equivalent for relational schemas [11].

Moreover, the implication from generic to internal dominance is strict if schemas contain key dependencies. However, it remains open whether the implications from calculus to generic dominance, and from internal to absolute dominance are strict.

5.2 Comparison

Let $\Gamma = (\Sigma, \Phi)$ and $\Gamma' = (\Sigma', \Phi')$ be two schemas. The proof of the following theorem can be found in [16].

Theorem 1. If $\Gamma \preceq \Gamma'(calc)$, then $\Gamma \sqsubseteq \Gamma'$. If $\Gamma \sqsubseteq \Gamma'$, then $\Gamma \preceq \Gamma'(abs)$.

There exist schemas Γ and Γ' such that $\Gamma \preceq \Gamma'(gen,int,abs)$ but $\Gamma \not\sqsubseteq \Gamma'$ (and hence $\Gamma \not\preceq \Gamma'(calc)$). For example, consider the following schemas.

SCHEMA1 $\stackrel{\text{def}}{=}$ (**sort**   *city*
            axiom $(\exists x, y)\neg(x = y)$)
SCHEMA2 $\stackrel{\text{def}}{=}$ (**sort**   *town*).

A SCHEMA1-instance is a set containing at least two cities, while a SCHEMA2-instance could be a singleton set. Hence SCHEMA1 is logically stronger than SCHEMA2. A map M from SCHEMA1-instances to SCHEMA2-instances could map every SCHEMA1-instance to the identical SCHEMA2-instance. On the other hand, a map M' from SCHEMA2-instances to SCHEMA1-instances could map every SCHEMA2-instance containing at least two towns to the identical SCHEMA1-instance; and map every singleton SCHEMA2-instance to the SCHEMA1-instance where *city* is assigned the set $\{SF, LA\}$. Since these two maps are both $\{SF, LA\}$-generic, and $M' \circ M$ is the identity map on SCHEMA1-instances, we conclude that SCHEMA1 $\preceq$ SCHEMA2(gen,int,abs). However, any schema transformation from SCHEMA1 to SCHEMA2 will have to map *city* to *town*. The only function symbol in SCHEMA1 is $=_{city}$. If it is mapped to $=_{town}$, then the image of the SCHEMA1-axiom is not a SCHEMA2-constraint. If it is mapped to an equivalence relation $\simeq$ other than $=_{town}$, then the image of the SCHEMA1-axiom cannot be true in any singleton SCHEMA2-instances. In either case, the schema transformation cannot be constraint-preserving, and hence SCHEMA1 $\not\sqsubseteq$ SCHEMA2.

This example tells us that Hull's notion could find dominance relationships between schemas that are not naturally related through dominance relationships: a schema should not be capable of storing more information if we reduce its capability of storing constraints. Our notion rules out such unnatural dominance relationships.

There also exist schemas Γ and Γ' such that $\Gamma \sqsubseteq \Gamma'$ (and hence $\Gamma \preceq \Gamma'(abs)$) but $\Gamma \not\preceq \Gamma'(int,gen,calc)$. For example, consider the following schemas.

SCHEMA3 $\stackrel{\text{def}}{=}$ (**extend** ATOM
            function $R_1(\_, \_, \_)$: *atom, atom, atom* $\rightarrow$ *bool*
            axiom $R_1(x, y, z) \wedge R_1(x, y', z') \rightarrow y = y' \wedge z = z'$)
SCHEMA4 $\stackrel{\text{def}}{=}$ (**extend** ATOM
            function $R_2(\_, \_)$: *atom, atom* $\rightarrow$ *bool*)

and a schema transformation from SCHEMA4 to SCHEMA3 that maps R_2 to the SCHEMA3-term $(\exists x)R_1(x, y, z)$. In other words, R_2 is the projection of R_1 on non-key columns. It is easy to show that the schema transformation is information-preserving, and hence SCHEMA4 $\sqsubseteq$ SCHEMA3. However, any map from SCHEMA4-instances to SCHEMA3-instances will have to invent as many distinct values as the the number of true tuples in R_2, up to $|atom|^2$, for the key column of R_1. For any fixed finite Z, we can find a set $atom$ such that $|atom| + |Z| < |atom|^2$, and a SCHEMA4-instance in which the number of true tuples in R_2 is $|atom|^2$. Hence the map cannot be Z-internal for a fixed finite Z, and SCHEMA4 $\npreceq$ SCHEMA3(int,gen,calc).

This example tells us that there are natural dominance relationships between schemas that are not captured by Hull's notion: the capability of storing information in a non-keyed schema should be increased by adding a key column. Our notion captures such natural dominance relationships.

Notice that the SCHEMA1-axiom is not a key dependency, while the SCHEMA3-axiom is. The above examples also show that calculus dominance is strictly more restrictive than information preservation, which is in turn strictly more restrictive than absolute dominance. Moreover, information preservation is not comparable to generic or internal dominance. Hence, when constraints are not limited to key dependencies, we have solved an open problem posed by Hull:

Corollary 2. *Calculus dominance is strictly more restrictive than generic dominance. Internal dominance is strictly more restrictive than absolute dominance.*

6 Applications

6.1 Redundancy Removal

Given two schemas $\Gamma = (\Sigma, \Phi)$ and $\Gamma' = (\Sigma', \Phi')$ where $\Gamma \equiv \Gamma'$, we say that Γ' is less redundant than Γ if Σ' contains fewer or simpler signature symbols than Σ, or Φ' contains weaker axioms than Φ. In this case, we could replace Γ by Γ' to achieve a more concise representation of the same information. Consider the following schemas in the relational model:

SCHEMA5 $\overset{\text{def}}{=}$ (**extend** ATOM
   function $R_1(\_,\_,\_), R_2(\_,\_,\_)$: $atom, atom, atom \to bool$
   axiom $R_1(x, y, z) \wedge R_1(x, y', z') \to y = y' \wedge z = z'$
   $R_2(x, y, z) \wedge R_2(x, y', z') \to y = y' \wedge z = z'$
   $R_1(x, y, z) \to (\exists y')R_2(x, y', z))$

SCHEMA6 $\overset{\text{def}}{=}$ (**extend** ATOM
   function $R_1'(\_,\_)$: $atom, atom \to bool$
   $R_2'(\_,\_,\_)$: $atom, atom, atom \to bool$
   axiom $R_1'(x, y) \wedge R_1'(x, y') \to y = y'$
   $R_2'(x, y, z) \wedge R_2'(x, y', z') \to y = y' \wedge z = z'$
   $R_1'(x, y) \to (\exists y', z')R_2'(x, y', z')).$

A schema transformation from SCHEMA5 to SCHEMA6 could map R_1 to the SCHEMA5-term $R_1'(x, y) \wedge (\exists y')R_2'(x, y', z)$. A schema transformation from SCHEMA6 to SCHEMA5 could map R_1' to the SCHEMA6-term $(\exists z)R_1(x, y, z)$. It is not hard to verify that SCHEMA5 $\equiv$ SCHEMA6. Compared to SCHEMA6, SCHEMA5 has more redundancy because the third column of R_2 is redundantly stored as the third column of R_1. Hence replacing SCHEMA5 by SCHEMA6 removes this redundancy. This schema transformation has been proposed in the literature [8, 17].

6.2 Schema Integration

Let $\Gamma_i = (\Sigma_i, \Phi_i)$ for $1 \leq i \leq n$ be n schemas such that Σ_i and Σ_j are union-compatible for $1 \leq i, j \leq n$. When we integrate these schemas into one, the first step is to identify the semantic relationships between them. Suppose that the semantic relationships are expressed over Σ_i for $1 \leq i \leq n$, and possibly an additional signature Σ'; and consist of a set of $(\bigcup_{i=1}^{n} \Sigma_i \cup \Sigma')$-sentences Φ'. An integration of Γ_i, for $1 \leq i \leq n$, is a schema $\Gamma = (\Sigma, \Phi)$ such that

$$(\bigcup_{i=1}^{n} \Sigma_i \cup \Sigma', \bigcup_{i=1}^{n} \Phi_i \cup \Phi') \equiv \Gamma.$$

Thus, schema integration can be viewed as applying information-preserving schema transformations to the union of component schemas and their semantic relationships to improve the quality of the integrated schema (e.g., to remove redundancy). Consider a schema specification similar to LIBRARY2 of Section 2.2:

LIBRARY2$'$ $\stackrel{\text{def}}{=}$ (**extend** LIBRARY1, SET(AUTHOR))
           function *authored-by(_)*: *book* $\rightarrow$ *set(author)*
           axiom $\neg(authored\text{-}by(x) = \{\})$
                $(\exists x)(y \in authored\text{-}by(x)))$.

Suppose that we integrate LIBRARY2 and LIBRARY2$'$. The semantic relationship between them can be expressed as

$$x \in author\text{-}of(y) \leftrightarrow y \in authored\text{-}by(x).$$

Intuitively, the two schemas contain the same information represented differently. Hence their union is redundant: the many-to-many relationship between authors and books is represented by two multi-valued maps that are inverses of each other. It is not hard to verify that the union of LIBRARY2 and LIBRARY2$'$ together with the above semantic relationship is equivalent to LIBRARY3 of Section 2.2. Hence LIBRARY3 can be taken as their integration. This schema transformation has been proposed in the literature [18].

6.3 Schema Translation

Given two schemas Γ and Γ', a schema transformation $\sigma\colon \Gamma \to \Gamma'$ is a translation from Γ to Γ' if $\Gamma \equiv \Gamma'$.

Schema translation between different data models is not any more difficult than that within the same data model, because our schema formalism really blurs the difference between data models: data models differ in the data types they support. So we could have a schema specified in a mixture of data models, e.g., LIBRARY4 of Section 4.1 is in a combination of complex-object and entity-relationship models.

As an example of schema translation, suppose that we extend LIBRARY3 of Section 2.2 with an additional axiom $name(x) = name(y) \to x = y$, which can then be translated to the following schema in the relational model:

$$
\begin{aligned}
\text{LIBRARY3}' \stackrel{\text{def}}{=} (&\textbf{extend} \quad \text{STRING, INTEGER} \\
&\textbf{sort} \quad s_1, s_2 \\
&\textbf{function } R_1(\_,\_)\colon s_1, string \to bool \\
&\phantom{\textbf{function }} R_2(\_,\_)\colon s_2, integer \to bool \\
&\phantom{\textbf{function }} R(\_,\_)\colon s_1, s_2 \to bool \\
&\textbf{axiom} \quad R_1(x,y) \wedge R_1(x,z) \to y = z \\
&\phantom{\textbf{axiom} \quad} R_2(x,y) \wedge R_2(x,z) \to y = z \\
&\phantom{\textbf{axiom} \quad} (\exists y) R_1(x,y) \\
&\phantom{\textbf{axiom} \quad} (\exists y) R_2(x,y))
\end{aligned}
$$

through the schema transformation

$$
\left\{
\begin{aligned}
&book \mapsto s_1, isbn \mapsto x, title \mapsto \{y | R_1(x,y)\}, \\
&author \mapsto s_2, name \mapsto x, year\text{-}of\text{-}birth \mapsto \{y | R_2(x,y)\}, \\
&authorship \mapsto R(x,y)
\end{aligned}
\right\}.
$$

Notice that the images of *title* and *year-of-birth* are always total and evaluate to singleton sets, because of the LIBRARY3'-axioms. Also notice that the inclusion dependencies from the two columns of R to the first columns of R_1 and R_2 respectively are satisfied automatically through sort constraints and the last two LIBRARY3'-axioms. Similar schema translations from the entity-relationship model to the relational model have been proposed in [14].

7 Conclusion

We have developed a formal basis of correct schema transformations. In particular, schemas are formalized as ADTs, schema transformations are formalized as signature interpretations, and correct schema transformations are formalized as information-preserving signature interpretations.

Compared with existing approaches, our formalism captures transformations of all schema components, making it possible to transform uniformly constraints and queries along with structures. In addition, our formalism captures schema transformations between different data models as easily as those within the same data model.

We have compared in detail our notion of information preservation with the most widely used correctness criteria—Hull's notion of relative information capacity. Information preservation is strictly less restrictive than calculus dominance, strictly more restrictive than absolute dominance, and incomparable to generic or internal dominance. Moreover, our notion captures more schema transformations that are natural, and fewer schema transformations that are unnatural, than Hull's notion. We have also solved an open problem with Hull's notion—calculus and internal dominance are, respectively, strictly more restrictive than generic and absolute dominance.

Our work lays the foundation of a transformational framework of schema manipulations. Popular transformations of common ADTs can be encoded as transformation rules and proven correct once. Schemas specified with common ADTs can be simplified, restructured, and translated by applying these rules repeatedly. As examples, we have shown the correctness of some common schema transformations that have been proposed in the literature.

Acknowledgment

The author thanks Richard Hull for valuable discussions and comments, which helped improve the presentation of this paper.

References

1. S. Abiteboul and R. Hull. Restructuring hierarchical database objects. *Theoretical Computer Science*, 62:3–38, 1988.
2. Y. Bar-Hillel and R. Carnap. An outline of a theory of semantic information. In Y. Bar-Hillel, editor, *Language and Information*, chapter 15, pages 221–274. Addison-Wesley, 1964.
3. C. Batini, M. Lenzerini, and S. B. Navathe. A comparative analysis of methodologies for database schema integration. *ACM Computing Surveys*, 18(4):323–364, December 1986.
4. C. Beeri. Theoretical foundations for OODB's — a personal perspective. *IEEE Data Engineering Bulletin*, 14(2):8–12, June 1991.
5. C. Beeri. New data models and languages — the challenge. In *Proceedings of the Eleventh ACM Symposium on Principles of Database Systems*, pages 1–15, 1992.
6. P. Buneman, S. Davidson, and A. Kosky. Theoretical aspects of schema merging. In *Proceedings of the Third International Conference on Extending Database Technology*, 1992.
7. M. A. Casanova, L. Tucherman, A. L. Furtado, and A. P. Braga. Optimization of relational schemas containing inclusion dependencies. In *Proceedings of the Fifteenth International Conference on Very Large Data Bases*, pages 317–325, 1989.
8. M. A. Casanova and V. M. P. Vidal. Towards a sound view integration methodology. In *Proceedings of the Second ACM Symposium on Principles of Database Systems*, pages 36–47, 1983.

9. H. B. Enderton. *A Mathematical Introduction to Logic*. Academic Press, 1972.

10. J. Goguen and J. Meseguer. Order-sorted algebra I: Equational deduction for multiple inheritance, overloading, exceptions and partial operations. *Theoretical Computer Science*, 105:217–273, 1992.

11. R. Hull. Relative information capacity of simple relational database schemata. *SIAM Journal of Computing*, 15(3):856–886, August 1986.

12. R. Hull and C. K. Yap. The format model: A theory of database organization. *Journal of the ACM*, 31(3):518–537, July 1984.

13. A. Klug. Calculating constraints on relational expressions. *ACM Transactions on Database Systems*, 5(3):260–290, September 1980.

14. V. M. Markowitz and A. Shoshani. Representing extended entity-relationship structures in relational databases: A modular approach. *ACM Transactions on Database Systems*, 17(3):423–464, September 1992.

15. R. J. Miller, Y. E. Ioannidis, and R. Ramakrishnan. Schema equivalence in heterogeneous systems: Bridging theory and practice. *Information Systems*, 19(1):3–32, January 1994.

16. X. Qian. Correct schema transformations. Technical Report SRI-CSL-95-08, Computer Science Laboratory, SRI International, July 1995.

17. A. Rosenthal and D. Reiner. Tools and transformations—rigorous and otherwise—for practical database design. *ACM Transactions on Database Systems*, 19(2):167–211, June 1994.

18. S. Spaccapietra and C. Parent. View integration: A step forward in solving structural conflicts. *IEEE Transactions on Knowledge and Data Engineering*, 6(2):258–274, April 1994.

19. D. Tsichritzis and F. Lochovsky. *Data Models*. Prentice-Hall, 1982.

20. J. D. Ullman. *Principles of Database and Knowledge Base Systems*, volume 1. Computer Science Press, 1988.

21. V. M. P. Vidal and M. Winslett. Preserving update semantics in schema integration. In *Proceedings of the Third International Conference on Information and Knowledge Management*, pages 263–271, 1994.

22. M. Wirsing. Algebraic specification. In J. van Leeuwen, editor, *Handbook of Theoretical Computer Science. Vol. B: Formal Models and Semantics*, chapter 13, pages 675–788. MIT Press/Elsevier, 1990.

Advanced DBMS

VALIDITY: Applications of a DOOD System

Oris Friesen,[1] Alexandre Lefebvre[2] and Laurent Vieille[2]

[1] Bull - VALIDITY, 13430 N. Black Canyon Hwy, Phoenix, AZ 85029-1310, U.S.A.
[2] Bull - VALIDITY, Rue Jean Jaurès, 78340 Les Clayes-sous-Bois, France

1 Introduction

The purpose of this short paper is to present an outline of VALIDITY, a Deductive and Object-Oriented Database (DOOD) system currently under development, together with a representative sample of its targeted applications.

As a DOOD system, VALIDITY combines deductive capabilities with the ability to manipulate complex objects (e.g., OIDs, inheritance, methods, etc.). It emphasizes declarative knowledge specification and logic-based tools. This emphasis turns out to offer unmatched characteristics for the development of new information systems.

First, the ability to declaratively specify knowledge as deduction and integrity rules brings *knowledge independence*. While traditional database management systems provide data independence (i.e., the ability to represent and manipulate data independently from the applications), deductive-based systems are able to represent and manipulate knowledge, such as deduction and integrity rules, independently from the applications.

Second, the logic-based languages of deductive databases enable advanced tools. For instance, explanation tools or tools checking the consistency of a set of rules can be developed using inference techniques specifically developed or adapted from previous works in Artificial Intelligence.

When compared to systems extending SQL technology, deductive systems offer more expressive declarative languages and cleaner semantics; they support logic-based tools; and they easily support SQL interfaces for co-existence with legacy applications and systems.

When compared to active database systems, deductive systems favor declarativity. For instance, an integrity rule can be expressed as one formula in a declarative database language; expressing the same integrity rule in Event-Condition-Action (ECA) rules typical of active databases would require one ECA rule for each event which may lead to an integrity violation. On the other hand, several ideas developed for active database systems (e.g., automatic integrity repairing – cf., the IDEA Esprit project) can be used to enrich deductive database systems; this is not developed here.

DOOD systems, and VALIDITY in particular, open up a new range of possibilities for the development of information systems. Applications that are suited include electronic commerce, rules-governed processes, knowledge discovery and concurrent engineering (see also *Applications of Logic Databases*, Kluwer Academic Publishers, edited by R. Ramakrishnan, 1995).

2 Overview of the VALIDITY System

VALIDITY provides: (1) a DOOD data model and language, called DEL (Data-log Extended Language); (2) an engine working along a client-server model; (3) a set of tools for schema and rule editing, validation and for querying.

The DEL data model provides object-oriented capabilities which are, in essence, similar to those provided by the ODMG data model. The DEL language includes both declarative and imperative features. The declarative features include deductive and integrity rules, with full recursion, stratified negation, disjunction, grouping and quantification. The imperative features allow functions and methods to be written.

The engine of VALIDITY integrates the traditional functions of a database (persistency, concurrency control, crash recovery, etc.) with the advanced deductive capabilities for deriving information and verifying semantic integrity. The lower-level component of the engine is a fact manager that integrates storage, concurrency control and recovery functions. The fact manager supports fact identity and complex data items. The concurrency control protocol goes beyond state-of-the-art locking techniques and integrates read-consistency technology, used in particular when verifying constraints. The higher-level component supports the DEL language and performs optimization, compilation and execution of statements and queries. The engine also supports an SQL interface permitting SQL queries and updates to be run on VALIDITY data.

VALIDITY provides tools for the management of deduction and integrity rules. Features of these tools include schema modeling, rule editing and maintenance, graphical querying, enhanced explanation and rule consistency checking. The key enabling element for the development of these tools is the solid foundation provided by the logic-based model.

Another important component of VALIDITY is DELite, a deductive wrapper for SQL systems. DELite supports a subset of DEL functionality (no constraints, no recursion, limited object capabilities, etc.) on top of commercial SQL systems. DELite facilitates the co-existence with legacy applications.

3 A Sample of VALIDITY Applications

There are various complementary ways to describe the benefits brought by VALIDITY to applications.

(1) *Knowledge independence* brings advantages in streamlining application development (multiple applications share rules managed by the database), application maintenance (changes in definitions and in regulations are more easily done) and ease-of-use (interactions are done through high-level tools enabled by the logic foundation). For instance, it simplifies the task of the application programmer who does not need to include tests in his application (defensive programming) to guarantee the soundness of his transactions.

(2) VALIDITY is able to express, manage and apply the business rules governing the various processes within a company: the rules governing the interaction between the various actors of a project can be managed and applied by

VALIDITY (see the "concurrent engineering" application); the rules expressing the business policies of a company with regard to its customers can be expressed in DEL and applied when sales people interact with customers (see the "electronic commerce" application); the rules expressing the legal regulations with which a process must comply, can be expressed as integrity rules (see the "rules-governed processes" application).

(3) VALIDITY is an ideal tool for applying software engineering principles to application development. It allows the formal specification of an application in the DEL language, which can then be directly compiled. This eliminates the error-prone step that most relational and entity-relationship methodologies require between specification and compilation.

3.1 Electronic Commerce

In the activity of electronic commerce, complex customer profiles have to be matched against target descriptions. The profiles are built from various data sources. Exceptional rules have to be introduced to deal with temporary cases or customization.

An application is currently under development with Next Century Media in the area of targeted advertising in an interactive television environment. Demographic data and viewing history compose the viewers' profiles. The advertisers rate their targets according to the available criteria.

Deduction rules describe the viewers' profiles. The matching process is also described by rules, and computed predicates deal with numeric computations. Advertisers can bring in their own viewer data and a mere rule addition takes them into account.

The declarative nature of DEL makes the formulation of the matching algorithm easy. This has proven to be a definite advantage, in the prototyping phase of the application as well as for the introduction of special matching rules.

3.2 Rules-Governed Processes

In a rules-governed process, well-defined rules define the actions to be performed, whether automatically or manually, in which case the system would give some guidance. The rules can either be formal and come from written regulations, or informal and reflect common practice.

An application prototype has been developed with the goal to handle the management of dangerous goods placed in containers, which is regulated by a large number of frequently changing regulations. Moreover, each harbor needs to customize the system to its own layout. Finally, the risks of accidents are well defined and need to be readily available to firemen in case of an incident, in order to identify the containers at risk.

The classes of dangerous materials are modeled as DEL classes. The possible locations for the containers are constrained by rules, which reflect the regulations. In the case of an incident, deduction rules identify potential accidents.

The main advantage of VALIDITY for this application has proven to be the ease in which new regulations are taken into account. This entails a productivity improvement in the development and maintenance of the application.

3.3 Knowledge Discovery

The goal of knowledge discovery is to find new data relationships by analyzing existing data. This is also sometimes called data mining; however, we do not mean here the automatic process of discovering relationships. The search process is guided by a knowledge worker, and requires an interactive, iterative process.

An application prototype has been developed for the Urban School Improvement Program, lead by the University of Illinois. This program is directed towards minority students and aims at discovering the factors that affect students' performance. The knowledge of those factors would allow corrective action.

Building the vignette with VALIDITY first consisted in building a database from multiple data sources. The original data had very few known relationships: in order to discover the factors that influence students' performance, the knowledge worker proceeds by building rules in DEL, and asking queries. The results of these queries entail the modification of the previous rules in order to re-direct the query, which often include the negation of query subparts. Rules are naturally recursive, as is the relationship between students that might have been in contact with other students.

A definite advantage of VALIDITY for knowledge discovery is the expressivity of the DEL language. Recursion is very limited in RDBMS, and negation, despite the "not in" construct of SQL, requires reformulating the query.

3.4 Concurrent Engineering

A concurrent engineering application deals with large amounts of centralized data, shared by several participants. While the design becomes more precise, the participants introduce the corresponding design decisions into the system. Inconsistencies in the design need to be detected as soon as possible, identified within the information system, and then forbidden later.

An application prototype has been developed in the area of civil engineering, based on discussions with the Center for Integrated Facility Engineering. The volume of data in a civil engineering project can be large. The participants, coming from specialized areas, are quite autonomous.

We have modeled the design data using the object-orientation power of the DEL language. When an inconsistency is detected, a new rule models the identified problem. This rule can be seen as a soft constraint. If later the participants have agreed on how to solve the inconsistency, the rule (soft constraint) is turned into a (hard) constraint simply by prefixing the formula with "not exists".

The ability of DEL to handle any closed formula as an integrity constraint has proven to be a definite advantage of VALIDITY. The nature of the language makes it easy to transform a deduction rule into an integrity constraint.

The Need for an Object Relational Model and Its Use

Daisy Bonjour

International Consultant ATG Cincom Europe South

Introduction

In order to better understand the reasons for introducing this new database management system technology, it is helpful to briefly review the evolution of database management systems from file systems through hierarchical, network, relational to most recently object-oriented database management systems.

As systems have evolved, the data management activities, such as concurrency control, authorization, etc., have been taken out of the developer's hands and put into the server itself. For example, while a file system forced the application programmer to implement concurrency by throwing locks in the application code, the first generation of database management systems (hierarchical, CODASYL, networked) provided automatic transaction management, automatic upgrading/downgrading of lock granularity for dynamic concurrency, powerful data navigation capabilities, etc.

In spite of the major benefits delivered by hierarchical, CODASYL and networked database management systems, the last decade watched a new generation of database management system –relational–dominate the database market for business data processing applications. The theory, implementation, and use of database systems became a major discipline of computer science. The simplicity of the relational data model, the dynamic management of a database, and the power of the SQL language for query processing have been accepted as vehicles for significant productivity enhancements in application development.

However, even as the acceptance of relational database systems spread, their limitations were exposed over the last decade by the emergence of various classes of new applications such as:

* multimedia systems
* statistical and scientific modeling and analysis systems
* geographic information systems
* engineering and design systems
* knowledge-based systems

The limitations of relational database systems exposed by these applications fall into two categories: data modeling and computational modeling. The data-modeling facilities that relational systems lack include those for specifying, querying and updating complex nested entities such as used in designing and engineering objects, and compound documents; arbitrary user-defined data types; frequently useful relationships, such as generalization and aggregation relationships; temporal evolution of data such as the temporal dimension of data, and versioning of data; and so on. The computation-modeling facilities that relational systems lack include the management of memory-resident objects for extensive pointer-chasing applications used for such things as the simulation of a computer-aided design; long-duration, cooperative transactions; and so on.

In order to solve the shortcomings of relational database systems, another fundamental advancement in database technology is required. The basis of this fundamental advancement is the object-oriented paradigm developed in object-oriented programming languages.

Object Oriented basis for database technology

Solutions to most of the difficulties related to the data-modeling of relational database systems are inherent in an object-oriented data model. Relational systems are designed to manage only limited types of data, such as integer, floating-point number, string, Boolean, date, time, and money. In other words, they are not designed to manage arbitrary user-defined data types. On the other hand, a central tenet of an object-oriented data model is the uniform treatment of arbitrary data types as well as the ability to add new data types. Further, an object-oriented data model allows the representation of not only data, and relationships and constraints on the data, as the relational data model does; but also the encapsulation of data and methods that operate on the data.

Another relational shortcoming is the lack of complex modeling which the object-oriented paradigm, through the notions of encapsulation and inheritance (reuse), inherently satisfies by reducing design difficulties and evolving very large and complex databases. The notions of encapsulation and inheritance are a key to further productivity gains in database application development.

However, the first generation of object-oriented database management systems were developed to provide transparency for object-oriented programming languages, and were designed initially as single user systems or as file systems with extensions to support concurrent environments. The lack of database management facilities in a first generation OO system is less of a problem in a small, static system. Moreover, first generation object-oriented systems are not able to scale up as the system has to support increasing numbers of users, diverse populations of users, growing data volumes, and high availability. As a persistent object store, a first generation database system fulfills its requirements. But, the requirements of a complete object-oriented database management system are distinguished by its database facilities (generally taken for granted in the relational world) and are fundamental for success for any shareable, reliable database system.

Unifying Relational and Object Oriented Data Models.

There is little debate today as to what the basic facilities of a database manager include: a DBMS separates the logical from the physical data storage, and automatically optimizes physical storage based on automatically captured statistics (and on "hints" from the database designer in the form of tunable DBMS parameters); a DBMS automatically enforces integrity constraints and cardinality; a DBMS provides a full authorization facility and automatically validates user access to the system; a DBMS provides on-line backup facilities and space recovery utilities, as well as automatic restart/recovery in the event of a crash; and a DBMS provides dynamic schema evolution to support non-stop mission-critical applications. All of these facilities are built-in, not layered in the interface, i.e., regardless whether access to the database is via Smalltalk, C++ or C or a query language or tool, they are automatic.

The limitations of the first generation of object-oriented data base management systems triggered database researchers to investigate and develop a second generation—object-relational database management systems.

Object-relational DBMSs were designed and built to provide ALL the benefits of the object-oriented paradigm (encapsulation, object identity, inheritance, methods, polymorphism, etc.) plus the best capabilities of pre-relational and relational database technology into a single engine. This architecture provides a formidable array of technical solutions for the most pressing problems faced by information technology organizations:

- pointer chasing to provide the high performance data navigation achieved with pre-relational database management systems.

- complete data and computational models. The object-relational data model supports all features engineered into mature relational database systems to support development of mission-critical applications. These features include full compliance to ANSI/ISO SQL92 database management language with extensions to support the object-oriented paradigm as proposed by ODMG93: updatable views, automatic query optimization, access authorization, dynamic schema evolution, automatic concurrency control, automatic recovery from crashes (including media crashes), triggers, client/server architecture, and more. In actuality, object-relational DBMS goes well beyond most conventional relational database systems in supporting such features as repeating groups, nested tables, etc.

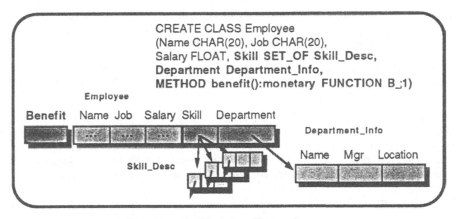

Relational Model   Extensions

- a powerful framework for uniform data management and application development support for virtually all types of multimedia data (e.g., text, images, audio, graphics, etc.), and even physical or logical devices associated with multimedia applications (e.g., scanners, fax machines, satellite links, video cameras and displays, etc.). The multimedia framework includes a built-in class hierarchy of multimedia data types and operations on them. The object-relational model also allows large unstructured data to be stored and managed in native operating system files, just as though they were inside the native object-relational database. It enables application developers to easily support virtually any type of input, output and storage device as an integral component of the data and application environment. Further, the multimedia framework is fully integrated with the query processing and transaction management components of the object-relational DBMS. Therefore, it supports queries against multimedia data and also maintains integrity for updates against multimedia data.

- inherently distributed, multidatabase management environment in which application programs using a single global view and a single database language can access multiple heterogeneous pre-relational, relational and object-oriented databases. Simply put, a distributed multidatabase is a database system that resides unobtrusively on top of existing database and file systems and presents a single database image to its users. It offers a significant improvement in productivity to application developers who develop mission-critical applications that require simultaneous reads and updates to multiple heterogeneous databases. This capability eliminates the need for application developers to use several different database interface languages and to deal laboriously with the schematic differences among multiple heterogeneous databases. Also, application developers no longer need to explicitly manage mutual consistency among multiple databases when simultaneously updating them within a single transaction. All the productivity, performance, multimedia data integration benefits and capabilities of the object-relational model carry over directly to new application development. This means the new object-oriented applications can be built using relational and pre-relational legacy databases.

Benefits of Object Relational Data Model.

The technological breakthrough that led to object-relational DBMS translates into numerous benefits for application developers:

First, because the object-relational data model offers a single database language, the application developers do not need to learn and use multiple external database interface languages to develop applications that require access to those databases.

Second, because the single database language of the object-relational model is based on ANSI/ISO SQL92 with object-oriented extensions, productivity of the application developers is almost immediate.

Third, because the data model (and database language of the object-relational DBMS is a natural outgrowth (extension) of the popular relational model and language, the application developers can take advantage of the object-oriented facilities of the object-relational DBMS to be even more productive. The object-relational data model in effect extends external relational databases with object-oriented data modeling and data management facilities.

Conclusion:

«The Object-Relational model subsumes all previous data models»

In summary, the object-relational model was designed to *subsume* the pre-relational, relational and object-oriented models by providing all the inherent capabilities of these models. This approach will provide developers with the capability of developing mission-critical applications in the challenging application domains where today's other database management systems have failed.

Persistence FrameWork™ from ATG Cincom Systems, Inc . includes one of the first commercially available
Object Relational database management system. Persistence FrameWork™ is one the primary building block of TOTAL FrameWork™.

TOTAL FrameWork™ is comprised of three primary building blocks:
The Assembly FrameWork™ , the WorkFlow FrameWork™ , and Persistence FrameWork™ , which were
developed using breakthrough object technology-based software and are fully integrated to create a powerful application assembly environment.

The WorkFlow FrameWork™ allows the intelligent flow of information to connect all tasks in a process, enforcing and automating the complete process. This component aligns IT with core business processes and reduces the lag time between business tasks, enabling a more productive, knowledgeable, and responsive workforce.

The Assembly FrameWork™ component of TOTAL FrameWork™ facilitates the assembly of highly flexible applications, enabling a quick response to market opportunities. Through the power of component-based technology, programmers can assemble customized applications that model the real-world business.

The Persistence FrameWork™ provides a single, global view to the organization's disparate information, leveraging existing systems and minimizing the disruption caused by adopting new technology. This repository allows the entire organization to work and share the same information.

Data Integration Using Self-Maintainable Views

Ashish Gupta[1] and H. V. Jagadish[2] and Inderpal Singh Mumick[2]

[1] Oracle Corporation
ashgupta@us.oracle.com
[2] AT&T Bell Laboratories
{jag,mumick}@research.att.com

Abstract. In this paper we define the concept of *self-maintainable* views – these are views that can be maintained using only the contents of the view and the database modifications, without accessing any of the underlying databases. We derive tight conditions under which several types of select-project-join are self-maintainable upon insertions, deletions and updates. Self-Maintainability is a desirable property for efficiently maintaining large views in applications where fast response and high availability are important. One example of such an environment is data warehousing wherein views are used for integrating data from multiple databases.

1 Introduction

Most large organizations have related data in distinct databases. Many of these databases may be legacy systems, or systems separated for organizational reasons like funding and ownership. Integrating data from such distinct databases is a pressing business need. A common approach for integration is to define an integrated view and then map queries on the integrated view onto queries on the individual systems. This model is not good for applications where response time is critical, or for decision support applications with complex queries. Further, in this model, the availability of the integrated view is the lowest denominator of the availabilities of all databases touched by a query. Finally, such query translation can become almost impossible when some of the underlying "databases" are actually flat files, or other non-relational systems.

We propose an alternative model, good for applications where fast response to queries and high availability are important: The integrated view is materialized and stored in a database. Queries on the view are then answered directly from the stored view. This approach involves the additional storage expense for the materialized integrated view. Also, we need to maintain the integrated view current as the underlying databases change. Maintaining the integrated database current requires efficient incremental view maintenance techniques.

Often, it may be expensive or impractical to obtain much more than just a periodic report of local updates from each underlying database. Even if an underlying database does not provide relational query support, one can require it to provide a log of changes it makes. Under such circumstances, it becomes crucial that the integrated view be *self-maintainable* (Self-M), meaning that view maintenance should be possible without requiring access to any underlying database, and without access to any information beyond the view itself and the log of the changes. Self-M can be used in data warehousing environments not only to maintain views efficiently but also to vaoid concurrency control problems faced by generic view maintenance strategies [Z+94].

We define the self-maintenance problem as the problem of maintaining a view in response to insertions, deletions, or updates (collectively referred to as modifications) using only the view and the set of changes to the referenced relations (without accessing the complete relations). We derive syntactic restrictions for SPJ view to be self-M. We show that view maintenance is easier when updates are modeled directly rather than as a set of deletions followed by insertions. The full version of this paper appears as [GJM94].

2 Background and Notation

We consider SPJ views, *i.e.*, SELECT-PROJECT-JOIN views written using SELECT-FROM-WHERE clauses. A SP (SELECT-PROJECT) view is a SPJ view with only one relation occurrence in the FROM clause.

Definition 1. (Distinguished Attribute) An attribute A of a relation R is said to be distinguished in a view V if attribute A appears in the SELECT clause defining view V.

Definition 2. (Updates) For a relation R that has a key, a tuple in R is said to be updated if one or more attributes of the tuple are assigned a value different from its original value. An update to tuple r that results in tuple r' is represented as $\mu(r, r')$.

For each of the three types of modifications (inserts, deletes, and updates) we identify classes of views that are self-M with respect to the modified relation R. We omit mentioning "with respect to modified relation R" when the context makes it clear that relation R is modified. Also, henceforth the phrase "with respect to R" implicitly assumes that R is used in the view under consideration.

Definition 3. (Self Maintainability with respect to a Modification) A view V is said to be self-M with respect to a modification type (insertion, deletion, or update) if for all database states, the view can be self-maintained in response to a modification of that type to the base relations.

Definition 4. (Local and Join Predicates) Consider a predicate $p(\bar{X})$ in the WHERE clause of a view. $p(\bar{X})$ is said to be a local predicate if all variables in $\bar{X}$ appear in a single relation in the FROM clause. Otherwise, $p(\bar{X})$ is said to be a join predicate.

Definition 5. (Derivation tree [RSUV89])(Informal) A derivation tree for a tuple t is a tree representation of the manner in which the tuple is derived from base relations. For a tuple t in a base relation, the derivation tree consists of a single node labeled with tuple t. For a tuple t in a view defined as a join between relations $R_1, \ldots, R_k$, a derivation tree consists of a root node labeled with the tuple t, and one child node for each of the tuples $(r_1 \in R_1, r_2 \in R_2, \ldots, r_k \in R_k)$ that join to derive tuple t.

Definition 6. (Tuple Derivation) Consider view V defined using relation R, and possibly other relations. A tuple r in R derives a tuple v in V if r appears in some derivation tree for tuple v.

In the paper we consider SP and SPJ views whose condition cannot, through algebraic manipulation, be rewritten in a form in which some conjunct (which itself could be a complex predicate) is either unsatisfiable or a tautology. Thus, there exists a database for which the view is non-empty. Unsatisfiable views are always empty and hence trivially self-M.

3   Self-Maintainable Views

Whether a view is self-M depends on both the definition of the view and on the type of modification, and also on other finer distinctions such as which attribute of a relation is updated, or the actual value of the modified attribute, or the presence of functional dependencies and other integrity constraints. In this paper we restrict ourselves to classifying self-maintainability with respect to the relation being modified, the type of modification, and key information.

Insertions Views are self-M for insertions only under very limited circumstances. We prove that it is not possible to self-maintain an SPJ (select-project-join) view joining at least two distinct relations upon an insertion into a component relation. Even a view involving a self-join of a relation with itself may not be self-M.

Theorem 7. *The self-maintainability of an SPJ view in response to insertions is decidable, and can be tested in time exponential in the number of self joins in the SPJ view.*

Proposition 8. *An SPJ view that takes the join of two or more distinct relations is not self-M with respect to insertions.*

Proposition 9. *All SP views are self-M with respect to insertions. An SPJ view defined using self-joins over a single relation R is self-M if every join is based on the key attributes of R.*

Deletions

Theorem 10. *An SPJ view V that joins one or more relations $R_1, \ldots, R_n$ is self-M with respect to deletions to R_1 if and only if, for every database instance, and for every occurrence of relation R_1 in the view definition, the following holds: Given a tuple t in view V, let a derivation tree for the tuple t use the tuple r in R_1 for the stated occurrence of R_1 in the view definition. Then, it is possible to identify the key of such a tuple r of R_1 from the tuple t and the view definition, without referring to the contents of any of the relations R_i.*

A sufficient condition for the conditions of Thm 10 to be true is when, for some key of relation R_1, each key attribute is either retained in the view, or is equated to a constant in the view definition. Then, given a tuple t in the view, we can identify the tuple r of R_1 from the key attributes.

Updates Updates have been modeled as deletions followed by insertions in previous view maintenance work. This model may lose information that could be useful for incremental view maintenance. Also, such a representation of an update means that a view is self-M with respect to updates only if the view is self-M with respect to both inserts and deletes. In fact, the following lemma may suggest that indeed the above conclusion holds for self-maintenance in response to updates.

Lemma 11. *Let V be an SPJ view, and R one of the relations in the* FROM *clause, such that there is at least one predicate on R. Then, the view maintenance problem for V in response to any insertion or a deletion into R can be reduced to the view maintenance problem for V in response to an update to R.*

However, a view may be self-M with respect to updates even it it is not self-M with respect to both insertions and deletions. By modeling an update directly, rather than as a deletion followed by an insertion, we retain the link between the deleted and inserted tuples. Therefore the attributes of the new tuple that needs to be inserted into the view may sometimes be obtained from the deleted tuple thereby enabling self-maintenance.

The information about the "deleted" view tuple that is retained by directly modeling updates facilitates self-maintenance in two respects: the conditions for self-maintenance becomes less onerous than in the case of simple insertions, so that many views that are not self-M with respect to insertions can be self-M with respect to updates; and the computational effort required to perform the insertion is decreased, whether or not the view is self-M.

Whether a view is self-M with respect to updates depends upon the attributes being updated. The following definition captures the property that enables self-maintenance.

Definition 12. (Exposed Variable) Given a view definition V, a variable, or equivalently, an attribute, A, of a relation used in the view definition is said to be exposed if it is involved in some predicate. A variable that is not exposed is called a unexposed variable.

A unexposed attribute does not affect the combinations of tuples that contribute to the view.

Theorem 13. *A SPJ view V that joins two or more distinct relations is self-M with respect to updates to relation R_1 if and only if either:*

- *The updated attributes are unexposed with respect to view V and are not distinguished with respect to view V, or*
- *The updated attributes are unexposed with respect to view V and V is self-M with respect to deletions to the relation R_1.*

4   Related and Future Work

View maintenance [BLT86, GMS93, GM95] has been generally studied as a problem to compute the changes to the view given the changes to the underlying relations, while having access to the view and the underlying relations.

[BCL89] defines a view to be *autonomously computable* with respect to a given update if the view can be maintained using only the materialized view for all database instances for only the given instance of the update. Autonomously Computability thus differs from self-M in that it considers a specific instance of the update, while self-M is defined over all possible updates. The update language of [BCL89] is more powerful – it permits deletions and updates to be specified using arbitrary conditions. In contrast, they do not consider views with self joins and do not use key information for deriving self-M conditions.

Future Work   This paper opens up a new area of work on view maintenance issues for data warehousing. How can functional dependencies, more general than keys, be used for for self-maintenance? How to self-maintain a *set* of views? How to self-maintain aggregate views?

5   Conclusions

An important application of the results is that they provide guidance to a designer on how to define views in the integrated database so that they may be maintained efficiently. Many times simply keeping an extra attribute can make a view self-M, and greatly reduce the maintenance work. Integrated views should be defined so as to be self-M for all expected modifications, if possible.

References

[BCL89] J. A. Blakeley, N. Coburn, and P. Larson. Updating Derived Relations: Detecting Irrelevant and Autonomously Computable Updates. *ACM Transactions on Database Systems*, 14(3):369–400, 1989.

[BLT86] J. A. Blakeley, P. Larson, and F. W. Tompa. *Efficiently Updating Materialized Views. SIGMOD 1986.*

[GJM94] A. Gupta, H. V. Jagadish, and I. S. Mumick. Data integration using self-maintainable views. Technical memorandum, AT&T Bell Laboratories, November 1994.

[GM95] A. Gupta and I. S. Mumick. Maintenance of Materialized Views: Problems, Techniques, and Applications. In *IEEE Data Engineering Bulletin, Special Issue on Materialized Views and Data Warehousing*, 18(2), June 1995.

[GMS93] A. Gupta, I. S. Mumick, and V. S. Subrahmanian. Maintaining Views Incrementally. In *Proceedings of ACM SIGMOD 1993 International Conference on Management of Data*, pages 157–167.

[LMSS95] J. Lu, G. Moerkotte, J. Schu, and V. Subrahmanian. Efficient maintenance of materialized mediated views. In *SIGMOD*, 1995.

[RSUV89] R. Ramakrishnan, Y. Sagiv, J. D. Ullman, and M. Vardi. Proof-tree Transformation Theorems and Their Applications. In *PODS*, 1989.

[Z+94] Y. Zhuge, H.Garcia-Molina, J. Hammer, and J. Widom. View Maintenance in a Warehousing Environment. In *SIGMOD 1995.*

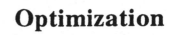

Optimization

Monet and its Geographical Extensions:
A Novel Approach to High Performance GIS Processing*

Peter A. Boncz, Wilko Quak, Martin L. Kersten

University of Amsterdam, CWI
{boncz,quak,mk}@fwi.uva.nl

Abstract

We describe Monet, a novel database system, designed to get maximum performance out of today's workstations and symmetric multiprocessors.

Monet is a type- and algebra-extensible database system using the Decomposed Storage Model (DSM) and employing shared memory parallelism. It applies purely main-memory algorithms for processing and uses OS virtual memory primitives for handling large data. Monet provides many options in memory management and virtual-memory clustering strategies to optimize access to its tables.

We discuss how these unusual features impacted the design, implementation and performance of a set of GIS extension modules, that can be loaded at runtime in Monet, to obtain a functional complete GIS server.

The validity of our approach is shown by excellent performance figures on both the Regional and National Sequoia storage benchmark.

1 Introduction

In recent years, consensus has been reached in the GIS community about the advantages of extensible database systems. In these systems, all data – thematic, geometric, and raster – is captured by a single datamodel. Queries containing both thematic and geometric primitives can be formulated in one language, and be optimized globally. Object-relational systems that extend their data- and query-model with GIS types and primitives are currently available [19, 5].

Storage and querying of geographic data in an extensible database system still poses severe performance challenges to current database technology. Data stored in a GIS is typically complex of nature (long polygons with topological inter-relationships) and large of size (raster data, sometimes even arriving in a continuous stream from satellites observing the earth).

The large datavolumes involved require the DBMS to use very efficient resource management strategies. Important aspects are I/O, multi-level cache performance, memory management and multiprocessor usage. Geographic query optimization requires an efficient use of spatial access paths and approximation

---

* Parts of this work were supported by SION grant no. 612-23-431

steps [3], and a way to extend the query optimizer with geometric knowledge [10].

In this article we present Monet [2], a novel database server, intended to serve as backend in various application domains. It has already achieved considerable successes in Data Mining [12] and for supporting O-O traversals[2].

We discuss how Monet's architectural features provide opportunities for algebraic optimization and parallelization of queries, and how we extended Monet with geographical primitives. The performance effectiveness and scalability of our approach is demonstrated by excellent results obtained on respectively the Regional and National Sequoia Benchmark.

Our work on Monet forms the lower layer of the MAGNUM project – underway since 1994 – that aims at building a high performance parallel GIS database system with ODMG compliant O-O technology, employing a spatial reasoning system for query optimization, and a state-of-the-art user interface.

2 Architecture of Monet

Monet is a novel database kernel under development at the CWI and UvA since 1994. Its development is based on both our experience gained in building PRISMA [1], a full-fledged parallel main-memory RDBMS running on a 100-node multi-processor, and on current market trends in database server technology.

Developments in personal workstation hardware are at a high and continuing pace. Main memories of 128 MB are now affordable and custom CPUs currently can perform over 50 MIPS. They rely more and more on efficient use of registers and cache, to tackle the ever-increasing disparity[3] between processor power and main memory bus speed. These hardware trends pose new rules to computer software – and to database systems – as to what algorithms are efficient. Another trend has been the evolution of operating system functionality towards micro-kernels, i.e. those that make part of the Operating System functionality accessible to customized applications. Prominent research prototypes are Mach, Chorus and Amoeba, but also commercial systems like Silicon Graphics' Irix and Sun's Solaris increasingly provide hooks for better memory and process management.

Given this background, we applied the following ideas in the design of Monet:

- *binary relation model*. Monet vertically partitions all multi-attribute relationships in Binary Association Tables (BATs, see Figure 1), consisting of [OID,attribute] pairs.
  This Decomposed Storage Model (DSM) [4] facilitates table evolution, since the attributes of a relation are not stored in one fixed-width relation. In a GIS setting, this means that Monet can easily choose to start maintaining

---

[2] For more details and actual information on Monet, see
  http://www.cwi.nl/cwi/projects/monet.html
[3] In recent years this disparity has been growing with 40% each year

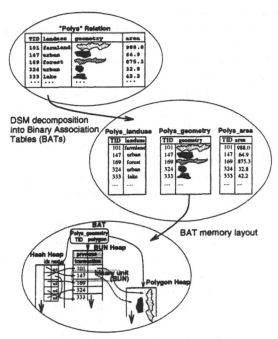

Fig. 1. An example of Monet's decomposed storage scheme, in a GIS-extended application

precomputed functions on a table with geometric data, by creating a new – separate – BAT with this information.

The price paid for DSM is small: the slightly bigger storage requirements are compensated by Monet's flexible memory management using heaps. The extra cost for re-assembling multi-attribute tuples before they are returned to an application, is negligible in a main-memory setting, and is clearly outweighed by saving on I/O for queries that do not use all the relation's attributes.

Finally, maintaining all attributes in a different table enables Monet to cluster each attribute differently, and to precisely advice the operating system on resource management issues, for each attribute according to its access path characteristics.

Figure 1 shows how relations are stored in BATs. The left column is referred to as *head*, the right column as *tail*. A BAT has at least 1 and at most 5 associated *heaps*, which form the basic memory structure of Monet. There is always a heap that contains the (fixed-size) atomic value pairs, called Binary UNits (BUNs). For atoms of variable size – such as string or polygon – both head and tail can have an associated heap (the BUNs then contain integer byte-indices into that heap). Finally, persistent search accelerators – for instance hash tables – may be stored in separate heaps, for both head and tail.

– *perform all operations in main memory.* Monet makes aggressive use of main memory by assuming that the database hot-set fits into main memory. All its primitive database operations work on this assumption, no hybrid algorithms are used. For large databases, Monet relies on virtual memory by mapping large files into it. In this way, Monet avoids introducing code to 'improve' or 'replace' the operating system facilities for memory/buffer management. Instead, it gives advice to the lower level OS-primitives on the intended behavior[4] and lets the MMU do the job in hardware.

Unlike other recent systems that use virtual memory [11, 21], Monet stores its tables in the same form on disk as in memory (no pointer swizzling), making the memory-mapping technique completely transparent to its main-memory algorithms.

Furthermore, Monet lets you specify a memory management strategy for each individual heap. Large heaps tend to be memory-mapped, while smaller heaps can be loaded in memory for speed. As for buffering strategies, BATs with a generally sequential access pattern can profit from DMA page prefetching, whereas this can be disabled for randomly accessed heaps.

 — *extensible algebra.* As has been shown in the Gral system [10], many-sorted algebras have many advantages in database extensibility. Their open nature allows for easy addition of new atomic types, functions on (sets of) those types. Also, an SQL query calculus-to-algebra transformation provides a systematic framework where query optimization and parallelization of even user-extended primitives becomes manageable. Monet's Interface Language (MIL) interpreted language with a C-like syntax, where sets are manipulated using a *BAT-algebra.*

The MIL has a sister language called MEL (Monet Extension Language), which allows you to specify extension modules. These modules can contain specifications of new atomic types, new instance- or set-primitives and new search accelerators. Implementations have to be supplied in C/C++ compliant object code.

 — coarse grained *shared-memory parallelism.* Parallelism is incorporated using parallel blocks and parallel cursors (called "iterators") in the MIL. Unlike mainstream parallel database servers, like PRISMA [1] and Volcano [9], Monet does not use tuple- or segment-pipelining. Instead, the algebraic operators are the units for parallel execution. Their result is completely materialized before being used in the next phase of the query plan. This approach benefits throughput at a slight expense of response time and memory resources.

A version of Monet designed to exploit efficiently distributed shared-nothing architectures is described in [20]. A prototype runs on IBM/SP1.

Monet's design overview is shown in Figure 2. The low-level table-handling code supplying BATs, persistency and concurrency is called GDK[5]. The top layers consist of the Monet *request-queue,* from which multiple *interpreter threads*

---

[4] This functionality is achieved with the mmap(), madvise(), and mlock() Unix system calls.

[5] the Goblin Database Kernel: a predecessor system.

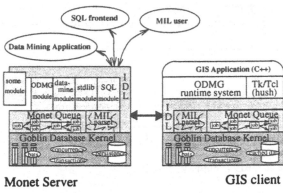

Monet Server   GIS client

Fig. 2. Monet Server and its Clients

can take jobs for execution. Some of the actual MIL primitives are kernel-primitives, though most of them are placed in extension modules, that can be dynamically loaded, configuring Monet to ODMG, Data Mining or GIS functionality.

The algebraic MIL interface has been wrapped in an IDL specification, which also allows flexible interoperability using the CORBA mechanism, and encapsulates operations executed remotely or locally. Clients can either be normal applications doing function-shipping, or peer-to-peer Monet systems. These typically are applications, which come with simplified server-layer, allowing them to cache and manipulate Monet tables locally (for data-shipping situations).

2.1 Algebraic Interface

Monet has a textual interface that accepts a set-oriented programming language called MIL (Monet Interface Language). MIL provides basic set operations (BAT-algebra) and a collection of orthogonal control structures, including mechanisms to execute tasks in parallel. The MIL interface is especially apt as target language for high-level language interpreters (SQL or OQL), allowing for rule-based algebra translation [10], in which parallel task generation is easy. Algorithms that translate relational calculus queries to BAT algebras can be found in [13, 20]

We show in an example what the MIL looks like. Consider the following object relational SQL query on the relation supply [comp#, part#, price]:

```
SELECT  company.name,
        company.telephone,
        supply.quantity
FROM    company, supply
WHERE   supply.comp# = company.comp# AND
        supply.part# = part_no AND
        supply.price < 0.50
```

In Monet's SQL frontend, the relational database scheme gets vertically decomposed into five tables named comp_name, comp_telephone, supply_comp,

152

supply_part and supply_price, where in each table the *head* contains an OID, and the *tail* contains the attribute value. The SQL query gets translated to the following MIL block:

```
{
    VAR m_supply, m_comp;
    VAR m_name, m_telephone, m_quantity;

    m_supply := SEMIJOIN(supply_part.SELECT(part_no),
                         supply_price.SELECT(0.0, 0.50));
    m_supply := MARK(m_supply);
    m_comp := JOIN(m_supply, supply_comp);
    [
        m_name       := JOIN(m_comp, comp_name);
        m_telephone  := JOIN(m_comp, comp_telephone);
        m_quantity   := JOIN(m_supply, supply_quantity);
    ]
    PRINT(m_name, m_telephone, m_quantity);
}
```

The variables created in the query cease to exist with the end of the sequential block ({}) in which they were created. The three last joins are placed in a parallel block ([]).

In all, the original double-select, single-join, three-wide projection SQL query is transformed in a sequence of 8 BAT algebra commands. The dot notation "a.oper(b)" is equivalent to function call notation "oper(a,b)". We describe in short the semantics of the BAT commands used:

BAT command	result
<AB>.mark	$\{o_i a | ab \in AB \wedge unique\_oid(o_i)\}$
<AB>.semijoin(CB)	$\{ab | ab \in AB, \exists cd \in CD \wedge a = c\}$
<AB>.join(CD)	$\{ad | ab \in AB \wedge cd \in CD \wedge b = c\}$
<AB>.select(Tl,Th)	$\{ab | ab \in AB \wedge b \geq Tl \wedge b \leq Th\}$
<AB>.select(T)	$\{ab | ab \in AB \wedge b = Tl\}$
<AB>.find(T)	$\{a | aT \in AB\}$

Note that JOIN projects out the join columns. The MARK operation introduces a column of unique new OIDs for a certain BAT. It is used in the example query to create the new – temporary – result relation.

3 Customizable Databases

When a database is used for more than administrative applications alone, the need for additional functionality quickly arises [17]. First of all, new application domains typically require – complex – *user-defined data-types*, such as for instance polygon or point. Secondly, one often needs to define new *predicates and functions* on them (intersect(p_1, p_2) or surface(p), for example). Also, new application domains often create a need for new *relational operators*, such as spatial join or polygon overlay. In order to evaluate queries using the new predicates, functions and relational operators, one needs new *search accelerators* (such as for instance R-Trees). Finally, applications using a database as backend want the option to perform certain application-specific operations near to the data. If a database server allows one to *link additional server code* on top of it, the communication penalties of creating a separate server process, encapsulating the database (a "client-level" server), can be avoided.

3.1 Other Systems

Postgres [19] and GeoSabrina [7] are typical examples of an extended relational systems, allowing for the introduction of new data types and access methods via prefixed ADT interfaces. This works fine for new datatypes, predicates on them, and their accelerators, but does not allow for addition of new relational operators. In recent years, database researchers have spent much effort on Object-Oriented databases. In these systems, the programmer has more control, but to the point that data independence is compromised and the system gets hard to debug [8]. Another effort to achieve customizability has been the "extensible-toolkit" approach, where a database can be assembled by putting together a set of "easily" customizable modules (see [6]). Putting together such a system remains a serious work, however. One of the most appealing approaches to the problem we find in the Gral system [10], which accepts a many-sorted algebra. Such an algebra can by its nature easily be extended with new operations.

3.2 Extensibility in Monet

Monet's extension system most resembles Gral, supporting new data types, new search accelerators, and user-defined primitives (embodying both new predicates and new relational operators).

Monet extensions are packaged in modules, that can be specified in the Monet Extension Language (MEL). It requires you to specify ADT interfaces for new atomic types and accelerators, together with mappings to implementation functions in C compliant object code for all ADT operations and user-defined primitives.

Both module-specification and implementation object-code are fed into the `Minstall` utility (one of several special-purpose utilities coming with the Monet server), that parses the specification, generates additional code, updates Monet's module tables, and stores the object files in the system directories.

Atomic Types The ADT interface for atomic types assures that GDK's built-in accelerators will work on user-defined types. For instance, one of the standard ADT operations is `AtomHash()`, which ensures that GDK's hash-based join works on BATs of any type. The ADT interface also contains routines to copy values to and from a heap, and to convert them to and from their string representations (for user interaction). Below we show how an atom can be specified, and which ADT operations should be defined:

```
ATOM <name> ( <fixed-size> , <byte-alignment> )
  FromStr  := <fcn>; # parse string to atom
  ToStr    := <fcn>; # convert an atom to string
  Compare  := <fcn>; # compare two atoms
  Hash     := <fcn>; # compute hash value
  Length   := <fcn>; # compute length of an atom
  Null     := <fcn>; # create a null atom
  Put      := <fcn>; # put atom in a BAT
  Get      := <fcn>; # get atom from a BAT
  Delete   := <fcn>; # delete atom from a BAT
  Heap     := <fcn>; # generate a new atom heap
END <name>;
```

In case of a fixed-sized atom, the `Put`, `Get` and `Delete` operations, perform the trivial task of updating some BUNs in the BAT. In case of a variable-sized atomic type, they have the additional task of updating the heap.

Search Accelerators GDK provides passive support for user-defined search accelerators via an ADT interface that maintains user-defined accelerators under update and I/O operations. The support is "passive" since basic GDK operations only use the built-in accelerators for their own acceleration. An ADT interface always incurs some implementation overhead, and bearing in mind that accelerators in Monet have to retain their efficiency under main-memory conditions, the canonical access path trio open(), findnext() and close() [19] was left out[6]. The ADT interface merely serves to ensure that an accelerator remains up-to-date under GDK operations.

```
ACCELERATOR <name>
  Build    := <fcn>; # build accelerator on a BAT
  Destroy  := <fcn>; # destroy accelerator
  Insert   := <fcn>; # adapt acc. under BUN insert
  Delete   := <fcn>; # adapt acc. under BUN delete
  Commit   := <fcn>; # adapt acc. for transaction commit
  Rollback := <fcn>; # adapt acc. for transaction abort
  Cluster  := <fcn>; # cluster a BAT on accelerator order
END <name>;
```

As mentioned earlier, each accelerator resides in an individual heap, and hence can be be made persistent on disk, mapped into virtual memory and assigned a buffering strategy.

New Primitives The MIL grammar has a fixed structure but depends on purely table-driven parsing. This allows for the run-time addition of new commands, operators, and iterators. Moreover, every user has an individual keyword-table, such that different users can speak different "dialects" of MIL at the same

---

[6] extension code that 'knows" the accelerator, typically accesses it with a C-macro or C++ inline function.

time. All system tables have been implemented as BATs and are accessible to the user via persistent variables for debugging purposes.

In order to do type-checking at the highest possible level, the MIL has been equipped with a polymorphism mechanism. A certain command, operation or iterator can have multiple definitions, with differing function signatures. Upon invocation, the Monet Interpreter decides which implementation has to be called, based on the types of the actual parameters.

```
COMMAND  <name> ( <type-list> )          : <type> := <fcn>;
ITERATOR <name> ( <type-list> )                  := <fcn>;
OPERATOR <name> ( <type> )                : <type> := <fcn>;
OPERATOR ( <type> ) <name> ( <type> ) : <type> := <fcn>;
```

The above shows the MEL syntax for specifying new primitives.

4 GIS processing in Monet

Using the Monet database kernel to support the GIS applications foreseen poses the following challenges on its design and implementation:

- putting optimization and extensibility together.
- efficiently dealing with huge data, while keeping overhead on small data low.

On the first point, our approach is to use Monet as a flexible GIS backend. Though this paper does not seek to investigate geographical query optimization, the BAT-operators for specifying memory management physical clusterings, and caching strategies (see Section 4.2) show that Monet provides many opportunities for doing so – using algebraic transformation techniques. In such an algebraic translation, the vertical decomposition using DSM also saves I/O, and provide a means for inter-operation parallelism [20].

4.1 Managing GIS data in main memory

Regarding the huge datavolumes, Monet's main-memory oriented approach may at first sight seem unsound. The below table shows the sizes and cardinalities of the Sequoia benchmark (as specified in [18]), and occupied space in datastructures of Monet.

On a workstation with 128 MB of main memory, Monet performs well until the database hot-set reaches 60 MB. Beyond that, the system will start swapping, until the BATs operated upon even exceed swappable memory.

Point			Polygon					
specification	monet	cardinality	specification	monet	cardinality			
2Mb	2.4Mb	60K	20Mb	39Mb	60K	Regional		
28Mb	13Mb	900K	300Mb	407Mb	900K	National		
300Mb		10M	3Gb		10M	World		
Graph			Raster					
specification	monet	cardinality	specification	monet	cardinality			
50Mb	-	300K	1Gb	900Mb	500M	Regional		
1Gb	-	6.5M	17Gb	15Gb	9G	National		
10Gb		65M	2Tb		1T	World		

SEQUOIA Benchmark Sizes

Still, one should bear in mind that GIS algorithms typically employ filtering steps, in which much smaller relations are used, before using the voluminous polygon or graph data [3].

Filtering algorithms in GIS use approximations, for example, minimum bounding rectangles (MBRs), for handling of polygon or graph data. Since a BUN consisting of a <OID, MBR> is 20 bytes long, we see that regional benchmark relations approximating the polygon and graph data would have sizes 1.2 Mb and 6 Mb, respectively, which can easily be handled in main memory. Even for the national benchmark these sizes are 18 Mb and 130 Mb, which – possibly with the help of some fragmentation – can also be made to work in a large main memory.

The above reasoning shows that the approximation steps on relatively large GIS data often can be performed in main memory. However, after the filtering steps, such algorithms still need to access the big tables, in order to perform the final steps on the filtered objects. It is clear that these tables cannot economically be held in main memory. Therefore we use virtual memory primitives, supplied by modern operating system architectures.

Memory Mapped Files In recent years, there has been an evolution of operating system functionality towards micro-kernels, i.e. those that make part of the OS functionality accessible to customized applications. Prominent prototypes are Mach, Chorus, and Amoeba, but also conventional systems like Silicon Graphics' IRIX and Sun's Solaris[7] provide hooks for better memory and process management.

Stonebraker discarded the possibility of using memory-mapped files in databases [16], on the grounds that operating systems did not give sufficient control over the buffer management strategy, and the fact that virtual management schemes waste memory. Now – a decade later – we think the picture has changed. Operating systems like Solaris and IRIX do provide hooks to give memory management advice (madvise), lock pages in memory (mlock[8]), invalidate and share pages of virtual memory. This is why recently interest of the database community in these techniques has revived [11].

Monet uses the virtual memory management system call mmap() to map big heaps into its main memory. The database table is mapped into the virtual memory as a range of virtual memory addresses. When addresses are accessed, page faults occur, and the pages are loaded when needed.

The only upper limit to the size of the tables is the virtual address space. Monet currently runs on Sun and SGI machines that have a 32-bit addressing scheme. This leads to an address space of 4 Gb, which for the present is enough. Future CPUs will be equipped with 64-bits addressing, like DEC's Alpha already is.

---

[7] These are the two platforms on which Monet is currently supported.
[8] One has to have Unix root permission for this.

4.2   Memory Management in Monet

The memory-mapping implementation technique has a number of advantages:

- it provides *flexibility*. Orthogonally of what is stored in a Monet heap, one can decide to memory-map it, or not. Additionally, for each heap one can specify a different buffering strategy, which can be one of:
    - *prefetch*. After a page-fault, get one disk cluster (64K of pages), and start an async readahead through DMA for the next cluster.
    - *random*. Just get the pages faulted on – no prefetching.
    - *sequential*. Similar to prefetch, but the touched pages are immediately marked for swapout.
- the scheme is completely *transparent* in Monet[9]. This allows for a seamless transition from main-memory processing to disk-based processing.
- it is *efficient* in loading database tables, since only the pages needed are loaded. Under page-swapping conditions it holds out better than normal memory, because the file will swap on itself, and is not copied to swap space. Also, when saving a memory-mapped file, the MMU hardware guarantees that only dirty pages are written.

Clustering on Memory Pages In effect, memory-mapped files bring Monet's approach back to the traditional, disk-based algorithms – but only where this is really necessary. This means, that in disk-dominated database configurations traditional methods such as clustering on a search accelerator order may be beneficial. Where in other systems this saves I/O, clustering will save page-faults in Monet. In Monet clustering is done by storing objects that are likely to be referenced at the time close to each other in memory – not necessarily, but probably, on the same disk-page. Remark that clustering can be performed orthogonally as an optional sorting operation (see Figure 3). It is transparent to Monet's main-memory algorithms, but will have an accelerating effect.

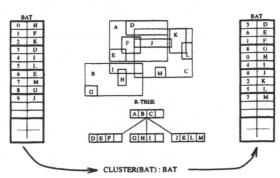

Fig. 3. Clustering BATs in Memory Pages

All three different types of heaps in a BAT can be clustered independently:

---

[9] recall that Monet's datastructures take the same form on disk as in main memory

- clustering *BUN-heaps*. The BUNs in a BAT can be clustered for optimal access via one of its associated accelerators. The result of the clustering depends on the accelerator-type. If, for instance, an R-Tree accelerator is used as access path, the resulting BUN-heap gets clustered spatially. In this case adjacent rectangles are likely to be on the same memory page. A hash-clustering ensures that items with the same hash value will be put together; this can significantly speed up equijoin operations.
- clustering *variable-sized atom heaps*. The variable-sized atoms of a BAT (which are stored in separate heap) can be clustered in the same order as the BUNs themselves. In some cases, however, it is better to cluster the BUN-heap and atom-heap differently, as we will see in the example of Section 4.2.
- clustering *search accelerator heaps*. Disk-page oriented systems use R^+ trees, putting effort in optimizing disk page occupancy, while minimizing tree-depth [15]. Monet is intended to be used in both disk-oriented as well as main-memory situations (in which simple algorithms tend to work best [14]). We solved this conflict by building a main-memory oriented R-Tree structure (with small nodes). For disk-dominated configurations we offer a clustering operation, that reorders a R-Tree, such that every memory page contains one subtree, which all together form the entire tree, where each dashed box contains about one disk-page of nodes (see Figure 4).

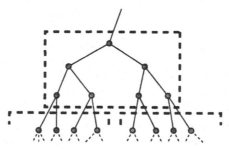

Fig. 4. Clustering R-Tree nodes on memory pages

Performance Effects of Clustering To give some idea of the impact of clustering on performance we have done some experiments with Query 6 of the Sequoia Benchmark (see Section 5). This query – which has a selectivity of about 1% – can be split into two parts: the first part selects all [OID,box] pairs within the given rectangle using an R-Tree. The boxes represent bounding boxes of polygons with the same OID. This query benefits from clustering of both the nodes in the R-Tree (in the way described above), and from clustering the [OID,box] BUNs on spatial proximity (R-Tree traversal order). The following table gives the results of this query with all possible clustering options:

time / #pageflt	nodecluster	no nodecluster
batcluster	0.234/30	0.775/89
no batcluster	0.388/39	0.843/97

The second part of Query 6 semijoins the selected OIDs with the [OID,polygon] BUNs, giving the requested set of polygons. Since Monet's semijoin is hash-based, it pays to cluster this BUN-heap, which contains only the OIDs – the polygons are in a separate variable-sized atom heap – on hash value. Because the OIDs were initially selected using the R-Tree, the polygon-heap can best be clustered on spatial proximity. This further reduced the number of page-faults on the semijoin from 336 to 274. So, we see here an example of a BAT, where the different heaps it consists of have differing optimal clustering orders.

Buffer Management Strategies On memory-mapped files, Monet uses OS hooks to give advice on OS paging cache strategies. We distinguish three ways of accessing a BAT – all of which prosper by a different caching strategy.

- If no index exists on a BAT, a sequential scan is the only way of accessing a BAT, the OS can be told that to prefetch pages[10] using DMA, and mark them for release immediately after.
- If a BAT is accessed via an index on which the BAT is clustered, it is likely that pages near a page accessed will be accessed in the near future. By telling the OS to prefetch pages in DMA (but not to release them!) speedup will be obtained.
- If a BAT is accessed via a non-clustered index, the prefetching of adjacent pages is useless, because the memory pages are accessed in random order. By telling the OS to expect random access, time wasted by prefetching unnecessary pages is saved.

Performance Effects of different Cache Strategies We ran Query 7 of the National Sequoia Benchmark (see Section 5) with different caching strategies, with the polygons clustered on R-Tree, or not:

Query 7	cluster	nocluster
random	2.29	2.35
prefetch	1.89	3.18

The above shows that in the nonclustered case, DMA *prefetching* is slower than *random* access (presumably because mostly unnecessary pages get fetched). In the clustered case, however, *prefetch* gives the best result, since spatially near polygons are stored in nearby memory pages.

Our results on clustering and buffer management prove that a database kernel, built on main-memory datastructures and algorithms, can indeed process huge data volumes (in a disk-bound setting), using modern OS virtual memory primitives.

---

[10] this is cheaper than generating page-faults one-at-a-time

5 Monet Implementation of the Regional and National Sequoia 2000 Benchmarks

To demonstrate the feasibility and effectiveness of our approach, we decided to run both the Regional and National Sequoia 2000 Storage Benchmarks [18]. Results on the Regional benchmark have been published for both research and commercial GIS database servers [5]. Our implementation of the National benchmark sets a new mile-stone for further developments in this area.

The implementation of the Monet GIS datatypes makes extensive use of MEL modules. Several modules were implemented to provide for the necessary primitives and search accelerators. The Sequoia Regional Dataset was obtained, and a National Dataset was created from it. Then, the Sequoia queries were translated to Monet's MIL interface and run. The modules and the experimentations are described below.

5.1 Extension Modules

To support the Sequoia Dataset, we have implemented Point, Box and Polygon atomic types. The former two consist of fixed-size records of integers. The polygon type is a variable-sized type: BAT's containing polygons will store them in an associated heap. We provided ADT operations for these atoms, as well as predicates on them (such as bool : Point_In_Box(p,b)).

To optimize access on queries involving spatial proximity, we chose to implement R-Trees [15]. Since Monet accelerators must perform well in both main-memory as disk-based settings, we chose the most simple, lightweight approach, complemented by clustering operations to optimize on page-faults. Algebra-operations like RTREEselect() where added that use these R-Trees to optimize, in this case, an overlap-select. Similarly, Quad-Trees [15] were implemented, for fast access to points.

Rasters were implemented as unary tables: these are BATs which have the void type any in one of the columns. We interpret such an unary as a 2-D mesh of tiles. The tiles are adjusted – depending on the atomsize – to occupy one diskpage, and from left to right, row by row. This raster functionality was created by defining new commands, operating on unary BATs, that in effect perform raster-loads and -clippings.

All extensions were packaged in a set of MEL modules, from which an excerpt is shown below:

```
MODULE Box;
    ATOM Box(16,4);
        TOSTR    = BOXtoStr;
        FROMSTR  = BOXfromStr;
        COMP     = BOXcomp;
        DEL      = BOXdel;
        HASH     = BOXhash;
        NULL     = BOXnull;
```

```
      PUT      = BOXput;
      GET      = BOXget;
      LENGTH   = BOXlength;
      HEAP     = BOXheap;
   END;
END Box;

MODULE RTree;
   USE Box;
   ACCELERATOR RTree ( Box );
      BUILD    = RTREEmake;
      DESTROY  = RTREEdestroy;
      INSERT   = RTREEinsert;
      SAVE     = RTREEsave;
   END;

   OPERATOR (bat[any,ibox]) Join (bat[ibox,any])
         : bat(any,any)  = RTREEjoin;
   COMMAND RTreeSelect( bat[any,ibox], ibox )
         : bat(any,ibox) = RTREEselect;
   COMMAND RTreeCluster( bat[ibox,any] )
                         = RTREElogiccluster;
   COMMAND RTreeClusterNodes( bat[ibox,any] )
                         = RTREEfysiccluster;
END RTree;
```

5.2 Test Configuration

The Regional sequoia Dataset consists of point-, polygon-, directed graph- and raster-data about the State of California. We generated a National benchmark out of this data, by creating a grid of 5×3 States of California. We also expanded the queries with a factor 15, that is, our National Benchmark queries select on regions that are 15 times as big as the Regional selections, etc.[11]

Our benchmark platform was a Sparc 20, at 60 Mhz, 1MB secondary cache, with 128 MB of main memory. It has a Seagate ST15150W disk with 5Gb capacity, a throughput of 20Mbyte/s throughput and 0.85 msec access time. The client was a Sun IPX, connected to the server by 10Mbit/s ethernet. In this article, we compare our numbers with results published on Postgres, Illustra and Paradise [5]. The configuration described there has a CPU about twice slower, a disk with roughly twice less throughput, and 1.0 msec access time. For this reason, we hardware corrected their numbers for comparison purposes with a factor 0.6. This factor was taken by assuming that Sequoia performance is 50% I/O and 50% CPU bound, giving equal weight to differences in random access time and throughput. Of course, this is only a rough comparison: in random-access

[11] detailed information about the Sequoia Dataset scripts, the queries, and results can be found on
http://www.cwi.nl/projects/monet/sequoia/.

queries, we expect Monet to perform relatively better, whereas CPU bound results may be a bit inflated.[11]

5.3 Query Results and Analysis

The below table gives the results of the Sequoia queries:

Query 1: Database load				
	Monet National	Monet Regional	Paradise Regional	Illustra Regional	Postgres Regional
total	37190	712	2204	3506	5299
raster	34580	590			
point	656	14.5			
poly	1954	107			

Monet National			Monet Regional			Para- dise	Illus- tra	Post- gres
Query 2: Select a raster for a given wavelength and rectangle, ordered by ascending time.								
cold	warm	hot	cold	warm	hot	cold	cold	cold
45.5			3.7	3.0	1.4	8.0	8.9	8.2
Query 3: Select a raster for a given time and rectangle, and calculate an average on the wavelengths for each cell.								
cold	warm	hot	cold	warm	hot	cold	cold	cold
14.2			0.87	0.75	0.38	1.20	2.88	3.44
Query 4: Select a raster for a given time, wavelength band and rectangle. Lower the resolution of the image by a factor 64 and store it in the DBMS.								
cold	warm	hot	cold	warm	hot	cold	cold	cold
2.4	1.6	1.2	0.24	0.18	0.09	0.36	1.44	0.78
Query 5: Find all points with a given name.								
cold	warm	hot	cold	warm	hot	cold	cold	cold
0.10	0.08	0.00	0.09	0.08	0.00	0.12	0.60	0.54
Query 6: Find all polygons intersecting a rectangle.								
cold	warm	hot	cold	warm	hot	cold	cold	cold
5.8	5.3	1.6	2.1	1.1	0.2	4.3	12.5	22.0
Query 7: Find all polygons larger than a certain size, and within a specific circle.								
cold	warm	hot	cold	warm	hot	cold	cold	cold
1.90	0.90	0.06	0.51	0.39	0.01	0.42	0.49	21.3
Query 8: Show the landuse/landcover in a 50km quadrangle surrounding a given point.								
cold	warm	hot	cold	warm	hot	cold	cold	cold
5.0	2.9	0.2	1.6	0.7	0.3	5.7	14.5	37.9
Query 9: Find the raster data for a given landuse type in a study rectangle for a given wavelength band and time.								
cold	warm	hot	cold	warm	hot	cold	cold	cold
14.7	0.7	0.4	1.4	0.2	0.0	1.7	0.7	1.7
Query 10: Find the names of all points of a specific vegetation type and create this a a new DBMS object.								
cold	warm	hot	cold	warm	hot	cold	cold	cold
			4.7		1.4	-	0.4	196.2

The measured times, presented throughout this article are in seconds of elapsed time.[12] The table presents three times for both the National and Regional measurements:

- *cold:* the tables involved in the query have not been accessed since server startup.
- *warm:* the tables involved in the query have been accessed, but for a query that involved different data instances. This time captures typical database browsing access.
- *hot:* the same query was run as just before. This number characterizes execution time in a purely main-memory situation.

All Sequoia relations were vertically partitioned into separate <relation>_<attribute> BATs having OIDs in the head-columns, and a Sequoia attribute in the tail column.

The OID head-columns of all BATs had a hash-index built on them. The BUN-heaps of all BATs were clustered on these hash-tables, except for the Points_location BAT, which was clustered on the Quad-Tree indexing the points.

During polygon creation, we computed bounding box approximations for all polygons. On this Polys_bboxes BAT, an R-Tree was built, with which the polygon-heap of the Polys_geometry was clustered.

Monet's default buffering strategy on memory-mapped heaps is *random*. Since GIS data is large, we chose to memory-map all heaps of all BATs for both the Regional and the National Benchmark. The *prefetch* strategy was applied only to take advantage of clustering: on the tree-indices, and the polygon-heap (which was clustered on R-tree).

Query 2 requires the result to be exported back to the client. This was done by writing the resulting rasters to a disk on the client with NFS.

Most time in Query 1 (database load) is spent on parsing the ASCII files, making this query CPU bound. The high performance is achieved mainly by DSM, making the construction of index structures cheap, since the tuples involved are small. We should add, though, that the fast results are a bit offset by the fact that our topological datastructures were not yet finished, so we did not have to import graph data (and consequently we did not perform Query 11 either – but neither did the other systems).

The fast performance on raster queries show the benefit of a low overhead system. Raster data for each time and wavelength band was stored in a separate – equally sized – raster, amounting to a total of 130 unary BATs. Since we did not have sufficient disk space to generate all 130 rasters for the National benchmark,

---

[12] Interestingly, our larger memory (128MB vs 32MB) was no factor of influence, due to the simple selection-character of the Sequoia queries. The biggest memory user was Regional Query 6 with 3.0 MB of loaded memory plus 1.2 MB in memory mapped pages. Only database import takes more memory: point query 1 takes 26 MB.

the national raster queries accessed a subset of them multiply, calling a memory-flush utility between accessing them during query execution.[11]

As for the polygon- and point-queries, our results show that simple main-memory algorithms, enhanced by clustering and specific cache strategies on individual heaps, give good performance, even on very large datasets. More data than described here was obtained, but is omitted here because of space limitations.[11]

Note that we did not use Monet as a main-memory system here: no data was preloaded whatsoever. Our "cold" times therefore present the worst-case behaviour; when Monet's performance becomes disk-bound. This made a fair comparison with other systems possible. If we had used the potential of our 128 MB (e.g. by preloading all search accelerator heaps), thus blending main-memory with disk-bound processing, "cold" times would improve dramatically towards the "hot" numbers.

As a final point, we think that the Sequoia benchmark has limitations in both the simplicity of the queries – providing no need for complex optimization – and lack of serious thematic data, that would make relations even wider. A more complex benchmark would favor our algebraic approach, and wider relations would let Monet save even more I/O using its Decomposed Storage Model.

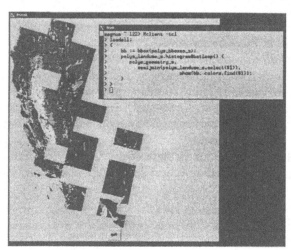

Fig. 5. Provisional GEO-Monet Interface

6   Future Work

In the short term, our current provisional interface (Figure 5), just allows for drawing maps using algebraic commands – and zooming in/out with the mouse. It will be replaced soon by the GIS client depicted in Figure 2, that provides a better interface and caches results for supporting browsing sessions.

Our future actions involve further development of a full-fledged geometric and topological reasoning system on top of the current framework. Extension with CPU-intensive routines also requires further investments in parallel execution.

An OQL query optimizer and graphical user-interface are under development by other members of the MAGNUM project. This work takes place in the context of our ODMG compliant persistent programming system, that uses Monet and its – geographical – extensions as a backend.

7   Conclusions

We describe Monet, a MMDBMS that employs OS virtual-memory and buffer management primitives when large data volumes exceed main-memory. Its novel architecture presents a response to the trend of increasing main-memory sizes in custom hardware, that can be contrasted with the approach of just equipping a conventional DBMS with a large cache. To test the performance and extensibility of our system, we wrote GIS modules and ran the Sequoia benchmarks. Our implementation of the 15 GB National benchmark sets a new mile-stone for future developments in this area.

Monet uses of virtual memory primitives to avoid overhead typically induced by a DBMS tuple-manager. Its flexible storage structures (Decomposed Storage Model) and efficient (lightweight) algorithms, make it a highly efficient main-memory system, as shown by the "hot" Sequoia results. The "cold" experiments present the proof of concept for the employed OS techniques: Monet also obtains excellent results when huge datavolumes degrade performance to disk-bound processing.

Holding more and more data memory-resident will make performance gradually shift from Monet's "cold" towards the "hot" performance, thus enabling to blend main-memory with disk-bound processing – a desirable property in times where many application domains are moving around the brink of the two situations.

Acknowledgements

We thank the members of the database research group of CWI and UvA for their continual support in making Monet a viable DBMS. The challenges posed by the MAGNUM project members have been a stimulus to prove our case.

References

1. P. M. G. Apers, C. A. van den Berg, J. Flokstra, P. W. P. J. Grefen, M. L. Kersten, and A. N. Wilschut. PRISMA/DB: A parallel main memory relational DBMS. *IEEE Trans. on Knowledge and Data Eng.*, 4(6):541, December 1992.
2. P. A. Boncz and M. L. Kersten. Monet: An impressionist sketch of an advanced database system. In *Proc. IEEE BIWIT workshop, San Sebastian (Spain).*, July 1995.
3. T. Brinkhoff, H. Kriegel, R. Schneider, and B. Seeger. Multi-step processing of spatial joins. In *23 ACM SIGMOD Conf. on the Management of Data*, pages 197–208, June 1994.

4. G. Copeland and S. Khoshafian. A decomposition storage model. In *Proc. ACM SIGMOD Conf.*, page 268, Austin, TX, May 1985.

5. David J. DeWitt, Navin Kabra, Jun Luo, Jignesh M. Patel, and Jie-Bing Yu. Client-server Paradise. In *Proceedings of the 20th VLDB Conference, Santiago, Chile.*, pages 558–569, September 1994.

6. et al. Carey,M. and DeWitt,D. The EXODUS extensible DBMS project: An overview. In *In 'Readings in Object-Oriented Database Systems*.

7. et al. G.Gardarin and M.Jean-Noël. Sabrina, a relational database system developed in a research environment. In *Technology and Sciences of Informatics*. AFCET-Gauthier Villard - John Willey and Sons Ltd., 1987.

8. et al. Neuhold,E. and Stonebraker,M. Future directions in DBMS research. *ACM SIGMOD RECORD*, 18(1), March 1989.

9. G. Graefe. Encapsulation of parallelism in the volcano query processing system. In *19 ACM SIGMOD Conf. on the Management of Data, Atlantic City*, May 1990.

10. R. H. Guting. Gral: An extensible relational database system for geometric applications.

11. D. Lieuwen H. V. Jagadish, R. Rastogi, A. Silberschatz, and S. Sudarshan. Dali: A high performance main memory storage manager. In *Proceedings of the 20th VLDB Conference, Santiago, Chile.*, pages 48–59, September 1994.

12. M. Holsheimer, M. L. Kersten, and A. Siebes. Data Surveyor: searching for nuggets in parallel. In *Knowledge Discovery in Databases*. MIT Press, Cambridge, MA, USA, 1995.

13. S. Khoshafian, G. Copeland, T. Jagodits, H. Boral, and P. Valduriez. A query processing strategy for the decomposed storage model. In *Proc. IEEE CS Intl. Conf. No. 3 on Data Engineering, Los Angeles*, February 1987.

14. T. J. Lehman and M. J. Carey. A study of index structures for main memory database management systems. In *Proceedings of the 12th VLDB Conference, Kyoto*, August 1986.

15. H. Samet. *The Design and Analysis of Spatial Data Structures*. Addison Wesley, 1990.

16. M. Stonebraker. Operating system support for database management. *Communications of the ACM*, 14(7), July 1981.

17. M. Stonebraker. Inclusion of new types in relational database systems. In *Proc. IEEE CS Intl. Conf. No. 2 on Data Engineering, Los Angeles*, February 1986.

18. M. Stonebraker, J. Frew, K. Gardels, and J. Meredith. The Sequoia 2000 storage benchmark. In *19 ACM SIGMOD Conf. on the Management of Data, Washington,DC*, May 1993.

19. M. Stonebraker and G. Kemnitz. The POSTGRES next-generation database management system. *Comm. of the ACM, Special Section on Next-Generation Database Systems*, 34(10):78, October 1991.

20. C. A. van den Berg and M. L. Kersten. An analysis of a dynamic query optimisation scheme for different data distributions. In J. Freytag, D. Maier, and G.Vossen, editors, *Advances in Query Processing*, pages 449–470. Morgan-Kaufmann, San Mateo, CA, 1994.

21. Seth J. White and David J. DeWitt. Quickstore: A high performance mapped object store. In *ACM SIGMOD Conf. on the Management of Data*, pages 395–406, May 1994.

Optimizing Queries with Aggregate Views

Surajit Chaudhuri[1] and Kyuseok Shim[2]

[1] Hewlett-Packard Laboratories, 1501 Page Mill Road, Palo Alto, CA 94304, USA
[2] IBM Almaden Research Center, 650 Harry Road, San Jose, CA 95120, USA

Abstract. Complex queries, with aggregates, views and nested subqueries are important in decision-support applications. Such queries are represented as multi-block queries where a query block may be a view definition containing aggregates or a correlated nested subquery. Beyond transformations that propagate predicates across blocks, the problem of optimizing such queries has not been addressed adequately. In this paper, we show how such queries can be optimized in a *cost-based* fashion. The crux of our solution is a careful treatment of group-by and aggregation operators that occur among views.

1 Introduction

Complex queries, with views containing aggregates and nested subqueries, are important in decision-support applications (e.g., see TPC-D benchmark). *Cost-based* optimization of such queries cannot be handled by most of the existing optimizers.

An *aggregate view* is a SQL Select-Project-Join query with a group-by clause In this paper, we address the problem of cost-based optimization of queries that consists of joins among base relations and aggregate views, possibly followed by a group-by (See Figure 3).

The problem of optimizing queries containing aggregate views is not only a key problem in its own right, but it also directly bears upon the problem of optimizing queries with nested subqueries. This follows from the past work in *flattening* to handle an important class of queries with nested subqueries (*join-aggregate* queries), pioneered by Kim [Kim82] (cf. [GW87, Day87, Mur92]). The result of Kim's transformation on a query with nested subqueries is a query that is a join[3] of base tables and one or more aggregate views. Thus, using Kim's transformation, the result of optimizing queries containing aggregate views can be used for optimizing an important class of queries with correlated nested subqueries [CS96].

Unfortunately, the techniques for optimizing queries with aggregate views have been limited to propagating predicates across query blocks [MFPR90, LMS94] to reduce the cost of optimizing each query block. However, subsequent to this preprocessing, each query block is optimized *locally* using the optimization algorithm for SPJ queries. What's missing is the ability to enumerate plans that

---

[3] In some cases, such transformations may introduce outerjoins.

considers joining relations that occur in *different query blocks*. This requires deferring aggregation after join. On the other hand, we must also consider the opportunities of taking advantage of possible data reduction effect of early aggregation.

In this paper, we present *transformations* as well as *optimization algorithms* for queries with aggregate views. We propose the *pull-up transformation* that makes it possible to reorder relations that belong to different query blocks. The key idea is to defer evaluation of group-by operators of aggregate views so that the relations across the query blocks may be joined before the group-by operators are applied. This transformation complements the previously studied *push-down transformation* that has the opposite effect, i.e., the latter pushes down a group-by even if in the given query, the evaluation of the join precedes the evaluation of the group-by.

In the second part of the paper, we present *optimization algorithms*. The challenge is to incorporate the pull-up transformation as well as push-down transformations in optimizers so that it is possible to pick a plan in a cost-based fashion. This problem has been only partially addressed in prior work [CS94]. Incorporating these transformations interacts with the problem of join ordering. We present an extension of the dynamic programming based join enumeration algorithm that can be adapted by many commercial optimizers. Our proposed algorithm enumerates a richer execution space beyond the traditional style of optimizing each query block *locally*. Furthermore, our cost-based optimization algorithm is guaranteed to pick a plan that is *no worse* than the traditional optimization algorithm. In summary, the paper presents an approach to optimizing queries that contain aggregate views in a cost-based fashion. Our approach, in conjunction with flattening algorithms, also provides a solution to the problem of optimizing complex queries containing nested subqueries.

In Section 3, we define the pull-up transformation and Section 4 reviews the push down transformations. The optimization algorithm is described in Section 5. In each section, we will discuss appropriate relevant work.

2 Preliminaries

Let us consider a SQL query of the following form:

```
(Q1) Select All <columnlist> AGG1(b1)..AGGn(bn)
     From    <tablelist>
     Where   cond1 and ... and condn
     Group By col1,..colj
     Having agg_cond1 and.. and agg_condk
```

SQL semantics [ISO92] require that `<columnlist>` must be among `col1,..colj`. The `Having` clause contains predicates that refer to the aggregated columns of the query. In the above notation, `AGG1..AGGn` represent *aggregate functions*. An aggregate function can be built-in or user-defined (without side-effects), e.g., `Sum(colname)` and `Standard_deviation(colname)`.

If each of the tablename in `<tablelist>` is a base table, then we refer to the above query as a *single block query*. Thus, a single-block query has the form $G(V)$ where G is a group-by operator and V is a SPJ query. To simplify the presentation, we assume that every aggregate view is also a single-block query, the database contains no NULLs and there are no outerjoins in the query. In the full version of our paper, we show how to relax these restrictions [CS96].

We can view our queries algebraically in terms of operators. An *operator tree* reflects the partial order on evaluation of operators in a query. In this paper, we use the term operator tree and *execution plan* alternatively. In this paper, we will consider *join* and *group-by* operators. A join operator is specified by naming relations it joins and a list of join predicates. Likewise, a set of *grouping columns* and a set of *aggregating columns* are associated with each group-by operator. Thus, the set of columns {b1,..bn} and the set of columns {col1,..colj} are the aggregating and grouping columns respectively. Additional annotations of a group-by operator include names of aggregating functions and predicates in the `Having` clause. We do not view projection as an explicit operator. Instead, we assume that each join as well as each group-by operator has an associated list of projection columns. Finally, we will use the notion of a *legal* operator tree, which corresponds to a syntactically correct algebraic expression [CS96].

3 Pull-up Transformation: Reordering Across Query Blocks

If each view is a SPJ query, then a query consisting of a join among such views and base tables is traditionally *reduced* to a single-block query and optimized. However, if an aggregate view contains a group-by operator, then the traditional reduction techniques do not apply. Our proposal for the pull-up transformation makes it possible to defer evaluation of a group-by until after a join although the former precedes the latter in an operator tree. A sequence of pull-up transformations may result in collapsing a multi-block query into a single-block query where traditional techniques fail. We introduce the intuition behind the transformation using the example below.

Example 1. Let us ask for employees below the age of 22 and who earn more than the average of the department salary. The query A1 computes the average salary of each department. Next, in the query A2, this average salary is compared with the salary of each employee.

```
(A1): A1(dno, Asal) AS              (A2): select e1.sal
        select e2.dno, avg(e2.sal)          from emp e1, A1 b
        from emp e2                         where e1.dno = b.dno and
        group by e2.dno                        e1.age < 22 and
                                               e1.sal > b.Asal
```

An alternative way to execute this query will be to identify employees under 22 years old and for each one of them to compute the average salary of the department they work in. Then, the average salary can be compared with the salary of the employee.

```
(B): select e1.sal
     from emp e1, emp e2
     where e1.dno = e2.dno and
           e1.age < 22
     group by e2.dno, e1.eno, e1.sal
     having e1.sal > avg(e2.sal)
```

Note that if there are many departments but few employees are younger than 22 years, then the query B may be more efficient to evaluate than A1 and A2. However, if there are few departments but many employees below 22 years old, then execution of A1 and A2 may be significantly less expensive. ∎

In the above example, A1 is an aggregate view and the query A2 is a join between an aggregate view and a base table. The query A2 cannot be flattened using traditional techniques. However, the query B, which is a single-block query equivalent to A2, results from an application of the pull-up transformation on A1 and A2.

We now formally define the pull-up transformation in terms of execution plans (i.e., operator trees). Let us consider the execution plans P1 and P2 in Figure 1. In the figure, R1 & R2, J1 & J2, and G1 & G2 are base (or derived) tables, join nodes and group by operators, respectively. By applying a pull-up transformation to the execution plan P1, we defer the group-by and obtain an equivalent plan P2.

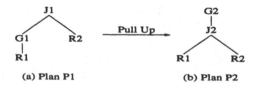

Fig. 1. Pulling Up a Group-By operator

We note that for each distinct tuple of values corresponding to grouping columns of G1 and each distinct tuple of R2 that matches the join predicate, the plan P1 produces a tuple. Therefore, to ensure equivalence we preserve the key columns of R2 until application of the group-by operator G2 and make the grouping columns of G2 to be the union of the grouping columns of G1 and the key columns of R2. Therefore, in P2, J2 includes key columns of R2 in its projection columns as well as aggregating columns in G1. Every join predicate on the aggregated columns of G1 needs to be deferred as a condition in the Having clause of the group-by operator G2 in the new plan. We can now state the formal statement of the transformation:

Definition 1. Given a legal operator tree P1 (Figure 1), the *pull-up transformation* produces a legal operator tree P2 (Figure 1) where

1. The projection columns of $G2$ are the same as that of $J1$.
2. The set of grouping columns of $G2$ is the union of grouping columns of $G1$, projection columns of $J1$ (except aggregated columns of $G1$), and a primary key of $R2$.
3. All aggregating columns of $G1$ that are among projection columns of $J1$ appear as aggregating columns of $G2$.
4. All join predicates in $J1$ involving aggregated columns in $G1$ appear as predicates in the **Having** clause of $G2$.
5. The join predicates of $J2$ are the join predicates of $J1$ that involve no aggregated columns of $G1$.

In [CS96], we formally establish that the trees $P1$ and $P2$ are equivalent. Observe that the transformation makes use of the *key* columns of $R2$. In the absence of a declared primary key, the query engine can use the internal *tuple id* as a key. In case the join $J1$ is a foreign key join, then the primary key of $R2$ does not need to be explicitly included in the grouping columns of $G2$. The statement of the above transformation assumes that *P1* and *P2* are legal plans. Therefore, the specification of plan $P2$ in the above definition is only partial. Thus, the definition also implies additional constraints, e.g., the projection columns of $J2$ include the key columns of $R2$ and columns of $R1$ and $R2$ on which there are predicates involving aggregated values computed in $G1$.

Successive group-by operators can arise in the transformed query if the original query has a group-by on an aggregate view or, if the query is a join between two aggregate views. Execution of such successive group-by operators can be combined under many circumstances.

It should be noted that the paper by Dayal [Day87] briefly touches on the idea of using keys for pull-up. Ganski-Wong [GW87] implicitly used a restricted form of pull-up for the specific class of Join-Aggregate queries that they optimized. These are special instances of the pull-up transformations defined above. Likewise, the transformations used Recently, [YL95, GHQ95] independently proposed variants of the pull-up transformation. A detailed description including the necessary generalizations of pull-up transformation for outer-joins and a quantitative analysis of the transformation is forthcoming in [CS96].

Advantages and Disadvantages of Pull-Up

The main advantage of pulling up a group-by operator is to allow more reordering among the relations that participate in the view definition. We can summarize the benefits as:

(1) Reduced Cost of Group-By: If the join is selective, deferring the group-by can take advantage of the selectivity of the join predicate.

(2) Increased Execution Alternatives: More access paths may be available for executing the join, thereby reducing the cost of the join.

On the other hand, pull-up is not a heuristic that should be used universally. Thus, pushing down group-by operators may result in significantly better performance:

(1) Increased Cost of Join: Application of a group-by reduces the size of the relation participating in the join. By deferring the group-by, the cost of the join may be increased.

(2) Reduced Selectivity of Join: The join predicates that use the aggregated column need to be deferred since an aggregation can take place only when the group-by is executed (at which point these predicates are evaluated as **Having** clauses).

(3) Increased Size of Projection Columns: Since the width of the relation, after join, can be increased by postponing group-by, the sizes of the intermediate relation can be larger. This can have profound effect on the cost of future operations on the relation.

4 Review of Push-Down Transformations

Push-down transformations are used to do the aggregation before we have completed processing all the joins. We will discuss two variants of the transformation. We refer the readers to [CS94, CS96] (cf. [GHQ95, YL94, YL95]) for further details, including conditions of applicability.

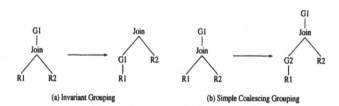

Fig. 2. Push Down Transformations of Group By

4.1 Invariant Grouping

The invariant grouping transformation is illustrated in Figure 2(a). Such a transformation moves a group-by operator past a join. In the figure, R_1 and R_2 need not be base relations but can represent a subquery (i.e., roots of subqueries). The invariant grouping property has the advantage that the **Having** clause can be pushed down.

For the invariant grouping transformations, we can define the notion of the *minimal invariant set*. Let us assume that the given single-block query is $G(V)$ where V is the SPJ query and G denotes the group-by operator. Let successive sound applications of invariant grouping result in an equivalent query $G(V') \bowtie$

$(V - V')$ but no further applications of invariant grouping transformation is possible on $G(V')$. Then, the set of relations in V' is called the minimal invariant set of $G(V)$.

Example 2. Let us consider the following query. The query computes the average salary for each department whose budget is less than 1 million dollars.

```
(C): select e.dno, avg(e.sal)
     from emp e, dept d
     where e.dno = d.dno and
           d.budget < 1m
     group by e.dno
```

Then, the query can be alternatively processed by invariant grouping transformation as follows:

```
(D1): D1(dno, Asal) AS           (D2): select e1.dno, e1.Asal
      select e.dno, avg(e.sal)         from D1 e1, dept d
      from emp e                       where e1.dno = d.dno and
      group by e.dno                         d.budget < 1m
```

The minimal invariant set of the query C consists of the singleton relation emp. ∎

4.2 Simple Coalescing Grouping

Like invariant grouping, the simple coalescing grouping property is a transformation that enables performing group-by early. However, instead of *moving* a group-by, the effect of simple coalescing is to *add* group-by operators. Thus, as in Figure 2, a new group-by operator G_2 has been added while G_1 has retained its original position. Intuitively, G_1 acts to coalesce groups that are created by G_2. While the effect of successive applications of invariant grouping transformation results in moving the group-by operator to a smaller (by query size) query, the effect of successive applications of simple coalescing results in *adding* group-by operators over smaller queries. The conditions for applicability of such a transformation require that the aggregating functions in the given query (i.e., in G_1) satisfy the property of being *decomposable*, e.g., we must be able to subsequently coalesce two groups that agree on the grouping columns.

5 Optimization Algorithms for Queries with Aggregate Views

Since neither pull-up nor push-down transformation always reduces the cost of execution, they must be applied judiciously. Furthermore, the applications of the transformations interact with ordering of the joins in the query. The purpose of this section is to provide an algorithm for *cost-based* optimization of queries containing aggregate views.

The optimization algorithm that we present minimizes IO cost. This is a reasonable criteria in the context of decision-support applications where the volume of stored data (such as obtained at a point of sale) is large. The algorithms can be adapted to optimize a weighted combination of CPU and IO cost. The cost model is assumed to satisfy the principle of optimality. The specific details of the cost model are not germane to the discussion here. Since many of the commercial optimizers use dynamic-programming based algorithm pioneered by [SAC+79] for optimizing single-block SPJ queries, we decided to ensure that our proposed extensions extend such optimizers with relative ease. However, the technique can be adapted to other optimization architectures as well.

We can summarize the key design goals of the optimization algorithms as follows:

- Expanded search space of execution to take into account pull-up and push-down transformations.
- Ability to limit the extent of search in a systematic fashion.
- A guarantee that our algorithm produces a plan that never does worse than the traditional optimizer.

In order to build our intuition, we begin by considering the enumeration algorithms for two simple cases. The first case corresponds to the problem of optimizing a single block SQL query containing group by. The second case corresponds to the case of optimizing a query that contains exactly one aggregate view V_1. The key ideas in these enumeration schemes are combined to produce the optimization algorithm for the general case. We begin by reviewing the traditional approach.

Notation

The class of queries for which we present optimization algorithms has the form shown in Figure 3:

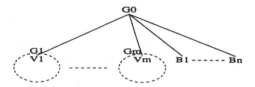

Fig. 3. Canonical Form of Query

- Every aggregate view Q_i consists of a select-project-join expression with a Group By clause and possibly a **Having** clause. Thus Q_i is of the form $G(g_i, A_i)(V_i)$ where V_i is a SPJ expression and $G(g_i, A_i)$ is a group-by operator in which g_i denotes the grouping columns and A_i denotes the information on aggregation functions and the aggregating columns. We will informally denote $G(g_i, A_i)$ by G_i. Since V_i is a SPJ query, we will also interchangeably denote the set of relations in it by V_i. Thus, if $V_i = \sigma_{R_1.a < R_2.b}(R_1 \bowtie R_2)$ then, we use V_i to represent the set of relations $\{R_1, R_2\}$ as well.

– A query consists of a join among aggregate views and base tables i.e., join among $Q_1, .., Q_m, B_1, .., B_n$ where each Q_i is an aggregate view and each B_i is a base relation. The query may contain a Group By $G(g_0, A_0)$ and a Having clause. The set of relations $\{B_1, .., B_n\}$ and the set of view definitions $\{Q_1, .., Q_m\}$ will be denoted by $\mathcal{B}$ and $\mathcal{Q}$ respectively.

5.1 Traditional Approach

Given a query as in Figure 3, most of today's optimizers represent this query as multiple query blocks with data-flow among the blocks (e.g., QGM representation in [PHH92]). Optimizing transformations are applied on this query representation. Examples of such transformations are that of propagating predicates from one query block to another [LMS94, PHH92]. Note that if the views did not have any aggregates, then the query is reduced to a single block query. As stated earlier, when the query contains a join among aggregate views, the query *cannot* be reduced to a single-block query by traditional preprocessing transformations.

The traditional optimization technique for queries with aggregate views, consists of *two phases*:

1. Optimize each aggregate view Q_i locally using the traditional optimization algorithm for SPJ queries that determines a linear join order.
2. Determine a linear join order among relations in $\mathcal{B}$ and relations corresponding to view definitions in $\mathcal{Q}$, treating relations in the latter set as base relations.

Thus, traditional optimization of queries with aggregate views repeatedly uses the algorithm for optimization of single block SQL with no group by. We describe this traditional algorithm next.

Single Block SQL with No Group By (SPJ Query): Traditionally, the execution space for SPJ queries has been limited to linear orderings of joins. The aim of the optimizer is to produce an execution plan of least cost from the above space. The well-known algorithm [SAC$^+$79] to choose an optimal linear ordering of joins in the query uses dynamic programming. A query (say Q) is viewed as a *set* of relations (say, $\{R_1..R_n\}$) which are *sequenced* during optimization to yield a join order. The optimization algorithm proceeds stage-wise, producing optimal plans for subqueries in each stage. Thus, for Q, at the i-th stage ($2 \le i \le n$), the optimizer produces optimal plans for all subqueries of Q of *size i* (i.e., subqueries that consist of join of i relations). Consider a subquery Q' of size $i+1$. The steps in the function *Enumerate* are followed to find its optimal plan.

Function *Enumerate*
1. **for all** R_j, S_j s.t $Q' = S_j \cup \{R_j\}$ **do**
2. $p_j := joinPlan(optPlan(S_j), R_j)$
3. **end for**
4. $optPlan(Q') := MinCost_j(p_j)$

In steps 1 and 2, all possible ways in which a plan for Q' can be constructed by extending an optimal plan for a subquery of size i (i.e., S_j) are considered. The function *joinPlan* creates the plan for joining a base relation with another intermediate (or a base) relation. Thus, access methods and choice of join algorithms are considered in *joinPlan*. In step 4, $MinCost$ compares the plans constructed for Q' and picks a plan with the least cost. It can be shown that the above algorithm is optimal with respect to the execution space of linear join ordering. We refer the reader to [SAC+79] for details.

5.2 Single Block SQL with Group By

In case of a single block SQL query with a group by, the traditional algorithm ignores the presence of the group-by node during join ordering except that the grouping columns are considered as interesting orders. the algorithm does not incorporate the push-down transformations. However, push-down transformations strongly interacts with join ordering [CS94]. This motivates our definition of a new execution space and a search algorithm that incorporates the effect of these transformations during the join ordering phase.

Execution Space: The traditional execution space for this class of queries consists of all linear join orders. The group-by is executed after processing all joins. Instead, we will consider all linear ordering of *joins and group-by* nodes as the execution space, i.e., some or all of the joins may succeed execution of the group-by. We refer to such executions as *linear aggregate join trees*. This expanded execution space enables applications of push-down transformations that result in placement of group-by early as well as introduction of additional group by nodes (i.e., invariant grouping and simple coalescing respectively). For example, the plans in Figure 4 represent linear aggregate join trees.

Search Algorithm: The complexity of exhaustively searching the space of linear aggregate join trees to determine the optimal plan is significant. Accordingly, we proposed a a *greedy conservative* heuristic to modify the traditional optimization algorithm *Enumerate* [CS94].

Greedy conservative heuristic has two components. First, it changes Step 2 of *Enumerate* so that linear aggregate join trees are considered. Next, it tells us how to pick a plan from the set of linear aggregate join trees considered in Step 2 of *Enumerate*. The key feature of greedy conservative heuristic is that these choices are made *locally*, thus preventing an explosion in the space of solutions searched.

We modify Step 2 in *Enumerate* to consider an early application of a group-by operator (whenever semantically correct). (1) $joinplan(optplan(S_j), R_j)$ (2)

$joinplan(G(optplan(S_j)), R_j)$ (or, $joinplan(optplan(S_j), G(R_j))$) where G designates an application of a group-by. Note that since we are concerned with
one-sided pull-down transformations, only one of the plans in (2) will be a candidate plan.

Next, we choose only one of the plans in (1) and (2). If Plan (2) is cheaper
and if the width of computed relation corresponding to Plan (2) is no more than
that of Plan (1), then Plan (2) is chosen. Otherwise, Plan (1) is chosen. It can
be shown that since the number of tuples in (1) is *at least* as many as in (2), and
our cost model is IO-only, the chosen plan is no worse than the traditional plan.
It was shown in [CS94], analytically as well as experimentally, that the modified
search algorithm results in very moderate increase in search space while often
producing significantly better plans.

5.3 Query with one Aggregate View

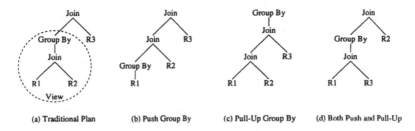

(a) Traditional Plan   (b) Push Group By   (c) Pull-Up Group By   (d) Both Push and Pull-Up

Fig. 4. Alternative Executions by Pushing and Pulling up Group-By

In this section, we consider the case where there is a single aggregate view, i.e.,
$m = 1$ in Figure 3. Using the notation introduced in Section 5, we denote the
aggregate view as $Q_1 = G_1(V_1)$.

Traditionally, the two-phase optimization algorithm in Section 5.1 uses the
enumeration algorithm described in that section for optimizing each query block.
By adopting the greedy conservative heuristic, we can improve upon the two-
phase algorithm since we can search the space of linear aggregate join trees
instead of linear join trees for each individual block. Thus, the above modification
enables considering pushing down G_1 on relations in V_1 (henceforth denoted by V
in this section) of the query in Figure 3. Thus, given a query with one aggregate
view as shown in Figure 4 (a), the alternative plan (b) in Figure 4 can be explored
by this simple approach. Likewise, in the second phase, we can consider plans
that push-down G_0 on the single-block query consisting of relations in B (i.e.,
the base tables that do not appear in view) and the view Q_1 treated as a base
table.

However, when we have an aggregate view, there are more opportunities for
optimization:

1. We can apply the *pull-up transformation* to consider execution plans where we join relations in V with those in B before performing the group-by G_1. Such an alternate execution plan is shown in Figure 4 (c). Observe that such a pull-up may result in *combining* G_0 and G_1.

2. If V' is the *minimal invariant set* of V (Section 4.1), then we can also consider enumerations where relations in $V - V'$ are treated like relations in B for enumeration. As a consequence, not only are new reordering before processing the group-by G_1 as in Figure 4 (d) possible, but it is now also possible to push down G_0 into relations in $V - V'$.

We now formally describe the execution space that considers these additional possibilities.

Execution Space: The syntactic structure of a plan considered for each single-block query is a linear aggregate join tree. If V' is the minimal invariant set of the single aggregate view $Q_1 = G_1(V)$, then the query in Figure 3 is equivalent to $G_0(G_1(V') \bowtie B')$ where $B' = B \cup (V - V')$. Intuitively, V' designates the minimal subset of relations in Q_1 such that G_1 may be placed only after all joins among relations in V' are taken. Therefore, additional linear aggregate trees can be considered by applying pull-up transformation, i.e., joining some other relations in B' with V' before applying G_1. Let $\chi(V', W)$ be the single block query equivalent to $G_1(V') \bowtie W$ obtained by applying the pull-up transformation to defer execution of G_1 until after all relations in the set W are joined with relations in V'. In other words, $\chi(V', W)$ has the form $G_1'(V' \bowtie W)$. The details of G_1' and join columns and predicates depend on the pull-up transformations.

The *execution space* of the query in Figure 3 is the union of the linear aggregate join execution spaces of the single-block SQL query consisting of G_0, relations $B' - W$ and the intermediate relation corresponding to the query $\chi(V', W)$ for *every* choice of $W \subseteq B'$. Thus, the execution space is $\bigcup_W \mathcal{E}_W$ where $\mathcal{E}_W$ represents the space of linear aggregate trees of the query $G_0(\chi(V', W) \bowtie (B' - W))$ where $\chi(V', W)$ is treated as a base relation.

We can consider the following three cases of $\chi(V', W)$ for different choices of W:

(i) $W = V - V'$: This pulled-up query corresponds to the aggregate view V in the original query, where the aggregate views can be locally optimized. This will allow us to consider plans like that in Figure 4 (b).

(ii) $W \supset V - V'$: Instead of optimizing the aggregate view, an "extended" aggregate view is optimized where the latter includes (base) relations from B to take advantage of selectivities of their join predicates. This allows us to consider the plan in Figure 4 (c). In particular, if $W = B' - V'$, then that corresponds to reducing the query to a *single-block query* (using the pull-up transformation).

(iii) $W \not\supseteq V - V'$: This sub-case corresponds to combining invariant grouping push-down and pull-up since we have included relations from B (pull-up) while excluding some relations that are in $V - V'$ (push-down) before doing the group-by. This allows us to explore a plan such as in Figure 4 (d).

Search Algorithm: Like the traditional approach, we have a two phase optimization algorithm. Thus, we pick a plan for $\chi(V', W)$ for every possible choice of W. Since $\chi(V', W)$ is a single block SQL query, we use the greedy conservative heuristic based enumeration algorithm of Section 5.2. However, we do not need to optimize $\chi(V', W)$ separately for each choice of W. While optimizing for $\chi(V', B')$, we can also generate the subplans for the joins of relations in the set $V' \cup W$ for every $W \subseteq B'$. For this step, we use the algorithm of [SAC$^+$79] with modification for greedy conservative heuristic to incorporate push-down transformations. However, in order to produce the plan for $\chi(V', W)$, we may need to extend the plan that has been picked for the join of the relations in the set $V' \cup W$, by applying a group-by. This is necessary since the latter may involves a group-by which may need to be applied on the chosen plan for $V' \cup W$.

We now turn to the second step of the two-phase enumeration. In this step, for each W, we consider the optimal linear order among relations in $B' - W$ as well as for the intermediate relation corresponding to $\chi(V', W)$. Note that during this step, the single block enumeration using the greedy conservative heuristic is applied once again. Furthermore, sub-plans generated for choices of W are shared.

To summarize, the search algorithm consists of the following key steps: (a) generate the query $\chi(V', B')$ (b) do a single block optimization of $\chi(V', B')$ (c) choose a plan for $\chi(V', W)$ from plans generated in Step (b) with the possible extension of adding G_1 and (d) optimize the single block query (with group-by G_0) consisting of relations in $B' - W$ and $\chi(V', W)$ for each choice of W.

We note that the plan generated by our search algorithm produces a plan no worse than the two-phase execution of a traditional optimizer. This follows from two observations: (a) Our search space includes the traditional execution strategy ($W = V - V'$) which corresponds to optimizing the given aggregate view locally. (b) Quality of plans produced by greedy conservative heuristic is no worse than the optimal plan produced by the traditional enumeration for optimizing each single query block.

Practical Restrictions on the Search Space: The size of the search space is extremely sensitive to the application of pull-up transformation. Thus, we do not pull-up a relation through a view unless they share a predicate. Furthermore, allowing *any* subset of relations in B' to be pulled-up may lead to a large search space. Another source of explosion in the search space is due to the fact that all possible orderings of relations in $\chi(V', W)$ are considered. We provide two techniques to restrict the search space significantly. First, we consider a *k-level pull-up* in which no partial plan may involve more than k applications of pull-up, where k is a constant independent of the size of the query. Next, we may consider only a syntactic subset of all linear aggregate join execution plans for each $\chi(V', W)$. A detailed description appears in [CS96].

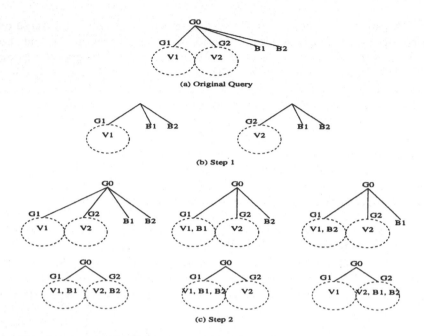

Fig. 5. Steps of Query Optimization

5.4 Query with Multiple Aggregate Views

We now sketch the enumeration algorithm for the general case where there may be multiple aggregate views in the query as in Figure 3. The key idea in the generalization is *not* to consider join reordering among relations that belong to the minimal invariant sets (See Section 4.1) of aggregate views. The reason to exclude such possibilities is to restrict a potential explosion of search space since such reordering leads to considering all possible linear ordering among group-by operators $G_1, .G_m$ [CS96].

Adopting the notation of the previous section, let us denote the minimal invariant set for V_i by V_i'. We note that relations that are in $\bigcup_{1 \le i \le m}(V_i - V_i')$ can be treated like relations in $\mathcal{B}$ and can be freely reordered. Accordingly, we define an augmented set

$$\mathcal{B}' = \mathcal{B} \bigcup_{1 \le i \le m} (V_i - V_i')$$

The execution space of the query is similar to that in the last section. Each V_i' may be pulled through a subset of (disjoint) relations from $\mathcal{B}'$ and locally optimized. In the second phase, optimization of the query consisting of the join among such pulled-up views (considered now as base relations) and the remaining relations in $\mathcal{B}'$ is addressed.

Thus, in the first phase, we choose plans for each $\chi(V_i', W_i)$, where $W_i \subseteq \mathcal{B}'$. The execution space and search strategy for obtaining plans for $\chi(V_i', W_i)$ are as in the previous section. In the second phase of the two-phase optimization, we define the execution space of the query to be the linear aggregate join orders for the relations $B' - \Sigma_l W_l$ and the intermediate relations $\chi(V'_i, W_i)$, where $1 \le i \le m$ and each W_i is disjoint from W_j whenever $i \ne j$.

The two steps of our optimization are illustrated in Figure 5. In the figure, for simplicity, we assumed that the original query consists of two aggregate views and $V_i = V'_i$ (and therefore, $B = B'$). In Step 1, we optimize each "extended" aggregate view as in the previous section. Thus, in our example, this step generates a plan for each of the following queries while optimizing for V_1 (and a similar set for V_2):

$$\mathcal{V}_1 = \{V_1, (V_1, B_1), (V_1, B_2), (V_1, B_1, B_2)\}$$

These set of plans correspond to pulling up each subset of the relations in B. In Step 2, we now consider possible linear orderings that result for each choice of a query U_1 from $\mathcal{V}_1$ and a query U_2 from $\mathcal{V}_2$ (as long the choices are consistent). For example, we will consider linear orderings of relations corresponding to $\{(V_1, B_1), V_2, B_2\}$.

As in the previous section, we can show that that the above search space produces a plan no worse than the traditional optimizer. The strategies for reducing the search space that are described in Section 5.3 apply as well.

6   Concluding Remarks

We have shown how queries containing views with aggregates may be optimized in a cost-based fashion. We developed a pull-up transformation that forms the basis for reordering two relations that are not in the same query block. In conjunction with push-down, the pull-up transformation forms the basis for optimizing queries with aggregate views. Effective incorporation of these transformations needs an *optimization algorithm*. This problem is specially challenging due to interaction between the join and the group-by operator. We showed how the traditional enumeration algorithm that is used widely in commercial setting can be extended.

The optimization algorithms that we presented in this paper provide several options. The traditional optimization algorithm can be augmented with greedy conservative heuristic for an immediate improvement by virtue of using push-down transformations. Pull-up transformations extend the execution space and provide opportunities for join reordering across query blocks. We proposed an enumeration algorithm to incorporate the transformations and indicated how such enumeration algorithm can be augmented by pruning techniques to reduce the search space. We guarantee that the chosen plan is no worse than that produced by the traditional optimization algorithm. Finally, our transformations and optimization algorithms apply not only to queries with aggregate views but also to queries with nested subqueries.

References

[CS94]   S. Chaudhuri and K. Shim. Including group-by in query optimization. In *Proc. of the 20th VLDB Conference*, Santiago, Chile, Sept 1994.

[CS96]   S. Chaudhuri and K. Shim. Complex queries: A unified approach. Technical report, Hewlett-Packard Laboratories, Palo Alto, In preparation, 1996.

[Day87]   U. Dayal. Of nests and trees: A unified approach to processing queries that contain nested subqueries, aggregates, and quantifiers. In *Proc. of the 13th VLDB Conference*, Brighton, August 1987.

[GHQ95]   A. Gupta, V. Harinarayan, and D. Quass. Aggregate-query processing in data warehousing environments. In *Proc. of the 21th VLDB Conference*, Zurich, Sept 1995.

[GW87]   Richard A. Ganski and Harry K. T. Wong. Optimization of nested SQL queries revisited. In *Proc. of the ACM SIGMOD*, San Francisco, May 1987.

[ISO92]   ISO. *Database Language SQL ISO/IEC*. Document ISO/IEC 9075, 1992.

[Kim82]   W. Kim. On optimizing an SQL-Like nested query. *ACM TODS*, Sept 1982.

[LMS94]   A. Y. Levy, I. S. Mumick, and Y. Sagiv. Query optimization by predicate move-around. In *Proc. of the 20th VLDB Conference*, Santiago, Chile, Sept 1994.

[MFPR90]   Inderpal Singh Mumick, Sheldon J. Finkelstein, Hamid Pirahesh, and Raghu Ramakrishnan. Magic is relevant. In *Proc. of the ACM SIGMOD*, Atlantic City, May 1990.

[Mur92]   M. Muralikrishna. Improved unnesting algorithms for join aggregate SQL queries. In *Proc. of the 18th VLDB Conference*, Vancouver, Canada, August 1992.

[PHH92]   H. Pirahesh, Joseph M. Hellerstein, and Waqar Hasan. Extensible/rule based query optimization in starburst. In *Proc. of the ACM SIGMOD*, San Diego, May 1992.

[SAC+79]   P. G. Selinger, M. M. Astrahan, D. D. Chamberlin, R. A. Lorie, and T. G. Price. Access path selection in a relational database management system. In *Proc. of the ACM SIGMOD*, Boston, June 1979.

[YL94]   W. P. Yan and P. A. Larson. Performing group-by before join. In *Proc. of International Conference on Data Engineering*, Houston, Feb 1994.

[YL95]   W. P. Yan and P. A. Larson. Eager aggregation and lazy aggregation. In *Proc. of the 21st VLDB Conference*, Zurich, Sept 1995.

Translating OSQL Queries into Efficient Set Expressions

Hennie J. Steenhagen   Rolf A. de By   Henk M. Blanken

Department of Computer Science, University of Twente
PO Box 217, 7500 AE Enschede, The Netherlands
{hennie,deby,blanken}@cs.utwente.nl

Abstract. Efficient query processing is one of the key promises of database technology. With the evolution of supported data models—from relational via nested
relational to object-oriented—the need for such efficiency has not diminished, and
the general problem has increased in complexity.

In this paper, we present a heuristics-based, extensible algorithm for the translation of object-oriented query expressions in a variant of OSQL to an algebra extended with specialized join operators, designed for the task. We claim that the
resulting algebraic expressions are cost-efficient.

Our approach builds on well-known optimization strategies for the relational model, but extends them to include relations and more arbitrary sets as values. We pay
special attention to the most costly forms of OSQL queries, namely those with full
subqueries in the SELECT- or WHERE-clause. The paper builds on earlier results
[17, 18].

1   Introduction

Currently, the ODMG group is working on the standards for object-oriented database
management systems [3]; the ODMG proposal includes a description of an object query
language named OQL, which is an SQL-like language. How to implement such a language, i.e. the subject of efficient query processing in object-oriented database systems,
is an important research topic. This paper studies the translation of a prototype object-
oriented SQL language (OSQL) into an algebra supporting complex objects. We believe that, as for the relational model, set-orientation is an appropriate query processing
paradigm for object-oriented models also. Set operators allow to apply techniques such
as sorting or hashing to improve performance. The goal is to obtain algebraic expressions that have good performance.

Important features of object-oriented data models are object identity, inheritance,
the presence of complex objects, and the possibility to define methods. In our opinion,
SQL languages for object-oriented models can be considered as an extension of SQL
languages for extended nested relational models [15]. Common features are the presence of complex objects and the orthogonality of language design. In the implementation of OSQL, precisely these features are of major importance. The work presented here
is meant to serve as the basis for the implementation of OSQL. Specific object-oriented
features can be handled as an addition or an extension. For example, the presence of object identity allows to speed up join algorithms [16]. We remark that, in our framework
[1], methods are written using OSQL instead of some general purpose programming language. Hence, method calls in a query can be textually substituted by their OSQL definition, allowing for additional optimization.

We study the transformation of nested OSQL queries. In [17], we showed that in complex object models it is impossible to transform arbitrary nested queries into flat join queries. As a solution, we introduced the nestjoin operator. In [18], we described a general approach to handle nested queries; here, we are more concrete and present a translation algorithm. Related to our work is that of [5], in which optimization of nested O_2SQL queries is discussed.

In Section 2, we briefly describe the language used and in Section 3 we discuss our approach to the transformation of nested OSQL queries. Next, in Section 4, the main steps of the algorithm are described, and a basic set of rewrite rules and an initial rewrite strategy is given. It becomes clear that, in order to obtain an efficient result, (multi-variable) parameter expressions have to be split. Heuristics are needed to guide the process of splitting expressions; these are presented in Section 5. In Section 6, we compare our work with that of others and, finally, Section 7 gives conclusions and discusses future work.

2 Preliminaries

We work within one language. The type system of our language is that of the nested relational model, extended in the sense that, besides relation-valued attributes, arbitrary set-valued attributes are allowed as well. The language consists of SQL-like constructs such as collect and quantifiers, which allow for nesting (the OSQL part of the language), and of pure algebraic operators such as set operators and join (the logical algebra part of the language). Below, we give the definitions of the main operators used in this paper.

$$
\begin{aligned}
\text{Collect} \quad & \Gamma[x : f(x) \mid p(x)](e) && = \{f(x) \mid x \in e \land p(x)\} \\
\text{Semijoin} \quad & e_1 \underset{x_1, x_2 : p(x_1, x_2)}{\ltimes} e_2 && = \{x_1 \mid x_1 \in e_1 \land \exists x_2 \in e_2 \bullet p(x_1, x_2)\} \\
\text{Antijoin} \quad & e_1 \underset{x_1, x_2 : p(x_1, x_2)}{\triangleright} e_2 && = \{x_1 \mid x_1 \in e_1 \land \not\exists x_2 \in e_2 \bullet p(x_1, x_2)\} \\
\text{Nestjoin} \quad & e_1 \underset{x_1, x_2 : f(x_1, x_2) \mid p(x_1, x_2); a}{\triangle} e_2 && = \{x_1 ++ \langle a = X \rangle \mid x_1 \in e_1 \land X = \\
& && \qquad \{f(x_1, x_2) \mid x_2 \in e_2 \land p(x_1, x_2)\}\}
\end{aligned}
$$

The collect operator Γ is simply a syntactic variant of the SELECT-FROM-WHERE construct of SQL:

$$\text{SELECT } f(x) \text{ FROM } x \text{ IN } e \text{ WHERE } p(x) \equiv \Gamma[x : f(x) \mid p(x)](e)$$

We have two special forms of Γ-expression:

1. $\Gamma[x : f \mid true](X) \equiv \alpha[x : f](X)$ which is also known as the map operator, and
2. $\Gamma[x : x \mid p](X) \equiv \sigma[x : p](X)$ which is also known as the selection operator.

The nestjoin operator was introduced in [17]. The operator is a combination of join and grouping and was introduced to avoid problems with dangling tuples. Parameters of the nestjoin operator are a predicate p, a function f, and a label a. Each tuple in the left-hand join operand is concatenated with the unary tuple $\langle a = X \rangle$; the set X consists of the right-hand operand tuples that satisfy p, modified according to function f.

In addition to the operators listed above, we have the standard set operators union, difference, and intersection, the tuple constructor $\langle a_1 = e_1, \ldots, a_n = e_n \rangle$, tuple projection $x[L]$, which is denoted as x_L, projection π, join $\bowtie$, nest ν and unnest μ, etc. The **except**-construct can be used as a shorthand for explicit tuple construction. Let t denote the unary tuple $\langle a = 1 \rangle$, then we have: t **except** $(a = 2, b = 3) = \langle a = 2, b = 3 \rangle$. The **except**-construct is used to modify attribute values, or to extend tuples with new attribute values. Predicates of the language may be arbitrary Boolean expressions, involving set comparison operators and quantifier expressions $\exists x \in X \bullet p$ and $\forall x \in X \bullet p$.

In this paper, capitals X, Y, Z are used to denote table expressions, i.e. base tables or set expressions with base table operands only. The expression $FV(e)$ stands for the set of free variables that occur in some expression e. Operators collect, select, map, and quantifiers $\exists$ and $\forall$ are called *iterators*.

3 Approach

In translation, the goal is to remove nested iterator occurrences as much as possible, by rewriting into efficient join expressions.

SQL languages offer the possibility to formulate nested queries, i.e. queries that contain subqueries (nested query blocks). In the relational model, a subquery operand is a base table or another subquery. In the translation to relational algebra, subqueries are removed by transforming nested queries into join queries. Transformation into join queries is advantageous because the join can be implemented such that its performance is better than pure nested-loop execution expressed by a nested query. Also for nested relational and object-oriented systems, the set-oriented paradigm seems appropriate. Though navigation has been considered as the prevailing method to access object-oriented databases in the past, recently more attention has been paid to set-oriented access methods, like pointer-based joins [16].

In a language such as OSQL, arbitrary nesting of query blocks may take place, in the SELECT- as well as in the WHERE-clause. The operands of nested query blocks may be base tables or set-valued attributes (or other subqueries); the two forms of iteration may alternate in arbitrary ways. The goal in translation is to achieve set-orientation, i.e. to remove nested iteration as much as possible. Nested iteration can be removed in two different ways:

Unnesting of Expressions Unnest rules may be applied either to the top level expression, moving nested base table occurrences to the top level, or to nested expressions, introducing nested set operations with base table and/or set-valued operands.

Unnesting of Attributes Set-valued attributes can be unnested using the operator μ, and nested later on, if necessary, using ν.

Depending on the expression concerned, one or more options may be appropriate. In this paper, we do not consider the option of attribute unnesting; it can be treated independently and easily incorporated into our transformation algorithm. We present some example equivalences:

Example 1 From Nested Expressions to Joins

1. $\sigma[x : \exists y \in Y \bullet x.a = y.a](X) \equiv X \underset{x,y:x.a=y.a}{\Join} Y$

2. $\alpha[x : \langle a = x.a, c = \Gamma[y : y.c \mid x.a = y.a](Y) \rangle](X) \equiv$
   $\alpha[v : \langle a = v.a, c = v.ys \rangle](X \underset{x,y:y.c|x.a=y.a;ys}{\Delta} Y)$

3. $\alpha[x : \Gamma[y : x.a + y.a \mid y.b = 1](Y)](X) \equiv$
   $\alpha[v : v.ys](X \underset{x,y:x.a+y.a|true;ys}{\Delta} \sigma[y : y.b = 1](Y))$

The left-hand side of the expressions above express a pure nested-loop execution strategy. By rewriting into join expressions, other implementation options come within reach.

We strive to achieve an efficient translation, i.e. to obtain logical algebra expressions that have reasonable performance. In our opinion, query optimization should not be restricted to the phases of algebraic rewriting and plan compilation; optimization should play a role in all phases of query processing. Simple, standard algorithms for translating the user language (either SQL or calculus-like) into the algebra may result in very inefficient expressions [19]. The inefficiency introduced in the translation phase is assumed to be reduced in the phase of logical optimization. This is quite a hard task, because in a pure algebraic context, in which information about the original query structure is scattered throughout the expression, it becomes difficult to find the proper optimization rules and to control the sequence of rule application [14]. To support this claim, we invite the reader to transform the expression:

$$((\sigma[x : p(x)](X) \times Y) \cup (X \underset{x,y:q(x,y)}{\Join} Y)) \div Y$$

into:

$$X - \sigma[x : \neg p(x)](X) \underset{x,y:\neg q(x,y)}{\Join} Y$$

using algebraic rewrite rules only. Both expressions are translations of the expression:

$$\sigma[x : \forall y \in Y \bullet p(x) \vee q(x,y)](X)$$

The first uses division to handle the universal quantifier, the second set difference. In our opinion, it is better to try to achieve a 'good' translation right away than to try to rewrite inefficient algebraic expressions afterwards.

4 Translation

In this section, we present our basic transformation rules. We restrict ourselves in that we discuss nested iteration only. We do not consider nested occurrences of set (comparison) operators, i.e., we leave them as they are.

The input to the transformation is a collect expression $\Gamma[x : f \mid p](e)$. Recall that the collect is the syntactic equivalent of the SQL SELECT-FROM-WHERE construct. The expressions f, p, and e may be arbitrary, containing other collects and/or quantifier expressions. Operands of nested iterators may be tables as well as set-valued attributes. The goal is to remove nested collects and quantifiers by rewriting into join operators. We want to achieve an efficient translation, i.e., we try to (1) avoid Cartesian products as much as possible, (2) push through predicates and functions, and (3) give preference to cheap operators, given a choice.

The basic rewrite algorithm consists of two steps: standardization and unnest. *Standardization* involves composition and predicate transformation. In *unnest*, subqueries are removed from parameter expressions by the introduction of join operators. The two steps are described in more detail below.

4.1 Standardization

Standardization involves composition and predicate transformation. In composition, collect operands and quantifier range expressions that are iterator expressions are transformed into table or attribute expressions; composition means the combination two iterators into one. As in the relational context, composition is needed because the user/system-prescribed order of operations (evaluation of predicates and functions) is not necessarily the most efficient. In addition, composition may offer additional optimization opportunities. We deal with the three iterators Γ, $\exists$, and $\forall$, therefore, we need the following rules:

Rule 1 Composition

1. $\Gamma[x : f(x) \mid p(x)](\Gamma[x : g(x) \mid q(x)](X)) \equiv \Gamma[x : f(g(x)) \mid p(g(x)) \wedge q(x)](X)$
   Note that the right-hand side contains the common subexpression $g(x)$.
2. $\exists x \in \Gamma[x : f(x) \mid p(x)](X) \bullet q(x) \equiv \exists x \in X \bullet p(x) \wedge q(f(x))$
3. $\forall x \in \Gamma[x : f(x) \mid p(x)](X) \bullet q(x) \equiv \forall x \in X \bullet \neg p(x) \vee q(f(x))$

The output of the phase of composition is a possibly nested collect expression in which the operand of each iterator is either a base table, a set-valued attribute, or a set expression (union, product), but not an iterator expression.

In the relational context, predicates usually are rewritten into Prenex Normal Form (PNF). After transformation into PNF, the matrix of the PNF expression can be optimized [11]. However, in [2], it is proposed to use a different normal form for predicates, namely the Miniscope Normal Form (MNF), in which quantifier scopes do not contain subexpressions that do not depend on the quantifier variable itself. Allegedly, MNF allows for a better translation, i.e. a translation with better results. As we will see, rewriting into MNF is one example of the generally beneficial rewrite strategy to remove local constants from iterator parameter expressions; therefore, we rewrite into MNF, according to the rules of [2].

4.2 Unnest

Below, we present a basic set of rewrite rules for the transformation of nested expressions into join or product expressions. We present rules that are generally valid: they can be applied to arbitrary subexpressions occurring at arbitrary levels. In Section 4.3 and Section 4.4, we discuss the restrictions placed on rule application and the rewrite strategy adhered to, respectively.

Whenever quantifiers occur in predicates between blocks, we may apply the rewrite rules presented below, translating nested expressions with quantification into relational join (product, join, semi-, or antijoin) operations. Existential quantification can be removed by the introduction of a semijoin, regular join or product operator:

Rule 2 Unnesting Existential Quantification

1. $\Gamma[x : f \mid \exists y \in Y \bullet p(x,y)](X) \equiv \Gamma[x : f \mid true](X \underset{x,y:p(x,y)}{\ltimes} Y)$

2. $\Gamma[x : f(x) \mid \exists y \in \sigma[y : p(x,y)](Y) \bullet q(x,y)](X) \equiv$
   $\quad \Gamma[v : f(v_X) \mid q(v_X, v_Y)](X \underset{x,y:p(x,y)}{\bowtie} Y)$

3. $\Gamma[x : f(x) \mid \exists y \in Y \bullet p(x,y)](X) \equiv \Gamma[v : f(v_X) \mid p(v_X, v_Y)](X \times Y)$

Universal quantification can be removed by introducing an antijoin or a product and a division operator:

Rule 3 Unnesting Universal Quantification

1. $\Gamma[x : f \mid \forall y \in Y \bullet p(x,y)](X) \equiv \Gamma[x : f \mid true](X \underset{x,y:\neg p(x,y)}{\triangleright} Y)$

2. $\Gamma[x : f \mid \forall y \in Y \bullet p(x,y)](X) \equiv \Gamma[x : f \mid true]((\Gamma[v : v \mid p(v_X, v_Y)](X \times Y)) \div Y)$

For expressions that contain nested collect operators, we have the following equivalence rules (these are explained below):

Rule 4 Unnesting Collect

1. $\Gamma[x : E(x, \Gamma[y : f \mid p](Y))](X) \equiv \Gamma[v : E(v_X, v.ys)](X \underset{x,y:f|p;ys}{\triangle} Y)$

2. $\Gamma[x : E(x, Y)](X) \equiv \Gamma[v : E(v_X, v.ys)](X \underset{ys}{\triangle} Y)$

In our language, we have at our disposal the complex object equivalent of the relational Cartesian product, namely the *nested Cartesian product*, which consists of a nestjoin operator with join predicate *true* and nestjoin function identity:

$$X \underset{x,y:y|true;a}{\triangle} Y \equiv X \times \{\langle a = Y\rangle\}$$

(A product expression $X \triangle_{x,y:y|true;a} Y$ may be abbreviated as $X \triangle_a Y$.) Consider Rule 4(2) above. The left-hand side of this rule is a collect, of which parameter expression E (an abbreviation of some expression $f \mid p$) contains a subexpression Y, which may be a base table, a subquery, a set expression, etc. Y may be removed from E by the introduction of the nested product $X \triangle_{ys} Y$. In the collect expression, now having as operand the nested product instead of table X, expression Y is replaced by the newly formed set-valued attribute ys. In addition, the occurrences of outer loop variable x must be adapted to account for the fact that the outer loop no longer iterates over X, but over the nested product, which has an additional attribute. The expression v_X delivers the original tuple value of x. Note that $v_X.a$, with a an arbitrary label, is equivalent to $v.a$. We give an example:

Example 2 Nested Product

$\Gamma[x : x \mid x.c \subseteq \sigma[y : x.a = y.a](Y)](X) \equiv$
$\quad \Gamma[v : v_X \mid v.c \subseteq \sigma[y : x.a = y.a](v.ys)](X \underset{ys}{\triangle} Y)$

So any (closed) nested table expression can be moved to the top level by the introduction of a nested Cartesian product. A nested product expression can be looked upon as the equivalent of the relational project-select-product expression. Like its relational equivalent, it is highly inefficient; it can be considered as the Most Costly Normal Form [12]. A nested product expression can be optimized by pushing through predicates and functions. However, we choose for a better translation rule. Consider Rule 4(1), the left-hand side of which denotes a collect that contains a nested collect expression. Nested collect expressions can be removed from collect parameter expressions (and from quantifier scopes as well) by the introduction of a (proper) nestjoin instead of a nested product. We give an example of this rule:

Example 3 Nestjoin

$$\Gamma[x : x \mid x.c \subseteq \sigma[y : x.a = y.a](Y)](X) \equiv$$
$$\Gamma[v : v_X \mid v.c \subseteq v.ys](X \underset{x,y:y|x.a=y.a;ys}{\Delta} Y)$$

4.3 Restrictions on Rule Application

The rules given above may be applied at will: at nested levels, to expressions concerning base table as well as set-valued attribute operands, etc. Theoretically, the only restriction on rule application is that it is not allowed to introduce free variables—specifically, it holds that the left join variable may not occur free in the right hand join operand. Also, whenever an unnesting rule is applied at top level, then it must hold that predicates and functions do not contain free variables other than the (nest)join variables themselves; if a rule is applied at nested levels, variables from higher levels may occur free in function and/or predicate. However, in practice we require that join predicates are closed dyadic formulas. As an exception, a nestjoin predicate may be missing (equivalent to true), whenever a dyadic nestjoin function is present.

Also, in theory, join predicates may be arbitrary expressions. Join predicates may contain set operators, iterators, as well as base table occurrences. For example, it is perfectly legal to write $X \bowtie_{x,y:x.a \in y.c} Y$, or even $X \bowtie_{x,y:x.a \in \Gamma[z:z|p(x,y,z)](Z)} Y$. Though work is being done on the efficient implementation of joins with complex join predicates, e.g. [9, 10], present join implementation techniques are not capable of handling complex join predicates; these probably will be handled by nested-loop execution after all. We therefore require that join predicates consist of atomic terms only. Atomic terms are comparisons between attribute values and/or constants of atomic type. Note that, consequently, join predicates do not contain base table occurrences.

Finally, in theory nestjoin functions may be arbitrary expressions as well. However, we require that nestjoin functions do not contain base table occurrences, precisely because the purpose of unnesting is to move base tables occurrences to the top level.

So, in practice we require that (1) join predicates are closed dyadic formulas that consist of atomic terms only, (2) nestjoin functions do not contain base table occurrences.

4.4 Rewrite Strategy

We propose the following initial rewrite strategy. Whenever possible, we push through predicates and functions to joins and join operands. Rules for pushing through predicates to regular joins and join operands can be found for example in [7]. In an extended version of this paper [19], we present rules for pushing through operations (predicates and functions) to nestjoin operands.

In unnesting, we use a top-down strategy, recursively joining outermost iterator operand with next inner, if possible. We first consider pairs of table expressions, then pairs of table expressions and set-valued attributes, and finally pairs of set-valued attributes. In other words, first we try to join the top level operand, which is a table, with each of the nested base table occurrences in the query, in order of nesting level. Next, we take the next inner iterator operand that is a base table, and follow the same procedure. After having considered each pair of base tables, we consider joining pairs of tables and set-valued attributes, and finally pairs of set-valued attributes. In case there is a choice, with multiple subqueries, the order of unnesting is arbitrary. We prefer partial joins (semi- and antijoin) to the regular join, and the regular join to the nestjoin. In the first instance, we avoid Cartesian products; these are introduced only if everything else has failed. The advantage of a top-down unnesting strategy is that the level of nesting in the algebraic expression is kept to a minimum. We give an example. Assume we have the following query:

$$\alpha[x : \Gamma[y : \sigma[z : x.a = z.a \wedge y.b = z.b](Z) \mid x.a = y.a](Y)](X)$$

or, equivalently:

$$\alpha[x : \alpha[y : \sigma[z : y.b = z.b](\sigma[z : x.c = z.c](Z))(\sigma[y : x.a = y.a](Y))](X)$$

We first join X and Y. Next, Z is joined with the top level nestjoin result, and finally, we introduce a local join between set-valued attributes ys and zs. The full rewriting is shown below:

Rewriting Example 1

$$\alpha[x : \alpha[y : \sigma[z : y.b = z.b](\sigma[z : x.a = z.a](Z))(\sigma[y : x.a = y.a](Y))](X)$$
$$\equiv \alpha[v : \alpha[y : \sigma[z : y.b = z.b](\sigma[z : v.a = z.a](Z))(v.ys)](X \underset{x,y:y|x.a=y.a;ys}{\Delta} Y)$$
$$\equiv \alpha[w : \alpha[y : \sigma[z : y.b = z.b](w.zs)](v.ys)]((X \underset{x,y:y|x.a=y.a;ys}{\Delta} Y) \underset{v,z:z|v.a=z.a;zs}{\Delta} Z)$$
$$\equiv \alpha[w : \alpha[t : t.yzs](v.ys \underset{y,z:z|y.b=z.b;yzs}{\Delta} w.zs)]((X \underset{x,y:y|x.a=y.a;ys}{\Delta} Y) \underset{v,z:z|v.a=z.a;zs}{\Delta} Z)$$

Whenever the operands of nested iterators are set-valued attributes instead of base tables, the result may contain nested joins.

5 Splitting Expressions

Given our set of rewrite rules presented above for unnesting quantifiers and collects (together with rules for pushing through operations to join (operands)), and given our restrictions concerning join predicates, often the only option will be to introduce (nested) Cartesian products, because predicates and functions do not have the right format. For example, consider the expression:

$$\Gamma[x : \Gamma[y : y \mid p(x,y) \wedge \exists z \in Z \bullet q(x,z) \wedge r(y,z)](Y) \mid true](X)$$

The nested collect predicate is not atomic, so we cannot use the rule for unnesting a collect. Also, the quantifier cannot be removed because it does not occur at the top level. Before we can apply the unnesting rules, the predicate has to be rewritten. Splitting of expressions enables us to introduce joins instead of Cartesian products. Below, we present equivalence rules used in splitting.

5.1 Equivalence Rules

Rules for splitting predicates are the following:

Rule 5 Splitting Predicates

1. $\Gamma[x : f \mid p \wedge q](X) \equiv\equiv \Gamma[x : f \mid q](\sigma[x : p](X))$
2. $\Gamma[x : f \mid p \vee q](X) \equiv \Gamma[x : f \mid p](X) \cup \Gamma[x : f \mid q](X)$
3. $\exists x \in X \bullet p \wedge q \equiv \exists x \in \sigma[x : p](X) \bullet q$
4. $\forall x \in X \bullet p \vee q \equiv \forall x \in \sigma[x : \neg p](X) \bullet q$

Expressions that denote function results can be split of as well. Let Θ denote either Γ, $\forall$, or $\exists$. For reasons of convenience, in the rules given below quantification $\forall x \in X \bullet p$ and $\exists x \in X \bullet p$ is written as $\forall[x : p](X)$ and $\exists[x : p](X)$, respectively. Expression $E(s_1, \ldots, s_n)$ denotes an iterator parameter expression E with subexpressions $s_1, \ldots, s_n$.

Rule 6 Splitting Functions

1. Let x not occur free in E outside of g, then:
   $\Theta[x : E(g(x))](X) \equiv \Theta[x : E(x)](\alpha[x : g(x)](X))$
2. Let x not occur free in E outside of instances of the form $g_i(x)$, then:
   $\Theta[x : E(g_1(x), \ldots, g_n(x))](X) \equiv$
   $\quad \Theta[x : E(x.a_1, \ldots, x.a_n)](\alpha[x : \langle a_1 = g_1(x), \ldots a_n = g_n(x)\rangle](X))$
3. Let X be a table, and let label a not occur in the schema of X, then:
   $\Theta[x : E(x, g(x))](X) \equiv \Theta[v : E(v_X, x.a)](\alpha[x : x \text{ except } (a = g(x))](X))$

We give an example illustrating each of the above rules:

Example 4 Splitting Functions

1. $\sigma[x : \exists y \in Y \bullet x.a = y.b + y.c](X) \equiv \sigma[x : \exists y \in \alpha[y : y.b + y.c](Y) \bullet x.a = y](X)$
2. $\sigma[x : \exists y \in Y \bullet x.a = y.a \wedge x.b = \mathrm{COUNT}(y.c)](X) \equiv$
   $\quad \sigma[x : \exists y \in \alpha[y : \langle a = y.a, b = \mathrm{COUNT}(y.c)\rangle](Y) \bullet x.a = y.a \wedge x.b = y.b](X)$
3. $\sigma[x : \forall y \in Y \bullet \mathrm{COUNT}(x.c) > y.a](X) \equiv$
   $\quad \Gamma[v : v_X \mid \forall y \in Y \bullet v.a > y.a](\alpha[x : x \text{ except } (a = \mathrm{COUNT}(x.c))](X))$

The syntactic form of the unnest rules, together with the restrictions posed on their application requires that predicates and functions are split to be able to introduce joins instead of products. Given our rewrite strategy and unnest rules, the way predicates are split determines the form of the result, w.r.t. join order and type of join operators present. We need heuristics to guide the splitting of predicates and functions. Below, we present some of the heuristic rules that can be used to achieve a better translation.

5.2 Heuristics

Given a choice, expressions are split such that the cheapest (most restrictive predicate, less costly function) expression part is evaluated first. Iterator parameter expressions can be classified according to the number of variables that occurs free (constant, monadic, dyadic, multi-variable), and the presence of other iterators (simple versus complex). The following nested expression will serve as the leading example in this section:

$$\sigma[x : \exists y \in Y \bullet \exists z \in Z \bullet p_1(x) \wedge p_2(y) \wedge p_3(x, y) \wedge p_4(z) \wedge p_5(x, z) \wedge p_6(y, z)](X)$$

We remark that we have chosen the above example just for illustration purposes—it looks relational, but the same nesting pattern can be achieved with collects instead of quantifiers. Assume that X, Y, and Z are base tables and that all predicates p_i are atomic.

We note that the selection predicate is in PNF, and that the matrix of the PNF expressions contains conjuncts that do not depend on one or both quantifier variables. The predicate therefore is rewritten into MNF, as proposed in [2]:

$$\sigma[x : p_1(x) \wedge \exists y \in Y \bullet p_2(y) \wedge p_3(x, y) \wedge \exists z \in Z \bullet p_4(z) \wedge p_5(x, z) \wedge p_6(y, z)](X)$$

A comparable transformation that concerns a map operator is the following:

$$\alpha[x : \alpha[y : x.b + y.b](Y)](X) \equiv \alpha[x : \alpha[y : x + y.b](Y)](\alpha[x : x.b](X)) \quad \text{(Rule 6(1))}$$

The subexpression $x.b$ does not depend on the inner map variable y, so it can be evaluated outside of the scope of y. The above transformation corresponds to the idea of pushing through a projection. Even if attribute names occur at different nesting levels, projections can be pushed through:

$$\alpha[x : \langle a = x.a, c = \alpha[y : x.b + y.b](Y) \rangle](X) \equiv$$
$$\alpha[v : \langle a = v.a, c = \alpha[y : v.b + y.b](Y) \rangle](\alpha[x : \langle a = x.a, b = x.b \rangle](X)) \quad \text{(Rule 6(2))}$$

We see that in a complex object model, as in the relational model, it is only necessary to preserve those attributes that are needed in subsequent computations. Subexpressions of parameter expressions that are constant w.r.t. the corresponding iterator variable, i.e. subexpressions in which the iterator variable does not occur free are called *local constants*. We have a first heuristic transformation rule:

Heuristic Rule 1 Local constants are removed from iterator parameter expressions as much as possible.

To remove independent subformulas from predicates we use the descoping rules (possibly others are needed too, see[2]):

Rule 7 Descoping Let $x \notin FV(p)$, then:

1. $\exists x \in X \bullet p \wedge q(x, y) \equiv p \wedge \exists x \in X \bullet q(x, y)$
2. $\exists x \in X \bullet p \vee q(x, y) \equiv p \vee \exists x \in X \bullet q(x, y)$[1]

To obtain independent subformulas, the technique of quantifier exchange may be of help. For functions, we use the rules for splitting of functions as given in Rule 6. Note that w.r.t. quantifier scopes, independent subformulas can be removed completely. W.r.t. functions, this is not possible—in the above map transformation, the inner map still contains the local constant x.

Second, another type of constant expression is one in which no variables from higher levels occur free; this type of expression is called an *global constant*. Global constants are evaluated independently, which becomes possible by naming them by means of a local definition facility:

---

[1] Because variables are range-restricted, we have to take into account the possibility of empty ranges. The correct transformation is:

if $X = \emptyset$ **then** *false* **else** $p \vee \exists x \in X \bullet q(x, y)$

For reasons of simplicity, we assume quantifier ranges are never empty.

$$\sigma[x : \exists y \in \sigma[y : p(y)](Y) \bullet q(x,y)](X) \equiv$$
$$\sigma[x : \exists y \in Y' \bullet q(x,y)](X) \text{ with } Y' = \sigma[y : p(y)](Y)$$

Heuristic Rule 2 Global constants are named with a local definition facility.

We return to our leading example. We notice two monadic conjuncts at the top level, i.e. $p_1(x)$ and the quantifier expression itself, and also two at a nested level, namely $p_2(y)$, and $p_4(z)$. Monadic expressions often can be pushed through to the corresponding iterator operand, thereby possibly creating global constants that can be evaluated independently:

$$\sigma[x : \exists y \in \sigma[y : p_2(y)](Y) \bullet p_3(x,y) \wedge$$
$$\exists z \in \sigma[z : p_4(z)](Z) \bullet p_5(x,z) \wedge p_6(y,z)](\sigma[x : p_1(x)](X)) \text{ (Rule 5)}$$

Heuristic Rule 3 Monadic expressions are evaluated first, if possible.

An example of Heuristic Rule 3 that concerns the map operator is the following:

$$\alpha[x : \alpha[y : x.b + y.b](Y)](X) \equiv \alpha[x : \alpha[y : x.b + y](\alpha[y : y.b](Y))](X) \text{ (Rule 6(1))}$$

Again, the above example deals with pushing through a projection. Notice however, that also very complex functions can be pushed through.

As mentioned, both p_1 as well as the top-level quantifier expression are monadic predicates; we made the assumption that predicate p_1 is atomic. Given a choice, it seems advantageous to evaluate expressions that do not contain iteration before the ones that do, i.e. to evaluate expressions in order of their respective nesting level. Whenever the nesting level is the same, we may choose an arbitrary evaluation order, or invent some other heuristic rule.

Heuristic Rule 4 Expressions are evaluated in order of nesting level.

So far so good. We have discussed constant and monadic expressions, and now we have to decide what to do with dyadic and multi-variable parameter expressions. Joins are binary operators, so dyadic expressions are candidates for join predicates and functions. In our example expression, we notice dyadic conjuncts p_3, p_5, and p_6 that mutually link the base tables that occur in the query. It is tried to split multi-variable predicates and functions as needed, i.e., as prescribed by the unnesting strategy. Whenever we investigate the possibility of joining two tables A and B, we search for maximal closed expressions of the proper format that refer to attributes of A and B.

Heuristic Rule 5 Predicates and functions are split as prescribed by the unnesting strategy.

In the relational model, predicates involve atomic attribute comparisons only, and multi-variable selection predicates and also quantifier scopes can be split easily. In a complex object model, we may have arbitrary functions as well as predicates, and splitting of multi-variable expressions is not always possible (consider for example the expression $\sigma[z : x.a \cup z.a = y.a](Z)$).

Nested collects can be removed independent from the nesting level, but quantification can be removed only by joining adjacent operands, i.e., in which the one operand occurs nested immediately within the other (or within a conjunction of predicates). Because we prefer flat joins above nestjoins, before starting the top-down unnesting procedure, we first try to introduce (nested) flat joins between base table expressions as much as possible. It is required that the nested join expressions are closed, to be able to move them to the top level. Given the example query:

$$\alpha[x : \sigma[y : p(x,y) \wedge \exists z \in Z \bullet q(x,z) \wedge r(y,z)](Y)](X)$$

we note an existential quantifier nested within a selection. Therefore, we split the multi-variable quantifier scope as needed, and first introduce a nested join between Y and Z:

Rewriting Example 2

$$\alpha[x : \sigma[y : p(x,y) \wedge \exists z \in Z \bullet q(x,z) \wedge r(y,z)](Y)](X)$$
$$\equiv \alpha[x : \sigma[y : p(x,y) \wedge \exists z \in \sigma[z : r(y,z)](Z) \bullet q(x,z)](Y)](X) \text{ (Rule 5(3))}$$
$$\equiv \alpha[x : \sigma[v : p(x,v_Y) \wedge q(x,v_Z)](Y \underset{y,z:r(y,z)}{\bowtie} Z)](X) \text{ (Rule 2(2))}$$

Heuristic Rule 6 Before starting the top-down unnesting procedure, we introduce closed flat join expressions at nested levels, if possible.

We now summarize the foregoing:

- Whenever possible, global constants are named, local constants are removed, and monadic subexpressions are pushed through, in order of nesting level. In addition, predicates and functions are pushed through to joins and join operands, whenever possible.
- We unnest, top down. We first join tables, then tables and set-valued attributes, and finally set-valued attributes. However, to handle nested quantification properly, we first try to introduce closed flat (nested) join operations. To enable the introduction of real joins instead of Cartesian products, parameter expressions are split as needed.

The above rewrite strategy is a starting point, i.e., in many cases it may be better to modify the strategy in one way or another.

5.3 Discussion

Traditionally, determination of the join order is done cost-based. We stress that in a complex object model with set-valued attributes that supports an algebra that contains a rich variety of (join) operators such a cost-based optimization may be hard to do. First, the proper algebraic equivalence rules have to be found. Second, the process of algebraic rewriting is difficult to control. By means of heuristic translation rules we try to achieve an algebraic expression that has performance that is not too bad right from the start.

The search space for an optimal join order is restricted. First, links between tables may be missing—we do not want to introduce Cartesian products. Second, iterator operands may be tables, as well as set-valued attributes, which cannot be moved to the top level. Whenever an iteration with an attribute operand is cast between iterators with table operands, the result may contain nested joins. Also, the links between tables may be of a different nature, i.e., predicate and/or function, and the creation of predicate links between operands may be preferable to the establishment of function links. It is not clear what constitutes an optimal join order, from the viewpoint of logical optimization, i.e. not taking into consideration physical database characteristics. Generally speaking, it seems reasonable to assume that:

- Set operators are better than iterator expressions.
- Partial joins (semi- and antijoin) are better than regular joins, which in turn are better than Cartesian products. A flat join is better than a nestjoin.[2] Also, predicate links are better than function links, and atomic links are better than complex ones.
- Top-level operations are better than nested ones.
- Table operations are better than operations on set-valued attributes.

But is a nested semijoin better or worse than a top-level join? We remark that it is not always easy to judge expressions on relative performance without the use of a more or less detailed cost model. For example, returning to our example, assume that operand Y is not a base table, but the set-valued attribute c of table X. We simplify our example:

$$\sigma[x : \exists y \in x.c \bullet p_3(x,y) \land \exists z \in Z \bullet p_5(x,z) \land p_6(y,z)](X)$$

The expression contains predicates that mutually link all three iterator operands. Existential quantifiers may be exchanged to move the attribute iterator inside, but this is not a generally valid strategy. We may choose to join X with Z at the top level, and then to execute a nested quantification:

$$\sigma[v : \exists y \in x.c \bullet p_3(v_X,y) \land p_6(y,v_Z)](X \underset{x,z:p_5(x,z)}{\bowtie} Z)$$

Also, it is possible to join table Z with attribute c at a nested level:

$$\sigma[x : \exists v \in (x.c \underset{y,z:p_6(y,z)}{\bowtie} Z) \bullet p_3(x,v_Y) \land p_5(x,v_Z)](X)$$

The former is likely to be better than the second, because in the second tuples of Z are replicated for each matching tuple in attribute c, for each (set) value c. However, the performance of both expressions depends on join methods used, join selectivities, the respective cardinalities of join operands, etc.

6 Related Work

The work presented here follows that done on the translation and optimization of relational SQL. Basically, there are two ways of optimizing SQL: (1) the rewriting of SQL expressions themselves [13], and (2) translation of SQL into relational algebra [4], followed by algebraic rewriting. The underlying idea is that nested-loop expressions should be transformed into set expressions that do not contain nested operators. The important difference with the work presented here is that (1) we have to deal with nesting in the SELECT-clause, which is not allowed in relational SQL, and (2) the presence of set-valued attributes, which is non-relational as well. SQL languages proposed for complex

---

[2] This is questionable: a nestjoin does not suffer from data replication, but is not commutative like the regular join.

object models usually are orthogonal languages; the problem of choosing an algebra for, and of translation into the algebra of such a language is much more complicated.

The work presented in [5] and [6] has much in common with ours. In [6] a binary grouping operator is defined that differs slightly from the nestjoin in the sense that the join function is applied to the *set* of matching right-hand operand tuples, not to the elements themselves. This has as a consequence that nested expressions with so-called projection dependency, which involve a free variable occurring in a SELECT-clause, cannot be unnested. Generally speaking, the algebraic operators and the (algebraic) equivalence rules of [6] are similar to ours. However, in this paper, we consider queries with arbitrary nesting levels, incorporating nested iterators with set-valued attribute operands.

In [17], we showed that in complex object models, the regular, i.e. flat relational join operator does not suffice for the unnesting of nested queries. To solve this problem, we introduced the nestjoin. In [18], we presented a general strategy for unnesting. We proposed to use relational (join) operators whenever possible, and to use the nestjoin otherwise. In this paper, the general strategy outlined in [18] is made mode concrete. Starting from a basic set of transformation rules, we have discussed what can be done to achieve efficient algebraic expressions. We use heuristic rules to determine an initial join order, and to push through predicates and functions.

7 Conclusions and Future Research

In this paper, we have presented a heuristics-based, extensible algorithm for the translation of nested OSQL queries into efficient join expressions. Queries that involve nested quantifier expressions are translated using relational algebra operators. For the translation of nested queries that cannot be translated into flat join queries, the nestjoin operator is used, which is a combination of join and grouping. During translation, predicates and functions are pushed through as far as possible. We have presented a general framework that can easily be extended.

The main problem in the translation of nested OSQL queries is to find a good unnesting strategy. We have proposed a top-down unnesting strategy that minimizes the nesting level in nestjoin expressions. Our goal is to rewrite nested expressions into algebraic expressions such that expensive operators (e.g. Cartesian products), nested base table occurrences, and nested joins are avoided as much as possible.

How to achieve the above goal in the best possible way is topic of further research. A (heuristic) cost model may be needed to guide the transformation of nested queries; such a cost model is much more complex than the heuristic model used in logical optimization in the relational context, that merely prescribes to push through selections and projections. Other topics of future research for example are how to deal with nested set (comparison) operators, how to implement nested joins, and how to deal with more complex join predicates.

References

1. Balsters, H., R.A. de By, and R. Zicari, "Typed Sets as a Basis for Object-Oriented Database Schemas," *Proceedings ECOOP*, Kaiserslautern, 1993.

2. Bry, F., "Towards an Efficient Evaluation of General Queries: Quantifier and Disjunction Processing Revisited," *Proceedings ACM SIGMOD*, Portland, Oregon, June 1989, pp. 193–204.
3. R.G.G. Cattell, ed., *The Object Database Standard: ODMG-93*, Morgan Kaufmann Publishers, San Mateo, California, 1993.
4. Ceri, S. and G. Gottlob, "Translating SQL into Relational Algebra: Optimization, Semantics, and Equivalence of SQL Queries," *IEEE Transactions on Software Engineering*, 11(4), April 1985, pp. 324–345.
5. Cluet, S. and G. Moerkotte, "Nested Queries in Object Bases," *Proceedings Fourth International Workshop on Database Programming languages*, New York, Sept. 1993.
6. Cluet, S. and G. Moerkotte, "Classification and Optimization of Nested Queries in Object Bases," manuscript, 1994.
7. Elmasri, R. and S.B. Navathe, *Fundamentals of Database Systems*, Benjamin/Cummings Publishing Company Inc., 1989.
8. Graefe, G., "Query Evaluation Techniques for Large Databases," *ACM Computing Surveys*, 25(2), June 1993, pp. 73–170.
9. Hellerstein, J.M. and A. Pfeffer, "The RD-Tree: An Index Structure for Sets," Technical Report #1252, University at Wisconsin at Madison, October 1994.
10. Ishikawa, Y., H. Kitagawa, and N. Ohbo, "Evaluation of Signature Files as Set Access Facilities in OODBs," *Proceedings ACM SIGMOD*, 1993, pp. 247–256.
11. Jarke, M. and J. Koch, "Query Optimization in Database Systems," *ACM Computing Surveys*, 16(2), June 1984, pp. 111–152.
12. Kemper, A. and G. Moerkotte, "Query Optimization in Object Bases: Exploiting Relational Techniques," in: *Query Processing for Advanced Database Systems*, eds. J.-C. Freytag, D. Maier, and G. Vossen, Morgan Kaufmann Publishers, San Mateo, California, 1993.
13. Kim, W., "On Optimizing an SQL-like Nested Query," *ACM TODS*, 7(3), September 1982, pp. 443–469.
14. Nakano, R., "Translation with Optimization from Relational Calculus to Relational Algebra Having Aggregate Functions," *ACM TODS*, 15(4), December 1990, pp. 518–557.
15. Pistor, P. and F. Andersen, "Designing a Generalized NF^2 Model with an SQL-Type Language Interface," *Proceedings VLDB*, Kyoto, August 1986, pp. 278–285.
16. Shekita, E.J. and M.J. Carey, "A Performance Evaluation of Pointer-Based Joins," *Proceedings ACM SIGMOD*, Atlantic City, May 1990, pp. 300–311.
17. Steenhagen, H.J., P.M.G. Apers, and H.M. Blanken, "Optimization of Nested Queries in a Complex Object Model," *Proceedings EDBT*, Cambridge, March 1994, pp. 337–350.
18. Steenhagen, H.J., P.M.G. Apers, H.M. Blanken, and R.A. de By, "From Nested-Loop to Join Queries in OODB," *Proceedings VLDB*, Santiago de Chile, September 1994.
19. Steenhagen, H.J., *Optimization of Object Query Languages*, Ph.D. Thesis, University of Twente, October 1995.

Data Mining and Warehousing

Knowledge Discovery from Epidemiological Databases

Gérard Pavillon

INSERM and Université Versailles-St Quentin - Laboratoire PRISM
44, chemin de ronde - 78110 Le Vésinet, France
Tel.: 34 80 24 62 Fax: 34 80 24 29 - e-mail: pavillon@tolbiac.inserm.fr

Abstract: ARC II is a learning system that allows to discover relationships from symbolic data. The learning strategy is based on probabilistic induction and produces dependence relationships between a fact and a set of facts. The system also takes into account dated facts or events in order to produce causal relationships between an event (effect), and a set of facts (cause) including at least one event. Relationships are represented under the form of uncertain production rules. The algorithm ensures that (1) the rules are complete, i.e. that the premises include all known relevant facts and (2) the rules are elementary, i.e. no irrelevant fact belongs to the premises. ARC II has been applied to the analysis of medical data.

Keywords: Knowledge Discovery, Induction, Dependence and Causal Relationships

1. Introduction

This paper presents ARC II, an inductive learning system that produces dependence rules from examples using a probabilistic approach. It tackles two problems.
(1) Firstly, the system can discover both dependence relationships and causal relationships. Causal relationships are a special kind of dependence because they bring extra knowledge : the production of the effect by the cause. In some domains, it is fundamental to make the difference between the two types of dependence. In the medical field for instance, it is obvious that the dependence relationship "lung neoplasms are more frequent among men" is quite different and less informative than the causal relationship "smoking can cause lung neoplasm".
(2) Secondly, the system produces complete and elementary rules: all and only the relevant facts are included in the premises of the rule. ARC II uses a example-driven algorithm that allows to take into account all relevant facts and it discards all the facts that do not modify the level of dependence. This property determines the quality of the knowledge base produced: rules are neither too specific nor too general in regard of the examples and of the dependence.

2. Dependence Relationships and Causal Relationships

The probabilistic dependence allows to establish relationships between facts on the basis of their probability. When facts are dated, a time-oriented dependence can be computed, which allows to establish the direction of the causal relationship.
Let $p(a)$, be the probability of a fact a to occur, and $p(a \cdot b)$ the probability of two facts a and b to occur together, a and b are dependent if and only if $p(a \mid b) \neq p(a)$, with

$$p(a \mid b) = \frac{p(a \cdot b)}{p(b)}$$

the conditional probability of a given b. This dependence is positive when p (a | b) > p (a), which means that the probability of a increases when b occurs. Conversely, the dependence is negative when p (a | b) < p (a). The dependence can be more or less important, and a measure of its strength is given by |p (a | b) - p (a)|. The dependence between two non-empty sets of facts can be defined in the same way. Relationships between facts as "to smoke" and "lung cancer" or "to be a male" and "prostate disease" are examples of dependence relationships.

A dependence relationship between facts expresses a "static link" between facts as in the example where "prostate disease" is related to the fact "to be a male", or it reveals a causal relationship between a cause and an effect as in the example "smoking" and "lung cancer". A causal relationship also implies dependence between facts, but this dependence is oriented from the cause to the effect. This direction of the relationship cannot be deduced from the mere dependence between cause and effect and the time dimension needs to be added : the cause necessarily predates the effect. This supposes that cause and effect are dated events, then the dependence is the probability of effect e given cause c when cause c predates effect e. Formally, let e_t be a probabilistic event occurring at time t and p (e_t) the probability of this event, event $c_{t'}$ is a presumptive cause of event e_t if and only if [Suppes70]:

(1) $t' < t$
(2) $p (c_{t'}) > 0$
(3) $p (e_t \mid c_{t'}) \neq p (e_t)$

Like a dependence relationship, a causal relationship can be either positive or negative depending on the sign of (p ($e_t \mid c_{t'}$) - p (e_t)). An example of negative causal relationship is "vaccination decreases the probability of the disease it prevents".

A particular aspect of causality is the multiplicity of causes. Indeed, an effect is seldom due to a single cause : it does not rain just because there are clouds in the sky, everyone who smokes does not get lung neoplasm. The cause is usually a set of component causes co-operating to produce an effect. Two types of component causes can be characterised. For instance, if the causal relationship involving the effect "neoplasm of prostate" is studied, the conditional probability can be very different if it is computed out of males and females or only out of males, since the neoplasm of prostate only affects males. The fact "to be a male" is a part of the cause as it is a necessary condition of the studied causal relationship and as it modifies the dependence. However it cannot be considered as the cause, with a common meaning, of the effect "neoplasm of prostate". This leads to distinguish two types of component causes.

(1) Conditions which are part of the cause as they help to precise dependence. These conditions cannot produce the effect by themselves. They remain unchanged during the observation period : they are a state of the world.

(2) Events which are dated modifications of the observed world.

The definition of a causal relationship entails that at least one component cause is an event and that the effect is an event.

3. Arc II Learning Algorithm

The ARC II algorithm discovers dependence and causal relationships from examples. An example E is a set of facts and a fact f_i is an attribute with value i. Relationships are represented by uncertain rules of the form: A_i -> f_j (μ) where the premises A_i are a conjunction of facts, the conclusion f_j is a fact and μ is the conditional probability of f_j given A_i.

Any fact in the examples base is a candidate conclusion. For a given conclusion, ARC II can find all the possible premises that contain all the relevant facts and only the relevant facts. Such rules are called *complete* (all the known relevant facts are included in) and *elementary* (the sole relevant facts appear in the condition).

For causal rules the same representation is used with two particularities : (1) the conclusion of the rule must be an event and the premises must contain at least one event, (2) the conditional probability is computed taking into account the time orientation between cause (the premises) and effect (the conclusion).

The complexity of the algorithm is approximatively $O(m.e^3)$, where m is the number of facts in an example and e the number of examples.

4. Rule Characteristics

The rule characteristics are all the pieces of information that can assist in selecting and using the rule. In the following we shall consider a rule $\{A_i, c_j\}$, where A_i are the premises and c_j the conclusion. Five characteristics can be attached to each rule.

(1) The nature of the rule. Since ARC II can produce both dependence rules and causal rules, they must be differentiated.

(2) The sign of dependence. This is the sign of $(p (c_j \mid A_i) - p (c_j))$.

(3) The certitude factor of the conclusion. It is the conditional probability $p (c_j \mid A_i)$.

(4) The a priori probability of the conclusion $p (c_i)$.

(5) The usefulness of the rule is the probability of the premises $p(A_i)$: a high probability of the premises means that the rule will be frequently applied.

5. Application of Arc II

ARC II was implemented using the Prolog II+ language on a MacIntosh IIci computer. It produces simple, complete and elementary dependence rules and causal rules with their characteristics. The application domain concerns the analysis of the chain of diseases leading to death among patients with AIDS. This type of study, called multiple causes of death analysis, is difficult to undertake due to the important number of possible sequences. This application is based on the data of a survey on a representative sample of AIDS deaths that occurred in France during the year 1992. The examples base includes 2932 cases and 20 attributes were studied: 3 conditions and 17 events. The conditions are: sex and 2 risk factors (homosexuality and drug addiction). The events are the diagnoses of hospitalisation during the last year preceding death. ARC II has produced a number of rules, which allows us to draw up a card of the main dependencies between ten diseases as represented in Fig 1. For the sake of simplicity, these relationships do not include the associated conditions (sex, risk factor). In addition ARC II discovered two presumptive causal rules between cytomegalovirus and kaposi sarcoma on the one hand, and between cytomegalovirus and atypical mycobacterium on the other hand. The first relationship involving kaposi sarcoma has already been mentioned in other studies[Abrams91][Dover91], even if no confirmation of the causal role of the cytomegalovirus has been provided at present.

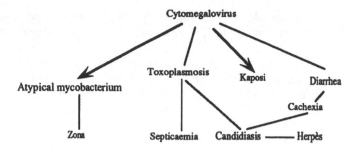

Fig 1. Main dependencies between diseases

6. Conclusion

ARC II is a learning system that uses a probabilistic induction method to discover dependence rules and causal rules. These rules are complete and elementary and they are described by a set of characteristics. This type of system is useful in several ways: the rules can be used as high level description of data, they can be used in knowledge bases or, in a multimodel approach of machine learning, the system can be used as a basic learning module providing knowledge for the higher levels.

References

[Abrams91] D.I. Abrams, *Acquired Immunodeficiency Syndrome and Related Malignancies: a Topical Overview,* Seminar in Oncology, Vol 18, n° 5, pp 41-45, 1991

[Clark89] P. Clark, T. Niblett, *The CN2 Induction Algorithm.* Machine Learning 3: 261-283, 1989

[Dover91] J.S. Dover, *Cutaneous Manifestations of Human Immunodeficiency Virus Infection. Part I,* Archives of Dermatology, Vol 127, pp 1383-1391, 1991

[Michalski90] R. S. Michalski, Y. Kodratoff, *Research in Machine Learning: Recent Progress, Classification of Methods and Future Directions.* Machine Learning: an Artificial Intelligence Approach, Vol III, pp 3-30, 1990

[Pavillon95] G. Pavillon, *ARC II: Un Algorithme d'Apprentissage par Induction Probabiliste,* Thèse de Doctorat, Paris VI, 1995

[Piatestky91] G. Piatestky-Shapiro, *Discovery, Analysis, and Presentation of Strong Rules.* Knowledge Discovery in Databases, AAAI Press / The MIT Press, 229-248, 1991

[Quinlan86] J.R. Quinlan, *Induction of Decision Trees.* Machine Learning 1, pp 81-106, 1986

[Smyth91] P. Smyth, R.M. Goodman, *Rule Induction Using Information Theory.* Knowledge Discovery in Databases, AAAI Press / The MIT Press, 159-176, 1991

[Suppes70] P. Suppes, "A Probabilistic Theory of Causality", Acta Philosophica Fennica, Fasc XXIV, 1970

System Issues

Scalable Update Propagation in Epidemic Replicated Databases

Michael Rabinovich, Narain Gehani, and Alex Kononov

AT&T Bell Laboratories
600 Mountain Ave,
Murray Hill, NJ 07974

Abstract. Many distributed databases use an *epidemic* approach to manage replicated data. In this approach, user operations are executed on a single replica. Asynchronously, a separate activity performs periodic pair-wise comparison of data item copies to detect and bring up to date obsolete copies. The overhead due to comparison of data copies grows linearly with the number of data items in the database, which limits the scalability of the system.

We propose an epidemic protocol whose overhead is linear in the number of data items being copied during update propagation. Since this number is typically much smaller than the total number of data items in the database, our protocol promises significant reduction of overhead.

1 Introduction

Data replication is often used in distributed systems to improve system availability and performance. Examples of replicated systems abound and include both research prototypes (e.g., [5, 14]) and commercial systems (e.g., [8, 10]).

Many of these systems use an *epidemic* [4] approach to maintain replica consistency. In this approach, user operations are performed on a single replica. Asynchronously, a separate activity (termed *anti-entropy* in [4]) compares version information (e.g., timestamps) of different copies of data items and propagates updates to older replicas.

Epidemic protocols exhibit several desirable properties: user requests are serviced by a single (and often a nearby) server; update propagation can be done at a convenient time (i.e., during the next dial-up session); multiple updates can often be bundled together and propagated in a single transfer.

A significant problem with existing epidemic protocols is the overhead imposed by anti-entropy. This overhead includes periodic pair-wise comparison of version information of data item copies to decide which copy is more recent. It therefore grows linearly with the number of data items in the system. This limits the scale the system can achieve without significant performance degradation.

It might appear that a simple solution to this problem exists where each server would accumulate its updates and periodically push them to all other replicas, without any replica comparison. However, the following dilemma arises. If recipients of the updates do not forward them further to other nodes, then full responsibility for update propagation lies with the originating server. A failure of this server during update propagation may leave some servers in an obsolete state for a long time, until the originating server is repaired and completes the propagation. On the other hand, forwarding updates by servers to each other would create a lot of redundant traffic on the network.

In this paper, we propose a different solution to the anti-entropy overhead problem. We present a protocol that, like existing epidemic protocols, performs periodic comparison of version information of replicas to determine which replicas are out-of-date.

Unlike existing epidemic protocol, our protocol detects whether update propagation between two replicas of the *whole database* is needed in constant time, independently of the number of data items in the database. Moreover, when update propagation is required, it is done in time that is linear in the number of data items to be copied, without comparing replicas of every data item. Typically, the number of data items that are frequently updated (and hence need to be copied during update propagation) is much less than the total number of data items in the database. Thus, our protocol promises significant reduction of overhead.

Our protocol is based on *version vectors*, first proposed in [12] to detect inconsistencies between replicas of a data item and widely used for various purposes in distributed systems. In existing replicated systems based on version vectors, a server i associates a *version vector* with every data item replica x_i stored on this server. This vector (described formally later in the paper) records in its j-th component the number of updates originally performed by server j and reflected in x_i. By comparing the version vectors of two copies of a data item, the system can tell which of the two is more recent. Therefore, the older replica can catch up, e.g., by copying the newer replica. As other existing epidemic protocols, version vector-based protocols impose significant overhead on the system due to pair-wise comparison of version information (version vectors in this case) of data item replicas.

The initial idea behind our protocol is simple: associate version vectors with the entire database replicas, instead of (or, in fact, in addition to) replicas of individual data items. Then, perform anti-entropy between replicas of entire databases. Anti-entropy would compare the version vectors of two database replicas to detect in constant time whether update propagation between replicas of *any* data item in the database is required, and if so, infer which data items must be copied by looking at these version vectors and database logs.

There are two main challenges in implementing this idea. First, our goal to limit update propagation time dictates that only a constant number of log records per data item being copied can be examined or sent over the network. However, the number of log records is normally equal to the number of updates and can be very large. This problem required an interesting mechanism for log management.

The second problem is due to the mismatch between managing version vectors at the granularity of entire database replicas and maintaining replica consistency at the granularity of individual data items. Specifically, our idea implies that update propagation is always scheduled for all data items in the database at once. In contrast, existing version vector-based protocols allow update propagation to be scheduled differently for each individual data item. While it is not feasible to provide different schedules for *each* data item in the database, the ability to, say, reduce the update propagation time for some key data items is important. Thus, we must allow nodes to obtain a newer version of a particular data item at any time, in addition to normally scheduled update propagation. We call these data items, obtained by direct copying outside the normal update propagation procedure, *out-of-bound* data items. Out-of-bound data violates certain ordering properties of updates on a node, which are essential for the correctness of our protocol.

We deal with this problem by treating out-of-bound data completely differently from the rest of the data. When a node copies a data item out of bound, it does not modify its database version vector or database logs. Instead, it creates parallel data structures: an *auxiliary* data item and an auxiliary log. The node then uses the auxiliary copy for servicing user operations and requests for out-of-bound copying of this data item from other nodes. At the same time, the node uses the "regular" copy of the data item for scheduled update propagation activity. In addition, a special *intra-node update propagation* procedure ensures that updates from the auxiliary log are eventually applied to the regular copy without violating the update orderings required by the protocol. When the regular copy catches up with the auxiliary copy, the latter is discarded.

This separation of out-of-bound and "regular" data is achieved at the expense of additional costs, both in storage for keeping auxiliary data and in processing time for intra-node update propagation. Thus, the assumption behind our protocol is that the number of out-of-bound data items is small relative to the total number of data items.

A secondary contribution of this paper is that it explicitly specifies correctness criteria for update propagation, separately from correctness criteria for database transactions. This allows formal reasoning about correct propagation independently from the data consistency guarantees provided by the system.

2 The System Model

We assume a collection of networked servers that keep databases, which are collections of data items. A database can be replicated (as a whole) on multiple servers. We will refer to an instance of a database (data item) kept on an individual server as a *replica* or *copy* of the database (data item). For simplicity, we will assume that there is a single database in the system. When the system maintains multiple databases, a separate instance of the protocol runs for each database.

Different replicas of a data item are kept consistent using an epidemic protocol: user operations are serviced by a single server; asynchronously, updates are propagated throughout the network by an anti-entropy process. In addition to periodically scheduled update propagation, a server may obtain a newer replica of a particular data item at any time (*out-of-bound*), for example, on demand from the user.

Update propagation can be done by either copying the entire data item, or by obtaining and applying log records for missing updates. For instance, among commercial systems, Lotus Notes uses whole data item copying, while Oracle Symmetric Replication copies update records. The ideas described in this paper are applicable for both these methods. We chose whole data copying as the presentation context in this paper.

The protocol is targeted towards applications where the number of data items copied during update propagation is small compared to the total number of data items. In other words, the fraction of data items updated on a database replica between consecutive update propagations is in general small. Another assumption for the workload is that relatively few data items are copied out-of-bound.

We do not make any assumptions about the level of replica consistency guaranteed by the system. The system may enforce strict consistency, e.g., by using tokens to prevent conflicting updates to multiple replicas. (In this approach, there is a unique token associated with every data item, and a replica is required to acquire a token before performing any updates.) Or, the system may use an optimistic approach and allow any replica to perform updates with no restrictions. In the latter approach, when conflicting updates are discovered, they are resolved in an application-specific manner (which often involves manual intervention).[1]

Neither do we assume anything about the transactional model supported by the system. The system may use two-phase locking [2] on an individual server while relying on optimism for replica consistency. The system can also choose to provide guaranteed serializability of transactions by executing on top of a pessimistic replica

---

[1] We do not get into the discussion of tradeoffs between optimistic and pessimistic replica management. The ideas we present here are equally applicable to both approaches.

control protocol. (See [2] for the serializability theory in replicated systems.) Finally, the system may not support any notion of multi-data-item transactions at all (like Lotus Notes, [9]).

Finally, to simplify the presentation, we assume that the set of servers across which a database is replicated is fixed.

2.1 Correctness Criteria

We assume that actions performed by individual nodes are atomic. In particular, any two updates or an update and a read on the same data item replica are executed in some serial order. Thus, all updates reflected in a replica form a serial *history* $h = \{op_1, \ldots, op_n\}$, according to the order in which these updates executed.

To reason about correctness of update propagation, we need a few definitions.

Definition 1 Inconsistent data item replicas. Let x_A and x_B be two replicas of a data item x. x_A and x_B are called *inconsistent* or *in conflict* if there are updates op_i and op_j such that x_A reflects update op_i but not op_j, while x_B reflects op_j but not op_i.

Definition 2 Older and newer data item replicas. x_A is called *older* or *less recent* than x_B (and x_B is called *newer* or *more recent* than x_A) if the update history of x_A is a proper prefix of the update history x_B. A replica of a data item is called *obsolete* if there is a newer replica of the same data item in the system.

We assume the following correctness criteria for update propagation.

1. Inconsistent replicas of a data item must be eventually detected.
2. Update propagation cannot introduce new inconsistency. In other words, data item replica x_i should acquire updates from x_j only if x_j is a newer replica.
3. Any obsolete data item replica will eventually acquire updates from a newer replica. In particular, if update activity stops, all data item replicas will eventually catch up with the newest replica.

3 Background: Version Vectors

Version vectors were proposed in [12] to detect inconsistency among replicas in distributed systems, and have been widely used for various purposes in distributed systems. We describe some existing applications of version vectors in the review of related work (Section 8).

Consider a set of servers, $\{1, \ldots, n\}$, that keep copies of a data item x. Denote x_i to be the copy of x kept by server i. Every server i maintains a *version vector* $v_i(x)$ associated with its copy of x. This version vector has an entry (an integer number) $v_{ij}(x)$ for each server j that keeps a copy of the data item.

The rules for maintaining version vectors are as follows. Upon initialization, every component of the version vector of every replica of the data item is 0.

When a server i performs an updates of data item x_i, it increments its "own" entry (i.e., $v_{ii}(x)$) in its version vector for x_i.

When server i obtains missing updates for x from a server j (either by copying the whole data item or by obtaining log records for missing updates), i modifies $v_i(x)$ by taking the component-wise maximum of $v_i(x)$ and $v_j(x)$: $v_{ik}^{new}(x) = \max(v_{ik}^{old}, v_{jk})$, $(1 \leq k \leq n)$.

The following fact about version vectors has been shown [11].

Theorem 3. *At any time, $v_{ij}(x) = u$ if and only if i's replica of x reflects the first u updates that were made to this data item on server j.*

In particular, these corollaries hold:

1. If two copies of the same data item have component-wise identical version vectors, then these copies are identical.
2. For two replicas of the data item, x_i and x_j and some server k, let $v_{ik} < v_{jk}$ and $v_{jk} - v_{ik} = u$. Then, x_i has seen u fewer updates performed on server k and reflected on x_j. Moreover, these missing updates are the last updates from server k that were applied to x_j.
3. A copy x_i is older than a copy x_j iff (a) version vector $v_i(x)$ is component-wise smaller or equal to $v_j(x)$, and (b) at least one component of $v_i(x)$ is strictly less than the corresponding component of $v_j(x)$. ($v_j(x)$ is said to *dominate* $v_i(x)$ in this case).
4. Copies x_i and x_j are inconsistent iff there exist k and l such that $v_{ik}(x) < v_{jk}(x)$ and $v_{il}(x) > v_{jl}(x)$. We will call two version vectors with this property *inconsistent* version vectors.
   Indeed, this means that x_i has seen some updates (made on server l) that x_j has not received; at the same time, x_i has not seen some updates made on server k and reflected in x_j.

Given these facts, update propagation can be done by periodically comparing version vectors of pairs of data item replicas and either doing nothing (if both replicas have identical version vectors), or bringing the older replica up-to-date, or flagging a conflict.

4 Data Structures

This section describes the data structures and some utility functions used by the protocol. This is followed by the description of the protocol in the next section.

Consider a system with n nodes replicating a database. As before, every node i maintains an item version vector (IVV) for every data item x_i in i's replica of the database. Additional data structures are described in the rest of this section.

4.1 Database Version Vectors

Our protocols associate version vectors with entire replicas of databases. These version vectors are referred to as *database version vectors*, or *DBVV*, as opposed to data item version vectors, or *IVV*, described in Section 3. DBVV is similar in many ways to IVV, except its components record the *total* number of updates performed on corresponding servers to *all* data items in the database replica.

More formally, node i keeps a database version vector V_i with n components, where n is the number of nodes maintaining a replica of the database, with the following maintenance rules.

1. Initially, all components of V_i are 0.
2. When node i performs an update to any data item in the database, it increments its component in the database version vector: $V_{ii}^{new} = V_{ii}^{old} + 1$.
3. When a data item x is copied by i from another node j, i's DBVV is modified to reflect the extra updates seen by the newly obtained copy of the data item: $V_{il}^{new} = V_{il}^{old} + (v_{jl}(x) - v_{il}(x))$, $1 \le l \le n$, where $v_{km}(x)$ is the mth component of the IVV associated with data item x on node k.

To get an intuition behind the last rule, consider an arbitrary node l. x_i has seen $v_{il}(x)$ updates originally performed by l, and x_j has seen $v_{jl}(x)$ such updates. Our protocol will copy x from j to i only if x_j is more recent. Thus, $v_{il}(x) \leq v_{jl}(x)$, and the additional number of updates seen by x_j that were originated on l is $(v_{jl}(x) - v_{il}(x))$. Once i copies the value of x_j, the total number of updates originated on l and seen by all data items in i's database increases by this amount. Therefore, component V_{il} of ith DBVV must increase accordingly.

4.2 The Log Vector

Node i maintains a *log vector* of updates, L_i. Each component, L_{ij}, records updates performed by node j (to any data item in the database) that are reflected on node i. The order of the records in L_{ij} is the same as the order in which j performed the updates.

Records are added to the log when node i performs updates to non out-of-bound data items. New records can also be added to the log when they are obtained from the source node during update propagation.

A log record has a form (x, m), where x is the name of the updated data item, and m is the value of V_{jj} that node j had at the time of the update (including this update). Recall from Section 4.1 that V_{jj} counts updates performed by j. So, m gives the sequence number of the update on node j. Note that log records only register the fact that a data item was updated, and not information to re-do the update. Thus, these records are very short.

The key point is that, from all updates performed by j to a given data item that i knows about, only the record about the *latest* update to this data item is retained in L_{ij}. Hence, when a new record (x, m) is added to L_{ij}, the existing record referring to the same data item is discarded.

To do this efficiently, all records in L_{ij} are organized in a doubly linked list (see Figure 1). An array of pointers $P(x)$ is associated with every data item x_i. Its component P_j contains the pointer to the existing record in L_{ij} referring to x. When a new record (x, m) is added, the following *AddLogRecord* procedure is executed:

AddLogRecord(node number j, record $e = (x, m)$):
  The new record e is linked to the end of log L_{ij};
  The old log record referring to the same data item is located in constant
      time using pointer $P_j(x)$ and un-linked from the log;
  Pointer $P_j(x)$ is updated to point to the newly added record.

Note that every log L_{ij} may contain at most one record per data item in the database. Thus, the total number of records in the log vector is bounded by nN, where n is the number of servers and N is the number of data items.

4.3 Auxiliary Data Items and IVVs

When a data item x is copied out-of-bound (i.e., outside the normal update propagation), a separate *auxiliary* copy of this data item, x' is created. A auxiliary copy has its own version vector, which is called auxiliary IVV.

Node i performs all updates to x on its auxiliary copy, while update propagation continues using regular copies. When regular copies "catch up" with auxiliary copies, the latter are discarded.

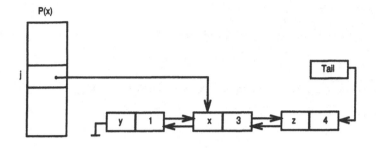

(a) The structure of log component L_{ij}.

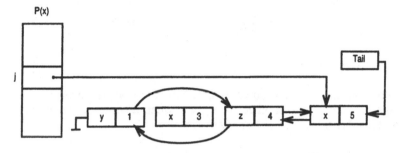

(b) The structure of L_{ij} after adding record (x,5).

Fig. 1. The structure of a log component.

4.4 The Auxiliary Log

The *auxiliary log*, AUX_i, is used to store updates that i applies to out-of-bound data items. Records in the auxiliary log are of the form $(m, x, v_i(x), op)$, where x is the name of the data item involved, $v_i(x)$ is the IVV that the auxiliary copy of x had at the time the update was applied (*excluding* this update) and op is the operation executed (e.g., the byte range of the update and the new value of data in the range). Thus, unlike records in the log vector, auxiliary log records contain information sufficient to re-do the update, and hence they can be much bigger. However, these records are never sent between nodes.

The auxiliary log must be able to support efficiently (in constant time) a function *Earliest(x)* that returns the earliest record in AL_i referring to data item x. Also, we must be able to remove in constant time a record from the middle of the log. These requirements can be easily satisfied with a list structure of the auxiliary log. The details are straightforward and are omitted.

We will often refer to auxiliary data items, their IVVs, and the auxiliary log as auxiliary data structures, as opposed to the rest of the node state, which will be called regular data structures.

```
SendPropagation(i, V_i):
    if V_i dominates or equals V_j {
        send "you-are-current" message to i and exit;
    }
    for k = 1 to n {
        if (V_jk > V_ik) {
            D_k = Tail of L_jk containing records (x, m) such that m > V_ik;
        else
            D_k = NULL;
        }
    }
    send D and a set S of data items referred to by records in D to i;
end
```

Fig. 2. The *SendPropagation* procedure.

5 The Protocol

The protocol consists of procedures executed when a node performs an update, when it propagates updates from another node j, and when it copies a later version of a data item from another node (out-of-bound copying).

5.1 Update Propagation

Update propagation is done between a recipient node i and a source node j using exclusively regular data structures, regardless of prior out-of-bound copying that might have taken place between the two nodes. For instance, if i had previously copied a newer version of data item x from j as an out-of-bound data and its regular copy of x is still old, x will be copied again during update propagation.[2]

When node i performs update propagation from node j, the following steps are executed:

(1) i sends V_i to j. In response, j executes *SendPropagation* procedure in Figure 2. In this procedure, j compares the received version vector with V_j. If V_i dominates or equals V_j, there is no need for update propagation, and the protocol terminates.

Otherwise, j builds a *tail vector*, D, whose kth component contains log records of updates performed by node k that node i missed, and list S of data items referred to by these records. Note that only regular (non-auxiliary) copies of data items are included into S. j then sends D and S to i. In addition, with every data item x in S, j includes its IVV $v_j(x)$.

(2) When i receives the response from j with D and S, it executes *AcceptPropagation* in Figure 3. It goes through data items from S. For every such data item x_j, i compares x_j's version vector, $v_j(x)$, with the version vector of its local copy of x, $v_i(x)$.

If $v_j(x)$ dominates $v_i(x)$, i adopts the received copy and modifies V_i according to the DBVV maintenance rule 3. Otherwise, i alerts the system administrator that copies x_i and x_j are inconsistent and removes all log records referring to x from all log tails

---

[2] In other words, out-of-bound copying never reduces the amount of work done during update propagation.

```
AcceptPropagation(D, S):
    for every x_j in S {
        if v_j(x) dominates v_i(x) {
            adopt x_j from S as a new regular copy x_i;
            v_i(x) := v_j(x);
        else
            declare x_i and x_j inconsistent;
            remove records referring to x from D;
        }
    }
    for each tail D_k from D {
        for every record r from D_k (going from the head of D_k to tail) {
            AddLogRecord(k,r);
        }
    }
end
```

Fig. 3. The *AcceptPropagation* procedure.

in D (preserving the order of the remaining records). Note that we do not consider the case when $v_i(x)$ dominates $v_j(x)$ because this cannot happen (see Section 7).

Finally, i appends log tails from the tail vector to the corresponding logs of its log vector, using the *AddLogRecord* procedure from Section 4.2.

Note that removing records that refer to conflicting data items from the tail vector may be an expensive operation. However, this is done only if conflicts are found (which is supposed to be an extraordinary event).

(3) i performs *intra-node update propagation* on Figure 4 to see if any updates accumulated in the auxiliary log can be applied to regular data item.

For every data item x copied in step 2, if auxiliary copy x' exists, i compares the IVV of the regular copy, $v_i(x)$, with the IVV stored in record *Earliest(x)*, the earliest auxiliary log record referring to x.

If both are identical, the operation from this record is applied to the regular copy. All actions normally done when a node performs an update on the regular copy of a data item are executed: $v_{ii}(x)$ and V_{ii} are incremented by 1, and a log record (x, V_{ii}) is appended to L_{ii}. Finally, the auxiliary record *Earliest(x)* is removed from auxiliary log.

If $v_i(x)$ and the IVV of the *Earliest(x)* record conflict, there exist inconsistent copies of x, and conflict is declared.[3]

The whole process is repeated until either the next earliest auxiliary record has version vector that dominates or conflicts $v_i(x)$, or until the auxiliary log contains no more records referring to x. ($v_i(x)$ can never dominate a version vector of an auxiliary record.) In the latter case, the final comparison of the regular and auxiliary IVVs is done to see whether the regular copy of x has caught up with the auxiliary copy. If so, the auxiliary copy of x can be deleted. (We do not check here whether or not the regular and auxiliary IVVs conflict, deferring conflict detection to the *AcceptPropagation* procedure.)

---

[3] In fact, the nodes where inconsistent replicas reside can be pinpointed: if the above version vectors conflict in components k and l, then nodes k and l have inconsistent replicas of x.

```
IntraNodePropagation:
    for every data item x copied during execution of AcceptPropagation {
        if auxiliary copy of x, x'_i, exists {
            let e = Earliest(x);
            let v_e(x) and op_e be version vector and update operation from e;
            while e ≠ NULL and v_i(x) = v_e(x) {
                apply op_e to x_i;
                v_ii(x) = v_ii + 1;
                V_ii = V_ii + 1;
                append log record (x, V_ii) to L_ii;
                remove e from AUX_i;
                e = Earliest(x)
                let v_e(x) and op_e be version vector and update operation from e;
            }
            if e = NULL {
                if v_i(x) dominates or is equal to v_i(x') {
                    remove auxiliary copy x'_i;
                }
            }
            else
                if v_i(x) conflicts with v_e(x) {
                    declare that there exist inconsistent replicas of x;
                }
        }
    }
end
```

Fig. 4. The *IntraNodePropagation* procedure.

5.2 Out-of-bound Data Copying

A node i in our protocol can obtain a newer version of an individual data item from any server j at any time. This can be done in addition to regular update propagation of Section 5.1 that causes *all* data at the recipient node to catch up with the data at the source. As already mentioned, data items obtained by direct copying, outside the normal update propagation procedure, are called out-of-bound data items.

Upon receiving an out-of-bound request for data item x, j sends the auxiliary copy x'_j (if it exists), or the regular copy x_j (otherwise), together with the corresponding IVV (auxiliary or regular). Auxiliary copies are preferred not for correctness but as an optimization: the auxiliary copy of a data item (if exists) is never older than the regular copy.

When i receives the response, it compares the received IVV, $v_j(x)$, with its local auxiliary IVV (if auxiliary copy x'_i exists) or regular IVV (otherwise). If $v_j(x)$ dominates, then the received data is indeed newer. Then, i adopts the received data item and IVV as its new auxiliary copy and auxiliary IVV. If $v_j(x)$ is the same as or dominated by the local IVV (auxiliary or regular, as explained above), the received data item is actually older than the local copy; i then takes no action. If the two IVVs conflict, inconsistency between copies of x is declared.

Note that no log records are sent during out-of-bound copying, and the auxiliary log of the recipient is not changed when the old auxiliary copy of x is overwritten by the new data.

5.3 Updating

When a user update to data item x arrives at node i, i performs the operation using auxiliary data structures (if the auxiliary copy of x exists), or regular data structures (otherwise). In the first case, i applies the update to the auxiliary copy x', appends a new record $(x, v_i(x'), update)$ to the auxiliary log, and then modifies the auxiliary IVV: $v_{ii}(x') = v_{ii}(x') + 1.$.

In the second case, i applies update to the regular copy x; modifies IVV of the regular copy and DBVV: $v_{ii}(x) = v_{ii}(x) + 1$, $V_{ii} = V_{ii} + 1$; and then appends a log record (x, V_{ii}) to L_{ii}.

6 Performance

The procedure *AddLogRecord* is executed in the protocol only when the data item x mentioned in the record being added is accessed anyway. Thus, the location of $P(x)$ is known to *AddLogRecord* for free, and the procedure computes in constant time.

The additional work done by the protocol in the procedure for updating a data item (beyond applying the update itself) takes constant time.

For the rest of this section, we assume that the number of servers is fixed and the size of data items is bounded by a constant. With these assumptions, out-of-bound copying is done in constant time (again, beyond accessing the data items themselves).

Now consider update propagation. In the *SendPropagation* procedure, computing tails D_k is done in time linear in the number of records selected. Since only the records corresponding to updates missed by the recipient are selected, each D_k is computed, at worst, in time linear to the number of data items to be sent (denoted as m). Thus, the total time to compute D is $O(nm)$, where n is the number of servers. Under the assumption that n is fixed, the time to compute D is linear in m.

An interesting question is time to compute set S, which is the union of data items referenced by records in D_k, $1 \leq k \leq n$.

To compute S in $O(m)$, we assume that every data item x has a flag *IsSelected*. The location of this flag is recorded in the control state associated with x. As already mentioned, whenever a log record x is added to the log, the corresponding data item is accessed. Then, the location of x's *IsSelected* flag can be added to the log record at the constant cost.

Then, when *SendPropagation* procedure adds a log record to D_k, the *IsSelected* flag of the corresponding data item x is accessed in constant time. If its value is *"NO"*, the data item is added to S and x's *IsSelected* flag is flipped to *"YES"*. The next time a record referencing x is selected (for a different tail D_l), it will not be added to S. Once computation of D is complete, S will contain the union of data items referenced in records from D_k.

Now, for every data item x in S, its *IsSelected* flag is flipped back to *"NO"*. This takes time linear in the number of data items in S.

Therefore, the total time to compute *SendPropagation* is $O(m)$. In addition, the message sent from the source of propagation to the recipient includes data items being propagated plus constant amount of information per data item. (This information includes the IVV of a data item and the log record of the last update to the data item on every server; recall that regular log records have constant size.)

Finally, the *AcceptPropagation* procedure, in the absence of out-of-bound copying, takes $O(m)$ time to compute (in addition to accessing data items to adopt newer versions received). We conclude that in the common case, the total overhead for update propagation is $O(m)$.

The cost of *IntraNodePropagation* is clearly dominated by the cost of re-applying updates accumulated by the auxiliary copy to the regular copy. This cost is linear in the number of accumulated updates and, depending on the number of such updates, may be high. However, our protocol assumes that few data items are copied out-of-bound. Then, even if overhead imposed by an out-of-bound data item is high, the total overhead is kept low. (Note that *IntraNodePropagation* is executed in the background and does not delay user operations or requests for update propagation or out-of-bound copying from other nodes.)

7 Proof of Correctness

Definition 4 Transitive update propagation. Node i is said to perform update propagation transitively from j if it either performs update propagation from j, or it performs update propagation from k after k performed update propagation transitively from j.

Theorem 5. *If update propagation is scheduled in such a way that every node eventually performs update propagation transitively from every other node, then correctness criteria from Section 2.1 are satisfied.*

Proof. See [13].

8 Related work

In this section, we compare our work with existing approaches. Several epidemic protocols have been proposed for replica management. The common feature of existing systems is that they perform anti-entropy and maintain replica consistency at the same data granularity level. Then, as the number of data items grows and the overhead imposed by anti-entropy becomes too large, the existing systems must either schedule anti-entropy less frequently, or increase the granularity of the data (e.g., use a relation instead of a tuple as a granule) to reduce the number of data items.

Neither option is too desirable: the first causes update propagation to be less timely and increases the chance that an update will arrive at an obsolete replica; the second increases the possibility of "false sharing" where replicas are (needlessly) declared inconsistent while the offending updates were actually applied to semantically independent portions of the data item.

Our protocol, on the other hand, decouples the data granularity used for anti-entropy from the granularity used to maintain replica consistency. This enables the system to perform anti-entropy efficiently at the granularity of the entire database, while maintaining replica consistency at the granularity of individual data items.

In the next subsection, we compare our approach with the Lotus Notes system, a commercial epidemic system that is not based on version vectors. The special attention we pay to show how a Lotus Notes-like system would benefit from our approach is partially due to the wide usage of Lotus Notes in practice. We then consider Oracle Symmetric Replication approach in Section 8.2, and replicated database and file systems that employ version vectors in Section 8.3.

8.1 Lotus Notes Protocol

The Lotus Notes protocol [8] associates a *sequence number* with every data item copy, which records the number of updates seen by this copy. Similar to our protocol, Lotus assumes that whole databases are replicated, so that anti-entropy is normally invoked once for all data items in the database. Each server records the time when it propagated updates to every other server (called the last propagation time below).

Consider two nodes, i and j, that replicate a database. Let i invoke an instance of anti-entropy to compare its replica of the database with that of server j, and catch up if necessary. Anti-entropy executes the following algorithm.

1. When node j receives a request for update propagation from i, it first verifies if any data items in its replica of the database have changed since the last update propagation from j to i. If no data item has changed, no further action is needed. Otherwise, j builds a list of data items that have been modified since the last propagation. The entries in the list include data item names and their sequence numbers. j then sends this list to i.
2. i compares every element from the received list with the sequence number of its copy of the same data item. i then copies from j all data items whose sequence number on j is greater.

This algorithm may detect in constant time that update propagation is not required, but only if no data item in the source database has been modified since the last propagation with the recipient. However, in many cases, the source and recipient database replicas will be identical even though the source database has been modified since the last update propagation to the recipient. For instance, after the last propagation between themselves, both nodes may have performed update propagation from other nodes and copied some data modified there. Or, the recipient database may have obtained updates from the source indirectly via intermediate nodes.

In these cases, Lotus incurs high overhead for attempting update propagation between identical database replicas. At the minimum, this overhead includes comparing the modification time of every data item in the source database against the time of the last update propagation. Thus, it grows linearly in the number of data items in the database.

In addition, the first step of the algorithm will result in a list of data items that have been modified or obtained by j since the last propagation. This list will be sent to i, who then will have to perform some work for every entry in this list in step 2. All this work is overhead.

In contrast, the protocol proposed in this paper *never* attempts update propagation between identical replicas of the database. It always recognizes that two database replicas are identical in constant time, by simply comparing their DBVVs.

Moreover, even when update propagation is required, our protocol does not examine every data item in the database to determine which ones must be copied. It makes this determination in time proportional to the number of data items that must actually be copied.

Finally, Lotus update propagation protocol correctly determines which of two copies of a data item is newer only *provided the copies do not conflict*. When a conflict exists, one copy is often declared "newer" incorrectly. For example, if i made two updates to x while j made one conflicting update without obtaining i's copy first, x_i will be declared newer, since its sequence number is greater. It will override x_j in the next execution of update propagation. Thus, Lotus protocol does not satisfy the correctness criteria of Section 2.1.

8.2 Oracle Symmetric Replication Protocol

Oracle's Symmetric Replication protocol [10] is not an epidemic protocol is a strict sense. It does not perform comparison of replica control state to determine obsolete replicas. Instead, it uses a simple approach outlined in the Introduction of this paper. Every server keeps track of the updates it performs and periodically ships them to all other servers. No forwarding of updates is performed.

In the absence of failures, this protocol exhibits good performance. However, a failure of the node that originated updates may leave the system in a state where some nodes have received the updates while others have not. Since no forwarding is performed, this situation may last for a long time, until the server that originated the update is repaired. This situation is dangerous, not only because users can observe different versions of the data at the same time, but also because it increases the opportunity for user updates to be applied to obsolete replicas, thus creating update conflicts.

Our protocol has similar to Oracle performance of update propagation in the absence of failures: it only copies those data items that need to be propagated, executing no work per every data item in the database. However, our protocol does not have the above-mentioned vulnerability to failures during update propagation. If the node that originated updates fails during update propagation (so that some but not all servers received new data), the system will discover this during a periodic comparison of database version vectors on surviving nodes. Then, the newer version of the data items will be forwarded from nodes that obtained it before the failure to the rest of nodes.

The price our protocol pays for this, the periodic comparison of database version vectors, is very small.

8.3 Protocols Using Version Vectors

To our knowledge, version vectors were first introduced in the Locus file system [12] and have been used in several epidemic distributed database and file systems. Version vectors have also been used to prevent out-of-order delivery of causally related messages in a distributed system [3, 6].

The Ficus replicated file system [5] (a descendant of Locus) divides anti-entropy activity into update notification and replica reconciliation processes. Each node i periodically notifies all other nodes about files updated locally. Other nodes then obtain the new copy from i. This notification is attempted only once, and no indirect copying from i via other nodes occurs.

Reconciliation then makes sure that updates have been properly propagated by periodically comparing version vectors of different file replicas and detecting obsolete or conflicting copies. Reconciliation is done on a per data item basis and involves comparing version vectors of every file.

Thus, update propagation in Ficus involves examining the state of every data item, which our protocol avoids. While overall performance of this system is less affected by this than performance of Lotus Notes (since reconciliation may run less frequently because most updates will be propagated by update notification mechanism), our approach would still be beneficial by improving performance of update propagation when it does run.

In Wuu and Berntein's protocol [15], anti-entropy is done by nodes exchanging *gossip messages* [9, 7]. A gossip message from j to i contains log records of updates that j believes are missed by i, and version vector information describing the state of j as well as the extent of j's knowledge about the state of other nodes in the system.

The Two-phase Gossip protocol [7] improves [15] by sending fewer version vectors in a gossip message. It also describes a more general method for garbage-collecting log records. Agrawal and Malpani's protocol [1] decouples sending update logs from sending version vector information. Thus, separate policies can be used to schedule both types of exchanges.

The important difference between our protocol and the three protocols above is that the latter perform anti-entropy on the per data item basis, and each invocation involves at least one comparison with the (old) version vector of the recipient copy. Thus, their total overhead is at least linear in the total number of data items.[4]

The protocol proposed in [9] uses version vectors to enforce causally monotonic ordering of user operations on every replica. If an operation arrives out of order, it is delayed until the previous operations arrive. A client stores the version vector returned by last server it contacted and uses it to ensure causal ordering of operations when it connects to different servers.

This approach was extended further in [14]. The protocol of [14] provides more levels of consistency. It also allows to localize consistency control to an individual *session* between a client and the system, independently of other sessions.

These two protocols concentrate on taking advantage of weak-consistency models to improve availability and performance of user operations. Anti-entropy in these systems, as in other existing protocols, is done at the same data granularity as consistency control.[5] Thus, the overhead for anti-entropy in these systems grows, again, linearly with the total number of data items.

9 Conclusion

In this paper, we addressed the scalability issues in epidemic replicated databases. The epidemic approach to replica management is attractive because user operations are serviced by a single (and often a nearby) server, update propagation can be done at a convenient time (i.e., during the next dial-up session), and multiple updates can often be bundled together and propagated in a single transfer.

However, existing epidemic protocols impose overhead that grows linearly with the number of data items in the database. This limits the size of the database that the system can handle without significant performance degradation.

In contrast, the protocol proposed in this paper imposes overhead that is linear in the number of data items that actually must be copied during update propagation. Since this number is usually much lower than the total number of data items in the database, our protocol promises significant reduction of overhead.

A secondary contribution of this paper is that it explicitly specified correctness criteria for update propagation, separately from correctness criteria for database transactions. This allows one to reason formally about correct propagation regardless of the data consistency guarantees provided by the system to the users.

Finally, we showed how some commercial replicated databases could benefit from our protocol and compared our approach with existing research proposals.

---

[4] In fact, this overhead is even greater because these protocols compare the recipient version vector with every record in the log to be sent. So the overhead is linear in the number of data items plus the number of updates exchanged.

[5] The protocol of [14] uses a database as the granule for consistency control; it does not specify how anti-entropy is done. As already mentioned, doing consistency control at a coarse granularity reduces overhead but increases the possibility of false sharing.

Acknowledgments

The authors thank Garret Swart for reading the paper and verifying its claims about the Oracle replication scheme. We would also like to thank Julie Carroll, Aaron Watters, and Stacey Marcella for their comments.

References

1. D. Agrawal and A. Malpani. Efficient dissemination of information in computer networks. *The Computer Journal*, 6(34), pp. 534-541, 1991.
2. P. A. Bernstein, V. Hadzilacos, and N. Goodman. *Concurrency Control and Recovery in Database Systems*. Addison-Wesley, Reading, Mass., 1987.
3. K. Birman, A. Schiper, and P. Stephenson. Lightweight causal and atomic group multicast. *ACM Trans. on Comp. Sys.* Vol. 9, No. 3, pp. 272-314, August 1991.
4. A. Demers, D. Greene, C. Hauser, W. Irish, J. Larson, S. Shenker, H. Sturgis, D. Swinehart, and D. Terry. Epidemic algorithms for replicated database maintenance. In *Proc. of the 6th Symp. on Principles of Distr. Computing*, pp. 1-12, 1987.
5. R. G. Guy, J. S. Heidemann, W. Mak, T. W. Page, G. J. Popek, G. J. Rothmeier. Implementation of the Ficus replicated file system. In *Proc. of Usenix Summer Conf.*, pp. 63-71, 1990.
6. C. Fidge. Timestamps in message-passing systems that preserve the partial ordering. In *Proc. of the 11th Australian Computer Science Conf.*, pp. 56-66, 1988.
7. A. Heddaya, M. Hsu, and W. Weihl. Two phase gossip: managing distributed event histories. *Information Sciences*, 49, pp. 35-57, 1989.
8. L. Kawell Jr., S. Beckhardt, T. Halvorsen, R. Ozzie, and I. Greif. Replicated document management in a group communication system. Presented at the 2d Conf. on Computer-Supported Cooperative Work. September 1988.
9. R. Ladin, B. Liskov, L. Shrira, and S. Ghemawat. Providing high availability using lazy replication. *ACM Trans. on Computer Systems*, 4(10), pp. 360-391, November 1992.
10. Oracle 7 Distributed Database Technology and Symmetric Replication. Oracle White Paper, April 1995.
11. D. S. Parker, G. J. Popek, G. Rudisin, A. Stoughton, B. J. Walker, E. Walton, J. M. Chow, D. Edwards, S. Kiser, and C. Kline. Detection of mutual inconsistency in distributed systems. *IEEE Trans. on Software Eng.* 9(3), pp. 240-246, May 1983.
12. G. Popek, B. Walker, J. Chow, D. Edwards, C. Kline, G. Rudisin, and G. Thiel. LOCUS: A network transparent, high reliability distributed system. In *Proc. 8th Symp. on Operating Systems Principles*, pp. 169-177, 1981.
13. M. Rabinovich, N. Gehani, and A. Kononov. Scalable update propagation in epidemic replicated databases. AT&T Bell Labs Technical Memorandum 112580-951213-11TM, December 1995.
14. D. Terry, A. Demers, K. Peterson, M. Spreitzer, M. Theimer, and B. Welch. Session guarantees for weakly consistent replicated data. In *Proc. of the Int. Conf. on Parallel and Distributed Information Systems*, 1994.
15. G. T. Wuu and A. J. Bernstein. Efficient solution to the replicated log and dictionary problems. In *Proc. of the 3d ACM Symp. on Principles of Distr. Computing*, pp. 233-242, 1984.

Database Support for Efficiently Maintaining Derived Data *

Brad Adelberg and Ben Kao and Hector Garcia-Molina

Abstract. Derived data is maintained in a database system to correlate and summarize base data which record real world facts. As base data changes, derived data needs to be recomputed. A high performance system should execute all these updates and recomputations in a timely fashion so that the data remains fresh and useful, while at the same time executing user transactions quickly. This paper studies the intricate balance between recomputing derived data and transaction execution. Our focus is on efficient *recomputation strategies* — how and when recomputations should be done to reduce their cost without jeopardizing data timeliness. We propose the *Forced Delay* recomputation algorithm and show how it can exploit *update locality* to improve both data freshness and transaction response time.
Keywords: derived data, view maintenance, active database system, transaction scheduling, update locality.

1 Introduction

Active rule-based systems are often employed in dynamic environments to monitor the status of real-world objects and to discover the occurrences of "interesting" events. For instance, a military radar system can track aircraft and signal alerts when a dangerous pattern appears. A program trading application, for example, monitors the prices of stocks and other commodities, looking for good opportunities. Figure 1 illustrates the major components of such systems. The dynamic environment is modeled by a set of *base data* items stored within a database system. The environment is monitored (e.g., through sensors or humans reporting information); any changes are captured by a stream of *updates* to the base data.

In addition to the base data, the system very often contains *derived composite data*. This is data that indirectly reflects the state of the outside environment, and can be computed from the base data. For example, the S&P 500 stock index represents the aggregate price of 500 U.S. stocks (the base data in this case). In a robot arm control application, readings from sensors (base data) may be used to estimate the weight of the object being lifted by the arm. We say that the composite data (such as a financial composite index, the estimated weight of the object held by a robot arm) is *derived* from the base data (such as a stock price,

* This work was supported by the Telecommunications Center at Stanford University, by Hewlett Packard and by Philips. This work was also supported by an equipment grant from Digital Equipment Corporation.

a sensor reading) collected directly from the environment. The computations for derived data are expressed as *rules* that specify how changes to the base data should be reflected on the derived data. As we will study in this paper, these rules can be triggered and executed in a variety of ways, leading to derived data with varying degrees of "up to dateness."

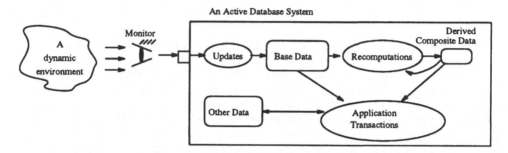

Fig. 1. A high level model for the derived data maintenance problem.

Both base and derived data are accessed by *application transactions* that generate the ultimate actions taken or decisions made by the system. For instance, application transactions may request the purchase of stock, move a robot arm, or initiate defensive action against enemy aircraft. Application transactions can be driven by user requests, or in other cases by triggers that identify certain conditions in the base or derived data. Notice that updates to base data or recomputations for derived data may also be run as transactions (e.g., with some of the ACID properties). In those cases, we refer to them as update transactions and recomputation transactions. When we use the term transaction alone, we are referring to an application transaction.

Application transactions can be associated with one or two types of timing requirements: transaction timeliness and data timeliness. Transaction timeliness refers to how "fast" the system responds to a transaction request, while data timeliness refers to how "fresh" the data read is, or how closely in time the data read by a transaction models the environment. Satisfying the two properties poses a major challenge to the design of the underlying database system. This is because the requirements pose conflicting demands on system resources. Some of the reasons why update and recomputation loads can be very high are as follows:

– Very large numbers of base data items may be involved. For example, there could be thousands of sensors in a power network, and there are about 300,000 financial instruments in the U.S. market alone.
– Recomputing a derived item may be expensive. To compute the theoretical value of a financial option price, for example, requires computing the cumulative distribution of the standard normal function and the natural log function.

- The base data update rate can be very high. For example, a financial database that keeps track of the prices of U.S. financial instruments may receive more than 500 updates per second during peak time [CB94].
- Recomputations can have high fan-in and fan-out. A derived data item may depend on a large numbers of base data items i.e., high *fan-in*. For example, the S&P 500 index is derived from a set of 500 stocks. When any one of these base data items changes, the derived data has to be updated, so the recomputation is triggered very frequently. Similarly, a base data item may be "popular" in the sense that it is used to derive a number of derived data items, i.e., high *fan-out*. For example, a pixel value is used to calculate a number of pair-wise co-occurrence probabilities; IBM stock price is being used in a number of composite indices and many other stock options.

This problem of heavy update and recomputation arose in our experience with STRIP. STRIP is a main-memory resident soft real-time database system implemented at Stanford. One of the applications driving our system is program trading. In our experiments, STRIP maintains a database of stock prices and various composite indices on which trading transactions are run. The system is driven by a real-time trace of price quote updates. We found that recomputing the composite indices triggered by the updates represents a major load to the system, and indeed, trading transactions are often significantly delayed due to the heavy update and recomputation activities.

Thus, in these systems we believe that the central problem is the efficient installation of updates and the recomputations they trigger. This problem appears to be more critical than the scheduling of transactions which has traditionally received a lot of attention in the real-time database literature [Ram93]. In a previous study [AGMK95], we have looked at the scheduling problem of updates and transactions and suggested efficient algorithms that can improve transaction timeliness without sacrificing data timeliness. In that study, our focus was on the update process (how to maintain the base data efficiently and up-to-date), and the semantics of data *staleness* (when data should be considered out-of-date). In this paper, we focus instead on the recomputation process, developing and evaluating algorithms for triggering and scheduling recomputations efficiently. One major difference between the two studies is that, as we have argued, recomputations could be much more expensive than simple updates. They may require more data accesses, more computation cycles, and in some cases, one update could trigger multiple recomputations. Recomputations thus have an even more marked effect on the two timeliness properties than updates do.

Even though recomputations consume substantial system resources, there is one feature, *locality*, in our favor. As we will see later, the recomputation strategies we propose will take advantage of this property whenever possible to significantly reduce loads and improve data timeliness. Intuitively, update locality here means that when a base item is updated, it is very likely that the same item or a *related* one will be updated soon thereafter. For example, a stock price update indicates that there is an interest in its trading. The same stock is therefore likely to be the subject of further trading activities and have its price changed again. In Section 2 we will show that the locality property is very marked in practice. Our recomputation schemes will thus attempt to delay recomputations slightly, so that several related base updates can be combined in a single recomputation. The challenge is to accomplish this without severely affecting the timeliness of the derived data.

There are a number of studies related to the derived data maintenance problem (e.g., [BLT86, BCL86, Han87, AL80, RK86, SF90]). Most of these studies assume the relational model and focus on maintaining *materialized views* expressible by relational algebra and some basic aggregate functions such as "sum" and "average". While materialized views can be considered as a special case of derived data, our study covers the more general case in which recomputing the value of a derived item can be arbitrarily complicated. Where appropriate, we will incorporate techniques from view maintenance to improve performance.

2 Update Locality

Many applications that deal with derived data exhibit update locality: an update to a base item is quickly followed by updates to the same or related items. By related we mean that the later updates trigger the same recomputation(s) that the first one did. Locality occurs in two forms: time and space. Updates exhibit time locality if related updates occur in bursts. Since base data models the physical environment, an update on a base data item often signals the "movement" of a modelled object. In many cases, this motion generates a burst of updates to the same base item over a period of time. For example, a stock price update usually indicates trading activity on that stock. Further related updates are therefore likely to arrive soon. As a representative example, Figure 2 shows the inter-arrival distribution of the stock price updates of General Electric Co. on January 3, 1994. In this trace there were 3240 updates on G.E. stock over a trading period of about 31,000 seconds. The average update arrival rate is therefore about one every 10 seconds. If there were no correlation in update arrivals, the inter-arrival time would be exponentially distributed (memoryless). This hypothetical exponential distribution (with mean 10 seconds) is also shown in Figure 2. We see that the actual distribution is much more "skewed" than the exponential one. For example, about 700 out of the 3240 updates occur within 1 second of a previous update, which is about twice as many as the exponential distribution predicts. Thus, the graph clearly illustrates the time locality of the updates.

The other form of locality is space locality: when base item b, which affects derived item d, is updated, it is very likely that a related set of base items, affecting d, will be updated soon (so space locality also requires time locality). For example, if the reading of a temperature sensor changes, it indicates that the surrounding temperature is changing. Under normal conditions, readings of other temperature sensors close to the first would change too. Each of these updates could trigger the same recomputation, say for the average room temperature.

Update locality implies that recomputations for derived data occur in bursts.

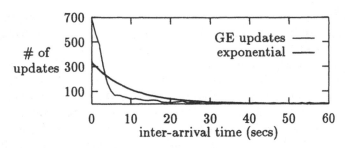

Fig. 2. Inter-arrival distribution of the stock price updates of G.E. on 94/1/3.

Recomputing the affected derived data on every single update is probably very wasteful because the same derived data will be recomputed very soon, often before any application transaction has a chance to read the derived data for any useful work. Instead of recomputing immediately, a better strategy might be to defer a recomputation by a certain amount of time and coalesce the same recomputation requests into a single computation. How to do this effectively will be studied in Section 4.

3   Recomputation and Temporal Correctness

As argued in Section 1, there is a fundamental tradeoff between performance and data correctness. Thus, before we discuss efficient schemes for recomputing derived data, we need a solid definition of what correctness means, both for its consistency and timeliness aspects. In this section we will first review existing notions for consistency and timeliness, and will argue that they are too rigid for the applications we are considering. Instead we will suggest a new notion that we believe succinctly captures correctness for our environment, and show how it leads to concise and intuitive metrics for both transaction and data timeliness.

ACID transactions are the traditional way of guaranteeing data consistency, in our case, guaranteeing that the derived data is consistent with the base data. To achieve consistency, recomputations for derived data are folded into the triggering update transactions. Unfortunately, running updates and recomputations as coupled transactions is not desirable in a high performance, real time environment. It makes updates run longer, blocking other transactions that need to access the same data. Indeed, [CJL91] shows that transaction response time is much improved when *events* and *actions* (in our case updates and recomputations) are decoupled into separate transactions.

Thus, we will assume that recomputations are decoupled from update transactions. This flexibility of course means that consistency can be compromised. For example, if a stock price is updated and the transaction to recompute a composite that includes the stock is delayed, a transaction that reads both the stock and composite values will see an inconsistent set. In many of the applications we are considering, application transactions can cope with such inconsistencies. Still, we believe that is desirable to have a handle on how frequently application transactions encounter inconsistencies, and the metric we propose later on provides an indirect measure of this.

Beyond consistency, data *timeliness* is the second critical correctness notion. For instance, say the system chooses to never update base or derived data even as the external world changes. The data could be completely consistent but still incorrect. Thus, we also need a measure that captures the timeliness of the data.

The real-time database community has proposed definitions of *temporal consistency* which quantify both the consistency and the timeliness of data but they focus on environmental variables that change continuously (e.g. temperature sensors). For this study, since we consider only base data that changes at discrete points in time in response to external events (e.g. stock prices) we believe that the previous definitions are not appropriate. The extended version of this paper [AKGM95] explains the distinction in more detail.

To formulate our new notion of temporal correctness, we define the behavior of an "ideal" system. It is intended only as a yardstick by which to measure the correctness of "real" systems.

Definition 1 (instantaneous system) *An instantaneous system applies base updates and performs all necessary recomputations as soon as an update arrives, taking zero time to do it.*

Definition 2 (temporally correct system) *In a temporally correct system, an application transaction requesting at time t the value of object o (base or derived) is instantaneously given the value that o would have in an instantaneous system.*

The last definition does *not* state that in a temporally correct system data can never be stale or inconsistent. It only states that no transactions can *read* stale or inconsistent data. For base data, this definition is equivalent to the *unapplied update* staleness criteria used in [AGMK95]: base data is temporally correct iff there are no updates that would change its value that have arrived at the database but have not been applied.

Clearly, it is very hard to build a system that is temporally correct. Instead, our goal is to quantify how much a real system deviates from the ideal, temporally correct system. A real system can deviate in two ways: by sometimes letting transactions read data not in the instantaneous system, or by delaying the completion of the read operation.

Regarding the first type of deviation, a transaction can read three types of data. Let $v_s(o, t)$ be the value of object o read by a transaction at time t in system s, where s is either I for the instantaneous system or R for a real system. At time t_1 a transaction T reads object o_i from R. The read is

correct: iff $v_R(o_i, t_1) = v_I(o_i, t_1)$,
stale: iff the read is not correct but $v_R(o_i, t_1) = v_I(o_i, t_0)$ where $t_0 < t_1$,
erroneous: iff the read is neither correct nor stale.

Figure 3 shows an example using two base data items b_1 and b_2 and a derived item d which is defined as their sum. The times t_1, t_2, t_3 are when an external variable being modelled by b_1 or b_2 changes value. Each × indicates a change in database state. For this example, both the real and ideal systems are assumed to update their base data as soon as updates arrive, so only one set of base data is shown in the figure. For the derived data, the real system experiences a delay between updates to base data and recomputation. Just before time t_1, a transaction reading d_R would get the value 5, which is identical to the value in the instantaneous database, d_I. If a transactions tries to read d (d_R in the figure) just after time t_1, however, it will still read the value 5. This is a stale read since the same transaction would read the value 6 in the ideal system. Notice that in the terms of our previous discussion of correctness, if a transaction had read both d and either b_1 or b_2, we would have called this an example of inconsistency. Using instantaneity as the correctness definition, it is impossible to read inconsistent data without at least one item being stale. Thus our new definition allows us to measure both the consistency *and* timeliness of the data read by transactions in one metric: the percentage of transaction that read stale data, p_{stale}. This is the metric we will use to evaluate scheduling algorithms in Section 6.

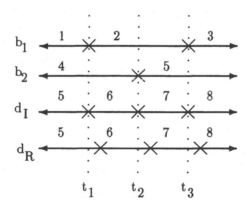

Fig. 3. Derived data example

The second way in which a real system may deviate from a temporally correct one is by delaying reads. In particular, notice that a system can force p_{stale} to zero by delaying transactions that attempt to read stale data until the necessary recomputations have been performed. Thus we need a second metric to quantify the delays experienced by transactions. In this paper we use the average transaction response time, s_q. Notice that s_q measures delays caused by both recomputation delays and excessive system loading. We believe that these two metrics, p_{stale} and s_q, succinctly capture how much a real system deviates from the ideal one. Also, both metrics are intuitive and relevant to the high level behavior that users are interested in.

We stress that p_{stale} is not a metric that can be measured on a running system. It can, however, be measured in a simulation that tracks the database state of both the instantaneous system and the real system. Thus, p_{stale} is used at system design time, to develop algorithms and to select parameter values that yield acceptable p_{stale} and s_q values.

There is a fundamental tradeoff between p_{stale} and s_q, i.e., a system may reduce p_{stale} by delaying transactions that were going to read stale data. However, in order to exploit this tradeoff, the system must be able to determine when a transaction is about to read stale data, or at least when it is *likely* that a read will be stale. In the rest of this section we discuss mechanisms for this.

One approach is to mark relevant derived data as stale whenever an update arrives for base data. In the above example, when the update for b_1 arrives at time t_1, the database marks both b_1 and d stale. When transaction T attempts to read either, the database will see that they are marked as stale and can then restart or delay T as desired. A lazy approach is also possible: When a derived object is read, check the timestamps of all of its base data to see if any is more recent than it. The relative performance of the two approaches will depend on the ratio of reads to writes, as well as the fan-in.

In either case the database needs to know the relation between the base and derived data (i.e., which base data affects which derived data). For our experiments we will assume the existence of an exact dependency graph that gives the precise set of objects read and written by a rule. In some experiments, this graph will be used to block transactions that are about to read stale data (if our main goal is to make $p_{stale} = 0$). In others, the graph is simply used by the simulator to measure the percentage of transactions that read stale data.

4   Algorithms

In this section we describe the algorithms for derived data management. Each algorithm can be characterized by its approach to the following five issues. Our focus in this paper is on the last three issues, but we include the first two for completeness.

1. *Relevancy testing.* One technique for reducing recomputation load is to check in advance if an incoming update affects derived data at all; if it does not, the update can be ignored. Blakely originally proposed this technique in the context of materialized views [BLT86, BCL86]. For example, consider a view V defined as $V(A, B) = \Pi_{A,B}(R_1(A, C, D) \bowtie R_2(C, B))$ where R_1 and R_2 are two base relations and A, B, C, and D are attributes. If a tuple is inserted to R_1 whose values on the A and C attributes are the same as another tuple already in the relation, then the newly inserted tuple will not affect V and is considered *irrelevant* to the view. Since relevancy testing is only possible in a few applications, for our performance studies we assume that relevancy testing is not used.

2. *Decoupled Transactions.* As discussed in Section 3, recomputations may be performed within or outside the context of the transactions performing the

base data updates. We believe that decoupled recomputations are best for a high performance system, so in this paper we only consider this type of recomputation.

3. *Incremental Recomputations.* Recomputations can be performed more efficiently if they are done incrementally [Han87] [RCBB89]. Instead of fully recomputing a derived item by reading the values of all of the base data items it depends on, it is recomputed using its old value and the set of changes to the base data since its last recomputation. Significant performance gain, due to fewer data accesses and shorter computation, can usually be achieved. This performance improvement is especially marked for derived data with large fan-in. One problem with incremental recomputation though is that not all functions can be computed incrementally. For those that can, additional information may have to be kept. For example, to recompute the variance of a set of values incrementally requires one to know about the average of the square of the values too. In our study, we will consider both incremental (I) and full recomputation (F).

4. *Batching.* As discussed earlier, batching can also reduce the cost of recomputations. The idea is to coalesce several updates into a single recomputation. Batching can be performed in one of the following ways:

   (a) *No Batching (NB):* Recomputation transactions are created when an update transaction commits, one per each derived item that the update affects. Often referred to as an *eager* approach.

   (b) *On Demand (OD):* Derived data is only recomputed when it is invalid (or stale) and a read is attempted. This approach is also referred to as *lazy* or *deferred* recomputation, and has been studied with regard to view maintenance ([Han87, AL80, RK86, SG90, SJGP90]). On-demand has limited applicability in active systems. In particular, it cannot be used for recomputations that must trigger an application transaction or alerts. For the remaining recomputations, OD requires a dependency graph so that when derived data is read, it can be determined if it is stale and if so, what recomputations must be triggered. In spite of these limitations, we still include it in this study for the cases when it can be used.

   (c) *Periodic (P):* A recomputation transaction is periodically invoked for each derived object.

   (d) *Periodic or On Demand (POD):* This is a combination of periodic recomputation and the on demand approach. Derived data is recomputed periodically unless a transaction tries to access it and finds that it is invalid, in which case it is recomputed immediately.

   (e) *Forced Delay (FD):* When an update u on a base item is applied, a recomputation transaction r is generated for each affected derived data, say d. The recomputation r, however, is not released until a fixed time after update u commits. During the delay, further updates to base data of d will not generate new recomputations.

5. *Block on Stale Data.* Our final issue deals with whether the system tries to minimize p_{stale} by blocking reads when it believes that the data is stale. As discussed in Section 3, a blocking system (BL) keeps a dependency graph to detect possible stale reads. A non-blocking system (NBL) always lets application transactions read data.

We will use the notation X/Y/Z to identify a particular algorithm, where X is either I (incremental) or F (full recomputation), Y is the batching scheme (NB, OD, P, POD, FD), and Z is either BL (blocking) or NBL (non-blocking). Due to space limitations we do not consider further the periodic schemes -/P/- and -/POD/-. We believe that these schemes are dominated by forced delay. Furthermore, it is usually hard to select a good recomputation period. If it is set too short, the recomputation load is high and s_q (transaction response time) becomes too high. If it is set too long, data becomes stale and p_{stale} grows. Also, we do not consider -/OD/NBL algorithms: if we do a recomputation on demand when a read occurs, it is supposedly so that transaction reads the new value, so a blocking strategy is most natural.

Having categorized the algorithms we will evaluate, in the rest of this section we will briefly discuss some implementation issues related to how these various options interact with each other. The derived data is defined through rules; each rule specifies (a) an update event of a base data object, (b) a condition, and (c) a recomputation procedure. For incremental recomputations (I), the procedure needs the old and the new values of the updated base object. Since the recomputation may be delayed, when the update occurs the system generates a *delta record* that specifies the old and new information. This record is then given to the recomputation procedure when it eventually runs. For full recomputations, delta records are not necessary; the procedure reads whatever data it needs from the database to derive the new values.

When incremental recomputation procedures are batched together, the corresponding delta records are combined into a *delta set*. Thus, a single instance of the recomputation procedure is eventually fired; it takes as input the delta set, and from it computes the new derived values for the entire batch of updates. For this to work, the code in the recompute procedure must know how to handle delta sets, and furthermore, the programming environment in which it was developed should have facilities for accessing the various components in delta sets. In [AKGM95] we suggest some programming structures to facilitate the writing of recomputations based on delta sets.

Delta records and delta sets need to be saved until the recomputation takes place. In most cases, the storage requirements are small and the information can be kept in main memory. (If a failure occurs and memory is lost, the derived data can be computed from the base data directly.) However, in some cases, the storage requirements could be non-trivial. In particular, with on-demand recomputation, if a derived object is updated frequently but not read for a long period of time, the delta set could become large. Similarly, for a high fan-out base object, its delta record must be included in the delta set of many derived objects until these are read, leading again to large sets. We could deal with this problem with a modified on-demand scheme that delays recomputation until a read occurs or until the delta set becomes too large. Since this modified scheme could deal with growing delta sets without significant performance impact, in our performance evaluations we simply assume that delta sets fit in main memory.

5 Performance Model

In order to compare the different algorithms for scheduling recomputations, we define a performance model that specifies the structure of the database, its interaction with the external world, and how transactions are processed. The model is developed in the context of a program trading application. The model is driven by an actual trace of stock price changes. However, the recomputations and application transactions are synthetic, generated to approximate a realistic environment. To isolate the key issues for derived data management, without becoming lost in irrelevant details, we have made simplifying assumptions about the application and about the database system as described below.

Data and Transactions The relationship between data and transactions in our model mirrors the system shown in Figure 1. We ignore the "other data" from the figure and instead concentrate on the base data, in this case stock data, and the derived data. There is an object for each stock being tracked, which stores many details about the stock (e.g. last price, trade volume, daily high and low). The stock base data is then used to calculate a number of derived objects such as composite averages and theoretical option prices. There are three types of transactions in this system:

updates are write only transactions that change the value of one stock object. For our experiments, the updates that are generated correspond to actual stock trace activity taken from the TAQ database provided by the New York Stock Exchange. Both the arrival time of each update and the stock that is changed are real values from a day of trading.

recomputations are transactions that calculate the value of derived objects using the stock data. Both the fan-in, the number of base objects which are read, and the fan-out, the number of derived objects which are updated, are simulation parameters. The recomputations are actually fired according to the algorithm under consideration (Section 4).

queries are read only transactions that are generated by users of the system. They can read both base and derived data, but modify neither. They are assumed to have Poisson arrival.

We assume that updates to base data are installed using the *updates first* scheme of [AGMK95]. In this scheme, updates are queued separately from other transactions, and are executed in FIFO order with highest priority. Recomputations and queries are combined into a second class which is also scheduled in FIFO order, but only if no update transactions are queued. If an update arrives while a recomputation or a query is being processed, the running transaction will not be preempted. We believe that this updates-first scheme is the most appropriate for the program trading application because of its data driven nature. (Actually, [AGMK95] reports that a *split updates* scheme could be superior, but we do not use it here since it requires partitioning the data by importance to the application.)

Storage Model The database is composed of N_{stocks} stock objects and $N_{derived}$ derived objects. We assume that the entire database cannot fit in main memory and so must be stored on disk. For simplicity, we do not model the disk caching scheme in detail. Instead, we define the probability that a desired page will already be present in memory to be determined by the parameter p_{cache_hit}. If the page is not present, an I/O will have to be performed which will take io_{lookup} or io_{access} milliseconds for index page reads or data page reads respectively. Log writes will usually be to main memory as well, but when a page fills it requires io_{write_log} milliseconds to write it. We assume that the disk can only service one request at a time, so additional requesters must wait for the current request to finish before starting. The waiting transactions are maintained in two FIFO queues: one for updates and one for other transactions. Updates are always serviced first for I/O, just as in CPU scheduling.

Fan-in/Fan-out Scenarios In the introduction, we discussed the fan-in and fan-out of derived data. We have chosen to study the effects of the two properties separately in our simulations. We have therefore defined two scenarios to study, each focusing on only fan-in or fan-out.

In the first scenario, we test the performance of the scheduling algorithms when computing derived data that have high fan-in, such as composite indices. Each of the $N_{derived}$ derived objects is computed from N_{fan_in} stock objects. For each derived object, the required stocks are chosen randomly from all of the stocks but weighted by the number of occurrences of each stock in the trace. For example, a stock that appears 500 times is twice as likely to be used in a derived object as one that appears 250 times. We feel this is a reasonable approach because the most important companies (for predicting general economic and industry specific trends) are also the companies that are most heavily traded.

The second scenario tests the performance of the scheduling algorithms when computing derived data such as theoretical option prices which have moderate fan-out. The fan-in of the derived objects is set to 1 which means that each is computed from only one stock object. The fan-out, defined as $\overline{N_{fan\_out}}$, is the average number of derived objects computed from each stock. The actual number of derived objects computed from each stock depends on the the number of occurrences of the stock in the trace as in scenario 1. For example, a stock that appears 500 times will have twice as many objects derived from it as one that appears 250 times. We feel this is a reasonable approach because the most heavily traded companies are also the ones with the most options (and other derivatives) traded.

Metrics and Parameters We only use three metrics to evaluate the scheduling algorithms. The two primary metrics, $\overline{s_q}$ and p_{stale}, were motivated and described in Section 3. The third metric, $\overline{N_r}$, is the average number of recomputes per second and is provided to help explain system behavior.

The values of the simulation parameters were chosen as reasonable values for a typical workstation. Where possible, we have performed sensitivity analysis of key parameter values. The simulator is written in **DeNet** [Liv90]. Each simulation experiment (generating one data point) ran for approximately 2 hours of simulated time, driven by the stock price trace data. The simulation parameters are detailed in Table 1.

Description	Parameter	Value
# of instructions executed per second	ips	100×10^6
# of instructions to find one data object	cpu_{lookup}	500
# of instructions to check condition of rule	$cpu_{check\_condition}$	500
# of instructions to compute derived value (fixed)	$cpu_{compute_f}$	5000
# of instructions to compute derived value (incremental)	$cpu_{compute_i}$	1000
# of instructions to perform query excluding I/O time	cpu_{query}	1000000
# of instructions to begin a transaction	$cpu_{start\_transaction}$	7500
# of instructions to commit a transaction	$cpu_{commit\_transaction}$	7500
# of instructions to begin an update	cpu_{start_update}	1500
# of instructions to commit an update	cpu_{commit_update}	1500
I/O time (ms) to find one data object	io_{lookup}	10
I/O time (ms) to access one data object	io_{access}	10
I/O time (ms) to write log record	io_{write_log}	1
I/O cache hit rate	p_{cache_hit}	0.99
query arrival rate	λ_q	50.0
mean # of stock objects read by query	μ_s	50
S.D. of # of stock objects read by query	σ_s	3
mean # of derived objects read by query	μ_d	5
S.D. of # of derived objects read by query	σ_d	1
mean # instructions to perform query	μ_q	1000000
S.D. of # instructions to perform query	σ_q	100000
# of stock objects	N_{stocks}	10000
# of derived objects	$N_{derived}$	200
fan-in	N_{fan_in}	100
average fan-out	N_{fan_out}	2

Table 1. Scheduler baseline settings

6 Results

In this section we present selected results from our simulations. Our goals are to compare the various algorithms with respect to our performance metrics (Section 5), and to study how the characteristics of the derived data affect the timeliness of both data and transactions. By evaluating the system under different settings, we are able to address questions such as: Which algorithm is best under which conditions, and what is the best delay value for the Forced Delay strategy to balance data timeliness with recomputation cost? To answer the second question, we fill experiment with four versions of the Forced Delay scheme. They are denoted as FD(d) where d is the value of the delay (t_{delay}).

We focus first on derived data with high fan-in in Section 6, followed by the fan-out case in Section 6. All of the experiments described in this section were run with the parameter values described in Table 1 unless otherwise stated. Additional results, including various sensitivity analyses, are described in [AKGM95].

Effects of fan-in To begin, we examine the performance of algorithms I/-/NBL (incremental recomputation without block on stale reads). This means that recomputations are not expensive and applications are allowed to read stale derived data. To compare the algorithms under different loads we vary the fan-in of the derived data (e.g. the number of stocks used to compute a composite index). By varying fan-in, we can control how many base data items a derived object depends on, and thus the frequency that the derived data is recomputed. Figure 4(a) shows how the different algorithms maintain the timeliness of the data. As expected, $p_{stale} = 0$ under OD because transactions that try to read stale data cause a recompute to be triggered, thereby refreshing the derived data as they read. Also, the no batching scheme (NB), which releases a (decoupled) recomputation transaction immediately after an update, keeps derived data relatively fresh: less than 1 in 10 queries tries to read a derived data object in the small window between update and recompute. The FD algorithms, which force the delay to be larger, exhibit higher rates of p_{stale} in direct relation to the size of t_{delay}. Even with a small delay, p_{stale} is around 60%. Even though sometimes queries are reading stale data under FD, we remark that under the non-blocking scenario, transactions are *allowed* to read stale data. Also, the stale data which is read is not very old. Since queries arrive randomly, the average age of a stale item is $\frac{t_{delay}}{2}$ (at most 1.5 seconds in our experiments). This delay is probably dwarfed by the time it takes an update to arrive at the database itself. (Stock price information is entered by hand at terminals on the exchange floor, so the time between a trade and the update for that trade will be many seconds.)

We now look at the number of recomputations the database has to perform per second, $\overline{N_r}$. It was our claim in Section 2 that delaying and batching recomputes that exhibit locality would significantly reduce the number of necessary recomputes. Figure 4(b) supports this. Even a small delay, such as a quarter of a second, reduces N_r by half or more. FD(3.0), which has the longest delay, reduces the number of recomputes by over an order of magnitude when $N_{fan\_in} = 150$. More importantly, notice that NB does not handle large fan-in well. As is seen in the figure, NB requires 50% more recomputations when N_{fan_in} is increased by 50%. The Forced Delay schemes however, effectively absorb the added recomputation load caused by high fan-in situation. FD(3.0), for example, keeps the recomputation rate to 50 per second over the range of fan-in shown.

As seen in Figure 5(a), the savings in recomputation effort by batching di-

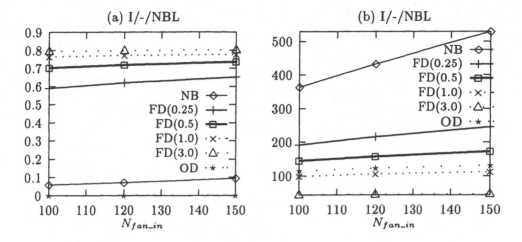

Fig. 4. Effects of N_{fan_in} on p_{stale}(a) and $\overline{N_r}$(b) with baseline settings.

rectly relate to a reduction in query response time, s_q. More recomputations mean more contention for resources, both CPU and I/O, which in turn means longer delays for queries. When $N_{fan\_in} = 150$, queries take 50% longer under NB than they do under the other algorithms. By allowing queries to read slightly out-of-date data, the FD algorithms significantly improve query response time. This s_q improvement is significant but not as large as the difference in N_r seen in the previous graph. The reason is that with incremental recomputation, most of the work in the system is generated by queries so that even a large reduction in the recomputation load does not have a huge effect on the total system load (and hence waiting times). In systems where the recomputation work dominates the system (e.g., high fan-in, large number of derived items, full recomputation) the ratio of s_q between NB and FD would approach the N_r ratio. Such an example is shown in next section on complete recomputation.

In the case where no stale reads are allowed and queries must block if they read stale data (I/-/BL), the conclusions about query response time change dramatically. For FD with a large t_{delay}, we expect that service time will be very long since a query that tries to read stale data will have to wait $\frac{t_{delay}}{2}$ on average. Figure 5(b) illustrates this effect. FD(3.0) has a query response time of over 5 seconds which implies that it is waiting for more than one derived object to be recomputed. Figure 5(b) clearly shows that FD with large delays is inappropriate for applications that do not allow stale reads. (FD still has good throughput though, because it reduces the number of necessary recomputes; hence it lowers the system load. The recompute graph is not shown since it is identical to figure 4(b).)

In conclusion, OD seems to outperform the other algorithms in satisfying both data and transaction timeliness: Stale data is never read, and transaction response time is kept low by recomputing only if necessary. In systems where lazy recomputation is possible, therefore, OD appears to be the best choice. However, in data-driven systems OD will not work (Section 4) because alerts will not be sent unless a query reads the relevant derived item. In these cases the choice is between NB and FD. If the application can tolerate reads of slightly stale data, FD with a small delay (in this experiment, 0.25 or 0.5 seconds) is a good tradeoff between data and transaction timeliness. Finally, for cases where data timeliness is extremely important, NB should be chosen over FD.

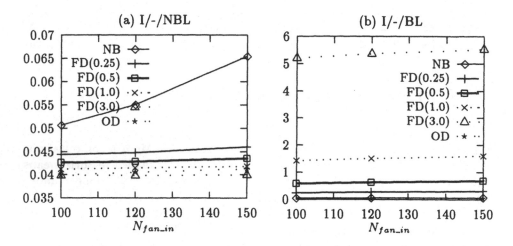

Fig. 5. Effects of N_{fan_in} on query response time.

Effect of Complete Recomputation When recomputation is full (F/-/NBL), the cost to perform a single recomputation rises in direct proportion to the fan-in. This impacts the performance of the database in two ways. First, since recomputation becomes much more expensive relative to query processing, we would expect that algorithms that reduce N_r will show even greater gains in s_q than in the previous section. Second, since both the number of recomputes and the cost per recompute increase with N_{fan_in}, we would expect that the system load (CPU and I/O) will increase drastically. Figure 6 supports this. The database using NB starts to overload with $N_{fan\_in} < 20$, far lower than the 100-150 range used in the incremental experiments. Due to the high loading of the system, reducing the amount of recomputation work yields large benefits in query response time: Switching from NB to FD(0.25) allows the system to handle 30% more fan-in (which also translates to 30% more recomputation load). The heavy load also causes NB, which under moderate loading maintains data timeliness well, to degrade below the performance of the FD algorithms. For example, in Figure 6(b), p_{stale} under NB goes up from 1% to 60% as fan-in increases. This is due to long queueing time that causes long delay to recomputation transactions.

As in the incremental case, OD performs very well in both metrics and across the entire range of fan-in. In conclusion, in systems with complete recomputation or with heavy loading, OD should be used if possible. If OD is not appropriate, FD is a clear winner over NB.

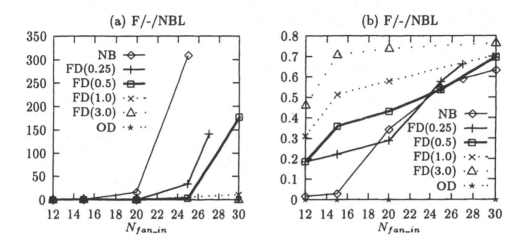

Fig. 6. Effects of N_{fan_in} on s_q(a) and p_{stale}(b) with complete recomputes and high I/O contention.

Effects of fan-out In this section we discuss the performance of the algorithms when maintaining derived data with fan-out instead of fan-in. Due to space constraints, we only report a few results and direct the reader to the technical report for more details [AKGM95]. The relative performance of the algorithms is similar to that of the fan-in experiments: OD and NB do the best job maintaining data timeliness, whereas FD and OD best maintain transaction timeliness. One difference: the FD algorithms keep the derived data far fresher than with fan-in since each derived object only becomes stale when the value of a particular base object changes, so the relative rate of invalidation is much lower. Another difference is that the query response time of NB is not as bad as with fan-in although it is clear that s_q is growing fastest for NB and that at larger values of N_{fan_out} the difference will widen. In conclusion, for maintaining fan-out data, OD is the best choice if it is applicable. If not, FD with a low delay is again a good compromise choice.

7 Conclusions

Management of derived data is a critical task in real-time database systems. In this paper we have presented and analyzed a variety of schemes for managing this derived data, balancing the needs for up-to-date data with those for processing cycles for application transactions. Our results indicate that a good general-purpose strategy is to delay recomputations slightly (Forced Delay), to allow batching of related recomputations. A lazy, On-Demand strategy can perform even better for those applications where derived data does not trigger application transactions. Incremental recomputations are best (with either of the above schemes), but again, are only feasible in some cases.

Since batching of incremental recomputations is so beneficial (reduces processing load while still keeping data relatively fresh), we believe that systems need to provide good support for this. The extended version of this paper [AKGM95] describeds how a standard ECA rule system can be augmented to do so. The STRIP real-time database system we are currently implementing is incorporating such facilities for incremental and batched recomputations.

References

[AGMK95] B. Adelberg, H. Garcia-Molina, and B. Kao. Applying update streams in a soft real-time database system. In *SIGMOD Proceedings*, 1995.

[AKGM95] B. Adelberg, B. Kao, and H. Garcia-Molina. Database support for derived data. Technical report, Stanford University, 1995. Available by anonymous ftp from db.stanford.edu in /pub/adelberg/1995.

[AL80] M. Adiba and B. Lindsay. Database snapshots. In *VLDB Proceedings*, 1980.

[BCL86] J. A. Blakely, N. Coburn, and P. Larson. Updating derived relations: Detecting irrelevant and autonomously computable updates. In *Proceedings of the 12th VLDB Conference*, pages 457–66, 1986.

[BLT86] J. A. Blakely, P. Larson, and F. W. Tompa. Efficiently updating materialized views. In *SIGMOD Proceedings*, 1986.

[CB94] M. Cochinwala and J. Bradley. A multidatabase system for tracking and retrieval of financial data. In *VLDB Proceedings*, 1994.

[CJL91] M. Carey, R. Jauhari, and M. Livny. On transaction boundaries in active databases: A performance perspective. *IEEE Transactions on Knowledge and Data Engineering*, 3(3):320–36, 1991.

[Han87] E. Hanson. A performance analysis of view materialization strategies. In *SIGMOD Proceedings*, 1987.

[Liv90] M. Livny. DeNet user's guide. Technical report, University of Wisconsin-Madison, 1990.

[Ram93] K. Ramamritham. Real-time databases. *Distributed and Parallel Databases*, 1(2):199–226, 1993.

[RCBB89] A. Rosenthal, S. Chakravarthy, B. Blaustein, and J. Blakely. Situation monitoring for active databases. In *VLDB Proceedings*, 1989.

[RK86] N. Roussopoulos and H. Kang. Preliminary design of ADMS ±: A workstation-mainframe integrated architecture for database management systems. In *VLDB Proceedings*, 1986.

[SF90] A. Segev and W. Fang. Currency-based updates to distributed materialized views. In *Data Engineering Proceedings*, 1990.

[SG90] A. Segev and H. Gunadhi. Temporal query optimization in scientific databases. *IEEE Data Engineering*, 13(3), sep 1990.

[SJGP90] M. Stonebraker, A. Jhingran, J. Goh, and S. Potamianos. On rules, procedures, caching and views in database systems. In *SIGMOD Proceedings*, 1990.

Optimal Multi-Block Read Schedules for Partitioned Signature Files*

Paolo Ciaccia

DEIS - CIOC-CNR - University of Bologna - Italy
pciaccia@deis.unibo.it

Abstract. Queries on partitioned signature files, namely Quick Filter (QF), can lead to retrieve from disk a large number of blocks, depending on the specific query pattern. In order to reduce the overall retrieval time, we consider *multi-block read schedules* that, provided contiguous allocation of blocks of the file on disk surface is guaranteed by the storage system, transfer more than one block at a time. We show that, for any signature query and buffer size, there always exists an optimal schedule whose reads all have the same size, and that such a *constant size* (CS) schedule can be determined in a time logarithmic in the number of blocks to be retrieved. We then provide analytical results for the expected performance of QF using CS schedules and compare QF with other, sequential-based, signature file organizations. Finally, we suggest how our approach can also be of interest for other file organizations based on multi-attribute hashing.

1 Introduction

Many file organizations have been designed to efficiently support partial match and/or range queries, that lead to retrieve from disk a (possibly large) set of *qualifying blocks*, that is, those blocks containing at least one record that satisfies the query. The traditional strategy (or *schedule*) for retrieving these qualifying blocks, conveniently called the *1-block-per-read* (1BPR) schedule, is to issue a separate read request for each of them, as usually assumed by database optimizers to evaluate the costs of access plans [SAC+79, CM93].

When some of the qualifying blocks are contiguously stored on the disk surface, and enough buffer space is available in main memory, an alternative strategy is to merge the read requests for such blocks into a single one. This can reduce the total I/O retrieval time because of the minor number of positioning operations involved. For this read strategy, hereafter termed the *1-run-per-read* (1RPR) schedule, a suitable metrics to evaluate performance is the number of distinct runs (i.e. sequences) of contiguously-stored qualifying blocks [Jag90].

Both 1BPR and 1RPR schedules only transfer to main memory qualifying blocks. Since in typical disk devices the positioning time (=seek time + rotational delay) is (much) higher than the transfer time of a block, it makes sense to also consider read schedules that transfer non-qualifying blocks, in order to merge distinct read requests into a single one. Of course, a trade-off exists between positioning time and transfer time, since attempting to reduce the former usually leads to increase the latter [SLM93].

---

* This work has been partially supported by Italian CNR, under contract no. 94.00388.CT12, and by ESPRIT LTR project no. 9141, HERMES (Foundations of High Performance Multimedia Information Management Systems).

In this paper we consider the optimal read schedule problem for queries on *partitioned signature files* [LL89], namely Quick Filter (QF) [ZRT91, CZ93]. Typical queries supported by signature files are partial match queries, where the user specifies a certain number of *query terms* (search keywords) and is returned all the objects containing all such terms.

In order to avoid searching the whole signature file, QF partitions signatures into fixed-size *buckets*, and stores into a same bucket all the signature having the same *key* value, where the key of a signature is simply a subset of its bits. The major advantages of QF with respect to other signature file organizations, such as those performing a *vertical* partitioning of signatures [LF92], are the low insertion costs and the high efficiency in processing queries with many terms. However, when only a few terms are specified in the query, a high percentage of buckets is likely to be retrieved, which can deteriorate performance in case the 1BPR schedule is adopted.

In this work we provide a theoretical analysis of the access patterns arising from queries on QF, and show how they can be formally characterized and used to efficiently determine the cost of an optimal multi-block read schedule, whose more remarkable property is to have all reads of the same size, therefore termed a *constant size* (CS) schedule. As a second major contribution we provide an average-case analysis for CS schedules, that we then use to compare performance of QF and other signature file organizations (namely QF using only the 1BPR schedule, sequential, and bit-sliced). This shows that CS schedules substantially improve QF performance.

The rest of the paper is organized as follows. In Section 2 we provide some background on Quick Filter. In Section 3 we formalize the problem, showing how signature queries on QF lead to a more general class of access patterns, called z-GDT sequences. The determination of optimal read schedules is the subject of Section 4. In Section 5 we present an average-case analysis of the behavior of CS schedules. Section 6 presents simulation results and a comparison of QF with other signature file organizations.

2 Quick Filter

Quick Filter (QF) [ZRT91] is a partitioned signature file organization [LL89, Fal90] that organizes signatures into fixed-size *buckets*. Signatures are generated using the *superimposed coding* method, which works as follows [FC87]. First, for each object to be indexed, a set of T terms, such as attribute values, keywords, etc., is obtained. Each of these terms yields a *term signature*, that is, a binary string of length f where v bits are randomly set to 1 by using v independent uniform hash functions, and the others are 0. Term signatures are then superimposed (i.e. OR-ed together) to yield the object signature (see Figure 1). Object signatures are organized by QF into NB

Term	Term signature
signature	100 101 000 010
access	010 100 010 100
method	110 100 010 000
Object signature	110 101 010 110

Fig. 1. Superimposition of term signatures yields the object signature. $T = 3$ terms, $f = 12$ bits, and $v = 4$ bits.

buckets by using the principle of *linear hashing* [Lit80], which dynamically adapts NB to the number of signatures in the file (see [ZRT91] for full details). Without loss of generality, consider the case $NB = 2^k$. Then, QF takes the k-bit *suffix* of signature s, denoted $s^{[k]}$, as the *key* of both s and the bucket where s has to be stored.

When processing a *query signature*, q, obtained by superimposing the signatures of the query terms, only those buckets whose key *includes* the key of q – i.e. the buckets whose key has a 1 in all the positions where the query key has a 1 – need to be accessed. Letting $w(\cdot)$ denote the *weight* function, which returns the number of bits set to 1 in its bit vector argument, it can be verified that, when $NB = 2^k$, exactly $2^{k-w(q^{[k]})}$ buckets qualifies for q, where $q^{[k]}$ is the k-bit suffix (key) of query q. As a second step, signatures in *qualifying buckets* are matched against q according to the same inclusion criterion. Finally, for each qualifying signature the corresponding data object is retrieved and, since *false drops* are possible, each retrieved object is checked to verify if it indeed contains the query terms [Fal90].

The simplest way to map (logical) buckets of QF to (physical) disk blocks, which exploits the underlying linear hashing organization, is to assign the bucket with key $s^{[k]}$ to the block with address $(s^{[k]})_2 \in [0, NB - 1]$.[1] In the general case, let $k = \lceil \log_2 NB \rceil$. According to linear hashing, the disk address of the bucket where s is stored is $(s^{[k]})_2$ if $(s^{[k]})_2 < NB$, otherwise it is $(s^{[k-1]})_2$.

Example 1. Figure 2 shows a QF file for signatures of size $f = 12$, with $NB = 8$ buckets ($k = 3$). The query q = (100000010010) has key $q^{[3]} = 010$, and selects the buckets with keys 010, 011, 110, and 111, which correspond to disk blocks 2,3,6, and 7, respectively. □

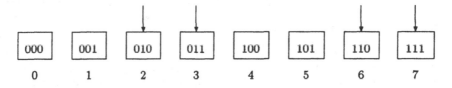

Fig. 2. The query q = (100000010010), whose key is $q^{[3]} = 010$, selects the 4 buckets pointed by arrows. Decimal values are the addresses of blocks to which buckets are mapped to.

Analysis of QF performance [CZ93] reveals that, when $NB = 2^k$, a signature query of weight $w(q) = w_f$ selects, on the average:

$$2^k \left(1 - \frac{w_f}{2 \times f}\right)^k \tag{1}$$

buckets, which can result in a lot of I/O operations in the case of *low-weight* queries, i.e. those arising when only a few search terms are specified, and if qualifying buckets are retrieved one at a time (1BPR schedule). For instance, if $NB = 1,024$ ($k = 10$), $f = 512$ bits, and $w(q) = 50$, about 620 buckets satisfy the query. Assuming that an I/O operation requires 10 msecs., the response time is about 6 seconds.

3 Problem Formalization

Consider a QF file stored on $NB = 2^k$ contiguous blocks of a device characterized by an average positioning (= seek + rotational delay) time T_{pos} and a transfer time

---

[1] Without loss of generality, we assume that a bucket corresponds to a single block, that is, we do not consider multi-block buckets.

(per block) T_{trans}, a main memory buffer of B blocks, and a signature query $\mathbf{q}$ with suffix $\mathbf{q}^{[k]}$. Let $BRS(\mathbf{q}^{[k]})$ denote the *block response set*, that is, the set of blocks corresponding to qualifying buckets for query $\mathbf{q}^{[k]}$. What is the optimal way, in terms of elapsed I/O time, to retrieve all the blocks in $BRS(\mathbf{q}^{[k]})$? Let $\delta(\mathbf{q}^{[k]})$ be a read schedule that consists of N_{pos} read operations, with the i-th read retrieving $N_{trans}(i) \leq B$ contiguous blocks. Letting $T_{pos} = P \times T_{trans}$, the *cost* of schedule $\delta(\mathbf{q}^{[k]})$ can then be expressed in terms of transfer units as:

$$Cost(\delta(\mathbf{q}^{[k]})) = \sum_{i=1}^{N_{pos}} (P + N_{trans}(i)) \tag{2}$$

on the assumption that each read request incurs the same positioning time.

3.1 The z-GDT Access Patterns

A general approach to determine an optimal schedule for reading an arbitrary set of n blocks is derived in [SLM93], where it is shown how exact solution, with $O(n^2)$ complexity, requires finding a shortest path on a graph whose nodes correspond to qualifying blocks. In our case, however, we can derive a more efficient ($O(\log n)$) algorithm by exploiting the regularity of access patterns of signature queries, which is a remarkable improvement especially in the case of large files. For the sake of generality, we develop our formal arguments with reference to an abstract model of queries, where each query Q is assumed to select 2^z blocks of the file, for some $z \geq 0$. This model includes signature queries on QF, with $z = k - w(\mathbf{q}^{[k]})$ and $Q = \mathbf{q}^{[k]}$, as well as partial match queries on multi-attribute hash files (see Section 7).

Let $a_1, a_2, \ldots a_{2^z}$ be the addresses of the blocks in $BRS(Q)$, with $a_i < a_{i+1}$ ($i \in [1, 2^z - 1]$). Let $d_i = a_{i+1} - a_i$ denote the i-th *inter-block distance*, and let $\mathbf{d} = (d_1, d_2, \ldots, d_{2^z-1})$ be the ordered sequence of such distances. We are interested in so-called *z-growing distance tree* (z-GDT) sequences, which are recursively defined as follows:

1. ($z = 0$) The empty sequence $\mathbf{d} = ()$ is the (unique) 0-GDT sequence.
2. If $\mathbf{d}$ is a z-GDT sequence ($z \geq 0$) then the sequence $(\mathbf{d}, D_{z+1}, \mathbf{d})$ is a $(z+1)$-GDT sequence iff $D_{z+1} \geq d_i$, for each $d_i \in \mathbf{d}$.
3. No other sequence is a z-GDT sequence.

The sequence $\mathbf{D} = (D_1, D_2, \ldots, D_z)$ is called the *trace* of the z-GDT sequence. For the 0-GDT sequence the trace is empty, $\mathbf{D} = ()$. In a z-GDT sequence the maximum number of distinct d_i values is z, which is attained iff all the D_j's are distinct. In general, we have $D_j \leq D_{j+1}$, as it can be derived from point 2 above. It can be easily verified that a sequence $\mathbf{d}$ of length $2^z - 1$ is a z-GDT sequence iff

$$d_{2j-1} = d_{2j-1+m \times 2^j} \quad \forall j \in [1, z], m \in [0, 2^{z-j} - 1] \quad \text{and}$$
$$d_{2j-1} \leq d_{2j} \quad \forall j \in [1, z-1]$$

If $\mathbf{d}$ is a z-GDT sequence, the j-th value of its trace is $D_j = d_{2j-1}$ ($j \in [1, z]$).

Example 2. Consider a query Q that selects the 8 blocks $5, 7, 10, 12, 17, 19, 22, 24$. The sequence of inter-block distances is therefore $\mathbf{d}(Q) = (2, 3, 2, 5, 2, 3, 2)$. This is a 3-GDT sequence, with trace $\mathbf{D}(Q) = (2, 3, 5)$, since $D_1 = d_1 = d_3 = d_5 = d_7$, $D_2 = d_2 = d_6$, $D_3 = d_4$, and $d_1 \leq d_2 \leq d_4$ also holds. $\square$

A z-GDT sequence can be represented by a binary tree with $z + 1$ levels, whose leaves are at level 0 and correspond to qualifying blocks. The trace value D_j is assigned to each of the 2^{z-j} nodes at level j ($1 \leq j \leq z$). It represents the inter-block distance

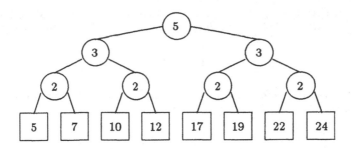

Fig. 3. Tree representation of the 3-GDT sequence $\mathbf{d} = (2, 3, 2, 5, 2, 3, 2)$ of Example 2.

between the rightmost leaf (block) in the left subtree of the node and the leftmost leaf in the right subtree (see Figure 3). The reason why z-GDT sequences are of interest to Quick Filter is due to the fact. that the access pattern of any signature query is a z-GDT sequence.[2]

Lemma 1. *Let* $\mathbf{d}(\mathbf{q}^{[k]})$ *be the sequence of distances between the blocks in* $BRS(\mathbf{q}^{[k]})$. *Then,* $\mathbf{d}(\mathbf{q}^{[k]})$ *is a* z-*GDT sequence, with* $z = k - w(\mathbf{q}^{[k]})$.

Example 3. Consider a signature query $\mathbf{q}$ with suffix $\mathbf{q}^{[6]} = (010101)$. The 8 qualifying buckets have keys

$$010101, 010111, 011101, 011111, 110101, 110111, 111101, 111111$$

Converting to block addresses, we obtain the access pattern: $21, 23, 29, 31, 53, 55, 61, 63$, for which it is $\mathbf{d}(010101) = (2, 6, 2, 22, 2, 6, 2)$, that is, a 3-GDT sequence with trace $\mathbf{D}(010101) = (2, 6, 22)$. □

4 Optimal Read Schedules for QF

In this section we exploit the regularity of access patterns of z-GDT sequences (consequently of queries on QF) to derive basic properties of optimal schedules. In doing this, we will consider only so-called *regular schedules* [SLM93], having the following three properties:

1. No two read operations overlap, that is, no block is read more than once.
2. Each read operation starts from a qualifying block and ends with a qualifying block.
3. The read requests are in ascending order of starting block address.

As shown in [SLM93], any optimal schedule for reading an arbitrary set of blocks satisfies the first two properties, whereas the last property just discards from the analysis schedules which are equivalent to a regular schedule up to a permutation of read requests. In the following it has therefore to be understood that "schedule" actually means "regular schedule".

We start with the case of unlimited buffer size, and derive a general form for the cost expression of an arbitrary schedule.

---

[2] Due to space limitations, analytical results are stated without proof. The interested reader can refer to [Cia95] for full details.

Lemma 2. *Let $\mathbf{D}(Q) = (D_1, D_2, \ldots, D_z)$ be the trace of the z-GDT sequence of query Q. The cost of any schedule for reading the blocks of $BRS(Q)$ can be expressed as:*

$$Cost(\delta(Q)) = \alpha_0(P+1) + \sum_{j=1}^{z} \alpha_j \times D_j \tag{3}$$

where α_0 is the number of read operations and the α_j coefficients are integers that satisfy the constraint:

$$\sum_{j=0}^{z} \alpha_j = 2^z \quad \text{with} \quad 0 \le \alpha_j \le 2^{z-j} \quad (j = 0, 1, \ldots, z) \tag{4}$$

Conversely, any expression of the form given in Eq. (3) and that satisfies constraint (4) defines the cost of a schedule.

Example 4. Consider the query Q with trace $\mathbf{D}(Q) = (2, 3, 5)$ of Example 2, and the $\delta(Q)$ schedule consisting of $\alpha_0 = 3$ reads, reading qualifying blocks $(5, 7, 10)$, (12), and $(17, 19, 22, 24)$, respectively (see also Figure 3). $Cost(\delta(Q))$ can be written as:

$$Cost(\delta(Q)) = 3P + (6 + 1 + 8) = 3(P + 1) + (5 + 7) = 3(P + 1) + (3 \times 2 + 2 \times 3)$$

which has the form of Eq. (3), and satisfies constraint (4), with $\alpha_1 = 3$, $\alpha_2 = 2$, and $\alpha_3 = 0$. Intuitively, the schedule, besides reading blocks in $BRS(Q)$, also reads 3 "gaps" of size 2 and 2 "gaps" of size 3. □

Among the set of regular schedules, those having all the reads of the same size, called *constant-size* (CS) schedules, are particularly relevant in the case of z-GDT sequences. Referring to the tree representation of z-GDT sequences, level γ ($\gamma \in [0, z]$) of the tree corresponds to a CS schedule consisting of $2^{z-\gamma}$ reads, each corresponding to a node at level γ and retrieving all the blocks (leaves) in the subtree rooted at that node.

Lemma 3. *The cost of the $\delta(Q, 2^{z-\gamma})$ CS schedule that executes $2^{z-\gamma}$ reads ($\gamma \in [0, z]$) is given by:*

$$Cost(\delta(Q, 2^{z-\gamma})) = 2^{z-\gamma}(P+1) + \sum_{j=1}^{\gamma} 2^{z-j} \times D_j \tag{5}$$

where each read request transfers $1 + \sum_{j=1}^{\gamma} 2^{\gamma-j} \times D_j$ blocks.

Example 5. Consider the trace $\mathbf{D}(Q) = (2, 3, 5)$ of Example 2, and assume $\gamma = 2$. Since $z = 3$, the CS schedule consists of $2^{3-2} = 2$ reads. The size of each read is, according to Eq. (5), computed as $(1 + 2^{2-1} \times 2 + 2^{2-2} \times 3) = 8$. This is immediately derivable from the tree representation in Figure 3, by first choosing any node at level 2, then summing all the values in its subtree, and finally adding 1. □

Although Lemma 3 can be used to determine the costs of CS schedules for arbitrary z-GDT sequences, signature queries provide the way for a more direct approach, for which the computation of the trace $\mathbf{D}(\mathbf{q}^{[k]})$ is not needed.

Lemma 4. *The cost of a CS schedule $\delta(\mathbf{q}^{[k]}, 2^{z-\gamma})$ that executes $2^{z-\gamma}$ reads ($\gamma \in [0, z]$) for retrieving the 2^z qualifying blocks in $BRS(\mathbf{q}^{[k]})$ is given by:*

$$Cost(\delta(\mathbf{q}^{[k]}, 2^{z-\gamma})) = 2^{z-\gamma}\left(P + 1 + \sum_{j=1}^{\gamma} 2^{b_j}\right) \tag{6}$$

where b_j is the position of the j-th rightmost 0 in $\mathbf{q}^{[k]}$, and with each read request that transfers $1 + \sum_{j=1}^{\gamma} 2^{b_j}$ blocks.

Example 6. Consider the query suffix $q^{[6]} = (010101)$ of Example 3, whose trace is $\mathbf{D}(010101) = (2,6,22)$, and whose 0's are in positions $b_1 = 1$, $b_2 = 3$, and $b_3 = 5$. The costs of the 4 CS schedules, derived either from Eq. (5) or directly from Eq. (6), are:

γ	n. of reads $(2^{3-\gamma})$	$Cost(\delta(010101, 2^{3-\gamma}))$
0	8	$8(P+1)$
1	4	$4(P+3) = 4\left(P+1+2^1\right)$
2	2	$2(P+11) = 2\left(P+1+2^1+2^3\right)$
3	1	$1(P+43) = 1\left(P+1+2^1+2^3+2^5\right)$ □

The importance of CS schedules is due to the following major result.

Theorem 5. *Let $\delta(Q, \alpha_0)$ be any schedule that uses α_0 reads. If the schedule is not CS, then, for each value of P, there exists at least one CS schedule whose cost is not greater than $Cost(\delta(Q, \alpha_0))$.*

Proof (sketch): The number of reads of a schedule that is not CS can be expressed as $\alpha_0 = 2^{z-\gamma} + \beta$, where $\gamma \in [1, z-1]$ and $0 < \beta < 2^{z-\gamma}$. Complete proof in [Cia95] shows that it is impossible to have

$$Cost(\delta(Q, \alpha_0)) < \min\{Cost(\delta_1(Q, 2^{z-\gamma})), Cost(\delta_2(Q, 2^{z-\gamma+1}))\}$$

when the α_j coefficients are subject to constraint (4) and the D_j trace values are non-decreasing.   □

Theorem 5 implies that *it suffices to consider only the $z+1$ CS schedules*, since one of them will be surely optimal. We can precisely characterize their optimality ranges as follows.

Theorem 6. *Consider a query Q whose trace is $\mathbf{D}(Q) = (D_1, D_2, \ldots, D_z)$. Furthermore, let $D_0 = 1$ and $D_{z+1} = \infty$. Then, the CS schedule $\delta(Q, 2^{z-\gamma})$ is optimal for Q if*

$$P + 1 \in [D_\gamma, D_{\gamma+1}] \qquad (\gamma \in [0, z]) \tag{7}$$

and its cost is

$$Cost(\delta(Q, 2^{z-\gamma})) \in [2^{z-\gamma} \times D_\gamma + \sum_{j=1}^{\gamma} 2^{z-j} \times D_j, 2^{z-\gamma} \times D_{\gamma+1} + \sum_{j=1}^{\gamma} 2^{z-j} \times D_j] \tag{8}$$

At a qualitative level, this confirms the intuition that, as the ratio of positioning time to transfer time increases, schedules executing less reads are more and more convenient. It also shows that the cost of an optimal schedule is a monotonically increasing function of such a ratio, that is, augmenting P always leads to an increase of I/O costs.

When 2 trace values are equal, that is $D_\gamma = D_{\gamma+1}$, then, from condition (7), the number of CS schedules that needs to be considered is decreased by 1. More in general, let $\mathbf{D}(q^{[k]})$ be the trace of the $q^{[k]}$ suffix of the signature query q. Then $D_j = D_{j+1}$ iff $b_{j+1} = b_j + 1$, that is, the j-th and the $(j+1)$-th 0's of $q^{[k]}$ are contiguous. In general, let M be the number of sequences of maximal length of contiguous 0's in $q^{[k]}$. It then follows that the number of possibly optimal CS schedules for $q^{[k]}$ is $M+1$ if $b_1 = 0$, and M otherwise.

Example 7. Consider the suffix $q^{[4]} = (1001)$. This selects the 4 buckets with keys 1001,1011,1101, and 1111, that is, $d(1001) = (2,2,2)$, and $\mathbf{D}(1001) = (2,2)$. Here $D_1 = D_2$ since $b_2 = 2 = b_1 + 1$. The costs of the 3 CS schedules are:

γ	n. of reads $(2^{z-\gamma})$	$Cost(\delta(1001, 2^{z-\gamma}))$
0	4	$4(P+1)$
1	2	$2(P+3)$
2	1	$1(P+7)$

It can be seen that no value of P is such that $2(P+3) < \min\{4(P+1), 1(P+7)\}$. When $P < 1$ the first schedule is the optimal one, whereas when $P > 1$ the minimal cost is obtained from the third schedule. On the other hand, when $P = 1$, all the 3 schedules yield the same cost. □

4.1   The Case of Limited Buffer Size

When the buffer size, B, is finite all the schedules that transfer, at least once, more than B blocks with a single read cannot be considered. Schedules which satisfy the constraint imposed by the buffer size are called *feasible* schedules. The following result generalizes Theorem 5, showing that an optimal feasible CS schedule always exists.

Theorem 7. *Let B be the buffer size and $\delta(Q, \alpha_0)$ be a feasible schedule that uses α_0 reads. If the schedule is not CS, then, for each value of P, there exists at least one feasible CS schedule whose cost does not exceed $Cost(\delta(Q, \alpha_0))$.*

Proof (sketch): As in the proof of Theorem 5, we consider a schedule $\delta(Q, \alpha_0)$ whose number of reads is $\alpha_0 = 2^{z-\gamma} + \beta$ ($\gamma \in [1, z-1]$, $0 < \beta < 2^{z-\gamma}$). The heart of the proof consists in showing that, if $\delta(Q, \alpha_0)$ is a feasible schedule, then so both CS schedules $\delta_1(Q, 2^{z-\gamma})$ and $\delta_2(Q, 2^{z-\gamma+1})$ are. Then Theorem 5 applies. □

Theorem 6, defining the optimality ranges of CS schedules, can be immediately adapted to the case of a finite buffer size in a rather intuitive way: when the optimal read size exceeds B, it suffices to consider the largest γ value (i.e. the minimum number of read operations) leading to a feasible CS schedule.

Example 8. Consider again the query suffix $q^{[4]} = (1001)$ and the 3 CS schedules of Example 7. If $B = 5$, say, and $P > 1$, the third schedule, executing a single read of size 7, cannot be applied. Since each of the 2 reads of the second schedule has size 3, this is a feasible schedule. Furthermore, since $2(P+3) < 4(P+1)$ when $P > 1$, the second schedule is the optimal one. □

5   Expected Cost of Optimal Schedules

How much can performance be improved, on the average, when optimal CS schedules are adopted? In this section we analytically evaluate the expected performance of QF with respect to a generalized storage model, where contiguous allocation is provided in terms of *clusters* (extents), each cluster consisting of $C = 2^c$ blocks, for some $c \geq 0$. Thus, each read request can retrieve only blocks within the same cluster. This model reduces to the one considered in previous sections when $c \geq k = \log_2 NB$. On the other hand, setting $c = 0$ corresponds to the case where only the 1BPR schedule can be applied.

We first deal with the case where no limitation on the size of the reads is present, that is, $B \geq C$ holds. Consider a QF file spanning 2^k blocks, thus stored in 2^{k-c} clusters, numbered $0, 1, \ldots, 2^{k-c} - 1$. Cluster 0 will consists of blocks with addresses in the range $[0, 2^c - 1]$, cluster 1 of blocks with addresses in the range $[2^c, 2^{c+1} - 1]$, and so on. In general, let $s^{[k:c)}$ denote the part of $k - c$ bits of the suffix $s^{[k]}$ of signature s from which the last c bits are removed, and let $s^{[c]}$ be the remaining suffix of c bits. Then, the block storing signature s is part of cluster $(s^{[k:c)})_2$, and its *relative address* within this cluster is $(s^{[c]})_2$.

Example 9. Let $k = 10$ and $c = 3$, so that each of the 2^7 clusters consists of 8 contiguous blocks. Bucket with key 0011101101 will be mapped to block $(0011101101)_2 = 237$, which belongs to cluster $(0011101)_2 = 29$. Within the cluster, the relative address of the block is $(101)_2 = 5$. Clearly, it is $237 = 29 \times 8 + 5$. □

Given a signature query with weight $w(q)$, the aspects which determine, according to our model, the expected I/O cost are the (expected) number of clusters with at least one qualifying block, also called *qualifying clusters*, and the (expected) cost of retrieving the qualifying blocks in a qualifying cluster. The partitioning of blocks into equal-sized clusters leads to the following result, which furtherly reduces the complexity of determining an optimal schedule:

Lemma 8. *Given a query* q, *the set of qualifying buckets is evenly partitioned into* $2^{(k-c)-w(q^{[k:c]})}$ *groups, each corresponding to a qualifying cluster. Each group, consisting of* $2^{c-w(q^{[c]})}$ *buckets, is such that the sets of relative addresses of corresponding blocks is the same in each qualifying cluster.*

In other terms, $q^{[k:c]}$ determines the qualifying clusters, whereas $q^{[c]}$ determines the qualifying blocks in such clusters. Then, it immediately follows that, for a fixed $q^{[c]}$ suffix, *the optimal read schedule will consists of* $2^{(k-c)-w(q^{[k:c]})}$ *identical sub-schedules, each retrieving qualifying blocks from a qualifying cluster*. Therefore, the expected cost of processing a query q with weight $w(q) = w_f$ can be expressed as:

$$E[Cost(\delta(q))|w(q) = w_f] = E\left[2^{(k-c)-w(q^{[k:c]})} \times Cost(\delta(q^{[c]}))|w(q) = w_f\right] \quad (9)$$

Both $w(q^{[k:c]})$ and $w(q^{[c]})$ are (non-independent) random variables. Using results in [CZ93], showing that $w(q^{[k]}) = w(q^{[k:c]}) + w(q^{[c]})$ approximately behaves as a binomial random variable,[3] we can rearrange the above cost expression, and after some combinatorial manipulation obtain:

$$E[Cost(\delta(q))|w(q) = w_f] = 2^{k-c}\left(1 - \frac{w_f}{2 \times f}\right)^{k-c} \times \quad (10)$$

$$\times \left[\sum_{w_c \leq c}\binom{c}{w_c}\left(\frac{w_f}{f}\right)^{w_c}\left(1 - \frac{w_f}{f}\right)^{c-w_c} E[Cost(\delta(q^{[c]}))|w(q^{[c]}) = w_c]\right]$$

The factor outside square brackets, which closely resembles Eq. (1), represents the expected number of qualifying clusters, whereas the factor within square brackets provides a cost estimate for the retrieval of the qualifying blocks in a qualifying cluster.

In order to gain insights on the behavior of QF, Eq. (10) suggests to evaluate the expected cost of an optimal (sub-)schedule, conditional on the weight of the $q^{[c]}$ suffix. Unfortunately, a simple expression for this expected cost cannot be derived, because of the way optimality of CS schedules depend on the value of the P device parameter.

Example 10. Assume that the cluster size is $C = 2^4$, and that expected cost for the case $w(q^{[c]}) = 2$ is needed. Figure 4 shows, for each of the 6 possible query suffixes, the corresponding trace, costs of optimal CS schedules, and optimality ranges. The expected cost is a piece-wise linear function of P, with 6 distinct slopes. □

---

[3] Actually, $w(q^{[k]})$ is a hypergeometric random variable, and the binomial approximation leads to slightly overestimate I/O costs, since it underestimates the value of suffix weight.

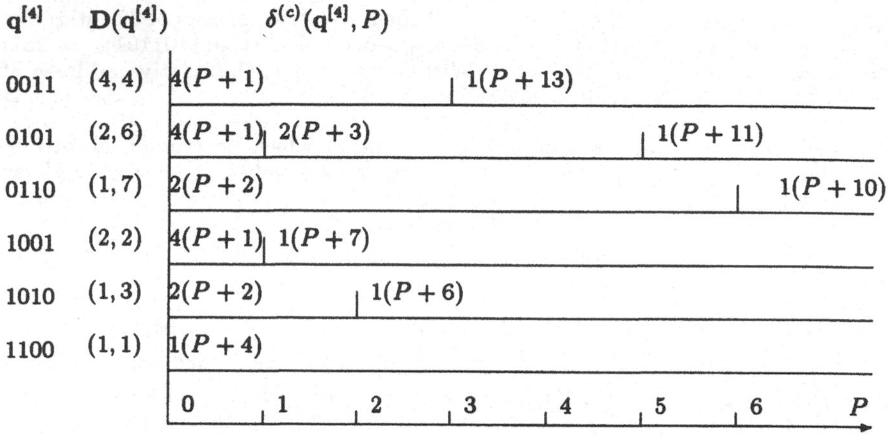

$q^{[4]}$	$D(q^{[4]})$	$\delta^{(c)}(q^{[4]}, P)$			

Fig. 4. Optimal schedules for the 6 $q^{[4]}$ query suffixes of weight $w(q^{[c]}) = 2$. The cluster size is $C = 2^4$. The optimality range of each schedule extends rightward from the vertical tick mark on its left. If no tick mark appears on the right of a schedule, the schedule is optimal for any larger value of P.

In order to come out with some useful, although approximate, analytical result, we first consider the case where, for each query suffix, the optimal schedule always consists of a single read request. This is an appropriate model for "slow" devices (i.e. for high values of P) and/or small clusters. Indeed, when P exceeds a certain value (this is 6 in Figure 4) all the optimal schedules consist of a single read request. Because of Theorem 6, this threshold value, denoted P_{z_c}, equals the highest D_{z_c} trace value minus 1, where $z_c = c - w_c$ and all the traces of length z_c are considered. P_{z_c} can be expressed as:

$$P_{z_c} = \begin{cases} 0 & \text{if } z_c = 0 \\ 2^{c-1} - 2^{z_c-1} = 2^{c-1}\left(1 - 2^{-w_c}\right) & \text{if } z_c > 0 \end{cases} \qquad (11)$$

Then, if $P \geq P_{z_c}$ the determination of the optimal schedule is immediate, and a simple closed formula for the expected cost can be derived.

Lemma 9. *Let $P \geq P_{z_c}$, and let $w(q^{[c]}) = w_c = c - z_c$. The expected cost for retrieving with a single read all the qualifying blocks in a qualifying cluster is:*

$$E[Cost(\delta(q^{[c]}))|w(q^{[c]}) = w_c, P \geq P_{z_c}] = P + 1 + (2^c - 1)\left(1 - \frac{w_c}{c}\right) \qquad (12)$$

After substituting in Eq. (10) and simplifying we obtain:

$$E[Cost(\delta(q))|w(q) = w_f] = 2^{k-c}\left(1 - \frac{w_f}{2 \times f}\right)^{k-c}\left[P + 1 + (2^c - 1)\left(1 - \frac{w_f}{f}\right)\right] \qquad (13)$$

Example 11. Consider the schedules in Figure 4, and assume that $P \geq 6$. Evaluation of Eq. (12), with $c = 4$ and $w_c = 2$, predicts that the expected cost equals $P + 1 + 15/2 = P + 51/6$. This correctly equals the average cost of the 6 schedules executing a single read. □

As a second step, we consider the more general case where each query suffix of weight $w(q^{[c]}) = w_c$ is processed by a CS schedule consisting of $2^{z_c - \gamma} > 1$ reads, where

$z_c = c - w_c$ and the value of $\gamma \in [1, z_c - 1]$ is the same for all query suffixes (the case $\gamma = 0$ corresponds to the 1BPR schedule, whose cost is $2^{z_c}(P+1)$, and the case $\gamma = z_c$ is just Eq. (12)). This clearly provides an upper bound of the expected cost.

The derivation of the result is rather complex, in that it amounts to solve the following combinatorial problem: considering all the suffixes of c bits with z_c 0's, what is the expected value, for a fixed γ, of the sum $\sum_{j=1}^{\gamma} 2^{b_j}$ (see Lemma 4 and Eq. (6) in Section 4), where b_j is the position of the j-th rightmost 0 in the suffix?

Theorem 10. *The expected cost of a CS schedule $\delta(q^{[c]}, 2^{z_c-\gamma})$ is:*

$$E[Cost(\delta(q^{[c]}), 2^{z_c-\gamma})|w(q^{[c]}) = w_c] = \tag{14}$$
$$2^{z_c-\gamma}\left(P+1+\frac{\sum_{y=\gamma}^{c-z_c+\gamma}\binom{c-1-y}{z_c-1-\gamma}\binom{y-1}{\gamma-1}(2^y-1)}{\binom{c}{z_c}}\right)$$

5.1 Expected Cost with Limited Buffer Size

With a limited buffer size, $B < C$, we can still use Theorem 10, provided that each query whose suffix has weight $w(q^{[c]}) = w_c$ can be processed by a feasible $\delta(q^{[c]}, 2^{z_c-\gamma})$ CS schedule. A simple feasibility condition on the value of γ is derived as follows. Lemma 4 asserts that each read of a $\delta(q^{[c]}, 2^{z_c-\gamma})$ CS schedule transfers $1 + \sum_{j=1}^{\gamma} 2^{b_j}$ blocks (see Eq. (6)). The size of a read is therefore maximized when the z_c 0's are in the leftmost positions of $q^{[c]}$, which yields:

$$1 + \sum_{j=1}^{\gamma} 2^{c-z_c-1+j} = 1 + 2^{c-z_c}(2^\gamma - 1)$$

Clearly, if this value is less than or equal to B, we are guaranteed that *each* $q^{[c]}$ query suffix with z_c 0's can be processed by a feasible schedule that executes $2^{z_c-\gamma}$ reads. Therefore, all the $\delta(q^{[c]}, 2^{z_c-\gamma})$ CS schedule are feasible if γ satisfies:

$$2^\gamma \leq \left\lfloor \frac{B-1}{2^{c-z_c}} + 1 \right\rfloor = \left\lfloor \frac{B-1}{2^{w_c}} + 1 \right\rfloor \tag{15}$$

6 Simulation Results

In this section we provide simulation results aiming to quantify improvements obtainable by the application of CS schedules with respect to the 1BPR schedule. All the results are somewhat pessimistic, in that they rely on the cost upper bounds derived in the previous section.

We start by considering how the ratio of positioning time to transfer time influences the cost of retrieving blocks of a qualifying cluster, for a certain value of the weight of the $q^{[c]}$ query suffix. When $P \geq P_z = 2^{c-1}(1 - 2^{-w_c})$ holds, a single read retrieving all the qualifying blocks constitutes the optimal schedule, and Eq. (12) applies. In the general case, Eq. (12) only provides a (non tight) upper bound that can be improved by using the results of Theorem 10. For each value of P, we therefore select the number of reads that minimizes the expected cost (but not necessarily the cost of a single query), as predicted by Eq. (14). Results are shown in Figure 5, for the case of clusters of 16 blocks (i.e. $c = 4$), whereas Figure 6 shows relative cost savings for the case of clusters of 64 blocks. In both cases it is evident how CS schedules can substantially lower I/O

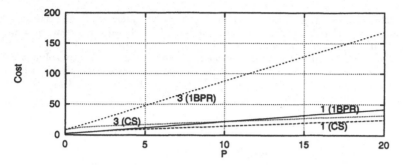

Fig. 5. Performance of QF with 1BPR and CS schedules with clusters of 16 blocks. Each graphs refers to a specific value of z_c, the number of 0's in the $q^{[4]}$ query suffix.

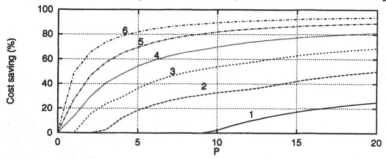

Fig. 6. Percentual cost savings of CS schedules with respect to the 1BPR schedule in the case of clusters of 64 blocks. Each curve refers to a different value of z_c.

costs, especially for low values of the weight of the $q^{[c]}$ query suffix. Indeed, this is the situation where performance of QF, using the 1BPR schedule, is known to deteriorate. This is also made evident in Figure 7, where overall costs are evaluated as a function of the query weight, $w(q)$, for the specific case $P = 10$.

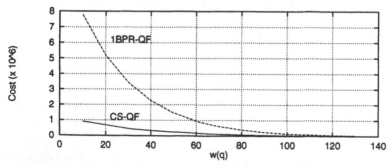

Fig. 7. I/O costs for the 1BPR schedule (label 1BPR-QF) and CS schedules (label CS-QF). The file consists of 2^{20} blocks (i.e. $k = 20$), grouped into 2^{14} clusters of size 64 on a disk with parameter $P = 10$. Signatures have length $f = 256$ bits.

As to the effects that a limited buffer size has on the average performance, Figure 8 shows how results in Figure 6 change when $B = 16$, that is 1/4-th of the cluster size. The most evident difference is in correspondence of high-weight query suffixes (namely $z_c = 1, 2$ in the figure), which cannot benefit at all of CS schedules, since there are specific instances for which the qualifying blocks are far apart in the cluster. This is a limit of our analytical model, as developed in Section 5.1, which is not able to take into account that feasible CS schedules indeed exist for many specific high-weight query suffixes (although not for all of them). However, this appears to be a minor weakness of the model, since it is known that high-weight queries are already efficiently processed by the 1BPR schedule.

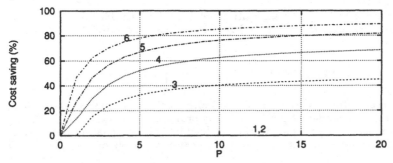

Fig. 8. Percentual cost savings of CS schedules with respect to the 1BPR schedule in the case of clusters of 64 blocks, when the buffer size is $B = 16$ blocks. Each curve refers to a different value of z_c.

In [SLM93, Section 5.1] an asymptotic analysis has been developed for the case there termed "unlimited gaps, limited buffer size". The analysis applies when qualifying blocks are uniformly distributed over the file address space, which is not the case with QF, since the probability of a block to qualify is proportional to the weight of its key. According to Eq. (3) in [SLM93], the expected cost of reading qualifying blocks in a qualifying cluster can be evaluated as (we have changed their notation for obvious reasons):

$$E[Cost_{SLM}(\delta(q^{[c]})|w(q^{[c]}) = w_c] = 2^{z_c} \frac{P + B - (2^{w_c} - 1)\left(1 - (1 - 2^{-w_c})^{B-1}\right)}{1 + (B - 1)2^{-w_c}} \quad (16)$$

Figure 9 contrasts the estimates obtained from Equations (14) and (16), as applied to the situation already considered in Figure 8. Positive values in the figure denote that estimates based on the uniformity assumption are higher than those of our model. Since our model actually provides an upper bound on expected costs, it appears that the uniformity assumption is not adequate, especially for rather "fast" devices (i.e. $P \leq 10$) and low values of the query key weight.

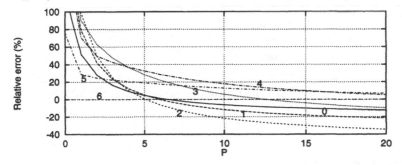

Fig. 9. Percentual relative errors of the model based on the uniform distribution assumption. Each curve refers to a different value of z_c.

254

6.1 QF, Sequential, and Bit-Sliced Organizations

We conclude this section by providing a comparison of some well-known signature file organizations. The analysis assumes the presence of clusters of C contiguous blocks, a buffer size of at least C blocks, and a file of N signatures of f bits each. The size of each block is BS bits.

The simplest organization is the sequential one, here denoted SSF (Sequential Signature File), for which the I/O cost is independent of the query weight and can be evaluated as:

$$Cost_{SSF}(\mathbf{q}|w(\mathbf{q}) = w_f) = \left\lceil \frac{N}{C \times BS/f} \right\rceil \times (P + C) \qquad (17)$$

The *Bit-Sliced* organization (BSSF) [LF92] vertically partitions signatures into f files, each corresponding to a specific bit position. Query processing takes place by retrieving only the bits in the files corresponding to the 1-valued bits in the signature query, since this is enough to determine whether a signature satisfies the query or not. The cost is then evaluated as:

$$Cost_{BSSF}(\mathbf{q}|w(\mathbf{q}) = w_f) = w_f \times \left\lceil \frac{N}{C \times BS} \right\rceil \times (P + C) \qquad (18)$$

Consider the case where $BS = 2^{15}$ bits (4 Kbytes), $C = 64$, and $P = 10$. Since we have assumed $B \geq C$, we need at least 256 Kbytes of buffer memory. The number of signature is $N \approx 2 \times 10^8$, each of $f = 512$ bits. Assuming an average storage utilization of 0.75, the QF organization requires $NB = 2^{22}$ buckets. Figure 10 shows the typical behavior of the considered organizations. Similar results have also been reported in [ZRT91], but only considering 1BPR schedules for all the organizations. Since both SSF and BSSF can easily take advantage of contiguous allocation of blocks, by simply reading C blocks at a time, comparison with QF using 1BPR schedule would highly penalize the latter. Our model, on the other hand, shows how CS schedules can make Quick Filter competitive even in storage systems which provide contiguous allocation of blocks.

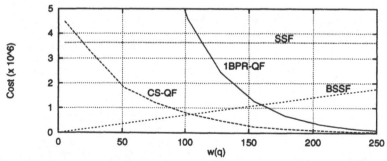

Fig. 10. I/O costs of: QF using the 1BPR schedule (1BPR-QF), QF using CS schedules (CS-QF), sequential organization (SSF), and bit-sliced organization (BSSF). See text for details on parameter values.

7 Concluding Remarks

In this paper we have analyzed the problem of deriving optimal strategies (schedules) to read from disk a set of blocks of a partitioned signature file organization, namely Quick

Filter. Results show that the problem has a logarithmic complexity in the number of blocks to be retrieved. Analysis of expected behavior of so-called CS schedules then provides the means to compare QF with other signature file organizations.

We have built our work on the key idea of exploiting the regularity of access patterns (z-GDT sequences) generated by signature queries. In this light, our approach is of interest also for the analysis of other file organizations as well.

For instance, consider a file whose records are stored in disk blocks by means of a multi-attribute hash function. In this setting each attribute value of record $\mathbf{r} = (r_1, \ldots, r_i, \ldots, r_n)$ yields, by applying a $h_i()$ hash function, a string of k_i bits. These string are then combined (e.g. by concatenation or bit interleaving) to obtain the address of the block where $\mathbf{r}$ has to be stored. Any partial match query that specifies values for a subset of the n attributes is therefore a string of length $k = \sum_{i=1}^{n} k_i$, whose bits have value 1, 0, or ? (unspecified). Then, it is not difficult to see that, for any partial match query, the corresponding access pattern is a z-GDT sequence, with z equal to the number of unspecified bits in the query, to which all the analyses in this paper apply.

References

[Cia95] P. Ciaccia. Optimal multi-block read schedules for partitioned signature files. Technical Report UBLCS-95-13, University of Bologna, Dept. of Computer Science, August 1995.

[CM93] P. Ciaccia and D. Maio. Access cost estimation for physical database design. *Data and Knowledge Engineering*, 11(2):125–150, 1993.

[CZ93] P. Ciaccia and P. Zezula. Estimating accesses in partitioned signature file organizations. *ACM Transactions on Information Systems*, 11(2):133–142, April 1993.

[Fal90] C. Faloutsos. Signature-based text retrieval methods: A survey. *Data Engineering*, 13(1):25–32, March 1990.

[FC87] C. Faloutsos and S. Christodoulakis. Description and performance analysis of signature file methods for office filing. *ACM Transactions on Office Information Systems*, 5(3):237–257, July 1987.

[Jag90] H.V. Jagadish. Linear clustering of objects with multiple attributes. In *Proceedings of the 1990 ACM SIGMOD International Conference on Management of Data*, pages 332–342, Atlantic City, NJ, May 1990.

[LF92] Z. Lin and C. Faloutsos. Frame-sliced signature files. *IEEE Transactions on Knowledge and Data Engineering*, 4(3):281–289, June 1992.

[Lit80] W. Litwin. Linear hashing: a new tool for files and table addressing. In *Proceedings of the 6th VLDB International Conference*, pages 212–223, Montreal, Canada, August 1980.

[LL89] D.L. Lee and C.-W. Leng. Partitioned signature files: Design issues and performance evaluation. *ACM Transactions on Office Information Systems*, 7(2):158–180, April 1989.

[SAC+79] P. G. Selinger, M. M. Astrahan, D. D. Chamberlin, R. A. Lorie, and T. G. Price. Access path selection in a relational database system. In *Proceedings of the 1979 ACM SIGMOD International Conference on Management of Data*, pages 23–34, May 1979.

[SLM93] B. Seeger, P.-A. Larson, and R. McFayden. Reading a set of disk pages. In *Proceedings of the 19th VLDB International Conference*, pages 592–603, Dublin, Ireland, August 1993.

[ZRT91] P. Zezula, F. Rabitti, and P. Tiberio. Dynamic partitioning of signature files. *ACM Transactions on Information Systems*, 9(4):336–369, October 1991.

Applications

Amalgamating SGML Documents and Databases*

Masatoshi Yoshikawa[1], Osamu Ichikawa[2], Shunsuke Uemura[1]

[1] Graduate School of Information Science, Nara Institute of Science and Technology
8916-5 Takayama, Ikoma, Nara 630-01, Japan
[2] Semiconductor Research Center, Matsushita Electric Industrial Co., Ltd.
3-1-1 Yagumo-Nakamachi, Moriguchi, Osaka 570, Japan

Abstract. We propose a uniform and flexible mechanism to make reference links from SGML documents to database objects. In addition to typical document logical structures such as sections and paragraphs, our mechanism allows arbitrary character strings in documents as source of these links. By using this mechanism, SGML attributes and their values of marked-up words can be transparently stored as database attributes, and we can establish hyperlinks between keywords in documents, which reflect relationships between the corresponding database objects. Also, we present a query language to retrieve SGML documents which are coupled with databases in this manner. The query language does not assume a particular database schema; instead, it utilizes DTD graphs, representing element structures of DTDs, as virtual schemas.

1 Introduction

During the past few years, SGML[6] has been gaining its popularity in wide area including (electronic) publishing, CALS and digital libraries. One of the most popular application of SGML is HTML used in WWW (World Wide Web). Two major components of an SGML document are a DTD (Document Type Definition) and a document instance. The DTD represents a grammatical rule of logical structure of documents, while the document instance is a document which conforms to the DTD. The document instance has, in addition to its contents, embedded tags to represent the logical structure and other attached information. A major goal of SGML is to provide a framework to expedite the processing, exchange and reuse of documents by making use of the logical structure of texts. Since database technologies play a crucial role to attain this goal, SGML databases are emerging as an important research area[5, 11].

Storing SGML documents by taking advantage of their logical structures makes it possible to retrieve texts not only by content-based but also by structure-based queries. Early studies in this direction include works of Macleod[10, 9].

---

* The first author was supported in part by International Information Science Foundation. The research by the second author was done while he is at Nara Institute of Science and Technology. E-mail addresses: yosikawa@is.aist-nara.ac.jp, ichikawa@vdrl.src.mei.co.jp, uemura@is.aist-nara.ac.jp

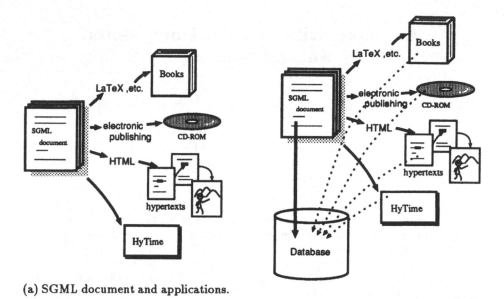

(a) SGML document and applications.

(b) Reference mechanism from SGML
documents to database objects.

Fig. 1. Enhancing the SGML functionality.

More recently, Christophides et. al. [2, 3] developed a query language, which
extends O_2SQL, to retrieve document instances. This query language assumes
an O_2 schema which is enhanced to represent DTDs. Another approach is the
introduction of a new data type for structured texts into data models. Blake et.
al.[1] proposed extensions to SQL2 by introducing data types and functions for
structured text. Also, Yan et. al.[13] proposed the integration of a structured
text retrieval system with an object-oriented database system.

Past researches in this area have mainly focused on the development of 1)
database schemas to store SGML documents based on their logical structure,
and 2) query languages to retrieve text components satisfying search conditions.
Such development is an important step to achieve efficient storage and operation
of large amount of SGML documents.

However, since SGML is a highly versatile language, there exist enormous
potentialities of applying database technologies in other aspects of SGML document processing which include creation, editing and application. Also, the final
usage of SGML documents is out of the scope of the standard, and is open to
application programs. In other words, SGML documents are "half-finished products", and application programs for specific purposes produce "final products"
in a form such as books, CD-ROMs, hypertext and etc. (see Figure 1(a)). Hence,
by enhancing the functionality of SGML documents as "half-finished products",

every "final product" can enjoy the enhanced functionality.

Our premise is that one important enhancement is to provide a general mechanism to establish reference links from SGML documents to database objects (see Figure 1(b)). In this paper, we propose a uniform and flexible mechanism to establish reference links from components of SGML documents to database objects. The components of SGML documents here might be arbitrary character strings as well as document elements. With this reference mechanism, (a part of) SGML attributes and their values can be uniformly managed by databases, or inversely, database attributes can be incorporated as (virtual) SGML attributes. Hence, deep amalgamation between SGML documents and databases is realized. As far as we know, no other research in literature proposed such reference mechanism between SGML documents and database objects, which allows references from arbitrary character strings in texts.

To provide users with a tool with which they can easily specify these reference links in a uniform manner, we introduce a new logical layer on top of SGML framework. Using the notion of *virtual element markup* on this layer, users can uniformly build wide varieties of reference links among SGML documents and databases, which include static/dynamic links to database objects and to document elements.

We have also developed a query language which fully exploits the deep amalgamation of SGML documents and databases established by above mentioned link mechanism. The proposed query language can express complex queries of which search condition may be any combinations of qualifications on documents' logical structures (such as sections and paragraphs), documents' contents, links and/or database attributes. Queries return document elements and/or database objects. The query language also can be used to express dynamic links mentioned above. Such dynamic links are very flexible in that destinations change with the current status of database instance and/or document sets. Another important feature of the query language is that it does not assume a particular database schema nor database model; instead, it utilizes DTD graphs, representing the logical structures of elements in DTDs, as virtual schemas.

Furthermore, compatibility is another notable feature of our framework. Firstly, the link mechanism proposed in this paper is designed to be "upward compatible" to the SGML standard. Hence, existing SGML documents can be "upgraded" in our framework by making very minor modification to DTDs. Secondly, since our query language does not assume a particular database schema, our general idea can be applied to other schemas and query languages for structured documents proposed so far. Since our proposal is "orthogonal to" the trend of many other researches in this area, we expect the combination of our mechanism and other research results would yield synergistic effects.

In the rest of the paper, Section 2 gives an overview of SGML. Section 3 presents underlying assumptions of our discussion, and classifies links we consider. In Section 4, detailed discussions are given to establish links from arbitrary character strings in SGML documents to objects stored in databases. Section 5 illustrates a wide range of queries expressed using our query language. Section 6

```
<!DOCTYPE article    [
<!ELEMENT article    -- (title, author+, abstract, section+)>
<!ATTLIST article    id    ID      #IMPLIED>
<!ELEMENT section    -- (title, p*, subsectn*)>
<!ATTLIST section    id    ID      #IMPLIED>
<!ELEMENT subsectn   -- (title, p+, subsectn*)>
<!ELEMENT title      -- (#PCDATA)>
<!ELEMENT author     -- (#PCDATA)>
<!ELEMENT abstract   -- (#PCDATA)>
<!ELEMENT p          -- (#PCDATA)>
<!ATTLIST p          idref IDREFS #IMPLIED>
<!ENTITY  RDB        "Relational Database">
]>
```

Fig. 2. An example DTD.

presents both static and dynamic reference link mechanism between document elements. The dynamic references utilize the query language given in Section 5.

2 SGML

SGML (Standard Generalized Markup Language)[4, 12] is an international standard markup language (ISO 8879[6]), which allows the description of structures and attributes of documents. SGML documents basically consist of two components: DTDs and document instances[3]. A DTD (Document Type Definition) defines the grammar to which the logical structure of corresponding document instances must conform. DTDs are defined for each type of documents, such as doctoral thesis, technical report, manual, and so on. In general, many document instances are created according to the logical structure defined by a DTD; hence, DTDs have some analogy with database schemas, and document instances with database instances. We illustrate these two components using examples in more detail.

- A DTD (Figure 2) consists of the following three parts:
  - *Element declaration* which declares elements to form document instances, and defines the element name and content model (i.e. logical structure) of each element.
  - *Attribute list declaration* which defines, for each element, SGML attributes, their declared values (or "domain" in database terminology), default values.

---

[3] Document instance is a terminology used in the ISO standard. In literature, terms "marked document" or "marked text" are also used.

```
<!DOCTYPE article SYSTEM "article.dtd">
<article><title>Structured Documents</title>
<author> ... </author><author> ... </author>
<abstract> ... </abstract>
<section><title>Introduction</title>
<p>SGML is the language based on the ... </p></section>
<section><title>Basic Concepts</title>
<subsectn><title>Generalized Markup Languages</title>
<p>The first generalized markup language is ... </p>
<p>In 1986, ISO ... <p>
...
</subsectn></section>
...
</article>
```

Fig. 3. An example document instance.

- *Entity declaration* which defines entities such as (long) character strings and another documents.
- A document instance (Figure 3) is a document embedded with markups such as tags and entity references. Tags are used to specify the starting and ending positions of logical structures such as chapters and sections. Tags are delimited by a start-tag(<) and an end-tag(>). Entity references are used to refer to other documents or predefined (long) strings which appear many times in the document with a short reference name. SGML parsers replace entity reference names in SGML documents by corresponding entities.

In document instances, SGML *attributes* are described within start-tags. The usage of SGML attributes is unrestricted. We can roughly classify the usage of SGML attributes as follows:

1. SGML attributes whose values are independent of the position of the tag's occurrence (i.e. context) in a document instance. For example, age in <person age=20>Hiroyuki Kato</person> falls into this category.
2. SGML attributes whose values are dependent on the context. For example, figid in <figure figid='piechart1'> has a value specific to each occurrence of the element <figure>. type in <div1 type='section'> is another example of such attribute.

In SGML, links between document elements are built using ID/IDREF. SGML attributes which have the declared value ID are used to give a unique identifier to each element. These identifiers are referred from SGML attributes with declared value IDREF.

3 Links among SGML Documents and Databases

In general, a link may have many anchors, and traversal between anchors may be bidirectional[7]. In this paper, however, we assume that links have exactly two anchors and that traversal is unidirectional; hence, we will use terms "source" and "destination" instead of "anchor". In SGML, the source of links in document instances must be elements defined in DTDs. However, in the link mechanism proposed in this paper, any character strings in documents can become link sources. The links among documents and databases we deal with in this paper can be classified along with the following two dimensions:

1. links of which destination is database[4] objects v.s. links of which destination is document elements
2. static links v.s. dynamic links

Among others, links referencing to database objects have not been extensively studied in literature so far. Utilizing this type of links, SGML attributes whose values are independent of the context can be stored in databases, and can enjoy its advantages (i.e. easy maintenance of value update, concurrency control, indexing and etc.) Inversely, database attributes can be incorporated into SGML documents. In both cases, a mechanism can be provided to make these database attributes be viewed as if they were ordinary SGML attributes. Also, schema evolution in the underlying database is reflected to the SGML attributes without changing DTDs. One interesting application of this reference link is hyperlink systems reflecting keywords' (partial) semantics which is managed in databases. Various (indirect) hyperlinks among keywords in documents can be built based on the relationships among corresponding database objects. In Section 4, we focus our attention to links of which destination is database objects.

As for the links to documents, SGML supports static links using ID and IDREF, but not dynamic links. In Section 6, we propose dynamic links using queries in our query language.

4 Links to Database Objects Using Virtual Element Markup

In this section, we first explain the difficulties in realizing links to database objects within the framework of SGML. Then, we introduce a notion of *virtual element markup* to uniformly specify flexible links to database objects.

---

[4] In general, SGML documents might also be stored in databases (i.e. "Database" in Figure 1(b)). Although our discussion in this paper applies to such situations as well, we assume, without loss of generality, that databases we consider does not store SGML documents.

4.1 Storing Data in SGML Attributes

In this subsection, we present the method to describe the properties of real-world entities using SGML attributes, and reveal problems of this method.

For example, some attributes of a person named "Kato" can be described as:

<person ssn=1234567 age=20 address="Nara">Kato</person>   (1)

Similarly, the population of the city "Nara" can be recorded as:

<city population=240000>Nara</city>   (2)

Of course, specifying every pairs of SGML attribute names and values for each occurrence of the tagged contents "Kato" and "Nara" in structured documents will be a cumbersome task. The entity declaration below, which is a part of a DTD, will ease the task. With this declaration, each occurrence of &hkato; and &nara; (i.e. entity references) in document instances is replaced by the character strings (1) and (2), respectively.

```
<!ENTITY hkato "<person ssn=1234567
                  age=20 address="Nara">Kato</person>">
<!ENTITY nara "<city population=240000>Nara</city>">
```

However, the management of attribute values within the SGML framework described above has the following problems:

Problem 1: The update of SGML attribute value(s) cause the rewriting of entity declaration in DTD, and re-parsing of every document instance which refers to the entities rewrote. This scenario is, of course, unrealistic.

Problem 2: In SGML, element names and their attributes must be declared in DTD before document instances are created. However, element names and their attributes in element markups (1) and (2) have exactly same semantics as classes and attributes of object-oriented databases. It is quite unlikely to be able to predict all classes and attributes of real-world objects referred in (unlimited number of) document instances.

4.2 Referencing Database Objects Using a General Element

The SGML attribute values in element markups (1) and (2) do not depend on the occurrence position of tags which contain those attributes. Therefore, a natural solution to resolve the Problems 1 and 2 is i) to store these SGML attribute values and element names such as person and city in databases; and ii) to provide a mechanism to refer from tags in document instances to the corresponding database objects. To resolve the Problem 2, we need to use a single element name, say "dbobject", for referring to database objects. Using dbobject, element markups (1) and (2) can be represented as follows:

<dbobject type = person   oid = 1234>Kato</dbobject>   (3)
<dbobject type = city   oid = 2345>Nara</dbobject>   (4)

The SGML attribute oid in the element markups (3) and (4) holds the OIDs of "Kato" and "Nara" in the underlying database, respectively. Let us assume the attributes of the person type in the underlying database be ssn, age and address. By preparing an SGML application program which, given the element markup (3), generates the SQL sentence "SELECT * FROM person WHERE oid= 1234", we can virtually provide users with the information of (1) in texts. By providing query results in this way, each dbobject elements can possess the attribute values stored in databases as if they were defined as SGML attributes. In this way, we can refer to any types of database objects by using the single general element dbobject in a uniform manner.

Again in this case, we can use entity declarations to refer to long character strings like (3) and (4) by short reference names. For this purpose, each dbobject element is declared in DTD; for example the element markup (3) might be declared as:

```
<!ENTITY hkato
    "<dbobject type = person  oid = 1234>Kato</dbobject>">
```

With this entity declaration, each occurrence of &hkato; in document instance is replaced by the character string (3).

As stated earlier, we assume that SGML documents which conforms to our proposing framework are created from scratch. However, upgrading existing SGML documents to make them able to refer database objects is also very easy. The required modifications to DTDs are the following very simple ones:

1. Insert the element and attribute declarations of the newly introduced tag dbobject.
2. Define dbobject in the root element of DTDs using the "inclusion" facility of SGML (+(dbobject) in Figure 4). By defining as "inclusion", dbobject elements can appear in any position within document instances conforming to the DTD.

The DTD after these modifications[5] is presented in Figure 4. Note that these modifications do not affect existing document instances at all unless we do not utilize the added functionality of referencing database objects. Otherwise, if we want to use this functionality, the modification to document instances is just to insert dbobject tags to appropriate positions.

4.3 Virtual Element Markup

In the last subsection, we have described a basic machanism for building links from arbitrary character strings in SGML documents to database objects. The mechanism still has the following problems in flexibility and easiness of use:

1. Parameterization of tagged contents (i.e. character strings.)

---

[5] The role of the SGML attribute "sgmlatt" is explained in Subsection 4.3.

```
<!ELEMENT root --
              ( ···, ···  ) +(dbobject)>
              ···
<!ELEMENT dbobject -- (#PCDATA)>
<!ATTLIST dbobject type     CDATA #REQUIRED
                   oid      CDATA #REQUIRED
                   sgmlatt  CDATA #IMPLIED>
```

Fig. 4. The DTD to refer to database objects.

The same real-world object is often denoted by different character strings depending on their occurrence positions. For example, a person may be denoted as "Kato" in one position and as "H. Kato" in another position within a single document. With the mechanism described in the previous subsection, we need to declare as many entities as different character strings.

2. The functionalities of the ordinary SGML should not be restricted. Specifically, we should be able to declare SGML attributes whose values are dependent on the occurrence of tags.

3. The information on links to database objects should be shared among SGML documents.

In this subsection, we will introduce the notion of *virtual element markup* to cope with these problems.

Firstly, we cannot meet the requirement 1 mentioned above within the SGML framework because the entity reference of SGML does not provide the functionality of parameterizing character strings. It is also difficult to meet the requirement 2 by simply extending the mechanism presented in the last subsection within the SGML framework. Therefore, we will introduce a new logical layer on top of the SGML framework. Users can logically create and view SGML documents in this new layer, and those SGML documents are translated to fit into the ordinary SGML framework.

The notation of element markups in this new logical layer is similar to ordinary element markups; "<<" and ">>" are used for tag open and close delimiters instead of "<" and ">". The general notation is as follows:

$$\texttt{<<ven } a_1 = v_1 \cdots a_n = v_n \texttt{>>A<</ven>>}$$

ven is a *virtual element name* which is a mnemonic name of a database object. $a_1, \cdots, a_n$ are SGML attribute names of **ven** whose values are dependent on the occurrence position of the tag (Hence these attributes cannot be stored in the underlying database). $v_1, \cdots, v_n$ are values of $a_1, \cdots, a_n$, respectively. Also, A is a content. By enclosing a content with a pair of start-tag and end-tag in this way, we can nest virtual element markups as ordinary SGML element markups.

For example, assume that we use "Kato" to represent, in one context, a person having oid **1234**, and "H. Kato" in another context. Then, these representations are denoted as (5) and (6), respectively.

$$\texttt{<<hkato>>Kato<</hkato>>} \tag{5}$$

$$\texttt{<<hkato>>H. Kato<</hkato>>} \tag{6}$$

Furthermore, if we want to specify an SGML attribute only for (5), we can use the following notation.

```
<<hkato comment = "...">>Kato<</hkato>>
```

We call document instances containing virtual element markups *raw document instances*. The correspondence between virtual element names and OIDs are stored in a separate dictionary file. This dictionary has the following three attributes:

1. **ven**: virtual element name
2. **type**: type of corresponding database object
3. **oid**: oid of corresponding database object

A preprocessor translates, by looking up the dictionary, raw document instances into document instances and entity declarations in a "common entity file" (see Figure 5). As illustrated in Figure 5, the SGML attribute "sgmlatt" in Figure 4 is used to accommodate SGML attributes and values which appear in virtual element markups.

5 Query Language

We have designed a query language which fully exploits the link mechanism between SGML documents and databases. Besides querying logical structures of SGML documents, the amalgamation mechanism presented in the previous section allows us to retrieve documents based on the information stored in underlying databases. In this section, we will sketch our query language using some examples. The query language does not assume a particular data model; instead it utilizes DTD graphs, representing logical structure of elements, as virtual schemas. A DTD graph is a directed graph of which nodes represent elements in a DTD, and edges represent the logical structure of elements (see Figure 6.)

5.1 Queries on Logical Structures of Documents

Q1 (content-based query): *Find the title and the first author of articles of which abstract contains 'SGML' and 'HyTime'.*

```
SELECT   <title>, <author>[1]
FROM     <article>
WHERE    <abstract> contains 'SGML' and 'HyTime'
```

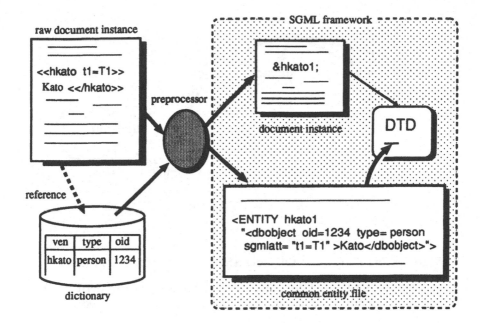

Fig. 5. The architecture of virtual element markup.

In FROM clause, we specify element names to specify the search range. In SELECT clause and WHERE clause we can use descendant elements (in the corresponding DTD graph) of those specified in FROM clause. Elements defined by occurrence indicator("+" or "*") are specified by "[ ]" notation in the query language. contains predicate is used to perform pattern matching of character strings.

Q2 (path expression): *Find the title and the abstract of articles containing 'OODBMS' in the third paragraph of the second subsection of the first section.*

```
SELECT  <title>, <abstract>
FROM    <article>
WHERE   <section>[1].<subsectn>[2].<p>[3] contains 'OODBMS'
```

In Q2, element names are concatenated by dot notation to represent parent-child relationship in DTD graph.

Q3 (incomplete path expression): *Find all titles in articles.*

```
SELECT    a..<title>
FROM      <article> a
```

The ".." notation represents a path in DTD graph. The result of this query is a set of titles reachable from the root of <article>. This example demonstrates that users can pose a query without exact knowledge of documents' logical structure.

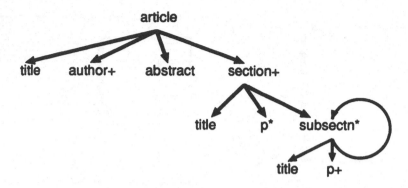

Fig. 6. A DTD graph.

5.2 Queries on Database Objects through SGML Attributes

By amalgamating structured documents and databases, we can perform the various queries on documents using information which is stored in databases.

Q4: *Find the title, the author and his/her age of articles of which abstract contains 'database'.*

```
SELECT <title>, <author>, <author>.(person).age
FROM   <article>
WHERE  <abstract> contains 'database'
```

In this query, (person) matches with <dbobject> elements of which value of SGML attribute **type** is **person**. Note that **age** is an attribute of underlying databases. We can retrieve databases attribute values through document elements in this manner.

Q5: *Find pairs of the title of an article and the name of a city such that the city is mentioned somewhere in the article and has more than 500,000 population.*

```
SELECT <title>, a..(city).name
FROM   <article> a
WHERE  (city).population > 500,000
```

In this query, **name** and **population** are attributes of underlying databases. This query retrieves document elements (i.e. <title>) and database values (i.e. a..(city).name) based on a search condition on database values.

6 Link Mechanism among Documents

In Section 4, we have proposed a fundamental mechanism to uniformly make a reference from arbitrary character strings in SGML documents to database

```
<!ATTLIST dbobject    type     CDATA   #REQUIRED

                      oid      CDATA   #IMPLIED

                      sgmlatt  CDATA   #IMPLIED

                      id       ID      #IMPLIED

                      idref    IDREFS  #IMPLIED

                      dids     CDATA   #IMPLIED>
```

Fig. 7. Attribute declaration of the element dbobject.

objects. In this section, we turn our attention to hyperlinks between SGML document elements. First, we will briefly present static links which utilize the cross-reference mechanism of ID/IDREF in SGML. Then, we illustrate dynamic links which use query language presented in Section 5. The destinations of dynamic links presented here may change depending on the information of the underlying databases as well as document structures and contents. Finally, we will extend virtual element markup to include links to document elements.

6.1 Static Link Using ID/IDREF

In SGML, links between document elements are built using ID/IDREF. To utilize this functionality, we extend the SGML attribute declaration shown in Figure 4 to include SGML attributes id and idref. The attribute list declaration after this extension is shown[6] in Figure 7. Note that dbobject element now has the following two SGML attributes for reference purpose:

- oid: for references to database object.
- idref: defined with the declared value IDREFS, for references to document elements.

The hyperlinks using ID/IDREF feature are static links whose destinations are fixed.

6.2 Dynamic Link

In this subsection, we will illustrate dynamic links to document elements using queries in the query language presented in Section 5. Queries which return a set of document elements can be used for dynamic links. In general, the returned set dynamically change depending on the set of document instances as well as the underlying database instance. We need to introduce a new SGML attribute,

---

[6] Figure 7 also includes the attribute dids which will be explained in Subsection 6.2.

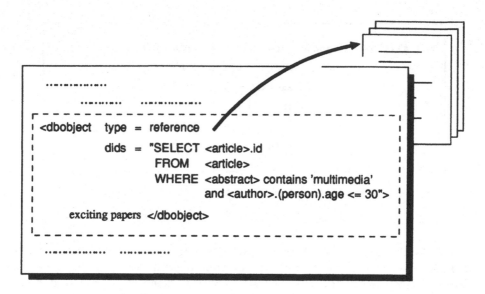

Fig. 8. Dynamic link using dbobject.

which holds a query sentence as its value, into **dbobject** element. The SGML attribute named "**dids**", which stands for "dynamic IDs", in Figure dbobject-ididref is used for this purpose.

Figure 8 illustrates a dynamic link using both document structures and the underlying database information. This example shows a hyperlink from inside a SGML document to the documents such that 1) the abstract contains the word " multimedia" and 2) at least one of the authors' age is less then 30, Note that the condition 1) is concerned with the document structure (and contents), whereas the condition 2) is concerned with the document structure and the information stored in the underlying database. Since the authors' age changes year by year, the set of documents obtained as the destination of this hyperlink may dynamically change.

6.3 Virtual Element Markup for Document Hyperlink

Although dynamic links described in Subsection 6.2 are useful mechanism, specifying a long SQL sentence as shown in Figure 8 for each occurrence of the link in documents is a tedious task. Therefore, we will extend the notion of virtual element markup introduced in Subsection 4.3 to cover (both static and dynamic) hyperlinks between SGML documents. With the notion of virtual element markups and dictionaries, we can succinctly specify hyperlinks in documents with short virtual element names.

As described in Subsection 4.3, the dictionary has attributes **ven**, **type** and **oid**. We now introduce a new attribute in this dictionary, which represents doc-

ven	type	oid	id
tanaka	person	1234	s1.2
d-cars	car	select ⋯	–
expapers	reference	–	SELECT <article>.id FROM <article> WHERE contains 'multimedia' <author>.(person).age <= 30
⋮	⋮	⋮	⋮

Fig. 9. An example dictionary.

ument elements' ID(s) referred from **dbobject** elements. An example dictionary is given in Figure 9. The attribute **oid** in this dictionary holds either an oid to statically specify a database object or an SQL sentence to dynamically specify oid(s). Whereas the newly introduced attribute **id** holds either ID(s) to statically specify document elements referred from **dbobject** or an SQL sentence to dynamically specify ID(s). Each attribute takes **null** value if there are no elements or objects to refer.

For example, if the above dictionary was defined, the dynamic link shown in Figure 8 can be specified succinctly as:

$$\texttt{<<expapers>>exciting papers<</expapers>>} \qquad (7)$$

The preprocessor replaces each occurrence of the virtual element markup (7) with the **<dbobjct>** element shown in Figure 8.

7 Conclusion

We have proposed a uniform and flexible reference mechanism among SGML documents and database objects. By using the notion of virtual element markup, we can specify wide range of links in a uniform manner. These include static/dynamic links to database objects or document elements. We also have developed a query language which can fully exploit the amalgamation of SGML documents and databases.

Although we illustrated, in Section 6, dynamic linking mechanism using our query language, the basic idea is independent of the query language used.

We are now developing, using HyTime, a link mechanism which extends the one proposed in this paper. The extension includes bidirectional traversal and high independence of database schema and SGML documents.

Acknowledgements

The authors are grateful to Dr. Yoshiharu Ishikawa, Mr. Hiroyuki Kato and other members of Laboratory for Database and Media Systems, NAIST, for their constructive discussions.

References

1. G. E. Blake, M. P. Consens, I. J. Davis, P. Kilpeläinen, E. Kuikka, P.-Å. Larson, T. Snider, and F. W. Tompa. Text / Relational Database Management Systems: Overview and Proposed SQL Extensions. Technical Report CS-95-25, UW Centre for the New OED and Text Research, Department of Computer Science, University of Waterloo, June 1995.
2. V. Christophides, S. Abiteboul, S. Cluet, and M. Scholl. From Structured Documents to Novel Query Facilities. In *Proc. ACM SIGMOD International Conference on Management of Data*, pages 313–324, May 1994.
3. V. Christophides and A. Rizk. Querying Structured Documents with Hypertext Links using OODBMS. In *Proc. of ACM European Conference on Hypermedia Technology (ECHT'94)*, pages 186–197, September 1994.
4. Charles F. Goldfarb. *The SGML Handbook*. Clarendon Press, Oxford, 1990.
5. Gaston H. Gonnet. Tutorial: Text Dominated Databases, Theory Practice and Experience. In *Proc. ACM Symp. on Principles of Database Systems*, pages 301–302, May 1994.
6. ISO 8879: 1986. *Information Processing – Text and Office System – Standard Generalized Markup Language (SGML)*, Oct. 15 1986.
7. ISO/IEC 10744: 1992. *Hypermedia/Time-based Structuring Language (HyTime)*, 1992.
8. I. A. Macleod. A Query Language for Retrieving Information from Hierarchic Text Structures. *The Computer Journal*, 34(3):254–264, 1991.
9. Ian A. Macleod. Storage and Retrieval of Structured Documents. *Information Processing & Management*, 26(2):197–208, 1990.
10. Ron Sacks-Davis, Timothy Arnold-Moore, and Justin Zobel. Database Systems for Structured Documents. In *Proc. of the International Symposium on Advanced Database Technologies and Their Integration*, pages 272–283, October 1994.
11. Eric van Herwijnen. *Practical SGML*. Kluwer Academic, 2nd edition, 1994.
12. Tak W. Yan and Jurgen Annevelink. Integrating a Structured-Text Retrieval System with an Object-Oriented Database System. In *Proceedings of the Twentieth International Conference on Very Large Databases*, pages 740–749, Santiago, Chile, 1994. Industrial Case.

Indexing Nucleotide Databases for Fast Query Evaluation

Hugh Williams   Justin Zobel

Department of Computer Science, RMIT,
GPO Box 2476V, Melbourne 3001, Australia
{hugh,jz}@cs.rmit.edu.au

Abstract

A query to a nucleotide database is a DNA sequence. Answers are similar sequences, that is, sequences with a high-quality local alignment. Existing techniques for finding answers use exhaustive search, but it is likely that, with increasing database size, these algorithms will become prohibitively expensive. We have developed a partitioned search approach, in which local alignment string matching techniques are used in tandem with an index. We show that fixed-length substrings, or intervals, are a suitable basis for indexing in conjunction with local alignment on likely answers. By use of suitable compression techniques the index size is held to an acceptable level, and queries can be evaluated several times more quickly than with exhaustive search techniques.

1 Introduction

Nucleotide databases such as GenBank [4] store strings representing sequences of nucleotide bases, each string annotated by a natural language description of the function of the sequence. These databases are used to assist molecular biologists to determine the biochemical function and chemical structure of query strings, and to investigate the evolutionary history of organisms. A query is a sequence of nucleotide bases whose properties are not fully known; answers are nucleotide sequences that exhibit local similarity to the query.

Most of the existing tools for matching queries to answers exhaustively compare the query with each of the sequences in the database. However, with the increasing number of users and the rapid increase in the number of stored sequences in genomic databases, exhaustive searching techniques are becoming prohibitively expensive because of the volume of data to be processed for each query. Conventional databases use indexing to provide fast access to relevant data. In particular, indexing has been shown to work well for information retrieval [17, 18], which has marked similarities to genomic retrieval: in both domains a typical query returns a large set of responses, most entries in the database exhibit some degree of similarity to the query, and matches are approximate rather than exact.

A difficulty in indexing for genomic databases is deciding what to index. Perhaps the most obvious approach, which is the option we have pursued in our research, is to index the distinct *intervals* occurring in the sequences, where an interval is a sequence of n bases for some fixed integer n. Having decided to index intervals, however, an effective mechanism is required for query evaluation. Moreover, since almost every base in a sequence is the start of an interval, the index must contain an entry for each base in the database, potentially a massive overhead on the data itself.

In this paper we describe the successful application of inverted file indexing to nucleotide databases. To address the problem of index size we have adapted compression techniques developed for text indexing [12]. The query evaluation technique used is an adaptation of a method that can be used for pattern matching for lexicons of names and English words [22, 23], which we call the CAFE method. The CAFE method is a combination of coarse searching, via an index, and fine searching, on the sequences the index has identified as likely answers. To achieve efficient retrieval from nucleotide databases, we have developed several modifications to the CAFE method used for general strings. Even with compression the index is unacceptably large, so we have used heuristics to further reduce index size. Because of the length of the stored strings, simply identifying which strings are likely matches does not sufficiently reduce query evaluation time; it is also necessary to store extra information in the index to identify where in the string a similar region can be found.

Our experiments show that the CAFE method can efficiently find answers using an index of moderate size. Although our implementation is only preliminary—for example, it uses a simple but slow local alignment algorithm—answers can be located in a fraction of the time used by the current exhaustive techniques.

The paper is organised as follows. Nucleotide databases are introduced in Section 2. Indexing and compression is discussed in Section 3. Local alignment is discussed in Section 4. In Section 5 we introduce the CAFE method for searching nucleotide databases, and show experimental results in Section 6. Conclusions are presented in Section 7.

2 Nucleotide Databases

Genetic material, or DNA, stores complete instructions for all the cellular functions of an organism. DNA is strings of a four-character alphabet, known as the *nucleotide bases*, represented by A, C, G, and T. The bases are arranged into *sequences*; a typical example is shown in Figure 1. In addition to the nucleotide bases, there are several standard wildcard characters used to represent different possible substitutions in a nucleotide sequence. For example, B is used to represent the permitted substitution of either C, G, or T, but not A, into a sequence. The most common wildcard is N, which represents any base.

A significant proportion of nucleotide sequences *transcribe*, or synthesise, proteins. The synthesis of proteins uses 3-base combinations, known as *codons*, to transcribe amino acids, which in turn are combined to create proteins. A *gene* is a region in a nucleotide sequence that codes a protein that performs a cellular function.

```
CTCAAGGCGCACTCCCGTTCTGGATAATGTTTTTTGCGCCGACATCATAAC
GGTTCTGGCAAATATTCTGAAATGAGCTGTTGACAATTAATCATCGAACTA
GTTAACTAGTACGCAAGTTCACGTAAAAAGGGTATCCA
```

Fig. 1. Nucleotide structure of a gene from *E. coli*

There are several public nucleotide databases. Three of the larger repositories are GenBank [4], the DNA Databank of Japan, and the European Molecular Biology Laboratory database [16]. Additionally, there are several single-species databases, such as the Portable Mouse Genome Database [21]. We use GenBank as the source of test data for our experiments; the structure and data in GenBank is similar to that of other nucleotide sequence databases.

GenBank stores sequence data generated through the human genome initiative, which not only focuses on the human genome, but also on model organisms such as the bacteria *E. coli*, the fruit-fly *D. melanogaster*, the nematode *C. elegans* and yeast *S. cerevisiae* [5, 6]. Currently GenBank contains around 300 million nucleotide bases and is doubling in size every 21 months [1]. The average sequence length is around 1,000 bases, with sequences ranging from 10 to 700,000 bases in length. Data within GenBank is, in some cases, duplicated through the submission of identical and, rather more frequently, overlapping sequences. Additionally, there is a small but significant error rate, both as a result of sequence determination errors and of data entry errors [1].

Nucleotide sequences for the same function can have varied structure, the distance in structure dependent on the evolutionary distance of the two organisms. Frequently, these regions derive from a common ancestor sequence, so that identification of the existence of *homology*, or similarity, through sequence comparison of these regions can shed light on the evolutionary history, biochemical function, and chemical structure of these molecules. A primary use of GenBank is for querying for such similarities.

3   Indexing and Compression

An inverted index has two components: a *search structure* for storing each distinct indexed value or *index term*; and for each index term an *inverted list*, which contains an entry for each occurrence of the index term in the database.

For indexing nucleotide data, we suggest that an appropriate choice of index term is the *intervals* occurring in each sequence, where the intervals are overlapping substrings of some fixed length n; choice of n is discussed later. (Intervals are also known as n-grams and n-mers.) For example, if n is 3 then the intervals of ACCTGTC are ACC, CCT, CTG, TGT, and GTC. Indexing on fixed-length substrings has been successfully used in pattern-matching for large lexicons [22, 23], a domain that is however rather different: strings in lexicons are typically around

10 characters, not thousands of characters, and similarity is total rather than local.

A simple inverted index would list, for each distinct interval, the ordinal numbers of the sequences containing that interval. Thus an inverted list for an interval might be

101 109 217 412 980 1013 ...

indicating that the interval occurs in the 101st sequence, the 109th sequence, and so on. Since, potentially, each base in each sequence is the start of a distinct interval, there could be an entry in the index for each base in the database; thus care must be taken to ensure that the index size is acceptable. To address this problem we have employed index compression techniques used for text databases [12] and string indexing [22, 23], which in these domains reduce index size by around a factor of 6.

The principle of the index compression is as follows. If the ordinal numbers in each list are sorted, differences can be taken between adjacent numbers, yielding small positive integers that can be effectively represented in a variable-length code. For example, the inverted list above becomes, after taking of differences,

101 8 108 195 568 33 ...

Appropriate coding schemes include the data-independent Elias codes [7] or the parameterised Golomb codes [8]. We have, in our current preliminary implementation, used the Elias gamma and delta codes, which are as follows. In the gamma code, a positive integer x is represented by $1 + \lfloor \log_2 x \rfloor$ in unary (that is, $1 + \lfloor \log_2 x \rfloor$ 0-bits followed by a 1-bit), followed by the binary representation of x less its highest bit. Thus 9 is represented by 0001001. In the delta code, x is represented by $1 + \lfloor \log_2 x \rfloor$ in gamma, followed by the binary representation of x less its highest bit. Thus 9 is represented by 00100001. In both schemes, 1 is represented by 1, that is, is represented in one bit. Gamma is more efficient for small numbers and delta for large.

The Elias codes yield acceptable compression and fast decoding, but better performance in both respects is possible with Golomb codes [13]. We would expect a production implementation to have indexes of around 80% of the size of those reported in Section 6, and query evaluation times would also be reduced.

As we explain later, query evaluation can be simplified if we store, in addition to ordinal sequence numbers, positions in each sequence at which each interval begins. Since an interval can occur several times in a sequence, we must also store a count of the number of occurrences. Thus the inverted list for an interval might be

101 (3: 46, 738, 754) 109 (1: 37) ...

indicating that the 101st sequence contains the interval three times, at offsets 46, 738, and 754; and that the 109th sequence contains it once, at offset 37. Differences can be taken between adjacent offset values, again allowing compression, so that the list would be represented as

101 (3: 46, 692, 16) 8 (1: 37) ...

Our experiments revealed that compression greatly reduced index size, but, unfortunately, also revealed that even with compression the resulting indexes were
unacceptably large.

We therefore used heuristics to further reduce index size. One heuristic was
to limit indexing of wildcards. We expand wildcards prior to indexing, so that
intervals with a wildcard are indexed several times, but sequences of wildcards
lead to geometric explosion; and long sequences of the wildcard N are common.
We therefore decided not to index any interval with more than one wildcard.
We also decided to not index any interval occurring in more than $x\%$ of the
sequences; small x leads to small indexes and fast query evaluation. This process,
of discarding frequent intervals, is known as *stopping*. Experiments with stopping
are reported in Section 6.

Nucleotide data can also be compressed, saving both storage space and query
evaluation time, since the cost of decompression can be offset by the reduction
in data fetch time. Some nucleotide search tools, such as BLAST [2], use a lossy
compression scheme in which wildcards are replaced by a random base. We
describe elsewhere a lossless compression scheme that requires only around 0.5%
more space than lossy compression [20]. We use this method in the experiments
described below.

4   Searching of Nucleotide Databases

GenBank is manually indexed, with DNA sequences labelled by natural-language
descriptors, according to their perceived importance. For example, an author
may classify a sequence according to the presence of a coding region, whilst
ignoring repeating series of nucleotide groups. Despite the obvious limitations
of manual indexing, the use of natural language allows queries on aspects of
nucleotide data that cannot be readily inferred from sequences themselves.

Queries on GenBank nucleotide sequence data are a nucleotide sequence for
comparison to the GenBank data. A typical query returns a ranked list of nucleotide sequences, along with pertinent data including the species, GenBank
accession number and the natural language descriptor. To determine which nucleotide sequences in GenBank are related to a query sequence requires a numerical estimate of the similarity of each sequence in GenBank to the query
sequence. A similarity function can be used to compute a similarity estimate for
every string in the database, allowing identification of the top t strings. Similarity, in the case of nucleotide sequences, is the degree of homology between
substrings of each string, based on the order and identity of nucleotide bases.
In other words, matching algorithms identify, within strings, regions that are
highly similar.

There are several common tools for comparison of nucleotide sequence data
with that stored in GenBank, all of which exhaustively scan the database,
comparing a query sequence to each sequence entry. These algorithms include

BLAST [2], Lipman and Pearson's FASTA [15] and the parallel algorithm BLAZE. All three are variations on Pearson and Lipman's original FASTP [10]. BLAST, the *Basic Local Alignment Search Tool*, is, of the systems available for general-purpose hardware, the fastest and most widely-used suite of tools for searching GenBank. It has had considerable effort invested in its development and is highly optimised. In our discussions and comparisons we focus on the version of BLAST for direct nucleotide to nucleotide comparisons, known as BLASTN.

Local Alignment

Searching algorithms for estimating the distance between two nucleotide strings must provide a numerical estimate of the similarity of two strings. Related sequences contain highly similar regions, but are often largely dissimilar overall. Thus, for example, techniques to fine-search lexicons of English words do not apply to this domain; fine searching of nucleotide sequences is the task of identifying homologous regions in two sequences, that is, *local alignment*. Local alignment is used to identify regions within two strings that are similar regardless of: the similarity of the strings as a whole; of where the regions occur in the two strings; and of their respective lengths.

Local alignment is based on a computationally intensive dynamic programming algorithm, first described by Needleman and Wunsch [19]. For two sequences of 1000 bases, local alignment can take around a day on a fast, general-purpose single-CPU machine [5]. The Smith-Waterman algorithm is a variation on the standard calculation of local alignment that recursively finds the maximum quality alignment between two strings [19]. For two strings $s = s_1 \cdots s_n$ and $t = t_1 \cdots t_m$, the maximum quality alignment consists of two initial segments $p^i = s_1 \cdots s_i$ and $q^j = t_1 \cdots t_j$, where $i \leq n$ and $j \leq m$, such that the distance $d(p^i, q^j)$ is calculated as:

$$d(p^i, q^j) = \max \begin{cases} d(p^{i-1}, q^j) + weight(p_i, \phi) & \text{("deletion of } p_i\text{"),} \\ d(p^{i-1}, q^{j-1}) + weight(p_i, q_i) & \text{("substitution of } p_i \text{ by } q_j\text{"),} \\ d(p^i, q^{j-1}) + weight(\phi, q_j) & \text{("insertion of } q_j\text{"),} \\ 0 & \text{("no alignment exists")} \end{cases}$$

Initial values are $d(p^i, q^0) = 0$ and $d(p^0, q^j) = 0$. At the fourth choice the algorithm terminates rather than award a negative score. The use of positive scores for matches and negative scores for deletions, insertions, and substitutions ensures that substring length is a weighted factor in local alignment, thus preventing meaningless alignments such as two sequences of one nucleotide each. The algorithm calculates the optimal alignment between all p^i and q^j by extending shorter alignments one base at a time. The optimal alignment of two sequences AATGCATG and AAGTAG can be represented as shown in Figure 2, where a match is represented by a vertical bar and an insertion by a dash.

As DNA is composed of two antiparallel strands, in which each A in one strand is mapped to T in the other and each G mapped to C, queries and sequences in GenBank can be from either strand. Local alignment algorithms

Sequence 1:	A	A	T	G	C	A	T	G
Sequence 2:	A	A	-	G	T	A	-	G

Fig. 2. Optimal local alignment between AATGCATG and AAGTAG

need, in effect, to inspect each sequence twice, once for direct match and once for the antiparallel strand match. We have not used complement match in the results described in this paper, but for most algorithms, including ours, it approximately doubles query evaluation time.

We assume in this paper that local alignment is a matching of bases. Local alignment can instead use intervals of fixed length, for example codons, measuring similarity with a distance matrix [3], but we have not pursued this option.

BLAST

Altschul et al. propose heuristics in BLAST to deal with the computational complexity of dynamic programming algorithms. BLAST deals with the high computational overhead of both an exhaustive database search and local alignment through heuristics that find "ungapped, locally optimised ranked sequence alignments" [2]. BLAST does not allow for the insertion or deletion of bases, but only for the substitution of one base for another. This heuristic has some merit, as both deletions and insertions cause the meaning of a nucleotide sequence, in terms of the three-letter codons that transcribe amino acids, to be completely lost; it seems a reasonable compromise to ignore sequence alignments that require significant mutations. Note however that sequence errors can be insertions or deletions, so that some matches will be missed.

Using exhaustive search, BLAST matches all the intervals in a query sequence against all the intervals in each subject sequence. The only exceptions are intervals that occur frequently in the database; that is, BLAST uses stopping. In the event of a hit—where each of the n bases in both substrings corresponds exactly—a comparison is made between the regions surrounding the hit in the query and subject sequences. A deterministic finite automaton is used as a pattern matching tool, the approach used in the Knuth-Morris-Pratt [9] string-matching algorithm.

The BLAST system is very fast indeed, able to process millions of bases per second on current hardware. However, in principle an indexed system should be even faster, because there is no need to inspect the entire database: an index can provide direct access to likely matches, drastically reducing the volume of data to be inspected. We describe application of indexes in the next section.

5 The CAFE Searching Method

Our aim is to reduce the cost of matching without affecting the quality of answers returned. To achieve this we propose partitioning the searching process into two components: a coarse search based on an index is used to select candidate strings that have the potential to be good answers, then a fine search through these candidates is used to decide which of the candidates is best. We call this coarse-and-fine approach the CAFE method.

The motivation for using an index is to reduce the amount of data processed and to reduce CPU costs. The cost is the need to store the index, the potential saving is that fetching of a limited volume of index information should enable us to identify a limited number of sequences as likely answers, thus reducing both disk traffic and the computation required to resolve a query. Local alignment is computationally expensive, and, with only a few sequences to inspect, CPU time should be dramatically reduced.

Coarse searching involves retrieval of the inverted lists corresponding to unstopped intervals in the query string. To select the top k sequences, we determine which sequence identifiers appear most frequently in the inverted lists, a computationally inexpensive operation involving the union of the inverted lists of the intervals occurring in the query sequence; the highest ranked sequence being that which has the greatest number of intervals in common with the query sequence. Formally, this ranking can be expressed as the $count(s, t)$ of intervals that the query string s and the subject string t have in common:

$$count(s, t) = |I(s) \cap I(t)|$$

where $I(x)$ is the set of intervals in string x. This scheme is rather simplistic as offsets are not used, nor is sequence length considered. Note that index processing is a highly parallelisable process.

A query can have hundreds or even thousands of unstopped intervals, potentially leading to slow query evaluation. We observed that, for long queries in particular, the inverted lists for the more frequent intervals tend not to introduce high-quality matches. An effective optimisation is therefore to sort the intervals by increasing frequency, then cease processing of inverted lists at some point. We are still investigating this optimisation.

Those sequences that fall within the top k according to frequency of occurrence of query intervals are presented to a fine searching algorithm for ranking against each other. Large values of k ensure that more strings that contain intervals in common with the query are presented for ranking to the fine search mechanism. However, the larger the value of k, the larger the heap required to store and sort the nucleotide strings, the greater the overhead in fine searching amongst the candidates, and the greater the time required to evaluate queries.

Exhaustive search methods such as BLAST return all sequences whose similarity exceeds an arbitrary statistical threshold. The CAFE method returns the best k sequences, regardless of their similarity values, for an arbitrary k. We do not believe that either approach is preferable in practice.

Fine Searching

Having selected, using our coarse interval search, k sequences, we require a fine searching mechanism to rank the k sequences and present the top t answers to the user.

We have already asserted, through the use of an index, that two strings will only be considered to be similar if they contain common intervals. Implicit in this assertion is the assumption that it is reasonable to only attempt local alignments that begin with the alignment of a common interval. It is here that offsets are valuable: knowledge of where the matching interval begins in the query sequence and in the candidate answer means that we can begin local alignment immediately. This is particularly attractive in the context of genomic databases, as some sequences are of over 100,000 bases. In preliminary experiments we did not use offsets, but despite the reduction in index size found query evaluation to be somewhat slow. Offsets can also be used to refine the coarse ranking, by identifying good regions within candidates.

We have found Smith-Waterman local alignment to be prohibitively expensive, even with the smaller number of alignments required after coarse searching. Therefore, we chose to use a similar local alignment method to that of BLAST, with a scoring algorithm that does not include deletion or insertion and therefore does not permit gap insertion. Altschul et al. [2] have found the scoring weights of +5 for a match and −4 for a mismatch effective and we use them in our algorithm.

As local alignment begins with an alignment of two common intervals, we award an initial score equal to the length of the interval times the hit score; for example, with an interval of length 8 and match score of +5, the initial score is 40. We proceed by attempting to match the bases immediately to the left and right of the matching interval, keeping a cumulative score of matches and mismatches. We continue this hit extension, comparing successive bases from the query and subject in both directions on either side of the matching interval, rewarding matches and penalising mismatches. A simple extension to the basic algorithm is to abandon any hit extension that is an overlap of a previously attempted alignment; any such hit extension almost always results in the same alignment as previously attempted, and thus can be abandoned.

Our simple local alignment algorithm is much slower than that used by BLAST, which uses multi-base mappings and an automaton generated from the query. Our local alignment could be improved in similar ways, leading to even better performance than that reported below; we estimate that, in a production implementation, total evaluation time would fall to around one-half of the current figures.

Search Parameters

Nucleotide sequence data has four possible token values, A, C, T, and G. Thus, for intervals of length 2, there are only 16 possible combinations. Indexes formed on intervals of length 2 are therefore unlikely to be discriminating, with all of the

16 combinations likely, through chance, to receive many votes for any nucleotide string. Using the interval local alignment scheme, most of these matches when extended will be false matches. Consequently, interval-based methods are slow for short intervals.

If we chose an interval length of 1, and extended all matches between the query and the subjects, we are guaranteed to find the optimal alignment (neglecting insertions and deletions) between the query and the database. As we increase interval length, our index becomes less sensitive. For example, with a interval length of 10, we are guaranteed to only find alignments that contain 10 or more bases which align perfectly between the query and subject strings. There is, therefore, a trade-off between interval length and sensitivity. In the experiments below we used interval lengths of 8, 9, and 10.

Other parameters of search are the number of answers, as discussed above, and heuristics for abandoning local alignments.

6 Results

For our comparison of DNA retrieval techniques described we used a subset of the complete GenBank collection.[1] This collection was around half of the GenBank database, and contained the mammalian, primate, rodent, and miscellaneous vertebrate and invertebrate databases. It contained approximately 109 million nucleotide bases in 87,683 sequences, with an average sequence length of 1,243. We chose this collection as it contained known reasonable similarities to some of the query sequences we used, as well as a fair spread of organisms and sequence types. In total, including textual descriptions, it occupied 484 Mb.

Queries came from a variety of sources. Some were sequences obtained from users who work regularly with GenBank. Other queries were sequences in Gen-Bank that are known to have both close and distant matching sequences. In total, there were 14 queries. Average length was 299 bases, the shortest was 88, and the longest was 880.

Tests were carried out on a Sun SPARC Model 512 under light load. The interval search structure and some ancillary tables were held in main memory. The test collections and the inverted lists were held on disk.

Space Utilisation

We show in Table 1 the impact on of varying interval length and stopping factor x on index size. The in-memory structures largely consist of the search structure of distinct indexed intervals. Increase in n dramatically increases the size of the search structure, but 13 Mb in memory is not excessive on current hardware, particularly since the search structure can be shared between all active users.

As can be seen, the index of 8-base intervals is much smaller than the other indexes, but as we show below is also rather slow. Even aggressive stopping has

---

[1] Flat-file, release 87.0, 15 February 1995.

Interval length n	Stopping factor x	Inverted lists (Mb)	In-memory structures (Mb)
8	1.5	160.0	0.6
9	0.7	211.0	2.8
10	0.2	238.3	11.8
10	0.3	300.5	13.0
10	0.8	367.1	13.6

Table 1. Inverted file index size

not, to our surprise, had a marked impact on index size of 10-base intervals. We are currently testing whether index size can be further reduced without effect on the ability of the CAFE method to find matches. Note that, even though these indexes are large, they are smaller than the set of GenBank entries being indexed.

The time required to construct these indexes depended on n and x, but was typically 4 to 8 hours. Use of high-performance algorithms for index construction would substantially reduce this time [11].

Speed

A summary of the results of using fine searching techniques on the test collection is presented in Table 2. For the CAFE method we tuned the parameters of local alignment so that the first 10 answers were almost identical to those returned by BLAST. The BLAST utility used was BLASTN, for which $n = 11$ was chosen because it is the default setting in the current implementation. It is not practical to use $n = 11$ for the CAFE method on our hardware, but note that increasing n has an adverse effect on the quality of answers; the BLAST default was reduced from $n = 12$ to $n = 11$ for this reason.

Use of 8-base intervals led to query evaluation that was only 3 times faster than BLASTN for the CAFE method, because the intervals had longer inverted lists and there was a corresponding increase in local alignments during fine-searching.

For $n = 9$ and above, the speed of CAFE increased dramatically. For $n = 10$, the CAFE method was around 7 to 11 times faster than BLASTN, and as discussed above we believe that significant further improvements in speed are possible. We believe that the cost of having an index is well worthwhile when it results in such speed gains. Note that these results use our method for compression of nucleotide data [20]; uncompressed query evaluation is about 25% slower.

Use of stopping might mean that some good answers are not found, but we do not believe this to have been a problem in practice. First, the stopping regime used was similar to that of BLAST, and there are typically hundreds of unstopped intervals in each query. Second, we have conducted preliminary experiments on a small database with a test query set and relevance judgements, and have found that CAFE and BLAST perform about equally well at finding good matches.

Technique	Parameters	Elapsed time (avg sec per query)
CAFE	$n = 8, x = 1.5$	11.5
	$n = 9, x = 0.7$	4.3
	$n = 10, x = 0.2$	2.4
	$n = 10, x = 0.3$	3.1
	$n = 10, x = 0.7$	4.1
BLASTN	$n = 8$	35.1
	$n = 10$	28.0
	$n = 11$	11.2

Table 2. Evaluation time for query evaluation techniques

Other researchers have considered the use of an index for searching nucleotide databases. Altschul et al. [2], the authors of BLAST, tested an index of intervals of 12 bases, but found it too slow; no details are provided. We would expect an index of 12-base intervals to be fast, but to have a huge search structure. Myers describes a trie-based algorithm [14] in which, in this application, the trie represents all distinct intervals of $\log_4 N$, where N is the number of bases in the database. We would not expect such an algorithm to be effective in practice. Trie traversal algorithms require a random access for each node—in this case, for each base in an interval. The size of a trie for such data is at least two pointers and possibly as many as four for each distinct interval in the database, and the structure of a trie makes compression difficult. For our data, the interval length would be 13 or 14, giving a structure of at least half a gigabyte, in addition to which must be stored a list of occurrences for each interval, that is, a set of inverted lists. The problems of trie structures for string matching are also discussed by Moffat and Zobel [12].

7 Conclusions

We have shown that queries to nucleotide databases can be evaluated more quickly via indexes than by exhaustive search. Although this result would not be surprising for general databases, to our knowledge there has been no previous successful attempt to use an inverted file to index a nucleotide database. Our success is due to several innovations: the CAFE separation of the search into coarse and fine searching, application of compression to inverted lists, and use of heuristics to reduce index size and query evaluation time.

Our implementation is only preliminary, particularly in contrast with BLAST, but nonetheless the CAFE method is several times faster. On our small test database, of just over 100 Mb, BLAST query evaluation was typically 3 to 11 times slower than CAFE and we would expect that CAFE relative performance would further improve with increasing database size.

Several improvements to our algorithms are possible. We believe that the coarse search can be improved by making further use of offsets to reduce the volume of sequence data inspected and by optimising the index decompression; our current implementation is somewhat slower than, for example, that of the MG text database system [12]. Run-time stopping may also lead to significant improvements. The fine search can be made substantially faster by adoption of local alignment techniques like those used in BLAST. Compression of the stored sequences should also lead to a significant increase in query evaluation speed. These savings will be in addition to the excellent times already observed.

Acknowledgments

We would like to thank Craig Primmer, a geneticist at the Swedish University of Agricultural Sciences (Uppsala). This work was supported by the Australian Research Council, the Cooperative Research Centre for Intelligent Decision Systems, an Australian Postgraduate Award, and the Collaborative Information Technology Research Institute CITRI.

References

1. S. Altschul, M. Boguski, W. Gish, and J. Wootton. Issues in searching molecular sequence databases. *Nature Genetics*, 6:119–129, 1994.
2. S. Altschul, W. Gish, W. Miller, E. Myers, and D. Lipman. Basic local alignment search tool. *Journal of Molecular Biology*, 215:403–410, 1990.
3. S.F. Altschul. A protein alignment scoring system sensitive at all evolutionary distances. *Journal of Molecular Evolution*, 36:290–300, 1993.
4. D. Benson, D.J. Lipman, and J. Ostell. GenBank. *Nucleic Acids Research*, 21(13):2963–2965, 1993.
5. M.J. Cinkosky, J.W. Fickett, P. Gilna, and C. Burks. Electronic data publishing in Genbank. *Science*, 252:1273–1277, 1991.
6. F. Collins and D. Galas. A new five-year plan for the US human genome project. *Science*, 262:43–46, 1993.
7. P. Elias. Universal codeword sets and representations of the integers. *IEEE Transactions on Information Theory*, IT-21(2):194–203, March 1975.
8. S.W. Golomb. Run-length encodings. *IEEE Transactions on Information Theory*, IT–12(3):399–401, July 1966.
9. D.E. Knuth, J.H. Morris, and V.R. Pratt. Fast pattern matching in strings. *SIAM Journal of Computing*, 6:323–350, 1977.
10. D.J. Lipman and W.R. Pearson. Rapid and sensitive protein similarity searches. *Science*, 227:1435–1441, 1985.
11. A. Moffat. Economical inversion of large text files. *Computing Systems*, 5(2):125–139, Spring 1992.
12. A. Moffat and J. Zobel. Self-indexing inverted files for fast text retrieval. *ACM Transactions on Information Systems*. (To appear).
13. A. Moffat and J. Zobel. Parameterised compression for sparse bitmaps. In *Proc. ACM-SIGIR International Conference on Research and Development in Information Retrieval*, pages 274–285, Copenhagen, Denmark, June 1992.

14. E.W. Myers. A sublinear algorithm for approximate keyword searching. *Algorithmica.* (To appear).
15. W.R. Pearson and D.J. Lipman. Improved tools for biological sequence comparison. *Proc. National Academy of Science*, 85:2444–2448, 1988.
16. C.M. Rice, R. Fuchs, D.G. Higgins, P.J. Stoehr, and G.N. Cameron. The EMBL data library. *Nucleic Acids Research*, 21:2967–2971, 1993.
17. G. Salton. *Automatic Text Processing: The Transformation, Analysis, and Retrieval of Information by Computer.* Addison-Wesley, Reading, Massachusetts, 1989.
18. G. Salton and M.J. McGill. *Introduction to Modern Information Retrieval.* McGraw-Hill, New York, 1983.
19. D. Sankoff and J.B. Kruskal, editors. *Time Warps, String Edits, and Macromolecules: The Theory and Practice of Sequence Comparison.* Addison-Wesley, Reading, Massachusetts, 1983.
20. H. Williams and J. Zobel. Practical compression of nucleotide databases. In *Proc. Australian Computer Science Conference*, pages 184–193, Melbourne, Australia, 1996.
21. R.W. Williams. The portable dictionary of the mouse genome: a personal database for gene mapping and molecular biology. *Mammalian Genome*, 5:372–375, 1994.
22. J. Zobel and P. Dart. Finding approximate matches in large lexicons. *Software—Practice and Experience*, 25(3):331–345, March 1995.
23. J. Zobel, A. Moffat, and R. Sacks-Davis. Searching large lexicons for partially specified terms using compressed inverted files. In *Proc. International Conference on Very Large Databases*, pages 290–301, Dublin, Ireland, 1993.

Version Management for Scientific Databases

I-Min A. Chen[1], Victor M. Markowitz[1],
Stanley Letovsky[2], Peter Li[2], and Kenneth H. Fasman[2]

[1] Information and Computing Sciences Division
Lawrence Berkeley National Laboratory, Berkeley, CA 94720
[2] Division of Biomedical Information Sciences
Johns Hopkins University, Baltimore, MD 21205

Abstract. Scientific databases are used to accession objects representing the results of scientific inquiry, such as genes and DNA sequences. These objects must have stable identifiers that can be used as references in scientific papers and other databases. The requirement for stable object identifiers, however, conflicts with the tendency of scientific data to evolve over time. We present in this paper version management facilities that allow scientific databases to achieve a balance between stable object identifiers and evolving data.

1 Introduction

Scientific databases are increasingly being used to accession objects representing the results of scientific inquiry, such as genes and DNA sequences. Accessioning involves providing these objects with stable identifiers that can be included as references in publications (e.g., journal papers) and other scientific databases. This requirement for stable object identifiers can conflict with the tendency of scientific data to evolve over time. By the time a scientist tracks down the scientific object recorded in the database, this object may have disappeared, or changed to the point where it no longer supports the claims made in the associated publications. The traditional literature does not have this problem; a paper once published remains unchanged, even if its claims have been refuted by later papers. A printed paper, however, cannot indicate to scientists whether the claims in the paper were subsequently refuted. Conversely, a database can maintain data representing the current view of scientific observations; however maintaining the stability of references to database objects as the underlying scientific data evolve is a problem.

In this paper, we present version management facilities that allow scientific databases to achieve a balance between stable object identifiers and evolving data, by providing support for:

1. maintaining stable object identifiers, where an identifier represents a particular state in the history of that object but is not rendered meaningless by changes to the object;
2. reconstructing the change history of objects in order to support queries that involve past as well as current object versions;

3. merging objects when they are discovered to represent the same real-world entity;

4. splitting an object that is found to represent more than one real-world entity.

Although these facilities are examined in the context of scientific databases, they can be applied in non-scientific database environments as well.

Versions have been examined in numerous papers dealing with general version management (e.g., [4, 7, 18, 19, 22]), or with versioning for special applications such as office information systems [2], engineering databases [9], CAD applications [1, 6, 13, 15, 16], and multimedia databases [20, 21]. However, the version management facilities mentioned above are not addressed by the versioning mechanisms described in the literature.

The first problem considered in this paper regards keeping track of current (*default*) object versions. Default versions are convenient for supporting generic (rather than version specific) references [4, 16, 19]. For example, suppose that a clinical syndrome, *breast cancer*, is associated with gene *brca1*. If the syndrome references a specific version of *brca1*, then each time *brca1* is revised as new information about the gene is discovered, a new version of the *breast cancer* syndrome needs to be created in order to reflect the change in the referenced gene. If other objects refer to *brca1*, then they may also need to be revised. The concept of default versions allows modeling this situation in a more efficient way using a *generic reference* from syndromes to the current versions of genes. In order to reconstruct a past database state at time t, the default versions of all versioned objects must be recorded so that past generic references to a versioned object x can refer to the default version of x at time t instead of referencing the last specified default version of x. We show in this paper that reconstructing the change history of objects in the context of generic references requires maintaining a history of default versions in addition to, and separate from, the history of each version.

The second problem addressed in this paper involves managing versions in class hierarchies. Version management for class hierarchies has to take into account the fact that an object can belong to multiple classes and therefore its versions can involve values of both local and inherited attributes. For example, consider data on authors of scientific references and citations. Let class AUTHOR be a subclass of class PERSON, and suppose that at time t_1 PERSON contains a version of object p; at time t_2, p becomes an object of class AUTHOR, and a new version of p is created. The version of p before t involves only the values of the attributes of PERSON, while the version of p after t involves the values of the attributes of both PERSON and AUTHOR. We show that if an object x belongs to multiple classes of a class hierarchy, then determining the values of all the versioned attributes of x at any given time t, requires a mechanism for combining versions of x across the classes containing x.

Finally, we consider the requirement for version derivations spanning different objects. The versioning mechanisms discussed in the literature do not support merging versions of different objects into a version of another object, or splitting a version of an object into versions of new objects. Such object merging and splitting is required for modeling the evolution of database objects representing imperfectly known real-world entities, such as those resulting from scientific observations.

Consider, for example, a class GENE representing genes and having an attribute, Location, representing the location of the gene on a chromosome. Let *brca* be an object of GENE: gene *brca* has two versions, v and v', where v' is created in order to record a change of Location and is derived from v. A gene that was initially considered a distinct object can subsequently turn out to be a conflation of two genes. For example, suppose that it is discovered that *brca* represents in fact two genes, *brca1* and *brca2*. This can be represented in the database by splitting version v' of *brca* into two new versions of *brca1* and *brca2*, respectively. We propose version management facilities that allow modeling version merging and splitting across different objects.

The rest of the paper is organized as follows. Section 2 briefly describes an object data model that supports selective versioning (i.e., non-versioned and versioned attributes) as well as generic and specific version references. Version defaults are examined in section 3. Version management in class hierarchies is discussed in section 4. In section 5 we examine the version management facilities that support version derivations across different objects. Section 6 contains concluding remarks.

2 An Object Data Model with Versions

In this section, we review the main constructs of an object data model whose non-versioned part is closely related to other semantic [11, 12] and object data models [3]. The version constructs of this data model follow [19].

Objects in our object data model are uniquely identified by object identifiers (oids), are qualified by attributes, and are classified into classes. A subset of the attributes associated with a class is specified as the external object identifier (ID). A class can be defined as a subclass of other (super) classes, where a subclass *inherits* the attributes of its superclasses. Examples of object classes are shown in Fig. 1.

Attributes can be *simple* or consist of a *tuple* of simple attributes (e.g., Location of GENE). A simple attribute can have a single value, a set of values, or a list of values, and can be *primitive*, if it is associated with a system-provided data type, or *abstract*, if it takes values from object classes (e.g., References of BOOK).

The attributes of an object class can be partitioned into *non-versioned* and *versioned* attributes. Non-versioned attributes represent stable object properties (e.g., SSN of PERSON), while versioned attributes represent evolving object properties of an object (e.g., Address of PERSON). A versioned abstract attribute can have a *generic reference* to current (default) object versions (e.g., References of BOOK) or a *specific reference* to specific object versions (e.g., Studies of SCIENTIST).

The structure of non-versioned objects in an object class is defined below.

```
OBJECT CLASS PERSON
  ID: SSN
  ATTRIBUTE              SSN: CHAR(11)              not null
  ATTRIBUTE              Name: CHAR(50)
  VERSIONED  ATTRIBUTE Address: CHAR(150)
OBJECT CLASS SCIENTIST isa PERSON
  VERSIONED  ATTRIBUTE Rank: CHAR(50)
  VERSIONED  ATTRIBUTE Studies: set-of specific GENE
OBJECT CLASS GENE
  ID: Name
  ATTRIBUTE              Name: CHAR(10)             not null
  VERSIONED ATTRIBUTE  Location (Chromosome, Position): (CHROMOSOME,INT)
OBJECT CLASS CHROMOSOME
  ID: Number
  ATTRIBUTE              Number: CHAR(2)            not null
OBJECT CLASS BOOK
  ID: ISBN
  ATTRIBUTE              ISBN: CHAR(30)             not null
  ATTRIBUTE              Title: CHAR(150)
  VERSIONED  ATTRIBUTE References: set-of GENE
```

Fig. 1. Examples of Object Classes

Definition 1. Let O be an object class and x be an instance of O. Then $x = (oid(x), val(x))$, where $oid(x)$ is the globally unique object identifier of x and $val(x)$ is the value of x. $oid(x)$ takes values from a class of object identifiers. $val(x)$ has the form $(A_1 : A_1(x), \ldots, A_n : A_n(x))$, where A_j, $1 \leq j \leq n$, is the name of an attribute of O, and $A_j(x)$ denotes the value of attribute A_j for x and is defined as follows:

1. If A_j is a simple attribute then: (i) if A_j is a primitive attribute then $A_j(x)$ consists of a value, a set of values, or a list of values of the data type associated with A_j, or (ii) if A_j is an abstract attribute taking values from class O_k, then $A_j(x)$ consists of one element, a set of elements, or a list of elements from $\{ oid(y) \mid y \in O_k \}$.
2. If $A_j = (A_{j_1}, \ldots, A_{j_n})$, then $A_j(x)$ consists of a tuple, a set of tuples, or a list of tuples of the form $[A_{j_1}(x), \ldots, A_{j_n}(x)]$, where each component $A_{j_k}(x)$, $j_1 \leq j_k \leq j_n$, consists of an element of the form defined in 1 above.

A version of an object x consists of the values of the non-versioned attributes for x (common to all versions of x) and the values of versioned attributes for a specific version of x. An object with multiple versions has a *default* version which is selected from the set of versions for that object.

The structure of versioned objects in an object class is defined below.

Definition 2. Let O be a versioned object class and x be an instance of O. Then $x = (oid(x), val(x), \{ (vid(x_i), vval(x_i)) \})$, where $oid(x)$ is the globally unique object identifier of x, $val(x)$ is the non-versioned value of x, $vid(x_i)$ is a unique version identifier for version x_i of x, $vval(x_i)$ is a versioned value for version x_i of x. $oid(x)$ and $val(x)$ are defined as in Definition 1 above. $vid(x_i)$ takes values from a class of version identifiers. $vval(x_i)$ has the form $(A_1 : A_1(x_i)$, ..., $A_n : A_n(x_i))$, where A_j, $1 \leq j \leq n$, is the name of a versioned attribute of O, and $A_j(x_i)$ denotes the value of A_j for version x_i and is defined as follows:

1. If A_j is a simple versioned attribute then: (i) if A_j is a primitive attribute then $A_j(x)$ consists of a value, a set of values, or a list of values of the data type associated with A_j, or (ii) if A_j is an abstract attribute taking values from class O_k, then $A_j(x_i)$ consists of one element, a set of elements, or a list of elements from $\{ (oid(y), vid(y_m)) \mid y \in O_k, y_m$ is a version of $y \}$.
2. If $A_j = (A_{j_1}, ..., A_{j_n})$, then $A_j(x_i)$ consists of a tuple, a set of tuples, or a list of tuples of the form $[A_{j_1}(x_i), ..., A_{j_n}(x_i)]$, where each component $A_{j_k}(x_i)$, $j_1 \leq j_k \leq j_n$, consists of an element of the form defined in 1 above.

A version x_v of x is defined as $(oid(x), val(x), vid(x_v), vval(x_v))$.

Version Management. Keeping track of object versions involves maintaining the following additional non-versioned system (i.e., system provided) attributes, for each object instance, x, where the values of these attributes are included in $val(x)$:

1. **defaultVersion** (x) consists of the identifier(s) of the default version(s) of x;
2. **deleteDate** (x) indicates the date/time x was marked as deleted.

The following versioned system attributes are also maintained for each version x_v of x, where the values of these attributes are included in $vval(x_v)$:

1. **fromDate** (x_v) indicates the date/time x_v was created;
2. **preVer** (x_v) consists of the identifier(s) of the predecessor version(s) of x_v;
3. **vdeleteDate** (x_v) indicates the date/time x_v was marked as deleted.

We assume that versioned objects and their versions are not physically deleted from the database, but only marked as (logically) deleted.

Version management data change as a result of data manipulations, such as creating a new version, editing or deleting an object, etc, or version operations such as setting a version default. The operations needed for version management include (t_{now} denotes the current date/time):

1. $x = $ **new**() for creating a new versioned object, x, together with its first version, x_0; $val(x)$ includes: **defaultVersion**$(x) = vid(x_0)$, **deleteDate**(x) = null; $vval(x_0)$ includes **fromDate**$(x_0) = t_{now}$, **preVer**(x_0) = null, **vdeleteDate**(x_0) = null.
2. $x_v = $ **new**($x_{i_1}, x_{i_2}, ..., x_{i_m}$), for creating a new version of object x, x_v, from one ($m = 1$) or several ($m > 1$) versions of x; $val(x)$ does not change; $vval(x_v)$ includes **fromDate**$(x_v) = t_{now}$, **vdeleteDate**(x_v) = null, **preVer**(x_v) consists of $vid(x_{i_1}), ..., vid(x_{i_m})$.
3. **ldelete_object**(x) for logically deleting instance x; **deleteDate**(x) and **vdeleteDate**(x_i) for all versions x_i of x are set to t_{now}.

4. **set_default**(x, x_v) for setting version x_v as the default version of x; **defaultVersion**(x) is set to $vid(x_v)$.

In addition, version management is involved in retrieval operations in a versioned database. We consider in this paper two such operations:

1. **get_all**($oid(x)$) for retrieving all versions of object x.
2. **get**($oid(x)$ [,$vid(x_v)$]) for retrieving version x_v of object x; if $vid(x_v)$ is not specified, then the default version of x is retrieved.

3 Default Versions

We consider in this paper versioned databases that require maintaining a lossless and consistent object history. We assume that all objects have at least one (initial) version, and that versioned objects and their versions are not physically removed (deleted) from the database. Object history losslessness guarantees recoverability of past states, while its consistency regards the validity of object references in each (i.e., past or current) database state. Thus, a database state at a given time t involves only references between objects and object versions that are not logically deleted at t; however, logical deletion of objects and object versions preserves past references to these objects and object versions.

The state of a versioned database is defined below.

Definition 3. A database state at (past or current) time t, $DS(t)$, consists of all objects, x, that are not logically deleted at t, (i.e., **deleteDate**(x) $> t$ or **deleteDate**(x) is null) and their versions, x_i, such that:

1. x_i is not logically deleted at t, that is, **vdeleteDate**(x_i) $> t$ or **vdeleteDate**(x_i) is null;
2. x_i has been created before or at t, that is, **fromDate**(x_i) $\leq t$; and
3. the attribute values for x_i are specified as specified in Definition 2 of section 2, where the value of a versioned abstract attribute of x, A, with generic reference to default (current) versions of objects in class O, consists of the version identifiers of the default versions of O objects at time t.

We examine in the rest of this section the problem of determining the default object versions at a given time t in a versioned database.

In a versioned database, usually one or more versions are selected from the set of versions of an object as its *default* versions. For simplicity, we assume below that at any given time t, an object can have only one default version. The default version of an object x is not necessarily the last one created, and it can be changed by setting another version as the new default for x.

Generic references to a versioned object automatically refer to its default version and are not invalidated when the referenced object or its default version are modified. Thus, the versions of an object x referencing the default version of object y are not affected by changes of y, including the replacement or deletion of the default of y. It is important to note, however, that the value of a versioned attribute with a generic reference depends on the time the value is evaluated. Consider two instances of object classes BOOK and GENE, as shown in Fig. 2, where BOOK has versioned attribute References referencing default (current) versions of GENE. For example, at time t_4 version x_2 of instance x of BOOK references default version y_4 of instance y of GENE (see Fig. 2). At a previous time, t (e.g., between t_0 and t_2), another version of x, x_0, was referencing the default version(s) of y at t rather than referencing the default version of y at t_4. Thus, at time t_1, x_0 could have referenced version y_0, y_1, or y_2 of y, depending on which one of these versions was the default version of y at t_1. Consequently, the history of default versions for each object needs to be maintained in order to infer the database state at any given time. If only one default version is allowed for each versioned object at any given time (as it is usually done), the default version history is linear (i.e., totally ordered), as shown in Fig. 2.

Default Version Management. Keeping track of the history of default versions for an object x requires maintaining an additional non-versioned tuple system attribute, defaultHistory [defaultVer, defaultStart, defaultEnd], where:

1. defaultVer (x) identifies a (current or old) default version of x, x_v;
2. defaultStart (x_v) indicates the date/time version x_v was selected as default version;
3. defaultEnd (x_v) indicates the date/time version x_v ceased to be a default version.

For example, the default history for GENE y is characterized as follows:
   defaultVer y_0: defaultStart = t_0, defaultEnd = t_1;
   defaultVer y_2: defaultStart = t_1, defaultEnd = t_3;
   defaultVer y_3: defaultStart = t_3, defaultEnd = t_4;
   defaultVer y_4: defaultStart = t_4, defaultEnd = null.

With the history of default versions properly maintained, a versioned database state at any given time t can be easily determined. The default version for an

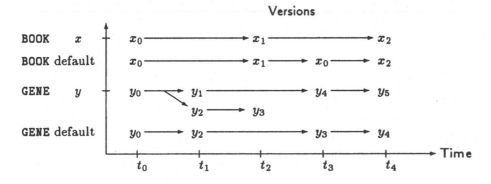

Fig. 2. Default Versions

object x at time t is the version x_v in the default history of x that has a pair (defaultStart(x_v), defaultEnd(x_v)) satisfying the following condition:

defaultStart(x_v) $\leq t$ and (defaultEnd(x_v) = null or defaultEnd(x_v) > t).

For example, for the objects and versions shown in Fig. 2, database state $DS(t_1)$ consists of instance x of BOOK with version x_0, and instance y of GENE with versions y_0, y_1 and y_2, where version x_0 of x references version y_2 of y, the default version of y at t_1.

4 Versions in Class Hierarchies

We examine in this section version management for objects belonging to multiple classes of a class hierarchy.

Consider an object class, O_i, and let x be an object of O_i. Suppose that changes to attribute values of x, where these attributes are associated directly with (i.e., are not inherited from) O_i, lead to the creation of a new version of x only in O_i, even if x belongs to other classes (e.g., a subclass of O_i). The following example shows that such a versioning mechanism is not sufficient for determining the state of x at a given time, t, that is, the values of all the attributes of x, including its inherited attributes, at t.

<u>Example 1.</u> (Fig. 3.) Consider class PERSON with versioned attribute Address, and subclass SCIENTIST of PERSON, with versioned attributes Rank and Studies.

Suppose that initially (i.e., at time t_0) instance x (version x'_0) is a PERSON object but not a SCIENTIST object. Subsequently (at time $t_1 > t_0$), x becomes a SCIENTIST object (version x''_0). Note that x'_0 and x''_0 have different creation times and involve different attribute values of x.

Later (at time $t_2 > t_1$), the Studies value of x changes and therefore a new version (x''_1) of x in SCIENTIST is created, but without creating a new version of x in PERSON. Then (at $t_3 > t_2$), the Address value of x changes and therefore a new version (x'_1) of x in PERSON is created, without creating a new version of x in SCIENTIST. Finally (at $t_4 > t_3$), the Rank value of x changes and therefore a new version (x''_2) of x in SCIENTIST is created.

Assuming that versions of an object x belonging to a class O_i involve only the values of the attributes associated directly with (i.e., not inherited by) O_i, if x belongs to multiple classes, O_i, $1 \leq i \leq m$, of a class hierarchy, then the state

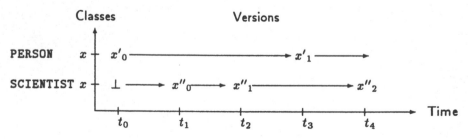

Fig. 3. Local Versions in Example 1

of x must be characterized by its versions in these classes. Note that version management data for versions of x in different classes must be maintained separately. However, some version management data (e.g., defaultVersion) must be synchronized across the classes of a class hierarchy. For the versions shown in Fig. 3, for example, it may not make sense to set version x'_1 as the default of PERSON x and version x''_0 as the default of SCIENTIST x.

Global Versions. An object belonging to multiple classes of a class hierarchy can be viewed as having *global* versions that involve all the attributes associated with these classes, where a global version of an object x is defined as the association of x versions that are local to the classes containing x. Note that a local version of x can be involved in several global versions of x.

Example 2. (Fig. 4.) Consider classes PERSON and SCIENTIST from the previous example. Suppose that initially (i.e., at time t_0) x is a PERSON (global version x_0, local version x'_0), but not a SCIENTIST object. Later, at time t_1, x becomes a SCIENTIST object (local version x''_0). A new global version, x_1, is defined as the association of local versions x'_0 and x''_0.

Subsequently, at time t_2, the Studies value of x changes and therefore a new local version, x''_1, of x in SCIENTIST is created; a new global version, x_2, is defined as the association of x'_0 and x''_1. At t_3, the Address value of x changes and therefore a new local version x'_1 of x in PERSON is created; global version x_3 is defined as the association of x'_1 and x''_1. Finally, at t_4, the Rank value of x changes and therefore a new local version, x''_2, of x in SCIENTIST is created; global version x_4 is defined as the association of x'_1 and x''_2.

Version Management. Version management data, such as the values of system attributes defaultVersion and preVer, refer to global versions. Similarly, version operations such as version creation and retrieval, refer to global versions.

Let x be an object belonging to multiple classes of a class hierarchy. A version of x local to a class in this hierarchy, x_i, continues to be identified by a unique version identifier, $vid(x_i)$ (see Definition 2 of section 2), while a global version of x, x_k, is identified by a global version identifier, $gvid(x_k)$.

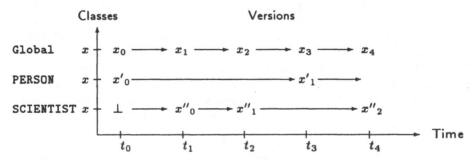

Fig. 4. Global and Local Versions in Example 2

The following additional version data are kept for each global version x_k of x: $\{ (gvid(x_k), lvid(x_k)) \}$, where $gvid(x_k)$ identifies global version x_k and $lvid(x_k)$ consists of the set of identifiers for the local versions associated with x_k. A global version of an object x is constructed by combining its associated local versions, as discussed below.

Creating, editing, deleting, and retrieving global versions involve creating, editing, deleting, and retrieving one or several local versions. Thus, retrieving (the attribute values of) a global version x_k of an object x, involves retrieving the local versions whose identifiers are associated with $gvid(x_k)$. For example, suppose that x_4 is the default global version of x in example 2 (see Fig. 4). Then $get(oid(x))$, which retrieves the default global version of x, consists of retrieving version x'_1 of PERSON and version x''_2 of SCIENTIST and then constructing x_4 from the attribute values of x'_1 and x''_2.

Alternative ways of maintaining global versions of an object x include:

(i) Keeping different identifiers for local and global versions, so that for a global version x_k associated with local versions x_{i1}, ..., x_{im}, $gvid(x_k)$ and $vid(x_{ij})$, $1 \leq j \leq m$, are distinct. This alternative requires maintaining global version identifiers and their association with local version identifiers, but limits local version creation to the classes associated with the attributes affected by a change.

(ii) Using common identifiers for local and global versions, so that $vid(x_i)$ would identify both local version x_i and the global version associated with x_i. This alternative involves a simpler version maintenance (and simpler version operations), but may entail data duplication. For an object instance x, for example, changes of the versioned attributes of x in class O_i, entail creating a new global version of x, x_n, identified by $vid(x_n)$, a new local version of x in O_i as well as new local versions in each class containing x, all identified by $vid(x_n)$.

5   Extended Version Derivations

Traditionally, different objects in a versioned database, that is, objects with distinct identifiers, are considered to represent different entities in the underlying application. In such a database, versions can be derived only from other versions of the same object and can be tracked back to one initial version of that object. If the version derivation for each object is represented by a directed acyclic graph (DAG),[3] then such DAGs have single roots representing the first version of each object, and DAGs representing versions of different objects are disconnected.

Traditional version derivation is not adequate to model the evolution of scientific database objects that often represent imperfectly known real-world entities.

---

[3] The nodes in the DAG represent versions and directed edges represent the derivation of the versions represented by their end nodes, from the versions represented by their start nodes.

In molecular biology, for example, it is not uncommon that two genes identified by distinct methods, and therefore represented by different objects in the database, are eventually found to be identical; or that experimental results indicate that what has been considered to be a single gene, represented by a single object in the database, is in fact a conflation of two genes. Modeling the evolution of scientific database objects representing such entities requires an extended version derivation.

Extended Version Derivations. The purpose of extended version derivations is to allow (i) creating (deriving) new objects in a class from versions of other objects in the same class, and (ii) setting versions of certain objects as defaults of the objects they have been derived from. Accordingly, the version management data associated with each object x of a versioned class O is modified as follows:

1. preVer (x_0) (predecessor of the initial version of x) can be either null or can consist of one or several pairs of the form $(oid(y), vid(y_i))$, where for each y, y belongs to O, y_i is a version of y, and $oid(y) \neq oid(x)$;
2. defaultVersion (x) (the default version for x) can either be null or consist of one or several pairs of the form $(oid(y), vid(y_i))$ or $(oid(y), *)$, where for each y, y belongs to O, y_i is a version of y, and '$*$' stands for defaultVersion(y).

Version Management. In order to support extended version derivation, the operations for creating new objects and for setting defaults (see section 2) must be extended as follows;

1. $x = \text{new}([y_i, \ldots, z_j])$ creates a new versioned object of class O, x, together with its first version, x_0; y_i, $\ldots$, z_j, represent versions of other objects of O, y, $\ldots$, z; $val(x)$ includes: defaultVersion$(x) = vid(x_0)$, and deleteDate(x) = null; $vval(x_0)$ includes: fromDate$(x_0) = t_{now}$, vdeleteDate (x_0) = null, and preVer(x_0) which is either null or (if y_i, $\ldots$, z_j, are specified) consists of $(oid(y), vid(y_i))$, $\ldots$, $(oid(z), vid(z_j))$. Attribute values for x can be selected from the corresponding attribute values of $y_i, \ldots, z_j$, or can be assigned new values.
2. set_default(x, y, y_i) sets the version identified by the pair $(oid(y), vid(y_i))$ as the default version of x, where either $oid(y) = oid(x)$ or preVer (y_0) contains $(oid(x), vid(x_k))$, and x_k is a version of x;
   set_default$(x, y, *)$ sets the default version of y as the default version of x (so that whenever the default version of y is changed, the new default version of y becomes the default version of x), where preVer (y_0) contains $(oid(x), vid(x_k))$, and x_k is a version of x.

If an object y in class O is derived from another object of O, x, then specific references to (old) versions of x are allowed. However, whether generic references to current default versions of x are allowed or not can be application specific, and include the the following alternatives:

(i) x is not affected by the creation of a new object y from x, and therefore generic references to default (current) versions of x are allowed; these generic references refer to versions of x identified by the values of defaultVersion(x);

(ii) after the creation of a new object y from x, x is not considered valid anymore, and therefore references to default (current) versions of x are disallowed; or

(iii) the creation of a new object y from x is considered to represent the replacement of x by y, and therefore generic references to default versions of x automatically refer to the default version of y.

Alternative (i) is straightforward. Alternative (ii) can be carried out by setting defaultVersion(x) to null. Alternative (iii) can be carried out by setting defaultVersion(x) to $(oid(y), *)$, by set_default($x, y, *$).

Operations get_all and get will take into account the extended version management data. For example, suppose that object x has versions x_0, x_1 and x_2, and that at time t a new object y (version y_0) is derived from x_2. If alternative (ii) above is followed, then get_all($oid(x)$) returns x_0, x_1 and x_2, while get($oid(x)$) returns null. If alternative (iii) above is followed, then get_all($oid(x)$) returns x_0, x_1, x_2 and y_0, while get($oid(x)$) returns y_0.

Object Merging and Splitting. Version derivations spanning different objects allow modeling new operations based on objects, such as the object merging and object splitting discussed below.

Consider two instances of class GENE, instance x with versions x_0 and x_1, and instance y with versions y_0, y_1, and y_2, as shown in Fig. 5. Suppose that eventually instances x and y are found to represent the same gene. Then objects x and y can be *merged* into a new object, z, of GENE, by creating its initial version (z_0) from version x_1 of x and version y_2 of y. Note that version z_0 can be specified with non-versioned attribute values that are different from the non-versioned attribute values of x and y, can preserve (some of) the non-versioned attribute values of x or y. Note also that specifying a new version in this example involves specifying attribute values for the new version by possibly selecting versioned attribute values from x or y, or by assigning new values to the versioned attributes. A special case of object merging consists of creating a new version of an existing object, x, from another version of x and versions of other objects, such as y: this represents merging objects such as y, into x.

Similarly, consider an instance of class GENE, x, with versions x_0 and x_1, as shown in Fig. 6, and suppose that it is discovered subsequently that in fact x

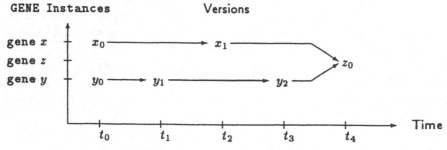

Fig. 5. Example of Merging Versions of Different Objects

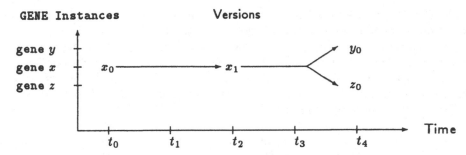

Fig. 6. Example of Splitting a Version into Versions of New Objects

represents a conflation of two genes. Then, x can be split into two new instances of class **GENE**, y and z, by creating these instances from version x_1 of x (see Fig. 6). A special case of version splitting is object cloning, where a version of a single new object, y, is created from a version of an existing object x.

Object merging and splitting can be used to correct the database representation of entities that cease to be current in the underlying application and therefore are superseded by other (current) entities. Object merging and splitting can be achieved using the extended **new** operation discussed above. The default of the merged or split object can be set as the default of the new objects created by merging or splitting, so that generic references to objects representing past objects will automatically point to current (default) versions of objects representing current objects.

For example, in Fig. 6, both y_0 and z_0 are versions of new objects created (derived) from version x_1 of object x. The default of object x, can be set to null, or can consist of the default version of y, the default version of z, or both. For version merging, the default of the merged objects (e.g., x and y in the example above) can be set to null or to the default of the object created by merging, z.

6 Concluding Remarks

While addressing general object version management problems, the facilities discussed in this paper were developed in order to support versioning in scientific (e.g., molecular biology, epidemiology) databases.

Part of the version management facilities presented in this paper have been incorporated into an object data model underlying a suite of data management tools used for developing scientific databases [5]. Since numerous scientific databases[4] are developed with commercial relational database management sys-

---

[4] For example, the Genome Data Base (GDB) at the Johns Hopkins School of Medicine, the Genome Sequence Data Base (GSDB) at the National Center for Genome Resources, the Protein Data Bank (PDB) at Brookhaven National Laboratory, Flybase at Harvard University, and the Mouse Genome Database (MGD) at Jackson Laboratory.

302

tems (DBMSs),[5] these facilities were implemented using relational constructs. Scientific databases often contain large amounts of data, therefore object versioning can lead to a substantial increase in their size and thus degrade their performance. We are currently experimenting with alternative relational implementations of the version management facilities discussed in this paper. where the overhead entailed by version management cannot be allowed to degrade the performance of the underlying databases.

Acknowledgements. The work of I-Min A. Chen and Victor M. Markowitz was supported by the Office of Health and Environmental Research Program of the Office of Energy Research, U.S. Department of Energy under Contract DE-AC03-76SF00098. The work of Stanley Letovsky, Peter Li, and Kenneth H. Fasman was supported in part by DOE award number DE-FC02-91ER61230. We want to thank the anonymous referees for their valuable suggestions.

References

1. Ahmed, R., Navathe, S.B. Version Management of Composite Objects in CAD Databases. *Proceedings of the ACM SIGMOD Conference* (1991), 218–227.
2. Banerjee, J. et al. Data Model Issues for Object-Oriented Applications. *ACM Transactions on Office Information Systems* 5, 1 (January 1987), 3–26.
3. Bancilhon, F., Delobel. C., Kanellakis, P. Building an Object-Oriented Database System: The Story of O_2. Morgan Kaufmann Publishers, Inc. (1992).
4. Beech, D., Mahbod, B. Generalized Version Control in an Object-Oriented Database. *Proceedings of the 5th International Conference on Data Engineering* (1988), 14–22.
5. Chen, I.A., Markowitz, V.M.: An Overview of the Object-Protocol Model (OPM) and the OPM Data Management Tools. Information Systems 20, 5 (1995) 393–417. Additional information available on the World Wide Web at http://gizmo.lbl.gov/opm.html.
6. Chou, H.-T., Kim, W. A Unified Framework for Version Control in a CAD Environment. *Proceedings of the 12th International Conference on Very Large Data Bases* (1986), 336–344.
7. Dadam, P., Lum, V., Werner, H.-D. Integration of Time Versions into a Relational Database System. *Proceedings of the 10th International Conference on Very Large Data Bases* (1984), 509–522.
8. Date, C.J. Referential Integrity, in *Relational Database – Selected Writings.* Addison-Wesley (1986).
9. Dittrich, K.R., Lorie, R.A. Version Support for Engineering Database Systems. *IEEE Trans. on Software Engineering* 14, 4 (April 1988), 429–437.
10. Goodman, N. An Object-Oriented DBMS War Story: Developing a Genome Mapping Database in C++. In W. Kim (ed.), *Modern Database Management: Object-Oriented and Multidatabase Techniques*, ACM Press (1994), 216–237.

---

[5] For large archival scientific databases, commercial relational DBMSs are often considered more robust and efficient than object-oriented and object-relational DBMSs. See [10] for an account of problems encountered developing a scientific database with an object-oriented DBMS.

11. Hammer, M., McLeod, D. Database Description with SDM: A Semantic Database Model. *ACM Trans. on Database Systems* **6**, 3, (September 1981), 351–386.
12. Hull, R., King, R. Semantic Database Modeling: Survey, Applications, and Research Issues. *ACM Computing Surveys* **19**, 3 (September 1987), 201–260.
13. Käfer, W., Schöning, H. Mapping a Version Model to a Complex-Object Data Model. *Proceedings of the 8th International Conference on Data Engineering* (1992), 348–357.
14. Katz, R.H., Chang, E., Bhateja, R. Version Modeling Concepts for Computer-Aided Design Databases. *Proceedings of the ACM SIGMOD Conference* (1986), 379–386.
15. Katz, R.H., Chang, E. Managing Change in a Computer-Aided Design Database. *Proceedings of the 13th International Conference on Very Large Data Bases* (1987), 455–462.
16. Katz, R.H. Toward a Unified Framework for Version Modeling in Engineering Databases. *ACM Computing Surveys* **22**, 4 (December 1990), 375–408.
17. Kim, W., et al. Composite Object Support in an Object-Oriented Database System. *Proceedings of the OOPSLA '87 Conference* (1987).
18. Klahold, P., Schlageter, G., and Wilkes, W. A General Model for Version Management in Databases. *Proceedings of the 12th International Conference on Very Large Data Bases* (1986), 319–327.
19. Sciore, E. Versioning and Configuration Management in an Object-Oriented Data Model. *VLDB Journal* **3** (1994), 77–106.
20. Woelk, D., Kim, W., Luther, W. An Object-Oriented Approach to Multimedia Databases. *Proceedings of the ACM SIGMOD Conference* (1986), 311–325.
21. Woelk, D., Kim, W. Multimedia Information Management in an Object-Oriented Database System. *Proceedings of the 13th International Conference on Very Large Data Bases* (1987), 319–329.
22. Zdonik, S.B. Version Management in an Object-Oriented Database. *Proceedings of the International Workshop on Advanced Programming Environments* (1986), 405–422.

Temporal Databases

First-Order Queries over Temporal Databases Inexpressible in Temporal Logic*

David Toman[†] and Damian Niwiński[‡]

Department of Computer Science, University of Toronto
Toronto, Ontario M5S 1A4, Canada

Institute of Informatics, Warsaw University
Banacha 2, 00-950 Warsaw, Poland

Abstract. Queries over temporal databases involve references to time. We study differences between two approaches of including such references into a first-order query language (e.g., relational calculus): explicit (using typed variables and quantifiers) vs. implicit (using a finite set of modal connectives). We also show that though the latter approach—a first-order query language with implicit references to time—is appealing by its simplicity and ease of use, it cannot express all queries expressible using the first one in general. This result also settles a longstanding open problem about the expressive power of first-order temporal logic. A consequence of this result is that there is no first-order complete query language subquery-closed with respect to a uniform database schema, and thus we cannot use temporal relational algebra over uniform relations to evaluate all first-order definable queries.

1 Introduction

In the last several years, various languages for querying temporal databases have been proposed in the literature. The first-order query languages can be divided into two main categories:

1. query languages based on a two-sorted version of relational calculus, e.g., TSQL2 [20] or TQUEL [19], and

2. query languages based on an extension of the relational calculus or algebra by temporal operators, e.g, HRDM's historical relational algebra [6], temporal relational algebra [23], etc.

These two approaches have been often considered equivalent in expressive power, e.g., in [23], where the temporal relational algebra based on an extension of the relational calculus by temporal operators has been proposed as a basis for first-order completeness of temporal query languages. This assumption was based on a well-known property of propositional temporal logic:

---

* Preliminary version of the results has been presented at the *Pre-PODS'95 Workshop on Theory of Constraint Databases*, TR UNL-CSE-95-08.

† Research conducted while this author was at the Dept. of Comp. and Info. Science, Kansas State University, Manhattan, KS 66506, U.S.A., david@cis.ksu.edu.

‡ Supported by Polish KBN grant 2 P301 009 06.

Proposition 1.1 (Kamp's Theorem) *Propositional temporal logic has an expressively complete set of temporal connectives over linear orders.*

This means that the propositional temporal logic has the same expressive power as the monadic first-order logic over linear orders. This result has been established by Kamp [15] for complete linear orders, later extended by Stavi [22] for all linear orders, and reproven several times using various proof techniques, e.g, [10, 14]. In this paper we show that this correspondence does *not* generalize to the relationship between the First-order Temporal Logic (FOTL) and the Two-sorted First-order Logic (2-FOL). The query languages based on 2-FOL are strictly more expressive than the languages based on FOTL *for any finite set of temporal connectives* defined over a (dense) linear order. We show that FOTL cannot express a large class of queries that involve references to several time instants, like equality of database relations at two different time instants. The result can be interpreted as

> *Temporal query languages cannot be simultaneously subquery-closed[1] and first-order complete.*

Such a result has strong implications for the design of temporal query languages: essentially all subquery-closed relational algebra-like languages are incomplete, while all complete relational calculus-like languages do not preserve closure. This is a problem from the implementation point of view: while the subquery-closed query languages are easier to implement, essentially because all intermediate results in a bottom-up query evaluation have the same structure as database relations, there are first-order queries that cannot be formulated in such languages. Despite this drawback, FOTL was used as a basis of temporal query languages [23] or for specification of temporal integrity constraints [3, 4, 5, 17]. The main reason for this choice is a simpler and more efficient implementation that does not generalize to full FOTL. The design of an expressively complete Temporal Relational Algebra requires an unbounded number of temporal attributes in the relations to guarantee completeness and preserve closure of products [21]. However, such solution does not allow to store the intermediate results needed to evaluate the query in a uniform temporal database as auxiliary relations. In addition to the separation of FOTL from 2-FOL we show several other results, especially:

1. Expressive equivalence of the *future* temporal logic and the *full* temporal logic, i.e., with both future and past temporal connectives [12] does not generalize to the first-order case.
2. Expressive completeness cannot be achieved using more general temporal logic, e.g., the many-dimensional first-order temporal logic [13].

Note also that we restrict our attention solely to the first-order languages. Thus any higher-order properties (e.g., the *even cardinality* property of relations given in [25]) are not expressible in either 2-FOL or FOTL.

---

[1] Assuming closure with respect to the database schema, where all the temporal relations, including derived ones, have exactly one temporal attribute or, in general, a bounded number of such attributes. This is a natural restriction imposed on virtually all practical temporal databases [21], e.g., on the timestamp relations in TSQL2 or TQUEL.

The rest of the paper is organized as follows: Section 2 introduces the formal definition of the temporal database and first-order temporal query languages over such databases. Section 3 introduces a model-theoretic games that allow us to study the expressive power of FOTL. In Section 4 we use these games to show our main result: FOTL⊊2-FOL. Section 5 shows several other non-expressibility results that can be established using games. In the last section of this paper we summarize the obtained results and conclude with the directions of further research.

2 Temporal Structures and Query Languages

In this section we define the precise notion of a temporal database as a temporal structure. We also define two query languages based on extensions of the first-order relational calculus.

2.1 Temporal Databases as Temporal Structures

The standard relational database can be viewed as a model-theoretic structure. For any given database schema the structure contains a finite relation over the database domain for every relational symbol in the database schema, together with the relations defined on the domain itself such as equality (such relations can be thought as *built-in* relations and their interpretation is fixed). It is also well known that relational calculus queries over such database can be thought of as formulas in a first-order language over the same set of symbols.

This model can be naturally extended to a *temporal relational database model* by augmenting every relation symbol in the database schema by an additional attribute that holds the time instant at which the original tuple is true. This extension is formally introduced in [2] and can serve as a unifying platform for various alternative approaches to the definition of temporal databases [7]. Similarly to the standard relational case such temporal databases can be treated as model-theoretic structures, in this case two-sorted.

The temporal structures considered in this section are built from the following three basic building blocks:

1. a first-order signature $\langle \rho_1, \ldots, \rho_n \rangle$ and a first-order structure $\langle T; \rho_1^T, \ldots, \rho_n^T \rangle$ to serve as the *temporal domain*.
2. a first-order signature $\langle p_1, \ldots, p_l \rangle$ and a first-order structure $\langle D; p_1^D, \ldots, p_l^D \rangle$ to serve as the *data domain* of the database.
3. a single-sorted set of predicate symbols $\langle r_1, \ldots, r_m \rangle$; the arity of the symbol r_i is v_i. This choice defines the *database schema* for our temporal database.

This arrangement abstracts from the particular choice of the data and temporal domains and thus allows a wide range of applications of the proposed method.

In the rest of this section we use γ to denote the signature $\langle \rho_1, \ldots, \rho_n \rangle$ of the temporal domain, δ for the signature $\langle p_1, \ldots, p_l \rangle$ of the data domain, and σ for the signature $\langle r_1, \ldots, r_m \rangle$ of the database schema.

Definition 2.1 (Uniform Temporal Database) *Let* $\langle T, \rho_1^T, \ldots, \rho_n^T \rangle$ *be a temporal domain (signature γ), $\langle D; p_1^D, \ldots, p_l^D \rangle$ a data domain (signature δ), and $\sigma = \langle r_1, \ldots, r_m \rangle$ a database schema. We define R_i to be two-sorted relation symbols of the sort $T \times D^{v_i}$ for each r_i in the database schema σ. We call R_i the uniform temporal extension of r_i. A temporal signature*

$$\tau = \langle \rho_1, \ldots, \rho_n, p_1, \ldots, p_l, R_1, \ldots, R_m \rangle$$

is a two-sorted signature composed of γ, δ, and the temporal extensions of all the symbols in σ. We define a temporal database $\mathcal{A}$ to be a two-sorted τ-structure

$$\mathcal{A} = \langle T, \rho_1^T, \ldots, \rho_n^T; D, p_1^D, \ldots, p_l^D; R_1^{\mathcal{A}}, \ldots, R_m^{\mathcal{A}} \rangle$$

such that the sets $\{(x_1, \ldots, x_{v_i}) : \mathcal{A} \models R_i(t, x_1, \ldots, x_{v_i})\}$ are finite for every $t \in T$ and $0 < i \leq m$. The extensions $R_i^{\mathcal{A}}$ of R_i in $\mathcal{A}$ define the interpretation of the symbols r_i in the database schema for every element of the time domain, formally:

$$r_i(c_1, \ldots, c_{v_i}) \text{ holds at time } t \text{ iff } \mathcal{A} \models R_i(t, c_1, \ldots, c_{v_i})$$

for $r_i \in \sigma$, $t \in T$, and $c_i \in D$.

Note that the interpretations of the predicate symbols, connected solely with the temporal domain (e.g., $<$) or the data domain (e.g., $=$), is fixed, while the interpretation of the symbols R_i depends on the actual contents of the database.

Example 2.2 Let $\langle Q; < \rangle$ be the temporal domain (dense linearly ordered rationals), $\langle D; = \rangle$ the data domain, and ρ the database schema consisting of a single binary relation $\rho = \langle$ salary $\rangle$ holding employee IDs and salaries. Then the temporal structure representing such a temporal database is defined as

$$\text{DB} = \langle Q, <^Q; D, =^D; \text{Salary} \rangle$$

where the fact *x has salary y at time t* is encoded by

$$\text{salary}(x, y) \text{ holds at time } t \text{ in DB} \iff \text{DB} \models \text{Salary}(t, x, y)$$

Note that the relations $<^Q$ and $=^D$ have fixed meanings for the given domains, e.g., $<^Q$ is the linear order on Q and $=^D$ is the diagonal on D. On the other hand the interpretation of the relation Salary depends on the actual *contents* of the database. The relation Salary is infinite in general, but the sets $\{(x, y) : \text{Salary}(t, x, y)\}$ are finite for every fixed $t \in T$.

2.2 First-order Query Languages

The choice of a first-order query language over such extension is not as straightforward: obviously we can use the two-sorted relational calculus or equivalently the two-sorted first-order logic (2-FOL) to express queries over such structures. The disadvantage of such a solution is that it refers to the *augmented* database schema rather than to the original schema. Moreover, all the references to *time* are explicit—we use variables and quantification over the time domain.

A more elegant solution is to use the first-order temporal logic (FOTL)—the single-sorted first-order logic augmented with a finite set of *temporal connectives* like 'sometime in the past' or 'always in the future'. This solution is preferable for two reasons: first, it refers to the *original* database schema rather than to the extended schema. However, the main advantage of this solution is that the references to time and to all the properties of the underlying temporal domain are *encapsulated* inside the temporal connectives added to the language—all the references to time are *implicit*.

We define two query languages over the uniform temporal databases represented by the τ-structures from Definition 2.1:

1. the two-sorted first-order logic language $\mathcal{M}$ and
2. the first-order temporal logic language $\mathcal{T}$.

The definition of the first language is a straightforward extension of the definition of standard Relational Calculus [24]. Let t_i be variables of sort T and x_i be variables of sort D.

Definition 2.3 *Let γ be the signature of the temporal domain and δ the signature of the data domain. A two-sorted FOL language $\mathcal{M}(\gamma, \delta)$ over the database schema σ is defined by the BNF rule:*

$$M ::= R(t_j, x_1, \ldots, x_{v_i}) \mid \rho(t_1, \ldots, t_{w_k}) \mid$$
$$p(x_1, \ldots, x_{u_i}) \mid M \wedge M \mid \neg M \mid \exists x_i.M \mid \exists t_i.M$$

where R is the temporal extension of r for $r \in \sigma$, $\rho \in \gamma$, and $p \in \delta$.

The semantics of the formulas in this language is the standard first-order Tarskian semantics. Note that the database schema is *monadic* with respect to the sort T, i.e., the predicate symbols in the database schema have always exactly one distinguished argument of sort T. To preserve the *closure* of the query language we restrict the set of the *valid* queries to $\mathcal{M}$-formulas that have exactly one free variable over sort T, so the result of the query can be stored in the temporal database itself. It is easy to see that the closure has been achieved artificially, and that not all $\mathcal{M}$ formulas are valid queries. Moreover, subformulas of a valid query in $\mathcal{M}$ may not be valid queries themselves.

Example 2.4 Consider the formula

$$\exists t_1, t_2.t_1 < t < t_2 \wedge \forall x.P(t_1, x) \iff P(t_2, x).$$

This formula defines the query *"find all the intervals such that P contains exactly the same values on both the ends of each of the intervals"*. Clearly, this is a valid $\mathcal{M}$ query. However, the subformula

$$\forall x.P(t_1, x) \iff P(t_2, x)$$

is not a valid query as it contains two free variables of sort T: t_1 and t_2. Moreover, in Section 4 we show that there is no $\mathcal{M}$ formula with the property that all its subformulas are valid queries and that expresses the original query.

In the definition of the second query language we need to be more careful. The language is defined in two steps: first the temporal connectives are defined. Note that the definition of the temporal connectives is independent of both the data domain and the database schema. The definition of the temporal connectives is purely syntactical and depends only on the chosen temporal domain. The semantics of the connectives is defined by a translation to 2-FOL (cf. Definition 2.10). This approach differs from the usual definition of such connectives given in [10] or [11], that is based on the intended semantics and uses truth tables.

Definition 2.5 (Temporal Connective) *Let γ be the signature of the temporal domain and*

$$O ::= \rho(t_1, \ldots, t_{w_k}) \mid O \wedge O \mid \neg O \mid \exists t_i.O \mid X_i$$

where X_i are predicate variables and $\rho \in \gamma$. A (k-ary) temporal connective *(over γ)* is an O-formula with exactly one free variable t_0 and k free predicate variables $X_1, \ldots, X_k$. We denote such connective by $\omega(X_1, \ldots, X_k)$. Let $\Omega(\gamma)$ denote a finite set of (names for) temporal connectives over γ.

The superscripts t_i denote explicitly the temporal contexts of the appropriate subformulas that the temporal connective glues together.

Definition 2.6 *If every quantification in a temporal connective $\omega \in \Omega(\gamma)$ is of the form $\exists t_i.(\rho(t_0, t_i) \wedge O)$ then ω is a ρ-restricted temporal connective.*

Example 2.7 We can express the usual temporal connectives given in [13] in the temporal signature $\langle < \rangle$ of linear orders as follows:

$$X_1 \,\text{until}\, X_2 \triangleq \exists t_2.t_0 < t_2 \wedge X_2 \wedge \forall t_1(t_0 < t_1 < t_2 \to X_1)$$
$$\Diamond X_1 \triangleq \exists t_1.t_0 < t_1 \wedge X_1$$
$$\Box X_1 \triangleq \forall t_1.t_0 < t_1 \to X_1$$

Similarly we can express the past temporal connectives **since**, $\blacklozenge$, and $\blacksquare$. Note that the connectives **until**, $\Diamond$, and $\Box$ are $>$-restricted while the connectives **since**, $\blacklozenge$, and $\blacksquare$ are $<$-restricted. We call the temporal logics that use only the $>$-restricted (the $<$-restricted) temporal connectives the *Future* FOTL (the *Past* FOTL), respectively.

The second step in the definition of the temporal extension to the language of first-order logic is straightforward: we augment the syntax of the FOL over the signatures of the data domain and the database schema by a finite set of temporal connectives:

Definition 2.8 *Let $\Omega(\gamma)$ be a finite set of temporal connectives over γ and δ be the signature of the data domain. A First-order Temporal Logic Language $\mathcal{T}(\Omega(\gamma), \delta)$ over the database schema σ is defined by the BNF rule:*

$$F ::= r(x_1, \ldots, x_{v_i}) \mid p(x_1, \ldots, x_{u_i}) \mid \omega(F_1, \ldots, F_k) \mid F \wedge F \mid \neg F \mid \exists x.F$$

for $r \in \sigma$, $p \in \delta$ and $\omega \in \Omega(\gamma)$.

In the rest of the section we use $\mathcal{M}$ and $\mathcal{T}$ in place of $\mathcal{M}(\gamma, \delta)$ and $\mathcal{T}(\Omega(\gamma), \delta)$, respectively.

Definition 2.9 *We say that $\mathcal{T}$ is a Propositional Temporal Logic (PTL) if all the relations in the database schema σ are 0-ary.*

It is easy to see that all the $\mathcal{T}$-formulas can be naturally embedded into the language of $\mathcal{M}$-formulas. This embedding also defines the semantics of the $\mathcal{T}$-formulas relatively to the semantics of $\mathcal{M}$:

Definition 2.10 (Embedding of $\mathcal{T}$ into $\mathcal{M}$) *Let Embed be a mapping of formulas in the language $\mathcal{T}(\Omega(\gamma), \delta)$ to the language $\mathcal{M}(\gamma, \delta)$ defined as follows:*

$$\begin{aligned}
\text{Embed}(r_i(x_1, \ldots, x_{v_i})) &= R_i(t_0, x_1, \ldots, x_{v_i}) \\
\text{Embed}(p_i(x_1, \ldots, x_{v_i})) &= p_i(x_1, \ldots, x_{v_i}) \\
\text{Embed}(F_1 \wedge F_2) &= \text{Embed}(F_1) \wedge \text{Embed}(F_2) \\
\text{Embed}(\neg F) &= \neg \text{Embed}(F) \\
\text{Embed}(\exists x.F) &= \exists x. \text{Embed}(F) \\
\text{Embed}(\omega(F_1, \ldots, F_k)) &= \omega^*(\text{Embed}(F_1)[t_0/t_1], \ldots, \text{Embed}(F_k)[t_0/t_k])
\end{aligned}$$

where ω^* is the (O-)formula denoted by ω in $\Omega(\gamma)$ and $F[t_0/t_i]$ is a substitution of t_i for t_0 in F.

In the following development we assume that all the $\mathcal{T}$-formulas are merely restricted $\mathcal{M}$-formulas, i.e., $\mathcal{T} \subseteq \mathcal{M}$. The translation of all $\mathcal{T}$-formulas yields a valid 2-FOL query as Embed(φ) has only one free variable of sort T, namely t_0. Thus, the translation of $\mathcal{T}$-formulas preserves the closure of the query language. Note that the translation of every subformula of the original formula has this property as well. This is obviously not true for subformulas of an arbitrary $\mathcal{M}$-formula even if the original formula is a valid query (cf. Example 2.4).

Example 2.11 Using the temporal database from Example 2.2 we can formulate the following queries in both FOTL and 2-FOL:

personal ID of everyone whose salary was negative

$\blacklozenge \exists y.\mathrm{salary}(x,y) \wedge y < 0$

$\exists t_1.t_1 < t_0 \wedge \exists y.\mathrm{Salary}(t_1,x,y) \wedge y < 0$

personal ID of everyone whose salary has decreased

$\exists y_1, y_2 \blacklozenge (\mathrm{salary}(x,y_1) \wedge \blacklozenge \mathrm{salary}(x,y_2)) \wedge y_1 < y_2$

$\exists y_1, y_2 \exists t_1 (t_1 < t_0 \wedge \mathrm{Salary}(t_1,x,y_1) \wedge \exists t_2.t_2 < t_1 \wedge \mathrm{Salary}(t_2,x,y_2)) \wedge y_1 < y_2$

This example also illustrates why the use of FOTL is easier than the use of 2-FOL: in FOTL we do not have to introduce any of the variables t_i—the references to time are encapsulated in the temporal connectives, e.g., $\blacklozenge$.

It is easy to see the essential difference between the full 2-FOL language $\mathcal{M}$ and the temporal extension to the first-order logic $\mathcal{T}$: each of the subformulas of a $\mathcal{T}$-formula is associated with exactly one temporal context represented by the variable t_0 in the translation to $\mathcal{M}$. Moreover the context can be changed only using a temporal connective. This distinction comes into the play when the temporal connectives, which are merely quantifiers over sort T, and the quantifiers over sort D are interleaved in a single formula.

It is quite clear that any two τ-structures distinguishable by a $\mathcal{T}$-formula φ are also distinguishable by a $\mathcal{M}$-formula, namely Embed(φ). However, two τ-structures distinguishable by a $\mathcal{M}$-formula may not be distinguishable by any $\mathcal{T}$-formula. In Section 4 we find concrete examples of structures that are distinguishable by a $\mathcal{M}$-formula but not distinguishable by any $\mathcal{T}$-formula.

3 Ehrenfeucht-Fraïssé Game for Temporal Logic

Our situation is slightly more complicated, as we try to separate FOTL *from* first-order logic, i.e., we try to show that there are 2-FOL formulas that define properties not definable in FOTL.

The rules of the game are modified to match exactly the syntactic restrictions placed on the temporal formulas by Definitions 2.5 and 2.8. The modification captures precisely the expressive power of FOTL. An easy way of thinking about the compatibility of variables is by considering the scopes[2] of variables defined by the expansion of the temporal connectives: The restrictions imposed on the scopes of the individual variable names in the formula Embed(φ) for $\varphi \in \mathcal{T}$ can be depicted as follows:

---

[2] The parts of the syntactic tree of the formula, where the variable in question can legally appear.

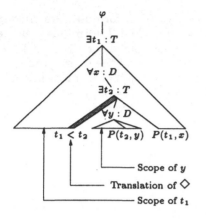

The diagram is a graphical representation of the scopes of the individual variables of the sort T. We can easily see that the scope of the variable t_1 is not the whole subformula rooted by $\exists t_1 : T$ (as it would be in a 2-FOL formula). The scope of t_1 extends only to the point where other temporal connective (e.g., $\Diamond$, represented by the shaded area) is encountered. While t_1 can still be used in the *body* of this connective (i.e., in the expansion of its definition—$t_1 < t_2$), it cannot be used in the subformula rooted by this connective, e.g., in $P(t_2, y)$.

Fig. 1. Restriction on the scopes of the individual temporal variables.

Example 3.1 Figure 1 shows the restrictions on the scopes of the individual variables in the translation Embed(φ) for an FOTL formula φ.

In general the variables x and y can appear together as arguments of an atomic formula only if their scopes *intersect*. Note that this restriction does not have any impact on pairs of variables of sort D. This is very natural as the restrictions are connected solely with the sort T. The following definitions give a precise definition of a combinatorial game, that captures the expressive power of FOTL (similarly to the game for First-order logic in [8, 9]):

Definition 3.2 (Game for Temporal Logic) *Let A and B be two τ-structures, $a = (a_1, \ldots, a_k)$ and $b = (b_1, \ldots, b_k)$ sequences of A-elements and B-elements (respectively), and $n \in N$. A round of the game $T_n((A, a), (B, b))$ consists of an ordered sequence of n moves $(a_{k+1}, b_{k+1}), \ldots, (a_{k+n}, b_{k+n})$ of the form "PLAYER I chooses an element in the carrier of either A or B and PLAYER II chooses an element in the carrier of the other structure". Both the players must obey the following rules:*

1. *the corresponding elements a_i and b_i must be of the same sort, and*
2. *the pair (a_1, b_1) must be of sort T.*

We say that i (i.e., i-th move) is a data move if both a_i and b_i are of sort D, and that i is a temporal move if both elements are of sort T.

We call the pair (a_1, b_1) the initial temporal context, and the vectors a and b the initial assignment.

The vectors $a = (a_1, \ldots, a_k)$ and $b = (b_1, \ldots, b_k)$ are used to handle the open formulas of $\mathcal{M}$ (cf. Theorem 3.10). Except for the additional rules, the game for temporal logic is the same as the Ehrenfeucht-Fraïssé game for first-order logic [18]. The first rule enforces the sort compatibility of the individual moves in the game—this is a natural requirement for the many-sorted structures (we can assume that the relations are empty if the arguments do not match the required sorts). The second rule is needed to define the initial temporal context, the subsequent moves are then relative to this context. Note that a closed temporal

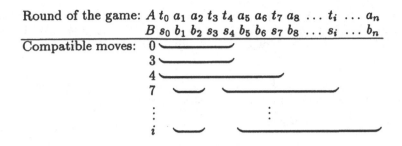

Fig. 2. A round of the game and the scopes of the temporal moves.

logic formula still has one free variable of sort T that represents the initial temporal context (cf. the semantic definition of the temporal logic in section 2 or [13]).

Besides the rules of the game itself we need to define the winning condition for the game for temporal logic. Here we use the observation from Example 3.1:

Definition 3.3 (Compatible Moves) *Let $T_n((A, a), (B, b))$ be a round of the game for temporal logic and i and j two moves in the game, such that i precedes j in T_n $(i < j)$. If at least one of:*

1. *i and j are data moves,*
2. *i is a data move and j is a temporal move,*
3. *i is the last temporal move preceding the data move j,*
4. *i and j are both temporal moves, and all the moves between i and j are temporal moves,*
5. *i and j are both temporal moves, and i is the last temporal move preceding j such that there is a data move between i and j*

holds, then we say that the moves i and j are compatible. A set of moves S is self-compatible if every two elements in S are compatible.

This definition is related to the definition of the temporal connectives and Example 3.1. The blocks of consecutive temporal moves in T_n correspond to a temporal connective or several subsequent temporal connectives with the same number of nested quantifiers over T. The compatibility criterion exactly matches the compatibility of the scopes of the corresponding variables in a formula of $\mathcal{T}$:

Example 3.4 Figure 2 shows a round of the game $T_n((A, t_0), (B, s_0))$ on the structures A and B. The lower part of the figure shows moves compatible with the individual temporal moves in this particular round of the game. It is easy to see that compatibility of moves in the game exactly corresponds to scopes of variables in $\mathcal{T}$-formulas. Note that in the case of 2-FOL, the scopes of the individual variables would extend to the rightmost edge of the figure—the n-th column.

Definition 3.3 implies the following restrictions on the winning condition of the game for temporal logic:

Definition 3.5 *Let* $a = (a_1, \ldots, a_k)$ *for* $a_i \in A$, $b = (b_1, \ldots, b_k)$ *for* $b_i \in B$, *and* $T_n((A, a), (B, b))$ *be a round of the game for FOTL of length* n. *We say that* PLAYER II *wins the round of the game for FOTL if the following conditions hold:*

1. *for any* $p_i \in \delta$ *and any* $k_1, \ldots, k_{u_i}$ *such that* $0 < k_j \leq n + k$ *where all* k_j *are data moves such that* $\{k_1, \ldots, k_{u_i}\}$ *is self-compatible*

$$A \models p_i^A(a_{k_1}, \ldots, a_{k_{u_i}}) \iff B \models p_i^B(b_{k_1}, \ldots, b_{k_{u_i}})$$

2. *for any* $\rho_i \in \gamma$ *and any* $k_1, \ldots, k_{w_i}$ *s.t.* $0 < k_j \leq n + k$ *where all* k_j *are temporal moves such that* $\{k_1, \ldots, k_{w_i}\}$ *is self-compatible*

$$A \models \rho_i^A(a_{k_1}, \ldots, a_{k_{w_i}}) \iff B \models \rho_i^B(b_{k_1}, \ldots, b_{k_{w_i}})$$

3. *for any temporal extension* R_i *of* $r_i \in \sigma$ *and any* $k_0, \ldots, k_{v_i}$ *s.t.* $0 < k_j \leq n+k$ *such that* k_0 *is a temporal move where all* k_j *such that* $0 < j \leq v_i$ *are data moves and* $\{k_0, \ldots, k_{v_i}\}$ *is self-compatible*

$$A \models R_i^A(a_{k_0}, \ldots, a_{k_{v_i}}) \iff B \models R_i^B(b_{k_0}, \ldots, b_{k_{v_i}})$$

Otherwise we say that PLAYER I *wins the round of the game for temporal logic. If* PLAYER II *can always win the game* $T_n((A, a), (B, b))$ *we say that* PLAYER II *has a* winning strategy *for* $T_n((A, a), (B, b))$.

It is easy to verify that a winning strategy for PLAYER II defines an equivalence relation $\sim_{k,n}$ on the class of τ-structures, where k is the length of the initial assignment and n is the number of moves in the game T_n.

The connection between the games and formulas of FOTL is established as follows:

Definition 3.6 (Quantifier Depth) *We define function* $\mathrm{qd} : \mathcal{M} \to \mathcal{N}$

1. *If* φ *is atomic then* $\mathrm{qd}(\varphi) = 0$.
2. *If* φ *is* $\neg\phi$ *then* $\mathrm{qd}(\varphi) = \mathrm{qd}(\phi)$.
3. *If* φ *is* $\phi_1 \wedge \phi_2$ *then* $\mathrm{qd}(\varphi) = \max\{\mathrm{qd}(\phi_1), \mathrm{qd}(\phi_2)\}$.
4. *If* φ *is* $\exists x.\phi$ *or* $\exists t.\phi$ *then* $\mathrm{qd}(\varphi) = \mathrm{qd}(\phi) + 1$.

Definition 3.7 *Let* $\mathcal{L}_{k,n}$ *be set of all formulas* φ *of* $\mathcal{M}$ *such that* φ *is a subformula of* $\mathrm{Embed}(\psi)$ *for some* $\psi \in \mathcal{T}$, $|FV(\varphi)| = n$, *and* $\mathrm{qd}(\varphi) = n$.

In general the sets $\mathcal{L}_{k,n}$ are countably infinite, but we can always find a finite subset of this set that "represents" all the formulas in $\mathcal{L}_{k,n}$:

Lemma 3.8 *For each* $k, n \in \mathcal{N}$ *there is a finite subset* $\Phi_{k,n}$ *of* $\mathcal{L}_{k,n}$ *such that every formula* $\phi \in \mathcal{L}_{k,n}$ *is equivalent to a formula* $\varphi \in \Phi_{k,n}$. *Moreover, all free variables in* φ *are* $\{v_1, \ldots, v_k\}$.

Notation 3.9 *Let* $\varphi \in \Phi_{k,n}$ *be a formula and* $a = (a_1, \ldots, a_k)$ *a vector of elements from the carrier of a first-order structure* A. *Then we write*

$$A; a \models \varphi \text{ for } A \models \varphi[v_1/a_1, \ldots, v_k/a_k].$$

Note that the variables v_i *are the only free variables of* φ.

Theorem 3.10 *Let A and B be τ-structures, $a = (a_1, \ldots, a_k)$, $b = (b_1, \ldots, b_k)$ sequences of A-elements and B-elements (respectively) such that $a_1 \in T^A$ and $b_1 \in T^B$, and $n \in N$. Then*

$$(A, a) \sim_{k,n} (B, b) \iff \forall \varphi \in \Phi_{k,n} : A; a \models \varphi \iff B; b \models \varphi$$

Note also that if $(A, a) \sim_{1,n} (B, b)$ then the τ-structures A and B are indistinguishable by any closed $\mathcal{T}$-formulas of quantifier depth at most n over an arbitrary set of temporal connectives built using Definition 2.5 for a given initial temporal context a, b.

4 Structures indistinguishable by FOTL formulas

We prepared all the necessary techniques to show our main result: the language $\mathcal{T}$ is strictly less expressive than the language $\mathcal{M}$. We show that for a standard choice of the data domain being the set of uninterpreted constants with equality and a standard choice of a linearly ordered temporal domain:

- the propositional temporal logic has an expressively complete set of temporal connectives [10, 14, 15, 22], but
- there is no finite set of temporal connectives expressively complete in the first-order case.

This result implies that the choice of FOTL with arbitrary finite set of connectives as a basis of a *first-order complete* query language for temporal databases is not adequate, as there are first-order queries not expressible in this language. We prove this result in two steps:

1. First we show that the FOTL language $\mathcal{L}$ is strictly less expressive than the 2-FOL language $\mathcal{M}$ for a degenerate choice of the temporal domain: a set of elements *without* any structure on the elements, even equality (i.e., the signature of the temporal domain is empty) and the standard data domain of uninterpreted constants with equality.

2. In the second step we extend this result to all dense linear orders.

4.1 Time Domain: a Set

The first claim is proven as follows: Let ϵ be an empty signature, $\Diamond_\epsilon X_1 \equiv \exists t_1 . X_1$ be a temporal connective, and $\mathcal{T}(\Omega(\epsilon), =)$ be an FOTL language.

Lemma 4.1 *The propositional TL $\mathcal{T}(\{\Diamond_\epsilon\})$ is expressively complete with respect to the monadic 2-FOL $\mathcal{M}(\epsilon)$.*

P r o o f: By induction on the structure of $\varphi \in \mathcal{M}(\epsilon)$.

Note that in the propositional case the signature of the data domain is irrelevant.

Notation 4.2 *Let $\mathcal{S}_n^m = \{S_1, \ldots, S_k\}$ be the set of all m-element subsets of the n-element set $\{1, \ldots, n\}$.*

We prove that Lemma 4.1 does not generalize to the first-order case: the logic $\mathcal{T}(\Omega(\epsilon); =)$ is strictly less expressive than the logic $\mathcal{M}(\epsilon; =)$:

Theorem 4.3 *Let* $m, n \in N$ *such that* $n > m$. *We define* $P_n^m = \{(t, x) : x \in S_t \in \mathcal{S}_n^m\}$ *and* $R_n^m = \{(-t, x) : x \in S_t \in \mathcal{S}_n^m\}$. *Let*

$$\mathcal{A}_n = \langle Z; \{1, \dots, 2n\}, =; P_{n-1}^{2n}, R_n^{2n} \rangle \text{ and } \mathcal{B}_n = \langle Z; \{1, \dots, 2n\}, =; P_n^{2n}, R_n^{2n} \rangle$$

be two temporal structures (with the signature $\langle \epsilon; =; p/1, r/1 \rangle$*). Then*

1. $\mathcal{A}_n$ *and* $\mathcal{B}_n$ *can be distinguished by a* $\mathcal{M}$ *formula (of quantifier depth 3), but*
2. $\mathcal{A}_n$ *and* $\mathcal{B}_n$ *cannot be distinguished by any* $\mathcal{T}$ *formula of quantifier depth less or equal to* $n - 1$.

P r o o f: (1) Let

$$\varphi \equiv \exists t_1. \exists t_2. ((\exists x. P(t_1, x)) \wedge (\exists x. R(t_2, x)) \wedge (\forall x. P(t_1, x) \iff R(t_2, x)))$$

Clearly $\varphi \in \mathcal{M}(\epsilon, =)$, $\varphi \not\models \mathcal{A}_n$, and $\varphi \models \mathcal{B}_n$. To prove (2) we define a winning strategy for PLAYER II: Let $(a_1, b_1), (a_2, b_2), \dots, (a_k, b_k)$ be all the data moves and (t, s) the last temporal move in a prefix of a round of the game $\mathcal{T}_n$ that satisfies the winning condition. We show that every sequence of moves, shorter than n can be extended by one move. By case analysis (assuming PLAYER I picks an element from the carrier of the structure $\mathcal{A}_n$):

1. PLAYER I plays a data move $a \in \{1, \dots, 2n\}$ and $a = a_i$ for some $0 < i \le k$. Then PLAYER II responds by $b = b_i$.

2. PLAYER I plays a data move $a \in \{1, \dots, 2n\}$ and $a \ne a_i$ for all $0 < i \le k$. Then PLAYER II plays $b \in \{1, \dots, 2n\}$ such that $b \ne b_i$ for $0 < i \le k$ and if $(t, a) \in P_{n-1}^{2n}$ then $(s, b) \in P_n^{2n}$, otherwise $(s, b) \notin P_n^{2n}$. Similarly, if $(t, a) \in R_n^{2n}$ then $(s, b) \in R_n^{2n}$, otherwise $(s, b) \notin P_n^{2n}$. In all cases PLAYER II can find such a b as there are only $k < n$ elements chosen so far.

3. PLAYER I plays a temporal move $t' \in \{1, \dots, |\mathcal{S}_{n-1}^{2n}|\}$. Then PLAYER II plays $s' \in \{1, \dots, |\mathcal{S}_n^{2n}|\}$ such that $(t', a_i) \in P_{n-1}^{2n}$ if and only if $(s', b_i) \in P_n^{2n}$ for all $0 < i \le k$. Again, such a s' exists because $\mathcal{S}_n^{2n}$ contains all n-element subsets of $\{1, \dots, 2n\}$ and the number of data moves played so far is less than n. The choice may not be unique—in that case PLAYER II can choose arbitrarily as all the elements of T are indistinguishable in the signature ϵ.

4. PLAYER I plays a temporal move $t' \in \{-1, \dots, -|\mathcal{S}_n^{2n}|\}$. Then PLAYER II plays $s' \in \{-1, \dots, -|\mathcal{S}_n^{2n}|\}$ such that $(t', a_i) \in R_n^{2n}$ if and only if $(s', b_i) \in R_n^{2n}$ for all $0 < i \le k$. Similarly to the previous case, such a s' always exists.

Similarly, if PLAYER I chooses an element from the carrier of the structure $\mathcal{B}_n$, PLAYER II replies with an element from $\mathcal{A}_n$ using symmetric strategy. In all cases the new move does not violate the winning condition. The conclusion of this theorem follows from Theorem 3.10.

Corollary 4.4 *FOTL* $\mathcal{T}(\Omega(\epsilon), =)$ *is strictly less expressive than 2-FOL* $\mathcal{M}(\epsilon, =)$ *for an arbitrary finite set of connectives* $\Omega(\epsilon)$.

Theorem 4.3 and Corollary 4.4 also provide an example of when expressive completeness in the propositional case does not imply the existence of a complete set of connectives in the first-order case.

4.2 Time Domain: Dense Linear Order

To show a similar result for temporal logic over linear orders is more complicated. We need to account for the structure of the temporal domain. Consider the following definition:

Definition 4.5 *Let $(Q, <)$ be a linear order, S a finite set, $I \subseteq Q$ a non-trivial interval, and $f : I \to S$ a function. We say that f is dense over S if for every $s, t \in I$ such that $s < t$ and for every $x \in S$ there is $r \in I$ such that $s < r < t$ and $x = f(r)$.*

Clearly, for any dense linear order we can define functions dense over any finite codomain.

Lemma 4.6 *Let $(Q, <)$ be a dense linear order and $I \subseteq Q$ an open interval such that $|I| > 1$. Then for every finite set S there is a $f : I \longrightarrow S$ that is dense over S.*

Theorem 4.7 *Let $(Q, <)$ be a dense linear order, $f^I_{m,n} : I \longrightarrow S^m_n \cup \{\emptyset\}$ dense over $S^m_n \cup \{\emptyset\}$ for every non-trivial interval $I \subset Q$, and let J_1 and J_2 be two nontrivial, open, and disjoint intervals in Q. We define $P^m_n = \{(t, x) : x \in f^{J_1}_{m,n}(t)\}$ and $R^m_n = \{(t, x) : x \in f^{J_2}_{m,n}(t)\}$. Let*

$$\mathcal{A}_n = \langle Q, <; \{1, \ldots, 2n\}, =; P^{2n}_{n-1}, R^{2n}_n \rangle \text{ and } \mathcal{B}_n = \langle Q, <; \{1, \ldots, 2n\}, =; P^{2n}_n, R^{2n}_n \rangle$$

be two temporal databases. Then

1. *$\mathcal{A}_n$ and $\mathcal{B}_n$ can be distinguished by a $\mathcal{M}$ formula (of quantifier depth 3), but*
2. *$\mathcal{A}_n$ and $\mathcal{B}_n$ cannot be distinguished by any $\mathcal{T}$ formula of quantifier depth less than or equal to $n - 1$.*

Corollary 4.8 *FOTL $\mathcal{T}(\Omega(<), =)$ over a dense linear order $<$ is strictly less expressive than 2-FOL $\mathcal{M}(<, =)$ for an arbitrary finite set of connectives $\Omega(<)$.*

5 Additional Results

Using our technique we can prove several additional results about FOTL. Among other results, we show that the gap between FOTL and 2-FOL cannot be bridged using a more powerful version of FOTL—the weakness is inherent to the restriction on the maximal temporal arity (dimension) of the logic FOTL.

5.1 Separation of Future FOTL from FOTL

Using a similar technique as in Theorem 4.7 we can separate the *Future* FOTL with arbitrary future temporal connectives from the *full* FOTL $\mathcal{T}(\text{since}, \text{until})$. These two logics are expressively equivalent in the propositional case [12].

Lemma 5.1 *Let $(Q^+; <, 0)$ be a dense linear order with a left endpoint (0). Let $J \subset Q^+$ be a non-trivial open interval and $f^I_{m,n} : I \longrightarrow S^m_n \cup \{\emptyset\}$ be dense over S^m_n. We define $P^m_n = \{(t, x) : x \in f^J_{m,n}(t)\}$ and $R_n = \{(0, x) : 0 < x \leq n\}$. Let*

$$\mathcal{A}_n = \langle Q, <; \{1, \ldots, 2n\}, =; P^{2n}_{n-1}, R_n \rangle \text{ and } \mathcal{B}_n = \langle Q, <; \{1, \ldots, 2n\}, =; P^{2n}_n, R_n \rangle$$

be two temporal structures. Then

1. *The structures $\mathcal{A}_n$ and $\mathcal{B}_n$ can be distinguished by a $\mathcal{T}(\mathbf{since}, \mathbf{until})$ formula of quantifier depth 3, but*

2. $\mathcal{A}_n$ *and* $\mathcal{B}_n$ *cannot be distinguished by any future $\mathcal{T}$ formula of quantifier depth less or equal to* $n - 1$.

P r o o f: (1) Let $\varphi = (\Diamond \forall x.(p(x) \iff \blacklozenge r(x))) \in \mathcal{T}(\mathbf{since}, \mathbf{until})$. Clearly, $\varphi, 0 \not\models \mathcal{A}_n$ and $\varphi, 0 \models \mathcal{B}_n$.

(2) follows from observation that $f^I_{m,n}$ is dense over S^m_n (and thus PLAYER II can find an appropriate answer to every temporal move of the PLAYER I), and the fact, that the quantifiers in future FOTL formulas are restricted (this means that PLAYER I cannot return to *time* 0 once he played any other temporal move, as the sequence of temporal moves in a game for Future FOTL has to be non-decreasing sequence of elements of T).

5.2 Expressive Incompleteness for Many-dimensional FOTL

When using FOTL as a query language, we cannot express queries that reference two distinct time instants (in an essential way, cf. Section 4). This is due to the limitation on the number of temporal contexts passed to the individual subformulas of a FOTL formula. In [13] many-dimensional propositional temporal logics are studied. These logics can be easily modified to many-dimensional first-order temporal logics (k-FOTL, where k is the dimension of the logic). The main idea behind this approach is to allow k *temporal contexts* in all the temporal (sub-)formulas. Clearly, 2-FOTL can express the query from Theorem 4.3 (2) as exactly two temporal contexts are needed in this query. However, using our technique we can show that k-FOTL is strictly less expressive than $(k+1)$-FOTL and thus is also less expressive than 2-FOL for any $k > 1$.

Definition 5.2 (Many-dimensional Temporal Connective) *Let γ be a signature of the temporal domain, $k > 0$, and t_i be variables ranging over k-tuples of elements of T (time instants). Then*

$$O ::= \rho(t_1[j_1], \ldots, t_{w_k}[j_k]) \mid O \wedge O \mid \neg O \mid \exists t_i.O \mid X_i$$

where X_i are predicate variables, $\rho \in \gamma$, and $t_i[j]$ is the j-th component of the tuple variable t_i. A (n-ary) k-dimensional temporal connective (over γ) is an O-formula with exactly one free variable t_0 and n free predicate variables $X_1, \ldots, X_n$. We denote it by $\omega(X_1, \ldots, X_n)$ Let $\Omega(\gamma)$ denote a finite set of (names for) temporal connectives over γ.

Now we can define the language of k-FOTL exactly the same way as in the case of FOTL (cf. Definition 2.8). The semantics is also defined in the same way as in Definition 2.10 with a small "fix" to the base case:

$$\text{Embed}(r_i(x_1, \ldots, x_{v_i})) = R_i(t_0[1], x_1, \ldots, x_{v_i}).$$

The game for k-dimensional temporal logic is similar to the game for FOTL. The only difference is that for every temporal move we always pick k-tuples of elements of sort T instead of a single element. We have to guarantee that the winning condition is met for all *components* of every tuple move.

Note that we are still using the uniform temporal databases with relations monadic in the sort T. Clearly, a higher dimension of the base relations in the temporal sort leads to the separation result immediately. However, even with the restriction on the database relations we can prove the separation of the k-FOTL from $(k+1)$-FOTL.

Theorem 5.3 *Let*

$$\varphi := \exists t.\exists t_1, \ldots, t_k.\forall x(R(t,x) \iff \bigvee_{0<i\leq k} P(t_i,x))$$

Then φ is expressible in $(k+1)$-FOTL but not in k-FOTL.

P r o o f: That φ is not expressible by k-FOTL follows from a modification of Theorems 4.3 or 4.7. To show that φ is expressible in $(k+1)$-FOTL, consider following $(k+1)$-dimensional connectives:

$$\Diamond = \exists t_1.X_1$$
$$\uparrow\downarrow_i = \exists t_1.(t_1[1] = t_0[i] \land X_1) \qquad \text{for } 0 < i \leq k$$

Note that the variables t_i range over $(k+1)$-tuples of temporal elements. Then

$$\varphi \text{ is equivalent to } \Diamond\forall x(r(x) \iff \bigvee_{0<i\leq k} \uparrow\downarrow_i p(x))$$

which is a $(k+1)$-FOTL formula.

Thus the many-dimensional FOTL logics form a proper hierarchy with respect to their relative expressive power:

$$\text{FOTL} \subsetneq 2\text{-FOTL} \subsetneq \ldots \subsetneq (k-1)\text{-FOTL} \subsetneq k\text{-FOTL} \subsetneq \ldots \subsetneq 2\text{-FOL}$$

Note that for an arbitrary finite set of connectives we can find a k-FOTL that can express all the connectives for any $k \in N$. Also, from the previous results and [16], we know that

$$\text{Future-FOTL} \subsetneq \text{FOTL} \subsetneq \text{FOTL(now)} \subseteq 2\text{-FOTL}$$

On the other hand, the hierarchy of k-FOTL *approximates* 2-FOL:

Theorem 5.4 *Let ψ be a 2-FOL formula. Then there is a natural number k and a k-FOTL formula φ such that $\psi \equiv \varphi$.*

5.3 Temporal Relational Algebras

Previous results also show that every temporal relational algebra is strictly weaker the temporal relational calculus:

Theorem 5.5 *Let Γ be a first-order definable relational algebra over uniform relational types. Then the relational algebra queries over Γ cannot express all first-order queries.*

5.4 Ordered Data Domain

Theorems 4.3 and 4.7 hold even in the presence of the linear order on the data domain (which is a usual assumption in relational databases). The only difference is in the choice of the cardinality of the subsets of elements that are in the relations P and R. The subsets are chosen similarly to proof of Theorem 4.7. We choose the data domain to be $\{1, \ldots, 2^{n+1}\}$ and define the τ-structures by

$$A_n = \langle Q, <; D, =; P_{2^n-1}^{2^{n+1}}, R_{2^n}^{2^{n+1}} \rangle \quad \text{and} \quad B_n = \langle Q, <; D, =; P_{2^n}^{2^{n+1}}, R_{2^n}^{2^{n+1}} \rangle$$

The strategy for PLAYER II is essentially the same, as two linear orders with cardinalities 2^n and $2^n - 1$ cannot be distinguished by n data moves, and PLAYER I cannot pick more than $n - 1$ data moves in a round of the game for temporal logic of length n.

5.5   Fixed Data Domain

Corollary 4.8 may suggest that the logic FOTL is always strictly less expressive than 2-FOL in the first-order case. This is not true either:

Example 5.6 Consider the situation where D is a finite set of fixed size. In this case the proof of Lemma 4.7 will not work as we cannot build the structures $\mathcal{A}_n$ and $\mathcal{B}_n$ of arbitrary size. If, moreover, every element of D is denotable by a constant we can replace quantifiers over D as follows:

$$\forall x.\varphi = \bigwedge_{c \in D} \varphi[x/c] \qquad \exists x.\varphi = \bigvee_{c \in D} \varphi[x/c]$$

It is easy to see that this case is essentially the same as the case of propositional temporal logic. Note that the fixed size of the domain is a first-order property (i.e., it can be defined by a first-order theory of D). However, the size of the resulting formula depends on the size of D.

6   Conclusion

In this paper we have defined a model-theoretical game that captures the expressive power of k-FOTL in a very general setting—the definition is independent of the underlying signatures and theories. We have used this game to resolve several open questions about temporal logics. Our main result is the separation of FOTL from 2-FOL: 2-FOL is strictly more expressive than *any* variant of temporal logic over dense orders. Thus k-FOTL cannot be used as a basis for the design of a first-order complete temporal query language. We conjecture that the same results hold for the expressive power over all (sufficiently large) linear orders—the proof of Theorem 4.7 for discrete orders needs to be modified using a *restricted* density property that allows one to maintain the winning strategy for PLAYER II, but makes the order isomorphic to the standard linear order on integers. We can prove Theorem 4.7 for FOTL with unary temporal connectives over discrete linear orders. However, substantiating this claim in its full generality is the goal of ongoing research.

Future research in this area will concentrate on the following topics:

1. In the case of complete first-order query languages, new and more general implementation techniques need to be developed for handling the temporal information. The intermediate results of the query evaluation algorithms may be more complicated than allowed by the uniform database schema. Thus, such intermediate results cannot be stored in a uniform temporal database itself as auxiliary relations.

2. In the area of incomplete but subquery-closed temporal query languages the relationships between the different sets of temporal connectives need to be investigated. For many applications a limited number of simultaneous temporal contexts may be sufficient. This would allow the use of a sufficiently large set of temporal connectives tailored for the specific application.

3. The temporal databases are infinite structures in general. However, all the data stored in the database must be finitely representable. This restriction disallows the use of arbitrarily complex temporal databases (cf. Definition 2.1)[3]. Sufficient restriction on the class of allowed temporal databases may be sufficient to guarantee both the closure and completeness. We have seen that bounded number of elements in the data domain is such a restriction. Are there other (nontrivial) restrictions (especially on the temporal domain) that also guarantee both the closure and completeness?

7 Related Work

The separation is proven using a modification of the Ehrenfeucht-Fraïssé Games to capture the properties of Temporal Logic. In [14] pebble games have been used to show expressivity results for the *monadic logic* over linear orders. However, our results and techniques are different, as we are interested in the *first-order* temporal logics (and the corresponding 2-FOL). The method introduced in [14] is no longer sufficient as it cannot handle unrestricted quantification over the data sort. In [16] a restricted version of 2-FOTL was presented introducing the *now* connective that allows one to reset the temporal context of a subformula to the original evaluation point. This logic was also shown to be strictly stronger than FOTL. However, the technique used in [16] does not apply to temporal databases—the proof of the fact is carried out over first-order structures that cannot be finitely encoded as the contents of the *database relation(s)* is an infinite and coinfinite[4] *at every time instant*. Such sets cannot be represented over the data domain (as the theory of equality can finitely encode only finite and cofinite sets. A recent result [1] that separates FOTL with the **since** and **until** connectives from 2-FOL in the case of finite (sufficiently large) linear orders supports our conjecture. However [1] uses a counting argument in the proof and thus it does not generalize to arbitrary linear orders. Also, the relationship between this work and various sets of temporal connectives defined in [13] is not clear.

References

1. Abiteboul, S., Herr, L., Van den Bussche, J. Temporal Connectives versus Explicit Timestamps in Temporal Query Languages. (unpublished manuscript).
2. Chomicki J. Temporal Query Languages: a Survey. Proc. *International Conference on Temporal Logic*, July 1994, Bonn, Germany, Springer-Verlag (LNAI 827), pp. 506–534.
3. Chomicki J. Efficient Checking of Temporal Integrity Constraints Using Bounded History Encoding. In *ACM Transactions on Database Systems*, (20) 2, pp. 149–186. 1995.
4. Chomicki, J.,N iwinski, D. On the Feasibility of Checking Temporal Integrity Constraints. Proc. *12th ACM Symposium on Principles of Database Systems*, pp 202–213, 1993. (full version to appear in JCSS).

---

[3] Note that all the databases used in our proofs are finitely representable.

[4] I.e., its complement is infinite.

5. Chomicki, J., Toman, D. Implementing Temporal Integrity Constraints Using an Active DBMS. *IEEE Transactions on Knowledge and Data Engineering*, Special section on Temporal and Real-time Databases, Vol. 7, No. 4, 1995.

6. Clifford J., Croker A. The Historical Relational Data Model (HRDM) and Algebra based on Lifespans. In *Proceedings of the International Conference on Data Engineering*, pages 528–537, Los Angeles, CA, February 1987.

7. Clifford J., Croker A., Tuzhilin A. On Completeness of Historical Relational Query Languages. *ACM Transactions on Database Systems*, Vol. 19, No. 1, pp. 64–116, 1994.

8. Ehrenfeucht, A. An application of games to the completeness problem for formalized theories. *Fund. Math.*, 49:129–141, 1961.

9. Fraisse, R. Sur les classifications des systemes de relations. *Publ. Sci. Univ. Alger*, 1:1, 1954.

10. Gabbay D. Expressive Functional Completeness in Tense Logic. In Mönnich U. *Aspects of Philosophical Logic*, 91–117, 1981.

11. Gabbay D. The Declarative Past and Imperative Future: Executable Temporal Logic for Interactive Systems. In Banieqbal B., et al. (ed.) *Temporal Logic in Specification*, vol. 398, pp.409–448, Springer Verlag, LNCS 398, 1989.

12. Gabbay D., Pnueli A., Shelah S., Stavi J. On the Temporal Analysis of Fairness. Proc. *ACM Symposium on Principles of Programming Languages*, 1980.

13. Gabbay D., Hodkinson I., Reynolds M. Temporal Logic. Mathematical Foundations and Computational Aspects. Vol. 1. *Oxford Logic Guides* 28, Oxford Science Publications, 1994.

14. Immerman N., Kozen D. Definability with Bounded Number of Variables. Information and Computation 83, pp.121–139, 1989.

15. Kamp J.A.W. Tense Logic and the Theory of Linear Order. PhD thesis, University of California, Los Angeles, 1968.

16. Kamp J.A.W. On the Formal Properties of 'now'. *Theoria* 37:227–273, 1971.

17. Lipeck U.W., Saake, G. Monitoring Dynamic Integrity Constraints Based on Temporal Logic. *Information Systems*, 12(2):255–269, 1987.

18. Rosenstein J.G. Linear Orderings. Academic Press, New York, 1982.

19. Snodgrass R. T. The Temporal Query Language TQuel. *ACM Transactions on Database Systems*, 12(2):247–298, June 1987.

20. Snodgrass R.T., editor. *The TSQL2 Temporal Query Language*. Kluwer Academic Publishers, 674+xxiv pages, 1995.

21. Tansel A., Clifford J., Gadia S., Jajodia S., Segev A., Snodgrass R. Temporal Databases. Theory, Design, and Implementation. Benjamin Cummings 1993.

22. Stavi J. Functional Completeness over Rationals. Unpublished, Bar-Ilan University, Ramat-Gan, Israel, 1979.

23. Tuzhilin A., Clifford J. A Temporal Relational Algebra as a Basis for Temporal Completeness. Proc. *International Conference on VLDB*, 1990.

24. Ullman J. D. Principles of Database and Knowledge-base Systems, Vol. 1,2. Computer Science Systems, 1989.

25. Vardi M.Y. A Temporal Fixpoint Calculus. In *ACM Symposium on Principles of Programming Languages*, 1988.

Querying TSQL2 Databases
with Temporal Logic

Michael H. Böhlen[1], Jan Chomicki[2],
Richard T. Snodgrass[3], and David Toman[4]

[1]Dept. of Mathematics and Computer Science, Aalborg University
Fredrik Bajers Vej 7E, DK-9220 Aalborg Ost, Denmark, boehlen@iesd.auc.dk

[2]Department of Computer Science, Monmouth University
West Long Branch, NJ 07764, chomicki@moncol.monmouth.edu

[3]Department of Computer Science, University of Arizona
Tucson, AZ 85721, rts@cs.arizona.edu

[4]Department of Computer Science, University of Toronto
Toronto, Ontario M5S 1A4, Canada

Abstract. We establish an exact correspondence between temporal logic and a subset of TSQL2, a consensus temporal extension of SQL–92. The translation from temporal logic to TSQL2 developed here enables a user to write high-level queries which can be evaluated against a space-efficient representation of the database. The reverse translation, also provided, makes it possible to characterize the expressive power of TSQL2. We demonstrate that temporal logic is equal in expressive power to a syntactically defined subset of TSQL2.

1 Introduction

In this paper, we bring together two research directions in temporal databases. The first direction is concerned with temporal extensions to calculus-based query languages such as SQL (e.g., [GN93, NA93, Sar93]). The issues addressed include space-efficient storage, effective implementation techniques, and handling large amounts of data. This approach includes the consensus temporal query language TSQL2 [Sno95], whose practical implementations should be forthcoming. The second direction is concerned with defining high-level query languages with logical semantics, e.g., temporal logic [TC90, GM91, CCT94]. The advantages of using logic languages come from their well-understood mathematical properties [GHR94]. Logic languages are easy to use and make algebraic query transformation possible [CT95]. For instance, temporal logic has been proposed as the language of choice for formulating temporal integrity constraints and triggers [Cho95, CT95, GL93, LS87, SW95].

The semantics of temporal logic queries is defined with respect to sequences of database states [GHR94]. In temporal databases we do not want to construct and store all the states explicitly. Instead, various proposals have associated with each fact a concise description of the set of points over which the fact holds, such as a period[1] [NA93, Sar90, Sno87, Tan86] or a finite union of periods

---

[1] We use the term 'period' in this paper rather than the term 'interval' commonly used in temporal logic because the latter term conflicts with SQL INTERVALs, which are unanchored durations, such as 3 months.

[CC87, Gad88, Sno95]. We show here how to translate temporal logic queries into TSQL2, enabling the user to write high-level queries which will be evaluated against a space-efficient representation of the database. While translations of first order logic to SQL have been previously discussed [AHV95, VGT91], we know of no translations from temporal logic to a temporal query language.

We start with a discussion of the basic framework in Section 2. We define the syntax and semantics of the two languages in question, temporal logic and TSQL2. In Section 3 we give the mapping from temporal logic to TSQL2.[2] We conclude the section with an example and the discussion of some implementation issues. Section 4 discusses the reverse mapping, thereby relating the expressive power of (a subset of) TSQL2 and temporal logic.

2 Basic framework

Before comparing temporal logic and TSQL2 we have to set up a formal framework suitable to both languages. Time is considered to be *integer-like:* linear (totally ordered), discrete, bounded in the past, and infinite in the future. Our approach can be adopted to other kinds of time, e.g., dense, rational-like time, although some details of the mapping may in that case be different. We also take the *point-based* view which is predominant in the context of temporal logic. This view means that the truth-values of facts are associated with individual time points (also called instants). We assume a fixed time granularity.

We will consider only *valid-time*, which relates when facts are valid in reality [JCE+94]. In particular, *transaction time*, which relates when facts are stored in the database, is not considered.

2.1 Temporal logic

Temporal logic is an *abstract language*, i.e., a language which is defined with respect to abstract temporal databases [Cho94]. An *abstract temporal database*, in turn, is a database which captures the formal semantics of a temporal database without considering representation issues.

It is possible to view an abstract temporal database in several different but equivalent ways. We choose here the *timeslice* view (called *snapshot* in [Cho94]) in which every time instant is associated with a (finite) set of facts that hold at it. For integer-like time, this view leads to an infinite sequence of finite database states $(D_0, D_1, D_2, \ldots)$.

Example 1. Table 1 presents an example of an abstract temporal database, viewed as a sequence of states. The database represents information about Eastern European history, modeling the independence of various countries [Cho94]. Each fact indicates an independent nation and its capital. This relation will be used as a running example throughout the paper.

---

[2] An implementation of the translation from temporal logic to TSQL2 is publicly available at http://www.iesd.auc.dk/~boehlen/.

Year	Timeslice
1025	$\{indep('Poland`, `Gniezno`)\}$
...	...
1039	$\{indep('Poland`, `Gniezno`)\}$
1040	$\{indep('Poland`, `Cracow`)\}$
...	...
1197	$\{indep('Poland`, `Cracow`)\}$
1198	$\{indep('CzechKingdom`, `Prague`), indep('Poland`, `Cracow`)\}$
...	...
1995	$\{indep('CzechRepublic`, `Prague`), indep('Poland`, `Warsaw`),$ $indep('Slovakia`, `Bratislava`)\}$
...	...

Table 1. Eastern European history: the abstract temporal database

Syntax. Temporal logic extends first order logic with binary temporal connectives **since** and **until**, and unary connectives ● ("previous" or "yesterday") and ○ ("next" or "tomorrow"). Informally, A **since** B is true in a state if A is true for states between when B was true and now (this state). A **until** B is true in a state if A will be true into the future until B will be true.

As usual, other temporal connectives can be defined in terms of these, e.g.,

$\blacklozenge A \equiv$ **true since** A (A was true sometime in the past)

$\lozenge A \equiv$ **true until** A (A will be true sometime in the future)

$\blacksquare A \equiv \neg\blacklozenge\neg A$ (A was true always in the past)

$\square A \equiv \neg\lozenge\neg A$ (A will be true always in the future).

Example 2. Our first example is a query which does not relate different database states. The query

$$(\exists City)(indep('Poland`, City) \wedge \neg(\exists City2)indep('Slovakia`, City2))$$

determines all years when Poland but not Slovakia was an independent country, i.e., the times when the query evaluates to true.

Example 3. The second example relates different database states. The query

$$(indep('Poland`, City) \wedge City \neq `Cracow`) \textbf{ since } indep('Poland`, `Cracow`)$$

returns the name of the city that superseded Cracow as Poland's capital and the years when this city was the capital.

Example 4. Consider the query [Cho94, p.515] "list all countries that lost and regained independence" over the abstract temporal database shown in Table 1. This is formulated in temporal logic as:

$$(\exists S1, S2)(\blacklozenge indep(X, S1) \wedge \lozenge indep(X, S2) \wedge (\forall S)\neg indep(X, S)).$$

For a country and a year to result, the country will have been independent in the past, will be independent in the future, but is currently not independent.

Semantics. An abstract temporal database is a sequence $D = (D_0, D_1, D_2, \ldots)$ of database states. Every database state D_i contains a relation (relation instance) r for each relation schema R. We define the semantics of temporal logic formulas in terms of a satisfaction relation $\models$ and a valuation ν (a valuation is a mapping from variables to constants):

- $D, \nu, i \models A$ iff A is atomic and $A/\nu \in D_i$ (where A/ν is the result of applying ν to the variables of A),

- $D, \nu, i \models \neg A$ iff $D, \nu, i \not\models A$,

- $D, \nu, i \models A \wedge B$ iff $D, \nu, i \models A$ and $D, \nu, i \models B$, similarly for $\vee$ and $\Rightarrow$,

- $D, \nu, i \models (\exists X) A$ iff for some c, $D, \nu[X \leftarrow c], i \models A$ where $\nu[X \leftarrow c]$ is a valuation identical to ν except that it maps X to c,

- $D, \nu, i \models (\forall X) A$ iff for all c, $D, \nu[X \leftarrow c], i \models A$,

- $D, \nu, i \models \bullet A$ iff $i > 0$ and $D, \nu, i - 1 \models A$,

- $D, \nu, i \models \bigcirc A$ iff $D, \nu, i + 1 \models A$,

- $D, \nu, i \models A \text{ since } B$ iff $\exists j (j < i \wedge D, \nu, j \models B \wedge \forall k (j < k \leq i \rightarrow D, \nu, k \models A))$

- $D, \nu, i \models A \text{ until } B$ iff $\exists j (j > i \wedge D, \nu, j \models B \wedge \forall k (i \leq k < j \rightarrow D, \nu, k \models A))$

The answer to a temporal logic query A in D is the set $\{(\nu, i) : D, \nu, i \models A\}$. Thus, temporal logic may be viewed as a natural extension of relational calculus.

As indicated by the example queries on the previous page, temporal logic provides a convenient means of expressing rather involved English queries in a natural way. However, the state-based semantics of temporal logic does not suggest an efficient implementation of such queries. A period-based implementation, in which the period over which each fact was valid is used directly in the evaluation, promises much faster execution.

2.2 TSQL2

TSQL2 [Sno95] is the consensus temporal extension of SQL–92 and, therefore, we use it as our target database query language when translating temporal logic. A *valid-time relation* is a relation where tuples are implicitly timestamped with periods[3].

Example 5. Table 2 contains a concrete TSQL2 relation representing the abstract temporal database shown in Table 1.

---

[3] In this paper, we use a slight variant of TSQL2 named *Applied TSQL2* (ATSQL2) [BJS95]. ATSQL2 modifies TSQL2 in a few minor ways. ATSQL2 timestamps tuples with periods rather than with temporal elements; ATSQL2 adds support for duplicates (though we will consider only ATSQL2 queries that remove duplicates); and ATSQL2 changes the syntax of the valid clause. We use ATSQL2 because the semantics of that language has been formally specified; only an informal specification of the semantics of TSQL2 has been given. Other than these changes, the languages are similar, and we will continue to refer to them under the rubric TSQL2.

indep

Country	Capital	VALID
Czech Kingdom	Prague	$[1198, 1620]$
Czechoslovakia	Prague	$[1918, 1938]$
Czechoslovakia	Prague	$[1945, 1992]$
Czech Republic	Prague	$[1993, \infty]$
Slovakia	Bratislava	$[1940, 1944]$
Slovakia	Bratislava	$[1993, \infty]$
Poland	Gniezno	$[1025, 1039]$
Poland	Cracow	$[1040, 1595]$
Poland	Warsaw	$[1596, 1794]$
Poland	Warsaw	$[1918, 1938]$
Poland	Warsaw	$[1945, \infty]$

Table 2. Eastern European history: the concrete TSQL2 relation

Syntax. TSQL2 extends the query language of SQL–92 [MS93] with the following constructs:

1. Syntactic constructs to manipulate timestamps (e.g., extract the start and end point of a period, construct a period out of two time points, etc.)[4].

2. Temporal built-in predicates, which can be used in the WHERE clause in order to specify temporal relationships between pairs of periods. To be consistent with SQL2, the relationships below have a somewhat different meaning than the identically-named relationships in [All83]. Notation: P^- for BEGIN(P) and P^+ for END(P).

   - $P_1 = P_2$ iff $P_1^- = P_2^-$ and $P_1^+ = P_2^+$
   - P_1 CONTAINS P_2 iff $P_1^- \leq P_2^-$ and $P_1^+ \geq P_2^+$
   - P_1 MEETS P_2 iff $succ(P_1^+) = P_2^-$
   - P_1 OVERLAPS P_2 iff $P_1^- \leq P_2^+$ and $P_2^- \leq P_1^+$
   - P_1 PRECEDES P_2 iff $P_1^+ < P_2^-$

   Also, period endpoints can be compared directly using PRECEDES. In this way, all the relationships in [All83] can be expressed.

3. A valid clause, which can be placed in front of queries.[5] It is to specify whether a query expression should be evaluated with temporal semantics (no valid clause) or with standard Codd semantics (valid clause). Intuitively, temporal semantics corresponds to snapshot reducibility [Sno87] which means that, conceptually, the respective query is evaluated over every

---

[4] These features are briefly discussed where used the first time.

[5] The same syntactic extension is allowed for queries in the FROM clause defining a derived table. With auxiliary tables or views such queries can be rewritten so that the valid clause only occurs at "the outermost level".

snapshot of a temporal database. The valid clause comes in two different flavors. If it is of the form VALID SNAPSHOT, a snapshot relation is returned. Otherwise, it is of the form VALID *expr* in which case a valid-time relation is returned with valid-time defined by *expr*.

4. (PERIOD) may follow a query expression or a relation name in a from clause, specifying that the result be *coalesced*, that is, tuples with identical explicit attribute values whose valid-times overlap or are adjacent are merged into a single tuple, with a period equal to the union of the periods of the original tuples. As a side-effect, duplicates are eliminated. We use (PERIOD) throughout because temporal logic does not allow duplicates or uncoalesced periods.

5. Other facilities not relevant here, including temporal indeterminacy, schema evolution, user-defined granularities, and extensible literal syntax.

Semantics. TSQL2 has been given a formal denotational semantics that maps TSQL2 statements to (temporal) relational algebra expressions [BJS95].

Example 6. In order to determine the name of the city that superseded Cracow as Poland's capital (c.f., Example 3), different database states have to be related. In TSQL2 this means that we have to specify a valid clause (in order to override snapshot reducibility) and we also have to specify the required temporal relationship. This results in the following TSQL2 query Q_1:

```
VALID VALID(i1)
  SELECT i1.Capital
  FROM indep(PERIOD) AS i1, indep(PERIOD) AS i2
  WHERE i1.Country = 'Poland'
  AND i2.Country = 'Poland' AND i2.Capital = 'Cracow'
  AND VALID(i2) MEETS VALID(i1)
```

Example 7. The formulation of a query becomes even simpler if it can be answered by looking at single snapshots. In this case the user can simply ignore time when formulating a query, as illustrated in the following query Q_2, which determines all period(s) when Poland but not Slovakia was independent (c.f., Example 2):

```
(SELECT i1.Country
  FROM indep(PERIOD) AS i1
  WHERE i1.Country = 'Poland'
  AND NOT EXISTS (
    SELECT *
    FROM indep(PERIOD) AS i2
    WHERE i2.Country = 'Slovakia'))(PERIOD)
```

3 Mapping Temporal Logic to TSQL2

A mapping from temporal logic to TSQL2 is useful for two reasons. First it relates the two languages and, thus, their expressive power. Second it yields an efficient implementation for temporal logic formulas using a translation to

TSQL2 that efficiently encodes identical adjacent facts. Also TSQL2 queries can be optimized.

Before we can describe the actual mapping of temporal formulas to TSQL2 we need to establish a relationship between the databases over which our translation is well defined. Not every abstract temporal database can be represented as a TSQL2 database. For example, the database that has a single fact $p(a)$ in every even-numbered state and whose every odd-numbered state is empty cannot be represented in TSQL2.

Definition 1. Let $D = (D_1, D_2, \ldots)$ be an abstract temporal database. The *support* of a temporal logic formula A under a valuation ν is the set

$$\{i : D, \nu, i \models A\}.$$

The support for ground formulas (e.g., facts) does not depend on the valuation. The definition of the support allows us to define the class of abstract temporal databases we are interested in.

Definition 2. An abstract temporal database is *finitary* if it contains a finite number of facts and the support of every fact can be represented as a finite union of periods.

Proposition 3. *Every TSQL2 database represents a finitary abstract temporal database and every finitary abstract temporal database can be represented by a TSQL2 database.*

The previous observations are used to define the translation of temporal logic formulas to TSQL2 and prove its correctness. The translation uses an extension of existing methods for translating first-order logic formulas to SQL–92, e.g., [VGT91, AHV95, Wüt91] as one of its steps. We also give a syntactic criterion for identifying (a subset of) domain independent formulas of temporal logic.

3.1 Temporal Logic to TSQL2 Translation

The translation of temporal logic formulas to TSQL2 is defined by induction on the structure of the formula. Temporal logic formulas can be thought of as first-order formulas augmented by additional *temporal* connectives **since**, **until**, ●, and ○. This observation allows us to define the translation process in two steps:

1. mapping of temporal connectives, and

2. mapping of maximal sub-formulas not containing temporal connectives.

The whole translation procedure then works inductively on the structure of the given query: It first computes the TSQL2 equivalents of the maximal first-order subformulas of the query. The results are then used in the definitions of the translations of temporal connectives to TSQL2 views. These views then *replace* the original temporal subformula (by a virtual relation name). The process is repeated until the whole formula is translated.

We first describe the mapping of the temporal connectives to TSQL2. This mapping links the translations of the (essentially) first-order pieces of the original query together.

Mapping since and until. Figure 1 graphically illustrates the semantics of **since** and **until**. We have listed all possible temporal relationships [All83] be-

Temporal relationship between formulas A and B	Temporal logic formula F	Truth period of formula F
A ———— ; ———— B	A since B / A until B	$[\,]$ / $[\,]$
A ———— ; ———— B	A since B / A until B	$[\,]$ / $[\,]$
A ———— ; ———— B	A since B / A until B	$[succ(B^-), A^+]$ / $[A^-, A^+]$
A ———— ; ———— B	A since B / A until B	$[A^-, A^+]$ / $[A^-, pred(B^+)]$
A ———— ; ———— B	A since B / A until B	$[\,]$ / $[A^-, A^+]$
A ———— ; ———— B	A since B / A until B	$[A^-, A^+]$ / $[\,]$
A ———— ; ———— B	A since B / A until B	$[succ(B^-), A^+]$ / $[A^-, pred(B^+)]$
A ———— ; ———— B	A since B / A until B	$[A^-, A^+]$ / $[A^-, A^+]$
A ———— ; ———— B	A since B / A until B	$[succ(B^-), A^+]$ / $[A^-, pred(B^+)]$
A ———— ; ———— B	A since B / A until B	$[succ(B^-), A^+]$ / $[A^-, A^+]$
A ———— ; ———— B	A since B / A until B	$[succ(B^-), A^+]$ / $[A^-, pred(B^+)]$
A ———— ; ———— B	A since B / A until B	$[A^-, A^+]$ / $[A^-, pred(B^+)]$
A ———— ; ———— B	A since B / A until B	$[succ(B^-), A^+]$ / $[A^-, pred(B^+)]$

Fig. 1. Semantics of **since** and **until**

tween the truth periods of two formulas A and B. For each relationship we have determined the truth period of A **since** B and A **until** B respectively. (A^-/A^+ denotes the start/end point of the truth period of A.) More formally the truth periods of A **since** B and A **until** B are defined as follows.

A **since** B $\mapsto [max(A^-, succ(B^-)), A^+]$
$$\text{for } max(A^-, succ(B^-)) \le A^+ \text{ and } B^+ \ge A^-$$

A **until** B $\mapsto [A^-, min(A^+, pred(B^+))]$
$$\text{for } A^- \le min(A^+, pred(B^+)) \text{ and } A^+ \ge B^-$$

The reader may verify that these general expressions evaluated on any particular relationship given in Figure 1 result in the correct truth period.

These expressions can be translated to TSQL2 straightforwardly. The valid clause is used to specify the final timestamp (and to prevent snapshot reducibility), whereas the conditions are translated into appropriate WHERE clause conditions. More precisely, A **since** B is translated to[6]

```
VALID PERIOD(LAST(BEGIN(VALID(a0)),BEGIN(VALID(a1))+1), END(VALID(a0)))
  SELECT ...
  FROM A'(PERIOD) AS a0, B'(PERIOD) AS a1
  WHERE LAST(BEGIN(VALID(a0)),BEGIN(VALID(a1))+1) <= END(VALID(a0))
    AND BEGIN(VALID(a0)) <= END(VALID(a1))
    AND ...
```

whereas A **until** B is translated to

```
VALID PERIOD(BEGIN(VALID(a0)), FIRST(END(VALID(a0)),END(VALID(a1)))-1)
  SELECT ...
  FROM A'(PERIOD) AS a0, B'(PERIOD) AS a1
  WHERE BEGIN(VALID(a0)) <= FIRST(END(VALID(a0)),END(VALID(a1))-1)
    AND BEGIN(VALID(a1)) <= END(VALID(a0))
    AND ...
```

The SELECT list of the TSQL2 statements is determined from the free variables occurring in either A or B. Variables used in A and B give rise to further WHERE clause conditions. We get A' by applying the translation recursively to A and B' by applying the translation recursively to B.

Mapping ● **and** ○. The mapping of the connectives ●A and ○A is defined as follows: First we define the truth periods for ●A and ○A with respect to the truth period of A:

$$\bullet A \mapsto [succ(A^-), succ(A^+)]$$
$$\circ A \mapsto [pred(A^-), pred(A^+)]$$

The result is translated to TSQL2 using a definition of the corresponding valid-time clause that shifts the valid-time period by one in the appropriate direction. The translation for ●A looks like

```
VALID VALID(a0)+1
  SELECT ...
  FROM A'(PERIOD) AS a0
```

and the translation for ○A is

```
VALID VALID(a0)-1
  SELECT ...
  FROM A'(PERIOD) AS a0
```

The SELECT list is again obtained from the set of free variables in A, and A' is the TSQL2 translation of A.

---

[6] PERIOD(x,y) takes two timepoints x and y, and returns a period. BEGIN/END returns the start/end point of a period. FIRST and LAST return the minimum and maximum timepoint out of a pair of timepoints, respectively. Finally, we assume here that the valid-time is at a granularity of a year. Thus +1 is shorthand for +INTERVAL '1' YEAR and -1 for -INTERVAL '1' YEAR.

Mapping of first-order (sub-)formulas. The mapping of first-order formulas to relational algebra has been described in several papers and books, e.g., [VGT91, AHV95]. As our target language is (T)SQL2 rather than relational algebra, we map maximal first-order subformulas to directly to SQL [Wüt91], thereby exploiting the syntactic features of the latter and achieving efficient SQL queries.

3.2 Domain independence

Similarly to the first-order case [VGT91, AHV95], not all formulas expressible in temporal logic are domain-independent. We identify (a subset of) the domain-independent formulas of temporal logic using an extension of the syntactic criteria defined for first-order formulas.

Proposition 4. *Let φ be a temporal formula and* ALWD *be a domain-independence criterion for first-order formulas. If*

1. ALWD(FOL(φ)),
2. ALWD(FOL(A)) *and* ALWD(FOL(B)) *for every subformula of φ that has the form A* **until** *B or A* **since** *B, and*
3. ALWD(FOL(A)) *for every subformula of φ of the form op A where op is one of* $\{\blacklozenge, \diamondsuit, \blacksquare, \square, \bullet, \bigcirc\}$

where FOL *is a mapping that replaces all occurrences of temporal subformulas by (imaginary) database relations with the same sets of free variables, then φ is domain-independent.*

The domain-independence needs to be extended to the temporal domain as well. We need to show that every tuple in the result of our query is associated with a finite union of periods. However, it is easy to show that:

Theorem 5. *For any finitary temporal database and a fixed valuation the support of every temporal logic formula can be represented by a finite union of periods.*

Thus the application of boolean operators, temporal operators, and quantifiers preserves the *finitary* property of relations. This result shows that all the intermediate results can be represented by finite unions of periods (and thus evaluated properly using TSQL2).

3.3 Correctness of the translation

Proposition 4 guarantees that at every point of the transformation process we only have to deal with domain-independent formulas (i.e., all first order variables are range-restricted). Thus there are only finitely many valuations (for any finitary temporal database) at that point. Thus

Theorem 6. *For every temporal logic formula φ satisfying the assumptions of Proposition 4 and for every finitary abstract temporal database D the following*

diagram commutes:

$$
\begin{array}{ccc}
D & \xrightarrow{\;\;\varphi\;\;} & R \\
\downarrow & & \downarrow \\
D^{TSQL2} & \xrightarrow{\;\varphi^{TSQL2}\;} & R^{TSQL2}
\end{array}
$$

where D^{TSQL2} is the TSQL2 equivalent of D, φ^{TSQL2} is the translation of the temporal logic query φ, and R^{TSQL2} is the TSQL2 variant of the result of the query.

3.4 Deriving specialized mappings

Based on the translation of **since** and **until**, the mapping of other temporal connectives can be defined. While theoretically feasible such an approach may be cumbersome in practice as it leads to unnecessarily complicated TSQL2 statements.

Mapping ◆. We illustrate how the definition of **since** can be used to derive an efficient special purpose mapping for **◆**. The formula **◆**B is equivalent to **true since B**. Therefore we take the definition of A **since** B (Section 3.1) and substitute A by **true**. We notice that the truth period of **true** is the whole time line which means that `BEGIN(VALID(a0))` evaluates to 0 (beginning of time) and `END(VALID(a0))` evaluates to ∞ (end of time). After the obvious simplifications we obtain:

```
VALID PERIOD(BEGIN(VALID(a1))+1, TIMESTAMP 'forever')
   SELECT ...
   FROM B'(PERIOD) AS a1
```

which is considerably less complex than the original statement. Similarly, we can use the definition of **until** to derive a mapping for **◇**.

Mapping ■. For **■**A, one can rewrite it as $\neg$◆$\neg A$ and use the approach presented above. Unfortunately, this approach is not very practical as it may lead to formulas that cannot be translated (e.g., $\neg$◆$\neg p(X)$ versus **■**$p(X)$). Therefore we derive a TSQL2 translation for **■**A from the definition

$$
D, \nu, i \models \blacksquare A \text{ iff } \forall j (j < i \rightarrow D, \nu, j \models A)
$$

Assuming bounded time in the past, this can be easily expressed in TSQL2:

```
VALID PERIOD(BEGIN(VALID(a0)), END(VALID(a0))+1)
   SELECT ...
   FROM A'(PERIOD) AS a0
   WHERE BEGIN(VALID(a0)) = TIMESTAMP 'beginning'
```

By analogy, a special purpose mapping for $\Box A$ can be derived.

3.5 Example

Consider the query "list all countries that lost and regained independence" (Example 4) formulated in temporal logic as:

$$
(\exists S1, S2)(\blacklozenge indep(X, S1) \wedge \Diamond indep(X, S2) \wedge (\forall S)(\neg indep(X, S))).
$$

To simplify the illustration of the translation we break up the formula into a set of auxiliary rules (views):

$$aux\_view1(X, S1) \leftarrow \blacklozenge indep(X, S1).$$
$$aux\_view2(X, S2) \leftarrow \Diamond indep(X, S2).$$

$$(\exists S1, S2) aux\_view1(X, S1) \land aux\_view2(X, S2) \land (\forall S)(\neg indep(X, S)).$$

We translate the first rule to

```
VALID PERIOD(BEGIN(VALID(a0))+1, TIMESTAMP 'forever')
  SELECT a0.Country, a0.Capital
  FROM indep(PERIOD) AS a0
```

and the second rule to

```
VALID PERIOD(TIMESTAMP 'beginning', END(VALID(a1))-1)
  SELECT a1.Country, a1.Capital
  FROM indep(PERIOD) AS a1
```

The main query is then translated to

```
SELECT a2.Country AS Country
FROM aux_view1(PERIOD) AS a2, aux_view2(PERIOD) AS a3
WHERE a2.Country = a3.Country
AND NOT EXISTS (
  SELECT *
  FROM indep(PERIOD) AS a4
  WHERE a4.Country = a2.Country)
```

Note that this last step is identical to the translation from first order logic to SQL. Because temporal logic and TSQL2 handle the temporal dimension of snapshot-reducible queries automatically, the translation of temporal logic formulas that do not contain temporal connectives degenerates to the translation of first order logic to SQL.

4   Mapping TSQL2 to temporal logic

Establishing a mapping between TSQL2 and temporal logic is less important from a practical point of view than establishing the mapping in the other direction, as described in the previous section. However, the former mapping makes it possible to study the expressive power of TSQL2 as a query language.

Definition 7. A TSQL2 query is *pure* if:

1. It does not use aggregate operators.

2. Coalescing of periods is forced using (PERIOD). As a side-effect, this ensures that no duplicates are generated.

The idea is to use only those features of SQL that can be mapped to relational calculus or algebra.

Definition 8. A TSQL2 query is *local* if:

1. In every subclause of a SELECT, all the references of the form VALID(v) refer to a tuple variable v of the FROM clause of this particular SELECT. (There is

no similar requirement for nontemporal attributes.) This implies that nested SELECT clauses cannot refer to the valid-times of correlation names specified in the FROM clause of an enclosing SELECT.

2. The only arithmetic expressions in which VALID(v) can appear are of the form VALID(v) $\pm k$ for an integer k.

3. No VALID SNAPSHOT clauses appear.

Example 8. The following TSQL2 query is nonlocal.
```
(VALID VALID(a)
 SELECT * FROM a AS a
 WHERE NOT EXISTS
   (SELECT * FROM b AS b
    WHERE VALID(a) MEETS VALID(b) AND a.X=b.Z))(PERIOD)
```

Our mapping maps pure local TSQL2 queries to temporal logic formulas. Its main idea is illustrated by the following example.

Example 9. Consider the following (pure local) TSQL2 query.
```
(VALID PERIOD(BEGIN(VALID(b)),END(VALID(c)))
 SELECT *
 FROM a AS a, b AS b, c AS c
 WHERE VALID(a) OVERLAPS VALID(b)
   AND VALID(c) OVERLAPS VALID(b)
   AND a.X=b.Z)(PERIOD)
```

Assume that a has two attributes: X and Y, b one attribute Z, and c also one attribute W.

We extend previous notation to apply to tuple variables as follows: x^- denotes BEGIN(VALID(x)) and x^+ denotes END(VALID(x)). Based on the WHERE clause, period endpoints have to be partially ordered in the following way:

$$a^- \leq b^+ \wedge b^- \leq a^+ \wedge c^- \leq b^+ \wedge b^- \leq c^+.$$

Now consider all linear orders of endpoints that are consistent with the above partial order, for example, the linear order O_1:

$$a^- < c^- < b^- < c^+ < a^+ < b^+.$$

Given a linear order O, every period with endpoints that are successive elements in O is called *nondecomposable*. Notice that in each such period and for each fixed valuation the truth values of $a(X,Y)$, $b(Z)$ and $c(W)$ do not change. For each such period P in a given linear order O, denote by α_P^O the conjunction of $a(X,Y)$, $b(Z)$, and $c(W)$ or their negations that is true over all the points in P. The formula α_P^O will be called the *local characteristic* of the period P in O. For example, $\alpha_{[b^-,c^+]}^{O_1}$ is $a(X,Y) \wedge b(Z) \wedge C(W)$. We also define the *global characteristic* of P in a given linear order O as the temporal logic formula β_P^O that encodes the given linear order of endpoints and is true exactly over P. The order O_1 leads to the formula $\beta_{[b^-,c^+]}^{O_1}$ which is a conjunction of

$$(a(X,Y) \wedge b(Z) \wedge c(W)) \textbf{ until}$$
$$((a(X,Y) \wedge b(Z) \wedge \neg c(W)) \textbf{ until } (\neg a(X,Y) \wedge b(Z) \wedge \neg c(W)))$$

and

$$(a(X,Y) \wedge b(Z) \wedge c(W)) \text{ since}$$
$$((a(X,Y) \wedge \neg b(Z) \wedge c(W)) \text{ since } (a(X,Y) \wedge \neg b(Z) \wedge \neg c(W)))$$

The temporal logic formula corresponding to the query with **VALID** period P[7] is obtained as the conjunction of the nontemporal condition in the **WHERE** clause (here: $X = Z$) and the disjunction of all the formulas formulas β_P^O where O is a linear order consistent with the partial order given by the **WHERE** clause.

Theorem 9. *For every pure local TSQL2 query Q, there is a temporal logic formula ϕ_Q such that for every TSQL2 database D, a tuple $\bar{a}$ timestamped by an period i belongs to the answer of Q over D iff $D', \nu, t \models \phi_Q$ for every timepoint t in i (where D' is the abstract temporal database corresponding to D and ν is the valuation that maps the free variables of ϕ_Q to $\bar{a}$).*

Proof. (sketch) The formula ϕ_Q is defined inductively. For a base relation p with n attributes, ϕ_Q is just $p(x_1, \ldots, x_n)$ where $x_1, \ldots, x_n$ are different variables. For a **VALID** P ... **SELECT** where P is a nondecomposable period, ϕ_Q is obtained as a disjunction of all the global characteristics β_P^O where O is a linear order consistent with the partial order given by the **WHERE** clause, as in Example 9 (all of TSQL2 built-in temporal predicates can be handled in this way).

There are several additional points that need to be considered. First, there may be more than one possible partial order of endpoints obtained from the **WHERE** clause. The resulting formula is obtained then as a disjunction of formulas corresponding to individual partial orders. Second, the period in the **VALID** clause may be decomposable. Then the TSQL2 query may be viewed as a finite union of TSQL2 queries in which such periods are nondecomposable. Third, temporal expressions on the valid-times have to be handled in a special way. In every linear order, one needs to consider not only period endpoints but also the appropriate neighboring points (predecessors and successors). As a result, local characteristics may now contain also ● and ○. For instance, in Example 9 the local characteristic of the period $[succ(\mathsf{b}^-), \mathsf{c}^+]$ should be $a(X,Y) \wedge b(Z) \wedge c(W) \wedge \bullet b(Z)$ and the global characteristic should be changed similarly. Fourth, temporal constants, e.g., 2 can be encoded using ●. Namely, we define inductively the formula n_i which is true exactly in the state D_i:

$$n_0 \overset{\text{def}}{\equiv} \neg \bullet \text{true}$$
$$n_{i+1} \overset{\text{def}}{\equiv} \bullet n_i.$$

To deal with unanchored spans, e.g., "3 instants", we introduce sufficiently many (3 in the example) additional points associated with the formula **true** into the partial ordering and construct the local characteristic appropriately. Finally, anchored spans are dealt with using the combination of the above techniques. In all cases, one produces the characteristics in essentially the same way: by encoding the linear order in temporal logic.

Moreover, nontemporal conditions in the **WHERE** clause, **NOT**, and **EXISTS** are translated as in the standard translation from SQL to (domain) relational calculus. For the attributes not in the **SELECT** list, appropriate existential quantifiers

---

[7] If no **VALID** clause is present the intersection of all valid periods corresponding to the **FROM** list is assumed.

are added to the formula. Finally, **SELECT** without a **VALID** clause is translated using the standard translation from SQL to domain relational calculus.

The translation from temporal logic to TSQL2 presented in the previous section produces pure local TSQL2 queries. Thus:

Corollary 10. *Temporal logic and pure local TSQL2 have the same expressive power as query languages.*

There is a subtle point here: the above translation produces temporal logic formulas that are domain-independent. However, not every such formula satisfies the assumptions of Proposition 4 and is thus amenable to the translation back to TSQL2. We conjecture that this gap may be closed by providing a more sophisticated translation from temporal logic to TSQL2.

The following is a natural next question to ask: Is there a logical query language equivalent to full TSQL2? The lack of aggregates in temporal logic can be remedied by a syntactic extension of the language, along the lines of one proposed for relational calculus [Klu82]. The requirement of maximal periods is more fundamental. In fact, allowing noncoalesced periods calls for a temporal logic that is not point- but period-based [Tom95]. Thus in this case, there can be no translation from full TSQL2 to the temporal logic discussed in this paper, even for local queries.

The restriction to local queries is also critical. Pure TSQL2 has the same expressive power as two-sorted first-order logic in which there is a separate sort for time [Tom95]. It has been recently shown [AHVdB95, TN96] that temporal logic is strictly less expressive than the above two-sorted logic. Thus, there can be no translation from TSQL2 to temporal logic that works for all pure queries.

5 Summary

We have established an exact correspondence between temporal logic and a syntactically defined subset of TSQL2. The translation from temporal logic to TSQL2 allows the efficient implementation of temporal logic queries within a temporal database management system supporting TSQL2.

Future work includes extending the class of allowed temporal logic formulas (which will also require extensions to the translation to TSQL2), and extending temporal logic and the translation to support aggregates. Also interesting would be an adaptation of our approach to a dense domain. This would require first extending TSQL2 to such a domain, including support for half-open and open periods, and then extending the mapping introduced here. Finally, a translation from two-sorted first-order logic to TSQL2, which is of clear practical interest, seems considerably more complicated than the translation from temporal logic to TSQL2 given in the present paper.

References

[AHV95]   S. Abiteboul, R. Hull, and V. Vianu. *Foundations of Databases*. Addison-Wesley, 1995.

[AHVdB95] S. Abiteboul, L. Herr, and J. Van den Bussche. Temporal Connectives versus Explicit Timestamps in Temporal Query Languages (unpublished manuscript).

[All83]   J. F. Allen. Maintaining Knowledge about Temporal Intervals. *Communications of the ACM*, 16(11):832–843, 1983.

[BJS95]   M. H. Böhlen, C. S. Jensen, and R. T. Snodgrass. Evaluating and Enhancing the Completeness of TSQL2. Technical Report TR 95-5, Computer Science Department, University of Arizona, June 1995.

[CC87]   J. Clifford and A. Croker. The Historical Relational Data Model (HRDM) and Algebra based on Lifespans. In *Proceedings of the International Conference on Data Engineering*, pages 528–537, Los Angeles, CA, February 1987.

[CCT94]   J. Clifford, A. Croker, and A. Tuzhilin. On Completeness of Historical Relational Query Languages. *ACM Transactions on Database Systems*, 19(1):64–116, March 1994.

[Cho94]   J. Chomicki. Temporal Query Languages: a Survey. *Proceedings of the First International Conference on Temporal Logic*, pages 506–534, 1994.

[Cho95]   J. Chomicki. Efficient Checking of Temporal Integrity Constraints Using Bounded History Encoding. *ACM Transactions on Database Systems*, (20) 2, 149–186, 1995.

[CT95]   J. Chomicki and D. Toman. Implementing Temporal Integrity Constraints Using an Active DBMS. *IEEE Transactions on Knowledge and Data Engineering*, Vol. 7, No. 4, August 1995.

[EN94]   R. Elmasri and S. B. Navathe. *Fundamentals of Database Systems*. Benjamin/Cummings Publishing Company, 2nd edition, 1994.

[Gad88]   S. K. Gadia. A Homogeneous Relational Model and Query Language for Temporal Databases. *ACM Transactions on Database Systems*, 13(4):418–448, December 1988.

[GHR94]   D.M. Gabbay, I. Hodkinson, and M. Reynolds. *Temporal Logic: Mathematical Foundations and Computational Aspects*. Oxford University Press, 1994.

[GL93]   M. Gertz and U.W. Lipeck. Deriving Integrity Maintaining Triggers from Transition Graphs. In *Proceedings of the International Conference on Data Engineering*, 1993.

[GM91]   D. Gabbay and P. McBrien. Temporal Logic and Historical Databases. In *Proceedings of the International Conference on Very Large Databases*, 1991.

[GN93]   S. K. Gadia and S. S. Nair. Temporal Databases: A Prelude to Parametric Data. In A. Tansel, J. Clifford, S. Gadia, S. Jajodia, A. Segev, and R. T. Snodgrass, editors, *Temporal Databases: Theory, Design, and Implementation*, pages 28–66. Benjamin/Cummings Publishing Company, 1993.

[JCE⁺94] C. S. Jensen, J. Clifford, R. Elmasri, S. K. Gadia, P. Hayes, and S. Jajodia editors. A Glossary of Temporal Database Concepts. *ACM SIGMOD Record*, 23(1):52–64, March 1994.

[Klu82]   A. Klug. Equivalence of Relational Algebra and Relational Calculus Query Languages Having Aggregate Functions. *Journal of the ACM*, 29(3):699–717, 1982.

[LM93]   T. Y. C. Leung and R. R. Muntz. Stream Processing: Temporal Query Processing and Optimization. In A. Tansel, J. Clifford, S. Gadia, S. Jajodia, A. Segev, and R. T. Snodgrass, editors, *Temporal Databases: Theory, Design, and Implementation*, chapter 14, pages 329–355. Benjamin/Cummings Publishing Company, 1993.

[LS87]   U.W. Lipeck and G. Saake. Monitoring Dynamic Integrity Constraints Based on Temporal Logic. *Information Systems*, 12(3):255–269, 1987.

[MS93]   J. Melton and A. R. Simon. *Understanding the New SQL: A Complete Guide.* Morgan Kaufmann Publishers, Inc., San Mateo, CA, 1993.

[NA93]   S. Navathe and R. Ahmed. Temporal Extensions to the Relational Model and SQL. In A. Tansel, J. Clifford, S. Gadia, S. Jajodia, A. Segev, and R. T. Snodgrass, editors, *Temporal Databases: Theory, Design, and Implementation*, pages 92–109. Benjamin/Cummings Publishing Company, 1993.

[Sar90]   N. Sarda. Extensions to SQL for Historical Databases. *IEEE Transactions on Knowledge and Data Engineering*, 2(2):220–230, June 1990.

[Sar93]   N. Sarda. HSQL: A Historical Query Language. In A. Tansel, J. Clifford, S. Gadia, S. Jajodia, A. Segev, and R. T. Snodgrass, editors, *Temporal Databases: Theory, Design, and Implementation*. Benjamin/Cummings Publishing Company, 1993.

[Sno87]   R. T. Snodgrass. The Temporal Query Language TQuel. *ACM Transactions on Database Systems*, 12(2):247–298, June 1987.

[Sno95]   R. T. Snodgrass, editor. *The TSQL2 Temporal Query Language.* Kluwer Academic Publishers, 674+xxiv pages, 1995.

[SW95]   A.P. Sistla and O. Wolfson. Temporal Triggers in Active Databases. *IEEE Transactions on Knowledge and Data Engineering*, 7(3):471–486, June, 1995.

[Tan86]   A. U. Tansel. Adding time dimension to relational model and extending relational algebra. *Information Systems*, 11(4):343–355, 1986.

[Tom95]   D. Toman. Point-based vs. Interval-based Temporal Query Languages. TR-CS-95-15, Kansas State University, 1995.

[TN96]   D. Toman and D. Niwiński. First-Order Temporal Queries Inexpressible in Temporal Logic. Proc. *EDBT'96* (to appear), 1996.

[TC90]   A. Tuzhilin and J. Clifford. A Temporal Relational Algebra as a Basis for Temporal Relational Completeness. In *Proceedings of the International Conference on Very Large Databases*, 1990.

[VGT91]   A. Van Gelder and R.W. Topor. Safety and Translation of Relational Calculus Queries. *ACM Transactions on Database Systems*, 16(2):235–278, June 1991.

[Wüt91]   B. Wüthrich. *Large Deductive Databases with Constraints.* PhD thesis, Department Informatik, ETH Zürich, 1991.

A Formal Temporal Object-Oriented Data Model

Elisa Bertino [1]   *Elena Ferrari* [1]   *Giovanna Guerrini* [2]

[1] Dipartimento di Scienze dell'Informazione
Università di Milano - Milano, Italy
bertino@hermes.mc.dsi.unimi.it, ferrari@dsi.unimi.it

[2] Dipartimento di Informatica e Scienze dell'Informazione
Università di Genova - Genova, Italy
guerrini@disi.unige.it

Abstract. Although many temporal extensions to the relational data model have been proposed, there is no comparable amount of work in the context of object-oriented data models. This paper presents T_Chimera, a temporal extension of the Chimera data model. The main contribution of this work is to define a formal temporal object-oriented data model and to address on a formal basis several issues deriving from the introduction of time in an object-oriented context.

1 Introduction

Conventional database systems do not offer the possibility of dealing with time-varying data. The content of a database represents a *snapshot* of the reality in that only the current data are recorded, without the possibility of maintaining the complete history of data over time. If such a need arises, data histories must be managed at application program level, thus, making the management of data very difficult, if at all possible. To overcome this lack in the past years there has been a growing interest in extending data models with temporal capabilities [11]. Most proposals are temporal extensions of the relational data model [4, 6, 13], and can be classified in two main categories. The *tuple timestamping* approach uses normalized (1NF) relations in which special time attributes are added [13]. The *attribute timestamping* approach uses non-normalized (N1NF) relations and attaches time to attribute values [6]. Some common approaches [4, 6] view attribute values as partial functions from the time domain to the attribute value domain. On the contrary, research on temporal object-oriented databases is still in its early stage. Although various object-oriented temporal models have been proposed [14], there is no amount of theoretical work comparable to the work reported for the relational model. Moreover, the problems related to the introduction of time in an object-oriented context have never been discussed on a formal basis. By contrast, a great amount of theoretical research is being carried on in the area of non temporal object-oriented programming languages and databases, and theoretical foundations have been established [1]. Issues concerning type systems and type checking have been widely investigated in a non temporal object-oriented framework [9], but they have never been addressed in the framework of temporal object-oriented data models. In this paper we present the T-Chimera data model, a temporal extension of the Chimera object-oriented, deductive, active data model [8]. Chimera provides all concepts commonly ascribed to object-oriented data models, such as: object identity, complex objects, user-defined operations, classes and inheritance. The main contribution of this paper is to formally address several issues deriving from adding temporal capabilities to an object-oriented model. First, we introduce the notion of temporal type to handle in a uniform way temporal and non temporal domains. Then, we provide a formal definition of classes and objects, specifying the consistency of an object with respect to its class. Finally, a formal treatment of other features of the model, like object equality and inheritance is presented. This paper is organized as follows. In Section 2 we survey related work. Section 3 introduces T-Chimera types and values, while Sections 4 and 5 deal with classes and objects, respectively. Inheritance is considered in Section 6. Finally, Section 7 concludes the paper.

	[3]	[5]	[7]	[10]	[12]	[15]	[16]	Ours
o-o data model	Oodaplex	generic	Tigukat	MAD	generic	OSAM*	Oodaplex	Chimera
time structure	linear discrete	linear discrete	user-def.	linear discrete	linear discrete	linear discrete	user-def.	linear discrete
time dimension	valid	valid	valid + trans.	valid	valid + trans.	valid	arbitrary[1]	valid
values & objects	objects	objects	objects	objects	objects	objects	objects	both
class features	NO	NO	NO	NO	NO	NO	NO	YES
what is timestamped	attr.	attr.	arbitrary	objects	attr.	objects	arbitrary	attr.
temp. attr. values	funct.[2]	funct.[2]	sets of pairs	atomic valued[3]	lists of tuples	atomic valued[3]	funct.[2]	funct.[2]
kinds of attributes	temp. + imm.	temp. + imm.	temp. + imm.	temp. + imm.	temp. + imm.	temp. + imm.	temp. + imm.	temp. + imm + non-temp.
histories of obj. types	NO	YES	YES	NO	NO	NO[4]	YES	YES

Legenda:
[1] One time dimension is considered, it can be transaction or valid time.
[2] With *funct.* we denote functions from a temporal domain.
[3] Time is associated with the entire object state.
[4] The information can be derived from the histories of object instances.

Table 1. Comparison among temporal object-oriented data models

2 Related work

Table 1 compares some temporal object-oriented data models proposed in the literature. Some considered approaches are compared under a different perspective by Snodgrass [14]. In [14] the emphasis is on temporal object-oriented query languages, while we consider only data model characteristics. Moreover, in [14] only the temporal characteristics are compared, disregarding the object-oriented ones, whereas we consider both.

Most approaches focus on the temporal characteristics of the model and consider rather simple object models, for example none of them distinguishes values from objects, nor supports class features. Concerning the temporal aspects, most models support a linear discrete time structure[3], whereas only few model a user-defined hierarchy of time types. Two time dimensions are of interest in temporal databases: *valid* time (the time a fact was true in reality) and *transaction* time (the time the fact was stored in the database). Most models consider only the valid time. Some approaches associate a timestamp with the whole object state; others associate a timestamp with each object attribute often regarding the value of a temporal attribute as a function from a temporal domain to the set of legal values for the attribute. Another important characteristic is whether temporal, immutable and non temporal attributes are supported. A *temporal* (or historical) attribute is an attribute whose value may change over time, and whose values at different times are recorded in the database. An *immutable* attribute is an attribute whose value cannot be modified during the object lifetime[4], whereas a *non temporal* (or static) attribute is an attribute whose value can change over time, but whose past values are not meaningful, and are thus not stored in the database. Some models keep track of the dynamic links between an object and its most specific class. Indeed, an important dynamic aspect of object-oriented databases is that an object can dynamically change type, by specializing or generalizing its current one.

3 Types and values

In this section we introduce T_Chimera types and values. In the following we refer to Table 2 that summarizes the functions used in defining the model. For each function the table reports the name, the signature and the output[5].

3.1 T_Chimera types

We denote with $\mathcal{OI}$ a set of object identifiers, with $\mathcal{CI}$ a set of class identifiers, that is, class names, with $\mathcal{AN}$ a set of attribute names and with $\mathcal{MN}$ a set of method names.

---

[3] We consider time structure and time dimension as discussed in [14].

[4] Immutable attributes can be regarded as a particular case of temporal ones, since their value is a constant function from a temporal domain.

[5] The meaning of each function will be clarified in the remainder of the discussion.

Name	Signature	Output
T^-	$TT \rightarrow CT$	static type associated with a temporal type
π	$CI \times TIME \rightarrow 2^{OI}$	extent of a class at a given instant
$type$	$CI \rightarrow T$	structural type of a class
h_type	$CI \rightarrow T$	historical type of a class
s_type	$CI \rightarrow T$	static type of a class
h_state	$OI \times TIME \rightarrow V$	historical value of an object
s_state	$OI \rightarrow V$	static value of an object
$o\_lifespan$	$OI \rightarrow TIME \times TIME$	lifespan of an object
$c\_lifespan$	$OI \times CI \rightarrow TIME \times TIME$	lifespan of an object as a member of a class
$snapshot$	$OI \times TIME \rightarrow V$	state of an object at a given instant

Table 2. Functions employed in defining the model

In Chimera the existence of a finite set $BVT = \{B_1, \ldots, B_n\}$ of basic predefined value types is postulated, containing the types *integer*, *real*, *bool*, *character*
and *string*. Moreover, Chimera allows class names to be used in the definition
of types, as stated by the following definition.

Definition 1 (Object Types) [8] The set of Chimera object types OT is defined as the set of class identifiers CI. □

Chimera supports *structured types* such as sets, lists and records and allows
the use of class names in the definition of structured types.

Definition 2 (Value Types) [8] The set of Chimera value types VT is recursively defined as follows.

- the predefined basic value types are value types ($BVT \subseteq VT$);
- if T is a value type or an object type, then *list-of*(T) and *set-of*(T) are
  structured value types, indicated as list type and set type, respectively;
- if $T_1, \ldots, T_n$ are value types or object types and $a_1, \ldots, a_n$ are distinct elements of AN, then *record-of*($a_1 : T_1, \ldots, a_n : T_n$) is a structured value
  type, indicated as record type. □

The set of Chimera types CT is defined as the union of Chimera value types
VT and Chimera object types OT.

$T\_$Chimera extends the set of Chimera types with a collection of *temporal
types*, that allow to handle in a uniform way temporal and non temporal domains. For each Chimera type T, a corresponding temporal type, *temporal*(T),
is defined. First, the set BVT is extended with the type *time*. Intuitively, instances of type *temporal*(T) are partial functions from instances of type *time* to
instances of type T^6.

Definition 3 (T_Chimera Temporal Types) The set of $T\_$Chimera temporal types TT is defined as the set of types *temporal*(T), for each $T \in CT$. □

In $T\_$Chimera, temporal types can be used in the definition of structured
types, as stated by the following definition.

Definition 4 (T_Chimera Types) The set of $T\_$Chimera types T is defined
as follows.

- *time* is a $T\_$Chimera type (*time* $\in T$);
- the Chimera types are $T\_$Chimera types ($CT \subseteq T$);

---

[6] We elaborate on this informal definition in the following section.

- the temporal types are T-Chimera types $(TT \subseteq T)$;
- if T is a T-Chimera type then $list\text{-}of(T)$ and $set\text{-}of(T)$ are T-Chimera structured types;
- if $T_1, \ldots, T_n$ are T-Chimera types and $a_1, \ldots, a_n$ are distinct elements of $\mathcal{AN}$, then $record\text{-}of(a_1 : T_1, \ldots, a_n : T_n)$ is a T-Chimera structured type.

□

In the remainder of the discussion we use function: $T^- \colon TT \to CT$, which takes as argument a temporal type $temporal(T)$, and returns the corresponding static type T.

3.2 Values

For each predefined basic value type $\mathcal{B} \in \mathcal{BVT}$, we postulate the existence of a non-empty set of values, denoted as $dom(\mathcal{B})$. For instance, the domain of the basic value type $real$ is the set $\mathcal{R}$ of real numbers. Moreover, we assume as the domain of the type $time$ the domain $TIME = \{0, 1, \ldots, now, \ldots\}$, isomorphic to the set of natural numbers $\mathbb{N}$. Symbol '0' denotes the relative beginning, while now denotes the current time. Thus, we assume time to be discrete. An interval, denoted as $I = [t_1, t_2]$, is a set of consecutive time instants, including all time instants between t_1 and t_2, t_1 and t_2 included. A single time instant t can be represented as the time interval $[t, t]$, while $[,]$ denotes the null interval. The operators of union $(I_1 \cup I_2)$, intersection $(I_1 \cap I_2)$ inclusion $(I_1 \subseteq I_2)$ have the semantics of set operations. Moreover $t \in I$ is true if t is one of the instants represented by interval I. In the following, we use a set of disjoint intervals $I = \{[t_i, t_j], \ldots, [t_r, t_s]\}$ as a compact notation for the set of time instants included in these intervals.

Note that in T-Chimera oids in $\mathcal{OI}$ are handled as values. Thus, an object identifier i is a value of an object type in $\mathcal{OT}$. We consider as legal values for an object type c all the oids of objects belonging to c both as instances or as members[7]. The set of objects members of a class changes dynamically over time. Thus, to define the extension, that is, the set of legal values for T-Chimera object types, we introduce a function $\pi \colon CI \times TIME \to 2^{\mathcal{OI}}$, assigning an extent to each class, for each instant t. For each $c \in CI$, $\pi(c, t)$ is the set of the identifiers of objects that, at time t, belongs to c either as instances or as members.

Definition 5 (Type Legal Values) $[\![T]\!]_t$ denotes the extension of type T at time t.

- $null \in [\![T]\!]_t, \forall T \in T$;
- $[\![\mathcal{B}]\!]_t = dom(\mathcal{B}), \forall \mathcal{B} \in \mathcal{BVT}$;
- $[\![time]\!]_t = TIME$;
- $[\![c]\!]_t = \pi(c, t), \forall c \in CI$;
- $[\![set\text{-}of(T)]\!]_t = 2^{[\![T]\!]_t}$;
- $[\![list\text{-}of(T)]\!]_t = \{[v_1, \ldots, v_n] \mid n \geq 0, v_i \in [\![T]\!]_t, \forall i, 1 \leq i \leq n\}$;

---

[7] According to the usual terminology, an object is an *instance* of a class c, if c is the most specific class, in the inheritance hierarchy, to which the object belongs. If an object is an instance of a class it is also a *member* of all the superclasses of c.

- $[\![\text{record-of}(a_1 : T_1, \ldots, a_n : T_n)]\!]_t = \{(a_1 : v_1, \ldots, a_n : v_n) \mid a_i \in \mathcal{AN},$
  $v_i \in [\![T_i]\!]_t, \forall i, 1 \leq i \leq n\};$
- $[\![\text{temporal}(T)]\!]_t = \{f \mid f : \mathcal{TIME} \rightarrow \bigcup_{t' \in \mathcal{TIME}} [\![T]\!]_{t'} \text{ is a partial func-}$
  tion such that $\forall t'$ if $f(t')$ is defined then $f(t') \in [\![T]\!]_{t'}\}.$ □

Given an instant t the extensions of predefined basic value types are the elements of their corresponding domains, the extensions of classes are their explicit extents at time t, while the set of legal values of the structured types are defined recursively in terms of the legal values of their component types. The extension of a temporal type $temporal(T)$ is the set of partial functions from $\mathcal{TIME}$ (i.e, the set of legal values for type $time$) to the union of the sets of legal values for type T for each instant t' in $\mathcal{TIME}$. The value of a variable of type $temporal(T)$ can thus be represented as a set of pairs $(t, f(t))$, where f is a partial function, t is an element of $\mathcal{TIME}$ and $f(t)$ is the value of function f at time t. Usually, the value of a variable of type $temporal(T)$ does not change at each instant. Therefore, its value can be represented more concisely as a set of pairs $\{\langle \tau_1, v_1 \rangle, \ldots, \langle \tau_n, v_n \rangle\}$, where $v_1, \ldots, v_n$ are legal values for T, and $\tau_1, \ldots, \tau_n$ are time intervals, such that the variable assumes the value v_i for each instant in τ_i, $i = 1, \ldots, n$. We adopt this representation throughout the paper.

Example 1 Let t be an instant, i_1 and $i_2 \in \mathcal{OI}$ such that $i_1, i_2 \in \pi(person, t)$.
- $10, 100 \in [\![integer]\!]_t;$
- $\{i_1, i_2\} \in [\![set\text{-}of(person)]\!]_t;$
- (name: 'Bob', score:$\{\langle [1,100], 40 \rangle, \langle [101,200], 70 \rangle\}) \in$
  $[\![record\text{-}of(name : string, score : temporal(integer))]\!]_t.$ ◇

Definition 5 states the set of legal values for each T-Chimera type. In [2] we have defined a set of typing rules for values and we have proved their soundness and completeness.

4 Classes

A class in T-Chimera consists of two components: the *signature*, containing all the information for the use of the class and its instances, and the *implementation*, providing an implementation for the signature. A class can be *static* or *historical*. A class is static if all its c-attributes are static, that is, they do not have as domain a temporal type, it is historical otherwise[8]. Moreover, a *lifespan* is associated with each class, representing the time interval during which the class has existed. We assume the lifespan of a class to be contiguous. The class signature contains information about the attributes (name and domain) and the methods (name and type of input and output parameters) of its instances. Moreover, the signature contains similar information about c-attributes and c-methods. Since the objects belonging to a class vary over time, each class maintains the history of the objects instances or members of the class over time.

---

[8] Note that a static type may contain as a component a temporal type (cfr. Definition 4). For instance, $set\text{-}of(temporal(integer))$ is a legal T-Chimera type; we do not consider it a temporal type in that no track of the changes of its entire value over time is kept. Only the changes of its components are recorded.

The signature of a class is formally defined as follows[9].

Definition 6 (Class Signature) A class C is a 6-tuple $(c, type, lifespan, attr, meth, history)$, where

$c \in CI$ is the class identifier;

$type \in \{\texttt{static}, \texttt{historical}\}$ indicates whether the class is historical or static;

$lifespan \in (TIME \times TIME)$ is the lifespan of the class;

$attr$ is a set containing an item for each attribute of the class. Each item is a pair (a_name, a_type), where $a\_name \in AN$ is the attribute name and $a\_type \in T$ is the attribute domain.

$meth$ is a set containing an item for each method of the class. Each item is a pair (m_name, m_sign), where $m\_name \in MN$ is the method name and m_sign is the signature of the method, expressed as: $T_1 \times \ldots \times T_n \rightarrow T$, where $T_1, \ldots T_n, T \in T$, denote types of input and output parameters of the method, respectively.

$history \in V$, is a value containing the values for each c-attribute, plus two temporal values, representing the objects instances and members of C over time, respectively; $history$ is a record value $(a_1 : v_1, \ldots, a_n : v_n, ext : E, proper\text{-}ext : PE)$, where $a_1, \ldots, a_n$ are the names of the c-attributes of C, $v_1, \ldots, v_n$ are their corresponding values, E and PE are values of type $temporal(set\text{-}of(c))$. □

The temporal attributes ext and $proper\text{-}ext$ denote the set of the oids of objects members and instances, of the class, respectively, for each instant t of its lifetime. Obviously $PE(t) \subseteq E(t)$, $\forall t \in C.lifespan$, as all objects instances of a class at a given instant are also members of the class at the same instant. Function π (cfr. Table 2), is such that, for each class name c' and for each $t \in C.lifespan$, $\pi(c', t) = C.history.ext(t)$, where C is the class identified by c'.

Example 2 Consider a class *project*, whose instances are research projects. Suppose that objects of this class have as attributes a *name*, which is immutable during the project lifetime, an *objective* and a *workplan* whose variations over time are not relevant for the application at hand, and a *subproject* and some *participants*, for which the whole history must be maintained. Suppose that $i_1, \ldots, i_4 \in OI$, then the corresponding T-Chimera class signature is:

$c = project$

$type = \texttt{static}$

$lifespan = [\texttt{10}, \texttt{now}]$

$attr = \{(name, temporal(string)), (objective, string),$
$\quad\quad (workplan, set\text{-}of(task)), (subproject, temporal(project)),$
$\quad\quad (participants, temporal(set\text{-}of(person)))\}$

$meth = \{(add\text{-}participant, person \rightarrow project)\}$

$history = (average\text{-}participants: 20, ext : \{\langle[\texttt{10},\texttt{now}], \{i_1, \ldots, i_4\}\rangle\},$
$\quad\quad proper\text{-}ext : \{\langle[\texttt{10},\texttt{50}], \{i_1\}\rangle, \langle[\texttt{51},\texttt{now}], \{i_1, i_2\}\rangle\})$

Note that, the class *project* is a static class, since its only c-attribute *average-participants* is static. ◇

---

[9] Actually, each class has an associated *metaclass* to model in a uniform way object features and class features.

We now discuss the relationships between a class and its associated types. The identifier of a class C denotes the object type corresponding to C. Such object type is the type of the identifiers of the objects instances of C. Suppose that class C has as *attr* component the set: $\{(a_1, T_1), \ldots, (a_n, T_n)\}$, the following types can be associated with C.

- *Structural type.* It represents the type of the attributes of instances of C. It is defined by the record type $record\text{-}of(a_1 : T_1, \ldots, a_n : T_n)$.
- *Historical type.* It represents the type of the temporal attributes of instances of C. It is defined by the record type $record\text{-}of(a_k : T'_k, \ldots, a_m : T'_m)$. Let $\{(a_k, T_k), \ldots, (a_m, T_m)\}, 1 \leq k \leq m \leq n$, be the subset of *attr* consisting of all the pairs (a_i, T_i) such that T_i is a temporal type, then (a_i, T'_i) is such that $T'_i = T^-(T_i), \forall i = k, \ldots, m$.
- *Static type.* It represents the type of the static attributes of instances of C. It is defined by the record type $record\text{-}of(a_k : T_k, \ldots, a_m : T_m)$, where $\{(a_k, T_k), \ldots, (a_m, , T_m)\}, 1 \leq k \leq m \leq n$, is the subset of *attr* consisting of all the pairs (a_i, T_i), such that T_i is not a temporal type.

The notions of *structural*, *historical* and *static* types of a class will be used in the next section to check object consistency. We define three functions: *type*, h_type, s_type: $\mathcal{CI} \rightarrow \mathcal{T}$, taking as argument a class identifier c, and returning the structural, the historical and the static type of the class identified by c, respectively[10].

5 Objects

T_Chimera handles in a uniform way both historical and static objects. An object is historical if it contains at least one attribute with a temporal domain, it is static otherwise. Each object has a lifespan associated, representing the time interval during which the object exists. As for classes, we assume the lifespan of an object to be contiguous. Therefore, we do not consider a *reincarnate* operation [5]. Objects can be instances of different classes during their lifetime, but we can assume that for each instant in their lifespan, there exists at least a class to which they belong[11]. For example, an employee can be fired and rehired, but he remains instance of the class *person*, superclass of the class *employee*, till the end of its lifetime. Moreover, for each historical object the history of the most specific class to which it belongs during its lifespan is recorded. On the contrary, for each static object, only the class identifier of the most specific class to which it currently belongs is maintained.

Definition 7 (Object) An object o is a 4-tuple $(i, lifespan, v, class\text{-}history)$, where

$i \in \mathcal{OI}$ is the oid of o;

---

[10] Note that function h_type returns a null value when its argument is the identifier of a class whose instances are static, whereas function s_type returns a null value when its argument is a class whose instances only have temporal attributes.

[11] This class is the most general class (in the inheritance hierarchy) the object has ever belonged to.

lifespan $\in (\mathcal{TIME} \times \mathcal{TIME})$ is the lifespan of o;

$v \in \mathcal{V}$ is a value, containing the values of each attribute of o. It is a record value $(a_1 : v_1, \ldots, a_n : v_n)$, where $a_1, \ldots, a_n \in \mathcal{AN}$ are the names of the attributes of o and $v_1, \ldots, v_n$ are their corresponding values;

class-history stores information about the most specific class to which o belongs over time. It is a set $\{\langle \tau_1, c_1 \rangle, \ldots, \langle \tau_n, c_n \rangle\}$, where $\tau_1, \ldots, \tau_n$ are time intervals, $c_1, \ldots and c_n$ are class identifiers, such that c_i is the class identifier of the most specific class to which o belongs in τ_i, $1 \leq i \leq n$. □

If o is static, *class-history* records only the most specific class to which o currently belongs.

Example 3 Suppose that $i_1, \ldots, i_7 \in \mathcal{OI}$ and *project* $\in \mathcal{CI}$. The following is an example of T_Chimera object:

$i = i_1$

$lifespan = [10, \text{now}]$

$v = \{(name : \{\langle [10,\text{now}], \text{'IDEA'}\rangle\}), (objective : \textbf{'Implementation'}),$
$\quad (workplan : \{i_7\}), (subproject : \{\langle [10,45],i_4\rangle, \langle [46,\text{now}],i_6\rangle\}),$
$\quad (participants : \{\langle [10,80],\{i_2,i_3\}\rangle, \langle [81,\text{now}], \{i_2,i_3,i_5\}\rangle\}), \}.$

$class\text{-}history = \{\langle [10,\text{now}], project\rangle\}$

Note that, the above object is historical, since it contains some temporal attributes.

In a temporal context, several temporal constraints must be satisfied by object lifespans. To formalize these constraints we define function $o\_lifespan$: $\mathcal{OI} \rightarrow \mathcal{TIME} \times \mathcal{TIME}$, that given an oid i returns the lifespan of the object identified by i. Obviously, information about the historical extent of a class must be consistent with the class histories of the objects in the database, as stated by the following invariant.

Invariant 1 $\forall i' \in \mathcal{OI}, \forall c' \in \mathcal{CI}, \forall t \in \mathcal{TIME}$, let o be the object such that $o.i = i'$, C be the class such that $C.c = c'$, then

1. $i' \in C.history.ext(t) \Rightarrow t \in o\_lifespan(i')$;
2. $(\forall t \in \tau, i' \in C.history.proper\text{-}ext(t)) \Leftrightarrow \langle \tau, c' \rangle \in o.class\text{-}history$. △

Moreover, the lifespan of an object can be partitioned in a set of intervals, depending on the object most specific class. Indeed, during its lifetime an object can be member of different classes. Therefore, we introduce function $c\_lifespan$: $\mathcal{OI} \times \mathcal{CI} \rightarrow \mathcal{TIME} \times \mathcal{TIME}$, that given an oid i and a class identifier c, returns the interval representing the set of time instants in which i was a member of the class identified by c^{12}. The temporal constraints stated by the following invariant must be satisfied.

Invariant 2 $\forall i \in \mathcal{OI}, \forall c' \in \mathcal{CI}, \forall t \in \mathcal{TIME}$, then

1. $o\_lifespan(i) = \bigcup_{c \in \mathcal{CI}} c\_lifespan(i,c)$;
2. $t \in c\_lifespan(i,c') \Leftrightarrow i \in C.history.ext(t)$, where $c' = C.c$ [13]. △

---

[12] Note that $c\_lifespan(i,c) = \bigcup_{\langle \tau_i, c_i \rangle \in o.class-history, c_i \text{ subclass of } c} \tau_i$. Functions $o\_lifespan$ and $c\_lifespan$ are similar to those defined in [16].

[13] This also implies that $t \in c\_lifespan(i,c') \Leftrightarrow i \in [\![c']\!]_t$.

5.1 Consistency notions

Because of object migrations, the most specific class to which an object belongs can vary over time. Moreover, an object can be an instance of the same class in different, not consecutive, time instants. As an example, consider the case of an employee that is promoted to manager, (*manager* being a subclass of *employee* with some extra attributes, like *subordinates* and *official_car*). The other case is the transfer of the manager back to normal employee status. The migration of an object from a class to another can cause the addition or the deletion of some attributes from the object. The promotion of an employee to the manager status has the effect of adding the attributes *subordinates* and *official_car* to the corresponding object, while the transfer of the manager back to the employee status causes dropping the attributes *subordinates* and *official_car* from the corresponding object. If the attributes *subordinates* and *official_car* are static, they are deleted from the object. No track of their existence is recorded in the object when it migrates to the class *employee*. If they are temporal, the values they had when the object migrated to the class *manager* are maintained in the object, even if they are not part of the object anymore.

We require that each object must be a consistent instance of all the classes to which it belongs. In a context where objects can have both static and temporal attributes, the notion of consistency assumes a slightly different semantics with respect to its classical definition. Verifying the consistency of an object in a temporal context requires two steps. First the set of attributes characterizing the object for each instant t of its lifespan must be determined. Then, the correctness of their values must be checked. Note that, if we consider an instant t lesser than the current time, we are able to identify only the temporal attributes characterizing the object at time t, since for static attributes we record only their current values. Thus, for instants lesser than the current time, it only makes sense to check the correctness of the values of the temporal attributes of the objects. Therefore, we start by introducing the following definition.

Definition 8 (Meaningful Temporal Attributes) Let a be a temporal attribute of an object o. Let v be its value. Attribute a is said to be meaningful for o at time t, if t belongs to the domain of v. □

Note that, as the value of a temporal attribute is a partial function from $\mathcal{TIME}$ to the attribute value domain, its domain is the set of time instants for which the value is defined. We distinguish two kinds of consistency:

- *Historical consistency*. The values of the temporal attributes of the object at a given instant are legal values for the temporal attributes of the class.
- *Static consistency*. The values of the static attributes of the object are legal values for the static attributes of the class.

Consider an object $o = (i, lifespan, v, class\text{-}history)$, such that $v = (a_1 : v_1, \ldots, a_n : v_n)$. Therefore, given an instant $t \in o.lifespan$, the following values can be defined:

- *Historical value*. It is a record representing the values of the temporal attributes meaningful for the object at time t. Let $\{a_k, \ldots, a_m\}$, $1 \le k \le m \le$

n, be the subset of $\{a_1, \ldots, a_n\}$ consisting of all the names of the temporal attributes meaningful for o at time t. The historical value of o at time t is defined as $(a_k : v_k(t), \ldots, a_m : v_m(t))$, where $v_i(t)$ denotes the value of a_i at time t, $i = k, \ldots, m$.

- *Static value.* It is a record representing the values of the static attributes of the object. Its definition is analogous to that of the historical value, considering static attributes instead of the temporal ones.

Thus, we define two functions: $h\_state : \mathcal{OI} \times \mathcal{TIME} \rightarrow \mathcal{V}$, receiving an object identifier and an instant t, and returning the historical value of the object at time t; $s\_state : \mathcal{OI} \rightarrow \mathcal{V}$, receiving an object identifier, and returning the static value of the object. Note that when an object consists only of temporal attributes, h_state returns a snapshot of the value of the object attributes for a specified time instant. We are now ready to formally introduce the notions of *historical* and *static* consistency, by making use of functions h_type and s_type (cfr. Table 2).

Definition 9 (Historical Consistency) An object $o = (i, lifespan, v, class-history)$ is an historically consistent instance of a class c' at time t if $h\_state(o.i, t)$ is a legal value for the type $h\_type(c')$. □

Definition 10 (Static Consistency) An object $o = (i, lifespan, v, class-history)$ is a statically consistent instance of a class c', if $s\_state(o.i)$ is a legal value for the type $s\_type(c')$. □

The consistency of an object is checked only with respect to its most specific class. If an object is consistent with respect to its most specific class, it is consistent with respect to all its superclasses.

Definition 11 (Object Consistency) An object $o = (i, lifespan, v, class-history)$ is consistent iff the following conditions hold:

- For each pair $\langle \tau, c' \rangle$ in $o.class-history$, interval τ is contained in the lifespan of the class identified by c', that is, $\tau \subseteq C.lifespan$, where C is the class such that $C.c = c'$.
- For each pair $\langle \tau, c' \rangle$ in $o.class-history$, o is an historical consistent instance of c', for each instant $t \in \tau$.
- Let $\langle \tau, c \rangle$ be the (unique) element of $o.class-history$, such that $now \in \tau$. Object o must be a static consistent instance of class c. □

The above definition states that each object, for each instant t of its lifespan, must contain a value for each temporal attribute of the class to which it belongs at time t, and this value must be of the correct type. Moreover, at the current time also the consistency with respect to the static attributes must be checked. This notion of consistency allows to uniformly treat both static and historical objects. In the case of static objects, Definition 11 reduces to the traditional notion of consistency.

5.2 Object equality

Chimera, like most object-oriented systems, supports two notions of equality: *equality by identity* (meaning that the two objects are the same object), and *equality by value* (meaning that the two objects have the same attribute values). Equality by value can be further refined into: *shallow value equality*, which considers the equality of all the direct attributes of an object, and *deep value equality*, which considers in addition to the equality of the attributes, the equality of the attributes of objects which are recursively reached by means of oid references. A formalization of these concepts for the Chimera model can be found in [8]. Here, we consider only shallow value equality.

In a temporal context, we still have the classical notion of object identity, being the oid of an object a time invariant property.

Definition 12 (Equality by Identity) Two objects o_1 and o_2 are equal by identity iff they have the same object identifier, that is, $o_1.i = o_2.i$. ▫

Obviously, if two objects have the same oid, also all their other components are equal. Value equality is defined as follows.

Definition 13 (Value Equality) Two objects o_1 and o_2 are equal by value iff $o_1.v = o_2.v$. ▫

The above definition implies both the equality of the attribute values and of the attribute names and applies to both static and historical objects. For static objects, it simply reduces to the conventional notion of value equality, whereas for historical objects the equality of the whole history of temporal attributes is required.

In a temporal context, two further notions of value equality can be devised: *instantaneous-value equality* and *weak-value equality*. Two objects are instantaneously value equal if there exists an instant t in which their attributes have the same values. Two objects are weakly value equal if their attributes have ever had the same values, also in different instants. These notions of equality obviously make sense for historical objects consisting only of temporal attributes. Moreover, also historical objects containing static attributes can be compared under these types of equalities, but only at the current time, since we cannot reconstruct the value of static attributes at an instant t lesser than the current time. Finally, static objects can be compared only at the current time, too. Consider a function $snapshot : \mathcal{OI} \times \mathcal{TIME} \rightarrow \mathcal{V}$ that given an object identifier i' and an instant t "projects" the state of the object identified by i' at time t. This function returns a record value $(a_1 : v_1, \ldots, a_n : v_n)$ such that, for all j, $1 \leq j \leq n$: (i) if attribute a_j is static, $v_j = o.v.a_j$; (ii) if a_j is temporal, $v_j = o.v.a_j(t)$, where o is the object identified by i' ($o.i = i'$)[14]. For historical objects containing also static attributes and for static objects, we are able to reconstruct only the snapshot at the current time, thus in this case $snapshot(i,t)$ is undefined for $t \neq now$. For instance, referring to the object of Example 3, $snapshot(i_1, now) = (name :\text{'IDEA'},$ $objective :\text{'Implementation'}, workplan : \{i_7\}, subproject :i_6, participants : \{i_2, i_3, i_5\})$, whereas $snapshot(i_1, t)$, for $t \neq now$ is undefined.

Definition 14 (Instantaneous-value Equality) Two objects o_1 and o_2 are instantaneously value equal if there exists an instant $t \in o_1.lifespan \cap o_2.lifespan$ such that, $snapshot(o_1.i, t) = snapshot(o_2.i, t)$. ▫

---

[14] For historical objects containing only temporal attributes, the *snapshot* function coincides with the *h_state* function (cfr. Table 2).

Definition 15 (Weak-value Equality) Two objects o_1 and o_2 are weakly value equal if there exist two instants $t' \in o_1.lifespan$ and $t'' \in o_2.lifespan$, such that $snapshot(o_1.i, t') = snapshot(o_2.i, t'')$.   □

The usefulness of these notions of equality can be exemplified as follows. Referring to the class *project* of Example 2, two *project* objects having the same current state and the same history of modifications for *subproject* and *participants* attributes, are value equal. Two *project* objects having the same current value for all the attributes are instantaneous (and thus, weak) value equal.

6 Inheritance

Inheritance relationships among classes are described by an ISA hierarchy established by the user. We can suppose this information to be expressed as a partial order $\leq_{ISA}$ on the set of class identifiers $\mathcal{CI}$. Inheritance has two important implications: *substitutability*, that is, the property that each instance of a class can be used whenever an instance of one of its superclasses is expected; *extent inclusion*, that is, the property ensuring that the extent of a class is included in that of its superclasses.

6.1 Substitutability

A set of conditions must be satisfied by two classes related by the ISA relationship. These conditions are related to the fact that each subclass must contain all attributes and operations of all its superclasses. Inherited concepts may be redefined in a subclass definition under a number of restrictions. In Chimera the redefinition of the signature of an attribute is possible by specializing the domain of the attribute.

To formally define notions such as domain refinement, we have defined in [2] a subtype relationship $\leq_T$, similar to that introduced in most object-oriented data models, extended to temporal types by stating $temporal(T_2) \leq_T temporal(T_1)$ iff $T_2 \leq_T T_1$. The set T of types with the ordering $\leq_T$ is a poset. The following rule establishes refinement conditions for attribute domains in subclasses.

Rule 1 (Refinement of attribute domains) Let c_1 be a class, and a an attribute whose domain in c_1 is T. Let c_2 be a class such that $c_2 \leq_{ISA} c_1$. Attribute a in class c_2 can have as domain a type $T' \in T$ such that either (*i*) $T' \leq_T T$, or (*ii*) $T' = temporal(T'')$, $T'' \leq_T T$.   △

Rule 1 states that a non temporal attribute can be refined in a temporal attribute (on the same domain or on a most specific one), but not vice-versa. To ensure substitutability, however, we need to introduce a *coercion* function, since the value of a temporal attribute, which is a function from a temporal domain, cannot be substituted (from a typing viewpoint) by a value of a non temporal attribute, which is not a function. Suppose that class c_2 refines the non temporal domain of attribute a of its superclass c_1 in a temporal domain. Then, whenever an object o, instance of c_2, must be seen as an instance of c_1, the value of attribute a is "coerced" to $o.v.a(now)$, that is, the value of the function which is the value of the temporal attribute a at the instant now. The coercion function used is the *snapshot* function (cfr. Table 2). By considering a snapshot of the object at the instant now, the coerced value is $snapshot(o.i, now).a$. Note that this coercion is semantically meaningful. Indeed, in c_1 we are not interested in the history of the values taken by attribute a, but only in the last value of a.

6.2 Extent inclusion

At the extensional level, we require that in each database state the extent of a class is a subset of the extent of its superclasses.

Invariant 3 Given $c_1, c_2 \in \mathcal{CI}$, $c_2 \leq_{ISA} c_1$, and $c_1 = C_1.c$, $c_2 = C_2.c$, then

1. $C_2.lifespan \subseteq C_1.lifespan$;
2. $\forall t \in C_2.lifespan$, $C_2.history.ext(t) \subseteq C_1.history.ext(t)$;
3. $\forall i \in \mathcal{OI}$ $c\_lifespan(i, c_2) \subseteq c\_lifespan(i, c_1)$.   △

In Chimera a common superclass of all the classes does not exist. Therefore the hierarchy is a DAG, consisting of a number of connected components whose roots are the classes without superclasses, called *root classes*. Furthermore, since we consider objects which are instances of a unique class, the sets of oids in different hierarchies are disjoint. Consider a set of root classes $C_1, \ldots, C_m$ and an instant $t \in \mathcal{TIME}$, then Ext_i^t, $i = 1, \ldots, m$, denotes the extension of C_i at time t, which is the extent of the entire hierarchy rooted at C_i at this time. The following invariant must hold, stating that the sets of objects that have ever belonged to different hierarchies are disjoint, since an object cannot migrate over different hierarchies.

Invariant 4 Let $C_1, \ldots, C_m$ be the root classes of the ISA relationship, then for each i, j with $i \neq j$, $1 \leq i, j \leq m$, $\bigcup_{t \in \mathcal{TIME}} Ext_i^t \cap \bigcup_{t \in \mathcal{TIME}} Ext_j^t = \emptyset$.   △

7 Conclusions and future work

In this paper we have presented T-Chimera, an extension of the Chimera data model incorporating temporal capabilities. We have introduced the notion of temporal type and we have defined the set of legal T-Chimera values for each type. We have discussed the notion of object consistency and integrity and we have investigated problems related to inheritance and object identity in a temporal framework. This work can be extended in several directions. First, other features of Chimera, like methods, triggers and deductive rules will be extended with time. Issues such as termination and confluence will need to be re-visited when dealing with temporal triggers. Then, we plan to define a temporal integrity constraint language for Chimera allowing, among other things, to express constraints based on past histories of objects. We are also interested in investigating temporal object references and issues related to the query language and its typing. Time-dependent behavior is an interesting topic of future work, too. Finally, implementation issues will be investigated.

Acknowledgement. The authors wish to thank Claudio Bettini for useful preliminary discussions. Thanks are also due to the anonymous reviewers for their comments.

References

1. S. Abiteboul, R. Hull, and V. Vianu. *Foundations of Databases*. Addison-Wesley, 1995.
2. E. Bertino, E. Ferrari and G. Guerrini. A Formal Temporal Object-Oriented Data Model. Technical Report 141-95, University of Milano, 1995.
3. T. Cheng and S. Gadia. An Object-Oriented Model for Temporal Databases. In *Proc. of the Int'l Work. on an Infrastructure for Temporal Databases*, 1993.
4. J. Clifford and A. Crocker. The Historical Relational Data Model (HRDM) Revisited. In A. Tansel et al., editors, *Temporal Databases: Theory, Design, and Implementation*, pp. 6–26. Benjamin/Cummings, 1993.
5. J. Clifford and A. Croker. Objects in Time. In *Proc. 4th IEEE Int'l Conf. on Data Engineering*, pp. 11–18, 1988.
6. S.K. Gadia and S.S. Nair. Temporal Databases: A Prelude to Parametric Data. In A. Tansel et al., editors, *Temporal Databases: Theory, Design, and Implementation*, pp. 28–66. Benjamin/Cummings, 1993.
7. I. Goralwalla and M. Özsu. Temporal Extensions to a Uniform Behavioral Object Model. In *Proc. 12th Int'l Conf. on the Entity-Relationship Approach*, LNCS 823, pp. 110–121, 1993.
8. G. Guerrini, E. Bertino, and R. Bal. A Formal Definition of the Chimera Object-Oriented Data Model. Technical Report IDEA.DE.2P.011.01, ESPRIT Project 6333, 1994. Submitted for publication.
9. C. Gunter and J. Mitchell. *Theoretical Aspects of Object-Oriented Programming*. MIT Press, 1994.
10. W. Käfer and H. Schöning. Realizing a Temporal Complex-Object Data Model. In *Proc. of the ACM SIGMOD Int'l Conf.*, pp. 266–275, 1992.
11. N. Kline. An Update of the Temporal Database Bibliography. Proc. SIGMOD-RECORD, Vol. 22 Num. 4, 1993.
12. E. Rose and A. Segev. TOODM - A Temporal Object-Oriented Data Model with Temporal Constraints. In *Proc. 10th Int'l Conf. on the Entity-Relationship Approach*, pp. 205–229, 1991.
13. R. Snodgrass. The Temporal Query Language TQUEL. *ACM Transactions on Database Systems*, 12(2):247–298, June 1987.
14. R. Snodgrass. Temporal Object-Oriented Databases: A Critical Comparison. In W. Kim, editor, *Modern Database Systems: The Object Model, Interoperability and Beyond*. Addison-Wesley, 1995.
15. S. Su and H. Chen. A Temporal Knowledge Representation Model OSAM*/T and its Query Language OQL/T. In *Proc. 17th VLDB Conf.*, pp. 431–441, 1991.
16. G. Wuu and U. Dayal. A Uniform Model for Temporal and Versioned Object-Oriented Databases. In A. Tansel et al., editors, *Temporal Databases: Theory, Design, and Implementation*, pp. 230–247. Benjamin/Cummings, 1993.

The Web and Hypermedia

Dynamic Development and Refinement of HyperMedia Documents

Lois Delcambre[1], Catherine Hamon[2], Michel Biezunski[2], Radhika Reddy[1], Steven R. Newcomb[3]

lmd@cse.ogi.edu, hamon@hightext.com, michel@hightext.com, reddy@cse.ogi.edu, srn@techno.com

[1]Oregon Graduate Institute
Portland, Oregon
(503)690-1689

[2]High Text, S.A.R.L.,
Paris, France
(33) 1 42 05 93 15

[3]TechnoTeacher, Inc.
Rochester, New York
(716) 389 0964

1 Introduction

The Topic Map Architecture allows a collection of documents or other information objects to be semantically enriched through the definition of Topics and Topic Relations. The Topic Map is defined as part of the Conventions for the Application of HyTime[1] (CApH) Topic Navigation Module [1]. The CApH committee has been working for three years, chaired by Steven R. Newcomb [5] and sponsored by the Graphic Communications Association. The EnLIGHTeN Hyperdocument Navigation System, developed by High Text, S.A.R.L., implements part of the Topic Map Architecture.

The Topic Map can be viewed as combining the features of an independent index, glossary, and thesaurus much like the index at the back of a traditional, printed book, or the catalog of a library. But a Topic Map allows the user to dynamically place arbitrary terms of interest into the index and then link the term to any of the documents, according to the user's needs. The Topic Map document and all other document information objects collectively comprise a hyperdocument.

As an example, the Topic of "Person" is a HyTime link that might have a "Biography" anchor role. Through this anchor role, a person could then have as its anchors a paragraph in an encyclopedia, a section in a historical account, or an entire document, such as an autobiography, in the underlying collection of information objects. A Person might have another anchor role, for example "Citation" through which the person can be connected to any place where the person is mentioned. The Topic Map also allows the user to define Topic Relations, like a relation called Invented-by, that can connect two Topics, such as a Person with a Device.

A Topic Map provides more than the connections in an ordinary hyperdocument web because it defines Topics and Topic Relations at two levels. The Topic Map definition includes the declaration for Topic types and for Topic Relation types and the Topic Map instance allows the user to instantiate specific Topics and Topic Relations, according to these types. The Topic Map is represented as an SGML document (or a portion of an SGML document) and includes a Topic Map definition and a Topic Map instance. A Topic Map can be distributed over many documents (providing scalability) and any portion of a Topic Map can be inside a document whose primary purpose is not necessarily to contain a Topic Map. Such a contained Topic Map may (or may not) provide topic mapping service exclusively (or nonexclusively) to the document that contains it.

The Topic Map definition is analogous to a database schema, expressed in a simple Entity-Relationship Model. Continuing with the above example, given a Topic type of Person, the user could dynamically create Person Topic instances for Thomas Edison, Henri Pitot, and Alexander Graham Bell. The anchor roles for person, defined with the Person Topic type, are Biography and Citation. The anchor roles serve to differentiate the anchors for Thomas Edison in the collection of documents that describe him (for the Biography anchor role) and cite him (for the Citation anchor role). If a Device Topic type were defined in the Topic Map definition, then the Light Bulb could be entered as an instance of the Device Topic type. Finally, the Edison Topic instance and the Light Bulb Topic instance could be connected (in the Topic Map instance) by an instance of the Invented-By Topic Relationship type.

It is through the Topic Map definition that additional semantics are introduced. Rather than just providing links from one part of a document to the next like a regular hyperdocument, a Topic Map defines the reason or the meaning of the link. For the two anchors (i.e., the section and the paragraph in a standard Encyclopedia), the Topic Map tells us that they are both filling the anchor role of Biography for this Person.

The Topic Map Architecture is dynamic because new Topic and Topic Relation types, as well as individual Topic and Topic Relation instances can be introduced or changed at any time. The choice

---

[1]Hypermedia/Time-based Structuring Language (ISO/IEC 10744:1992)

of the anchors for each Topic can be changed as well. The hierarchical or other document structure is not changed because of the Topic Map definition and instance. This means that the individual documents in the collection can still be used for all of their original purposes: browsing, printing, etc. The Topic Map Architecture is unobtrusive: it does not require any alteration of the underlying documents.

The Topic Map Architecture is described below, in Section 2. Next, this paper describes how EnLIGHTeN can be used to create a Topic Map, in Section 3. The paper briefly discusses how a Topic Map compares to a conventional database schema in Section 4 and presents ideas for future work in Section 5.

2 Overview of the Topic Map Architecture

The Topic Map Architecture introduces a structure, represented as an SGML document, to represent both the Topic Map definition and the Topic Map instance. A simplified picture of the Topic Map Architecture is shown in Figure 1.

This figure shows the example described in Section 1. There are several documents in the Universe of Documents indicated as Document 1, Document 2, through Document n. Each document is shown as an SGML document; each document is self-contained. The Topic Map shows the two Topic types of Person and Device with corresponding instances in the Topic Map instance. The Topic Relation is defined in the Topic Map definition with one instance shown in the Topic Map instance.

The icon that looks like an envelope is meant to graphically indicate that a link end can contain multiple anchor addresses (either for a Topic or for a Topic Relation). The dashed lines from the envelopes to the Universe of Documents are meant to indicate the actual addresses of the anchors in the documents. The envelope may contain the address of an entire document (as indicated by the reference to Document 1). It may also contain an address of a portion of a document, as shown with dashed lines pointing into Document 2. Note that both Edison and the Light Bulb might point to the same anchor in Document 2. Then the two envelopes containing the address of the Citation

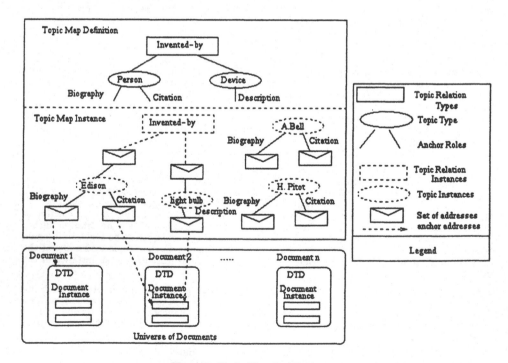

Figure 1: Topic Map Architecture

anchors for Edison and the address of the Description anchors for light bulb, might hold the same anchor address. When navigating through the Topic Map, if the anchor in Document 2 is pointed to by either of the Topics, the user can easily navigate back up to either of the Topics, to the next anchor (in either of the Biography or Description envelopes), or through the document.

3 Overview of EnLIGHTeN

The current implementation of EnLIGHTeN [2, 4] supports underlying information objects coded in SGML. EnLIGHTeN is built on top of the HyMinder HyTime Engine (Trademark of TechnoTeacher, Inc.); it uses a built-in SGML parser to import the hyperdocument into a database stored in proprietary format. Then the engine enforces the HyTime semantics (i.e., for the HyTime hyperlink and location address architectural forms) and resolves anchor addresses. Version 0.9.1 of EnLIGHTeN runs on Sun OS 4.1.x and on Linux 1.2.1 and provides the capability to navigate Topic Maps over a collection of SGML documents. Topic Relations are limited to binary relationships, although the definition of the Topic Map architecture supports n-ary relationships. The user interface allows the user to easily browse and navigate into the referenced documents, using the Topic Map instance, (e.g., by following the semantics of the anchor roles down, and, conversely, follow it upwards from documents to the corresponding Topic instances). For more information, contact either of the authors from HighText, S.A.R.L.

4 Comparison with Traditional Database Systems

A Topic Map definition is analogous to an Entity-Relationship Model where Topic types correspond to Entity types and Topic Relation types correspond to Relationship types. The Topic Map instance then, roughly corresponds to the extension of, e.g., a relational database that holds Topic instances and Topic Relation instances. There are a number of differences between these two models, however. Perhaps the most obvious is that the Topic instances, e.g., that represent Thomas Edison, are elaborated by arbitrary components of documents, through the anchors referenced on the anchor roles. The Topic instances are represented in the Topic Map only by a single attribute, in the database sense, called Topic Title. This is a character string, e.g., "Thomas Edison" used to represent the Topic instance. The cardinality of each link end (for Topics and Topic Relations) can be specified as either 1 or many (using the aggregate features of HyTime). The suggested form of a Topic Map is summarized in the Entity-Relationship Diagram shown in Figure 2. This figure presents a meta-model of a Topic Map, showing that individual Topic types may be related by Topic Relationships. The anchor addresses can be described by several mechanisms, including SGML IDs, coordinate locations, semantic locations (queries), URLs, etc., according to the HyTime location address module. Figure 2 presents the "suggested use" of a Topic Map; it is actually more general.

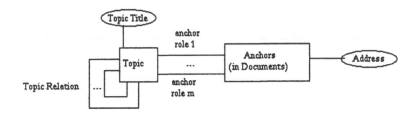

Figure 2: Suggested Modeling Capability of a Topic

The Topic Relation is not required to reference only Topics and it is not constrained to reference only a particular Topic type. For the example above, Invented-By can be defined as a Topic Relation but is not constrained to reference Person and Device Topic instances. The possibility of constraining a Topic Relation (to set the type for both ends) is possible by using a reference typing facility (the "reftype" attribute) defined by HyTime and is being considered by the CApH Committee to be explicitly added to the Topic Navigation Module. In general, the modeling capability of a Topic Map is more general and less strongly-typed than an Entity-Relationship diagram.

5   Plans for Future Work

The Topic Map Architecture will be completed and extended, taking into account the mechanisms for assigning properties to information objects, with the objective to interchange information about multiple topic maps. Current plans for the Topic Map Architecture are to submit it as an new project for an ISO standard. This should open an area for developing and extending existing tools, by various vendors, and could become a new arena for competition in the marketplace. Finally, research in progress is addressing the problem of integrating the Topic Map Architecture with database schemas to provide for information integration beyond traditional database schemas and to consider the possibility of database-style queries over documents based on the Topic Map [3].

References

[1] *CApH document.* ftp.techno.com.

[2] M. Biezunski. Modeling hyperdocuments using the topic map architecture. In *International HyTime Conference*, Vancouver, August 1995. available under HyTime conferences at http://www.techno.com.

[3] L. Delcambre and D. Maier. Content-based navigation on the national information infrastructure, NSF grant no. NSF-IRI 9502084.

[4] High Text Web Site: http://hightext.com. *Presentation of a demo of EnLIGHTeN.*

[5] S. R. Newcomb. SGML architectures, implications and opportunities for industry.

MATISSE: A Multimedia Web DBMS

Shel Finkelstein, ADB, Inc., Eric Lemoine and René Lenaers, ADB Europe
email: sfinkelstein@adb.com, elemoine@adb.fr and rlenaers@adb.fr
web: http://www.adb.com/ and http://www.adb.fr/

The explosion of content-rich uses of the World-Wide Web has changed the requirements for multimedia database management systems (DBMS). Relational database systems were not designed to meet these requirements, while object systems were not designed for the high performance multi-user environments necessitated by the Web. The MATISSE™ DBMS has the revolutionary architecture needed to meet these requirements, combining:

- A proven, high-performance, scaleable **server.**
- Intrinsic **versioning** eliminating the need for locking in typical read-only transactions.
- General data model capabilities for both standard and **multimedia** datatypes (image, text, audio, video, etc.) unified within the database.

SERVER: MATISSE was designed for large multi-user environments, and has been in use in such environments since 1992. A popular dictum is that databases should provide searching and accounting abilities for multimedia applications but should not be involved in delivering multimedia data to applications. This is because databases are usually slower than file systems for delivering large objects. But MATISSE can often *outperform file systems* because of its innovative architecture. MATISSE performance may scale with the number of disks used in the database (subject to other limits, such as CPU).

In MATISSE, the database and the log are the same, with no-overwrite storage. Objects from any classes are boxcarred into blocks together, as with Group Commit algorithms for logs. Blocks are written to the first available disk, close to the last place that disk was written (for dynamic clustering); for durability, replication may be used so they are written to the first two available disks. Large objects are automatically broken into blocks written to many disks in parallel (with read parallelism as well).

VERSIONING: Because MATISSE does not overwrite old data, previous versions are available for reading without locking. The high-performance contention-free benefits of this scheme for Web applications are obvious, particularly since serializability is not an issue in the usual sense in many Web applications (read-only, append-based, etc.).

MULTIMEDIA: MATISSE provides a flexible data model with classes, objects, attributes, relationships and methods. MATISSE objects are self-describing and general; we do not have a separate data storage for binary large objects (BLOBs). This multimedia store is excellent for representing content-rich Web standards such as HTML documents and MIME types. These may be indexed using MATISSE's powerful index mechanisms based on user-specified functions, which may span multiple classes; these have been used to index Web pages for searching.

Web pages may also invoke CGI programs which access databases. We also plan to expand abilities for Java™ bindings and efficient single message transaction updates, which will enhance the portability, transparency, ease-of-use and performance of Web applications using MATISSE.

Doing Business with the Web :
The Informix / Illustra Approach

Informix
Menlo Park, CA, United-States
http://www.informix.com

Presented by Brian Baker
Informix Software France
Les Collines de l'Arche
92057 Paris La Défense Cedex

Abstract

Illustra's Web DataBlade module is a comprehensive toolset for creating Web enabled database applications that dynamically retrieve and update Illustra database content. You can construct simple query front ends in a matter of minutes and powerful Web applications in just a few hours with the Web DataBlade module. The Illustra Web DataBlade makes it easy for you to take full advantage of the Illustra server's many important features, including extensible data types, an underlying rules system, and Time Travel capabilities, all of which make Illustra the database of choice for managing all types of content on the World Wide Web.

The Evolution of Content Management in Cyberspace

Over the past few years, with the introduction of the HTTP protocol and HTML technology, a paradigm shift has begun to revolutionize the way information is conveyed. Initially developed for ad hoc information access to the military and universities via the Internet, the Web has evolved from a collection of simple text files to a wide variety of interactive multimedia applications that support dynamic content management. This shift offers a number of benefits, from reduced costs for publishing information to the ability to collect customer feedback through intelligent Web applications.

Most first generation Web applications were simply a collection of HTML documents connected by hyperlinks. But as the requirement to access new and varied types of information grew, so did the complexity of HTML documents. Developers soon recognized the need to dynamically generate some portion of the HTML content. The Common Gateway Interface (CGI) was adopted for this purpose. With CGI, programmers build applications that generate static HTML and then access a data source to retrieve content to build the dynamic portion of the Application Page. This second generation approach requires that programmers develop proprietary CGI applications, usually in C or perl.

Second generation applications have a number of inherent problems : These applications do not handle rich data types well, or readily accept the introduction of new data types, such as HTML documents, PDF, VRLM, JPEG, and GIF, or audio.

Typically, rich types are managed as BLOBs (binary large objects), which need to be loaded into proprietary client applications to be processed. This is an inefficient process that exacts a high overhead. These applications do not provide any built-in mechanism for sophisticated analysis of the Web server log. This means, for example, that you cannot easily find out what types of information visitors to your Web site are retrieving, or how often visitors are logging in to the site. Instead, you are required to write your own analysis tools, or buy a third party product. Integrating the database server and Web server poses a formidable challenge. Creating proprietary CGI applications is time-consuming. Typically, such home-grown applications do not take advantage of the latest developments in Web server technology, or manage the database-Web server interface well.

The Solution - the Illustra ORDBMS and the Web DataBlade Module

Illustra solves all of these problems with the core Illustra ORDBMS and the Web DataBlade module. You can easily construct interactive, intelligent Web sites and other Web-enabled applications with Illustra's ORDBMS and Web DataBlade module. For example, through a catalog application customers choose from product categories - CDs, videos, electronic merchandise, and so forth. Each product listed in a category has a detailed description page that includes still images, video, and sound. Users can view categories of products, search for specific products, or insert new products into the database, tailoring catalogs to a specific vertical interest. At the same time, with the Illustra ORDBMS, a Web site administrator can analyze usage patterns and derive other important information about an application.

Illustra's Extensible Data Types for all Your Web Content

Today, Web applications need to manage and support rich data types such as images, graphics, formatted text, and audio samples. The Illustra object-relational DBMS, is the database of choice for managing the sophisticated content utilized by today's multimedia Web-enabled database applications. With the Illustra ORDBMS you are not restricted to the handful of data types found in ordinary database systems. Instead, you can define your own data types, or use additional data types and access methods provided through other Illustra DataBlade modules.

Creating Intelligent Home Pages

Instead of merely acting as a passive data repository, the Illustra ORDBMS is also an active, intelligent system capable of notification and analysis. This is accomplished through Illustra's rules system, programmed in easy to maintain industry-standard SQL. Illustra's rules system makes click stream analysis possible so that you can understand exactly who your customers are and how they view your application. Click stream analysis means that you can track where and how often a user clicks on a particular application area. With the feedback gathered through click stream analysis, you can build a business model around the usage of an application. You can, for example, give popular products more prominence in your application, or redesign an infrequently visited portion of your application. Rules also enable specified events to trigger notification messages. These events can include inventory running low or a new order being placed. Notification provides useful feedback in many application areas.

Managing Your Web Site Over Time

Illustra supports the creation of multiple versions of an object and its components through a unique feature called Time Travel. Time Travel can be used to build novel applications (such as the Graffiti Wall on Illustra's Web site), without the overhead of writing sophisticated application code. In Illustra, with archiving enabled, changes to an object do not destroy the old version of the object. Instead, new information is written and old information is archived. This old information is available online until the database administrator explicitly removes it. While the archive information is online, an application can ask for a query to be answered "as of" a certain time. This makes it possible for corporate home page administrators to maintain older versions of Application Pages and content without having to program in any special application logic. For application developers, this feature provides the benefits of version control by enabling developers to easily retrieve past versions of Application Pages. For users, Time Travel can provide quick access to information such as last week's prices in an inventory list, or last month's front page story from a news service.

Illustra Web DataBlade Module Overview

By reducing development and maintenance time, the Illustra Web DataBlade module frees you to focus on attracting new customers to your business. In standard Web database applications, most of the logic is in the CGI application, typically written in perl, Tcl, or C. Generally, this CGI application connects to a database, builds and executes SQL statements, and formats results. By providing complete integration between the Web server and the database, the Web DataBlade module eliminates the need to develop a proprietary CGI application to dynamically access database content.

Application Pages Simplify Development Effort

With the Web DataBlade module, instead of programming complex CGI code, you create Application Pages by using Web DataBlade tags. This enables you to write your own SQL statements directly in the HTML document, thus avoiding CGI scripting. Application Pages are stored in the database. When they are retrieved, the SQL statements are executed and the results are dynamically formatted. Because they are stored in the Illustra database, you can manage Application Pages over time, retrieving past versions, if desired. This method of Web-based application development provides an industry-compliant approach, that embeds the action language directly in the HTML document. Thus, you can extend application pages by programming with other action language tags, for example, by calling a Java applet. Web DataBlade tags provide a rich framework with which to manage SQL statements, format specifications for data retrieval, manage variables, implement error handling, and call system commands. Architecture of the Web DataBlade Module
The Web DataBlade module consists of two core pieces : the WebExplode function, and Webdriver, Illustra's CGI driver :

- WebExplode parses the Application Page. The Application Page is stored in the database. When WebExplode finds Web DataBlade tags, it issues SQL statements and formats the results based on your formatting instructions.

- Webdriver handles all aspects of database interface and enables you to customize Web applications based on information obtained from a configuration file, the CGI environment, URLs, and HTML forms. Webdriver manages the database connection and retrieval of the Application Page from the database. Webdriver's Application Page Builder, Figure 1, with its convenient graphical interface, is a Web DataBlade application that you can use to create, edit, delete, and execute HTML pages in Web applications.

Performance, Load, and Scalability

The Web DataBlade module also provides Webclient, a tool for managing high- load web sites. Webclient, which can be used as an alternative to Webdriver, is a CGI-based application that can be integrated into any proprietary API that supports CGI. Webclient optimizes connection management between the Web server and the Illustra database. Web site administrators can configure a predefined number of database connections, so that no matter how many CGI processes are invoked, the requests to the database are all managed and processed through these already-established connections. This feature means that administrators can customize their system configuration to optimize the underlying CPU architecture and efficiently handle peak loads.

How the Web DataBlade Works

The core functionality of the Web DataBlade module is the WebExplode function. Most applications designers will call this function through the Webdriver interface. Webdriver extracts an Application Page from the database by issuing an SQL select statement.WebExplode parses the results of the select, executes the embedded SQL statements and generates an Application Page, which is then rendered to the browser. Unlike parsing functions for other commercial products, WebExplode executes inside the Illustra server for high performance.

1. The Web browser queries the Web server with a form submission request or other query.

2. The Web server launches the client database application (Webdriver or Webclient).

3. Based on a defined set of parameters, the driver connects to the specified database as a specified user, and then selects a specified Application Page, stored as a row in a table.

4. WebExplode parses the extracted pages, executes the embedded queries, and then formats the results. This is accomplished within the database server.

5. Based on the results of WebExplode, an Application Page is placed in the database server memory space and returned to Webdriver (or Webclient).

6. Webdriver (or Webclient) renders the Application Page through the Web server to the client browser program.

With the Web DataBlade module, a Web-enabled database application becomes a collection of HTML pages containing embedded SQL statements stored in the database. A small (but powerful) set of database-oriented markup tags embed the SQL in the HTML. These Web DataBlade tags adhere to all the properties of SGML processing tags, and at the same time make it possible for you to embed any SQL statement within the Application Page.

Core Features of the Web DataBlade Module

- Embeds industry-standard SQL in HTML
- Is not server-dependent ; runs on any server
- Implements error handling
- Manages variable processing
- Supports conditional statements
- Provides a set of template examples
- Provides an application development tool for building Application Pages
- Stores and manages applications in database
- Works with all industry-standard Web servers.

Advanced Features of the Web DataBlade Module

- Scalable driver manages and handles high loads
- Set of server functions enables sophisticated application development
- Provides comprehensive error reporting and logging
- Maintains transactional integrity within an Application Page

Benefits of the Web DataBlade Module

Saves Time.

The Web DataBlade module enables rapid application development and maintenance. Application designers are freed from low-level coding work and can focus on application flow and design. Applications are structured modularly in HTML pages and are therefore easy to maintain.

Reduces Development Costs.

The Web DataBlade module eliminates costly hours of CGI interface programming in perl, C, or Tcl. With the Web DataBlade module, application designers with HTML and SQL knowledge can quickly build Web-enabled database applications. The Application Page Builder development tool provides an easy to use interface for assembling Application Pages.

Offers an Open Development Environment.

The Web DataBlade module works with all standard HTTP and standard Web servers. It runs on most UNIX platforms, and Microsoft Windows NT.

Benefits of Using Illustra for Web-Enabled Content Management

The Illustra ORDBMS offers the following unique benefits :

- Supports rich data types such as HTML, VRML, PDF, JPEG, GIF and audio, as well as traditional data types such as integer and text.

- Has the unique built-in capability to provide content search on all data types.

Illustra's rule system supports click-stream analysis in Web applications, and provides for events being triggered on select statements. With Time Travel you can now easily manage your application and content over time.

Conclusion

Illustra's Web DataBlade module provides application developers with a toolset for quickly creating attractive, media-rich, database-driven Web sites. The Web DataBlade module solves many of the problems inherent in previous generations of Web application development products, including difficulties surrounding the management of complex data types and the need to write proprietary CGI access and management code.

References

Colton, Malcolm. Multimedia Asset Management. Copyright, Illustra Information Technologies, 1995.

Introduction to Illustra, Illustra Information Technologies. Part # ILL0795-01Ill Illustra Web DataBlade User's

Guide, Release 2.1 Beta. Sept. 1995. Part # WEB-00-12-UG

Performance

A Hash Partition Strategy for Distributed Query Processing*

Chengwen Liu and Hao Chen

School of Computer Science, Telecommunications and Information Systems
DePaul University, Chicago, IL 60604, USA

Abstract. This paper describes a hash partitioning strategy for distributed query processing in a multi-database environment in which relations are unfragmented and replicated. Methods and efficient algorithms are provided to determine the sets of relations that can be hash partitioned, the copies of the relations to be partitioned and the partition sites, how the relations are to be partitioned and where the fragments are to be sent for processing. For a given query, there are usually more than one set of relations that can be hash partitioned. Among the alternatives, our algorithm picks the plan that gives the minimum response time. The paper also presents a simulation study that compares the hash partition strategy to the PRS strategy. The study shows that our strategy outperforms the PRS strategy.

1 Introduction

Relation partitioning has been used as a strategy for data allocation [12, 19], or dynamic query processing [4, 13, 15, 21] to achieve a high degree of parallelism among processing units and to improve response time. In [4], one of the relations referenced by a query is partitioned into equal-sized fragments, each fragment is sent to a computer processor, and all other relations are replicated in all computer processors. Since different computer processors may have different processing speeds and/or different access methods for accessing required data, equal-sized fragments may not balance the load of computer processors. This is considered in [21] to partition a relation into unequal-sized fragments for load balancing. However, since only one relation is partitioned, the gain due to this partitioning may not be significant when the number of relations referenced by a query is large. It is desirable to partition more relations into fragments to improve response time. In this paper, we propose a new hash partition strategy for partitioning two or more relations into fragments. The advantage to hash partition two or more relations into fragments and process subqueries at different sites is that a higher degree of parallelism among the processing sites can be achieved and the size of data involved in the processing at a site is smaller.

The idea of hash partitioning has been used previously for query processing [2, 5, 13, 14, 15]. In both [5] and [15], the relations are hash partitioned and pre-distributed among various different sites and the query processing strategy

---

* Research supported in part by Trilogy Technologies, Inc.

usually consists of determining the join order. In [2, 13, 14], two relations are dynamically partitioned into fragments for natural join. If a query references more than two relations, complete processing of the query may need the replication of all other referenced relations in all processors or repeated partitioning of the relations. What distinguishes our work from the previous partition strategies is that 1) for a given query, all sets of referenced relations that can be hash partitioned are considered before join processing and at least two referenced relations will be chosen to be hash partitioned; 2) a method that determines the copies of relations to be partitioned is provided for balancing the partition load; 3) the relations are partitioned into unequal-sized fragments for load balancing; 4) our system is a multi-database environment where data distribution is usually application dependent and permanent partitioning of relations may not be allowed.

The rest of this paper is organized as follows. In section 2, we give a brief description of the partition problem. Our new partition strategy and algorithms are given in section 3. The performance of our strategy is given and discussed in section 4. In section 5, we conclude the paper with the directions of future research.

2 Partition Problem

For a given query referencing no fragmented relation, a Partition and Replicate Strategy (PRS) algorithm was proposed in [21] to partition one of the referenced relations into a number of fragments and distribute the fragments to a number of sites so that the query can be processed in parallel at these sites. Before we describe the partition problem, an example is given to illustrate how the PRS algorithm works and how the new partition strategy improves response time.

Example 1 Let a query reference two relations R_1 and R_2 which are unfragmented and distributed between site 1 and site 2 as shown in Table 1. Assume that both sites have the same processing speed.

Relation	Total Tuples	Site 1	Site 2
R_1	12000	R_1	
R_2	10000		R_2

Table 1. Data Distribution for Example 1

If PRS algorithm is used, R_1 will be partitioned into two equal-sized fragments F_{11} and F_{12}. Fragment F_{12} is sent to site 2 and relation R_2 is sent to site 1. Then two joins, $F_{11} \bowtie R_2$ and $F_{12} \bowtie R_2$, will be processed in parallel at the two different sites. The union of the results of the two joins forms the answer to $R_1 \bowtie R_2$.

If we further assume that the join attribute has integer domain and has uniform distribution, then we can partition R_1 in such a way that F_{11} contains all the tuples whose join attribute values are odd numbers and F_{12} contains all the tuples whose join attributes are even numbers. Similarly, R_2 can also be partitioned into two fragments, F_{21} and F_{22}. Obviously, the following conditions hold:

$$F_{11} \bowtie F_{22} = \emptyset \qquad F_{12} \bowtie F_{21} = \emptyset$$

Thus, $R_1 \bowtie R_2$ can be processed by sending F_{12} to site 2 and F_{21} to site 1, and then process two joins, $F_{11} \bowtie F_{21}$ and $F_{12} \bowtie F_{22}$, at the two sites in parallel. The final result of $R_1 \bowtie R_2$ is the union of the results of the two joins. Compared with the PRS strategy, the join cost at each site is less since only one fragment of R_2, instead of the whole relation, is involved in the join. Furthermore, communication cost is also reduced because only F_{21} instead of R_2 needs to be transferred from site 2 to site 1. Clearly, the trade off is that the partition of R_1 may be slower since the join attribute needs to be checked to decide to which fragment a tuple belongs. In addition, partitioning R_2 also takes time. However, this is not a problem because it is performed at site 2 while R_1 is being partitioned at site 1. The time needed to compare the join attribute values also might not be a problem since in most present day systems, a data transfer involving secondary storage usually takes as long as, or longer than searching the block for desired data in main memory [17]. If we implement the partitioning in such a way that comparing the join attribute values of one block overlaps with the transfer of another block from disk to main memory, then the partition cost will be approximately the same as in the previous strategy. ∎

Example 1 shows that both R_1 and R_2 are partitioned into two fragments based on whether the value of the join attribute is odd or even. In general, a hashing function can be applied to the join attribute to decide which fragment a tuple should belong to [2, 18]. Furthermore, we need to determine which relations are to be partitioned, how they are partitioned, what are the processing sites, etc. We describe the partition problem in the rest of this section.

Definition 1 A relation R_i is hash partitioned on attribute A into d disjoint fragments $\{F_{ij}\}$, $1 \leq j \leq d$, if 1) $R_i = \cup_{1 \leq j \leq d} F_{ij}$; 2) $F_{ij} \cap F_{ik} = \emptyset$ for $j \neq k$; and 3) $\forall T \in F_{ij}$ $h(T.A) = c_j$, where $h()$ is a hash function and c_j is a constant for a given j. ∎

Suppose that $RR_Q = \{R_1, R_2, ..., R_n\}$ are the set of relations referenced by a query Q and none of them is fragmented. A subset PR of these relations will be chosen to be hash partitioned on their join attributes. Each relation contained in PR is partitioned into d disjoint fragments, for some integer d, by applying the same hash function to one of its join attributes. Then the fragments will be assigned to a set of d sites, called processing sites, in such a way that the fragments having the same hash address are assigned to the same site. The other relations, $WR = RR_Q - PR$, are replicated at each of the d sites. At each processing site, a subquery, which is the same as Q but referencing the fragments of the relations in PR and all the other relations in WR, is executed. The answer to Q is the union of the results to the subqueries at the d sites. The problem is to decide (1) the set of relations to be partitioned, i.e., PR, (2) the copy of the relation to be used, if multiple copies exist, (3) the set of processing sites, (4) the number of fragments of the relations are to be partitioned, and (5) the size of each of the fragments to be produced, such that the response time (in terms of both local processing cost and communications cost) is minimized. In the next section, we present methods and algorithms to solve these problems.

3 Partition Strategy

Our environment is based on the concept of shared-nothing [16] architecture in which processors do not share disk drives and random access memory. The sites over which a database is distributed are connected in a local area network (Ethernet). Each site is managed by a local DBMS. A given query is submitted to a front end system which parses the query and determines a strategy to process the query. The strategy usually consists of decomposing the query into several subqueries and assigning them to the local DBMSs at different sites. The front end system then waits for all the subqueries to finish executing. The partial results from the processing sites are then combined to produce the final result.

We assume that all queries are of the form

$$Q = \{target \mid qualification\}$$

where *target* is the list of projected attributes and *qualification* is the list of equijoined attributes. An attribute in a given query Q is called a *joining attribute* if it is included in the qualification part of the query. Let us denote by RR_Q the set of referenced relations, $J(R_1)$ the set of joining attributes of R_1 and P_Q the set of join predicates in a given query Q. For example, for the query

$$Q = \{R_1.A, R_2.B \mid R_1.A = R_2.A \wedge R_2.B = R_3.B\}$$

$RR_Q = \{R_1, R_2, R_3\}$, $J(R_1) = \{A\}$, $J(R_2) = \{A, B\}$, $J(R_3) = \{B\}$ and $P_Q = \{(R_1.A, R_2.A), (R_2.B, R_3.B)\}$.

3.1 Cost Model

The total cost of processing a subquery at a site p consists of the delay due to relation partitioning, the data communication cost and the local processing cost for the subquery at site p. These costs are described as follows.

Partitioning a relation consists of retrieving the relation from secondary memory, dividing it into fragments by applying the same hash function to one of its join attributes, and assigning buffers for the data to send to other sites. The partitioned relation needs to be transferred from secondary memory to the buffer only once. Dividing the relation into fragments can be performed by scanning the relation once. Thus for a relation to be partitioned, the partitioning cost is assumed to be monotonically increasing in the size of the relation to be partitioned and monotonically decreasing in the processing speed of the site where the relation is to be partitioned, but is independent of the number of partitions.

Since there are two or more relations to be partitioned and the relations may be partitioned at different sites in parallel, the partition delay PC for a query Q is the largest partition cost among the sites that participate in the partition processing.

The data communication cost DC is assumed to be a monotonically increasing (nondecreasing) in the amount of data transferred. It is assumed to be the same between any pair of sites. This assumption is consistent with those used in earlier processing algorithms.

The local processing cost LC for processing the subquery at a site p depends on the processing speed of the site p, whether the join is supported by fast access paths such as indexes, and size of the relations participating in the join. The cost is assumed to be monotonically increasing in the size of each of the relations to be processed and monotonically decreasing in the processing speed of a site. The reasons for choosing such a simplified cost function are the following: (1) The analysis given in [7] has demonstrated that a linear cost model is sufficiently robust to cover the usual join algorithms, including nested-loop join (with an indexed inner relation or without an index), hash join, and merge join. Note that sort-merge join is not linear in the cardinalities of the input relations. However, most systems do not use sort-merge join, since in situations where merge join requires sorting of the input, either hash join or nested-loop join is almost always preferable to sort-merge [6]. Linear cost models have also been evaluated experimentally for nested-loop and merge joins, and were found to be relatively accurate of the performance of a variety of commercial systems [3]. (2) Our front-end system has little control over the local database management systems, which are free to perform any local optimization. (3) Our front-end system which is intended for ad hoc queries has to produce a processing strategy quickly in response to the submitted query. If detailed information about the costs of operations is incorporated, it is likely that the front-end system will take a long time to produce the processing strategy.

The total cost of processing a subquery at a site, $COST$, is assumed to be the sum of the partition delay PC, the data communication cost DC and the local processing cost LC.

3.2 Alternative Sets of Relations that Can Be Hash Partitioned

Generally speaking, not all of the relations referenced by a query can be partitioned ($PR \subseteq RR_Q$) and there may be many alternatives for PR. For example, let a query be $Q = \{R_1.A, R_2.B \mid R_1.A = R_2.A \land R_2.B = R_3.B\}$. Then not all of the three relations can be partitioned since the first join predicate ($R_1.A = R_2.A$) requires R_2 be partitioned on attribute A and the second join predicate ($R_2.B = R_3.B$) requires R_2 be partitioned on attribute B. Clearly there is a conflict between these requirements. However, we can choose to partition R_1 and R_2 on attribute A and replicate R_3 at the processing sites. Yet another alternative is to partition R_2 and R_3 on attribute B and replicate R_1 at the processing sites. Therefore, the problem here is to decide which set of relations can be partitioned.

378

Definition 2 A set of relations, $PR = \{R_1, R_2, ..., R_r\} \subseteq RR_Q$, can be **hash partitioned** with respect to the query Q if each of the relations can be hash partitioned and

$$Ans(Q) = \cup_{j=1}^{d} Ans(Q_j)$$

where $Ans(Q)$ represents the answer of query Q and Q_j is the subquery derived by substituting each $R_i \in PR$ with F_{ij}. ∎

In order to find the set of relations to be hash partitioned, it is helpful to consider a query graph and a join graph.

Definition 3 $G_Q = (V_Q, E_Q)$ is a **query graph** of the query Q, where $V_Q = \{R \mid R \in RR_Q\}$, and $E_Q = \{(R, S) \mid \{R, S\} \subseteq RR_Q \land \exists A \in J(R) \land \exists B \in J(S) \land (R.A = S.B) \in P_Q\}$.

$G_J = (V_J, E_J)$ is a **join graph** of the query Q, where $V_J = \{R.A \mid R \in RR_Q \land A \in J(R)\}$, and $E_J = \{(R.A, S.B) \mid \{R, S\} \subseteq RR_Q \land A \in J(R) \land B \in J(S) \land (R.A = S.B) \in P_Q\}$. ∎

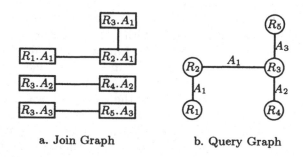

a. Join Graph   b. Query Graph

Fig. 1. Sample Query and Join Graph

In general, the join graph of a query consists of a set of connected components, each of which forms an equivalent class of the join predicates [22]. For example, Figure 1 gives the query graph and the join graph for the following query:

$$Q = \{R_1.A_2, R_2.A_4 \mid \quad R_1.A_1 = R_2.A_1 \land R_2.A_1 = R_3.A_1$$
$$\land R_3.A_2 = R_4.A_2 \land R_3.A_3 = R_5.A_3\}$$

A query Q is called *acyclic* either if its query graph is acyclic or it is equivalent to a query whose query graph is acyclic. Otherwise, query Q is called *cyclic* query [1]. For some cyclic query graphs equivalent acyclic query graphs exist. The algorithm to convert a cyclic query graph into an acyclic query graph can be found in [1, 11]. In the following we give a result which allows all the sets of relations, that can be hash partitioned for a given query, to be identified.

Proposition 1. *For an acyclic query Q, all the nodes of a component of the join graph form a set of relations that can be hash partitioned.*

3.3 Determine the Copies of the Relations to Be Partitioned

For a given set of relations PR to be partitioned, some relations in PR may have more than one copy. Therefore, for each relation in PR, we need to determine which copy should be used to obtain the best response time. This problem can be proven to be NP-Hard [20]. Therefore, instead of finding the optimal copies, the following heuristic is used to find a reasonable copy for each of the relations to be partitioned.

In order to simplify the problem, we consider the partition delay (time needed to do partitioning) rather than response time of the query. Since each site may have different processing speed, we define the normalized partition load (NPL) for site j as the total size of the relations to be partitioned at site j divided by the processing speed of the site.

Now the problem becomes to balance the partition load. Unfortunately, even for this reduced problem, there is no polynomial algorithm. As a result, the following greedy method is used. We first sort the relations to be partitioned into descending order of their sizes, i.e., $R_1 \geq R_2 \geq ... \geq R_p$. Then for each relation in the list, we arrange the copies of the relation in increasing order of normalized partition load. The first copy will be chosen and the NPL of the corresponding site is updated.

For a given set of relations $PR = \{R_1, R_2, ..., R_r\}$ to be partitioned, we use vector $CS = (CS_1, CS_2, ..., CS_r)$ to represent the distribution of the copies of the relations and vector $SP = (SP_1, SP_2, ..., SP_m)$ to represent the processing speeds of the sites, where m is the total number of sites. Specifically, CS_i is the set of sites that contain a copy of relation R_i and SP_j is the processing speed of site j. We also use $|R_i|$ to denote the size of R_i.

The following four steps are processed to determine the copies of the relations to be partitioned.

Step 1: For each site that contains a copy of relation(s) in PR, we initialize its NPL to 0.

Step 2: For any relation $R_i \in PR$, if R_i has only one copy, this copy of R_i will be chosen to be partitioned. Thus, the value, which is the size of R_i divided by the processing speed of the site that contains this copy, is added to the NPL of the corresponding site.

Step 3: The remaining relations to be partitioned are sorted in descending order of their sizes and stored in a list L. Relations having the same sizes are further ordered in ascending order of the number of copies.

Step 4: For every relation R_j (from first to last) in the above list, we first compute the estimated NPL' of every site in CS_j, where NPL' of a site is the sum of its NPL and the size of R_j divided by its processing speed, i.e., for site $k \in CS_j$, $NPL'_k = NPL_k + |R_j|/SP_k$. Secondly, the copy of R_j that situates at the site having minimum NPL' among the sites in CS_j will be chosen to be partitioned and the NPL of the site is updated to its NPL'.

Assume the number of copies of a relation at a single site is either 0 (not exist at this site) or 1 (there is a copy at the site). Then the copies of the relations to be partitioned can be represented as vector $CP = (S_1, S_2, ..., S_r)$, $1 \leq S_i \leq m$, where S_i $(1 \leq i \leq r)$ is the site containing the copy of R_i in PR to be partitioned. Let MAXNPL be the maximum NPL among the sites that participate in partition processing. After performing the above steps, both CP and MAXNPL can be obtained.

An algorithm based on the above steps and its performance study were given in [10]. The algorithm is called SH (Size Heuristic) algorithm since relations are considered in descending order of relation sizes. Another heuristic is to consider the relations in ascending order of the number of existing copies. The algorithm based on this heuristic is called CH (Copy Heuristic) algorithm. Both algorithms do not guarantee the optimal solution, but they are very efficient and effective as shown in [10].

3.4 Determine the Processing Sites

Given a set of relations $PR = \{R_1, R_2, ..., R_r\}$ and their copies $CP = (S_1, S_2, ..., S_r)$ to be partitioned, we want to determine the processing sites (and therefore the number of partitions). Let the total cost of processing the subquery at site p be T_{Q_p}. We define the partition weight at site p, denoted as $PW_p(PR, CP)$, to be $limit_{\sum_{i=1}^{r} |F_{ip}| \to 0} T_{Q_p}$, where $|F_{ip}|$ is the size of the fragment of R_i assigned to site p. Thus, the partition weight of a site is the overhead for partitioning the relations in PR and the cost for transferring and processing the other unfragmented relations $(R_{r+1}, ..., R_n)$ for the processing of the subquery at the site. If site p is to be used as a processing site, it will incur a total cost greater than its partition weight $PW_p(PR, CP)$.

An optimal way to assign fragments to a given set of sites is in such a way that each site will have the same total cost. It has been shown in [21] that:

1. If a site is not used as a processing site, then those sites with partition weights higher than or equal to that of the site should not be used as processing sites.
2. If a site is used as a processing site, then those sites with partition weights smaller than or equal to that of the site should also be used as processing sites.

Based on these two results, all the sites can be arranged in ascending order of partition weight. Consider site p, if site p is not a processing site, then sites $(p + 1)$ to the last site need not be considered; otherwise, site 1 to site p and possibly the next few sites will be processing sites.

Definition 4 Let OS be a set of processing sites. If the processing by hash partitioning each of the relations in PR into $|OS|$ number of fragments, one for each site in OS, at the given sites CP yields the optimal response time, then OS is an optimal set of processing sites. Each site in OS is an optimal processing site. ∎

It remains to determine whether a given site p is an optimal processing site. The minimum cost at site p is the partition weight at the site, i.e., T

$= PW_p(PR, CP)$. Suppose the tuples of the relations in PR are assigned to the preceding $(p-1)$ sites such that each of the $(p-1)$ sites has response time T. The following proposition states that site p is an optimal processing site if and only if the sum of the sizes of fragments of all relations in PR assigned to the first $(p-1)$ sites is less than the sum of the size of all relations in PR.

Proposition 2. *Let F_{ij} $(1 \leq i \leq r)$ be the part of relation R_i $(1 \leq i \leq r)$ assigned to site j $(1 \leq j \leq p-1)$ such that the total cost of site j $(1 \leq j \leq p-1)$ is the same as the partition weight of site p, i.e., $T_{Q_j} = PW_p(PR, CP)$. Site p is an optimal processing site if and only if*

$$SIZE = \sum_{j=1}^{p-1} \sum_{i=1}^{r} |F_{ij}| < \sum_{i=1}^{r} |R_i| \qquad (1)$$

To determine the set of optimal processing sites, we use the binary search technique. We first consider the middle site, the $(m/2)$th site (m is the total number of sites). If this is not an optimal processing site, then it is sufficient to consider the first $(m/2 - 1)$ sites. We then repeat the process by checking the $(m/4)$th site. If the $(m/2)$th site is an optimal processing site, then the $(3m/4)$th site will be examined. The BINSEARCH algorithm which determines the set of optimal processing sites and hence the number of fragments into which the relations in PR should be partitioned is given in Figure 2.

Algorithm BINSEARCH (low, high, result): determine the last processing site.

/* The relations to be partitioned is $PR = \{R_1, R_2, \ldots, R_r\}$, the copies of the relations to be partitioned is $CP = \{S_1, S_2, \ldots, S_r\}$, the optimal set of processing sites is 1 to result. */

IF (low > high) **THEN** result = high
ELSE
{
    MID $\leftarrow$ (low + high) / 2;
    FOR $j := 1$ **TO** MID-1
    {
        assign ρ_j% of $|R_1|, |R_2|, \ldots, |R_r|$ to site j such that
        $T_{Q_j} = PW_{MID}(PR, CP)$
    }
    IF $(\sum_{j=1}^{MID-1} \sum_{i=1}^{r} \rho_j \cdot |R_i| \geq \sum_{i=1}^{r} |R_i|)$ **THEN**
        BINSEARCH(low, MID-1, result)   /* search left half */
    ELSE
        BINSEARCH(MID+1, high, result)   /* search right half */
}

Fig. 2. The BINSEARCH Algorithm

3.5 A Partition Algorithm

In the previous subsections, methods are provided to determine the copies of the relations to be partitioned and the optimal processing sites for a given set of relations. The above methods can be applied to each set of relations that can be hash partitioned.

Here we provide an algorithm to find an efficient query processing plan by using hash partitioning. For a given query Q, we first divide the set of referenced relations, $RR = \{R_1, R_2, ..., R_n\}$, into a number of non-exclusive sets of relations that can be hash partitioned by constructing the join graph of the given query. Each maximum connected component of the join graph forms a set of relations that can be hash partitioned on their join attributes. We use PRR to represent the alternative sets of relations that can be hash partitioned, i.e., $PRR = \{PR_1, PR_2, ..., PR_q\}$, $1 \leq q \leq n - 1$. Each PR_i consists of a minimum of two relations and a maximum of n relations. The strategy of single site processing is also considered in our algorithm since it may be able to yield better response time for some queries.

Figure 3 is the sketch of the partition algorithm. In step (1), the best single site processing strategy is determined. In order to reduce execution time, we divide the set of sites S into two subsets: referenced sites RS (containing at least one copy of at least one of the referenced relations) and non-referenced sites NRS ($NRS = S - RS$). Let t be the fastest non-referenced site. It suffices to consider sites in $RS \bigcup \{t\}$ for the single site processing strategy since any other site would incur a larger response time than site t. In step (2), the join graph of the query is first constructed and then the alternative sets of relations that can be hash partitioned, i.e., PRR are determined. In step (3), the SH algorithm and the BINSEARCH algorithm are applied to each element of PRR to determine the copies of the relations to be partitioned and the processing sites. All sets in PRR are considered and the one yielding the best response time is chosen to be partitioned. The chosen relations, copies and processing sites are identified by $PRSET$, $COPY$ and $PSSET$ respectively.

3.6 Determine the Sizes of the Fragments

Given a set of relations $PRSET$ and their copies represented by $COPY$ to be partitioned, and the processing sites $PSSET$, we determine the sizes of the fragments to be assigned to the sites as follows.

The optimal assignment is to make each processing site have the same total cost. Thus for each processing site j,

$$T_{Q_j} = f(F_{1j}, F_{2j}, ..., F_{rj}) = C \quad for \ 1 \leq j \leq d \qquad (2)$$

where C is the total cost (and hence the response time) to be determined, r is the number of relations in the set $PRSET$, d is the number of processing sites in set $PSSET$ and F_{kj} is the fragment of relation R_k to be assigned to site j.

Algorithm PARTITION: determine the partition relations, copies and processing sites.
Input: Q /* a given query Q */
         S /* the set of all sites */
         CS /* each element CS_i is a set of sites that contain a copy of referenced relation R_i */
         SP /* Processing speeds of the sites */
Output: $PRSET, COPY$ and $PSSET$.

(1) Estimate the total time if the query is processed at a single site $k, k \in RS \bigcup \{t\}$;
Set **Bound** = the best estimated response time obtained at single site k;
Processing site $PSSET = \{k\}$.

(2) Construct the join graph of the query.
Determine the set PRR, which contains all alternative sets of relations that can be hash partitioned on their join attributes.

(3) For each set $PR_i \in PRR$, do the following:

(3.1) Apply SH(PR_i, CS, SP) algorithm to determine CP_i (the copies of the relations in PR_i to be partitioned) and $MAXNPL_i$ (maximum normalized partition load).

(3.2) Arrange all sites in RS in ascending order of partition weight $PW_p(PR_i, CP_i)$
(Note the maximum normalized partition load for partitioning the relations in PR_i is $MAXNPL_i$).

(3.3) Discard those sites with partition weight greater than or equal to **Bound**.

(3.4) Use binary search to determine the optimal processing sites for CP_i obtained in step (3.1).
low = 1, high = the number of sites remained after step (3.3);
BINSEARCH(low,high,result);

(3.5) Compute response time RT using the processing sites 1 to result, denoted by
$PS_i = \{1, ..., result\}$.   /* see Subsection 3.6 for details */

(3.6) IF ($RT <$ **Bound**) **THEN**
{
         Bound $\leftarrow RT$;
         $PRSET \leftarrow PR_i$;
         $COPY \leftarrow CP_i$;
         $PSSET \leftarrow PS_i$;
}

Fig. 3. The PARTITION Algorithm

Clearly, the above equations are not enough for solving the fragments. Thus, we assume that the fragments of the relations at site j satisfy

$$\frac{|F_{1j}|}{|R_1|} = \frac{|F_{2j}|}{|R_2|} = \cdots = \frac{|F_{rj}|}{|R_r|} = \rho_j \tag{3}$$

Therefore, we have the following equations:

$$g(\rho_1) = C, \quad g(\rho_2) = C, \quad ..., \quad g(\rho_d) = C \tag{4}$$

therefore,

$$\rho_1 = g^{-1}(C), \quad \rho_2 = g^{-1}(C), \quad ..., \quad \rho_d = g^{-1}(C) \tag{5}$$

Since

$$\sum_{j=1}^{d} \rho_j = \rho_1 + \rho_2 + \ldots + \rho_d = \frac{|F_{i1}|}{|R_i|} + \frac{|F_{i2}|}{|R_i|} + \cdots + \frac{|F_{id}|}{|R_i|}$$

$$= \frac{\sum_{j=1}^{d} |F_{ij}|}{|R_i|} = \frac{|R_i|}{|R_i|} = 1, \quad 1 \le i \le r. \tag{6}$$

We can solve for C by substituting (6) into (5) and therefore ρ_j ($1 \le j \le d$) can be determined. Thus we can solve for $|F_{ij}|$ ($1 \le i \le r, 1 \le j \le d$) by substituting ρ_j into (3). That is the sizes of the fragments are determined.

4 Performance of Our Algorithms

In order to study the performance of our partition strategy and compare to the PRS strategy, we define the improvement factor of our strategy to the PRS strategy as $((Y_p - Y_o)/Y_p) * 100\%$, where Y_p and Y_o are the response times obtained by applying the PRS strategy and our strategy respectively.

Experiments are set up as follows. The dimension of the initial data distribution for each experiment is $n * m$, where n, which changes from 2 to 10, is the number of relations, and m, which changes from 2 to 10, is the number of sites.

The range of the sizes of the relations is from 1K to 10K tuples. These sizes are relatively small compared to the sizes of nowaday databases. However, most queries have some types of restrictions that reduce the number of tuples for the join operation. In the experiment, the relative speed of the sites are represented by numbers from 1000 to 10000.

Since linear cost models are used for relation partitioning, data communication and local processing, the following two parameters are used to characterize the experimental environment. The first parameter is α, which is used to denote the ratio of partition cost to local processing cost. The smaller the value of α, the smaller the partition cost relative to local processing cost. The second parameter is β, which is used to denote the ratio of transmission cost to local processing cost. The smaller the value of β, the smaller the transmission cost relative to local processing cost.

We arbitrarily generated 400 initial data distributions for each given combination n (the number of referenced relations) and m (the number of sites). The two parameters are varied from 0.1 to 1.0 with increment of 0.1. Results of our algorithm and PRS algorithm are averaged over the 400 cases and recorded. Representative sets of experimental results are shown in Tables 2-4.

We first look at the impact of of the number of relations and the number of sites on the improvement factor. As shown in Table 2, the improvement factor increases rapidly initially as the number of sites increases, but slows down as the number of sites continues to increase. This can be explained as follows. When the number of partitioned fragments increases, there is more parallelism, but it also incurs more data communication cost because of sending data to more sites. Furthermore, each processing site needs to process not only fragments of

Number of	Number of Sites									
Relations	2	3	4	5	6	7	8	9	10	Average
2	26.5	38.0	47.1	51.4	56.8	59.0	63.9	65.1	65.7	52.6
3	23.3	34.5	42.4	45.0	49.2	51.7	53.6	55.0	57.1	45.8
4	19.0	24.3	35.6	36.0	40.1	42.5	43.7	45.5	46.1	37.0
5	16.1	20.6	30.0	30.4	34.6	37.6	38.3	40.1	41.7	32.2
6	15.2	18.9	29.1	28.6	32.5	36.4	37.2	38.2	40.0	30.7
7	13.3	17.6	27.2	28.1	31.6	34.6	35.0	37.2	38.6	29.2
8	12.8	17.0	26.5	26.9	31.1	33.3	34.8	36.0	36.8	28.4
9	11.4	16.4	25.2	24.3	29.5	32.0	32.9	34.6	35.4	26.9
10	10.9	15.2	21.7	22.0	25.5	28.5	30.0	32.3	34.0	24.5
Average	16.5	22.5	31.6	32.5	36.8	39.5	41.0	42.7	43.9	

Table 2. Performance of Our Algorithms with $\alpha = 0.2$ and $\beta = 0.2$

the partitioned relations but also all other unpartitioned relations referenced by
the query. Thus, even if the number of processing sites to approach infinity, the
fragments would be reduced to sizes close to zero, but the other unpartitioned
relations still need to be processed. So, after a certain number of sites, the benefit
of having additional sites is marginal.

Recall that for a query referencing n relations, the PRS strategy partitions
one relation and our algorithm partitions r ($2 \leq r \leq n$) relations. When the
number of referenced relations increases, the ratio of r/n decreases. Thus, the
relative savings on local processing cost due to partitioning decreases. Furthermore, relative partition delay may also increase since the chances that two or
more relations have to be partitioned at one site increase. As a result, the improvement factor decreases as the number of relations increases.

We also study the impact of the relative partition speed (α) and the relative
transmission speed (β). Table 3 shows the results for the case where the number
of referenced relations is 5, the value of β is 0.2 and the value of α changes from
0.1 to 1.0. Table 4 shows the results for the case where the number of referenced
relations is 5, the value of α is 0.2 and the value of β changes from 0.1 to 1.0.

	Number of Sites									
α	2	3	4	5	6	7	8	9	10	Average
0.1	19.7	24.4	32.5	32.8	37.0	38.9	39.5	41.1	42.7	34.3
0.2	16.1	20.6	30.0	30.4	34.6	37.6	38.3	40.1	41.7	32.2
0.4	9.8	13.5	23.4	24.7	29.2	34.0	34.8	36.9	38.6	27.2
0.6	4.8	10.0	16.7	24.2	25.9	29.0	29.7	31.9	33.9	22.9
0.8	0.0	8.8	13.3	21.5	24.1	26.4	26.9	27.9	29.0	17.5
1.0	0.0	5.4	9.3	18.1	21.9	22.2	22.8	23.9	27.1	16.7

Table 3. The Impact of α when β is fixed at 0.2

From tables 3 and 4, one can easily see that the improvement factor of our
strategy over the PRS strategy decreases as the value of α or β increases. However, the decreasing due to β is rather slow while that due to α is faster. This

	Number of Sites									
β	2	3	4	5	6	7	8	9	10	Average
0.1	16.3	21.9	30.3	30.6	34.9	37.9	38.6	40.3	42.0	32.5
0.2	16.1	20.6	30.0	30.4	34.6	37.6	38.3	40.1	41.7	32.2
0.4	14.9	19.9	29.7	30.2	34.4	36.9	38.0	39.7	41.1	31.6
0.6	14.6	19.6	29.0	30.1	33.8	36.4	37.8	39.2	40.4	31.2
0.8	14.3	19.2	28.6	29.9	33.4	35.9	37.3	38.6	39.9	30.8
1.0	13.7	19.0	28.2	29.4	33.1	35.3	36.9	37.7	39.4	30.3

Table 4. The Effect of values β

indicates that the partition cost has an important impact on the algorithm while the impact of communication cost is less significant.

5 Conclusion

We have presented a hash partitioning strategy and an algorithm for distributed query processing in a multi-database environment in which relations are unfragmented and replicated. For a given query, our algorithm first determines the alternative sets of relations that can be hash partitioned according to the join predicates. Since replicas of relations are allowed and determining the optimal copies of the relations to be partitioned is NP-hard, an efficient and effective heuristic approach is used. Since the sites are allowed to have variable processing speeds, a method is given to determine the set of optimal processing sites for the given copies of the relations to be partitioned. For each set of relations that can be hash partitioned, an execution plan can be generated by hash partitioning the relations in the set and replicating all the other referenced relations. Our algorithm considers all such plans and picks the one that gives the minimum response time.

Simulation experiments are conducted to evaluate the performance of our algorithm. In terms of response time, our hash partition strategy outperforms the PRS strategy. We also examine the impacts of the relative partition speed and the relative transmission speed. We find that the relative partition speed has a significant impact on the performance of our partition strategy while the impact of the relative transmission speed is not important.

The PRS algorithm have been validated in a realistic environment [8]. We plan to integrate our hash partition strategy into a multi-database distributed query processing system [9] and carry out performance study in a realistic environment.

References

1. Bernstein, P. A. and Chiu, D-M. W.: Using semi-joins to solve relational queries. *JACM*, Vol. 28, No. 1, pp. 25-40, Jan. 1981.

387

2. DeWitt, D. and Gerber, R.: Multiprocessor hash-based join algorithms. *Proc. of the 11th Int'l Conf. on Very Large Data Bases (VLDB)*, pp. 151-164, Stockholm, Aug. 1985.

3. Du, W., Krishnamurthy, R. and Shan, M. C.: Query Optimization in Heterogeneous DBMS. *Proc. of the 18th Int'l Conf. on VLDB*, Vancouver, Aug. 1992.

4. Epstein, R., Stonebraker, M. and Wong, E.: Distributed query processing in relational databases system. *Proc. 1978 ACM SIGMOD Conf.*, Austin, May 1978.

5. Ghandeharizadeh, S. and DeWitt, D. J.: A Multiuser Performance Analysis of Alternative Declustering Strategy. *Proc. 6th IEEE Int'l Conf. on Data Engineering*, pp. 466-475, Los Angeles, CA, Feb. 1990.

6. Hellerstein, J. M. and Stonebraker, M.: Predicate Migration: Optimizing Queries with Expensive Predicates. *Proc. 1993 ACM SIGMOD Conf.*, pp. 267-276, Washington, DC, May 1993.

7. Hellerstein, J. M.: Practical Predicate Placement. *Proc. 1994 ACM SIGMOD Conf.*, pp. 325-335, Minneapolis, Minnesota, May 1994.

8. Liu, C. and Yu, C.: Validation and Performance Evaluation of the Partition and Replicate Algorithm. *Proc. of the 12th IEEE Int'l Conf. on Distr. Comp. Sys.*, pp. 400-407, Yokohama, Japan, June 1992.

9. Liu, C. and Yu, C.: Performance Issues in Distributed Query Processing. *IEEE Trans. on Par. and Distr. Sys.*, Vol. 4, No. 8, pp. 889-905, Aug. 1993.

10. Liu, C. and Chen. H.: A Heuristic Algorithm for Partition Strategy in Distributed Query Processing. *ACM SAC96, Philidelphia, USA, Feb. 1996.*

11. Pramanik, S. and Vineyard, D.: Optimizing join queries in distributed databases. *IEEE Trans. on Soft. Engr.*, Vol. 14, No. 9, pp. 1319-1326, Sept. 1988.

12. Sacca, D. and Wiederhold, G.: Database partitioning in a cluster of processors. *ACM TODS*, Vol. 10, No. 1, pp. 29-56, Mar. 1985.

13. Sacco, Giovanni Maria: Fragmentation: A technique for efficient query processing. *ACM TODS*, Vol. 11, No. 2, pp. 113-133, June 1986.

14. Schneider, D. A. and DeWitt, D. J.: A Performance Evaluation of Four Parallel Join Algorithms in a Shared-Nothing Multiprocessor Environment. *Proc. 1989 ACM SIGMOD Conf.*, pp. 110-121, Portland, OR, June 1989.

15. Shasha, Dennis and Wang, Tsong-Li: Optimizing Equijoin Queries In Distributed Databases Where Relations Are Hash Partitioned. *ACM TODS*, Vol. 16, No. 2, pp. 279-308, June 1991.

16. Stonebraker, M.: The case for shared-nothing. *Data Base Engineering*, Vol. 9, No. 1, pp. 4-9, Mar. 1986.

17. Ullman, J. D.: Principles of Database Systems. *Computer Science Press, Inc.*, Rockville, MD, 2 edition, 1982.

18. Valduriez, P. and Gardarin, G.: Join and semijoin algorithms for a multiprocessor database machine. *ACM TODS*, Vol. 9, No. 1, pp. 133-161, Mar. 1984.

19. Wong, E. and Katz, R. H.: Distributing a database for parallelism. In *Proc. 1983 ACM SIGMOD Conf.*, pp. 23-29, San Jose, CA, May 1983.

20. Yu, C. T., Chang, C. and Chang, Y.: Two surprising results in processing simple queries in distributed databases. *Proc. 6th IEEE Int'l Computer Software and Application Conf.*, pp. 377-384, Chicago, IL, Nov. 1982.

21. Yu, C. T., Guh, K. C., Brill, D. and Chen, A. L. P.: Partition strategy for distributed query processing in fast local networks. *IEEE Trans. on Soft. Engr.*, Vol. 15, No. 6, pp. 780-793, June 1989.

22. Yu, C. and Sun, W.: Automatic knowledge acquisition and maintenance for semantic query optimization. *IEEE TKDE*, Vol. 1, No. 3, pp. 362-375, Sept. 1989.

Fine-granularity Locking and Client-Based Logging for Distributed Architectures

E. Panagos[1,2] and A. Biliris[2] and H.V. Jagadish[2] and R. Rastogi[2]

[1] Boston University
Computer Science Department
Boston, MA 02215
[2] AT&T Bell Laboratories
600 Mountain Avenue, Murray Hill, NJ 07974

Abstract. We present algorithms for fine-granularity locking and client-based logging where all transactional facilities in a distributed client-server architecture are provided locally. Multiple clients are allowed to concurrently modify different objects on the same page without synchronizing their updates. Each client has its own log disk where all log records for updates to locally cached data are written. Transaction rollback and client crash recovery are handled exclusively by the clients and local logs are not merged at any time. Clients can take checkpoints independently, and client clocks do not have to be synchronized.

1 Introduction

The proliferation of inexpensive workstations and networks has created a new era in distributed computing. At the same time, non-traditional applications, such as computer aided design (CAD), computer aided software engineering (CASE), geographic information systems (GIS), and office information systems (OIS), have placed increased demands for high-performance transaction processing on database systems. The combination of these factors creates significant performance opportunities in the design of modern client-server database systems.

Allowing clients to cache portions of the database in their local memory and retain their caches across transaction boundaries has been proven to be an effective way to reduce dependence on the server [26, 25, 4, 8]. However, existing client-server database systems do not adequately exploit client disk space. In particular, clients are not allowed to offer transactional facilities locally. The high cost of main memory and disks in the past made it more cost effective to increase the resources of the server rather than the resources of each client. In addition, client machines are not considered to have the same reliability and availability characteristics as server machines. This is because client machines may be connected to or disconnected from the network, or they may simply be turned off at arbitrary times.

Today, advances in hardware and software have resulted in both reliable network connections and reliable workstations that approach server machines regarding resources. Thus, client reliability concerns become less and less important. Concerns related to availability are more a function of the computing environment rather than of the technology. In many computing environments, such as corporate, engineering, computer aided design and manufacturing, and software development, client workstations are connected to the server(s) all the time. Of course, disconnection of these machines from the network for some reason does happen sporadically, but it can be handled in an orderly fashion. In such environments, allowing clients to offer transactional facilities locally will further reduce dependence on server resources and, thus, additional performance and scalability benefits will be gained.

In our previous work [20], we developed recovery algorithms for distributed data shipping architectures. These algorithms offer transactional facilities locally and use page-level locking. In this paper, we describe how local transaction management is carried out in a data shipping client-server architecture when fine-granularity locking is used. Our algorithms allow multiple clients to concurrently update different portions of the same database page. Each client writes log records to a local log file and logs are not merged at any time. The database state is recovered correctly even if the server and several clients crash at the same time, and if the updates performed by different clients on a page are not present on the disk version of the page, even though some of the updating transactions have committed.

The remainder of the paper is organized as follows. Section 2 states our assumptions about the distributed environment we assume when describing our algorithms. Section 3 describes our solutions to the problems associated with fine-granularity locking, and it presents our algorithms for client, server, and complex failures. We compare our work with relevant work that appears in the literature in Section 4 and, finally, we summarize in Section 5.

2 Terminology and Basic Assumptions

Transactions are executed in their entirety at the client where they are started. Data items referenced by a transaction are fetched from the server before they are accessed, and the unit of transfer is assumed to be a database page (this corresponds to the page server approach described in [6]). The buffer managers of the clients and the server follow the *steal* and *no-force* strategies [10]. Modified pages that are replaced from a client cache are sent to the server, and modified pages that are replaced from the server cache are written *in-place* to disk. Pages that were updated by a terminated transaction (committed or aborted) are not necessarily sent to the server before the termination of the transaction.

Concurrency control is based on locking and the server has a global lock manager (GLM) that employs the strict two-phase locking protocol. Each client has a local lock manager (LLM) that caches all acquired locks and forwards the lock requests that cannot be granted locally to the server. *Inter-transaction* caching [26, 25, 4, 8] of the cached pages and locks is supported, and the *callback locking* protocol [11, 13] is used for cache consistency. Fine-granularity locking is employed, and both shared and exclusive locks are retained by a client after a transaction terminates (whether committing or rolling back). For concreteness, we assume that the adaptive locking scheme presented in [3] is used. Cached locks that are called back in exclusive mode are released and exclusive locks that are called back in shared mode are demoted to shared.

Each database page consists of a header that among other information contains a *page sequence number* (PSN), which is incremented by one every time the page is modified by a transaction. The server initializes the PSN value of a page when this page is allocated by following the approach presented in [18] (i.e. the PSN stored on the space allocation map containing information about the page in question is assigned to the PSN field of the page).

The private log of each client is used for logging transaction updates, rolling back aborted transactions, and recovering from client crashes. Recovery is based on the *write-ahead log* (WAL) protocol and the ARIES [16] algorithm is employed. Log records are written to the private log before an updated page is replaced from the local cache and at transaction commit. Each client log manager associates with each log record a *log sequence number* (LSN), which is a monotonically increasing value. We assume that the LSN of a log record corresponds to the address of the log record in the private log file. Log records describing an update on a page contain among other fields the page id and the PSN the page had just before it was updated.

When the server receives a page P from some client, it merges the updates present on that page with the version of P that is present in its buffer pool. If there is no copy of P in its buffer pool, the server reads P from the disk first and then it applies the merging procedure. After the server merges two copies of the same page having PSN values PSN_i and PSN_j, respectively, it sets the PSN value of the page to be: $\max(PSN_i, PSN_j) + 1$. We add one to the maximum value to ensure monotonically increasing PSN values when two copies with the same PSN value are merged.

When a client triggers a callback for an object and the server sends the page P containing the object, the client installs the updates present on this object on the version of P that is present in its cache, if any. Similarly to the server merging procedure, the client sets the PSN of the page to be one greater than the maximum of the PSN values present on the two copies that are being merged. In this way, log records written for the same object by different clients contain monotonically increasing PSN values.

While presenting our algorithms, we assume that each client in the system writes log records for updates to pages in its own log file. We also assume that the crashed client performs restart recovery. However, our algorithms do not require that each client has a log file, nor do they require that the crashed client is the one that will recover from its failure. In particular, clients that do not have local disk space can ship their log records to the server. In addition, restart recovery for a crashed client may be performed by the server or any other client that has access to the log of this client.

3 Client-Based Logging

In this section, we first present our solutions to the recovery issues which arise when fine-granularity locking is used. Then, we present our algorithms for client, server, and complex crashes and, finally, we address issues related to log space management.

3.1 Recovery Issues in Fine-Granularity Locking

Using fine-granularity locking in a page server architecture raises the issue of managing concurrent client updates to the same pages. The *update-privilege* approach has been suggested for both shared-disks systems [17] and client-server architectures [18]. The idea is to serialize the updates by using an "update token," which is acquired before updating a page. However, this approach tends to be communication intensive due to the synchronization messages required for transferring the token and the pages that are often sent along with the transfer of the token.

A second approach is to permit multiple outstanding updates on a page and merge these updates when necessary. One way of merging these updates is by merging the log records generated for them [19, 2]. However, merging log records is an expensive and I/O intensive operation. An alternative solution is to merge the updated copies of a page. This solution involves CPU cost and usually no server disk I/O, and the price paid is only a little more book-keeping. This approach fits better with the cost parameters of a networked client-server system, and is the approach we follow here.

Merging updates that simply overwrite parts of objects residing on the same page, referred to as *mergeable* updates, is straightforward. However, updates that modify the structure of a page (by either changing the size of an object or creating new objects) cannot always be merged[3]. Consequently, only one client at a time should be allowed to perform non-mergeable updates. This is accomplished by acquiring an exclusive lock on the page whose structure is going to be altered.

Another challenge in fine-granularity locking is to be able to determine whether the updates of a log record are present on the page. When page-level locking is employed or when the update token approach is used, only one client at a time can update the PSN value of a page and write a log record containing this value. As a result, the PSN value of a page is enough to determine whether the updates of a log record are present on the page. According to the assumptions made in Section 2, the updates of a log record are present on a page when the PSN value of the page is greater than the PSN value stored in the log record.

However, when a page is updated concurrently by many clients, then some log records written for this page by these clients may contain the same PSN

---

[3] Object size modifications could be made mergeable by either using some forwarding mechanism or reserving in advance enough space to accommodate any future expansions of the object. We do not consider these alternatives any further in this paper.

value. Consequently, the PSN value of the page cannot be used to determine the log records that have their updates reflected on the page. Our solution to this problem consists of two parts. For handling client crashes, when a client sends a page to the server, either because of cache replacement or in response to a callback request, the server remembers the PSN value present on the page. In addition, the server remembers the PSN value present on the page the first time a client acquires an exclusive lock on the page or an object present on the page. As a result of the above technique, the following propery is guaranteed.

Property 1. The updates of a client record written for a page P are reflected on the copy of P present in the server's cache or on disk, when the PSN value stored in it is less than the PSN value the server remembers for P and this client.

For handling server crashes, the server forces to its log a *replacement* log record when it is about to write an updated page to disk. This log record contains the PSN value of the page and the list of the PSN values the server remembers for the clients that have updated the page, together with the ids of these clients. It can be easily proven that this solution has the following property.

Property 2. If the PSN value of a page P on disk is PSN_{disk} and the server's log contains a replacement log record for P whose PSN field is the same as PSN_{disk}, the PSN values stored in this log record determine the client updates that are present on the page. In particular, the updates of a client log record whose PSN value is less than the PSN value stored in the replacement log record for this client are present on the page.

Finally, because the same object may be updated by several clients before the page containing this object is written to disk, restart recovery must preserve the order in which these clients updated the object. This order corresponds to the order in which the server sent callback messages for the object, and it should be reconstructed during server restart recovery (Property 1 guarantees correct recovery in the case of a client crash). In order to be able to reconstruct the callback order, each client that triggers a callback for an exclusive lock writes a *callback* log record in its log. This log record contains the identity of the called back object, the identity of the client that responded to the callback, and the PSN value the page had when it was sent to the server by the client that responded to the callback request. Section 3.4 explains how the callback log records are used during server restart recovery.

3.2 Normal Processing

When the server receives a lock request for an object that conflicts with an existing lock on the same object or the page P conatining the object, it examines the following cases.

– *Object-level conflict.* If the requested lock mode is shared and some client C holds an exclusive lock on the object, C downgrades its lock to shared and sends a copy of P to the server, which forwards P to the requester. The same procedure is followed when the requested lock is exclusive. In this case, all clients holding conflicting locks release them, and they drop P from their cache if no other locks are held on objects residing on the page.

- *Page-level conflict.* All clients holding conflicting locks on P de-escalate their locks and obtain object-level locks; each LLM maintains a list of the objects accessed by local transactions, and this list is used in order to obtain object-level locks. After de-escalation is over, the server checks for object-level conflicts.

Clients periodically take checkpoints. Each checkpoint record contains information about the local transactions that are active at the time of the checkpointing. The checkpoint record also contains the dirty page table (DPT), which consists of entries corresponding to pages that have been modified by local transactions and the updates have not made it to the disk version of the database yet. Each entry in the DPT of a client C contains at least the following fields.

PID:	id of a page P
RedoLSN:	LSN of the log record that made P dirty

A client adds an entry for a page to its DPT the first time it obtains an exclusive lock on either an object residing on the page or the page itself. The current end of the log is conservatively assigned to the *RedoLSN* field. The *RedoLSN* corresponds to the LSN of the earliest log record that needs to be redone for the page during restart recovery. An entry is dropped from the DPT when the client receives an acknowledgment from the server that the page has been flushed to disk and the page has not been updated again since the last time it was sent to the server.

The server also takes checkpoints. Each checkpoint record contains the dirty client table (DCT), which consists of entries corresponding to pages that may have been updated by some client. Each entry in the DCT has at least the following fields.

PID:	id of a page P
CID:	id of client C
PSN:	P's PSN the last time it was received from C
RedoLSN:	LSN of the first replacement log record written for P

The server inserts a new entry into the DCT the first time it grants an exclusive lock requested by a client on either an object residing on the page or the page itself. The new entry contains the id of the client, the id of the page, the PSN value present on the page[4], and the *RedoLSN* field is set to NULL. The server removes an entry for a particular client and page from the DCT after

---

[4] If the client has the page cached in its local pool, the client sends the PSN value of the page when it requests an exclusive lock on an object residing on the page. It is that PSN that will be inserted in the DCT entry. Otherwise, the PSN value present on the page that is sent to the client is assigned to the new DCT entry.

the page is forced to disk, and the client does not hold any exclusive locks on wither objects residing on the page or the page itself.

Every time the server forces a page P to disk, it first writes a replacement log record to its log file. The replacement log record contains the PSN value stored on the page and all the DCT entries about P. If the *RedoLSN* field of the DCT entry about P is NULL, the LSN of the replacement log record is assigned to it.

When the server receives a page P that was either called back or replaced from the cache of a client C, it first locates the entry in the DCT that corresponds to C and P and sets the value of the *PSN* field to be the PSN value present on P. Next, the server merges the updates present on P, as explained in Section 2.

Transaction rollback is handled by each client. Furthermore, clients can support the savepoint concept and offer partial rollbacks. Both total and partial transaction rollbacks open a log scan starting from the last log record written by the transaction. Since updated pages are allowed to be replaced from the client's cache, the rollback procedure may have to fetch some of the affected pages from the server. When a client needs to access again a page that was replaced from its local cache, the server sends the page to the client together with the *PSN* value present in the DCT entry that corresponds to this client and the page in question. The client ignores the PSN value sent along during normal transaction processing.

3.3   Recovery From a Client Crash

When a client fails, its lock tables and cache contents are lost. The server releases all shared locks held by the crashed client and queues any callback requests until the client recovers. Transaction processing on the remaining clients can continue in parallel with the recovery of the crashed client.

During restart recovery, the crashed client installs in its lock tables the exclusive locks it held before the failure. The recovery of the crashed client involves the recovery of the updates performed by local transactions. Since each client writes all log records for updates to pages in its own log file, all the pages that had been updated before the crash can be determined by scanning the local log starting from the last complete checkpoint. These pages correspond to the entries of the DPT which is constructed during the analysis phase of the ARIES algorithm. However, according to Property 1 and the way the DCT is updated, only the pages that have an entry in the DCT need to be recovered.

Next, the client executes the ARIES redo pass of its log by starting from the log record whose LSN is the minimum of all *RedoLSN* values present in the entries of the DPT. A page that is referenced by a log record is fetched from the server only if the page has an entry in the DPT and the *RedoLSN* value of the DPT entry for this page is smaller than or equal to the LSN of the log record. When the page is fetched from the server, the server sends along the PSN value stored in the DCT entry that corresponds to this client and the client installs this PSN value on the page. The log record is applied on the page only when it corresponds to an update for an object that is exclusively locked and the PSN field of this record is greater that or equal to the PSN value stored on the page.

During the redo pass, callback log records may be encountered. These callback log records are not processed, according to the discussion presented in Section 3.1. After the redo pass is over, all transactions that were active at the time of the crash are rolled back by using transaction information that was collected during the ARIES analysis pass. Transaction rollback is done by executing the ARIES undo pass.

3.4 Recovery From a Server Crash

When the server crashes, pages containing updated objects that were present in the server cache at the time of the crash may have to be recovered. These pages may contain objects that were updated by multiple clients since pages are not forced to disk at transaction commit, or when they are replaced from the client cache, or when they are called back. During its restart recovery, the server has to (a) determine the pages requiring recovery, (b) identify the clients that are involved in the recovery of these pages, (c) reconstruct the DCT, and (d) coordinate the recovery among the involved clients.

The pages that may need to be recovered are those that have an entry in the DPT of a client and they are not present in the cache of this client. Although some of these pages may be present in the cache of some other client, it is wrong to assume that these pages contain all the updates performed on them before the server's crash. This is because fine-granularity locking is in effect. The server constructs the list of the pages that may require recovery, as well as the GLM tables, by requesting from each client a copy of the DPT, the list of the cached pages, and the entries in the LLM tables.

The clients that are involved in the recovery are identified during the procedure of determining the pages that require recovery. In particular, all clients that have an entry for a page in their DPTs and they do not have the page cached in their cache will participate in the recovery of the page.

Next, the server reconstructs its DCT. The construction of the DCT must be done in such a way that the state of a page with respect to the updates performed on this page by a client can be precisely determined. When a page is present in the cache of a client its state corresponds to the PSN value present on the page. When a page is not present in the cache of a client its state must be determined from the state of the page on disk and the replacement log records written for this page. In particular, the server executes the following steps.

1. Insert into the DCT entries of the form $< PID, CID, NULL, NULL >$ for all the pages that are present in the DPTs of the operational clients.
2. Read from disk all the pages that were determined to be candidates for recovery and remember the PSN values stored on them.
3. Update the NULL PSN and $RedoLSN$ entries in the constructed DCT in the following way:

   (a) Retrieve from the log the DCT stored in the last complete checkpoint and compute the minimum of the $RedoLSN$ values stored in this table.

(b) Scan the log starting from the above computed minimum and for each *replacement* log record that corresponds to a page P having an entry in the constructed DCT do the following:

    i. If the $RedoLSN$ value of the DCT entry for P is NULL then set its value to the LSN of this log record.

    ii. If the PSN value stored in the log record is the same as the remembered PSN value computed in Step 2, then replace the PSN fields of all entries in the DCT that correspond to the client ids stored in the log record with the corresponding PSN values present in the log record.

4. Request from each operational client the pages that are present in its cache and have an entry in the DPT of this client. The updates present on these pages are merged and the PSN fields in the DCT are updated accordingly.

Finally, the server coordinates the recovery of a page P by determining for each involved client C the state of each object residing on P which had been updated by many clients before the crash. This is done in the following way.

1. Each client C_i that has P in its cache scans its log and constructs a list, referred to as $CallBack_P$, of all the objects residing on P that were called back from C. The scan starts from the location corresponding to the $RedoLSN$ value present in the DPT entry about P. $CallBack_P$ contains the object identifiers and the PSN values present in the callback log records written for these objects and the client C. If multiple callback log records are written for the same object and the same client, the PSN value stored in the most recent one is stored in $CallBack_P$.

2. The server collects all $CallBack_P$ lists and merges all the entries referring to the same object by keeping only the entry containing the maximum PSN value. The resulting list is sent to C together with P and the PSN value present in the DCT entry.

Client C installs on P the PSN value sent by the server and starts its recovery procedure for P by examining all log records written for updates to P. The starting point of the log scan is determined from the $RedoLSN$ value present in the DPT entry for P. For each scanned log record, C does the following.

1. If the log record was written for an object belonging to the $CallBack_P$ list sent by the server, the log record applied to P only when the PSN value stored in it is equal to or greater than the object's PSN value present in the above list.

2. If the log record was written for an object that does not belong to the $CallBack_P$ list, then the log record is applied to P.

3. If the log record is a callback log record that was written for an object present in the $CallBack_P$ list, the log record is skipped. Otherwise, C requests P from the server and sends the CID and PSN values present in the log record along. C continues the recovery procedure after the server sends P and C merges the updates present on it with the copy it has in its cache.

When the server receives the request for page P from C in the above Step 3, it compares the PSN value sent against the PSN values stored in the DCT for the client CID. If the latter is greater or equal to the former, then the server will send P to C. Otherwise, the server will request P from CID and then forward P to C. This situation materializes when CID is recovering P in parallel with C. In this case, CID will send P to the server only after it has processed all log records containing a PSN value that is less than the PSN value C sent to the server.

3.5 Recovery From a Complex Crash

So far, we have presented our recovery algorithms for the case of a single client or server crash. However, the server may crash while a client is in the process of recovering from its earlier failure. Similarly, a client may crash while the server is in the process of recovering from its earlier failure. In this case, operational clients will recover their updates on the pages that were present in the server's buffer pool during the crash in the same way as in the server-only crash case. Crashed clients will recover their updates in a way similar to the client-only crash case. In particular, each crashed client will scan its local log starting from the last complete checkpoint and build an augmented DPT. The server will scan its log file, starting from the minimum $RedoLSN$ value present in the DCT stored in the last checkpoint record, and build the DCT entries that correspond to both the pages the crashed clients updated and the pages the operational clients had replaced. From the replacement log records and the PSN value present on each of these pages, the server will calculate the PSN value to be used while recovering those pages in the way explained in Section 3.4.

3.6 Log Space Management

Log space management becomes an issue when a client consumes its available log space and it has to overwrite existing log records. Since the earliest log record needed for recovering from a client and/or server crash corresponds to the minimum of all the $RedoLSN$ values present in the DPT of this client, the client can reuse its log space only when the minimum $RedoLSN$ is pushed forward. In the algorithms we have presented so far, the minimum $RedoLSN$ may be pushed forward only when an entry is dropped from the DPT. But, this may not be enough to prevent the client from not having enough log space to continue executing transactions.

Our solution to the above problem is the following. When a client sends a dirty page that is replaced from its local cache to the server, the client remembers the current end of its private log file. When the server forces the page to disk, it informs all clients that had replaced the page. These clients replace the $RedoLSN$ field of the DPT entry referring to the page that was forced to disk with the remembered end of the log LSN for the page. When a client faces log space problems, it replaces from its cache the page having the minimum $RedoLSN$ value in the DPT and asks the server to force the page to disk. If, however, the page is not present in the client cache, the client just asks the server to force the page to disk. If the client needs more log space, it repeats the above procedure.

4 Related Work

In the following sections, we compare our work sith relevant work in the areas of client-server, shared-disks, and distributed file systems.

4.1 Client-Server Systems

A comprehensive study of performance implications related to different granularities for data transfer, concurrency control, and coherency control in a client-server environment is presented in [3]. Unlike our scheme, the authors of the above study assumed that copies of all updated data are sent back to the server at transaction commit. While concurrent updates on the same page are handled by merging individual updates, no recovery algorithms are presented in [3].

In [7], a client-server architecture that exploits client disks for extending the in-memory cache is proposed. Even though that paper's main focus is on the performance of the different ways of integrating disks with memory caches, the authors also discuss issues related to recovery when pages modified by a committed transaction are not sent to the server as part of the commit protocol. In contrast to [7], we have investigated logging and recovery issues when clients are allowed to perform local logging and they do not send pages to the server at transaction commit.

Local disk space is also used in the architecture presented in [5]. In [5], local disks are used to store relational query results that are retrieved from the server. Transaction management is carried out exclusively by the server and all updates to the database are performed at the server. Our work differs significantly in that we permit clients with local disk space to offer transactional facilities to local transactions.

Versant [24], a commercially available OODBMS, also explores client disk space. In Versant, users can check out objects by requesting them from the server and store them locally in a "personal database." In addition, locking and logging for objects stored in a personal database can be turned off to increase performance. The checked out objects are unavailable to the rest of the clients until they are checked in later on. All modified and new objects in the client's object cache must be sent to the appropriate server so that changes can be logged at transaction commit. Our architecture is more effective since it avoids generating log records at commit time, and it allows local logging of updates.

In ARIES/CSA [18], clients send all their log records to the server as part of the commit processing. Similar to our work, ARIES/CSA employs a fine-granularity locking protocol, clients do not send modified pages to the server at transaction commit, and transaction rollback is performed by clients. However, client crashes are still handled by the server and clients are not allowed to update the same page simultaneously. Unlike our algorithms, client checkpoints in ARIES/CSA are stored in the log maintained by the server and server checkpointing requires synchronous communication with all connected clients.

4.2 Shared-Disks Systems

In [21], logging and recovery protocols are presented for a shared-disks architecture employing the *primary copy authority* (PCA) locking protocol. Under the PCA locking protocol, the entire lock space is divided among the participating nodes and a lock request for a given item is forwarded to the node responsible for the item. Although PCA is similar to our work, there are several important differences. Unlike PCA that supports only physical logging, our algorithms support both physical and logical logging. PCA employs the *no-steal* buffer management policy – only pages containing committed data are written to disk – which is argued to be an inflexible and expensive policy, especially when fine-granularity locking is used [16].

Like our algorithms, PCA allows pages to be modified by many nodes before they are written to disk. However, PCA uses page level locking and commit processing involves the sending of each updated page to the node that holds the PCA for the page. Furthermore, double logging is required for every page that is modified by a node other than the PCA node. During normal transaction processing, the modifying node writes log records in its own log and at transaction commit it sends all the log records for remotely controlled pages to the PCA nodes responsible for these pages. Our algorithms do not require updated pages to be sent to the owner nodes at transaction commit time, nor do they require log records to be written in two log files.

In [17] four different recovery schemes for a shared-disks architecture are presented and analyzed. The presented algorithms were designed to exploit the fast inter-node communication paths usually found in tightly-coupled data sharing architectures. Similar to these algorithms, our algorithms work with write-ahead logging recovery, the steal no-force buffer replacement policy, and fine-granularity locking. But, unlike these algorithms, which prohibit different nodes from updating the same page concurrently, our algorithms allow multiple nodes to update different parts of the same page in parallel. Further, our algorithms are not based on the assumption that the clocks of all the clients are perfectly synchronized. Finally, our algorithms do not force pages to disk when they are exchanged between nodes as it is done in the *simple* and *medium* schemes presented in [17], nor do they require merging of the private logs at any time. Private logs have to merged in the *fast* and *super-fast* schemes presented in [17] even in the case where only a single node crashes.

The *shared data/private log* recovery algorithm presented in [14] motivated our work. However, our recovery algorithms do not require a seamless ordering of PSNs, nor do they associate for each database page extra information with the space management sub-system. Unlike the algorithm presented in [14], which requires modified pages to be forced to disk before they are replaced from a node's cache, our algorithms let the cache replacement policy force a modified page to disk. In addition, our algorithms work with fine-granularity locking.

Rdb/VMS [22] is a data sharing database system executing on a VAXcluster. Earlier versions of Rdb/VMS employed an undo/no-redo recovery protocol that required, at transaction commit, the forcing to disk of all the pages updated by the committing transaction. More recent versions offer both an undo/no-redo and an undo/redo recovery scheme [15]. In addition, a variation of the callback locking algorithm, referred to as *lock carry-over*, is used for reducing the number of messages sent across the nodes for locking purposes. However, Rdb/VMS does not allow multiple outstanding updates belonging to different nodes to be present on a database page. Thus, modified pages are forced to disk before they are shipped from one node to another.

In Rdb/VMS, each application process can take its own checkpoint after the completion of a particular transaction. The checkpointing process forces to disk all modified and committed database pages. Unlike Rdb/VMS, our algorithms support different variations of *fuzzy checkpoints* [1, 9, 12]. Those checkpoints are asynchronous and take place while other processing is going on. Another important difference is that Rdb/VMS uses only one global log file. Consequently, the common log becomes a bottleneck and a global lock must be acquired by each node that needs to append several log records to the log.

4.3 Distributed File Systems

Coda [23] is a distributed file system operating on a network of UNIX work-stations. Coda is based on the Andrew File System [11] and cache coherency is based on the callback locking algorithm. However, the granularity of caching is that of entire files and directories. Coda's most important characteristic, which is closely related to our work, is that it can handle server and network failures and support portable workstations by using clients disks for logging. This ability is based on the *disconnected operation* mode of operation that allows clients to continue accessing and modifying the cached data even when they are not con-nected to the network. All updates are logged and they are reintegrated to the systems on reconnection.

However, Coda does not provide the same transactional semantics as our algorithms. In particular, failure atomicity is not supported and updates cannot be rolled back. Another important difference is that our algorithms guarantee that the updates performed by a transaction survive various system failures and they are altered only when a later transaction modifies them. Coda, on the other hand, guarantees permanence conditionally; updates made by a transaction may change if a conflict is discovered at the time these updates are being reintegrated into the system.

5 Conclusions

In this paper we have presented recovery algorithms that exploit client disk space to offer transactional facilities locally, while maintaining the transaction semantics associated with traditional database systems. The algorithms we have described work with fine-granularity locking and multiple clients can update concurrently different portions of the same page. The database state is recovered correctly even if several clients and the server crash, and even if the updates performed by different clients on a page have not been merged, even though some of the updating transactions have committed.

The key advantages of our algorithms are: (1) updated pages are not forced to disk at transaction commit time or when they are replaced from a client cache, (2) transaction rollback and client crash recovery are handled exclusively by the clients, (3) clients may recover the same page in parallel, (4) for objects that were updated by several clients, the synchronization log records preserve the ordering of updates, (5) private log files are never merged during the recovery process, (6) each client can take a checkpoint without synchronizing with the rest of the operational clients, and (7) client clocks do not have to be synchronized and lock tables are not checkpointed.

We believe that as the world becomes more and more distributed, it will become increasingly more important for all transaction facilities to be provided locally, even when data is shared in a global environment. In this paper, we have taken a step in this direction by showing how local logging, transaction commitment and recovery can be performed in a distributed architecture.

References

1. P. A. Bernstein, V. Hadzilacos, and N. Goodman. *Concurrency Control and Recovery in Database Systems*. Addison-Wesley, Reading, MA, 1987.

2. M. J. Carey, D. J. DeWitt, M. J. Franklin, N. E. Hall, M. McAuliffe, J. F. Naughton, D. T. Schuh, and M. H. Solomon. Shoring up persistent applications. In *Proceedings of ACM-SIGMOD 1994 International Conference on Management of Data*, Minneapolis, Minnesota, pages 383 – 394, May 1994.

3. M. J. Carey, M. J. Franklin, and M. Zaharioudakis. Fine-grained sharing in a page server OODBMS. In *Proceedings of ACM-SIGMOD 1994 International Conference on Management of Data*, Minneapolis, Minnesota, pages 359–370, May 1994.

4. M.J. Carey, M. Franklin, M. Livny, and E. Shekita. Data caching tradeoffs in client-server DBMS architectures. In *Proceedings of ACM-SIGMOD 1991 International Conference on Management of Data*, Denver, Colorado, pages 357–366, May 1991.

5. A. Delis and N. Roussopoulos. Performance and scalability of client-server database architectures. In *Proceedings of the Eighteenth International Conference on Very Large Databases*, Vancouver, British Columbia, pages 610–623, August 1992.

6. D. J. DeWitt, D. Maier, P. Futtersack, and F. Velez. A study of three alternative workstation-server architectures for object-oriented database systems. In *Proceedings of the Sixteenth International Conference on Very Large Databases*, Brisbane, pages 107–121, August 1990.

7. M. Franklin, M. Carey, and M. Livny. Local disk caching for client-server database systems. In *Proceedings of the Nineteenth International Conference on Very Large Databases*, Dublin, Ireland, pages 641–654, August 1993.

8. M. Franklin, M. Carey, and Livny M. Global memory management in client-server DBMS architectures. In *Proceedings of the Eighteenth International Conference on Very Large Databases*, Vancouver, British Columbia, pages 596–609, August 1992.

9. M. Franklin, M. Zwilling, C. Tan, M. Carey, and D. DeWitt. Crash recovery in client-server EXODUS. In *Proceedings of ACM-SIGMOD 1992 International Conference on Management of Data*, San Diego, California, pages 165 – 174, June 1992.

10. T. Haerder and A. Reuter. Principles of transaction oriented database recovery — a taxonomy. *ACM Computing Surveys*, 15(4):289–317, December 1983.

11. J. H. Howard, M. Kazarand,
    S. Menees, D. Nichols, M. Satyanarayanan, R. Sidebotham, and M. West. Scale

and performance in a distributed file system. *ACM Transactions on Computer Systems*, 6(1):51–81, February 1988.

12. H.V Jagadish, D.F. Lieuwen, R. Rastogi, A. Silberschatz, and S. Sudarshan. DALI: An extensible main memory storage manager. In *Proceedings of the 20th International Conference on Very Large Databases*, Santiago, Chile, September 1994.

13. C. Lamb, G. Landis, J. Orenstein, and D. Weinreb. The ObjectStore database system. *Communications of the ACM*, 34(10):51–63, October 1991.

14. D. Lomet. Recovery for Shared Disk Systems Using Multiple Redo Logs. Technical Report CLR 90/4, Digital Equipment Corp., Cambridge Research Lab, Cambridge, MA., Oct. 1990.

15. D. Lomet, R. Anderson, T.K. Rengarajan, and P. Spiro. How the Rdb/VMS data sharing system became fast. Technical Report CRL 92/4, Digital Equipment Corporation Cambridge Research Lab, 1992.

16. C. Mohan, D. Haderle, B. Lindsay, H. Pirahesh, and P. Schwarz. ARIES: A transaction recovery method supporting fine-granularity locking and partial rollbacks using write-ahead logging. *ACM Transactions on Database Systems*, 17(1):94–162, March 1992.

17. C. Mohan and I. Narang. Recovery and coherency-control protocols for fast intersystem page transfer and fine-granularity locking in a shared disks transaction environment. In *Proceedings of the Seventeenth International Conference on Very Large Databases*, Barcelona, Spain, pages 193–207, September 1991.

18. C. Mohan and I. Narang. ARIES/CSA: a method for database recovery in client-server architectures. *Proceedings of ACM-SIGMOD 1994 International Conference on Management of Data*, Minneapolis, Minnesota, pages 55–66, May 1994.

19. C. Mohan, I. Narang, and S. Silen. Solutions to Hot Spot Problems in a Shared Disks Transaction Environment. In *Proceedings of the 4th International Workshop on High Performance Transaction Systems*, September 1991. Also, in IBM Research Report RJ8281 (August 1991).

20. E. Panagos, A. Biliris, H.V. Jagadish, and R. Rastogi. Client-based logging for high performance distributed architectures. In *Proceedings of the 12th International Conference on Data Engineering*, New Orleans, Louisiana, February 1996. To appear.

21. E. Rahm. Recovery Concepts for Data Sharing Systems. In *Proc. 21st Int. Conf. on Fault-Tolerant Computing*, Montreal, June 1991.

22. T. Rengarajan, P. Spiro, and W. Wright. High availability machanisms of VAX DBMS software. *Digital Technical Journal 8*, pages 88–98, February 1989.

23. M. Satyanarayanan, K.J. Kistler, P. Kumar, M.E. Okasaki, E.H. Siegel, and D.C. Steere. Coda: A highly available file system for a distributed workstation environment. *IEEE Transactions on Computers*, 39(4), April 1990.

24. Versant Object Technology, Menlo Park, California. *VERSTANT System Reference Manual, Release 1.6*, 1991.

25. Y. Wang and L. A. Rowe. Cache consistency and concurrency control in client/server DBMS architecture. In *Proceedings of ACM-SIGMOD 1991 International Conference on Management of Data*, Denver, Colorado, pages 367–376, May 1991.

26. K. Wilkinson and M. A. Neimat. Maintaining consistency of client-cached data. In *Proceedings of the Sixteenth International Conference on Very Large Databases*, Brisbane, pages 122–133, August 1990.

Exploiting Persistent Intermediate Code Representations in Open Database Environments*

Andreas Gawecki   Florian Matthes

Universität Hamburg, Vogt-Kölln-Straße 30
D-22527 Hamburg, Germany
{gawecki,matthes}@informatik.uni-hamburg.de

Abstract. Modern database environments have to execute, store, analyze, optimize and generate code at various levels of abstraction (queries, views, triggers, query execution plans, methods, 4GL programs, etc.). We present TML, an abstract persistent intermediate code representation developed in the Tycoon[2] project to fully integrate static and dynamic code analysis and rewriting. TML is a continuation passing style (CPS) language which excels in its explicit, high-level representation of control and data dependencies. We formally define TML and its core rewrite rules which unify many well-known optimizing transformations. We also present Tycoon's innovative reflective system architecture which supports modular compile-time as well as global runtime optimizations. Moreover, we describe how this architecture enables optimizations across abstraction barriers in large modular persistent applications including embedded declarative queries.

1   Introduction and Motivation

The traditional focus of database language research has been on high-level languages for data access and manipulation (query languages, trigger definition languages, 4th generation languages, script languages) or on implementation-oriented languages which capture the characteristic operations of a specific target system at hand (relational algebra, object algebra, structural recursion, ...).

A closer look at tools working on such code representations like query and program optimizers reveals a large number of common tasks which at present are addressed with often incompatible technologies:

▷ Binding analysis: Which entity (table, index, view, function, method, variable, etc.) is denoted by an identifier? Are there multiple references to the same entity?

---

* This research is supported by ESPRIT Basic Research, Project FIDE, #6309 and by a grant from the German Israeli Foundation for Research and Development (*bulk data classification*, I-183 060).

[2] Tycoon: Typed Communicating Objects in Open Environments.

▷ Identifier substitution by a bound value or expression: View expansion, procedure or method inlining, constant folding, substitution of host programming language parameters, etc.

▷ Free variable analysis: Does a variable appear in a query predicate? Does a procedure depend on global variables? Does a query contain programming language variables? Are there independent subexpressions? Which base relations appear inside an integrity constraint?

After a decade of experience with building integrated database programming environments [Schmidt 1977; Mall *et al.* 1984; Schmidt and Matthes 1994] and successive versions of optimizers for their query languages [Jarke and Schmidt 1982; Jarke *et al.* 1982; Jarke and Koch 1984; Böttcher *et al.* 1986; Eder *et al.* 1991], we made the radical decision to replace special-purpose representations for queries, programs and scripts with a single, expressive *intermediate* language. We thereby avoid incompatibilities and redundancies arising from the repeated implementation of the above functionality.

In this paper, we present the Tycoon Machine Language (TML), the common abstract persistent intermediate code representation used for local compile-time as well as global runtime optimizations in the Tycoon system developed at the University of Hamburg. The development of TML was influenced heavily by continuation passing style (CPS) representations found in modern optimizing compilers for functional, imperative and object-oriented languages [Appel 1992; Kranz *et al.* 1986; Kelsey 1989; Teodosiu 1991; Gawecki 1992].

TML inherits the advantages of CPS representations which support a wide range of algorithmically-complete languages, multiple front-ends and back-ends and cross-language optimization. To address the specific needs of database environments, TML also supports optimizations based on runtime bindings to arbitrary complex values in the persistent store and mechanisms to work with persistent TML terms attached to executable code.

The paper is organized as follows: In section 2 we present the abstract syntax and semantics of the CPS-based intermediate representation TML. The core rewrite rules on TML terms are described in section 3. Examples are then given of innovative code optimization architectures which exploit the availability of persistent TML terms at runtime (section 4.1. A full description of TML and its rewrite rules can be found in [Gawecki and Matthes 1994; Kiradjiev 1994]. The paper ends with a perspective on future research work and on other innovative application domains for uniform persistent code and query representations in the spirit of TML.

2 The Tycoon Intermediate Representation TML

This section presents the CPS-based intermediate representation TML (Tycoon Machine Language) which is used for integrated program and query compilation, transformation and analysis, both at compile time and at runtime.

2.1 Advantages of CPS Intermediate Representations

Continuation Passing Style (CPS) is a powerful yet simple program representation technique. Using continuations, various control structures commonly found in programming languages such as conditionals, (non-block-structured) loops and exception handling can be expressed quite naturally. While this is also true for many other intermediate representations such as triples or quadrupels, the main advantage of CPS lies in the great reduction of the number of program constructs which have to be handled by the compile-time and runtime optimizer while preserving much of the structural information of the source language input.

CPS representations are well-suited for machine analysis by making the flow of control and of data explicit through the uniform use of one language construct: the procedure call. Since CPS does not have implicit procedure returns, this language construct can be viewed as a generalized goto with parameter passing [Steele 1978].

CPS has simple and clean semantics based on the λ-calculus. TML is effectively a call-by-value λ-calculus with store semantics. A number of predefined *primitive procedures* (section 2.3) operate on an implicit, hidden store.

CPS supports higher-order languages, i.e. languages where functions may take other functions as arguments. For example, the selection operation $\sigma_p(R)$ in relational algebra takes two arguments, a range relation R and a selection predicate p where p can be understood as a boolean function on the element type of R.

Like terms in the λ-calculus, CPS terms provide an integrated representation of code fragments and their associated data bindings. To meet the specific requirements of persistent languages and database languages, TML terms may contain simple literal values and object identifiers which denote arbitarily complex objects (tables, indices, ADT values) in the persistent Tycoon object store.

By representing programs in CPS, many well-known program and algebraic query optimization techniques become special cases of a few simple and general λ-calculus transformations. These transformations can be applied freely even in the presence of nonterminating computations and/or side-effecting calls to primitive procedures. This is due to the syntactical restrictions on CPS terms (see Sec. 2.2) which require actual parameters to function calls to be constants, variables or abstractions.

Six different node types are sufficient to represent the data structures for a TML tree. This simplicity facilitates the construction of compact language processors like compiler front ends, back ends and optimizers.

2.2 The Minimalistic Abstract TML Syntax

The complete abstract syntax of TML is defined in figure 1. The set of literal constants (*Lit*) includes simple values such as integers, characters and boolean values, as well as references (*object identifiers, OIDs*) to complex objects in the persistent object store. These *values* can be bound to language *variables* (identifiers) by means of an *application*. In the following example, an integer

```
lit ∈ Lit       Literal constants (including object identifiers)
t ∈ Temp        Temporary variables
c ∈ Cont        Continuation variables
prim ∈ Prim     Primitive procedures (procedure constants)
v    ::= t | c              Variables
val  ::= lit | v | abs      Values
abs  ::= λ(v_1..v_n) app    Abstractions, n ≥ 0
app  ::= (val_0 val_1..val_n)   Applications, n ≥ 0
     |   (prim val_1..val_n)
```

Fig. 1. Abstract Syntax for the Tycoon Machine Language TML

literal, a character constant and an object identifier are bound to variables i, ch and oid, respectively. These variables might be used as values within the body app of the λ-abstraction (which in turn must be an application):

```
(λ(i ch oid) app
  13
  'a'
  < oid 0x005b4780 >)
```

Abstractions are also values in TML, i.e. TML is a higher-order language. This means that abstractions may be bound to variables and that these variables may be used in the functional position of an application (val_0 on the right hand side of the production for app in figure 1). In TML, the body of an abstraction must be an application, and applications are surrounded by parentheses. Therefore, the scope of the abstraction is unambiguous. In the following example, an abstraction with a single formal parameter t is bound to the variable fn, and fn is used immediately within an application of the abstraction, whereby t is bound to an integer value:

```
(λ(fn) (fn 13)
  λ(t) app)
```

Although the semantics of TML is based on the general λ-calculus, well-formed TML programs must satisfy a number of additional constraints[3]:

1. A value used in the functional position of an application must, at runtime, evaluate to an abstraction. Furthermore, this abstraction must expect the same number of value and continuation arguments as the given application, and it must expect them in the same order[4]. This property is statically

---

[3] It is important to note that these constraints are never violated by any of the TML rewrite rules introduced in section 3.

[4] We currently investigate techniques for compiling and type-checking variable-length argument lists. These techniques would merely weaken the given well-formedness rule.

enforced by the compiler front end which performs the necessary type checking on the input to the TML code generator, rejecting any program which contains an application which might violate this rule.

2. Similarly, an application of a primitive procedure must obey the calling conventions of the primitive. Again, the compiler front end (which generates calls to primitive procedures) has to enforce this constraint on any input program.

3. Continuations may not *escape* (by binding them to value identifiers), therefore, continuations are not first-class values in TML. It is not possible to store continuations in data structures where they might be retrieved and applied subsequently. This restriction allows TML procedure calls to be compiled into efficient (stack based) procedure calls and returns on stock hardware, i.e. the main motivation behind this restriction lies in the target code generation techniques we use.

   Several CPS-based compilers support continuations as first class values [Appel 1992; Kranz *et al.* 1986; Kelsey 1989; Teodosiu 1991]. However, these compilers have to translate source language constructs which capture the current continuation, for example, the *call/cc* of SCHEME [Steele 1986], or the built-in polymorphic function *callcc* of ML.

4. Identifiers (value and continuation variables) may not be bound more than once (unique binding rule), i.e. an identifier may occur only once in at most one formal parameter list. For example, the following two TML code fragments are not allowed:

   $\lambda(x\ x)app$

   $\lambda(x)(\lambda(x)app\ val)$

   This means that the TML code generator has to use fresh identifiers for the parameter list of every new λ-abstraction. The TML optimizer (section 3) and the target code generator rely heavily on this property.

5. Abstractions which are used as values (that is, not as continuations and not in functional position of applications) may take an arbitrary number of value parameters, but they must take exactly two continuation parameters: one for the *normal* continuation (which receives the computed value) and one for the *exception* continuation (which is invoked if a runtime exception occurs).

Abstractions which are used as values correspond to first-class, user level procedures. In order to make the printed TML representation used in this paper more readable, these procedures (**proc** abstractions) are differentiated from continuations (**cont** abstractions) even though both have the same internal representation and the same semantics (λ-abstractions). The differentiation is based on a purely syntactic property of abstractions: a continuation does not take any other continuation as a parameter. Thus, the parameter lists of continuation abstractions do not contain any continuation variables. The following two syntactic equivalences reflect these considerations ($n \geq 0$):

$$\lambda(t_1..t_n)\,app \equiv \mathbf{cont}(t_1..t_n)\,app$$

$$\lambda(t_1..t_n\ c_e\ c_c)\,app \equiv \mathbf{proc}(t_1..t_n\ c_e\ c_c)\,app$$

2.3   Adaptability through Primitive Procedures

In TML, most of the "real work" needed to implement source language semantics (e.g. integer arithmetic, query evaluation) is factored out into primitive procedures which are not considered part of the intermediate language itself.

A typical set of primitive procedures used for the compilation of a fully-fledged imperative, algorithmically-complete polymorphic programming language (TL [Matthes and Schmidt 1992]) is listed in figure 2. By definition, each primitive calls exactly one of its continuation arguments tail-recursively, passing the result of its computation, if any. For example, some arithmetic primitives take two continuations: the *normal* continuation which receives the calculated result, and an *exception* continuation which is invoked if the primitive fails due to overflow or division by zero.

Although the set of predefined primitive procedures is typically chosen to be rather small, the set does not need to be minimal due to efficiency tradeoffs. Moreover, it is possible to add new primitive procedures in order to meet the specific needs of more specialized source languages (e.g., supporting multiple bulk data types or scientific or statistical databases). The easiest way to support such complex instructions in TML is to define new primitives which are mapped directly to corresponding abstract machine instructions during target code generation.

New primitive procedures can be defined at back end compile-time by providing the following information to the generic TML rewriting tools:

1. A function to generate target machine code for a given call. This function is used by the code generator to map TML primitive procedure calls into sequences of target machine instructions or calls to the underlying runtime system.
2. A meta-evaluation function to perform optimizations on TML nodes representing calls to this primitive procedure. This function is used by the optimizer to perform constant folding and dead code elimination. To give an example, the primitive procedure '+' has an associated function which is able to reduce the TML application node

    $(+ \ 1 \ 2 \ c_e \ c_c)$

    into an application of the continuation which represents *normal* (i.e. non-exceptional) execution with the result:

    $(c_c \ 3)$
3. A function to estimate the runtime cost of a given call (represented by a TML node) to the primitive procedure, measured in the number of instructions necessary to implement the primitive on an idealized abstract machine. This function is used by the optimizer to estimate the possible savings resulting from the inlining of a TML procedure containing calls to the primitive.
4. A collection of attributes useful for the optimizer, for example commutativity, side effect classes [Gifford and Lucassen 1986], and flags to enable or disable certain optimization rules. There is a default value for any of these attributes, representing the worst possible case (i.e no further information available) for the optimizer.

Note that exception handling is expressed in TML by passing continuations: Every function accepts an additional argument, the exception continuation, which is normally passed through to other functions called. To install a new exception handler, however, a new continuation function which handles exceptions in the callee's body is passed. The 'old' handler is stored automatically within the lexical environment.

$(p\ val_1\ val_2\ c_e\ c_c)$	integer arithmetic, $p \in \{+, -, *, /, \%\}$
$(p\ val_1\ val_2\ c_1\ c_2)$	integer comparison, $p \in \{<, >, <=, >=\}$
$(p\ val_1\ val_2\ c)$	bit operations on integers, $p \in \{<<, >>, \&, |, \hat{\ }, \tilde{\ }\}$
$(\text{char2int}\ val\ c)$	convert a byte to an integer value
$(\text{int2char}\ val\ c)$	convert an integer to a byte value
$(\text{array}\ val_1 \ldots val_n\ c)$	create a mutable array holding n object references
$(\text{vector}\ val_1 \ldots val_n\ c)$	create an immutable array
$(\text{new}\ val_1\ val_2\ c)$	create a mutable array holding val_1 object references, initialized with val_2
$(\$\text{new}\ val_1\ val_2\ c)$	create a mutable byte array holding val_1 simple byte values, initialized with val_2
$([]\ val_1\ val_2\ c)$	array access: indirect indexed load
$([]:=\ val_1\ val_2\ val_3\ c)$	array update: indirect indexed store
$(\$[]\ val_1\ val_2\ val_3\ c)$	byte array access
$(\$[]:=\ val_1\ val_2\ val_3\ c)$	byte array update
$(==\ val$	case analysis based on object identity with...
$\quad val_1 \ldots val_n \cdot$	values and...
$\quad c_1 \ldots c_n\ [c_{n+1}])$	branches (optional else branch)
$(Y\ \lambda(c_0\ val_1 \ldots val_n\ c)\ app)$	the Y combinator
$(\text{size}\ val\ c)$	array or byte array size (in slots)
$(\text{move}\ val_1 \ldots val_5\ c)$	move array contents
$(\$\text{move}\ val_1 \ldots val_5\ c)$	move bytearray contents
$(\text{ccall}\ val_{fmt}\ val_{cfn}\ c_1\ c_2)$	C language function call
$(\text{pushHandler}\ c_1\ c_2)$	Install continuation c_1 as a new exception handler, continue with c_2
$(\text{popHandler}\ c)$	Remove the topmost exception handler, continue with c
$(\text{raise}\ val)$	Raise exception

Fig. 2. TML primitives for the compilation of an imperative programming language

This approach makes control flow explicit even in the presence of exceptions, with the advantage that exception handling can be optimized immediately without special optimization rules. This becomes important when the optimizer is inlining functions which perform extensive exception handling, which is quite common in high-level value-oriented languages.

The primitive procedure Y is a multiple-value-return CPS version of the lambda-calculus fixed point operator. The abstraction given to the Y-primitive takes n abstraction arguments $v_1..v_n$ and a continuation abstraction c_0, and returns $n+1$ abstractions. As usual in CPS, this multiple-value-return is expressed by calling the continuation c with the desired return values.

The Y-primitive computes the least fixed point of its abstraction argument. This fixed point is a vector of mutually recursive procedures and/or continuations. In other words, the effect of the Y-primitive is that the $n+1$ abstractions $cont()app$ and $abs_1..abs_n$ are bound to the variables c_0 and $v_1..v_n$, respectively, and that these bindings are visible within the abstractions themselves. Moreover, the continuation $cont()app$ which is bound to c_0 is invoked tail-recursively (by Y) after all the recursive bindings have been established.

To give a simple example, a loop which iterates from 1 up to 10, written in the Tycoon Language as *for i = 1 upto 10 do f(i) end* is expressed in TML as follows:

```
(Y proc(c₀ for c)
    (c
      cont()                    ; continuation, bound to c₀
       (for 1)                  ; loop entry
      cont(i)                   ; loop head, bound to 'for'
       (> i 10 cc cont()        ; loop exit
       (f i ce cont(t1)         ; loop body
       (+ i 1 ce cont(t2)
       (for t2))))))))          ; recursion
```

As usual, cc and ce represent the current normal and the current exception continuation, respectively. The introduction of the Y-primitive obviates the need to extend the intermediate language with a special recursive binding operator similar to the letrec special form of SCHEME. A similar primitive is used in the ORBIT compiler [Kranz *et al.* 1986].

The set of TML primitives is described in more detail with additional examples in [Gawecki and Matthes 1994; Kiradjiev 1994].

3 Analysis and Rewriting of TML Intermediate Representations

We have organized the TML optimizer into two separate passes, namely a *reduction* pass and the *expansion* pass. During the reduction pass, a number of generic rewrite rules are applied to the TML tree until no more rules are applicable. Termination is guaranteed because each of the rewrite rules reduces the size of the TML tree if it is applied.

The subsequent expansion pass tries to substitute bound λ-abstractions (procedures or continuations) at the positions where they are applied. Effectively, this CPS transformation performs *procedure inlining* in terms of traditional compiler optimization or view expansion in database terminology. The decision whether a given use of a bound abstraction is to be substituted is based on a heuristic cost model similar to the one described by [Appel 1992].

When one or more abstractions are substituted during the expansion pass, there usually is the opportunity to perform more reductions on the TML tree (this is indeed the main reason why inlining is performed in programming languages at all), so each expansion pass is followed by a reduction pass. Likewise, the reduction pass may reveal new opportunities to perform expansions, so the two passes are applied repeatedly until no more changes are made to the TML tree. To guarantee the termination of this process even in obscure cases, a penalty is accumulated at each round of the reduction/expansion phases. The optimization process stops when this penalty reaches a certain limit.

In the following, we give a formal definition of the core TML rewrite rules. We present these rules using the notation

$$(precondition) :$$
$$A \xrightarrow{rule\ name} B$$

indicating that the TML expression A may be rewritten to the TML expression B if $precondition$ evaluates to true. By convention, an empty precondition evaluates to true.

A key feature of CPS-based representations is the fact that control and data dependencies are captured uniformly by the concept of bound variables (variable occurrences inside the scope of a binder). In the precondition, we denote the number of occurrences of a variable v in an TML expression E with $|E|_v$. This function is defined inductively on the abstract syntax of TML as follows:

$$|v|_v = 1$$
$$|lit|_v = 0$$
$$|prim|_v = 0$$
$$|v_1|_{v_2} = 0 \quad (v_1 \neq v_2)$$
$$|\lambda(v_1..v_n)\ app|_v = |app|_v$$
$$|(val_0\ val_1..val_n)|_v = \sum_{i=0}^{n} |val_i|_v$$

Similarly, on the right side of a TML rewrite rule, we use the notation $E[val/v]$ which denotes the expression E where every occurrence of the variable v is replaced by the value val. Name clashes cannot occur during substitution because each variable is bound only once in a TML tree (unique binding rule). This property is achieved by the α-conversion performed during TML code generation, and is never violated by any of the TML rewrite rules, except in one case: if, in an application of the substitution rule, the value substituted is an abstraction, the formal parameters of this abstraction occur temporarily at two different places within the TML tree. However, this does not do any harm because the first occurrence of the abstraction will be removed immediately (by an application of the rewrite rule $remove$) since the substituted variable is not referenced any more.

Variable substitution is defined inductively on the abstract syntax of TML as follows:

$$v[val/v] = val$$
$$v'[val/v] = v' \quad (v \neq v')$$
$$lit[val/v] = lit$$
$$prim[val/v] = prim$$
$$\{\lambda(v_1..v_n)\,app\}[val/v] = \lambda(v_1..v_n)\,\{app[val/v]\}$$
$$(val_0\,val_1..val_n)[val/v] = (val_0[val/v]\,val_1[val/v]..val_n[val/v])$$

Values bound to λ-variables may be substituted freely within the TML tree since, due to CPS, they are not allowed to contain nested primitive or function calls which may cause side effects in the store.

The complete set of the TML rewrite rules which is currently implemented as a part of the reduction pass is given below. The expansion pass uses a variant of the *subst* rewrite rule in order to perform procedure inlining. Although each individual rule is fairly simple, the combination of these rules is surprisingly powerful. Many of the well-known standard program optimizations like constant and copy propagation, dead code elimination, procedure inlining or loop unrolling are just special cases of these general λ-calculus transformations.

The *subst* rewrite rule replaces each occurrence of a bound variable v_i with the corresponding value val_i. Note that the precondition of this rule states that, if the value val_i is an abstraction, the variable v_i must be referenced exactly once. This precondition prevents the TML code from growing arbitrary large:

$$(val_i \notin Abs \vee |app|_{v_i} = 1):$$
$$(\lambda(v_1..v_i..v_n)\,app \xrightarrow{subst} (\lambda(v_1..v_i..v_n)\,app[val_i/v_i]$$
$$val_1..val_i..val_n) \qquad\qquad val_1..val_i..val_n)$$

The *remove* rewrite rule strikes out a bound variable v_i which is not referenced any more. The corresponding value val_i is also removed. Note that this is possible because, due to syntactical restrictions (cf. figure 1), val_i cannot be an application, and, therefore, cannot contain any calls to side-effecting primitive procedures:

$$(|app|_{v_i} = 0):$$
$$(\lambda(v_1..v_i..v_n)\,app \xrightarrow{remove} (\lambda(v_1..v_{i-1}\,v_{i+1}..v_n)\,app$$
$$val_1..val_i..val_n) \qquad\qquad val_1..val_{i-1}\,val_{i+1}..val_n)$$

The *reduce* rewrite rule simply removes applications of λ-abstractions which do not bind any variables:

$$(\lambda()\,app)\ \xrightarrow{reduce}\ app$$

The *η-reduce* rewrite rule removes unnecessary abstractions:

$$(\forall_{i=1...n}\ |val|_{v_i} = 0):$$
$$\lambda(v_1..v_n)(val\ v_1..v_n) \xrightarrow{\eta\text{-}reduce} val$$

The *fold* rewrite rule uses an evaluation function *eval* which knows details of the semantics of primitive procedures:

$$(prim\ val_1..val_n) \xrightarrow{fold} eval(prim, val_1, .., val_n)$$

Given an application of a certain primitive, it may be able to *meta-evaluate* the call, yielding a somewhat simpler TML tree than the original call. For example, if the evaluation function detects that a given call to a primitive will always compute the same value and invoke always the same continuation, it reduces the primitive call to an application of the continuation to the result. Typically, this is possible if some of the arguments are literal constants:

$$(+\ 1\ 2\ c_1\ c_2) \xrightarrow{fold\ +} (c_2\ 3)$$

To give another example, a call to the object identity primitive will fold if the value to be compared is identical to one of the case tags:

$$(==\ 2\ 1\ 2\ 3\ c_1\ c_2\ c_3) \xrightarrow{fold\ ==} (c_2)$$

If the *eval* function cannot perform any useful meta-evaluation, it simply returns the original call to the primitive.

The *case-subst* rewrite rule substitutes variables in case statements with the tag value of the corresponding branch:

$$\begin{array}{l}(==\ v \\ \quad val_1..val_n \\ \quad val_1^c..val_n^c)\end{array} \xrightarrow{case\text{-}subst} \begin{array}{l}(==\ v \\ \quad val_1..val_n \\ \quad val_1^c[val_1/v]..val_n^c[val_n/v])\end{array}$$

$$\begin{array}{l}(==\ v \\ \quad val_1..val_n \\ \quad val_1^c..val_n^c\ val_{n+1}^c)\end{array} \xrightarrow{case\text{-}subst} \begin{array}{l}(==\ v \\ \quad val_1..val_n \\ \quad val_1^c[val_1/v]..val_n^c[val_n/v]\ val_{n+1}^c)\end{array}$$

Finally, there are two rewrite rules which operate on calls to the primitive procedure Y. The *Y-remove* rewrite rule strikes out any recursive procedure which is not referenced from within the bodies of the other (mutually) recursive procedures, whereas the *Y-reduce* rewrite rule removes empty Y applications:

$$(|app|_{v_i} = 0 \wedge \forall_{i \neq j}\ |val_j|_{v_i} = 0):$$

$$\begin{array}{l}(Y\ \lambda(c_0\ v_1..v_i..v_n\ c) \\ \quad (c\ \mathbf{cont}()\ app \\ \quad abs_1 \\ \quad .. \\ \quad abs_i \\ \quad .. \\ \quad abs_n))\end{array} \xrightarrow{Y\text{-}remove} \begin{array}{l}(Y\ \lambda(c_0\ v_1..v_{i-1}\ v_{i+1}..v_n\ c) \\ \quad (c\ \mathbf{cont}()\ app \\ \quad abs_1 \\ \quad .. \\ \quad abs_{i-1} \\ \quad abs_{i+1} \\ \quad .. \\ \quad abs_n))\end{array}$$

$$(|app|_{c_0} = 0):$$

$$(Y\ \lambda(c_0\ c)(c\ \mathbf{cont}()\ app)) \xrightarrow{Y\text{-}reduce} app$$

4 Exploiting Persistent TML Representations

The TML intermediate representation and the TML rewrite rules described so far can be utilized fairly straightforward to build a static optimizer for a given source language and target architecture. Additionally, TML supports innovative code optimization scenarios which we describe in the following subsections.

4.1 Optimization across Abstraction Barriers

Today's applications are constructed incrementally, with heavy re-use of modular software components defined in shared program libraries or application frameworks. At the same time, many binding decisions are delayed until runtime. Abstraction barriers (module interfaces, class interfaces, schema layers) severely restrict the binding information available to local static program optimizers which become less effective with increasing modularization.

Effective optimization of highly modular languages and of database languages therefore requires the analysis and rewriting of CPS terms which have been declared and compiled in separate scopes (logical schema, physical schema, query modules, embedded query, application program), at different times and most often by different users.

In the following, we explain by an example how the Tycoon system achieves optimizations across abstraction barriers. Given a uniform representation of programs and queries, the "trick" to eliminate these abstraction barriers is (1) to wait until link or execution time, when all the bindings between the contributing parts of a persistent application are established (database schemata, application modules, program libraries, program parameters, etc.), and (2) to keep sufficiently abstract code and binding information until that point in time. Based on this approach it is rather straightforward to collect (via transitive reachability) all declarations which contribute to a given TML term (for example an embedded query) into a single scope (represented again as a TML term) and to invoke the TML optimizer to generate a globally optimized TML term.

Since the compiler (and, therefore, the optimizer) is an integral part of the Tycoon persistent programming environment, it is not difficult to call the Tycoon compiler at runtime.

For each exported source code function f in a compilation unit, the compiler back end augments the generated code for f with a reference to a compact persistent representation of the TML tree (Persistent TML, PTML) for f. At runtime, it is possible to map PTML back into TML, re-invoke the optimizer and code-generator, link the newly-generated code into the running program, and execute it (Fig. 3).

The mapping from PTML back to TML also returns the set of R-value bindings ([identifier, OID] pairs) established at runtime. These bindings correspond to free variables (module names, database names, table names, function names, constant names, etc.) in the source text and they naturally give rise to context-dependent, inter-procedure and inter-module optimizations (*optimization across abstraction barriers*).

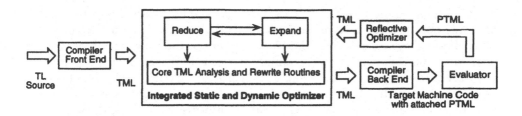

Fig. 3. Interaction between compilation, optimization and evaluation in the Tycoon system

To speed up repeated optimizations of (shared) functions, the optimizer attaches several derived attributes (costs, savings, ...) to the generated code which also become part of the persistent system state.

For example, the following Tycoon module *complex* exports a (hidden) abstract data type *complex.T* and encapsulated accessor functions *complex.x()*, *complex.y()*, ... on values of that type:

```
module complex export
  Let T = Tuple x,y :Real end
  let new(x,y :Real):T = tuple x y end
  let x(complex :T) :Real = complex.x
  let y(complex :T) :Real = complex.y
  ...
end
```

Here is a function *abs* which uses the functions exported from the module:

```
let abs(c :complex.T) :Real =
  sqrt(complex.x(c) * complex.x(c) + complex.y(c) * complex.y(c))
```

In the static context of this function, the implementation of the module (the binding to the module value) is not available. Only after module linkage (Tycoon has first class modules), the dynamic context of *abs* contains bindings to the exported function.

The programmer can obtain a (dynamically created) function *optimizedAbs* which is equivalent to the original function *abs* but which executes faster than the original by explicitly invoking the optimizer on *abs*:

```
let optimizedAbs = reflect.optimize(abs)
```

In our current implementation, the reflective dynamic optimizer inlines the bodies of *complex.x* and *complex.y*, i.e., *optimizedAbs* is equivalent to:

```
let optimizedAbs(c :complex.T) :Real = sqrt(c.x*c.x + c.y*c.y)
```

Finally, the optimized function which takes advantage of the particular encapsulated implementation of complex numbers can be applied:

```
optimizedAbs(complex.new(3 4))
```

The main extension which is necessary to be able to carry out this kind of dynamic optimization is to re-establish, in TML, the R-value bindings of global variables as they are stored in the *closure record* of the runtime representation of a given procedure. For the example above, this means that the values of the variables *complex*, '+', '*' and *sqrt* which are global to the function *abs* are fetched from the closure record of *abs* and are bound to the corresponding identifiers *before* the (original) body of *abs* is processed by the optimizer[5]:

```
proc(c_10 c_11)
   (λ(complex_6 *_7 +_8 sqrt_9)
      ([] complex_6 2 cont(t_12)          ; begin of the original body of abs
      (t_12 c_10 cont(t_13)
      ([] complex_6 2 cont(t_14)
      (t_14 c_10 cont(t_15)
      (*_7 t_13 t_15 cont(t_16)
      ([] complex_6 3 cont(t_17)
      (t_17 c_10 cont(t_18)
      (+_8 t_16 t_18 cont(t_19)
      ([] complex_6 3 cont(t_20)
      (t_20 c_10 cont(t_21)
      (*_7 t_19 t_21 cont(t_22)
      (sqrt_9 t_22 cont(t_23)
      (c_11 t_23))))))))))))))          ; end of the original body of abs
      <oid 0x005b4780>          ; value of module complex
      <oid 0x001b4044>          ; value of function '*'
      <oid 0x001b4024>          ; value of function '+'
      <oid 0x00993d28>)          ; value of function sqrt
```

Given these value bindings, the optimizer is able to perform substitution, constant folding and procedure inlining in the usual way, yielding a result which is equivalent to the above Tycoon code for *optimizedAbs*.

4.2 Towards Integrated Program and Query Optimization

There is a strong interest in improving the interface between query languages and programming languages. For example, the ODMG standard document explicitly states that "object database management systems provide an architecture which is significantly different than other DBMSs – they are a revolutionary rather than an evolutionary development. Rather than providing only a high-level language such as SQL for data manipulation, an ODBMS transparently integrates database capability with the application programming language" [Catell 1994].

Following this rationale, the syntax of many modern query languages allows programming language variables, function and method calls to appear in the

---

[5] This is a TML listing similar to the output of our TML pretty-printer. Note that, during α-conversion, each identifier name is appended with a unique number in order to distinguish it from any other identifier.

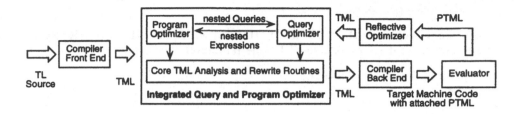

Fig. 4. Embedded Query Optimization

select and **where** clauses of SQL statements. Furthermore, the body of element-at-a-time iterators (**for each** statements) and of database triggers may refer to programming language statements. User-defined data types lead to further interaction between query expressions and programming language expressions.

Since traditional query optimizers do not have access to an abstract representation of these program fragments, they have to work under worst-case assumptions (dependencies between subexpressions, side-effects) or they have to rely on programmer-supplied information (commutativity, idempotence, side-effects) which is difficult to keep consistent in large, long-lived systems. In particular, current query representations do not cover any form of control flow (conditionals, case analysis, loops, exceptions) which is "inherited" through embedded programming language expressions.

Given an integrated database language where user-defined code and query expressions are fully integrated [Matthes and Schmidt 1991], query and program optimization have to interact closely (see Fig. 4): Whenever the program optimizer encounters an embedded query construct like a set-at-a-time (bulk) query or update, an element-at-a-time iterator, or a view definition, it invokes the query optimizer on the respective TML subtree with a TML environment which describes the global bindings (free variables) for that expression. Similarly, the query optimizer invokes the program optimizer to analyze and optimize nested programming language expressions which appear in query constructs (target list, selection predicate, iterator body). Again, binding information for free variables (e.g., range variables in queries or loop control variables in **for each** iterators) is passed along with the respective TML subtree. Recursive declarations of functions, values, or queries are represented uniformly through applications of the fixpoint combinator Y and do *not* lead to repeated traversals of TML terms.

In general, since the optimization of query expressions depends on runtime bindings (for example, knowledge about index structures), we have to delay query optimizations until runtime as described in the previous section. The translation of a declarative query construct embedded in the source language into a TML term is rather straightforward and resembles the usual approach of mapping a relational query 1:1 into a tree of algebraic operators [Ullman 1989].

For example, the SQL statement

select Target(x) **from** Rel x **where** Pred(x)

can be represented by the following TML term which uses the primitive procedures *project* and *select* as defined by the relational algebra:

```
(select λ(x ce cc) (Pred x ce cc)
  Rel
  ce
  cont(tempRel)
    (project λ(x ce cc) (Target x ce cc)
      tempRel
      ce
      cc))
```

The scope of the SQL correlation variable x is captured in TML by having two
λ-abstractions with the bound variable x in addition to the two continuation
variables ce and cc. The data dependency between the selection and projection
is made explicit by introducing a named variable *tempRel* in the continuation for
the selection which is then used as an argument to the projection. Since the variable ce which describes the current exception handler is simply passed through,
exceptions which are raised during selection or projection are propagated to the
enclosing block.

As can be seen in the simple example above, CPS focuses on data and control
dependencies, but leaves much freedom in the choice of the particular primitive
procedures to be used for the representation of declarative queries. Instead of
relational algebra operators, more general operators can be utilized, for example
the higher-order-functions proposed for the optimization of generalized queries
over multiple bulk types in [Trinder 1991; Breazu-Tannen *et al.* 1991; Fegaras
1994].

For a given set of primitive procedures, algebraic and implementation-oriented
query optimization rules can be expressed quite naturally in CPS, for example,
the simple equivalence $\sigma_p(\sigma_q(R)) \equiv \sigma_{p \wedge q}(R)$ can be written as:

$$
\begin{array}{ll}
(select & \xrightarrow{\ merge\text{-}select\ } \quad (select \\
\quad \lambda(r_1\ ce_1\ cc_1) & \qquad \lambda(r_1\ ce_1\ cc_1) \\
\quad\quad (q\ r_1\ ce_1\ cc_1) & \qquad\quad (p\ r_1\ ce_1 \\
\quad R & \qquad\quad\quad cont(t_1) \\
\quad ce & \qquad\quad\quad (q\ r_1\ ce_1 \\
\quad cont(tempRel) & \qquad\quad\quad\quad cont(t_2) \\
\quad\quad (select & \qquad\quad\quad\quad (and\ t_1\ t_2\ ce_1\ cc_1))) \\
\quad\quad\quad \lambda(r_2\ ce_2\ cc_2) & \qquad R \\
\quad\quad\quad\quad (p\ r_2\ ce_2\ cc_2) & \qquad ce \\
\quad\quad\quad tempRel & \qquad cc) \\
\quad\quad\quad ce & \\
\quad\quad\quad cc)) &
\end{array}
$$

In particular, scoping restrictions which limit the applicability of certain
rewrite rules are also directly expressible using the notation introduced in section

3. For example, if the variable x does not appear in the predicate p of the quantified expression $\exists x \in R : p$, this predicate is equivalent to $p \wedge (R \neq \oslash)$. This rule is written as follows, using CPS notation and the predefined procedures *and*, *exists* and *empty*:

$$(|p|_x = 0) :$$
$$(exists \qquad \xrightarrow{\text{trivial-exists}} (empty\ R$$
$$\qquad \lambda(x\ ce'\ cc')p \qquad\qquad ce$$
$$\qquad R \qquad\qquad\qquad \text{cont}(t_1)$$
$$\qquad ce \qquad\qquad\qquad (\lambda(ce'\ cc')p$$
$$\qquad cc) \qquad\qquad\qquad ce$$
$$\qquad\qquad\qquad\qquad \text{cont}(t_2)$$
$$\qquad\qquad\qquad\qquad (and\ t_1\ t_2\ ce\ cc)))$$

Note that the resulting TML tree will be further reduced and optimized using any other applicable rewrite rule.

5   Related Work

The issue of uniform intermediate code representations in database environments arose in the integration of program and query optimization.

Freytag [Freytag and Goodman 1989] investigated the problem of translating relational queries into iterative programs which are quite effectively simplified using a set of transformation rules. Queries are rewritten into nested applications of stream operators which are similar to our polymorphic higher-order iterator functions. The transformation process is based on purely algebra-based relational query specifications which may neither contain embedded (user-defined) function calls nor side effects.

Lieuwen and DeWitt [Lieuwen and DeWitt 1991] have applied loop trans-formations on queries written in the database programming language O++ [Agrawal and Gehani 1989] which provides constructs to iterate through a set in an unspecified order. Similar constructs can be found, for example, in Pascal/R [Schmidt 1977] and DBPL [Schmidt and Matthes 1994]. Lieuwen and DeWitt focus on the reordering of joins which are expressed via nested set iterations. Iterations may contain embedded function calls and output statements which constrain reorderings. However, they do not interact with the program opti-mizer. They have developed their own query tree representation which is quite different from the AST used by the compiler.

Breazu-Tannen et al. [Breazu-Tannen *et al.* 1991] propose a programming paradigm based on structural recursion on sets which comes close to both the semantic simplicity of the relational algebra and the expressive power of al-gorithmically complete programming languages. The authors suggest that this conceptual unification of queries and functional programs will contribute to the optimization problem.

The work which is most closely related to ours is described in [Poulovassilis and Small 1994]. This work investigates algebraic query optimization techniques for database programming languages in the context of a purely declarative functional language which supports sets as first-class objects. Within the language, it is possible to use user-defined functions as query predicates and as target expressions. Since the language is computationally complete, the possibility of non-termination and the construction of infinite data structures must be taken into account, while problems concerning side-effects are avoided. As in our framework, all optimizations can be fully exploited for all subexpressions of a query since no distinct languages are used to represent query trees and programming language expressions. In contrast to our work, the query language is not integrated into a general-purpose persistent programming environment.

6 Concluding Remarks

We have presented the syntax and generic rewrite rules for TML, a persistent intermediate code representation. We also reported on our experience building reusable TML analysis and rewrite tools to carry out the core tasks in symbolic code manipulation like binding analysis, identifier substitution, and free variable analysis. Due to its parameterization by user-defined primitive procedures, TML is virtually independent of the Tycoon language TL and Tycoon's bulk data library and can be tailored with little effort to other program or query languages. By utilizing TML, innovative optimizers like reflective code optimizers and integrated query and program optimizers can be constructed systematically.

The current version of the Tycoon system fully implements dynamic reflective optimization across abstraction barriers based on CPS representations as described in this paper. In particular the static and dynamic optimizers share the same code for TML analysis and rewriting. As described in more detail in [Kiradjiev 1994], performing local program optimizations on standard benchmarks for imperative programs (the Stanford Suite) do not yield a significant speedup in the Tycoon database programming language. The reason for this is the fact that even operations on integers and arrays are factored out into dynamically bound libraries and therefore not amenable to local optimization. However, a move to dynamic (link-time or runtime) optimization more than doubles the execution speed of the standard benchmarks as well as of most larger Tycoon programs we have experimented with (including the compiler itself, consisting of 98 modules containing more than 29,000 lines of high-level Tycoon code). On the down side, due to the space requirements for the additional persistent encoding of the TML tree for each function, the code size doubles at the same time (1.2MB vs. 600kB for the complete Tycoon system). We are currently investigating techniques to reconstruct a TML representation by examining the persistent executable code representation of a procedure, effectively inverting the target machine code generation process. In general, the TML tree reconstructed this way will not be isomorphic to the original TML tree which we currently encode in PTML. The interesting question is whether this has an impact on the possible optimizations, in particular in the presence of nested recursive function bindings.

More work is required to evaluate the effectiveness of query optimization exploiting the availability of a uniform program and query representation at runtime. We are also very interested in exploiting TML for other tasks in data-intensive applications, like code shipping in distributed systems [Mathiske et al. 1995], synchronization of persistent threads [Matthes and Schmidt 1994], access control and security issues [Rudloff et al. 1995].

References

Agrawal and Gehani 1989: Agrawal, R. and Gehani, N.H. Rationale for the design of persistence and query processing facilities in the database programming language O++. In *Proceedings of the Second International Workshop on Database Programming Languages, Salishan, Oregon,* June 1989.

Appel 1992: Appel, A. W. *Compiling with Continuations.* Cambridge University Press, 1992.

Böttcher et al. *1986:* Böttcher, S., Jarke, M., and Schmidt, J.W. Adaptive predicate managers in database systems. In *Proceedings of the Twelfth International Conference on Very Large Databases, Kyoto, Japan,* 1986.

Breazu-Tannen et al. *1991:* Breazu-Tannen, V., Buneman, P., and Naqvi, S. Structural recursion as a query language. In *Proceedings of the Third International Workshop on Database Programming Languages, Nafplion, Greece.* Morgan Kaufmann Publishers, September 1991.

Catell 1994: Catell, R.G.G., editor. *The Object Database Standard: ODMG-93.* Morgan Kaufmann Publishers, 1994.

Eder et al. *1991:* Eder, J., Rudloff, A., Matthes, F., and Schmidt, J.W. Data construction with recursive set expressions in DBPL. In *Proceedings of the Kiev East/West Workshop on Next Generation Database Technology,* volume 504 of *Lecture Notes in Computer Science,* April 1991.

Fegaras 1994: Fegaras, L. Efficient optimization of iterative queries. In Beeri, C., Ohori, A., and Shasha, D.E., editors, *Database Programming Languages, New York City, 1993,* Workshops in Computing, pages 200–225, 1994.

Freytag and Goodman 1989: Freytag, J.C. and Goodman, N. On the translation of relational queries into iterative programs. *ACM Transactions on Database Systems,* 14(1), March 1989.

Gawecki and Matthes 1994: Gawecki, A. and Matthes, F. The Tycoon Machine Language TML - an optimizable persistent program representation. FIDE Technical Report FIDE/94/100, Fachbereich Informatik, Universität Hamburg, Germany, July 1994.

Gawecki 1992: Gawecki, A. An optimizing compiler for Smalltalk. Bericht FBI-HH-B-152/92, Fachbereich Informatik, Universität Hamburg, Germany, September 1992. In German.

Gifford and Lucassen 1986: Gifford, David K. and Lucassen, John M. Integrating functional and imperative programming. In *Proceedings of the ACM Conference on Lisp and Functional Programming, Cambridge, Massachusetts, August 4-6, 1986,* pages 28–38, 1986.

Jarke and Koch 1984: Jarke, M. and Koch, J. Query optimization in database systems. *ACM Computing Surveys,* 16(2):111–152, 1984.

Jarke and Schmidt 1982: Jarke, M. and Schmidt, J.W. Query processing strategies in the Pascal/R relational database management system. In *Proceedings of the ACM-SIGMOD International Conference on Management of Data,* 1982.

Jarke et al. 1982: Jarke, M., Koch, J., Mall, M., and Schmidt, J.W. Query optimization research in the database programming languages (DBPL) project. *IEEE – Data Engineering,* pages 11–14, September 1982.

Kelsey 1989: Kelsey, R.A. Compilation by program transformation. Technical report, Yale University, Department of Computer Science, May 1989.

Kiradjiev 1994: Kiradjiev, P. Dynamische Optimierung in CPS-orientierten Zwischensprachen. Diplomarbeit, Fachbereich Informatik, Universität Hamburg, Germany, December 1994.

Kranz et al. 1986: Kranz, D., Kelsey, R., Rees, J., Hudak, P., Philbin, J., and Adams, N. ORBIT: an optimizing compiler for Scheme. *ACM SIGPLAN Notices,* 21(7):219–233, July 1986.

Lieuwen and DeWitt 1991: Lieuwen, Daniel F. and DeWitt, David J. Optimizing loops in database programming languages. In *Proceedings of the Third International Workshop on Database Programming Languages, Nafplion, Greece,* Nafplion, Greece, September 1991. Morgan Kaufmann Publishers.

Mall et al. 1984: Mall, M., Reimer, M., and Schmidt, J.W. Data selection, sharing and access control in a relational scenario. In Brodie, M.L., Myopoulos, J.L., and Schmidt, J.W., editors, *On Conceptual Modelling.* Springer-Verlag, 1984.

Mathiske et al. 1995: Mathiske, B., Matthes, F., and Schmidt, J.W. Scaling database languages to higher-order distributed programming. In *Proceedings of the Fifth International Workshop on Database Programming Languages, Gubbio, Italy.* Springer-Verlag, September 1995. (Also appeared as TR FIDE/95/137).

Matthes and Schmidt 1991: Matthes, F. and Schmidt, J.W. Bulk types: Built-in or add-on? In *Proceedings of the Third International Workshop on Database Programming Languages, Nafplion, Greece.* Morgan Kaufmann Publishers, September 1991.

Matthes and Schmidt 1992: Matthes, F. and Schmidt, J.W. Definition of the Tycoon Language TL – a preliminary report. Informatik Fachbericht FBI-HH-B-160/92, Fachbereich Informatik, Universität Hamburg, Germany, November 1992.

Matthes and Schmidt 1994: Matthes, F. and Schmidt, J.W. Persistent threads. In *Proceedings of the Twentieth International Conference on Very Large Data Bases, VLDB,* pages 403–414, Santiago, Chile, September 1994.

Poulovassilis and Small 1994: Poulovassilis, A. and Small, C. Investigation of algebraic query optimisation for database programming languages. In *Proceedings of the 20th International Conference on Very Large Databases, Santiago, Chile,* September 1994.

Rudloff et al. 1995: Rudloff, A., Matthes, F., and Schmidt, J.W. Security as an add-on quality in persistent object systems. In *Second International East/West Database Workshop,* Workshops in Computing. Springer-Verlag, 1995. (to appear).

Schmidt and Matthes 1994: Schmidt, J.W. and Matthes, F. The DBPL project: Advances in modular database programming. *Information Systems,* 19(2):121–140, 1994.

Schmidt 1977: Schmidt, J.W. Some high level language constructs for data of type relation. In *Proceedings of the ACM-SIGMOD International Conference on Management of Data, Toronto, Canada,* August 1977.

Steele 1978: Steele, Guy L. Rabbit: A compiler for SCHEME. Technical report, Massachusetts Institute of Technology, May 1978.

Steele 1986: Steele, Guy L. The revised[3] report on the algorithmic language Scheme. *ACM SIGPLAN Notices,* 21(12):37–79, December 1986.

Teodosiu 1991: Teodosiu, Dan. Hare: An optimizing portable compiler for Scheme. *ACM SIGPLAN Notices,* 26(1):109–120, January 1991.

423

Trinder 1991: Trinder, P. Comprehensions, a query notation for DBPLs. In *Proceedings of the Third International Workshop on Database Programming Languages, Nafplion, Greece.* Morgan Kaufmann Publishers, September 1991.

Ullman 1989: Ullman, J.D. *Database and Knowledge-Base Systems, vol. 2.* Computer Science Press, 1989.

Workflow Management

Providing High Availability in Very Large Workflow Management Systems[1]

M. Kamath
Dept. of Computer Science
University of Massachusetts
Amherst, MA 01003, USA
kamath@cs.umass.edu

G. Alonso
Institute for Information Systems
Database Group, ETH Zentrum
CH-8092 Zürich, Switzerland
alonso@inf.ethz.ch

R. Günthör
IBM European Networking Center
Vangerowstr. 18, 69115 Heidelberg
Germany
rgunthor@heidelbg.ibm.com

C. Mohan
IBM Almaden Research Center
650 Harry Road, San Jose, CA 95120
USA
mohan@almaden.ibm.com

Abstract

Workflow management systems (WFMS) support the modeling, coordinated execution and monitoring of business processes within an organization. In particular, very large workflow management systems are used in organizations with several thousand users, hundreds of thousands of process instances, and several thousand sites, all distributed over wide geographic areas. In these environments, failure of the WFMS or the underlying workflow database which stores the meta-information about the processes is not tolerable. This paper addresses the problem of providing high availability in workflow management systems by proposing a backup technique which ensures that execution of a process instance can be resumed at any point in time in the event of a failure. An essential characteristic of our backup scheme is that it allows the user to define different availability levels, reducing the cost of maintaining backups. The backup scheme is implemented using the workflow semantics, which we believe will (i) make it independent of the underlying workflow database, thus permitting the use of heterogeneous databases as primary and backup, (ii) reduce overheads, especially when compared to backup schemes provided by database systems.

1 Introduction

Workflow management systems (WFMS) enjoy an increasing popularity due to their ability to coordinate and streamline complex *business processes* within large organizations. The goal of WFMSs is to orchestrate the execution of business processes, ultimately being responsible for the control of the organization's activities. Thus, a WFMS becomes not just a support tool but an integral part of the organization. This is substantiated by the fact that the most likely candidates to use a WFMS are large corporations such as banks, insurance companies and telecommunication companies which need to coordinate several instances of a variety of business processes. Current customer requirements indicate that the number of potential users can be in the tens of thousands, the number of process instances in the hundreds of thousands and the number of sites in the thousands all distributed over a wide geographic area and based on heterogeneous systems. With these figures, continuous availability becomes a crucial aspect of any successful commercial WFMS. Though more than 70 workflow products exist in the market [Fry94], this is an issue that has been ignored by workflow developers, and to our knowledge, has not yet been addressed by research in the area of workflow management.

---

[1] This work was performed while M. Kamath, G. Alonso and R. Günthör were visiting scientists at the IBM Almaden Research Center

428

This paper reports ongoing research in the availability of WFMSs, as part of the research efforts of the *Exotica* project [MAGK95]. The research has been centered around *FlowMark* [IBMa, LR94], a WFMS from IBM. However our results can be easily generalized to any WFMS.

In this paper our focus will be on WFMSs that use a centralized database (work-flow database) to store meta-information about the business processes. They conform to the reference model developed by the Workflow Management Coalition [WfMC94] and typically handle *production* workflows [GHS95]. In environments where several workflow databases coexist, each of them typically stores a different subset of processes instances. If one database fails, all process instances running off that database will stop their execution. This behavior is unacceptable for several critical business processes which cannot be delayed. Hence the workflows database remains a single point of failure that may have grave consequences. To address this problem, our approach is to use process instance replication to guarantee that if the database where the particular instance resides fails, execution can be resumed elsewhere based on the replicated information.

The novelty of our approach is to use workflow semantics[2] as the basis for replication and backup, as opposed to low level constructs such as pages or log records used in traditional database backup techniques. The reasons are as follows:

- *Necessity for WFMSs that are database independent:* Relying on the backup facilities supplied by the underlying database ties the system to the platforms where such a database runs. Since we envision a system in which heterogeneous databases, even as different as relational and object-oriented to be used as backup for each other, low level techniques as those provided by database management systems cannot be used. By using application (workflow) level backup, the replication scheme becomes independent of the underlying platform, thus allowing the use of heterogeneous databases.

- *Need for flexibility in replicating process instance data:* In traditional database backup techniques, the units of exchange tend to be pages or log records [GMP90, BGHJ92, MTO93] which makes it difficult to control which data is actually being replicated. If such techniques are used to replicate data between two workflow databases, log records of changes to all objects, including those that correspond to static information about processes will be replicated. This is not really required and there can be excessive overheads when several hundred thousand processes run concurrently. Instead the overheads can be minimized by providing different availability levels (each having different overheads and degree of reliability) and exploiting workflow semantics to minimize the amount of information that is replicated.

The specific contributions of this paper are:

1. Provision for different availability levels by categorizing process instances as *normal*, *important*, and *critical*, each with its own backup approach.
2. A backup architecture and mechanism to efficiently use the resources available in a distributed workflow system to perform backup, *i.e.*, use the workflow servers and workflow databases to function both as a primary (for some process instances) and as a secondary (for some other process instances).

---

[2]From the perspective of the database that stores the meta-information, the WFMS is an application and hence workflow semantics can also be referred to as *application* semantics.

3. Backup algorithms to replicate process instance data for each of the above process instance categories during normal processing and when there are failures at the primary or backup site. These algorithms have been analyzed in a simple manner to show that they can scale for very large WFMSs.

The rest of the paper is organized as follows: in the next section we describe the basic ideas behind a WFMS and the backup requirements in WFMSs. A discussion on backup techniques and how they can be adapted to WFMS is presented in section 3. Section 4 discusses availability levels, the backup architecture and issues related to object state replication. In section 5 we introduce the necessary data structures, describe our backup algorithms. Section 6 concludes the paper.

2 Workflow Management

In this section we present some basic concepts of workflow management that are necessary for discussing particular aspects of the implementation of our replication and backup technique. Specific details of workflow management systems are described based on FlowMark. We then briefly discuss the requirements of high availability in WFMSs.

2.1 Workflow Model and Architecture

A common term used to refer to the work performed in large organizations is a *business process*, defined by the Workflow Management Coalition as "a procedure where documents, information or tasks are passed between participants according to defined sets of rules to achieve, or contribute to, an overall business goal" [WfMC94]. A *workflow* is a particular representation of a business process. The role of a *workflow management system*, WFMS, is the scheduling and coordination of all the activities encompassing a business process. This involves determining the order of execution, interacting with each activity's tools, establishing the data flow between activities, mapping activities to users, checking the timeliness of the execution, monitoring the progress and determining when a process has terminated. Though these concepts have been around for a number of years, the technology required to implement suitable systems has however been available only recently. Currently, there is a considerable amount of attention devoted to this area [GHS95, Hsu95, She94].

A workflow model is a description of a business process. For this purpose, the Workflow Management Coalition has proposed the following reference model [WfMC94]: A business process is represented by a schema that includes the *process* name, version number, start and termination conditions and additional data for security, audit and control. A process consists of several steps. Each step within a process is an *activity*, which has a name, a type, pre- and post-conditions and scheduling constraints. It also has a *role* and may have an *invoked application* associated with it. The *role* determines who will execute the activity. The *invoked application* is the tool to be used in the execution, which may range from computer programs to human actions with no specific tool, e.g., a meeting. Furthermore, activities use *relevant data* defined as the data passed to and produced by the activities. Relevant data have a name and type associated with them. The users of the system are represented in terms of *roles*. Finally, and for notational purposes, a specific invocation of a process is referred to as a *process instance*. For a given process, there can be many instances of it running concurrently. The instances have the same components and structure as the process.

The architectural components of the reference model are as follows. A *process-definition tool* is used to define the schema of each business process. A *workflow engine* creates a process instance, interprets the process schema and determines which activities are ready for execution. If an activity is to be performed by a role, then the

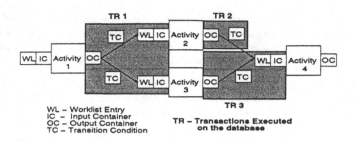

Figure 1: *Transactions Executed during Process Navigation*

eligible role is notified by placing the activity on the role's *worklist*. The role has to then select the activity for execution from the worklist using a *worklist-handler*. On the other hand, if the activity is to be performed automatically, then the workflow engine selects it for execution. If an application program is to be invoked to execute the selected activity, the workflow engine notifies an *application-agent* that exists at the location (node) where the program is to be invoked. The application agent then executes the program and returns the results of the program to the workflow engine.

For our study, we have selected FlowMark as the specific WFMS since its architecture closely resembles the architecture described by the reference model. FlowMark is based on a client-server architecture and uses an object-oriented DBMS as a central database to store meta-information about workflows. The meta-information consists of process scheme definitions and all runtime information related to active process instances. Besides the database, FlowMark is organized into four other components. The *FlowMark Server* acts as the workflow engine, the *Runtime Client* acts as the worklist-handler, the *Program Execution Client* acts as the application-agent, and the *Buildtime Client* acts as the process-definition tool. A single database usually acts as a repository to several workflow (FlowMark) servers.

Navigation is the procedure by which the server determines the next activities to execute. It takes place through transactional updates to the centralized database. Since the reference model does not provide implementation details, we describe navigation in the context of FlowMark since its model closely resembles the reference model. In FlowMark, the *flow of control*, which is specified by *control connectors* between activities, is the order in which these activities have to be executed. Each control connector has a state. Before the activity from where it originates finishes, the control connector is *unevaluated*. Once the activity terminates, the *transition condition* associated with the outgoing control connectors are evaluated and their state is set to TRUE or FALSE. Such transition conditions are boolean expressions involving data returned by activities in the output containers. For each activity there is an *input data container* and an *output data container* where the invoked application takes its input and places its output. The *flow of data*, specified through *data connectors*, corresponds to mappings between output data containers and input data containers and allows passing data from activity to activity.

The object representation of the modeling concepts discussed above is shown in Figure 1. The shaded areas represent sets of objects in the centralized database updated by different transactions. The interactions with the database in terms of transactions are as follows. Transaction TR_1 changes the state of activity 1, updates its output container, evaluates the control connectors leading to activities 2 and 3. If the start condition of the succeeding activities evaluates to true, then the input containers are populated and the activities are added to the appropriate worklists.

Transaction TR_2 is executed upon completion of activity 2 and performs much the same tasks as TR_1, except that activity 4 is not yet scheduled for execution. When activity 3 completes, it is transaction TR_3 that will schedule activity 4 if its starting condition evaluates to true.

2.2 Requirements of High Availability

In large enterprises, different departments or divisions should be able to use existing database platforms as repositories (workflow database) for their WFMS. As a result, an important requirement is that the WFMS and the backup mechanism should be database independent. Also from the perspective of the enterprise, certain processes are mission critical and more important than others. Replicating all data immediately for providing high availability can result in huge overheads especially when several thousand process instances are running concurrently. On the other hand, without replication the system becomes very vulnerable to database failures. Both of these solutions are unacceptable and hence another important requirement is flexibility in defining the availability requirements of different processes.

3 Adapting Database Backup Techniques to Workflows

In this section we present salient aspects of backup techniques developed for databases and discuss how some of the basic concepts can be adapted to workflow environments. This will help us focus on the specifics of our workflow semantics-based backup technique in the rest of the sections.

The basic ideas behind backup mechanisms are well known. Consider, for instance, Tandem's Remote Data Facility [Lyo90]. In this environment a server or group of servers, known as *primary*, use a single backup computer, known as *secondary*. Under normal operation, a client sends requests to the primary, and the log records generated at the primary are sent to the backup and applied to its state. Therefore, the backup is an exact replica of the primary and it is kept up to date, which allows the backup to take over almost immediately upon failure of the primary. This mode of operation in which the backup can take over immediately is known as *hot standby*. Note that the overhead incurred is high: a transaction takes place in the primary, log records are sent to the secondary, a transaction applies those log records in the secondary, and a 2 Phase Commit protocol (2PC) is used to guarantee the combined atomicity of both transactions. Note that since there are only two participants involved, the primary and the backup, some optimizations of 2PC can be implemented [SBCM95, GR93]. When using 2PC, this approach is known as *2-safe* and it is similar in some aspects to the very-safe case of [GR93]. Contrary to the 2-safe policy, the *1-safe* policy does not require the primary to wait for the secondary. It commits its transaction first and then propagates the log records to the secondary. There is, of course, the risk of data loss when the backup takes over but in practice the 1-safe policy is preferred over the 2-safe due to its lower overhead. Algorithms for the maintenance of remote copies under the 1-safe and 2-safe policies are discussed in [GMP90] and [BGHJ92] respectively.

In the case of workflow systems, we do not believe that the 1-safe option is viable always. In the case of traditional databases, since transactions are short and perform few changes, losing these changes may not be critical. In a WFMS, an update may correspond to the execution of very complex activities, making the loss of data unacceptable in many cases. Hence in this paper we will discuss only *variations of the 2-safe policy* to ensure that the take over by the backup does not require redo of work already completed.

A hot standby policy places a heavy burden on both the primary and the backup. When a dedicated machine is used as a backup, the load in the backup is not a major concern. However in our case, it is a concern since the backup is not a dedicated machine but a workflow server that is used both as a primary for some process instances and as a backup for some other process instances. This is done to effectively use the available resources. In some cases, quick take over by the backup may not be a key issue, allowing the backup to perform the updates asynchronously and therefore reducing the overhead due to replication. In the extreme case, the backup does not perform any updates unless it has to take over the operation of the primary. This is known as a *cold standby* policy. In this policy, the information sent from the primary is stored at the backup but not applied immediately. Obviously, the trade off is lower overheads at the primary during normal operation at the cost of a slower recovery at the backup in case of failures. To add flexibility to our design, we provide the user with the possibility of using both approaches: cold standby and hot standby.

Inconsistencies that can arise due to transaction dependencies during crash recovery are discussed in [FCK87, MHL+92]. However they are irrelevant in the workflow context since the execution states of different business processes are independent. Techniques to replicate data at a high level in the context of relational databases are discussed in [Gol94] where SQL calls are trapped at the primary and executed at the backup site. However, this is not a suitable approach since there are enormous overheads due to duplication of processing and different order of executions at the primary and backup can cause inconsistencies within a business process.

Coordinating the nodes of a distributed system that contain replicated data is discussed in [CS92] in the context of the D^3 model. The model provides schemes for choosing a coordinator and a new primary/backup in case of node failures. The model also has provision for load-balancing and for adding/removing nodes from the system without interruption of normal operation. Since these techniques can be directly adapted to WFMS, we do not discuss node coordination issues in the rest of the paper. Techniques that exploit parallelism in processing the log records at the backup, and schemes that allow new transactions to begin in parallel along with the takeover process are discussed in [MTO93]. These can be adapted to WFMS to speed up recovery. A disaster recovery scheme with options to choose the desired degree of data durability and service durability through different *insurance levels* and *readiness levels* on a per-transaction basis is discussed in [BT90]. However, the scheme is based on remote logging of data pages and cannot be used for process-instance replication since this can lead to higher overheads.

Apart from less overheads, another important requirement for our backup technique is the fact that it should be database independent. A workflow system is designed to run over multiple platforms and each server may be connected to an entirely different database, not only in terms of schema but also in terms of conceptual approach. Hence the assumption used in traditional backup techniques that the backup system is identical to the primary is no longer true in a WFMS. Therefore, we cannot rely on physical descriptions such as pages, segments or log records because they do not have any meaning across heterogeneous systems. The only entities that maintain their meaning from server to server are workflow objects, which are actually databases independent. Hence, to design a backup mechanism that can be implemented across heterogeneous systems and that minimizes the replication overheads, data replication must be performed at the application (workflow) level.

4 The Exotica Approach to High Availability in WFMSs

In this section we describe the details of our backup approach. Specifically we focus on availability levels, the backup architecture and issues related to object-state replication. Through the rest of the paper we use the following notation for the primary

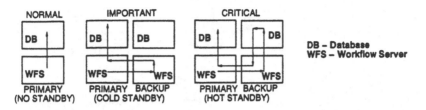

Figure 2: *Process Categories and Replication Policies*

and the backup. The primary and secondary copies of the workflow data are located at the primary and the secondary *databases* respectively. The workflow (FlowMark) servers that are connected to the primary and secondary database are termed as primary and secondary *servers* respectively.

4.1 Availability Levels — Cost-effective Backup of Process Instances

To provide an adequate level of flexibility in the design of workflows and to allow the user to specify when it is cost-effective to provide a backup for a given process, we define three process categories: *normal, important* and *critical*. We associate with each of them a different backup mechanism. From the many variations that are possible, we selected them since they are the most meaningful. These three *backup categories* are described below and the message exchanges they require are shown in Figure 2.

- **Critical**: similar to 2-safe with hot standby. When navigation takes place at the primary and workflow objects change their state, the new state is sent to the backup. The backup will update the corresponding local objects immediately.

- **Important**: similar to 2-safe with cold standby. For this type of processes, the procedure is identical to that followed for critical processes, except that the backup does not apply the new state immediately: the coordination is between the primary committing the navigation transaction and the backup committing the new state to stable storage. These changes can be applied to the database in an asynchronous and lazy fashion, thereby reducing the overheads both at the primary and the backup.

- **Normal**: processes of this type are not replicated at all. If forward recovery is provided, there is no data loss when there are server failures. However, execution cannot be resumed until the same server is back on line.

The particular category to which a process belongs is specified by the workflow designer. There are two possibilities. One is to associate a backup category with a process class. The other is to associate the backup category with the process instance. They are not mutually exclusive options, and they are orthogonal to the discussion here so we will not analyze them further. Finally, and since most workflow systems allow the nesting of processes, it is necessary to specify the semantics of the backup category for nested processes. For simplicity, we will assume that the subprocesses will *inherit* the category of the parent process, even if it has a different category on its own. In the rest of the paper we focus only on the critical and important process categories.

An alternative to availability levels is to have different WFMSs whose underlying workflow databases have different degrees of reliability and assign process instances dynamically to the WFMSs. We believe such alternatives do not provide the required flexibility and also increase resource requirements and system complexity.

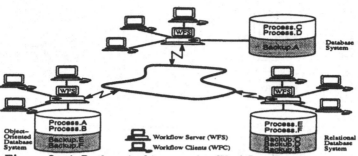

Figure 3: *A Backup Architecture for Workflow Environments*

4.2 Backup Architecture

Most WFMSs are based on a client/server architecture with the workflow server connected to a single workflow database. In a large enterprise, there are typically several servers and several databases, many of which could be heterogeneous in nature. A dedicated backup approach in such a highly distributed and heterogeneous environment would require a backup for every individual system. Hence it is not feasible to use a dedicated backup since the cost is too high. Therefore, in our implementation we do not architecturally distinguish a primary server from a backup. All workflow servers are used both as primary for some processes and as backup for others. This being the case, there is no guarantee that the backup server selected by the user will use the same type of database system as the primary. In fact, it is possible for the primary to be a relational database while the backup is an object-oriented database. Moreover, in our scheme, replication will take place on a per process instance basis, i.e., each active process instance has its own primary and backup, and thus, the notion of backup is not tied to the primary site but to each process instance. The actual decision of choosing which server will be the primary and which will be the backup is left to the user. This can also be done automatically using the techniques described in [CS92]. Another alternative to achieve this is to use load balancing algorithms, but this issue is beyond the scope of the paper. The architecture is summarized in Figure 3.

We will assume there is an underlying communication layer that provides the appropriate interface and mechanisms for the clients and servers to communicate. We will further assume that messages do not get lost and arrive uncorrupted. This same communication layer will perform failure detection.

4.3 Object State Replication

As discussed earlier, variations of 2-safe policies are to be used to avoid data loss. To reduce the overheads for processes run under this policy, we need to minimize the information exchanged between primary and backup servers. We also need to cope with the fact that the databases may be heterogeneous. Hence we need to replicate information that is significant to any database, regardless of the schema it implements. To accomplish all this, our approach is to send information only about state changes of workflow objects such as activities or connectors, instead of about the data structures over which they are implemented, i.e, we will only replicate the state of workflow entities. Another scheme to avoid data loss is to use the messages exchanged between the primary server and the clients. By replaying (not executing) the messages in the same temporal order at the backup server, the progress of a process can be easily recreated at the backup. However, this would require that the backup perform the navigation itself which may result in greater delays. Also, if the WFMS allows the modelling of time events to trigger activities, then it is not guaranteed that

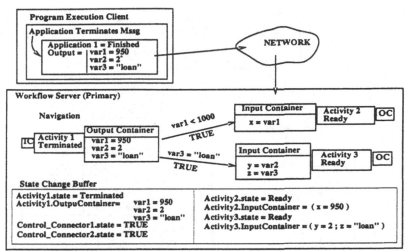

Figure 4: *Navigation at the Primary and State Changes*

replaying the messages on the backup results in the same workflow execution. Instead of using this, our approach takes advantage of the very clear set of components of a workflow specification and records the state changes in these components. There are only a few of these components that are relevant during the navigation procedures (see Figure 1), and they usually correspond to tangible database entities such as objects or records in a table. Therefore, it is possible to replicate the state of a process by recording the state changes of these entities at the primary database, sending those changes to the backup server and directly updating the state of the entities at the backup database. At the backup server, the state of an activity can be modified directly either through an SQL statement if it is a relational database, or through the corresponding method if it is an object-oriented database. This approach has the advantage of being faster (having reduced overheads) both at the primary and the secondary servers, especially when the number of entities involved is large. It has the disadvantage that a mapping is needed between the database schemas to guarantee that both sides refer to the same activity. These ideas are summarized in Figure 4.

When a client reports that a program has terminated, the server performs navigation as explained in Section 2. For each item - activities, containers, connectors - that changes its state, the new state is recorded in a buffer. When navigation is completed, this buffer contains all the changes that have occurred. This buffer is then sent to the backup. The information in this buffer is stored using the canonical representation explained in the next section. This representation is understood by all servers and can be mapped to the particular database in use.

5 Backup Algorithms for Providing High Availability

This section first introduces the data mappings/structures and then describes the backup algorithms.

5.1 Data Mappings between Primary and Backup — Canonical Representation

In many cases, the primary and the backup databases will have different schemas. Thus, a mechanism is needed to map entities between both databases. For instance, in object-oriented databases, objects reference each other by their OIDs. However, these OIDs are usually not visible to the user, hence a surrogate identifier must be used to refer to the object [WN94]. Moreover, even if the OIDs of objects were to be available, two databases will assign different OIDs to what is essentially the same

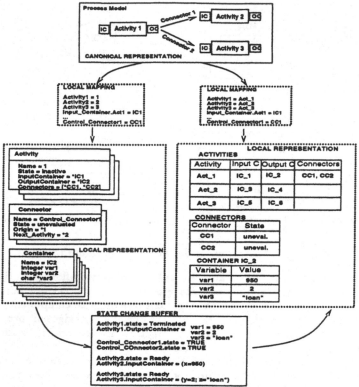

Figure 5: *Mappings between the different representations of a process*

object, one at the primary and one at the backup database. To solve this problem we rely, once more, on semantic information about the particular process instance.

Usually, in a workflow model only the process schemas/instances and activities have user assigned names. Connectors and data containers exist in relation to a particular activity or process instance, but usually have no names on their own. To be able to uniquely identify each component of the workflow, the system must supply a unique name such as "control connector j". This information is extracted from the definition of the workflow when it is compiled into a database schema. With this information, primary and backup databases can ensure consistency. Such a representation of a process is called a *canonical representation*. Note that it is different from the process model since it contains much less information, it is only a list of agreed upon names for the workflow entities. This canonical representation is chosen to optimize storage and communication overhead. Hence at both the primary and the backup servers a *local mapping* must exist between the canonical representation and the particular format of the database or *local representation*. These ideas are shown in Figure 5, where the *canonical representation* is mapped to hypothetical object-oriented and relational databases by supplying a correspondence to object identifiers or primary keys. Note that the state changes are transmitted using the canonical representation, and therefore will also have to be mapped to the local representation.

5.2 Hash Table

To organize the data about messages sent between the primary and secondary, so that it can be easily accessed whenever needed, we use a persistent open hash table

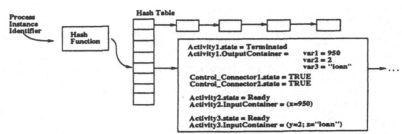

Figure 6: *Storage of State Changes in a Hash Table*

like the one shown in Figure 6. Each entry in the table corresponds to an executing process instance, and the messages are stored as a linked list. Using a hash table also obviates the need for reorganization as in the case of sequential logs. Such a hash table is maintained both at the primary and the backup workflow servers. When activities complete, these hash tables are updated and when a process completes, the corresponding entries are deleted.

When a failure occurs at the primary database, the backup database becomes the primary database and hence a new backup database must be selected. For important processes (instances), the information to restore processes to the same state they had at the primary server is found in the hash table. For critical processes we also keep the messages received with the state changes in the hash table. Therefore, for both critical and important processes the new backup can be established by sending the information stored in the hash table. Creating a new backup database, on the failure of the existing backup database is handled similarly. To further speed up the setting of a new primary/backup database, it may be possible to use database *loaders* [WN94]. However, their efficient use requires, for instance, to turn logging off, which would conflict with normal operations and many object-oriented databases do not provide such a feature. Hence, it is not yet clear if this is a feasible option. Exact details about how the hash table is maintained and used are provided in the next section while discussing the backup algorithm.

5.3 Backup Algorithm

Since we exploit workflow semantics to reduce replication overheads, instead of replicating all information, only the *canonical representation* of a process is replicated. Changes are packed into a buffer which is then sent to the backup server. The algorithms are associated with the following *system events: process initialization, normal execution, failure of the primary database, failure of the backup database, backup database creation*, and *site initialization*.

Process initialization is necessary to ensure that both the primary and the backup servers have the information they need about a process schema before starting to execute it. In existing WFMSs like FlowMark, which have no backup, the definition of a process model is compiled into a database schema. However, if a backup mechanism is in place this compilation cannot take place directly since at the point a process model is defined we don't know what the local representations (schemas) will be for each instance. Hence, when a process model is defined, we can only extract the canonical representation for it. If the number of process schemas and the number of platforms are numerous, then extracting the local mappings at compile time may not be efficient. Hence the actual local mappings and representations will be established when an instance is to be executed. The algorithm for this is shown in Figure 7.

During normal execution of a process instance, the algorithm used to replicate data from the primary to the backup is shown in Figure 8. The buffers are filled and

```
Process is defined; (* using buildtime client *)
Canonical representation is created and stored; (* at some server *)
User selects process for execution; (* from runtime client *)
  begin PROCESS INSTANCE CREATION;
    Canonical representation and process definition sent to primary and backup;
    Both at the primary and the backup servers:
      Canonical representation mapped to local representation;
      Local mapping generated;
      Entry in hash table created;
  end PROCESS INSTANCE CREATION;
Process instance is ready for execution;
```

Figure 7: *Algorithm for Process Initialization*

```
At the PRIMARY SERVER                    At the BACKUP SERVER
  At a client, a program terminates;
  Client sends message to primary server;
  Primary server performs navigation;
  Changes are recorded in a buffer;
  Buffer is stored in hash table;
  Buffer is sent to backup server;
                                        Backup server receives buffer;
                                        Buffer is stored in hash table;
                                        If process is critical then update
                                            backup database;
                                        Ack. sent to primary server
  Primary server concludes execution step;
```

Figure 8: *Algorithm for Replicating Data during Normal Processing*

sent to the backup when the transactions explained in Figure 1 are executed on the completion of activities. At the primary, the buffers are stored in the hash table so that in the event of a failure of the backup, a new backup can be quickly established by just resending the buffers stored in the hash table for this process instance.

Upon failure of the primary database the backup database is to be used. Since a single database acts as a repository to several workflow servers, a failure of this database does not imply that all workflow servers or clients have also failed. Also note that if the failure occurs only at the workflow server, the problem can be easily solved by starting another workflow server somewhere else and connecting it to the original database. Failure of a particular database is notified by the communication layer to all servers in the system. Upon receiving such a message, a workflow server must determine which of the active process instances in its own hash table were running at the failed database. When the database fails, the workflow servers connected to it cannot perform navigation. However, they are used as relay nodes so the backup server can contact the clients who were connected to the primary server. In this way, the failure of the primary database is transparent to the user. All the data is currently available at a different database at the backup, and messages are rerouted to reach the backup server instead of the primary server. Since the primary and the backup servers know about each other, this rerouting is easy to establish. The algorithm to handle the failure of primary database is shown in Figure 9.

If during normal operation a backup database fails, the primary server must halt the execution of all critical and important processes (instances) until a new backup database is established. The notification mechanism is the same as the one described

```
Backup server receives message informing of failure;
Backup server examines hash table to determine processes to take over;
Backup server creates a new backup database;
Original backup server becomes new primary server (so do the databases);
The following happens at the new primary (original backup):
  For critical processes:
      resume execution;
  For important processes:
      Retrieve changes from hash table;
      Apply changes to its own database;
      resume execution;
```

Figure 9: *Algorithm for Handling Failure of Primary Database*

```
Primary server receives message informing of failure;
Primary server examines hash table to determine the processes that need
  a new backup;
Primary server creates a new backup database;
Primary resumes execution;
```

Figure 10: *Algorithm for Handling Failure of Backup Database*

above. A server must identify which of its process instances were using the failed database as a backup. Each server maintains a table specifying which servers are connected to the backup database for the active process instances running at that server. This table is used for routing the state change buffers when navigation takes place. In case of failures of the backup database, the table is used to determine the affected process instances. The algorithm to handle the failure of backup database is shown in Figure 10.

In case of failures, either of the primary or the backup database, it is necessary to *create a new backup database*. The algorithm to locate a new backup database, initialize it and bringing it up to date is shown in Figure 11.

After a failure, the primary or the backup database will later recover. This may happen while a new primary/backup database is being established. It would be an obvious error to let the recovered database to resume execution because its actions will conflict with whoever has taken over. Hence, when a database recovers from a failure, the corresponding workflow server must check, for each process, whether someone has already taken over. The algorithm for site initialization is shown in Figure 12.

5.4 Garbage Collection

Of all the process categories, the one that will probably be used most is *important*. It provides data backup in case of failures without excessive overheads. The only problem with these processes is the space they require. If, to reduce the overhead at the backup server, changes are only applied when the backup server actually takes over the navigation from the primary server, the amount of state changes accumulated can be considerable. Hence, some garbage collection algorithm is necessary to keep the space manageable. All required information is available in the hash table we mentioned earlier. When a process instance terminates, the entry is discarded from the hash table, thus deallocating the space. The termination of a process instance can be easily detected by examining the state changes sent by the primary server or by having the primary server communicating this fact to the backup server. In either

```
+-----------------------------------------------------------------------+
| At the PRIMARY/                          At the new BACKUP SERVER      |
| old BACKUP SERVER                                                     |
|   Locate a new backup database;                                       |
|   Locate a workflow server connected                                  |
|     to that database;                                                 |
|   Send process definition to new                                      |
|     backup server;                                                    |
|                                          Receive process definition;  |
|   Send canonical representation to                                    |
|     new backup server;                                                |
|                                          Receive canonical representation; |
|                                          Canonical representation mapped |
|                                                to Local representation; |
|                                          Local mapping generated;     |
|                                          Entry in hash table created;  |
|                                          Send Acknowledgement;         |
|   Receive Acknowledgement;                                            |
|   Retrieve list of state changes                                      |
|     (database or hash table);                                         |
|   Send state change buffers from list;                                |
|   Change entries in hash table to                                     |
|     reflect new backup server mapping;                                |
|                                          Backup server receives buffers; |
|                                          Buffers are stored in hash table; |
|                                          If process is critical then apply |
|                                                changes to the backup database; |
|                                          Ack. sent to primary server   |
|   Process ready to resume execution;                                  |
+-----------------------------------------------------------------------+
```

Figure 11: *Algorithm for Creating a New Backup Database*

case, when the process instance has completed its execution, its copy at the backup server is no longer needed. Similarly entries that correspond to terminated processes are discarded from the hash table at the primary server as well. Also, as explained earlier in the algorithm, a recovering server has to discard all the processes whose execution has been resumed elsewhere using a similar procedure.

5.5 Analysis and Discussion

While performing data replication, two types of overheads are to be considered — overheads at primary/backup during normal processing and network overheads during normal processing. The most important among these as far as scalability is concerned are network overheads. We have reduced this as follows: By just replicating workflow specific information at the end of each activity instead of replicating log records of changes to each object, we considerably reduce the number of messages transmitted. Since we just ship output results of activities as name-value pairs, the size of the buffer is also reduced and hence the number of messages exchanged per buffer is reduced. We introduced the notion of availability levels and the associated process categories to reduce the overheads during normal processing both at the primary and the backup. Hence we expect workflow administrators/users to take full advantage of this option (especially the "important" category) to get scalability.

We described algorithms for message exchange between the primary and the backup workflow servers to handle failures of the workflow database. Wherever relevant, we addressed the special requirements of the different process categories. The algorithms do not rely on replication features offered by the database and hence allow the use of heterogeneous databases. Since we exploit workflow semantics and just

```
For primary processes active at the moment of failure:
    Locate the backup server of each process instance;
    Query the backup server for status;
    If backup server has taken over
            then Discard the process instance;
    else Notify backup server;
            Resume execution;
For backup processes active at the moment of failure:
Locate the primary server of each process instance;
Query primary server for status;
    If primary server has new backup
            then Discard the process instance;
    else Notify primary server;
            Resume execution;
```

Figure 12: *Algorithm for Site Initialization*

replicate the canonical representation, the replication overheads are minimized. Our backup technique is different from checkpointing schemes of fault-tolerant systems since we also have provision to handle failures at backup (which is usually ignored in fault-tolerant systems). Our algorithms are quite general and do not contain references to FlowMark-specific features and hence can be used to backup process data in any WFMS.

6 Conclusions

In the future, organizations will increasingly rely on WFMSs for their daily business activities. To make workflow technology successful, WFMSs should be able to work with heterogeneous systems and at the same time provide high availability. WFMSs are extreme example of applications where due to the environment in which they are embedded, traditional database approaches are not suitable to provide backup across heterogeneous systems and for replicating data to provide high availability. Hence we have proposed a set of new techniques that exploit workflow semantics to meet these objectives.

In this paper we introduced the notion of availability levels in the context of WFMSs and described a backup architecture and the necessary algorithms for efficiently maintaining backups of process data. The backup mechanism is based on the idea of replicating workflow information as opposed to replicating database structures. This allows us to implement backup over heterogeneous systems, i.e., over databases with different schemas and of different nature. The cost of replicating process instances is minimized by exchanging information only about changes that are relevant. Hence our algorithms can scale to very large WFMSs. By carefully analyzing the workflow semantics/requirements and comparing tradeoffs we have provided a practical solution for providing high availability in WFMSs. Future work includes a complete evaluation of some of the tradeoffs as well as a study of their impact on the overall performance and a prototype based on FlowMark.

Acknowledgements

This work was partially supported by funds from IBM Networking Software Division and IBM Software Solutions Division. We would also like to thank Prof. Divyakant Agrawal and Prof. Amr El Abbadi for their help in formulating some of the ideas described in this paper. Additional information about the Exotica project can be found at the URL http://www.almaden.ibm.com/cs/exotica/

442

References

[BGHJ92] A. Bhide, A. Goyal, H Hsiao, and A. Jhingran. An Efficient Scheme for Providing High Availability. In *Proc. of 1992 SIGMOD International Conference on Management of Data*, pages 236–245, May 1992.

[BT90] D. L. Burkes and R. K. Treiber. Design Approach for Real-Time Transaction Processing Remote Site Recovery. In *Proceedings of IEEE Compcon*, pages 568–572, 1990.

[CS92] D. D. Chamberlain and F. B. Schmuck. Dynamic Data Distribution (D^3)in a Shared-Nothing Multiprocessor Data Store. In *Proceedings of 18th VLDB Conference*, pages 163–174, Vancouver, British Columbia, 1992.

[FCK87] J. C. Freytag, F. Cristian, and B. Kaehler. Masking System Crashes in Database Application Programs. In *Proceedings of 13th VLDB Conference*, pages 407–416, Brighton, England, 1987.

[Fry94] C. Frye. Move to Workflow Provokes Business Process Scrutiny. *Software Magazine*, pages 77–89, April 1994.

[GMP90] H. Garcia-Molina and C. A. Polyzois. Two Epoch Algorithms for Disaster Recovery. In *Proc. of 16th VLDB Conference, Brisbane, Australia*, pages 222–230, 1990.

[GHS95] Georgakopolous D. and Hornick M. and Sheth A. An Overview of Workflow Management: From Process Modelling to Workflow Automation Infrastructure. *Distributed and Parallel Databases Journal*, 3(2):119–152, 1995.

[Gol94] R. Goldring. A Discussion of Relational Database Replication Technology. *InfoDB*, 8(1), 1994.

[GR93] J. Gray and A. Reuter. *Transaction Processing: Concepts and Techniques*. Morgan Kaufmann, San Mateo, CA, 1993.

[Hsu95] M. Hsu. Special Issue on Workflow Systems. *Bulletin of the Technical Committee on Data Engineering, IEEE*, 18(1), March 1995.

[IBMa] IBM. *FlowMark for OS/2: Managing Your Workflow*. Document No. SH19-8176-00, May 1994.

[LR94] F. Leymann and D. Roller. Business Processes Management with FlowMark. In *Proc. 39th IEEE Computer Society Int'l Conference (CompCon), Digest of Papers*, pages 230–233, San Francisco, California, February 28 – March 4 1994. IEEE.

[Lyo90] J. Lyon. Tandem's Remote Data Facility. In *Proc. of IEEE Compcon*, 1990.

[MAGK95] C. Mohan, G. Alonso, R. Günthör, and M. Kamath. Exotica: A Research Perspective on Workflow Management Systems. In [Hsu95].

[MHL+92] C. Mohan, D. Haderle, B. Lindsay, H. Pirahesh, and P. Schwarz. ARIES: A transaction recovery method supporting fine-granularity locking and partial rollbacks using write-ahead logging. *ACM Transactions on Database Systems*, 17(1), 1992.

[MTO93] C. Mohan, K. Treiber, and R. Obermarck. Algorithms for the Management of Remote Backup Data Bases for Disaster Recovery. In *Proc. of 9th International Conference on Data Engineering*, pages 511–518, 1993.

[SBCM95] Samaras, G., Britton, K., Citron, A., Mohan, C. Two-Phase Commit Optimizations in a Commercial Distributed Environment. In *Distributed and Parallel Databases Journal*, Vol. 3, No. 4, October 1995.

[She94] A.P. Sheth. On Multi-system Applications and Transactional Workflows, 1994. Collection of papers from Bellcore.

[WfMC94] The Workflow Reference Model. Workflow Management Coalition, December 1994. Accessible via: http://www.aiai.ed.ac.uk/WfMC/.

[WN94] J. Wiener and J. Naughton. Bulk Loading into an OODB: A Performance Study. In *Proceedings of the 20th VLDB Conference*, pages 120–131, Santiago, Chile, 1994.

Semantic WorkFlow Interoperability

F. Casati, S. Ceri, B. Pernici, G. Pozzi

Dipartimento di Elettronica e Informazione - Politecnico di Milano
Piazza L. Da Vinci, 32 - I20133 Milano, Italy
ceri/casati/pernici/pozzi@elet.polimi.it

Abstract. A workflow consists of a collection of activities which support a specific business process; classical examples range from claim management in an insurance company to production scheduling in a manufacturing company to patient care management and support within an hospital. In conventional workflow systems, each business process is separately specified and autonomously supported by a workflow management system, which drives and assists computer-supported activities. However, business processes often interact with each other; in particular, activities which are performed in the context of one process may influence activities of a different process in a way that, laying "between" the two processes, is quite difficult to formalize and understand.
Therefore, a new challenging area for research consists of studying the process of workflow interoperability, i.e. to focus on the interactions among workflows which are autonomously and separately specified, yet need each other's support. This paper is focused on the semantic specification of workflow interoperability, and provides a classification of "modes of interaction" and of the semantic properties of cooperating workflows. We introduce some topological properties of cooperative workflows, e.g. reachability, deadlock and starvation, and discuss "workflow integration", i.e. links established between workflows that allow us to view an integrated process from its component processes.

1 Introduction

Workflows are activities involving the coordinated execution of multiple tasks performed by different processing entities. A task defines some work to be done by a person, by a software system or by both of them. Specification of a workflow (**WF**) involves describing those aspects of its component tasks (and the processing entities that execute them) that are relevant to control and coordinate their execution, as well as the relations between the tasks themselves.

Information in a WF mainly concerns when a certain work task (**WT**) has to start, the criteria for assigning the WT to agents and which WTs it activates after its end; therefore, less emphasis is placed on the specification of the WT itself (which may be informally described and only partially automated), while the focus is on the WTs' coordination. Connections among WTs can be rather complex, and some of them may be run-time dependent. A Workflow Management System (**WFMS**) permits both to specify WFs and to control their execution. During a WF execution (enactment), a WFMS has to schedule WTs (including their assignment to users) on the basis of the (static) WF specifications and of the (dynamic) sequence of events signaling the completion of WTs and of generic events produced within the execution environment (including exceptions).

For the specification of WF behavior, we have presented in [8] a conceptual WF model, inspired by a rich literature on WF specification [1, 13, 15, 18, 21, 24, 25]. The model includes a large collection of constructs for specifying WT interactions, enables the specification of accesses to external databases, and supports preconditions and exceptions. All these concepts are formalized in a Workflow Description Language (WFDL), which is presented in [8] together with graphical notation for visualizing flow interconnections.

A critical problem in the conceptual characterization and understanding of WFs concerns the interoperability among different WFs, i.e. the interaction between WF applications which, although autonomously and separately designed, may interact. "Controlled interoperability" may translate into a fruitful interaction, whereas "unplanned interoperability" may cause problems such as deadlock, starvation, nontermination, or failure to terminate in the desired final state.

The problem of WF interoperability has many facets, ranging from technological issues about how to integrate different WFMS of different vendors on different platforms to the purely conceptual issues of specifying how the interaction should occur. This paper is focused on the semantic specification of WF interoperability, i.e. on the abstract specification of conceptual mechanisms by means of which WF interaction may be fully understood, and potential problems may be removed. Thus, we assume that several WFs are autonomously specified by means of the same conceptual model. In this context, all interoperability problems between WFs are confined within a conceptual context and relate to the semantics of WFs. This problem is quite similar to the problem of schema integration in conceptual databases, which occurs when designing applications on federated databases; and, with no surprise, we recognize not only similar problems, but also similar solutions. In particular, this paper progressively introduces a notion of WF integration that serves the purpose of explaining interactions among WF schemata, and a methodology for achieving integrated WF schemata.

1.1 Previous Related Work

Office modeling techniques [6] proposed the first descriptions of WFs as extensions of Petri Nets, flowcharts and production rules. Process modeling in the Software Engineering field brought to a closer relationship between modeling and enactment of processes: several WF specification languages [18, 13] and several process modeling tools to "animate" WFs [2] were introduced.

Interest in connecting WF systems to existing information systems has recently increased, in order to interconnect to existing data and to cope with large volumes of information. The challenge posed by WF management pushes towards removing some of the classical limitations of databases in the context of concurrency and transactional models [21]. Active rules were indicated as a particularly promising operational model for WFs [11, 27]: active rules for WT enactment are presented in [7, 9]. The field of WF interconnections and inter-actions, as well as that of exceptions and access to shared databases, still needs going into depth.

1.2 Paper Outline

In order to make this paper self-consistent, Section 2 summarizes the Workflow Conceptual Model presented in [8]. Section 3 introduces two examples of WF schemata that illustrate many of the issues arising in WF interoperability. Section 4 introduces several properties that may help understanding the collective behavior of WF enactments; these include all possible causes of nontermination and three possible interaction schemes: cooperation, competition, and interference. Section 5 discusses WF integration and gives some preliminary guidelines on how to achieve integration. Finally, Section 6 sketches out some final remarks.

2 Conceptual WorkFlow Model

The conceptual WF model enables the design of *WF schemata*, which contain the specifications of a collection of WTs and of the dependencies between them. This specification indicates which WTs should be executed, in which order, which agent may be in charge of them, and which operations should be performed on external databases. Intertask dependencies are specified using a restricted number of constructs: sequence, alternatives, parallelism such as *fork* and *join* [2, 11, 24]. The behavior of each WT is formally described by listing its preconditions, its actions, and its exceptional conditions during its execution. The peculiar feature of the proposed WF model is to enable, within WTs' conditions, actions, and exceptions, the manipulation of databases by means of standard SQL2 statements.

We call *WF instance* (or "WF case") any execution (enactment) of a WF schema: a WF may control the evolution of a given object which is relevant to an activity. For example, a WF schema may describe the process of a patient that needs a pacemaker and is periodically followed up: a WF case is created whenever a patient is admitted to an hospital and a pacemaker is implanted. Thus, several WF cases of the same WF schema may be active at the same time.

A WF schema is described by means of a **WorkFlow Description Language** (WFDL), defined in [8]. Each WF schema is composed of two sections: descriptions of flows, showing intertask relationships, and descriptions of WTs; each section starts with definitions of constants, types, variables, and functions. In WFDL, all types are either atomic types or records of atomic types. Definitions in the context of flow descriptions are global (visible to every WT in the WF), while definitions in the context of WTs are local; for details, see [8]. In both cases, variables exist only during an execution of the WF or WT instance, and are not visible outside the scope of a peculiar WT or WF instance.

The flow declaration may also refer to persistent data (**DB**) which are shared by all WF agents and possibly by agents of other WFs. These data are usually defined externally (i.e. they are part of the information system of the organization and their existence is independent of the particular WF being modeled); for the sake of simplicity, we use the relational data model to denote persistent data. DB manipulation and retrieval is the only way of exchanging data with other WFs. The complete description of the conceptual model can be found in [8].

2.1 WorkTask Descriptions

Each WT has five major characteristics:

- *Name*: a string identifying the WT.
- *Description*: few lines in natural language, describing the WT.
- *Preconditions*: a boolean expression of simple conditions which must yield a truth value before the actions in the WT can be executed. Simple conditions may either contain (conventional) boolean expressions in WFDL, or be based on the (boolean) query `exists` on a SQL2 statement, which is interpreted as `false` if the corresponding query is the empty relation, and `true` otherwise.
- *Actions*: sequence of statements in WFDL which serves as a *specification* of the intended behavior of the WT. WFDL actions describe data manipulations of temporary and persistent WF data occurring while the WT is active; therefore, WFDL includes instructions for getting input from agents, for manipulating the content of WT or WF variables, and for retrieving and manipulating shared databases (performed by means of SQL2 `update queries`).
  The user executing the WT has full freedom on the way the WT itself should be executed, provided that eventually the actions which are listed in its action part are performed.
- *Exceptions*: in every WT it is possible to specify a set of pairs `<Exception, Reaction>` to handle abnormal events: every time an exception is raised, the corresponding reaction is performed. An exception is a WFDL predicate, which may include time-related and query predicates. All exceptions are monitored by the WFMS; when they become true (possibly at the start of the WT), the exception is raised. A reaction is next performed by the WFMS to handle the exception. Reactions can be selected among a restricted set of options that includes `end` (imposes the termination of the WT), `cancel` (the WT is canceled), `notify` (a message is escalated to the person responsible for the WT) and a few others; a detailed description of available reactions is available in [8]. A typical exception is raised when a WT is not completed within a specified deadline, and a person is notified.

WTs are graphically represented by boxes, separated in four sections, giving the precondition, the name and description, the action, and the exception, respectively.

Each WT may be fully automated (i.e. when it can be performed by a software program or a machine) or be assigned to one agent. Note that we require each WT execution to be under control of one specific agent; this is a requirement that should be taken into account in designing WT granularity.

2.2   WorkFlow Descriptions

A WF description consists of several interconnections between WTs, which are formally defined in WFDL and also graphically described.

Two WTs may be directly connected by an edge, with the intuitive meaning that as soon as the first one ends, the second one is ready for execution. In all other cases, connections among WTs are performed by *routing tasks* (**RT**). RTs are classified into:

- *fork tasks* (**FT**), for initiating concurrent WT executions
- *join tasks* (**JT**), for synchronizing WTs after concurrent execution.

A FT is followed by many WTs, called *successors*. FTs are classified as:

- *Total*: after the FT is activated, all successors are ready for execution.
- *Non deterministic*: the fork is associated with a value k; the FT selects nondeterministically k successors for execution.
- *Conditional*: each successor is associated with a condition; the FT instantaneously evaluates conditions and only successor WTs with a **true** condition are ready for execution.
- *Conditional with mutual exclusion*: it adds to the previous case the constraint that only one condition can be **true**; thus, after the predecessor ends, if no condition or more than one conditions are **true** an exception is risen, otherwise one of the successors is ready for execution.

A JT is preceded by many WTs, called its *predecessors*. JTs are classified as:

- *Total*: JT is activated only after the end of all predecessors.
- *Partial*: the JT is associated with a value k; after the end of k predecessor WTs the JT is active. Subsequent ends of predecessor WTs have no effect.
- *Iterative*: the JT is associated with a value k; whenever k predecessor WTs end the JT is active. Iterative JTs are implemented by counting terminated WTs and resetting the counters to zero whenever a successor becomes ready. Iterative join with two predecessors and $k = 1$ is used to describe cycles.

The above values k may be associated with constants, variables, or functions expressed in WFDL; in the last two cases, their value becomes known at execution time.

Each WF schema has one start symbol and several stop symbols; the start symbol has one successor WT and each stop symbol has one predecessor WT. WFDL includes also modularization mechanisms (called "supertask" and "multitask") which are omitted from this paper [8]. Figure 1 represents the adopted graphical symbology for WF representation.

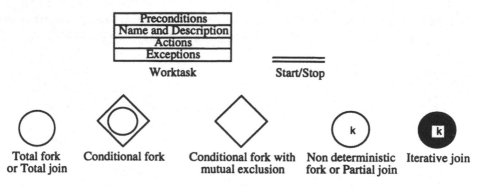

Fig. 1. Graphical symbols for flow interconnections.

2.3 WorkFlow Enactment

A conceptual WF schema describes the legal behaviors of WF executions, called **WF enactment**. An operational semantics of WF enactment is given, by means of active rules, in [9]. Each WF instance, or *case*, is explicitly initiated by an agent and is conducted by assigning WTs to agents according to the WF schema, until the final WTs are reached; at that point summary information about the case is recorded and the case is completed. We assume a WFMS architecture composed of two cooperative environments, one dedicated to WF coordination (*WF management environment*) and one to WT execution (*WT environment*). Details about the architectural environment in which WFs are executed are not of concern in this paper, and can be found in [8, 9].

Figure 2 depicts WT execution by means of a state-transition diagram. A WT becomes *ready* for execution either because it is the first WT of the case or due to the completion of some predecessors; the WF schema allows the WF manager to decide whether a given WT is *ready*. If the WT has no precondition or if the precondition is **true**, then the WT becomes *active*. If instead the WT's precondition is **false**, then the WT's state becomes *inhibited* and the WFMS waits for some external event which may change the truth value of the precondition before the WT becomes *active*. However, exceptional conditions may cause the WT termination from the *inhibited* state.

When a WT is *active*, its execution is controlled within the WT environment. Its state evolves into *executing* as soon as an agent starts operating on the WT (for instance, by opening a window on his screen which corresponds to the WT). The agent can suspend execution, by entering a *suspended* state, and then resume execution.

WT termination is represented by three exclusive states: a WT can be *ended* or *canceled*, in which case WF enactment continues by determining which WT, if any, becomes *ready* due to this event according to the WF schema; the two states are distinguished because in the former case the WT's activities are assumed to be positively accomplished, while in the second case the WT's activities are not accomplished. A WT can also be *refused* by its agent, in which case the WFMS

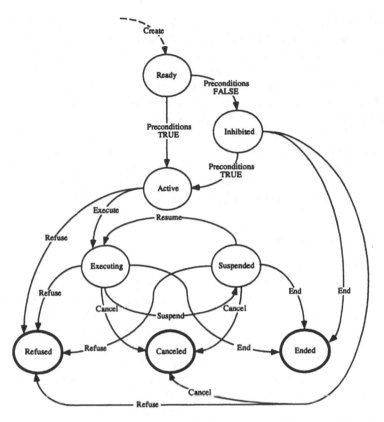

Fig. 2. State-transition diagram describing WT execution (*Refused, Canceled, Ended* are final states).

must re-assign it to a different agent. When a WT is *active, inhibited, executing,* or *suspended,* it can be forced to a final state by exceptions which are generated by the WFMS.

3 WorkFlow Interoperability

WF interoperability is concerned with defining the interaction which occurs between distinct cases. Complex interactions may indeed occur between cases of the same WF schema, thus yielding to interoperability issues which are internal to one specific WF application; however, the most difficult problems arise when the interaction occurs between cases from different WF schemata and are caused by applications which are independently and autonomously designed. In this paper, we focus on conceptual interoperability; we assume that each WF schema is described by means of the same WF model, described in Section 2.1 and 2.2, and that its enactment conforms to the rules given in Section 2.3.

The most relevant feature of the conceptual WF model as it concerns interoperability is that each case has no access to control variables of other cases, be them of the same WF schema or of a different schema. The only interaction which may occur between cases, documented on WF schemata, is by means of the access to shared databases. This feature occurs in practice, as WFMS are components of enterprise-wide information systems; as we will see, it enables us to identify and focus on a limited number of sources of interaction.

In order to introduce the problems of WF interoperability, we present two examples of tightly integrated WFs. We describe a patient management system, illustrating the sequence of activities performed by patients whose heart disease is cared by means of pacemakers, and a pacemaker management system, illustrating the process of acquiring, charging, implanting, maintaining, and replacing pacemakers. The two processes have a tight interoperability[1].

3.1 Patient Workflow

The precondition to start the WF case, i.e. to admit the patient Pt, states that a functioning pacemaker (PmFree.Status = ''OK'') must be available (recorded as a tuple in the table *PmFree*). The patient is then registered (get Pt) and assigned a pacemaker chosen among available ones (Pm1 = select-one ...). The chosen pacemaker Pm1 is no longer available to other patients (delete from PmFree ...).

Pacemaker Pm1 is then implanted into patient Pt; this activity, performed by clinicians in the operation room, is reflected in the WF just by a new record in the table Implanted indicating that the patient Pt is implanted with the pacemaker Pm1 and will have a follow-up visit after 90 days; two null attributes are reserved for the status of the patient, and status of the pacemaker.

After implant, a follow-up visit occurs every 90 days (adjustments to the visit day may be performed by nurses which directly access records of the *Implanted* table; emergencies are also taken care by nurses that may set the visit day to the current date and then schedule the visit as soon as possible). During a follow-up visit, the status of patients is recorded together with the date of the next visit; an exception may be caused by a failure of the pacemaker, that forces the WT to be suspended and exited with Status = fail. The Status is set to "Fail" also if the patient is not fine (e.g. he needs a more sophisticated pacemaker) or if the patient needs no pacemaker at all.

The WT *Need a pacemaker* states if the patient Pt needs a new pacemaker (get NeedAnotherPM). If no pacemaker is needed, WT *Explant* explants the old one (delete from Implanted ...). If instead a new one is needed, then the WT *Find a new pacemaker* is activated. As a precondition, it looks inside *PmFree* if there is another available functioning pacemaker: it selects a functioning pacemaker (Pm2 = select-one ...) and makes it no longer available to others (delete from PmFree ...). The old pacemaker is then explanted (delete from Implanted ...), and the patient Pt is associated with a new pacemaker

---

[1] This example was suggested by John Mylopoulos to Stefano Ceri in 1982 while doing research on script languages, long time ago ...

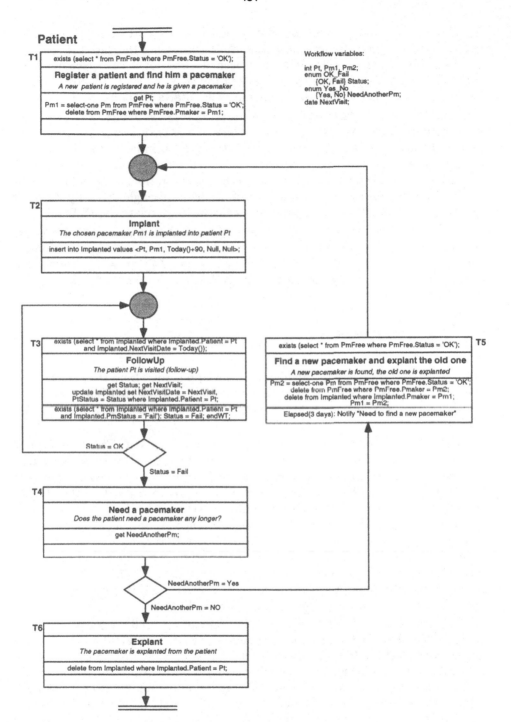

Fig. 3. Patient Workflow.

(by means of the assignment Pm1 = Pm2, which allows us to refer to the pacemaker currently implanted in the patient Pt by means of the variable Pm1). As an exception, when the patient Pt has been waiting for a new pacemaker for more than three days, a message is notified to the WT agent. Finally, the new pacemaker is implanted and the follow-up cycles starts again.

Note that the *Patient* WF requires several local variables: Pt, Pm1, Pm2, Status, NextVisit, NeedAnotherPm. Values of these variables cannot be accessed outside a specific WF case; indeed, the WFDL imposes that these variables be atomic so as to associate each case with a row of values, one for each variables, in a specific table describing the case evolution. This table can be accessed by WT execution environments if needed, although normally variables are used as parameters within procedure calls which activate the WTs.

All communication with the external environment, consisting of other cases, possibly enactments of different schemata, and of generic other applications, is performed by means of database tables PmFree and Implanted. In particular, PmFree is manipulated by the *Pacemaker* WF, which is described next.

3.2   Pacemaker Workflow

The *Pacemaker* WF gives the dual view of this application from the pacemaker's perspective. A pacemaker Pm is assembled, tested and inserted into *PmFree*. If the pacemaker is defective (Status = Fail), WT *Trash* trashes it and the WF ends.

After Pm is implanted into a patient, it is checked by WT *Check*, performed by the technicians who are responsible of the pacemaker functioning. Normally, each patient gets an appointment on the same date, and then is seen by clinicians and by technicians. Thus, in the same way as the *Follow-up* WT of the *Patient* WF, the precondition of WT *Check* requires that Pm is implanted and today is the next visit day. The result of the *Check* is encoded in the variable status, now referring to the pacemaker, which is entered into the suitable record of the *Implanted* table. Status of the pacemaker is set to "OK" if Pm is functioning correctly: otherwise Status is set to "Fail". If Status is "OK", WT *Check* is re-activated, where its precondition force next check to take place only at the next fixed day: if Status is "Fail", WT *Check* ends.

An exception of WT *Check* may force Status to "Fail", regardless of the functionality of Pm. In fact, if Pt is not fine, the exception is raised and the WT is forced to completion. In both cases (either a pacemaker failure or a change of the patient's care), technicians have no responsibility on the subsequent pacemaker explant, and their next WT aims at recharging and testing Pm after it has been explanted: as a precondition, Pm must be not implanted (not exists (select * ...)). After the recharge and the test, if the Status of Pm is "OK", the pacemaker waits for another implant into another patient (WT *Implant* of WF *Patient*): otherwise it is trashed and removed from the *PmFree* table.

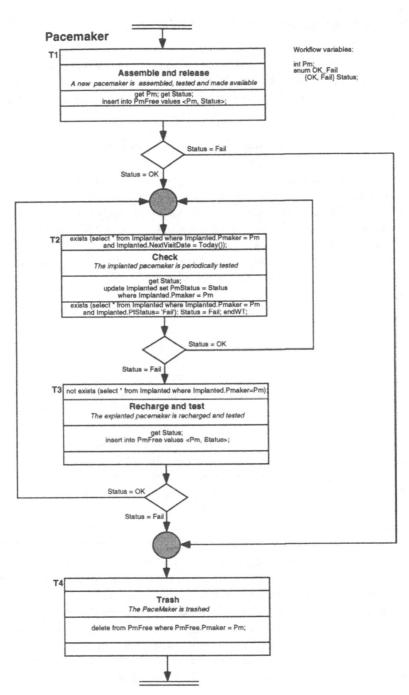

Fig. 4. Pacemaker Workflow.

4   Properties of Interacting Workflows

The above examples may be used in order to introduce several interoperability problems that may exist between WFs. Indeed, we will see that the above WFs exhibit a nice cooperation pattern, which can be formally studied and proved.

4.1   Properties of Enactments of a Single WF Schema

We first define properties that characterize the enactment of a single WF schema. Recall that there can be multiple concurrent case executions of the same WF schema, and that one case may cause multiple concurrent executions of the same WT. Therefore, we identify each case enactment by a *case-id* C_i, which is assigned at the start of the case by the WFMS, and each WT execution E_{ijk} by a triple *case-id, task-id, execution-number*, where the execution number k is progressively assigned for each execution of a given WT T_j within a given case C_i.

The following properties describe WT execution during a given case enactment:

- **Reachability**: a WT is reachable if it can be set to the *active* state during the course of a given case enactment. When a WF schema is compiled, all WTs should be reachable (or else they don't contribute to the WF); however, during enactment in general the set of reachable WTs for a given case reduces progressively.
- **Potential Termination**: a case potentially terminates iff at least one of its stop symbols is reachable. This property should always hold during enactment, otherwise the schema is incorrectly specified.
- **Mutual Exclusion**: two WTs of the same case are in mutual exclusion if they cannot be in the *executing* state at the same time.
- **Potential Parallelism**: two WTs of the same case are potentially parallel if they can be in the *executing* state at the same time.
- **Potential Precedence**: this relationship is a partial order between WTs $T_h <_{pp} T_k$ which holds when, in an arbitrary case enactment, T_h can be completed (*ended* or *canceled*) before T_k is made *ready*.
- **Absolute Precedence**: this relationship is a partial order between WTs $T_h <_p T_k$ which holds when, in all case enactments, T_h must be completed (*ended* or *canceled*) before T_k is made *ready*. If T_h and T_k can be activated multiple times, then absolute precedence applies to each WT execution for each case; therefore, $\forall\ i, j$, E_{ihj} should be completed before E_{ikj} is *ready*.

For example, in the *Patient* WF all WTs are reachable; the WT T_1 becomes unreachable once it is completed; no WTs can be potentially parallel; T_1 absolutely precedes T_6, and T_2 absolutely precedes T_4 and T_5.

4.2 Properties of Enactments of Different WF Schemata

Concurrent enactments of cases from different WF schemata are characterized by one additional identifier, the *schema-number*, which needs to be added in order to properly identify WTs (T_j^s), cases (C_i^s), and WT executions (E_{ijk}^s).

- **Condition-Action Dependency**: this relationship is a partial order between WTs $T_h^p <_{ca} T_k^q$, $p \neq q$, which holds when it is required that the WT execution T_h^p be *ended* within an arbitrary case before the precondition of T_k^q becomes true in another arbitrary case. The left hand side of the precondition may include multiple WTs when termination of anyone of them may cause T_k^q to become *ready*.
- **Case Binding**: it is a link established between case identifiers i and j when the condition-action dependency $T_h^p <_{ca} T_k^q$ occurs between specific WT executions E_{ihm}^p and E_{jkn}^q.
- **Activation Precedence**: this relationship is a partial order between WTs $T_h^p <_{ap} T_k^q$, $p \neq q$, which holds when T_h^p can become *active* before T_k^q.
- **Pseudo-Simultaneous Execution**: it is established between two WTs T_h^p and T_k^q, $p \neq q$, when it holds both $T_h^p <_{ap} T_k^q$ and $T_k^q <_{ap} T_h^p$ and they are not in mutual exclusion.
- **Task Binding**: it is a link established between case identifiers i and j when the pseudo-simultaneous execution of T_h^p and T_k^q occurs between specific WT executions E_{ihm}^p and E_{jkn}^q.

Given that the only information shared by different WF cases is stored within database tables, condition-action dependencies normally are established by means of queries in the precondition of T_k^q and database inserts or updates in the action of T_h^p. Similarly, the presence of the same precondition in two WTs T_k^q and T_h^p indicates that they could be pseudo-simultaneous, as the same external event may cause their simultaneous activation.

Bindings established between cases are normally associated with data sharing among the executions E_{ihm}^p and E_{jkn}^q. Although in many simple cases bindings between executions are *one-to-one* (e.g. one case C_i^p is bound to one case C_j^q and viceversa), indeed bindings may be also *one-to-many* and *many-to-many*.

In the *Patient* and *Pacemaker* WFs, condition-action dependencies are established from WTs {*Pacemaker.T1, Pacemaker.T3*} to WTs *Patient.T1* and *Patient.T5*. These dependencies establish case bindings, which intuitively correspond to the possibility of progressing both WFs which occur when a pair (*Pacemaker-Patient*) is identified. Such bindings are *one-to-one*; however, they evolve dynamically, as the same patient can dynamically receive multiple pacemakers, and similarly the same pacemaker may be implanted within many patients.

WTs *Patient.T3* and *Pacemaker.T2* (corresponding to the *Patient's FollowUp* and the *Pacemaker's Check*) are pseudo-simultaneous, due to the fact that they have the same precondition. Correspondingly, whenever they are executed a task binding is established between two executions of *Patient.T3* and *Pacemaker.T2*, respectively. These WT bindings indicate that indeed the two WTs of the different WF schemata are candidate for integration.

4.3 Properties Concerning Termination

The next properties concern the termination of cases in presence of interaction between cases.

- **Sufficience:** A set of WF schemata A, B ...N is sufficient on schema P iff all the WTs of P are condition-action dependent only from WTs of A, B ...N. Formally, if $task(F)$ denotes the set of WTs of a WF F, $dep(T_h^p)=\{T_k^q : T_h^p <_{ca} T_k^q\}$ denotes the set of all WTs on which T_h^p depends, and the symbol * denotes transitive closure, then the set A, B ...N is sufficient on a WF schema P if:
  $$\forall\, T_i \in task(P)(dep^*(T_i) \in (task(A) \cup task(B) \ldots \cup task(N)))$$
- **Starvation:** A WT T is in starvation, and thus the cases in which T is *ready* may be indefinitely held in wait, when the WTs of the set $dep(T)$ on which T depends are not evolving by providing sufficient data so as to satisfy the preconditions for all the above cases.
- **Deadlock:** two interacting WFs A and B could be in deadlock when they have two WTs T_a and T_b such that the former depends on the latter and viceversa, i.e. both $T_a \in dep(T_b)$ and $T_b \in dep(T_a)$ hold at the same time.

For instance, the set {*Patient-Pacemaker*} is sufficient (since all the condition-action dependencies of *Patient* are related to *Pacemaker* and viceversa); when no *Pacemaker* is available, WTs **Patient.T1** and **Patient.T5** are in starvation.

As an example of deadlock, consider two simple WFs *Invite* and *Propose*. The *Invite* WT is performed by a conference's chairman, who waits for someone to send him a proposal of a tutorial before inviting someone to give the tutorial. The *Propose* WT is performed by the company of potential speakers, expecting tutorial invitations before sending the corresponding abstracts. The two WFs are in deadlock, since they can indefinitely wait for each other. Note that a deadlock between WFs can be broken by external events; for instance, a colleague of the conference chairman could send the speaker's abstract to the chairman and propose him for the tutorial which an activity that is outside of the WF specifications.

4.4 Workflow Interactions

The following classification indicates the possible interaction schemes that may be identified between different WF schemata.

- *Cooperation:* Two WFs A and B cooperate iff their interaction is desired and foreseen. In this case, the WF administrator designs the WF schemata so that at given points A produces some data and, possibly at different points, B uses those data. Typical examples of cooperation are the producer-consumer and the client-server environments.

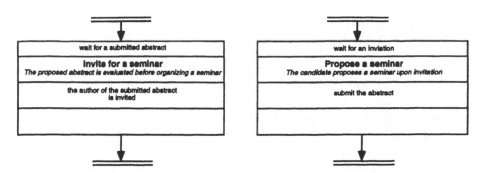

Fig. 5. Workflow deadlock: the two WFs are waiting for each other.

- *Competition:* Two WFs **A** and **B** compete iff their interaction is not desired but foreseen. In this case, the two WFs **A** and **B** could be executed correctly in a separated way, but a contemporary execution is not possible due to the limited number of available resources. A typical example of competition takes place when WFs **A** and **B** need two resources, **R1** and **R2**, and the resource pool **ResPool** has one item only.
- *Interference*: Two WFs **A** and **B** interfere iff the interaction is neither desired not foreseen. In this case, both **A** and **B** are correctly designed for a stand-alone execution but their synchronization is badly designed.

Clearly, in the *Patient-Pacemaker* example the cases of *Patient* and of *Pacemaker* cooperate, while the cases of *Patient* compete with each other for the assignment of pacemakers required by each patient.

5 Workflow Integration

WF integration aims at building an integrated frame representing two or more cooperative WF schemata, which indicates explicitly case and WT bindings. WF integration may lead to the identification and removal of interferences between WFs, and therefore can cause the redesign of some features of the component WFs. It is important to note, however, that WF integration is hereby proposed as a conceptual device, whereas each WF application remains managed by the WF management environment as explained in Section 2. Thus, the result of WF schemata integration is not another WF schema but only a frame in which interactions of the original schemata can be better understood.

Integrated frames collect WTs from various WF schemata, called its *component WFs*. They have the following features:

- There can be multiple start tasks, one for each component WF.
- New special tasks *link* and *unlink* are introduced to denote case bindings and unbinding. A link node has several incoming edges, representing component WFs, and one outgoing edge, representing the integrated frame; an unlink node has one incoming edge, representing the integrated frame, and several

outgoing edges, representing component WFs. Syntactically, along each path connecting a link node to a stop symbol there must be at least an unlink node.

- Most WTs are taken unchanged from anyone of the component schemata; however, they may be replicated on the integrated schema if this facilitates the schema merging.
- Bound WTs from component WFs are merged into one integrated WT, graphically represented by double frames. The name of bound WTs is given by the composition of names of the original WTs, preconditions and exceptions are composed by means of disjunction (to indicate that anyone of them applies to the bound WT) and actions are listed in sequence (to indicate that all actions of the bound WTs are eventually performed).

From a methodological viewpoint, the integrated frame is built by detecting condition-action dependencies and activation precedences, and deducing case and WT bindings from them. Case bindings are represented by link nodes. Once WF schemata are linked, the designer should consider each component WF and understand which WTs are performed within WF by preserving the binding (be them bound WTs or not), thus identifying a dual unlink node, that represents the logical point in the execution of the WF where case bindings is changed or no longer effective. Link-unlink nodes are paired; if component WFs remain linked until they reach their stop task, the unlink is simply added as the last node before all stop tasks.

5.1 Patient - Pacemaker Integration

In Figure 6, we illustrate the integration of the *Patient-Pacemaker* WFs. As already indicated in Section 3, condition-action dependencies are established from WTs {*Pacemaker.T1, Pacemaker.T3*} to WTs *Patient.T1* and *Patient.T5*. These dependencies establish the *one-to-one* case binding between the WFs, which intuitively matches the fact that a given patient has a given pacemaker implanted[2]. Case binding is represented by a link node which immediately follows the two WTs where the condition-action dependency is recognized; the link node delimits a portion of the integrated schema representing the binding of cases, which is represented by a gray shade in Figure 6.

After the implant operation, which is performed within the WF *Patient*, we recognize a WT which is candidate for merging. Indeed, as already noticed, WTs

---

[2] Note that in the proposed example case binding is very concrete case, as it corresponds to an "implant" operation (and similarly the unbinding corresponds to an "explant" operation). Normally, case binding is less evident, and it corresponds to using shared data which become relevant to several WF schemata. For instance, claim management from the viewpoint of an insurance company and of a lawyer company, where binding is due to the processing of the same claim; or reviewing process seen from the viewpoint of the editor and the referees, where binding is due to the processing of the same paper.

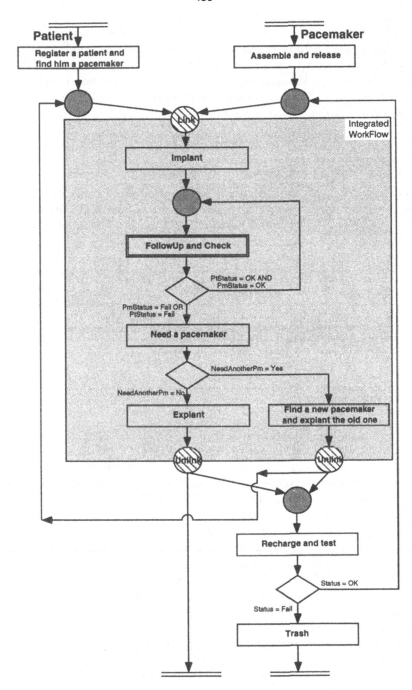

Fig. 6. Frame resulting from the integration of Patient and Pacemaker workflows

Patient. T3 and *Pacemaker. T2*, representing the patient's follow-up and the pacemaker's check, are pseudo simultaneous, have the same precondition (indicating that the patient is being visited during the current day), and physically happen one after the other, as the patient sees the doctor and the pacemaker technician during the same visit[3]. Their merge generates the *FollowUp and Check* WT of the integrated schema, which is associated with:

- The same precondition as its components (corresponding to the disjunction of identical predicates).
- The sequencing of follow-up and check activities.
- The removal of exceptions (we recognize that exceptions can actually be removed as they express within each WF the failure of the other WF; thus, WT variables `PtStatus` and `PmStatus` can simply be tested in disjunction at the end of the WT).

FollowUp and Check is executed until the `Status` of either the patient or the pacemaker is not `OK`. Then an explant becomes required. If the patient needs a new pacemaker, a new one is found before scheduling the explant operation, otherwise the explant has no prerequisites. In both cases, the explant operation brings as a consequence the unlink of the WF schemata, and delimits the "merged" area of the integrated WF schema.

6 Conclusions

The problems of WF integration have many aspects in common with schema integration in conceptual database design [4]. Indeed, schema similarities are searched, and entities are sometimes integrated by merging their contributions from various schemata. Name and type conflicts are common to schema integration and WF integration, and may lead to WT renaming and restructuring which are dual to schema integration activities. Properties such as transformational, mapping, and behavioral equivalence of conceptual schemata can also be extended to WFs. Therefore, we believe that this paper has opened a new promising area for research, which can be suitably attached by reusing competence already established for conceptual database design.

Another interesting analogy links WF interoperability to object-oriented interoperability. In the latter context, objects are described together with their messages (events) which may cause a change in their internal state; objects' coordination is achieved through the message passing mechanism, and the interoperability problem consists in understanding and/or designing a global system evolution. Some proposals in this direction are contained in the F-ORM model (Functionalities in Objects with Roles Model [12]), in which object modeling processes are introduced to facilitate coordination between interacting objects

---

[3] In the concrete case study that we are considering, the pacemaker checking is sometimes performed by a clinician.

aiming at achieving a common goal. The concepts of cooperation in object-orientation systems could thus be another source of design principles for formalizing WF integration, while keeping each WF relatively independent during the execution of its own WTs.

In future work we will deepen our analysis of theoretical properties of integrated WF schemata and will use such theory in the development of tools assisting the designer in WF analysis and integration.

References

1. Attie P., Singh M., Sheth A., Rusinkiewicz M., "Specifying and Enforcing Intertask Dependencies", *Proc. 19th VLDB Conf.*, Dublin, Ireland, 1993.
2. Bandinelli S., Fuggetta A., Ghezzi C., "Software Process Model Evolution in the SPADE Environment", *IEEE Transactions on Software Engineering*, December 1993.
3. Baralis E., Ceri S., Paraboschi S., "Modularization Techniques in Active Rule Design", Tech. Report IDEA.WP.003.01, Politecnico di Milano, Milano, Italy, Dec. 1994.
4. Batini C., Ceri S., Navathe S.B.: *"Conceptual Database Design: An Entity-Relationship Approach"*, The Benjamin-Cummings P.C., Redwood City, Ca, 1992.
5. Batini C., Lenzerini M., Navathe S.B.: "Comparison of Methodologies for Database Schema Integration", *ACM Computing Surveys*, 18:4, 323-364, Dec. 1986.
6. Bracchi G., Pernici B., "The Design Requirements of Office Systems", *ACM Trans. on Office Information Systems*, 2(2), April 1984.
7. Bussler C., Jablonski S., "Implementing Agent Coordination for Workflow Management Systems Using Active Database Systems", *Proceedings of the Fourth International Workshop on Research Issues in Data Engineering (RIDE-ADS '94)*, Houston, Texas, February 1994.
8. Casati F., Ceri S., Pernici B., Pozzi G., "Conceptual Modeling of Workflows", in *Object-Oriented and Entity-Relationship Approach* Int. Conf., Gold Coast, Australia, December 1995.
9. Casati F., Ceri S., Pernici B., Pozzi G., "Deriving Active Rules for Workflow Enactment", submitted for publication, 1995.
10. Ceri S., Fraternali P., Paraboschi S., Tanca L., "Active Rule Management in Chimera", in [27]
11. Dayal U., Hsu M., Ladin R., "Organizing Long-running Activities with Triggers and Transactions", *Proc. ACM SIGMOD*, 1990.
12. De Antonellis V., Pernici B., "Reusing Specifications through Refinement Levels", *Data and Knowledge Eng.*, vol. 15, 1995
13. Ellis C., Nutt G., "Modeling and Enactment of Workflow Systems", in *Application and Theory of Petri Nets*, M. Ajmone Marsan Ed., Lecture Notes in Computer Science 691, New York: Springer Verlag, 1993.
14. Ellis S., Keddara, K. and Rozenberg, G., "Dynamic Change within Workflow Systems", *ACM Conf. on Organizational Computing Systems* (COOCS 95), 1995.
15. Forst A., Kuhn E., Bukhres O., "General Purpose Work flow Languages", *Distributed and Parallel Databases*, vol. 3, n. 2, April 1995.
16. Francalanci C., Pernici B., "View Integration: a Survey of Current Developments", *Internal Report n. 93.053*, Dipartimento di Elettronica e Informazione, Politecnico di Milano, Milano, 1993.

17. Fraternali P., Tanca L.: "A Toolkit for the Design of Active Database Semantics", Dipartimento di Elettronica e Informazione, Politecnico di Milano, Technical Report 93-078, 1993.

18. Georgakopoulos D., Hornick M., Sheth A., "An Overview of Workflow Management: from Process Modeling to Workflow Automation Infrastructure", *Distributed and Parallel Databases*, vol. 3, n. 2, April 1995.

19. Gonzales-Quel L. A., Gonzales S., Perez M., "IDEA Technology Assessment Based on Workflow Applications. The Royal Life Application", *IDEA Rep. IDEA.DE.21S.001.01*, November 1994.

20. Hewlett Packard Company, "Workflow Module Programming Guide", Palo Alto, Ca, July 1994.

21. Hsu M. (ed.), Special Issue on Worflow and Extended Transaction Systems, *Data Engineering Bulletin*, 16(2), June 1993.

22. Krishnakumar N., Sheth A., "Managing Heterogeneous Multi-system Tasks to Support Enterprise-wide Operations", *Distributed and Parallel Databases*, vol. 3, n. 2, April 1995.

23. Paton N.W., Diaz O., Williams M., Campin J., Dinn A., and Jaime A: "Dimensions of Active Behaviour", in *Rules in Database Systems*, Norman W. Paton and M. Howard Williams (Eds), Springer-Verlag, 1993.

24. Rusinkiewicz M., Sheth A., "Specification and Execution of Transaction Workflows", in *Modern Database Systems: the Object Model, Interoperability, and beyond*, Kim W. (ed.), Addison-Wesley, 1994.

25. Sheth A., Rusinkiewicz M., "On Transactional Workflows", *Data Engineering Bulletin*, 16(2), June 1993.

26. Ullman, J.D., "Principles of Database and Knowledge Base Systems", 2 Volumes, Computer Science Press, Rockville, Maryland, 1989.

27. Widom J., Ceri S., "Active Database Systems", Morgan-Kaufmann, San Mateo, Ca, May 1995.

LabFlow-1: A Database Benchmark
for High-Throughput Workflow Management*

Anthony Bonner[1]
bonner@db.toronto.edu

Adel Shrufi[1]
shrufi@db.toronto.edu

Steve Rozen[2]
steve@genome.wi.mit.edu

[1] University of Toronto, Department of Computer Science, Toronto, ON, Canada
[2] Whitehead/MIT, Center for Genome Research, Cambridge, MA, USA

Abstract. Workflow management is a ubiquitous task faced by many organizations, and entails the coordination of various activities. This coordination is increasingly carried out by software systems called *workflow management systems* (WFMS). An important component of many WFMSs is a DBMS for keeping track of workflow activity. This DBMS maintains an audit trail, or event history, that records the results of each activity. Like other data, the event history can be indexed and queried, and views can be defined on top of it. In addition, a WFMS must accommodate frequent workflow changes, which result from a rapidly evolving business environment. Since the database schema depends on the workflow, the DBMS must also support dynamic schema evolution. These requirements are especially challenging in high-throughput WFMSs—*i.e.*, systems for managing high-volume, mission-critical workflows. Unfortunately, existing database benchmarks do not capture the combination of flexibility and performance required by these systems. To address this issue, we have developed *LabFlow-1*, the first version of a benchmark that concisely captures the DBMS requirements of high-throughput WFMSs. LabFlow-1 is based on the data and workflow management needs of a large genome-mapping laboratory, and reflects their real-world experience. In addition, we use LabFlow-1 to test the usability and performance of two object storage managers. These tests revealed substantial differences between these two systems, and highlighted the critical importance of being able to control locality of reference to persistent data.

1 Introduction

1.1 Overview

Workflow management is a ubiquitous task faced by many organizations in a wide range of industries, from banking and insurance, to telecommunications and manufacturing, to pharmaceuticals and health care (*e.g.*, [8, 14]). The task is to coordinate the various activities involved in running an enterprise. Increasingly,

---

* This work was supported by funds from the U.S. National Institutes of Health, National Center for Human Genome Research, grant number P50 HG00098, and from the U.S. Department of Energy under contract DE–FG02–95ER62101.

this coordination is carried out by a software system called a *workflow management system* (WFMS). The activities themselves may use a variety of software components, including files, databases, application programs, and legacy systems, which may run on a variety of hardware platforms and operating systems, which may be located at a variety of sites. For example, in a large genome laboratory, workflow management software knits together a complex web of manual and automated laboratory activities, including experiment scheduling and setup, robot control, raw-data capture, multiple stages of preliminary analysis and quality control, and release of finished results. Appropriate software is necessary to make coordination of these activities both intellectually manageable and operationally efficient, and is a prerequisite for high-throughput laboratories. This software includes a DBMS component for tracking and controlling workflow activity. This paper addresses the requirements of this DBMS.

LabFlow-1 is a benchmark that concisely describes the database requirements of a WFMS in a high-throughput genome laboratory. Although it is based on genome-laboratory workflow, we believe that LabFlow-1 captures the database requirements of a common class workflow management applications: those that require a *production workflow system* [12]. In production workflow, activities are organized into a kind of production line, involving a mix of human and computer activities. Examples in business include insurance-claim or loan-application processing. Production workflow systems are typically complex, high-volume, and central to the organizations that rely on them; certainly these characteristics apply to the laboratory workflow-management systems used in high-throughput genome laboratories. Many production workflows are organized around central materials of some kind, which the workflow activities operate on. Examples of central materials include insurance claims, loan applications, and laboratory samples. As a central material is processed, workflow activities gather information about it.

Production workflow systems include the class of *Laboratory Information Management Systems*, or LIMS (*e.g.*, [14]). LIMS are found in analytical laboratories in a wide range of industries, including pharmaceuticals, health care, environmental monitoring, food and drug testing, and water and soil management. In all cases, the laboratory receives a continual stream of samples, each of which is subjected to a battery of tests and analyses. Workflow management is needed to maintain throughput and control quality.

Much of the research on workflow management in computer science has focussed on developing extended transaction models for specifying dependencies between workflow activities, especially in a heterogeneous environment (*e.g.*, [11, 8]). However, the *performance* of WFMSs has so far received little attention. The need to study performance arises because commercial products cannot support applications with high-throughput workflows. As stated in [8],

Commercial workflow management systems typically support no more than a few hundred workflows a day. Some processes require handling a larger number of workflows; perhaps a number comparable to the number of transactions TP systems are capable of handling. For example, telecommunications companies currently need to process ten thousand service provisioning workflows a day, including a few thousand service provisioning workflows per hour at peak hours. Commercial workflow management systems are currently not capable of handling such workloads.

Note that each workflow may involve many transactions.

High-throughput workflows are also characteristic of large genome laboratories, like the Whitehead Institute/MIT Center for Genome Research (hereafter called "the Genome Center"). Workflow management is needed to support the Genome Center's large-scale genome-mapping projects [7]. Because of automation in instrumentation, data capture and workflow management, transaction rates at the Genome Center have increased dramatically in the last three years, from processing under 1,000 queries and updates per day in 1992 [9], to over 15,000 on many days in 1995. Of course, peak rates can be much higher, with a rate of 22.5 updates and queries per second recently observed over a 5-minute period. These rates are expected to increase by another order of magnitude in the near future if the Genome Center begins large scale sequencing of the Human genome [7]. Moreover, unlike the simple banking debit/credit transactions of some TPC benchmarks [17], these transactions involve complex queries, and updates to complex objects, such as arrays, sequences, and nested sets.

In this paper, we take a first step towards measuring the performance of workflow management systems. We do not attempt to study all the components that affect WFMS performance, such as networks, hardware platforms, and operating systems. Instead, we focus on one dimension of the problem: the performance of DBMSs that control and track workflow. Like other components, the DBMS can become a workflow bottleneck, especially in high-throughput applications.

1.2 DBMS Requirements

Workflow management has numerous DBMS requirements. First, it requires standard database features, such as concurrency control, crash recovery, consistency maintenance, a high-level query language, and query optimization. Workflow for advanced applications (such as laboratory workflow) also requires complex data types, as are found in object-oriented databases. A DBMS supporting production workflow management must provide this functionality on a mixed workload of queries and updates. In addition, it must provide two other features, which are characteristic of production workflow systems:

Event Histories. The DBMS must maintain an audit trail, or event history, of all workflow activity. From this history, the DBMS must be able to quickly retrieve information about any material or activity, for day-to-day operations. The history is also used to explore the cause of unexpected workflow results, to generate reports on workflow activity, and to discover workflow bottlenecks during process re-engineering. The DBMS must therefore support queries and views on an historical database. We note that many commercial laboratories are legally bound to record event histories. Salient examples include clinical drug trials and environmental testing.

Dynamic Schema Evolution. A hallmark of modern workflow management is that workflows change frequently, in response to rapidly changing business needs and circumstances [8]. Typically, a workflow will acquire new activities and existing activities will evolve. In both cases, the changed workflow generates new kinds of information, which must be recorded in the database. This requires changes to the database schema, preferably while the workflow is in operation (so-called *dynamic workflow modification*).

It is worth observing that because the database is historical and the schema is evolving, data at different points in the history will be stored under different schemas. Thus, an historical query or view may access data with many different schemas. This presents a challenge both to database design and to the formulation of queries and views. For instance, an application program may have to query an object's schema, as well as its value.

Existing database benchmarks do not capture the above requirements. This should not be surprising, as it has been observed by researchers working on OODBMS benchmarks that advanced applications are too complex and diverse to be captured by a single benchmark [4, 6]. A quick glance at several recent benchmarks illustrates their diversity of characteristics and requirements. For instance, the OO1, OO7 and HyperModel benchmarks [5, 4, 1] are concerned with the traversal of large graphs, which is a requirement of engineering and hypertext applications. In contrast, the SEQUOIA 2000 benchmark [19] is concerned with the manipulation of large sets of spatial and image data, such as those found in geographic information systems (GIS). The Set Query benchmark [15] is concerned with queries for decision support, including aggregation, multiple joins and report generation. (Such queries also arise in workflow management—for process re-engineering—but they are only part of the story.) Like these benchmarks, LabFlow-1 specifically targets a broad application area: workflow management. This application is characterized by a demand for *flexible* management of a stream of queries and updates, and of historical data and schema.

Unfortunately, many DBMSs do not yet fully support the requirements of production workflow systems as described above. Certainly, a surprising number of commercial products showed serious flaws in simple tests performed by the Genome Center in 1991. Fortunately, one can build a specialized DBMS that supports workflow on top of a storage manager that does not. This approach is taken at the Genome Center. Their specialized DBMS—called *LabBase* [16]—provides the needed support for event histories and schema evolution on top of an object storage manager. LabBase provides a historical query language, as well as structures for rapid access into history lists. It also transforms data from the user's database schema (which is dynamic) into the storage manager's schema (which is static). Besides providing support for workflow, this approach also provides portability, since different object storage managers can be "plugged into" the DBMS. In this way, we can test a wide range of existing storage managers. The benchmark implementation in this paper is based on this idea. We emphasize, however, that the LabFlow-1 benchmark does not depend on LabBase, which is an implementation detail. In the future, we hope to use our benchmark to test the support for workflow management in "off-the-shelf" DBMSs.

1.3 LabFlow-1

The LabFlow-1 benchmark is based on the data and workflow management needs of the Genome Center, and reflects their real-world experience. The benchmark has several goals. One goal is to provide a tool for the Genome Center to use in analyzing object storage managers for LabBase. Other goals are (*i*) to provide a general benchmark for databases supporting workflow-management systems, and (*ii*) to provide developers of next-generation DBMS technology with a set of requirements based on the characteristics of a real-world application domain. Developers of new technology often have few if any realistic applications against which to measure their systems. As with any benchmark, the challenge in designing LabFlow-1 was to create a database schema and workload that are realistic enough to be representative of the target class of applications yet simple enough to be feasibly implemented on a variety of systems.

Although LabFlow-1 is intended to be a general benchmark for DBMSs, this paper uses it to compare storage managers only. This is achieved by running the benchmark on versions of LabBase implemented on top of different storage managers, as described above. This paper compares ObjectStore (version 3.0) [13]. and Texas (versions 0.4 and 0.3) [18]. Compared to relational systems, these storage managers have been used in few production applications, so this analysis is interesting in its own right. Since they are a relatively novel technology, we compare these storage managers not only in terms of performance, but also in terms of client interface, tuning options, and system-administration facilities. In a similar fashion, LabFlow-1 can be used to compare other DBMS components, such as query optimizers and historical access structures.

Labflow-1 is a preliminary version intended for a single database user (hence the name). This choice arises from the architecture of the Genome Center's production DBMS, and also from a belief that it is useful to understand single-user performance before attempting to understand multi-user performance. We plan to develop in the future (*i*) multi-user and client/server workflow benchmarks, and (*ii*) benchmarks to evaluate and compare deductive database systems as query processors for workflow databases.

In sum, LabFlow-1 is the first version of a benchmark for DBMSs that control and track workflow. It is designed for applications with the following characteristics and requirements: high volume, mission critical workflows; frequent workflow change and process re-engineering; an audit trail of workflow activity; and complex-structured data. Due to space limitations, this paper can provide only an informal description of the benchmark. A detailed description can be found in [2], which is available by anonymous ftp. Benchmark software is also available at the same site.

2 Workflow in LabFlow-1

As noted above, an important component of many workflow management systems is a DBMS for tracking workflow. This DBMS maintains an audit trail, or event history, that records the results of each activity. Like other data, the event history can be indexed and queried, and views can be defined on top of it. In genome laboratories, the event history serves much the same function as a laboratory notebook: it records what was done, when it was done, who did it, and what the results were. All laboratory information management systems produce an event history. Managing this event history is the primary function of the DBMS, and the main subject of this paper. This section provides an overview of data and workflow management in LabFlow-1 from the perspective of the DBMS. To keep the discussion concrete, we frame it in terms of laboratory workflow and LabBase.

The database has two main kinds of object: *materials* and *steps*. In object-oriented terms, the database has a material class and a step class, with subclasses representing different kinds of materials and steps. Step and material instances (objects) are created in two distinct situations. (*i*) As the laboratory receives or creates new materials, new material instances are created in the database to represent them. (*ii*) Each time a material instance is processed by a workflow step, a new step instance is created in the database to represent the activity. The step instance records the results of the workflow step (*e.g.*, measurements of length and sequence) and the conditions under which the step was carried out (*e.g.*, temperature and salinity). In this paper, we often say "step" instead of "step instance," and "material" instead of "material instance."

As a material is processed by a workflow, more-and-more step instances are created in the database, all associated with the same material. These steps constitute the material's event history. Workflow steps are not always successful, however, and earlier steps sometimes have to be repeated. Thus, the event history of a material may contain several different (though similar) versions of a step. Usually, the most recent version is of greatest interest to scientists, since it represents the most up-to-date results. LabBase uses special-purpose storage and access structures to rapidly retrieve most-recent results from the event history of each material [2].

Notice that as described above, the database schema depends on the workflow. For each kind of workflow step, there is a class in the database, and for each measurement made by the step, the class has an attribute. Consequently, workflow changes are reflected in the database as schema changes. In particular, as laboratory steps change, the corresponding classes also change. For instance, if scientists decide that a particular step should measure more properties, then attributes must be added to the corresponding class in the database. Likewise, if scientists add a new step to the workflow, then a new class is added to the database schema. If scientists split a complex step into a combination of smaller steps, then new classes are introduced into the schema to represent the smaller steps.

The data representation described above is *event oriented*. That is, information about a step is kept in one place, but information about a material is scattered among different steps. This provides a straightforward record of laboratory activity, but an awkward representation of materials. In particular, retrieving information about a material requires a detailed knowledge of laboratory workflow. For each property of a material, one must know what step(s) measured its value. Moreover, because workflows change constantly, a detailed knowledge of workflow changes and workflow history are also needed.

To alleviate these problems, the database provides a view that is *material oriented*, *i.e.*, in which information is associated with materials, not steps. In the database, observed values (*e.g.*, sequence, length, and mass) are attributes of *steps*; while in the view, they are attributes of *materials*. Using the view, an application programmer can retrieve the length of a DNA segment without knowing what step measured the length. In this way, the view isolates the application programmer from the details of workflow and workflow change.

Defining this view is not a straightforward matter. For one thing, the view definition depends on the workflow and its history. For another, different instances of the *same* kind of material can have *different* attributes in the view. For instance, segments of DNA may or may not have a length attribute, depending on whether or not they were processed by a step that measured their length. Thus, the attributes (or type) of a material depend on the *history* of the material, as well as its class. This rather dynamic feature reflects the flexibility demanded by workflow management. These issues are addressed in [2], where we introduce structures that allow the view to be defined *independently* of the workflow, so that the view definition does not have to be changed each time the workflow changes.

3   Benchmark Database Schema

Like the OO1 benchmark [5] and the Sequoia 2000 benchmark [19], our benchmark is independent of the data model provided by the DBMS. We therefore describe the database schema abstractly, using an extended entity relationship (EER) diagram [20]. An EER diagram is an ER diagram extended with is-a links. The database itself can be implemented in any number of ways, possibly as a relational database or as an object-oriented database.

As shown in Figure 1, the EER diagram has two levels (separated by a dashed line). The top level is abstract, and is a partial specification of an event-history model [2]. The second level is concrete, and represents the workflow in particular laboratory projects. The top-level is the same for all laboratory projects, while the bottom level changes from project to project. In fact, because of schema evolution, the bottom level also changes during the lifetime of a single project, possibly many times.

In the laboratory, materials are processed by experimental steps. The top level of the EER diagram thus has two entities: material and step. material has two attributes: name, a human-recognizable name; and state, a workflow state. Step has two attributes: who, the name of the user (or program) that

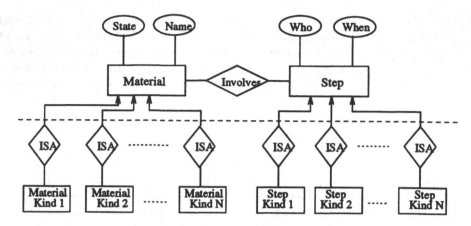

Fig. 1. An EER diagram for the benchmark schema

carried out the step; and **when**, the time and date at which the step was completed. Because of the **when** attribute, **step** data is historical. Each laboratory step involves at least one material, and each material is processed by at least one step. This is represented by the binary relation **involves**. Most queries in our benchmark require navigating between steps and materials via the **involves** relationship. The frequency of such queries arises because the database supports two mutually-dependent views of the data—a step-centered view, and a material-centered view—as described in Section 2. The **involves** relation allows data to be conveniently translated from one view to the other.

Different laboratory projects will involve different kinds of materials and different kinds of experimental steps. These appear as entities in the lower level of the ERR diagram. The two levels of the diagram are connected by is-a links. In object-oriented terms, each material kind is a subclass of **material** and inherits its two attributes, and each step kind is a subclass of **step** and inherits its two attributes. Each kind of material and step may also define its own attributes. The lower level of the EER diagram can be fleshed out in many different ways depending on the particular workflows being modeled. The benchmark provides a specific schema for this lower level [2]. It is a simplified version of schema used in production at the Genome Center.

In the rest of this paper, we adopt object-oriented terminology; we refer to entities as objects, where each object has a unique identifier; we refer to step kinds and material kinds as classes; and we say that objects are instances of classes.

4 Benchmark Database and Workload

The database for our benchmark is an event history or audit trail. We therefore need to provide a simple but realistic sequence of events, both to build the database and to serve as a workload for the benchmark. The issue of generating a realistic workload cannot be solved by generating a random sequence of simple events, as in TPC benchmarks. This would not capture the idea of materials flowing through a network of workflow stations. One solution would be to use a real database and a real workload from the Genome Center, generated during its day-to-day operations. We decided against this option because the resulting benchmark would be complex, hard to understand, and difficult to scale. Instead, our benchmark is based on a relatively simple workflow simulation [2]. This simulation models many of the important features encountered in real workflows at the Genome Center. For instance, the workflow has cycles, it has success and failure states, and it models multiple, co-operating production lines. As materials are processed by the workflow, each workflow activity produces a stream of database accesses, consisting largely of queries and inserts. These accesses are recorded as they arrive at the database, producing a *log* of database activity. Our benchmark is based on this log.

Starting from an empty database, the inserts in the log produce a constantly expanding database. Our benchmark monitors the performance of the DBMS as the database expands. Specifically, we perform measurements at three different database sizes: when the database is half the size of physical main memory, the same size, and twice the size. By defining measurement points in terms of memory size, the benchmark can be scaled up as memories grow. It is not hard to extend the benchmark to larger multiples of main memory, and we plan to do so in the near future. However, since this significantly increases the time required to run benchmark tests, we intentionally limited database size in this initial study.

At each database size, we identify an interval of 10,000 queries and updates from the database log. We augment each interval with a small number of report-generation queries, to simulate the contribution to the DBMS workload by administrative departments. The three augmented intervals then become three workloads, one for each database size. The derivation of these workloads from the database log is illustrated in Figure 2.

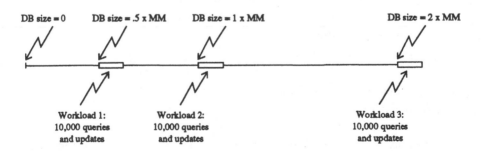

Fig. 2. The Derivation of Three Workloads from the Database Log

To generate the database log, we ran our workflow simulation against a version of LabBase that relies on ObjectStore for storage management. We allowed the simulation to continue until the file size of the database was slightly larger than 64Mbyte. We refer to the log resulting from this simulation run as the *initial log*. We then modified the initial log as follows:

• Based on periodic measurements of the size of the database file during the simulation run, we selected points within the log that correspond to database-file sizes of approximately 16Mbyte, 32Mbyte, and 64Mbyte. Since the benchmark machine has 32Mbyte of physical memory, these sizes are respectively 0.5, 1, and 2 times physical memory size.

• Starting at each of these three points in the log, we modified the subsequent sequence of 10,000 queries and updates. Specifically, we inserted queries to measure resource usage during execution of the log, and to measure resource usage for commits and for two read-only queries that simulate ad-hoc reporting activity. We also inserted queries to measure database size. We call each of the three modified sequences a *benchmark interval*.

• We removed all read-only queries that lay outside the benchmark intervals (in order to reduce the total amount of time needed to run the benchmark).

We call the result of the above modifications the *benchmark log*. The benchmark is run by executing LabBase with the benchmark log as input. Query output is saved in another file and compared between different benchmark runs to confirm consistent operation of the various versions of LabBase.

In more detail, the benchmark interval at each of the three database-file sizes consists of the following queries:

1. set baseline for resource usage
2. commit
3. get incremental resource usage
4. set baseline for resource usage
5. 10,000 queries and updates from the initial log
6. 2 report queries added to the log to simulate ad hoc queries
7. get incremental resource usage
8. set baseline for resource usage
9. commit
10. get incremental resource usage
11. get database size

In addition, at the start of the benchmark query stream, we inserted a single query to set the baseline resource usage. The benchmark thus records elapsed time, user cpu time, system cpu time, database size, and number of major page faults. All times are in seconds. Of these measurements, users will be most interested in elapsed time and database size. The other measurements are intended for database developers and debuggers.

5   Storage-Manager Comparisons

The purpose of our benchmark is to measure both the functional and the performance characteristics of DBMSs for managing workflow data. In the tests discussed here, we used several versions of the LabBase data server, which varied in storage management. The versions that we tested are:

1. OStore3—a version relying on ObjectStore (v3.0) [13] for storage management.
2. Texas.3—a version relying on the Texas storage manager (v0.3) [18] for storage management.
3. Texas.4—a version relying on the latest release (v0.4) of the Texas storage manager.
4. Texas.3+TC and Texas.4+TC— versions almost identical to Texas.3 and Texas.4 respectively, which use the same storage manager, but with additional object clustering implemented in client code.
5. Ostore3-mm, Texas.3-mm and Texas.4-mm—versions without any persistent storage management, and running entirely in main memory.

In a preliminary version of this paper we reported the results for Texas.3, but since then Texas.4 has been released. This new release employs a more efficient storage allocator that results in better data clustering and less internal fragmentation. In fact, the results for Texas.4, in terms of the elapsed time to run query 7, are comparable to those we obtained for Texas.3 with additional clustering, which clearly demonstrate the benefits of the new storage allocator. Although we conducted the same set of tests for both Texas.3 and Texas.4, some of the tests, such as Texas.4+TC and Texas.3-mm, gave similar results and did not lead to any new insights. Hence, they are not shown in Table 1. The complete set of test results can be found in [2]. Since much of the subsequent discussion applies to both Texas.3 and Texas.4, we often refer simply to Texas and its variants, Texas+TC and Texas-mm, without using version numbers.

The code running in the Ostore3-mm and Texas-mm tests was identical to that for the OStore3 and Texas tests, respectively, except that no persistent database was used. Technically, for the Ostore3-mm and Texas-mm tests all objects were allocated in the transient database. The consequence is that for Ostore3-mm, objects are allocated by `malloc`, whereas for Texas-mm the same allocator was used as for Texas and Texas+TC, since Texas uses its own version of `malloc` for both transient and persistent allocation.

ObjectStore and Texas present very similar interfaces to the programmer—their interface is essentially a persistent C++, in which C++ objects can be allocated in a persistent heap as well as in the familiar, transient heap. Both ObjectStore and Texas provide a distinguished mechanism for allocating objects on the persistent heap, but once an object is allocated all code that uses it can be oblivious of whether it is persistent or transient. The ObjectStore and Texas interfaces are so similar that out of approximately 11,000 lines of C++ code constituting the LabBase server, only a few hundred differ between the two storage managers. These differing sections are demarcated by precompiler directives (*e.g.*, `#ifdef`/`#endif` blocks.) Roughly speaking, the LabBase server implements the top level of the schema in Figure 1 (the part above the dashed line) directly in C++. Thus this part of the schema is compiled in. The lower level is implemented by making entries in a data dictionary, and is defined by database users at run time. The `involves` relation is implemented by keeping a (C++) pointer from each material instance to a list of pointers to those step instances that are related to the material by `involves`.

ObjectStore and Texas also both rely on pointer swizzling at page-fault time, as described in [18]. However, internally they are rather different. ObjectStore offers concurrent access with lock-based concurrency control implemented in a page server that mediates all access to the database.[3] Texas does not support concurrent access, and Texas programs access their database files directly.

Both the **OStore3** and **Ostore3-mm** versions used ObjectStore indexes. All the Texas versions used b-tree indexes supplied by the authors of the Texas storage manager (though not part of the standard Texas distribution).

5.1 Performance Comparison

The benchmark machines for the results reported here were Sun 4/50s (SPARC-station IPXs) running SunOS 4.1.*x*. The systems had 32Mbyte of main memory. The benchmark machine was not used for any other purpose during bench-marking, but the benchmarks were not run in single-user mode. For Texas the database file, the executable, and the log were allocated on one disk, while the system swap space was allocated on another. Because of licensing restrictions and the undesirability of disturbing our production ObjectStore-based applications, we kept the ObjectStore database file, log file, and page server on a separate machine, a SPARCstation 20. The ObjectStore cache file (an mmaped file used as temporary backing store by ObjectStore) was on the benchmark machine. We discuss the possible performance impact of these varying configurations later in this section. Table 1 summarizes the results for six different versions of the LabBase data server.

In each interval, query 7 measures resource usage for the 10,000 queries and updates from the initial log, plus the two additional queries that simulate ad hoc reporting queries. Query 11 measures database file size after a commit at the end of the benchmark interval.

At a nominal database size of approximately 0.5X main-memory size, all six versions of the LabBase data server consume similar resources, except for database-file size, which is greater in the Texas versions than in the OStore3 version. (Of course, database file size is not meaningful for the Ostore3-mm or Texas.4-mm versions.) The larger size of the Texas database file is due to a segregated allocation scheme that rounds object sizes up to approximately the

---

[3] Thus, when based on the ObjectStore storage manager, the LabBase server is what Carey et al. term a "client-level server" [3].

		Database Server Version					
		Persistent				Transient	
Intvl	Resource	OStore3	Texas.4	Texas.3+TC	Texas.3	Ostore3-mm	Texas.4-mm
0.5X	elapsed sec	1,424	1,474	1,469	1,402	1,384	1,471
	user cpu sec	1,381	1,452	1,449	1,385	1,364	1,450
	sys cpu sec	16	6	7	6	5	6
	majflt	329	571	468	397	463	683
	size (MB)	16.6	20.9	24.2	24.6	—	—
1X	elapsed sec	3,243	3,460	2,783	63,214	309,305	2,640
	user cpu sec	2,568	2,644	2,613	2,679	3,453	2,600
	sys cpu sec	137	83	15	2,958	20,981	8
	majflt	9,847	69,342	5,190	2,718,898	17,451,919	1,911
	size (MB)	33.8	41.5	48.2	48.8	—	—
2X	elapsed sec	7,057	n/a	n/a	n/a	n/a	n/a
	user cpu sec	4,711	n/a	n/a	n/a	n/a	n/a
	sys cpu sec	812	n/a	n/a	n/a	n/a	n/a
	majflt	153,742	n/a	n/a	n/a	n/a	n/a
	size (MB)	62.1	n/a	n/a	n/a	—	—

Table 1. Resource Usage for Six Storage-Management Schemes.

Elapsed time and user and system cpu were measured by SunOS's times (3V) function (system-V flavor). "majflt" was measured by getrusage (2), and is the number of "page faults requiring physical I/O" (i.e., major faults). All resource usage was measured at query 7, except for the size of database files, which was determined using stat (2V) at query 11. The column labeled "intvl" indicates a particular benchmark interval at 0.5, 1, or 2 times physical memory size.

nearest power of 2, and which for the object sizes in LabBase left a substantial proportion of allocated space unused.

Starting at a nominal database size of approximately 1X main-memory size all the Texas versions began to thrash, and performance decayed so quickly that it seemed unfruitful to allow the benchmark run to continue to the 2X benchmark interval. The data-server process, as observed by SunOS's ps (1), was almost continually in 'D' state (non-interruptible wait—presumably for disk I/O). The larger database size in the Texas versions (than in OStore3) cannot be the primary cause of the problem, because the number of hard page faults (majflt) measured at query 7 for OStore3 at the even larger file size at the 2X interval was only 153,742, as opposed to 2,718,898 for Texas.3 at the 1X interval. Even in the case of the more efficient Texas.4, there is an 8-fold increase in page faults as compared to OStore3 at the 1X interval. In our use of ObjectStore in previous implementations of the production version of LabBase, we saw the beginnings of thrashing behavior, so we employed ObjectStore's ability to assign objects to storage segments (instances of the os_segment class) in an attempt to achieve better locality of reference than would be achieved in a single persistent heap. The OStore3 implementation of LabBase uses four such segments, three of which contain relatively small amounts of frequently accessed data, and one of which contains a relatively large amount of infrequently accessed data.

To test the hypothesis that poor locality of reference was the chief cause of thrashing behavior in Texas, we ran the same data server as in OStore3, but without any persistent database, and consequently without the benefit of clustering based on the os_segment class; we called this test Ostore3-mm. To our surprise Ostore3-mm displayed far worse thrashing behavior than all the Texas versions, and we deemed it unfruitful (and infeasible) to continue the benchmark to the 2X interval. Seeking to understand why page-faulting behavior in Ostore3-mm was so much worse than in Texas, we analyzed the object sizes in Texas.3, and hypothesized that Texas's segregated storage allocator, with one exception, stored frequently-accessed objects in segments different from those storing rarely accessed objects. In other words, by accident Texas's allocation provided reasonable storage segmentation, with the exception of one putatively mis-allocated class of objects.

To test this hypothesis, we modified the Texas.3 code to pre-allocate extents of the putatively mis-allocated objects. (Texas does not presently offer a storage-segment mechanism.) The Texas.3+TC test uses this modified Texas.3 code. The results in Table 1 show that, at the 1X benchmark interval, paging activity is indeed substantially reduced, which resulted in better performance than both Texas.3 and Texas.4. However, as the size of the database continued to grow beyond the 1X interval, paging activity increased dramatically, with the result that we did not gather performance numbers for the 2X interval of the Texas.3 test. We are still seeking an explanation for this behavior.

We also ran the same data server as Texas.4 without any persistent database, in the test called Texas.4-mm. Because Texas.4-mm still relies on its own storage allocator for the transient heap, and in the absence of any commit overhead, this test displays performance at the 1X interval that is slightly superior to all other tests.

None of the measurements presented in Table 1 captures commit costs. The ObjectStore page server resided on a different machine from the LabBase data server during the benchmark OStore3 tests, and it was not feasible for us to relate resource usage in the ObjectStore page server to activities of a particular LabBase client because the server was also being used for production activities. Therefore the only meaningful figure we can report for commits is elapsed seconds, presented in Table 2. We report the results for Texas.4 only since the commit times for Texas.3 were inordinately high due to an inherent inefficiency that has now been fixed in Texas.4. (Commit times for Ostore3-mm and Texas.4-mm were of course 0, and are not shown.) It is interesting to observe that Table 2 shows that the commit times for the two systems depend on the amount of work committed. Clearly, in committing large amounts of work, OStore3 is more efficient than Texas.4 by almost a factor of two. Yet, Texas.4 performs as well as OStore3 for small amounts of work, and in fact outperforms it by the same factor at 1X main memory.

Intvl	Query	OStore3	Texas.4
0.5X	3	47	109
	10	8	11
1X	3	70	115
	10	21	12
2X	3	162	n/a
	10	22	n/a

Table 2. Elapsed Time for Commits (in seconds).

5.2 Functional Comparison

In contrast with commercial relational database management systems, there are huge differences in the functional and operational characteristics of today's object databases. Therefore a critical objective of our benchmark is to shed light on similarities and differences of such functional and operational characteristics. The interested reader is referred to [2] for a discussion of the similarities and differences between ObjectStore and the Texas Storage System. We compare the two systems along several dimensions: concurrency control, class libraries, tuning options, and database administration.

To summarize, our benchmark revealed significant differences among different storage managers and implementations of LabBase. The most notable difference between the storage managers was in facilities to control object allocation by storage segment, which critically affects performance of the benchmark application when the database size exceeds main-memory size. The benchmark also revealed significant differences in the time needed to perform commits in the two systems.

Acknowledgements: The authors gratefully acknowledge the support of the Whitehead Institute for Biomedical Research and the Whitehead/MIT Center for Genome Research for making this work possible. We also express our thanks to the developers of the Texas storage system.

References

1. T.L. Anderson, A.J. Berre, M. Mallison, H.H. Porter, and B. Schneider. The hypermodel benchmark. In *Proceedings of the International Conference on Extending Database Technology (EDBT)*, pages 317–331, Venice, Italy, March 1990.
2. A. Bonner, A. Shrufi, and S. Rozen. LabFlow-1: a database benchmark for high-throughput workflow management. Technical report, Department of Computer Science, University of Toronto, 1995. 53 pages. Available at ftp://db.toronto.edu/pub/bonner/papers/workflow/report.ps.gz.

3. M.J. Carey, D.J. DeWitt, M.J. Franklin, et al. Shoring up persistent applications. In *Proceedings of the ACM SIGMOD International Conference on Management of Data*, pages 383–394, Minneapolis, MN, May 1994.

4. M.J. Carey, D.J. DeWitt, and J.F. Naughton. The OO7 benchmark. Technical report, Computer Sciences Department, University of Wisconsin-Madison, January 1994. Available at `ftp://ftp.cs.wisc.edu/oo7/techreport.ps`.

5. R.G.G. Cattell. An engineering database benchmark. In [10], chapter 6, pages 247–281.

6. A. Chaudhri. An Annotated Bibliography of Benchmarks for Object Databases. *SIGMOD Record*, 24(1):50–57, March 1995.

7. *Communications of the ACM*, 34(11), November 1991. Special issue on the Human Genome Project.

8. D. Georgakopoulos, M. Hornick, and A. Sheth. An overview of workflow management: From process modeling to infrastructure for automation. *Journal on Distributed and Parallel Database Systems*, 3(2):119–153, April 1995.

9. Nathan Goodman. An object oriented DBMS war story: Developing a genome mapping database in C++. In Won Kim, editor, *Modern Database Management: Object-Oriented and Multidatabase Technologies*. ACM Press, 1994.

10. Jim Gray, editor. *The Benchmark Handbook for Database and Transaction Processing Systems*. Morgan Kaufmann, San Mateo, CA, 1991.

11. M. Hsu, Ed. Special issue on workflow and extended transaction systems. *Bulletin of the Technical Committee on Data Engineering (IEEE Computer Society)*, 16(2), June 1993.

12. Setrag Khoshafian and Marek Buckiewicz. *Introduction to Groupware, Workflow, and Workgroup Computing*. John Wiley & Sons, Inc., 1995.

13. Charles Lamb, Gordon Landis, Jack Orenstein, and Dan Weinreb. The ObjectStore database system. *Communications of the ACM*, 34(10):50–63, October 1991.

14. Allen S. Nakagawa. *LIMS: Implementation and Management*. Royal Society of Chemistry, Thomas Granham House, The Science Park, Cambridge CB4 4WF, England, 1994.

15. P. O'Neal. The set query benchmark. In [10], chapter 5, pages 209–245.

16. Steve Rozen, Lincoln Stein, and Nathan Goodman. Constructing a domain-specific DBMS using a persistent object system. In M.P. Atkinson, V. Benzaken, and D. Maier, editors, *Persistent Object Systems*, Workshops in Computing. Springer-Verlag and British Computer Society, 1995. Presented at POS-VI, Sep. 1994. Available at `ftp://genome.wi.mit.edu/pub/papers/Y1994/labbase-design.ps.Z`.

17. O. Serlin. The history of debit credit and the TPC. In [10], chapter 2, pages 19–117.

18. Vivek Singhal, Sheetal V. Kakkad, and Paul R. Wilson. Texas: an efficient, portable persistent store. In *Proceedings of the Fifth International Workshop on Persistent Object Systems (POS-V)*, San Minato, Italy, September 1992. Available at `ftp://cs.utexas.edu/pub/garbage/texaspstore.ps`.

19. M. Stonebraker, J. Frew, K. Gardels, and J. Meredith. The Sequoia 2000 storage benchmark. In *Proceedings of the ACM SIGMOD International Conference on Management of Data*, pages 2–11, Minneapolis, MN, May 1993.

20. T.J. Teorey, D. Yang, and J.P. Fry. A logical design methodology for relational databases using the extended entity-relationship model. *ACM Computing Surveys*, 18:197–222, June 1986.

Esprit Projects

Adaptive Parallel Query Execution in DBS3[*]

Luc Bouganim[(1,2)], Benoît Dageville[(2)], Patrick Valduriez[(1)]

(1) INRIA, Rocquencourt	(2) Bull OSS
78153 Le Chesnay, France	38432 Echirolles, France
Luc.Bouganim@inria.fr	B.Dageville@frec.bull.fr
Patrick.Valduriez@inria.fr	

1. Introduction

DBS3 (Database System for Shared Store) [1] is a parallel database system for shared-memory multiprocessors [7]. It has been implemented on an Encore Multimax (10 processors) and on a Kendal Square Research KSR1 (72 processors).

In a shared-memory architecture, each processor has uniform access to the entire database through a global main memory. Thus, the *parallel scheduler*, which allocates processors to the query's operations, has much freedom for balancing the query load onto processors. However, query response time can be hurt by several barriers which must be overcome by the scheduler: start-up time of parallel operations, interference and poor load balancing among the processors due to skewed data distribution.

In DBS3, we use static relation partitioning to reduce interference and for compile-time query parallelization and dynamic allocation of processors to operations, independent of the degree of partitioning, to control start up time and load balancing.

In this paper, we present the adaptive parallel query execution model of DBS3. A simple analysis outlines three important factors that influence the behavior of our model: skew factor, degree of parallelism and degree of partitioning. Then we reports on experiments with the 72-node KSR1 version of DBS3 with the relations cached in main memory. This main memory assumption is not a restriction of the model but a constraint of our KSR1 configuration which has a single disk.

2. Parallel Execution Model

In DBS3, the compilation phase takes an ESQL [5] query which is optimized [6] and parallelized [2]. The parallel execution plan produced by the compiler is expressed in Lera-par [3] and captures the operations and their control.

A Lera-par program is represented by a dataflow graph whose nodes are *operators* (like filter, join or map) and edges are *activators*. An activator denotes either a tuple (data activation) or a control message (control activation). In either case, when an operator receives an activation, the corresponding sequential operation is executed. Therefore, each activation acts as a sequential unit of work.

Lera-par's storage model is statically partitioned. Relations are partitioned by hashing on one or more attributes, and relation fragments are distributed onto disks. To obtain intra-operation parallelism, each operation of the execution plan, whose input is a partitioned relation, gets as many instances as fragments. *Pipelined* execution is expressed by using data activation between a producer operation and a consumer

* This work has been partially funded by the CEC under ESPRIT project IDEA.

operation, which can then operate in parallel as soon as the consumer gets activated
To manage activations, a FIFO queue is associated to each operation instance. There
are two kinds of queues. A triggered queue is associated to an operation triggered by a
control activation. It receives only one activation which starts the associated operation
(Figure 1). A pipelined queue is associated to an operation which receives one operand
in a pipeline fashion (Figure 2). In this case, each activation conveys one tuple and the
queue will receive as many activations as pipelined tuples.

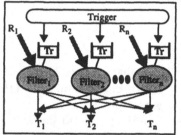

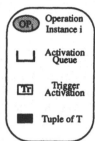

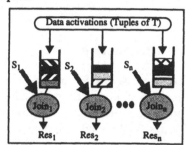

Figure 1: Triggered operation   *Figure 2: Pipelined operation*

In a shared-memory architecture, it is possible to decouple the implementation of the
parallel execution model from thread allocation. The typical thread allocation strategy
would assign a single thread per operation instance. Instead, we allocate a pool of
threads for the entire operation, independent of the operation instances (and of the
degree of partitioning). This is done by allocating the queues of an operation's
instances in a shared-memory segment so all the threads of a pool can access all
queues associated with the operation. Therefore, the threads can execute code for any
activation in order to increase load balancing.

This thread allocation strategy reduces the major barriers of parallel query execution
by offering several means to adapt to the execution context. First, we can define the
degree of parallelism independent of the degree of partitioning. Second, by controlling
the number of threads per pool, we can achieve better balancing of CPU power
between operations. Finally, each thread can dynamically choose in which queue to
consume activations which should yields good load balancing.

The default mode of queue consumption is random, i.e. the thread randomly chooses
one queue among the non empty ones associated with its operation. Thus, thread
utilization is maximum as long as activations are available. However, at operation end,
when there is no more activation, threads become idle as they terminate until the last
thread completes processing its activation.

Let us now consider an operation execution with a activations and n threads. P
indicates the average processing time for an activation. In the worst case, one thread
will consume the last activation when all other threads have terminated. During the
processing of this activation, one thread is active and thread utilization is minimum.

Let T_{ideal} be the ideal execution time for the operation, when all threads complete
simultaneously, and T_{worst} be the worst time. To compute v, the overhead of the worst
time, we have the following equation for T_{worst}:

$$T_{worst} = (1 + v) \times T_{ideal} = (1 + v) \times \left(\frac{a \times P}{n} \right)$$

The worst case scenario can be seen with two phases. In the first phase, all activations but the most expensive one are processed. Let P_{max} be the time to process the last activation (i.e. the most expensive one), the execution time for the first phase is:
$((a \times P) - P_{max})/n$:
The second phase corresponds to the processing of the last activation whose time is P_{max}. Thus, we can compute v as follows:
$$v \leq \frac{P_{max}}{P} \times \frac{(n-1)}{a}$$
This equation exhibits that the overhead depends on three factors: skew factor (P_{max}/P), degree of parallelism (n) and number of activations (a). For the latter, we have two interesting cases, depending on whether a is high or low:

The number of activation is high. This case corresponds to a pipelined operation with lots of tuples. a is then equal to the cardinality of the pipelined relation. Thus, v is quite small and the execution time of the operation is close to T_{ideal}.

The number of activation is low. This case corresponds to a triggered operation. The overhead due to skew can then be quite serious. A solution is to use a consumption strategy that reduces this overhead, like LPT (Longest Processing Time First) which processes the most expensive activations with highest priority.

3. Experiments

In these experiments, we use two relations of the Wisconsin benchmark, partitioned based on hashing. We use two Lera-par execution plan: IdealJoin which indicates a parallel join where both operands are partitioned on the join attribute in the same number of buckets, and AssocJoin where one operand must be dynamically repartitioned before the parallel join.

We have created many databases for which we have varied the tuple distribution within fragments. To determine fragment cardinality, we use a Zipf function [8] which can model skewed data distributions varying a factor between 0 (no skew) and 1 (high skew). Each database has two relations A and B' of 100K and 10K tuples, respectively, partitioned in 200 fragments. The query is executed on 10 threads.

In the case of AssocJoin, B' is redistributed, so 10K tuples move through the pipeline. The execution time measured is constant whatever the skew (Figure 3). Even in the worst case, the maximum deviation is small (3%). Thus, this experiment shows that we obtain an ideal execution time, independent of the skew factor.

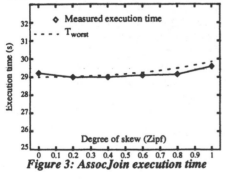

Figure 3: AssocJoin execution time

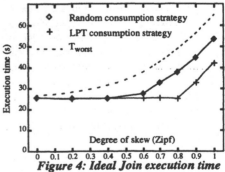

Figure 4: Ideal Join execution time

IdealJoin is a triggered operation. Thus, the number of activations is equal to the number of operation instances. Since the relation has 200 fragments, each fragment is relatively small which yields good load balancing (less than 2% overhead with respect to the ideal time). The inflection after 0.8 is due to the execution time of the longest activation. This is because after 0.8, the execution time of this activation is higher than the ideal time of the whole operation. Even if this activation is processed first (LPT), the operation response time is equal to the execution time of this first activation.

4. Conclusion

The barriers to parallel query execution are start-up time of parallel operations, interference and poor load balancing among the processors due to skewed data distribution. In this paper, we have described how these problems are addressed in DBS3, a shared-memory database system implemented on a 72-node KSR1 multiprocessor.

Our solution combines the advantages of static and dynamic partitioning. We use static partitioning of relations to reduce interference and dynamic allocation of processors to operations to reduce start-up time and improve load balancing. A major advantage of this solution is to be able to deal efficiently with skew by allowing each thread to dynamically choose which operation's instance it will execute. A performance analysis on our prototype with databases of the Wisconsin benchmark confirm these results.

More information on this work can be found in *http://rodin.inria.fr/bouganim*.

References

1   B.Bergsten, M. Couprie, P. Valduriez, "Prototyping DBS3, a shared-memory parallel database system". *Int. Conf. on Parallel and Distributed Information Systems*, Florida, USA, December 1991.

2   P. Borla-Salamet, C. Chachaty, B. Dageville, "Compiling Control into Database Queries for Parallel Execution Management". *Int. Conf. on Parallel and Distributed Information Systems*, Florida, USA, December 1991.

3   C. Chachaty, P. Borla-Salamet, M. Ward, "A Compositional Approach for the Design of a Parallel Query Processing Language", *Int. Conf. on Parallel Architectures and Language Europe*, Paris, France, June 1992.

4   B. Dageville, P. Casadessus, P. Borla-Salamet, "The Impact of the KSR1 AllCache Architecture on the Behaviour of the DBS3 Parallel DBMS", *Int. Conf. on Parallel Architectures and Language Europe*, Athens, Greece, July 1994.

5   G. Gardarin, P. Valduriez, "ESQL2, an Extended SQL2 with F-logic Semantics.", *IEEE Int. Conf. on Data Engineering*, Phoenix, Arizona, February 1992.

6   R. Lanzelotte, P. Valduriez, M. Zait, M. Ziane, "Industrial-Strength Parallel Query Optimization: issues and lessons", *Information Systems*, Vol. 19, No. 4, 1994.

7   P. Valduriez, "Parallel Database Systems: open problems and new issues.", *Int. Journal on Distributed and Parallel Databases*, Vol. 1, No. 2, 1993.

8   G. K. Zipf, *Human Behavior and the Principle of Least Effort: An Introduction to Human Ecology*, Reading, MA, Addison-Wesley, 1949.

IRO-DB : Making Relational and Object-Oriented Database Systems Interoperable[*]

Peter Fankhauser[1], Béatrice Finance[2], Wolfgang Klas[1]

[1] GMD-IPSI
Integrated Publication and Information
Systems Institute
Dolivostrasse 15
64293 Darmstadt - GERMANY

[2] Université de Versailles
Laboratoire PRiSM
45 Avenue des Etats Unis
78000 Versailles - FRANCE

email : fankhaus@darmstadt.gmd.de, Beatrice.Finance@prism.uvsq.fr, klas@darmstadt.gmd.de

1. Introduction

With the gradual shift from mainframe architectures to highly interconnected distributed architectures nowadays relevant information is spread over a large number of independent databases. These databases are *heterogeneous*, that is, they model their information with differences in data model, structure, and semantics, and they are *autonomous*, that is, they can independently change.

This paper presents the ESPRIT project IRO-DB (Interoperable Relational and Object-Oriented Databases -ESPRIT-III P8929)[3], which aims at the provision of appropriate tools to achieve interoperability between such pre-existing databases. In Section 2, we present IRO-DB user functionality focusing on the support of schema integration and the application programming interface. In Section 3, we give an overview of the IRO-DB architecture. In Section 4, we summarize the current state of implementation, and outline the further developments planned.

2. IRO-DB user functionality

A federated system [5] is composed of a collection of heterogeneous local databases where means are provided for shared access, without loosing the control over their data and without re-engineering their DBMS and applications. To share data, each participant exports all or part of its data schemas. Then, local information is shared through integrated schemas which allow users to get information stored and managed by local databases in a transparent way. Data schema and semantic heterogeneity of existing databases are overcome by using a common interchange data model. As pointed out in [5] an object-oriented data model can cover object-oriented and relational, as well as hierarchical and network modeling concepts. The data model chosen in IRO-DB is the one proposed by the Object Database Management Group (ODMG) [1] which is an extension of the OMG model for databases [4].

2.1. Schema integration

Using ODMG as a common interchange model only overcomes the data model heterogeneity between pre-existing databases. The local schemas still can model

---

[*] This work is initiated and partially supported by the European IRO-DB ESPRIT project. The project is developed in cooperation with GMD,FAW,GOPAS, IBERMATICA, EDS, EURIWARE, INTRASOFT and O2 Technology. PRiSM acts as a subcontractor of both Euriware and EDS.

overlapping or related information with differences in naming, scaling, structural granularity, and level of abstraction. The goal of schema integration is to merge the export schemas in such a way that this information is represented in a uniform way, as if there is only one integrated database. To accomplish this task, overlapping schema portions have to be identified, and appropriate transformations for their homogenization have to be specified. Furthermore, to allow for uniquely updating external data through the integrated schema, the transformations should avoid information loss.

Specifying such transformations intellectually is a highly burdensome and error-prone task. For this reason, we develop an Integrator's Workbench (IW) which assists database designers in constructing integrated schemas in a declarative way. It is based on an integration methodology [2], which specifically copes with heterogeneity arising from modeling overlapping information with different structural granularity. Figure 1 gives an example of such a difference, where once the *producer* of a *Part* is attached as a direct attribute in the first local schema, whereas in the second schema there exists a separate class *Company* for modeling a producer. On the other hand, the master production schedule *Emps* is modeled as an individual class in the first local schema, whereas its attributes *date* and *qty* are attached directly to *Parts* in the second schema.

IW now supports the integration of these two schemas as follows. Using a graphical schema editor, overlapping or related schema portions can be identified by simple selection. IW then automatically checks whether the selected portions can be integrated, and generates an integrated schema together with the appropriate transformations to instantiate it from data received from the local schemas. For the two local schemas shown in Figure 1, it suffices to identify the corresponding attributes *id*, *date*, *qty*, and *producer* (corresponding with *name*). On this basis, IW automatically selects the remaining portions of the schemas, asks the user whether *Part* in schema 1 shall also correspond to *Part* in schema 2, and generates an integrated schema, which can represent data received from the local schemas without information loss. In addition, the mappings to the underlying schemas are generated.

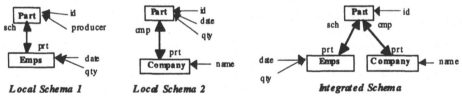

Local Schema 1   *Local Schema 2*   *Integrated Schema*

Figure 1: Example of an integrated schema without information loss.

2.2. Application Programming Interface

As stated in [1], "rather than providing only a high-level language such as SQL for data manipulation, an OODBMS transparently integrates database capability with the application language. This transparency obviates the need to explicitly copy and translate data between database and programming language representations, and supports substantial performance advantages through data caching applications". IRO-DB constitutes a Federated Object-Oriented Database System mediating between heterogeneous databases and integrated applications. It offers an application programming interface (API) based on ODMG proposal, called OML (Object Manipulation Language) which contains OQL embedded queries. OQL is an associative query language, extended with the object-oriented paradigm. OQL supports methods, complex structures and path traversals among relationships.

In IRO-DB, user interoperable applications are defined using OML. An OML program refers to the integrated schema. Figure 2 presents an OML/C++ user function defined on top of IRO-DB. The OQL query retrieves the "parts" identifiers which have been built after 1996 and their associated "emps" 1-1 relationship. The iterator is used to iterate over the result collection. Even if the "qty" property has not been retrieved for each "emps", it is possible to get this information by dereferencing the "ident" information. At the end of the program, the total quantity is printed.

```
void consult () {
        Set<Struct<Ref<PART>, Ref<EMPS>>> result;
        iterator<result> m;
        int sum = 0;
        OQL (result,"select struct( ref: p, ident: p.emps) from p in parts
                        where p.upd_date ≥ "01/01/96")
        m = result ->create_iterator (forward);
        While m->next() != NIL do sum := sum + m->next().ident->qty;
        cout << sum; }
```

Figure 2 : OML/C++ example.

To manage such a program, IRO-DB provides many services such as the global query processor to deal with OQL query against an integrated schema, and the interoperable object manager to deal with accesses and method calls against integrated objects. These two important services are responsible for delegating integrated object accesses to the appropriate remote databases.

3. IRO-DB Architecture

In this section we describe the overall architecture of IRO-DB. The architecture is organized in three layers as represented in Figure 3 [3].

At the *interoperable layer*, object definition facilities stand for specifying integrated schemas, which are integrated views of the federated databases. Views and export schemas are stored in a data dictionary. Object manipulation facilities include an embedding of OQL in the OML/C++ user language and modules to decompose global queries in local

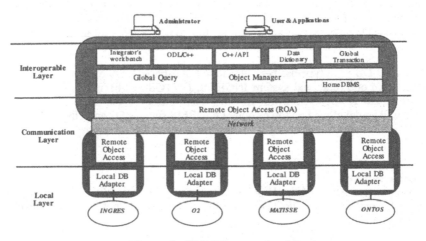

Figure 3 : IRO-DB general architecture.

ones (global query processor) and to control global transactions. Object definition and manipulation facilities are built upon the Home OODBMS. In IRO-DB, a tool called the *integrator workbench* is offered to help the database administrator in designing his/her integrated view.

The *communication layer* implements object-oriented remote data access services through the remote object access (ROA) modules, both on clients and servers. The system follows the standards for open system interconnection. Therefore, a client-(multi)server application protocol is the central component of the architecture, around which other components are organized. This protocol is a specialization of the RDA protocol for object-oriented databases. The external interface follows the SQL Access Group Call Level Interface recommendations [6], but extend it to handle objects.

The *local layer* is composed of a local database adapter. The local database adapter provides functionality to make a local system able to answer OQL queries on an abstraction of a local schema in term of ODMG schema (export schema). It manages the mapping between a local schema data types to the ODMG data types. It maps object identifiers and is responsible to evaluate OQL queries on the local site.

4. Conclusion

The functionality of IRO-DB can be summarized as follows:
- IRO-DB provides the ODMG interface at all product layers, i.e., at the interoperable layer, at the communication layer, and at the local layer. The benefit of using an upcoming standard is the foreseeable availability of ODMG-compliant interfaces for many commercial database management systems and as such to provide portability and reusability of applications.
- The Integrator Workbench offers design support for the definition of the integrated views derived from local database schemas which includes resolving of the various kinds of heterogeneities between existing databases, merging of data, and code generation for the integrated views.
- The C++/OML interface of IRO-DB transparently integrates heterogeneous database system services with the application programming language making it easy to use for application programmers.
- IRO-DB is a complete system providing access transparency to heterogeneous databases. It provides global query processing, global transaction management, object management, remote access to the existing databases, and local database adapters providing ODMG interfaces for local database systems.

A first IRO-DB prototype has been developed. It is based on one object-oriented system MATISSE and one relational system INGRES. ONTOS has been selected for this first prototype as the Home OODBMS. In the second phase of the project Local Database Adapters will be developed on top of other OODBMS such as O2 and ONTOS.

Acknowledgments:
IRO-DB is a joint effort of the IRO-DB consortium partners. Without the intensive and fruitful collaboration of the IRO-DB team the system would not be in its development stage as it is now.

References

[1] Cattell R.,"Object Databases:The ODMG-93 Standard", Book, Morgan &Kaufman, 1993.

[2] Fankhauser P., M. Kracker, E. Neuhold, "Semantic vs. Structural Resemblance of Classes", Special SIGMOD Record, issue on semantic issues in Multibase Systems, Vol. 20, n°4, ACM Press, 1991.

[3] Gardarin G. and al., "IRO-DB : A Distributed System Federating Object and Relational Databases", Object-oriented Multibase Systems, O. Bukhres and A. Elmagarmid Ed., Prentice Hall, 1995.

[4] Object Management Group, "Object Services Architecture", OMG document N° 92.8.4, OMG Ed., Framingham, USA, August 1992.

[5] Sheth A.P., Larson J.A, "Federated Database Systems for Managing Distributed, Heterogeneous and Autonomous Databases", ACM computing surveys, vol (22):3, 1990.

[6] "Data Management : SQL Call Level Interface (CLI), Snapshot, X/Open with SQL Access Group, X/Open Company Ltd.

Object Query Services for Telecommunication Networks

Jérôme Fessy[1], Yann Lepetit[2], Philippe Pucheral[1]

(1) Université de Versailles
45, avenue des Etats-Unis
78035 Versailles Cedex
e-mail: <Firstname.Lastname>@prism.uvsq.fr

(2) CNET
Route de Trégastel
22301 Lannion
e-mail: lepetit@lannion.cnet.fr

1. Introduction

For the time being, telecommunication networks are based on different standards, each of which adressing a specific purpose: provisioning of basic communication services (i.e., voice, data), network supervision and management, provisioning of added value services (i.e., free phone, credit card, mobile, videotext, web). This leads to a bad integration of new software and hardware technologies, multiplication of heterogeneous tools, bad network interoperability preventing to build sophisticated composed services and bad flexibility preventing to introduce easily new services.

To cope with these issues, the world-wide TINA consortium (grouping the main telecommunication operators and manufacturers) is defining a common Telecommunication Information Networking Architecture that will enable efficient introduction, delivery and management of telecommunications and networks services [1]. The TINA architecture is based on the ISO Open Distributed Processing (ODP) standard [7] which provides a general framework to design and engineer distributed networks and will capitalize on object oriented technology provided by OMG [8]. Future telecommunication networks, called Information Networks, will merge within this same unified architecture the different specialized networks already used by telecom operators. They pave the way to "information highways".

Information Networks increase the need to manage data shared by various applications like management services or communication services. To serve this purpose, France Telecom/CNET is contributing to TINA [2] to propose a data management framework for Information Networks. This work is the starting point for a join experiment from CNET and PRiSM laboratories on dedicated query services as a TINA auxiliary project.

Section 2 of this paper introduces the TINA requirements in terms of data management and query facilities. Section 3 presents the ODP viewpoints of the data management framework. Finally, Section 4 sketches the future industrial exploitation of this work.

2. Data Management Requirements in TINA

Data management is highly relevant for TINA. For example, Telecommunication Management Networks (TMN) manage entities like pieces of software or transmission devices. These entities are grouped in management information bases queried with telecom query facilities (CMIS: Common Management Information Service [5]). Within value added networks, many databases are also needed to store service information (e.g., credit card number, routing information or subscriber profile). Finally, new multimedia services based on a web approach will also require data management facilities. If these data management needs seem classical, the requirements imposed by the telecommunication environment are not: specialized telecom query languages, wide area distribution spanning countries, big number of fine grain data, federation and interworking with legacy telecom databases and real time constraints.

In the sequel, we call *Object Base* a group of objects which can be queried within the same querying space. Objects belonging to an Object Base can be either *Data Objects* (i.e., information chunks) or *Computational Objects* (i.e., application objects providing services accessible through interfaces). Queries can be expressed with classical or telecom query languages: OQL, SQL2,CMIS, X500 query. Object Bases can be managed by conventional DBMSs as well as by dedicated Query Managers.

3. ODP Viewpoints of the Data Management Framework

The ODP Model [7] describes a distributed system with five viewpoints: (i) the *enterprise* viewpoint is concerned with the definition of strategic and overall requirements of a system, (ii) the *information* viewpoint focuses on the conceptual aspect of a system, without bearing in mind its realization, (iii) the *computational* viewpoint represents the distributed system as seen by application programmers (applications are seen as computational objects providing interfaces), (iv) the *engineering* viewpoint is the concern of the operating systems and communications experts and (v) the *technology* viewpoint focuses on the technical components from which a system is built. We present below the data management framework which mainly deals with the information, computational and engineering ODP viewpoints.

3.1 Information viewpoint

Object Bases are modeled as Information Bases in accordance with the TMN approach. No restriction is placed on their representation in a real system (this choice is done at the computational level), on the means to manipulate them (query languages) and on the life time of their objects (persistent or transient). The semantics of Information Bases (conceptual schema) is defined with an extended version of the ISO GDMO specification language [6].

3.2 Computational viewpoint

An Object base is a group (TINA computational concept) of queryable objects (object data or computational objects) handled by an Object Base Manager. An Object Base Manager can be a DBMS, an OMG query manager as well as an ISO/ODMA multiple object request server [4]. The application objects using an Object Base rely on the services that the Object Base offers at interfaces and on the Object Base query language(s).

Interfaces: Several interface definition languages can be used: IDL from OMG, IDL from TINA (multiple interface objects). Queries are transmitted through these interfaces with location and access transparencies. Several query languages profiles will be provided: OQL and SQL for classical data management needs and CMIS for telecom needs. The long term objective is to promote a convergence between them.

Federation: The wide area distribution of our networks leads to partition Object Bases into autonomous Local Object Bases and Global Object Bases managed by federated managers. A special case of partitionning is the federation of standard DBMSs and real-time data managers providing reduced query facilities.

Transparencies: As any ODP computational interface, Object Base interfaces can be characterized by properties, such as Quality of Service or distribution transparencies. Programmers only express qualitative requirements (timing, performance, distribution hiding, security...) and are relieved from implementing the corresponding mechanisms. The query interfaces should provide the mandatory location and access transparencies.

Object base trading: The trader is an enhanced directory object enabling a client computational object to get interface references provided by server computational objects. In our context, it should enable to ask for an Object Base service (Object Base name, query language profile, ...). Assume two home Object Bases in a mobile network, one managing the French subscribers profiles while the other manages the English subscribers profiles. Depending on service properties (subscriber Universal Personal Number), the trader transparently selects the right interface.

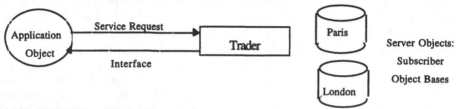

3.3 Engineering Viewpoint

The engineering viewpoint of TINA is based on a Distributed Processing Environment (DPE), that allows objects to advertise services through a registration process and allows other objects to access these services through a binding process. DPE can be seen as a specialization of the OMG CORBA platform [8] which provides engineering mechanisms to support the distribution of computational objects: IDL compilers and a communication mechanism (proxy, skeleton and locators), called Object Request Broker (ORB), by which objects interact. TINA implies the adjunction of trading services, some ODP transparencies and, in our context, a Telecom Oriented Query Service designed starting from OMG Object Query Service (OQS) proposals [9]. OQS provides a basic framework to manage distributed queries on an OMG platform. It is composed of two main types of engineering objects:

- The *query manager* which provides query interfaces to application objects. Queries are transmitted as string and results can be either a value transmitted back or the reference of a collection of queryable objects.

- The *collections* which can only be sequencially scanned and the *queryable collections* which can be queried through SQL or OQL.

The query management in a Telecom environment introduces specific requirements. First, the collections are managed by heterogeneous data managers like standard DBMSs supporting full query facilities and real-time collection managers supporting reduced query facilities. Real-time collection managers can be built on top of basic Object Managers like real-time DBMS engines, object managers or file systems. Second, certain query managers must support telecom query languages (as ISO/ODMA object request server). To deal with these requirements, query managers must provide common support to OQL,CMIS queries and must federate heterogeneous collection managers. Hence we propose a generic Telecom Query manager architecture pictured hereafter.

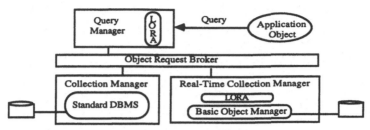

The major component of this architecture is a library of operators providing basic query facilities (e.g., filtering, join, path traversal) on collections of objects, independently of the physical storage of the collection extents. This library, called LORA (Language for Object Retrieval and Activation) [3], can be seen as a target executable complex object algebra for any query optimizer. Each collection manager exports some IDL interfaces and some associated services: objects, collections or queryable collections. A distributed query issued from an application object is decomposed by the query manager into sub-queries, each of which directed to a collection manager. If a sub-query is directed to a real-time collection manager and is beyond the capability of the basic object manager, the sub-query can be locally completed thanks to LORA. LORA can also be used by the query manager to aggregate the results of all sub-queries.

4 Conclusion

This paper provides an overview of data management requirements for future Information Networks. To match some of these requirements, a dedicated Telecom Object Query Service is being designed by CNET and PRiSM laboratories. During the next three years, a pre-industrial prototype of this query service will be realized as a TINA data auxiliary project on behalf of the CNET. The main waited results are a first validation of the data management framework proposed for TINA and a technical and practical skill enabling to derive later an industrial version of our prototype.

Acknowledgments

Special thanks are due to G. Gardarin and B. Finance for their contribution to this work.

References

[1] W.J. Barr, T. Boyd, Y. Inoue, "*The TINA initiative*" IEEE Communications Magazine, March 93.

[2] Y. Lepetit, F. Dupuy "*Data management in an ODP-conformant information networking architecture*", 4th TINA workshop, L'aquila, September 93.

[3] G. Gardarin, F. Machuca, P. Pucheral, "*OFL: A Functional Execution Model for Object Query Languages*", Proc. of the ACM SIGMOD Int. Conf. on Management of Data, San Jose, USA, May 1995.

[4] ISO/SC21/WG4/ N2151 "*Open Distributed Management Architecture: Management of event distribution and Multiple Object Requests*", Draft, May 95.

[5] ISO/IEC 9595 and CCITT/X710 "*Common Management Information Service: CMIS*", 1991.

[6] ISO/IEC 10165-4 and CCITT/X722 "*Guideline for the Definition of Managed Objects: GDMO*", 1992.

[7] ISO/IEC JTC1/SC 21 n 7524, "*Reference model of ODP Part 2 : Descriptive model*", Working document, February 1994.

[8] Object Management Group, "*The Common Object Request Broker: Architecture and Specification*", report 9305089, May 93.

[9] Object Management Group, "*Object Query Service specifications*", Itasca, Objectivity, Ontos, O2, Servio, Sunsoft, Sybase, Taligent, January 95.

Database Design

Accommodating Integrity Constraints During Database Design

Dimitris Plexousakis[1] and John Mylopoulos[2]

[1] Department of Computing and Information Sciences, Kansas State University,
Manhattan, KS 66506, USA. E-mail: dimitris@cis.ksu.edu
[2] Department of Computer Science University of Toronto, Toronto, Ont. M5S 1A4,
Canada. E-mail: jm@ai.toronto.edu

Abstract. We address the problem of maintaining the integrity of large knowledge bases using a compile-time transaction modification technique. The novelty of the approach lies in the adaptation of ideas from Artificial Intelligence (AI) planning research. Starting with the observation that solutions to the frame and ramification problems can be used during database transaction design time, we propose an integrity maintenance technique that modifies transaction specifications by incorporating into them conditions necessary of the constraints' satisfaction. Additions to the transactions' postconditions whose effect is to maintain the integrity constraints, are generated from a set of transaction specifications. Thus, the implications of constraints are realized by the transaction specifier and the effort of having to prove transaction safety is saved, since it is guaranteed by the correctness of the generation process.

1 Introduction

Integrity constraints specify the valid states of a data or knowledge base as well as its allowable state transitions [7]. Structural integrity constraints express properties of the data model used for representing knowledge. Semantic integrity constraints on the other hand, are user-defined and express properties of the domain being modeled. The maintenance of semantic integrity constitutes a major performance bottleneck in database management systems. The majority of commercial products do not provide but for the enforcement of very limited types of constraints. The maintenance of general constraints becomes the responsibility of the user submitting transactions to the database. In large, semantically rich knowledge bases the problem becomes even harder due to the large numbers of constraints and due to implicit updates caused by the presence of deductive rules. Compile-time processing of constraints and transactions aims at reducing the run-time cost associated with the enforcement of constraints, and is, in our view, a promising avenue for achieving acceptable performance.

The problem of integrity maintenance has received considerable attention in the literature of the past two decades. Most proposed techniques for integrity maintenance rely on monitoring by a generic application-independent program that verifies that updates do not violate semantic constraints [20],[15], [3], [10], [5], [22], [31], [24]. Another popular approach is based on maintenance by transactions [30], [8], [14], [4], [11]. The former technique relieves the user from the burden of implementing database transactions in a way such that no constraint is violated. The latter requires that the specification of updating transactions is given. Transactions are then modified so that database integrity constraints are guaranteed to hold in any executable sequence of transactions.

In our earlier work [22],[24] we presented a compile-time simplification method for knowledge bases, where integrity constraints, specified in a many-sorted temporal assertion language [18],[23], are specialized and simplified with respect to the anticipated transactions. In this paper, we undertake a dual approach, namely compile-time transaction modification in the context of knowledge bases containing (temporal) integrity constraints and deductive rules. In particular, we examine how transactions specified by means of *precondition-postcondition* pairs, can be modified so that the constraints they - directly or indirectly - affect are guaranteed not to be violated in the state resulting from transaction execution. Specifying database transaction by means of pre- and post-conditions, permits the database designer to express *what* the effect of transactions should be and not *how* this effect should be accomplished. Database transaction specifications, should be given in a formal notation that possesses both notational suitability and the capacity of supporting formal treatment. The formal specification language should be accompanied by the appropriate machinery for proving properties of specifications. We choose first-order (temporal) logic as the language for expressing transaction pre/post-conditions, constraints and rules. We address the problem of proving integrity maintenance by relating it to that of reasoning about actions [9] and elaborate on the impact that the *frame problem* [17] and *ramification problem* [6] have in transaction specifications.

In the majority of the existing methods for integrity constraint maintenance by transaction modification, the frame and ramification problems have either been ignored or bypassed by means of implicit assumptions that state that "nothing but what is explicitly declared to change in the update procedure does". Section 5 addresses the inadequacies of existing methods regarding the frame problem. Given a set of transaction specifications, the problem of succinctly stating that "nothing else changes" except the aspects of the state explicitly specified, has been called the *frame problem*. The *ramification* problem amounts to devising a way to avoid having to specify indirect effects of actions explicitly. Several attempts to solve these problems have appeared in the AI planning literature of the recent years. [13] presents a solution to the frame problem with application to database updates. The solution consists of systematically deriving a set of *successor-state* axioms that completely describe how *fluents*[3] can change truth value as a result of some action taking place. These axioms formulate closed-world assumptions for actions. A syntactic generator of successor-state axioms in the presence of binary constraints and stratified definitions of non-primitive fluents is proposed in [21]. We relate this solution to the problem of integrity maintenance. [1] and [2] show why the frame problem becomes particularly acute in object-oriented specifications where transactions are inherited and specialized from superclasses to subclasses. The arguments presented therein apply directly to the specification of database transactions in databases. The effects of rule evaluation or firing have to be accounted for and checked against integrity constraints. Moreover, transaction specifications can be specialized from superclasses to subclasses and conjoined to form complex transactions. The effects of specialized or synthesized transactions must be precisely characterized. To the best of our knowledge, there has not been any previous attempt to link the ramification problem with that of proving safety of transactions. In fact, a

---

[3] Fluents are predicates whose truth value may change from state to state [17].

solution of the ramification problem can suggest a strategy for integrity maintenance: transform the specifications of transactions to embody implications of constraints (these may be simpler formulae than the constraints themselves); if the new specifications are not met then the constraints are violated. Embodying the implications of constraints in transaction specifications means that the constraints need not be checked at run-time. The following example shows the rationale behind the use of ramifications for simplifying the task of proving transaction safety.

Example 1. Transaction *EnrollInCourse* records the enrollment of student *st* in course *crs*. *size* and *classlimit* are function symbols representing the class size and enrollment limit respectively, whereas *EnrolledIn* is a predicate symbol. We adopt the unprimed/primed notation to refer to the values of variables, functions or predicates immediately before and after the execution of the transaction.

EnrollInCourse (st, crs)   Precondition: $\neg EnrolledIn(st, crs)$ Postcondition: $size'(crs) = size(crs) + 1 \ \wedge \ EnrolledIn'(st, crs)$
Invariant: $\forall c / Course \ size(c) \leq classlimit(c)$

The precondition requires that the student is not already enrolled in the course, whereas the postcondition specifies the effect of the transaction on the final state: the size of the class is incremented and the predicate *EnrolledIn* becomes true of *st* and *crs*. The invariant requires that the size of a course should not exceed its limit. We can easily verify that, if the condition ($size(crs) + 1 \leq classlimit(crs)$) is conjoined with the postcondition, then no implementation that meets the augmented postcondition can violate the invariant. Indeed, the invariant follows as a logical consequence of the augmented postcondition, the invariant in the previous state and the assumption that in the state before transaction execution the invariants are known to be satisfied. As will be shown in the sequel, the derived addition to the postcondition is a ramification of (a form of) the invariant and the initial postcondition. This is different than simply conjoining constraints to the transaction postconditions [30]. Let us assume for a moment that the invariant had the form $\forall c / Course \ size(c) \leq classlimit(c) \wedge \psi$, where ψ does not mention predicate *EnrolledIn* or function *size*. Then, under the assumption that the invariant was satisfied before the transaction execution, the conjunct ψ can be eliminated since its satisfaction persists. A non-optimizing transaction modification technique, such as, e.g., in [30], would include ψ as a condition that would need to be conjoined with the postcondition.

Section 2 reviews the concept of *ramifications* and describes an extension to the solution to the frame and ramification problems proposed in [13],[1],[21] for the case of determinate transaction specifications. Section 3 presents the ramification method for transaction modification. The results are extended in section 4 to deal with multiple transactions, conjunction and inheritance of specifications. Section 5 reviews related work and discusses the integration of the proposed method in the database design process. Section 6 summarizes the results and outlines directions for further research.

2 Ramifications

In this section we provide the necessary background for the ramification method for transaction modification. In the first part we review the concept and properties of ramifications and, in the second, we describe the solution to the ramification problem for the class of deterministic transaction specifications. The bulk of the background material is based on [6] and [21] but is recast here in database terminology. Moreover, the results presented therein are extended as propositions 2.1 - 2.3 describe.

2.1 Background

Let us assume that a knowledge base, KB, comprises a set of ground literals representing facts true in KB, a set, R, of deductive rules and a set, I, of integrity constraints. Constraints and rules are expressed as range-restricted formulae of a many-sorted first-order logic in which we distinguish one sort, *Time*, for time points. We will refer to this logic as MSTL for short. Time is interpreted as being relative, linear, discrete, and unbounded. *Time* can be thought of as a set isomorphic to the integers.

Intuitively, a *ramification* of a formula ϕ is a formula N such that, N is inevitably true if ϕ is true [6]. This definition is amenable to different interpretations in different world models. If the world model in question - the knowledge base - is expressed as a first-order theory, then the concept of ramifications can be captured by first-order entailment. A formula ϕ is said to be in prenex normal form if it is of the form $\phi \equiv Q_1 x_1/S_1, \ldots, Q_m x_m/S_m\ \hat{\phi}$, where $Q_i \in \{\forall, \exists\}, i = 1, \ldots, m$, $S_1, \ldots, S_m$ are sorts and $\hat{\phi}$ is quantifier-free with free variables $x_1, \ldots, x_m$.

Definition 1 (*Ramification*). Given a knowledge base KB and a formula ϕ in prenex normal form with quantified variables $x_1, \ldots, x_m$, a formula N with free variables $y_1, \ldots, y_n$ among $x_1, \ldots, x_m$ is a ramification of ϕ in KB, if $KB \cup \{\phi\} \models \forall y_1, \ldots, \forall y_n N$.

Example 2. Consider the knowledge base[4] $KB = \{\forall x \forall y \forall z/Dom\ (A(x) \wedge C(y) \to D(x, y, z)\}$ and the formula $\phi \equiv \exists x \exists y (A(x) \wedge B(x, y) \wedge C(y))$. Then, the formula $N \equiv \forall z\ D(x^*, y^*, z)$ is a ramification of ϕ in KB since $KB \cup \{\phi\} \models N$.

It is easy to verify the following properties of ramifications:

1. If a ramification of a formula is known to be unsatisfiable, then the formula itself is unsatisfiable
2. Ramifications of formulae can reduce the search space for the formulae satisfaction
3. Transformations may be applicable to formulae ramifications but not to the formulae themselves

Hence, if there exists a way to systematically generate ramifications from a set of formulae, then the derived ramifications can be used for optimizing the evaluation of the formulae themselves.

Generating ramifications of a formula ϕ essentially involves augmenting a partial description of a state where ϕ holds with additional descriptions that stem from the knowledge of the consistency of the state. A procedure for generating ramifications may require an arbitrary amount of inferencing. From the

---

[4] For the sake of simplicity we assume that all variables range over the same sort *Dom*. Moreover, *-ed identifiers will denote Skolem constants.

semi-decidability of first-order entailment, it follows that the problem of finding ramifications is, in its generality, intractable. Tractability can be achieved by restricting the class of formulae for which ramifications are sought. For instance, the task is tractable for ordered conjunctions of literals [6]. Furthermore, not all derivable ramifications may be useful for simplifying the task of proving a formula. For that, the generator may be guided to derive only "useful" ramifications by providing appropriate input clauses. In fact, the solution to the ramification problem that we present in section 2.2 generates exactly those ramifications that are needed for proving the safety of transaction specifications.

The process of modifying a goal by conjoining it with additional constraints so that the reformulated formula is less expensive to check than the original one, has been termed *supersumption* in [6]. The methods proposed therein apply only to conjunctive formulae. It is easy to establish the soundness of supersumption for formulae in disjunctive normal form (DNF). Proposition 2.1 is a direct consequence of the definition of ramifications and proposition 2.2 follows from the properties of first-order entailment.

Proposition 2. If N is a ramification of ϕ in the knowledge base KB, and N is falsified in KB, then so is ϕ.

Proposition 3. Let ϕ be a formula in DNF, i.e. $\phi \equiv \bigvee_{i=1}^{n} \phi_i$, where each ϕ_i is a conjunction of literals. Let also N_i be a ramification of ϕ_i for each $i = 1, \ldots, n$ and $KB \models (\phi_i \Rightarrow N_i)$. Then, if for each $i = 1, \ldots, n$ $KB \models \neg N_i$, then $KB \models \neg \phi$.

According to proposition 2.2, given a formula in DNF, one can derive ramifications of the conjuncts of the formula and then test whether all ramifications are falsified. If this is the case, then the initial formula is falsified. This strategy is useful if one is interested in monitoring when a formula becomes violated rather than proving that it is always satisfied. As will be seen in the next section, this strategy is sufficient to monitor integrity constraint violations. The next corollary establishes the soundness of supersumption. This result establishes the correctness of the reformulation process as far as the satisfaction of the augmented formula is concerned.

Corollary 4 (*Soundness of Supersumption*). Let ϕ be the formula $Q_1 x_1, \ldots, Q_m x_m \hat{\phi}, Q_i \in \{\forall, \exists\}, i = 1, \ldots, m$, where $\hat{\phi}$ is quantifier-free in DNF with each of the variables $x_1, \ldots, x_m$, appearing in at least one of the disjuncts, and let N be a ramification of ϕ in the knowledge base KB. Then $KB \cup \{\phi\} \models Q_1 x_1, \ldots, Q_m x_m (\hat{\phi} \wedge N)$.

2.2 The Frame and Ramification Problems

In this section we sketch the solution to the frame and ramification problems for a class of constraints that encompasses static and transition constraints. The solution to the frame problem was initially proposed in [25] in the framework of situation calculus [17]. It was extended in [13] and [21] for dealing with the ramification problem as well. It relies on the automatic generation of complete characterizations of the conditions under which predicates or functions may change (truth) value as a result of transaction execution. Here we present an extension to the method of [21] for dealing with transition constraints.

The method generates *successor-state axioms* from a given set of *effect axioms*, in the presence of a limited class of constraints and definitions of non-primitive predicates. Effect axioms specify the direct effects of transactions on predicates. For instance, a direct effect of transaction *EnrollInCourse* (see example 1), is that the size of the course in which a student enrolls is incremented by 1. Successor-state axioms characterize all conditions under which predicates and functions may change value as a result of transaction execution. Such axioms serve as a formalization of a closed-world assumption about the transactions themselves rather than the knowledge base. Integrity constraints are of the form:

$$\forall x_1/S_1, \ldots, x_k/S_k, \forall t_1, t_2/Time$$

$$\phi(x_1, \ldots, x_k, t_1, t_2) \lor (\neg)p_1(x_1, \ldots, x_k, t_1) \lor (\neg)p_2(x_1, \ldots, x_k, t_2)$$

where, p_1, p_2 are $(k+1)$-ary predicates, intensional or extensional, $S_1, \ldots, S_k$ are object sorts and $\phi(x_1, \ldots, x_k, t_1, t_2)$ is a formula in which variables $x_1, \ldots, x_k, t_1, t_2$ occur free, if at all, and does not mention any predicate other than evaluable predicates. This class of constraints is an extension of the class of *binary constraints* of [21], since it allows the temporal variables to occur in evaluable predicates. It includes static constraints and transition constraints, i.e., constraints referring to two consecutive states of the knowledge base, but not general dynamic constraints. For example, the transition constraint specifying the property that an employee's salary can never decrease, can be specified by the formula

$$\forall e/Employee \ \forall s_1, s_2/Salary \ \forall t_1, t_2/Time$$

$$(s_1 < s_2) \lor \neg(t_1 < t_2) \lor \neg salary(e, s_1, t_1) \lor \neg salary(e, s_2, t_2).$$

A transaction T with parameters $\overline{x}$ is specified by a pair $(pre_T(\overline{x}), post_T(\overline{x}))$, where $pre_T(\overline{x})$, and $post_T(\overline{x}))$ denote the transaction pre- and post-condition respectively, both specified as well-formed formulae of MSTL. The solution assumes that deductive rules are not recursive. Moreover, they are assumed to be stratified. It also presupposes the existence of causal rules describing the direct effects of transactions. These causal rules are expressed by *direct effect axioms* which, for a transaction $T(\overline{x}) = (pre_T(\overline{x}), post_T(\overline{x}))$ have the form:

$$\forall \overline{x}/\overline{S} \ \forall t/Time \ (Occur(T(\overline{x}), t) \Rightarrow pre_T(\overline{x}, t) \land post_T(\overline{x}, next(t)))$$

where the term $next(t)$ denotes the state resulting from the execution of the transaction at time t. Given any transaction specification, the effect axioms are derived independently of any other specification. Hence, we can avoid having to specify the axioms in a reified[5] logic that interprets the predicate *Occur* outside a standard first-order interpretation. The above axiom can now be written as:

$$\forall \overline{x}/\overline{S} \ \forall t/Time \ T(\overline{x}, t) \Rightarrow pre_T(\overline{x}, t) \land post_T(\overline{x}, next(t)).$$

From the direct effect axioms we can systematically generate *positive* and *negative* effect axioms [2] for every predicate P that occurs in $post_T$, as described in the following steps.[6] The rationale is to describe concisely all conditions that are necessarily true when a predicate changes value from *False* to *True* (*True* to *False* respectively).

1. Construct the following positive and negative axioms:

   $$\forall \overline{x}/\overline{S} \ \forall t/Time \ (\neg P(\overline{x}, t) \land P(\overline{x}, next(t))) \land T(\overline{x}, t) \Rightarrow False)$$

   $$\forall \overline{x}/\overline{S} \ \forall t/Time \ (P(\overline{x}, t) \land \neg P(\overline{x}, next(t))) \land T(\overline{x}, t) \Rightarrow False)$$

2. If $post_T$ is $P(\overline{x}, next(t))$ ($\neg P(\overline{x}, next(t))$), add *True* as a disjunct to the positive (negative) effect axiom for P.

---

[5] In a reified logic formulae are considered as terms.

[6] We only show the derivation of effect axioms for predicates. Effect axioms for functions can be derived quite similarly.

3. If $post_T$ is of the form $\gamma(\overline{x}, t) \Rightarrow (\neg)P(\overline{x}, t)$, where γ does not contain terms referring to any time point except t, add a disjunct $\gamma(\overline{x}, t)$ to the positive (negative) effect axiom for P.

4. If $post_T(\overline{x})$ is of the form $\exists \overline{z}\ (\gamma(\overline{x}, \overline{z}, t) \Rightarrow (\neg)P(\overline{w}, next(t)))$, where $\overline{w}$ consists of constants and variables from $\overline{x}, \overline{z}$, then augment the positive (negative) axiom for P with a disjunct $\exists \overline{z}\ (\gamma(\overline{x}, \overline{z}, t) \wedge (\overline{x} = \overline{w}))$.

This process results in a set T_{ef} of effect axioms of the form:

$$\forall \overline{x}/\overline{S}\ \forall t/Time\ \neg P(\overline{x}, t) \wedge \neg \Phi_{1P}(\overline{x}, t) \Rightarrow \neg P(\overline{x}, next(t)) \quad (1)$$
$$\forall \overline{x}/\overline{S}\ \forall t/Time\quad P(\overline{x}, t) \wedge \neg \Phi_{2P}(\overline{x}, t) \Rightarrow P(\overline{x}, next(t))) \quad (2)$$

These axioms concisely describe how transactions directly affect the truth values of predicates. It remains to describe the indirect effects that are due to the presence of integrity constraints and deductive rules.

In addition to the effect axioms T_{ef}, the knowledge base is augmented with an axiomatization of time (T_{time}) formalizing the properties of discreteness and unboundedness, as well as unique name axioms (T_{una}) for predicates and functions. A new set T'_{ef} is obtained from T_{ef} by replacing each derived predicate occurring in an effect axiom by the disjunction of the bodies of the rules that define it. Since the set of deductive rules is assumed to be stratified, the process of replacing derived predicates by their definitions will terminate with all effect axioms mentioning only primitive predicates.

Let $C \equiv \forall \overline{x}/\overline{S}, \forall t_1, t_2/Time\ \phi(\overline{x}, t_1, t_2) \vee P(\overline{x}, t_1) \vee Q(\overline{x}, t_2)$ be a constraint that has to be satisfied at all times. Then, for each effect axiom of type (1) for P, the following axiom for Q is generated:

$$\forall \overline{x}/\overline{S}\ \forall t/Time\ \neg P(\overline{x}, t) \wedge \neg \Phi_{1P}(\overline{x}, t) \wedge \neg \phi(\overline{x}, t, next(t)) \Rightarrow Q(\overline{x}, next(t))$$

This axiom expresses the property that, if predicate P is known not to be true in the state prior to the execution of a transaction and constraint C is known to be satisfied in the same state, then, if the conditions that cause P to change truth value from $False$ to $True$ are not satisfied, $Q(\overline{x}, next(t)) \vee \phi(\overline{x}, t, next(t))$ has to be true in order for the constraint to remain satisfied in the state after the transaction execution. Symmetrically, for each effect axiom of type (1) for Q, generate the following axiom for P:

$$\forall \overline{x}/\overline{S}\ \forall t/Time\ \neg Q(\overline{x}, t) \wedge \neg \Phi_{1Q}(\overline{x}, t) \wedge \neg \phi(\overline{x}, t, next(t)) \Rightarrow P(\overline{x}, next(t))$$

The respective process takes place if the constraint contains negated predicates. Then, under the assumption that the given specifications characterize all transactions, we can generate the set T_{ss} of $successor$-$state$ $axioms$ as follows: Let $\Psi_P(\overline{x}, t) = \neg \Phi_{1Q}(\overline{x}, t) \wedge \neg \phi(\overline{x}, t, next(t))$ and $\Psi_{\neg P}(\overline{x}, t) = \neg \Phi_{2Q}(\overline{x}, t) \wedge \neg \phi(\overline{x}, t, next(t))$. $\Psi_Q(\overline{x})$ and $\Psi_{\neg Q}(\overline{x})$ are defined analogously. Then, the successor-state axiom for P is:

$$\forall \overline{x}/\overline{S}\ \forall t/Time\ \Psi_P(\overline{x}, t) \vee (\neg \Psi_{\neg P}(\overline{x}, t) \wedge P(\overline{x}, t))$$

Example 3. Example 1 showed the definition of transaction *EnrollInCourse* which affects the predicate *EnrolledIn* and the function *size*. Let us assume that another transaction, *DropCourse* is defined as follows:

DropCourse(st,crs)   **Precondition:** *EnrolledIn(st,crs)*   **Postcondition:** $size'(crs) = size(crs) - 1\ \wedge\ \neg EnrolledIn'(st,crs)$
Invariant: $\forall c/Course\ size(c) \leq classlimit(c)$

The generation process described in this section will generate the following successor-state axioms for *EnrolledIn* and *size*:

$\forall st/Student\ \forall crs/Course\ \forall t/Time\ \neg EnrolledIn(st, crs, t)\ \lor$
$\quad EnrolledIn(st, crs, next(t))\ \lor\ DropCourse(st, crs, t)$
$\forall crs/Course\ \forall t/Time\ (size(crs, t) = size(crs, next(t)))\ \lor$
$\quad \exists st\ EnrollInCourse(st, crs, t)\ \lor \exists st\ DropCourse(st, crs, t)$

Under the assumption that the transactions *EnrollInCourse* and *DropCourse* are the only ones affecting *EnrolledIn* and *size*, the above axioms characterize all conditions under which the predicate or function can change (truth) value as a result of transaction execution. Specifically, the first axiom expresses the property that if a student is enrolled in a course in the state prior to a transaction's execution but is not enrolled in the course after the transaction's execution, then it has to be the case that transaction *DropCourse* occurred and it cannot be the case that any other transaction may have occurred. The second axiom says that, if function *size* changes value because of transaction execution, then it is the case that either transaction *EnrollInCourse* occurred or transaction *DropCourse* occurred.

It has been shown in [13] that a set, T_{ss}, of successor-state axioms constitutes a solution to the frame and ramification problem if, for every predicate p, the condition $T_{una} \models \neg(\Psi_p \land \Psi_{\neg p})$ is satisfied. Moreover, the correctness of the syntactic generation has been proven in [13] and [21]. We are now in a position to state the relationship of the syntactic generation of successor-state axioms with ramifications of constraints. A similar result holds for the case in which predicates occur negated in the expression of a constraint. The proposition follows from the syntactic generation process.

Proposition 5. For a knowledge base KB and a constraint
$$I \equiv \forall \overline{x}/\overline{S}, \forall t_1, t_2/Time\ \phi(\overline{x}, t_1, t_2) \lor P(\overline{x}, t_1) \lor Q(\overline{x}, t_1, t_2)$$
the following entailment relation holds:
$$KB \cup \{I\} \models [(\neg \Phi_{1P}(\overline{x}, t) \land \neg \phi(\overline{x}, t, next(t))) \lor (\neg \Phi_{1Q}(\overline{x}, t) \land \neg \phi(\overline{x}, t, next(t)))]$$

The above result is significant to the problem of proving transaction safety, since it provides a way to produce systematically necessary conditions for the satisfaction of constraints in the state resulting from the transaction execution.

3 Integrity Maintenance by Transaction Modification

In this section we establish the relationship between the ramification problem and the maintenance of integrity constraints.

3.1 Ramifications and Integrity Maintenance

The problem of integrity maintenance is defined as follows: Given a knowledge base KB with constraint set I and a set of transaction specifications $T = \{T_1, \ldots, T_k\}$ with $T_i = (pre_i, post_i)$, can the set I be systematically partitioned into sets I_t, I_f, I_c so that: (a) constraints in I_t are *provably* maintained by T, (b) constraints in I_f are *provably* violated by some $T' \subseteq T$, and (c) constraints in I_c have to be checked after execution of some transactions in T but possibly in some simplified form? Since we are following a transaction modification approach, the problem is equivalent to transforming the set, T, of transactions into a set, T', of transactions with the property that, for each transaction T_i' in T', either $T_i' = T_i$ and T_i has been shown not to violate any of the integrity constraints, or T_i has been modified to T_i' and every implementation meeting its new specification cannot possibly violate any of the constraints in I.

Integrity constraints serve the role of invariants of transactions. Each transaction must maintain its invariants, i.e. not violate the relevant integrity constraints, in order to be accepted. The problem of proving that a transaction maintains its invariants is formalized in the following definition.

Definition 6 *Invariant Maintenance.* Let T be a transaction specification with precondition P, postcondition Q and invariant I. T is said to maintain invariant I, if $I \wedge P \Rightarrow (Q \Rightarrow I')$. where I' denotes the invariant in the state resulting after the transaction takes place.

Proving invariant maintenance is a difficult task since it requires theorem proving. Furthermore, the cost of undoing the transaction in case it is discovered to violate the invariants is high. A way to avoid checking whether transactions maintain their invariants is to augment their postconditions in a way such that the invariant is maintained as a result of meeting the postcondition. Such an augmented postcondition can be found by computing ramifications. The following discussion is based on a number of completeness assumptions. These assumptions specify that, firstly, all transaction specifications are known at the time that integrity constraints are specified and, secondly, that transaction invariants are known to be maintained in the state before the transaction execution. We discuss in the sequel how we can incrementally accommodate newly defined transactions.

We consider the single-transaction case first. Assume a transaction T specified by a pair (P, Q) of a precondition and a postcondition expressed in MSTL. Let I be an integrity constraint relevant to the transaction[7]. We need to find a formula N such that $KB \models (Q \wedge N \Rightarrow I')$, or equivalently that, $KB \models (Q \wedge \neg I' \Rightarrow \neg N)$. If $\neg N$ is a ramification of $Q \wedge \neg I'$ as computed by the syntactic generator, then the desired entailment relationship holds. This leads to the following theorem, whose proof follows from definitions 1, 6 and corollary 4:

Theorem 7. Let P and Q be the pre- and post-condition respectively of a transaction T. If I is an invariant of T and N is a ramification of $Q \wedge \neg I'$ computed by the syntactic generator of section 2.2, then the invariant is maintained in the state resulting after the execution of T if the postcondition $Q \wedge \neg N$ is met.

This result has significant impact to both the areas of procedure specification and constraint enforcement: if the process of suggesting additions to the postconditions of transactions can be automated, the transaction specifier actually realizes the implications of transaction invariants and the procedure implementor is saved the burden of finding ways to meet the postcondition in a way such that no invariant is violated. In fact, the implementor may not be familiar with all the invariants that a certain transaction may affect. The theorem also suggests a way of enforcing integrity constraints by requiring that updating transactions meet postconditions that embody implications of constraints: first, ramifications of the conjunction of the postcondition and the negation of the invariant instantiated in the state after transaction execution are computed; the negation of the computed ramifications is conjoined with the transaction postcondition to form a postcondition which should be met by the implementation in order not to violate the invariants. The fact that postconditions describe all the direct effects

---

[7] The notion of "relevance" is defined formally in the sequel.

of transactions can be exploited to simplify the formula of which ramifications are sought. Specifically, (truth) values of predicates or functions changed by the transaction can be assumed to be known in the state resulting from transaction execution. Hence, the (truth) values can be substituted for the predicates or functions and logical simplifications may be applicable. The invariants themselves need not be verified in the state resulting from the transaction execution since their satisfaction is guaranteed by the transformation process. Moreover, the ramifications generated may be simpler formulae than the invariants and hence, the transformation of postconditions can incur considerable savings in testing for the satisfaction of invariants. The following examples show the merits of the incorporation of ramifications into transaction specifications.

Example 4. Transaction *EnrollInCourse* was defined in example 1. In this example, we show the derivation of ramifications for postcondition augmentation, by rewriting the postcondition and invariant in MSTL. We first construct the conjunction of the postcondition Q and the negation of the invariant instantiated as follows:

$$\neg I' \equiv \neg(size(crs, t+1) \leq classlimit(crs))$$
$$\neg I' \wedge Q \equiv \neg(size(crs, t+1) \leq classlimit(crs)) \wedge (size(crs, t+1) = size(crs, t) + 1) \wedge EnrolledIn(st, crs, t+1)$$

By substituting *True* for $EnrolledIn(st, crs, t+1)$ and $size(crs, t)+1$ for $size(crs, t+1)$, $\neg I' \wedge Q$ becomes $\neg(size(crs, t)+1 \leq classlimit(crs))$. This formula is in fact a ramification of $\neg I' \wedge Q$ and can be computed as shown in section 2.2. According to theorem 7, it suffices to conjoin the negation of the ramification to the potscondition. The invariant is no longer needed for verifying the safety of transaction *EnrollInCourse*, since it is embodied in the new postcondition. The augmented transaction specification now becomes :

EnrollInCourse (st, crs)
Precondition: $\neg EnrolledIn(st, crs)$
Postcondition: $size'(crs) = size(crs) + 1 \wedge EnrolledIn'(st, crs) \wedge (size(crs, t) + 1 \leq classlimit(crs))$

The next example shows that certain ramifications can suggest that postconditions need not be modified in order to guarantee the invariants.

Example 5. (Special cases) The specification of transaction *DropCourse* was given in example 3. Intuitively, the invariant cannot be violated as a result of executing *DropCourse*, and hence the specification of the transaction need not be modified. In fact, the ramification generation process produces the Boolean constant *False* as a ramification of $\neg I' \wedge Q$. According to theorem 7, it suffices to augment the postcondition with the negation of the derived ramification, i.e., the Boolean constant *True*. This means that it suffices for the implementation to meet the initial postcondition in order to maintain the invariant.

The case in which the propositional constant *False* is derived as a ramification is of particular interest since, as the following corollary specifies, no change in the postcondition is needed in order to meet the invariant. The derivation of *True* as a ramification is only possible when the transaction specification is inconsistent. Hence, the process of generating ramifications can also discover inconsistent specifications that may have escaped the specifier's attention.

Corollary 8. If *False* is a ramification of $Q \wedge \neg I'$, then I' is maintained by a transaction meeting Q. If *True* is a ramification of $Q \wedge \neg I'$, then the transaction specification is inconsistent.

A valid question that arises is whether a similar approach where preconditions rather than postconditions of transaction specifications can be augmented so that the maintenance of the invariants is a result of the satisfaction of the transaction precondition. In general, the two approaches are not equivalent. They are equivalent only in the case where derived ramifications refer only to the state before the transaction execution. The following section shows an example of a transaction specification where the derived ramification refers to the state after the transaction's execution. It is, thus, unnatural to augment the precondition with a condition that refers to the state resulting from the transaction execution.

3.2 Dynamic Integrity Constraints

We would like to be able to propose similar augmentations to postconditions when the invariant refers to any number of states, both before and after a transaction takes place. In other words, we need to extend the method for the enforcement of dynamic integrity constraints. The solution to the ramification problem presented in section 2.2 does not deal with constraints more general than transition constraints. It is applicable in the cases where the checking of conditions over multiple consecutive states can be reduced to checking conditions over pairs of consecutive states. The extension of the method to general dynamic constraints is a topic of current research. Some initial results are given through examples of the use of ramifications for transactions that involve transition and general dynamic constraints. These examples also motivate the use of a temporal calculus for expressing transaction specifications.

Example 6. (*Transition constraints as transaction invariants*) Transaction *RaiseSalary* assigns an employee an increase to her salary.

RaiseSalary (emp, new_sal) **Precondition:** $\exists old\ salary(emp, old, T_b)$ **Postcondition:** $salary(emp, new\_sal, T_a)$
Invariant: $\forall e, s, s'/D\ \forall t, t'/T\ [salary(e, s, t) \wedge salary(e, s', t') \wedge (t \leq t') \Rightarrow (s \leq s')$

T_b and T_a are used to denote time points before and after the transaction respectively. They are parameters whose exact values are not known at transaction specification time[8]. For the purpose of deriving the successor state axioms, one needs to instantiate the time component of predicates referring to the state prior to the transaction with T_b. The time component of predicates referring to the state after the transaction are instantiated with T_a. The ramification derived is: $\neg(old^* > new\_sal)$. Its addition to the postcondition suffices to ensure the maintenance of the invariant.

For the sake of demonstrating the applicability of using ramifications with constraints strictly more general than the ones dealt with so far, we now switch

---

[8] These time points are not unique. It suffices that T_a is a time point at which the constraints have to be verified (before the transaction commits) and that T_b a time point before the transaction begins execution and at which it is known that the KB is in a consistent state.

to using first-order temporal logic (FOTL) [16] as the specification language.[9] FOTL allows one to express constraints referring to an arbitrary number of states. We need to assume, without loss of generality, that exactly one action can occur between two successive states of the knowledge base. Example 7 demonstrates why it is unnatural to consider augmentations of the precondition of a transaction in order to achieve the maintenance of invariants.

Example 7. (*General dynamic integrity constraints*) The formula expressing the property *"If $P(x)$, then sometime in the future $Q(x)$"* is an invariant for transaction *InsertP* that inserts a tuple (x, t) in the extension of base predicate P.

InsertP (x,t)
Precondition: *True*
Postcondition: $P(x,t)$

Invariant: $\forall x/D \; \forall t/Time \; [P(x,t) \Rightarrow \exists t'/Time \; (t' > t \wedge Q(x,t'))]$

In addition, assume that the knowledge base includes the following rules:

R_1: $\forall x/D \; \forall t/Time \; P(x,t) \rightarrow R(x,t+1)$
R_2: $\forall x/D \; \forall t/Time \; R(x,t) \rightarrow Q(x,t)$

Intuitively, after the transaction *InsertP* finishes execution, the knowledge base is in a consistent state, since the constraint is satisfied due to the implicit updates. Because of the presence of the rules, no precondition exists that will guarantee the invariant. The invariant however contributes to effects (ramifications) that can be used to eliminate the need for proving the invariant. We generate the ramifications as follows: the negated invariant is $\neg I' \equiv \forall t'[P(x,t) \wedge (Q(x,t') \Rightarrow (t' \le t))]$. From the postcondition and rule R_1 we derive $R(x,t+1)$. Using rule R_2, we can now derive $Q(x,t+1)$. Using the negated invariant and the postcondition we derive the ramification $N \equiv Q(x,t+1) \Rightarrow False \equiv \neg Q(x,t+1) \equiv False$. Hence, the invariant is maintained if the postcondition is met. Notice that it is unreasonable to include $Q(x,t+1)$ as a precondition to a transaction of which it is an implicit consequence. The constant $False$ is generated as a ramification by the syntactic generator by replacing the derived predicates that occur in $\neg I' \wedge Q$ by their definitions and then applying the steps described in section 2.2.

Albeit artificial, example 7 shows that dynamic constraints can have useful effects for transactions. Even in cases where the satisfaction of a constraint cannot be determined because the constraint refers to the yet undetermined future, the method yields a ramification that can be used in place of the original constraint. This is the case in example 7 if the rules are omitted. In this case, we cannot determine whether the constraint is satisfied. or violated, since it refers to the possibly infinite set of subsequent states. In this case, the method can propose a simpler condition, that is actually a ramification of the original constraint and the postcondition. The formula $N \equiv \neg \forall t' \; (t' \le t \vee \neg Q(x,t'))$ is derived and the new constraint that suffices to be verified is $\neg N \equiv \exists t' \; (t' > t \wedge Q(x,t'))$. It contains the property that has to be verified by the future states and can be treated as the original constraint would.

---

[9] Similar results can be obtained when transactions are specified in a FOTL with modal operators $\bigcirc$, $\square$ and $\Diamond$.

4 Extensions

In this section we present extensions of the ramification method for dealing with multiple constraints, multiple transactions, conjoining transaction specifications, and inheritance of specifications.

4.1 Multiple Transactions

The approach followed in the previous section is certainly applicable to the problem of reasoning about the set of constraints of a knowledge base in the presence of multiple transaction specifications. In this case all transaction specifications have to be taken into account since a constraint may be relevant to, or affected by, more than one transactions. The notion of relevance is based on that of *dependence*[22]. We assume that the specifications are given in first-order temporal logic. Moreover, we assume that no interleaving of transactions is allowed. A transaction is regarded as the only means of state change and is identified with its pre/post-condition pair.

Definition 9 (*Relevance*). A constraint I is relevant to a transaction $T = (pre, post)$ if *post* contains a literal on which some literal of I depends.

Definition 10 (*Direct Dependence*). A literal L directly depends on a literal K iff there exists a rule of the form $\forall x_1/C_1 \ldots \forall x_n/C_n$ $(F \rightarrow A)$ such that, there exists a literal in the body F of the rule unifying with K with mgu θ and $A\theta = L$. *(Dependence)* A literal L depends on literal K iff it directly depends on K, or depends on a literal that directly depends on K. A constraint/rule depends on a rule if its literal depends on the rule's conclusion literal.

An integrity constraint relevant to a set of transactions $\{T_i = (pre_i, post_i) | i = 1, \ldots, k\}$ has to be considered for the modification of each $post_i$, so that the execution of any T_i provably maintains the constraint. Hence, it suffices to repeat the process presented in section 3 for every T_i. The process may be optimized by reusing the derivation of ramifications for transactions that involve common predicates. The symmetric case, where a transaction specification is associated with more than one invariants, is dealt with by simply taking the conjunction of the invariants as the new invariant. Then the derived ramification depends on all invariants, provided that the union of the invariants is a satisfiable set.

4.2 Conjoining Transaction Specifications

The conjunction of specifications - denoted by the operator $||$ - is formed by conjoining the respective pre/post-conditions. Then, as theorem 11 suggests, it suffices to conjoin the ramifications of the two invariant-postcondition pairs, to guarantee that the invariant will be maintained if the new postcondition is met.

Theorem 11. Let $T_1 = (pre_1, post_1)$ and $T_2 = (pre_2, post_2)$ be two transaction specifications sharing invariant I. If there exist ramifications N_1 and N_2 which, if conjoined with the postconditions $post_1$ and $post_2$ guarantee the maintenance of I in T_1 and T_2 respectively, then $N_1 \wedge N_2$ is a ramification which, if conjoined with $post_1 \wedge post_2$ guarantees the maintenance of I in $T = T_1 || T_2$.

An important consequence of theorem 11 is the ability to accommodate new invariants without having to redo the entire process. Specifically, if a new invariant is to be added and is relevant to a transaction specification whose postcondition has already been augmented by computed ramifications, it suffices to verify that the new invariant does not introduce any contradiction, and, if this is the case, to generate ramifications of the new invariant and the postcondition. The new ramification can be conjoined with the previously derived ones, so that the new postcondition guarantees the invariants.

4.3 Inheritance of Transaction Specifications

In object-oriented specification languages, inheritance of transaction (*method*) specifications is traditionally accomplished by conjoining the superclass' method specification to that of its subclasses [27]. We examine whether ramifications derived for the superclass can be inherited by the subclasses.

Assume a transaction $T_2 = (pre_2, post_2)$ is a specialization of $T_1 = (pre_1, post_1)$ and that there exists a formula N_1 with the property $KB \models (post_1 \wedge N_1) \Rightarrow I$. The specification of T_1 is inherited by T_2. It is the responsibility of the specifier to ensure that neither of the conjunctions $(pre_1 \wedge pre_2)$ and $(post_1 \wedge post_2)$ is a contradiction. Then, according to theorem 11, if a ramification N_2 can be found, such that $KB \models (post_2 \wedge N_2) \Rightarrow I$, then augmenting $post_2$ with $N_1 \wedge N_2$ suffices to guarantee that the invariant will be maintained if the $post_2 \wedge N_1 \wedge N_2$ is met.

5 Discussion

In the majority of the existing methods for integrity constraint maintenance by transaction modification, the frame and ramification problems have either been ignored or bypassed by means of implicit assumptions that state that "nothing but what is explicitly declared to change in the update procedure does". Within AI however, the problems have long been recognized as common sense reasoning problems and several attempts towards their solution have appeared (e.g., [12], [26]). The solution presented by Reiter [25], combined and extended previous results, leading to the systematic solution on which this paper is based.

In [30], integrity constraints expressed as QUEL queries on relational databases are added as qualifications to transactions. The execution of the resulting transaction guarantees integrity preservation. However, no simplification of constraints takes place and the knowledge of their satisfaction prior to the update is not exploited. A set-oriented language for transaction specification is used in [11]. For each update and each constraint, a *weakest precondition* (*wp*) is derived so that, if *wp* is true in the state prior to the update, then the constraint is guaranteed to be true in the state resulting from the update. Although the derived weakest preconditions are frequently amenable to simplification, there is no systematic treatment of precondition optimization. The method is applicable to a limited class of static constraints only and there is no mention of derivations of weakest preconditions when multiple constraints are relevant to an update. Finally, although the authors claim that it is trivial to incorporate implicit updates, the machinery provided does not account for them. In [28], a general-purpose theorem prover employing heuristic rewrite rules is used for proving safety of transactions with respect to a set of static constraints. Implicit updates and dynamic constraints are not considered. Although safety of transactions is proved at compile-time, the theorem prover could take advantage of the knowledge of the updates taking part in the transaction in order to simplify the proof procedure and possibly suggest changes to the transaction specification. Although not discussed, the frame problem is implicitly dealt with by restricting attention to the predicates changed by transactions and by eliminating inertial terms from the theorems that have to be proven in order to verify integrity. The concept of *constraint protectors* discussed in [29] resembles that of constraint ramifications. Their generation however assumes the existence of a fairly general theory of lemmas that is independent of the transactions.

Dynamic integrity constraints specified in temporal logic are translated into transaction specifications in [14]. Constraints are translated into *transition graphs* and transformation steps that simulate the evaluation of the constraints on the graphs are applied. Transactions are specified in terms of pre/post-condition pairs and explicit frame assumptions. The transaction specifier has to supply all frame conditions explicitly. The specifications are then modified by incorporating conditions that represent the parts of the constraints that remain to be verified. Although, the transformation technique is sound, i.e., violations of constraints are detected, the transformations to transaction specifications introduce conditions that refer to the transition graphs instead of predicates occurring in constraints or transactions. It becomes unclear what the specifications of the transaction mean with respect to the database state. Moreover, the problem of implicit updates is not addressed.

The previous sections showed how the task of proving integrity maintenance can be assisted by the adaptation of a systematic solution to the frame and ramification problems. The method presented is applicable to a fairly large class of transaction specifications, namely that of determinate specifications, and a class of constraints that encompasses the types of constraints that are usually supported by commercial database systems and most research prototypes. Furthermore, the results extend to the case of object-oriented specifications and for the synthesis of specifications by conjoining existing specifications.

The process of designing a knowledge base can be assisted by a tool that, when given a set of transaction specifications, suggests modifications to the post-conditions so that the integrity constraints are provably maintained by any implementation meeting the modified specification. Moreover, inconsistencies in the specifications can be discovered. We argue that this form of feedback is crucial for the knowledge base design process, since it provides a systematic way of testing whether certain desirable aspects of a 'good' design can be achieved. It has to be noted that the results presented here are not tied to a particular specification language. A similar generation process can be devised for specifications given in a language like SQL or its extensions.

6 Conclusions

The contribution of the research presented in this paper is two-fold: it shows that the use of a solution to the frame and ramification problem can provide valuable feedback during the transaction design phase and suggests a new technique for integrity maintenance in large knowledge bases.

In particular, we have presented an adaptation of ideas from AI into the problem of maintaining the integrity of a knowledge base. We extended a systematic solution to the frame and ramification problem for simplifying - at compile time - the task of proving that transaction execution does not violate the integrity constraints. This becomes possible by the syntactic generation of successor state axioms which, for the case of determinate transaction specifications, completely characterize under which circumstances predicates or functions change value after a state transition. The complexity of the process of generating these axioms is polynomial in the number of predicates and functions in the constraints [13]. We extended the method to apply to a class of constraints which includes static and transition constraints. We showed that the introduction of new transaction specifications or new constraints can be accommodated incrementally. This technique can lead to the development of a tool which, as part of a knowledge base management system [19], will suggest additions to transaction postconditions, whose effect will be to maintain the invariants. This tool aims at assisting the knowledge base design process by providing feedback to the designer of transactions and by automating the task of verifying the safety of transactions.

Furthermore, a new technique for integrity constraint checking is suggested. Checking for the satisfaction of constraints after each transaction execution is saved for the constraints for which, it can be decided at compile-time that they remain provably true. Similarly, for those that are provably violated, the cost of undoing transactions is saved. Otherwise, a simpler condition sufficient for ensuring that constraints will not be violated is derivable. The proposed method is a promising avenue for achieving acceptable run-time performance for integrity maintenance in large knowledge bases.

We are currently investigating the possibility of devising similar syntactic generators for general dynamic constraints, as well as the application of additional optimization steps for generating simpler conditions that suffice to guarantee invariant maintenance. For the case of temporal constraints in particular, the minimization of the temporal information required to verify the constraints appears to be possible by using knowledge about the satisfaction of the constraints in the history of states up to the current state.

References

1. A. Borgida, J. Mylopoulos, and R. Reiter. And nothing else changes: The Frame Problem in Procedure Specifications. In *Proceedings of the 15th Int. Conference on Software Engineering*, 1993.
2. A. Borgida, J. Mylopoulos, and R. Reiter. The Frame Problem in Procedure Specifications. *IEEE Transactions on Software Engineering*, 1995. To appear.
3. F. Bry, H. Decker, and R. Manthey. A Uniform Approach to Constraint Satisfaction and Constraint Satisfiability in Deductive Databases. In *Proceedings of the Int. Conference on Extedning Data Base Technology*, pages 488–505, 1988.
4. S. Ceri and J. Widom. Deriving Production Rules for Constraint Maintenance. In *VLDB-90*, pages 566–577, 1990.
5. J. Chomicki. History-less Checking of Dynamic Integrity Constraints. In *8th Int. Conference on Data Engineering*, pages 557–564, Phoenix,AZ, 1992.
6. J. Finger. Exploiting Constraints in Design Synthesis. Technical Report STAN-CS-88-1204, Stanford University, 1988.
7. J. Florentin. Consistency Auditing of Databases. *Computer Journal*, 17(1):52–58, 1974.
8. G. Gardarin and M. Melkanoff. Proving Consistency of Database Transactions. In *Proceedings VLDB '79*, pages 291–298, 1979.
9. M. Ginsberg and D. Smith. Reasoning about Action I: A Possible Worlds Approach. In Matthew Ginsberg, editor, *Readings in Non-Monotonic Reasoning*, pages 433–463. Morgan Kauffmann, 1987.
10. M. Jeusfeld and M. Jarke. From Relational to Object-Oriented Integrity Simplification. In *Proceedings of DOOD-91*, pages 460–477, 1991.
11. M. Lawley, R. Topor, and M. Wallace. Using Weakest Preconditions to Simplify Integrity Constraint Checking. In *Proceedings of the Australian Database Conference*, pages 161–170, 1993.
12. V. Lifschitz. Towards a Metatheory of Action. In *Proceedings of the 2nd Int. Conference on Knowledge Representation and Reasoning*, pages 376–386, 1991.

13. F. Lin and R. Reiter. State Constraints Revisited. *Journal of Logic and Computation - Special Issue on Actions and Processes*, 1994.
14. U. Lipeck. Transformation of Dynamic Integrity Constraints into Transaction Specifications. *Theoretical Computer Science*, 76:115–142, 1990.
15. J. Lloyd, E. Sonenberg, and R. Topor. Integrity Constraint Checking in Stratified Databases. Technical Report 86/5, Department of Computer Science, University of Melbourne, 1986.
16. Z. Manna and A. Pnueli. *The Temporal Logic of Reactive and Concurrent Systems*. Springer Verlag, 1991. Vol. 1: Specification.
17. J. McCarthy. Some Philosophical Problems from the Standpoint of Artificial Intelligence. In B. Meltzer and D. Mitchie, editors, *Machine Intelligence 4*, pages 463–502. Edinburgh University Press, 1969.
18. J. Mylopoulos, A. Borgida, M. Jarke, and M. Koubarakis. Telos: Representing Knowledge about Information Systems. *ACM TOIS*, 8(4):325–362, 1990.
19. J. Mylopoulos, V. Chaudhri, D. Plexousakis, A. Shrufi, and T. Topaloglou. Building Knowledge Base Management Systems. *The VLDB Journal*, 1996. To appear.
20. J.-M. Nicolas. Logic for Improving Integrity Checking in Relational Databases. *Acta Informatica*, 18:227–253, 1982.
21. J. Pinto. *Temporal Reasoning in the Situation Calculus*. PhD thesis, Department of Computer Science, University of Toronto, 1994.
22. D. Plexousakis. Integrity Constraint and Rule Maintenance in Temporal Deductive Knowledge Bases. In *Proceedings of the International Conference on Very Large Databases*, pages 146–157, 1993.
23. D. Plexousakis. Semantical and Ontological Considerations in Telos: a Lanugage for Knowledge Representation. *Computational Intelligence*, 9(1):41–72, 1993.
24. D. Plexousakis. Compilation and Simplification of Temporal Integrity Constraints. In *Proceedings of the 2nd Int. Workshop on Rules in Database Systems*, pages 260–274, Athens, GR, September 1995.
25. R. Reiter. The Frame Problem in the Situation Calculus: A Simple Solution (Sometimes) and a Completeness Model for Goal Regression. In V. Lifschitz, editor, *Artificial Intelligence and the Mathematical Theory of Computation: Papers in Honor of John McCarthy*, pages 359–380. Academic Press, 1991.
26. L. Schubert. Monotonic Solution to the Frame Problem in the Situation Calculus: An Efficient Method for Worlds with Fully Specified Actions. In H. Kyberg, R. Loui, and G. Carlson, editors, *Knowledge Representation and Defeasible Reasoning*, pages 23–67. Kluwer Academic Publishers, 1990.
27. S. Schuman and D. Pitt. Object-Oriented Subsystem Specification. In L. Meertens, editor, *Program Specification and Transformation*, pages 313–341. Elsevier Science, 1987.
28. T. Sheard and D. Stemple. Automatic Verification of Database Transaction Safety. *ACM Transactions on Database Systems*, 14(3):322–368, 1989.
29. D. Stemple, S. Mazumdar, and T. Sheard. On the Modes and Meaning of Feedback to Transaction Designers. In *Proceedings of ACM-SIGMOD Int. Conference on the Management of Data*, pages 374–386, San Francisco, CA, 1987.
30. M. Stonebraker. Implementation of Integrity Constraints and Views by Query Modification. In *Proceedings of ACM-SIGMOD Int. Conference on the Management of Data*, pages 65–78, 1975.
31. Teniente, E. and Olivé, A. Updating Knowledge Bases While Maintaining Their Consistency. *The VLDB Journal*, 4(2):193–241, 1995.

Reasoning with Aggregation Constraints

Alon Y. Levy[1] and Inderpal Singh Mumick[2]

[1] AT&T Bell Laboratories
600 Mountain Avenue
Murray Hill, NJ 07974, USA.
levy@research.att.com
[2] AT&T Bell Laboratories
600 Mountain Avenue
Murray Hill, NJ 07974, USA.
mumick@research.att.com

Abstract. Aggregation queries are becoming increasingly common as databases continue to grow and provide parallel execution engines to enable complex queries over larger and larger amounts of data. Consequently, optimization of aggregation queries is becoming very important. In this paper we present a framework for reasoning with constraints arising from the use of aggregations. The framework introduces a constraint language, three types of inference rules to derive constraints that must hold given a set of aggregations and constraints in the query, and a sound and tractable inference procedure. The constraint language and inference procedure can be used by any system that deals with aggregations – be it constraint programming, databases, or global information systems. However, the prime application of aggregation reasoning is in database query optimizers to optimize SQL (or object-SQL) queries with grouping and aggregation. Our framework allows aggregation reasoning to be incorporated into an optimizer in a modular fashion, and we illustrate this through a detailed example.

1 Introduction

In advanced database applications (such as decision-support systems) we are witnessing a growing number of very complex queries. The complexity of these queries arises from the fact that they depend on many subqueries and views, each forming a query block in the query graph. The difficulty in optimizing such queries arises from the fact that the query blocks cannot always be merged (due to semantics of duplicates and aggregation), and therefore we cannot apply traditional cost-based plan optimizers which can only handle one query block at a time. In particular, query optimizers are especially ineffective in dealing with queries involving aggregation. At the same time, there is a realization by several parallel database vendors (e.g., Teradata) that optimization of aggregation queries is critical for their systems to scale to larger applications.

An important method of optimization is to rewrite the query so that predicates can be applied as early as possible. Predicate pushdown [Ull89] is a common and important optimization technique for pushing predicates down a query graph, into query blocks that are computed earlier during evaluation. Recently we described the *predicate move-around* algorithm [LMS94] that generalizes predicate pushdown. The key idea in predicate move-around is that the step of pushing predicates *down* the query graph should be preceded by a step in which predicates are pulled *up* the query graph. As a result, predicates that appear in one subtree of the graph can be applied in another subtree, if they are relevant.

A key requirement for such query rewrite algorithms is the ability to infer predicates on the attributes of a view from predicates on the attributes of the relations defining the view (for the pullup phase), or the other way around (for the pushdown phase). While making such inferences for views not involving aggregation is a well understood problem (e.g., see [Ull89]), the problem of making such inferences in the presence of aggregation is a largely open problem that has been considered only in simple cases [LMS94, RSSS94]. As a result, these techniques are unable to push predicates effectively in queries involving aggregation.

In this paper we present a general and principled approach to inferring predicates when views contain aggregation. Specifically, we make the following contributions:

- We describe a *constraint language* in which we can reason with constraints involving aggregation.
- We identify three different types of inferences that need to be made with aggregation constraints in order to use them for query optimization, and show how these inferences can be used to naturally extend query optimization algorithms.
- Finally, we describe algorithms for performing the three kinds of inferences.

Reasoning with aggregation constraints is important not only in query optimization, but also in logic programming, constraint programming, constraint databases, and global information systems [LSK95]. For example, in global information systems, the techniques for pushing constraints down a query graph are used in order to determine which of the many available external databases is *relevant* to a given query. Specifically, if the predicates on a relation R in the query are mutually exclusive with the integrity constraints describing an external source for R, then that source can be deemed irrelevant. For example, if we have a flight database, with the integrity constraint that the minimum flight cost is \$50, and the query asks how to get from NYC to Washington D.C. for less than \$40, then we can deem the flight database irrelevant.

Therefore, our first contribution, the constraint language, provides a basis for investigating the use of aggregation constraints in those domains as well. The problem of reasoning with aggregation constraints is a very broad one. Our second contribution is important because it identifies exactly the subset of the reasoning tasks that need to be addressed in order to use aggregation constraints in query optimization. These tasks are also important for the other areas mentioned above.

We begin with an example that illustrates the issues that arise in reasoning with aggregation constraints. Section 3 describes the constraint language we use and the different types of inferences which together form the framework within which reasoning about aggregation is done. Section 4 gives a detailed account of each type of inference rules. Section 5 shows how the reasoning framework and rules developed in Sections 3 and 4 can be used for query optimization. Related work is discussed in Section 6, and we conclude with Section 7.

2 Illustrative Example

Consider an example involving the relations described below. Phone numbers are broken into area code (AC), and the number (which includes the last 7 digits). The relation customers includes a tuple for each customer, specifying the area code, phone, name and membership level (regular, silver, or gold). The relation calls stores the calls placed on a telephone network over the last one year, including the From number (the source), the To number (destination), their length, and the date of the call.

calls(FromAC, FromTel, ToAC, ToTel, Date, Length)
customers(AC, Tel, OwnerName, MemLevel)

A marketing query Q is constructed from two views ptCustomers (potential customers for marketing plans) and wellCalled as follows. The view ptCustomers considers only the customers with membership level "silver", and for each, it computes the maximum length call placed to every area code and the earliest date on which a call is placed to the area code (using a MIN aggregation function defined over dates.) The view wellCalled computes for every area code the maximum length call placed to that area code amongst all the calls in the calls relation. The query Q tries to find the customers who have been making long calls to area codes, where the longest incoming calls (from anyone) have been relatively short. The query further wants these customers to have started calling into this area code a long time ago, so as to do a targeted mailing to long standing callers. The query thus chooses the tuples from the view ptCustomers for which:

- The maximum length call placed by the user to the area code is greater than 10 minutes (i.e., MaxLen > 10), and
- The maximum length call placed to the area code amongst all the calls in the calls relation is *less* than 100 minutes (i.e., MaxLen < 100), and
- The earliest call placed by the user to the area code was made before April 1, 1994 (i.e., MinDate < 1_Apr_1994),

(F): CREATE VIEW ptCustomers (AC, Tel, ToAC, MaxLen,MinDate) AS
        SELECT c.AC, c.Tel, t.ToAC, MAX(t.Length), MIN(t.Date)
        FROM customers c, calls t
        WHERE c.AC = t.FromAC AND
              c.Tel = t.FromTel AND
              c.MemLevel = "Silver"
        GROUPBY c.AC, c.Tel, t.ToAC .

(E): CREATE VIEW wellCalled (ToAC, MaxLen) AS
          SELECT t.ToAC, MAX(t.Length)
          FROM calls t
          GROUPBY t.ToAC .

(Q): SELECT p.AC, p.Tel, p.ToAC, p.MaxLen, p.MinDate,
      FROM wellCalled w, ptCustomers p
      WHERE w.ToAC = p.ToAC AND
              w.MaxLen < 100 AND
              p.MaxLen > 10 AND
              p.MinDate < 1_Apr_1994 .

A careful examination of the query reveals that it can be optimized by

- Applying the predicate "t.Length > 10" early on in the computation of the view wellCalled, prior to the aggregation step, so that we may write an optimized view:

    (Eo): CREATE VIEW wellCalled (ToAC, MaxLen) AS
              SELECT t.ToAC, MAX(t.Length)
              FROM calls t
              WHERE t.Length > 10   ⇐ *Inferred Predicate*
              GROUPBY t.ToAC .

- Applying the predicate "(t.Length > 10 OR t.Date < 1_Apr_1994)" early on in the computation of the view ptCustomers, prior to the join and aggregation step, so that we may write an optimized view:

    (Fo): CREATE VIEW ptCustomers (AC, Tel, ToAC, MaxLen,MinDate) AS
              SELECT c.AC, c.Tel, t.ToAC, MAX(t.Length), MIN(t.Date)
              FROM customers c, calls t
              WHERE c.AC = t.FromAC AND
                      c.Tel = t.FromTel AND
                      c.MemLevel = "Silver" AND
                      (t.Length > 10 OR t.Date < 1_Apr_1994) ⇐ *Inferred Predicate*
              GROUPBY c.AC, c.Tel, t.ToAC .

Empirical observation on several gigabytes of telephone call data has shown that 95% of the calls are under 10 minutes, and since the calls table only stores data for one year, it is likely that less than 10% of the stored calls are made prior to April 1, 1994. Thus, both the inferred predicates are very selective. The optimized query is thus expected to run an order of magnitude faster than the initial query.

Informally, the inference of the two predicates follows from the following observations. In the query, it will always be the case that w.MaxLen ≥ p.MaxLen, because w.MaxLen is the maximum length call for *all* calls, while p.MaxLen is the maximum length call placed by a single customer. Since the query requires that p.MaxLen > 10, it follows that only tuples of wellCalled for which w.MaxLen > 10 holds will be relevant to the query. Such tuples of wellCalled will be computed correctly if the predicate "t.Length > 10" is applied to calls before the aggregation operation. Similarly, since the query requires that (p.MaxLen > 10 AND p.MinDate < 1_Apr_1994), it follows that all the relevant tuples of ptCustomers can be computed even by applying the predicate "(t.Length > 10 OR t.Date < 1_Apr_1994)" before the aggregation step. This is because a tuple is relevant if the length is greater than 10 (therefore establishing that the customer makes long enough calls) *or* if the date is before April 1st, 1994 (establishing that the customer started calling early enough).

The optimized query uses the optimized views defined above; however the query statement itself is the same as before. Note that even though we have pushed predicates into the definitions of the views, in this example they still need to be applied in the query block (there are cases (see [LMS94]) in which applying the predicates earlier in the evaluation guarantees that they do not need to be applied later on).

Let us take a closer look at the kinds of inferences that we need to make to automate the above informal reasoning process in a principled fashion:

- First, we need to infer that the maximum length computed from the join of calls and customers is less than the maximum length computed from calls. This is because the maximum in the join is taken over a *subset* of the calls relation resulting from the join with the relation customers.
- Next, we need to infer that in the query, the maximum length from the view wellCalled is greater than the maximum from the view ptCustomers, i.e., w.MaxLen $\geq$ p.MaxLen. This is because w.MaxLen was obtained by grouping on a *subset* of the columns on which p.MaxLen was computed. (In particular, wellCalled grouped each area code, while the ptCustomers relation grouped each area code *and* customer).
- Finally, we need to infer that
  - If only tuples that satisfy w.MaxLen > 10 are relevant to the query, then the predicate t.Length > 10 can be applied on the relation calls in the computation of the view wellCalled.
  - If only tuples that satisfy (p.MaxLen > 10 AND p.MinDate < 1_Apr_1994) are relevant to the query, then the predicate ("t.Length > 10" OR t.Date < 1_Apr_1994) can be applied on the relation calls in the computation of the view ptCustomers. The conversion of a conjunction into a disjunction is counter-intuitive at first; however we must allow for the case where the two maximum length and the minimum date values that satisfy each predicate come from different tuples in the call relation.

In the first kind of inference, which we call *relation-to-view inference*, we infer relationships between the aggregates computed from a view and aggregates computed from the relations defining the view. In the second kind of inference, which we call *intra-relation inference*, we infer relationships between *different* groupby lists and aggregate functions applied to the *same* relation (or view). Finally, in the third kind of inference, which we call *view-to-relation inference*, we infer predicates that can be applied to the relations defining a view from predicates that will *ultimately* be applied to the view itself. These three kinds of inference fit naturally into query optimizers, such as the Starburst optimizer [PHH92] or the predicate move-around algorithm [LMS94]. Relation-to-view inferences are made in the predicate pullup phase of predicate move-around, and view-to-relation inferences are made in the pushdown phase. The intra-relation inferences are made in both phases, while taking the deductive closure of the predicates in a node of the query graph. We will show the actual inference steps in Section 5, after we define each of these inferences formally and then describe how to automate them.

3 Framework for Reasoning with Aggregation

As illustrated in the example above, using aggregation constraints for query optimization requires several different types of inferences to be made about them. In this section we explain formally these types of inferences. In the next section we explain how to perform each one.

As a basis for reasoning with aggregation constraints we need to define a *constraint language* in which we represent aggregation constraints and make inferences about them. Our language extends constraint languages used to reason about constraints that do not involve aggregation. In that case (e.g., as described in [Ull89, LS92, LMS94]), our constraints were of the form:

$$(\forall\ t \in R)\ t.A_1\ \theta\ t.A_2,$$

where R is some relation with attributes A_1 and A_2, t is a tuple variable quantified over all the tuples in R, and θ is one of the operators $\{\leq, <, =, \neq\}$. The meaning of such a constraint is that for every tuple in R the value of the attribute A_1 and the attribute A_2 satisfy the relation θ. We also have simpler constraints of the form $(\forall\ t \in R)t.A_1\ \theta\ c$, where c is a constant.

To extend the language, we note that aggregation constraints essentially introduce new functions that can be applied to attributes in a relation. For example, grouping the relation R by the attribute A_1 and computing the maximum of the values of the attribute A_2 essentially defines a unary function from a value x of attribute A_1 to the maximum value of attribute A_2 amongst all tuples with $A_1 = x$. In our language, we will denote this function by the symbol $f_{\{R,A_1,Max,A_2\}}$. Clearly, there are close relationships between the different functions we can define. For example, for any value x, $f_{\{R,A_1,Max,A_2\}}(x) \geq f_{\{R,A_1,Min,A_2\}}(x)$, that is, for any column, the maximum of the column will always be greater or equal to the minimum. The key behind our algorithm will consist of methods for inferring such relationships.

Formally, a function symbol in our language has the form: $f_{\{R,\bar{X},A,Y\}}$, where:

- R is a relation name (base or view relation).
- $\bar{X}$ is a subset of the attributes of the relation R, denoting the grouping attributes. $\bar{X}$ is called the grouping list.

- *A* is an aggregation function that is applied to the attribute *Y* of relation *R*. For the purpose of this paper, *A* will be drawn from the following set of five aggregation functions – {MIN, MAX, SUM, AVG, COUNT}.

The arity of such a function is the number of attributes in $\bar{X}$. The term $f_{\{R,\bar{X},A,Y\}}(x_1,\ldots,x_n)$ denotes the result of grouping the relation *R* on the columns of $\bar{X}$ that have values $x_1,\ldots,x_n$, and applying the aggregate *A* to the column *Y*.

Atomic constraints in our constraint language are of the form

$$(\forall\, t \in R)(\forall\, \bar{x})\ \tau_1\ \theta\ \tau_2,$$

where τ_1 and τ_2 are either

- constants,
- attributes of the tuple *t* (i.e., of the form *t.A*, where *A* is an attribute of relation *R*), or
- functional terms of the form $f_{\{R,\bar{X},A,Y\}}(\alpha_1,\ldots,\alpha_n)$, where the α_i's are either constants or attributes of the tuple *t*.

The set of variables appearing in τ_1 and τ_2 are $\bar{x}$. The meaning of such a formula is that for every tuple of *R* and values $\bar{a}$ for the variables $\bar{x}$, the formula $\tau_1[\bar{x}/\bar{a}]\theta\tau_2[\bar{x}/\bar{a}]$ holds, where $\tau[\bar{x}/\bar{a}]$ denotes the constraint resulting from replacing the variables $\bar{x}$ by $\bar{a}$ respectively. Note that an atomic constraint does not necessarily have to have both a tuple quantifier (i.e., $\forall\, t \in R$) and variable quantifiers (i.e., $(\forall\, \bar{x})$).

Definition 1. (Atomic and Functional Terms) A term that contains a function symbol, such as $f_{\{R,\bar{X},A,Y\}}$ is called a *functional term*; otherwise the term is a constant or an attribute of a tuple, and is called an *atomic term*.

Definition 2. (Ordinary and Aggregation Predicates) An atomic constraint in which both the terms τ_1 and τ_2 are atomic is called an *ordinary predicate*; otherwise the constraint involves at least one functional term and is called an *aggregation predicate*.

In this paper we consider constraints that are conjunctions of atomic constraints. An atomic constraint will be denoted by c_i, and the conjunction of atomic constraints would be denoted by ϕ. The language can also be generalized to more complex constraints (such as linear equations involving the terms). We say that a constraint is a *single-relation* constraint of relation *R* if its functional terms use only functions over *R*, and its tuple quantifier ranges over the tuples of *R* (if such a quantifier exists).

In order to use aggregation constraints for query optimization, we need to perform three kinds of inferences with expressions in our constraint language:

1. **Intra-relation inference:** This type of inference deduces predicates between functional terms of the *same* relation. For example, we can infer

$$(\forall\, x, y)\, f_{\{R,[A],Max,G\}}(x) \geq f_{\{R,[A,B],Max,G\}}(x, y)$$

since the maximum value of attribute G amongst all tuples with the same value for attribute A is guaranteed to be greater than the maximum value of attribute G amongst all tuples with the same value for attributes A and B.

As another example, from $(\forall t \in R)\,(R.B > R.C)$ we can infer that

$$(\forall x)\, f_{\{R,[A],Max,B\}}(x) > f_{\{R,[A],Max,C\}}(x).$$

Formally, we are given single relation constraints ϕ_1 and ϕ_2 of relation R, and the problem is to decide whether ϕ_1 is valid (i.e., whether $\models \phi_1$) or to decide whether $\phi_1 \models \phi_2$.

2. **Relation-to-view inference:** This type of inference deduces predicates between attributes and functional terms of a view and those of relations defining the view. For example, if V is defined by

```
CREATE VIEW V AS
SELECT E₁.A, E₁.B
FROM E₁, E₂
WHERE E₁.A = E₂.C
```

we can infer that $\forall x\, f_{\{E_1,A,Max,B\}}(x) \geq f_{\{V,A,Max,B\}}(x)$. This holds because the tuples of the view are a subset of the tuples in E_1, and therefore, the maximum values from V cannot be greater than the maximum values from E_1.

Formally, suppose the view V is defined using the relations $E_1, \ldots, E_m$. Let c be an atomic constraint involving the relation V and at least one of the relations $E_1, \ldots, E_m$. Let $\phi_1, \ldots, \phi_m$ be conjunctive constraints on the relations $E_1, \ldots, E_m$, respectively (i.e., every tuple in E_i must satisfy ϕ_i). The relation-to-view inference problem is to decide whether

$$\phi_1 \wedge \ldots \wedge \phi_m \models c.$$

3. **View-to-relation inference:** In this type of inference, we begin with a constraint c involving only the view V. This constraint represents the tuples of V that are relevant to the query (i.e., tuples of V not satisfying constraint c can be ignored without changing the result of the query). We use the constraint c to infer which tuples of the relations $E_1, \ldots, E_m$ (from which V is defined) are needed in order to compute the necessary part of V. For example, suppose V is defined from the view V_1 as follows:

```
CREATE VIEW V(A, C) AS
SELECT V₁.A, Max(V₁.B)
FROM V₁
GROUPBY V₁.A
```

Suppose that we have determined that only tuples of V that satisfy $5 \leq C \leq 10$ are relevant to the query. We can infer that we only need to compute tuples of V_1 that satisfy $B \geq 5$.

Formally, the view V is defined using the relations $E_1, \ldots, E_m$. We are given a single-relation constraint ϕ_V on the view V, and a single relation constraint ϕ_{E_i} on one of the relations E_i defining V. Let $V(G_1, \ldots, G_m)$ represent the result of computing V by substituting the expressions $G_1, \ldots, G_m$ for the relations $E_1, \ldots, E_m$. The view-to-relation inference problem is to decide whether the following equivalence holds:

$$\sigma_{\phi_V} V(E_1, \ldots, E_m) \equiv \sigma_{\phi_V} V(E_1, \ldots, \sigma_{\phi_{E_i}}(E_i), \ldots, E_m).$$

An optimization engine may restrict this inference problem to the case where ϕ_{E_i} is an ordinary predicate (does not involve any functional terms). The reason for this restriction is that if the constraints involve functional terms, then evaluating them may require performing additional aggregation operations. Such a predicate would then be classified as an expensive predicate, and it may be better not to push it down from a view into the referenced relations [HS93, Hel94].

4 Making Inferences with Aggregation Constraints

Recall that the inference problem in our constraint language is to decide whether a constraint c is entailed by a conjunction (possibly empty) of constraints $c_1 \wedge \ldots \wedge c_n$. To do so, we apply a general strategy, in which we begin with a set of constraints ϕ, initially containing $c_1, \ldots, c_n$, and apply a set of *inference rules* to add new constraints to ϕ. We apply the inference rules until no new constraints can be added to ϕ, and then, if $c \in \phi$, we will say that $c_1 \wedge \ldots \wedge c_n \models c$. To illustrate, consider the following example inference rules. We use the letters p and q to denote relations in the inference rules.

r_1 : **from** $(x \le y)$ and $(y \le z)$ **infer** $x \le z$.
r_2 : **from** $(\forall t \in p)(t.B \le t.C)$ **infer** $(\forall x) f_{\{p, [\mathcal{X}], Min, B\}}(x) \le f_{\{p, [\mathcal{X}], Min, C\}}(x)$
r_3 : $(\forall x) f_{\{p, [\mathcal{X}], Min, B\}}(x) \le f_{\{p, [\mathcal{X}], Max, B\}}(x)$

Suppose $R(A, B, C)$ is a relation, and we are given a constraint c_1 : $(\forall t \in R)(t.B \le t.C)$. Using rule r_2, we can infer

c_2 : $(\forall x) f_{\{R, A, Min, B\}}(x) \le f_{\{R, A, Min, C\}}(x)$

Using rule r_3 we can infer

c_3 : $(\forall x) f_{\{R, A, Min, C\}}(x) \le f_{\{R, A, Max, C\}}(x)$

Finally, using r_1, and the inferred constraints c_2 and c_3, we can infer

c_4 : $(\forall x) f_{\{R, A, Min, B\}}(x) \le f_{\{R, A, Max, C\}}(x)$

Therefore, we conclude that $c_1 \models c_4$.

In general, an inference rule has a set of *premises* and a set of *conclusions*. If we can find an instantiation of the premises of an inference rule in ϕ, then we can infer the corresponding instantiation of its conclusion and add it to ϕ.

Some inference rules, such as r_3, do not have any premises, and therefore their instantiations can always be added to ϕ. Such inference rules can be viewed as axiom schemas.

The worst case complexity of the inference procedure is $O(|r| \times |c|)$, where $|r|$ is the number of inference rules and $|c|$ is the number of different possible atomic constraints. The number $|c|$ is polynomial in the number of relations and is exponential in the arity of the relations (which tend to be small). In Section 5 we describe how to further speedup the inference process by focusing the application of the inference rules only to *needed* functional terms. The needed functional terms are determined by examining the structure of the query. In the following subsections we focus on the inference rules used and the principles underlying them. The following theorem holds for all the rules presented.

Theorem 3. *The inference procedure using the rules and axioms in Section 4 is sound, i.e., every predicate that is inferred can be applied without changing the result of the query. The inference can be done in time polynomial in the number of inference rules and functional terms.*

4.1 Relation-to-View Inferences

Recall that relation-to-view inferences are meant to infer relationships between terms involving a view V and terms involving the relations defining V, which we denote by $E_1, \ldots, E_n$. We assume that a view V can be defined from $E_1, \ldots, E_n$ using a combination of selection, projection, cross product, union, grouping and aggregation operations. In order to better understand the inference rules, we present rules that involve a single such operation at a time. Rules for more complex view definitions are obtained by composing these rules. We only present representative rules here. A more comprehensive list of rules appears in the full paper.

Projection: Let the view $V(\bar{X}_1)$ be defined by projecting arguments from the relation $E(\bar{X}_2)$, i.e., $\bar{X}_1 \subset \bar{X}_2$. For each set $\bar{X} \subset \bar{X}_1$, for each attribute $Y \in \bar{X}_1$, and for each aggregation function $A \in \{\texttt{MIN}, \texttt{MAX}\}$ we have the following rule:

$(L1):$ $(\forall \bar{x}) f_{\{V, \bar{x}, A, Y\}}(\bar{x}) = f_{\{E, \bar{x}, A, Y\}}(\bar{x}).$

That means that the minimum and maximum of a column do not change as a result of projection. If duplicates are preserved during projection, then the same holds for Count and Sum (hence for Avg). If duplicates are not preserved, then, for COUNT we have the following rule:

$(L2):$ $(\forall \bar{x}) f_{\{V, \bar{x}, \texttt{COUNT}, Y\}}(\bar{x}) \leq f_{\{E, \bar{x}, \texttt{COUNT}, Y\}}(\bar{x}).$

Selection: Suppose the view $V(\bar{X}_1)$ is defined by applying the selection c on the relation $E(\bar{X}_1)$. Then the following axioms will hold (for each $\bar{X} \subset \bar{X}_1, Y \in \bar{X}_1$):

$(L3):$ $(\forall \bar{x}) f_{\{V, \bar{x}, \texttt{MIN}, Y\}}(\bar{x}) \geq f_{\{E, \bar{x}, \texttt{MIN}, Y\}}(\bar{x}).$
$(L4):$ $(\forall \bar{x}) f_{\{V, \bar{x}, \texttt{MAX}, Y\}}(\bar{x}) \leq f_{\{E, \bar{x}, \texttt{MAX}, Y\}}(\bar{x}).$

(L5): $(\forall \bar{x}) f_{\{V, \bar{x}, \text{COUNT}, Y\}}(\bar{x}) \leq f_{\{E, \bar{x}, \text{COUNT}, Y\}}(\bar{x})$.

For example, the first rule says that the minimum can only increase as a result of selection. Note that we cannot say anything about the average of V. More inference rules can be stated for the cases where the selection predicate c is of a specific form (such as $Y \leq k$, where k is a constant). For example, when $Y \leq k$, the MIN values in the view V is equal to the MIN value from E.

Cross Product: Suppose $V(\bar{X}_1, \bar{X}_2)$ is defined by the cross product of $E_1(\bar{X}_1)$ and $E_2(\bar{X}_2)$, where $\bar{X}_1$ and $\bar{X}_2$ are disjoint sets of variables. Then, for each $\bar{X} \subset \bar{X}_1$ and $Y \in \bar{X}_1$, we have the following rules (similar rules hold for E_2):

(L6): $(\forall \bar{x}) f_{\{V, \bar{x}, \text{MIN}, Y\}}(\bar{x}) = f_{\{E_1, \bar{x}, \text{MIN}, Y\}}(\bar{x})$.
(L7): $(\forall \bar{x}) f_{\{V, \bar{x}, \text{MAX}, Y\}}(\bar{x}) = f_{\{E_1, \bar{x}, \text{MAX}, Y\}}(\bar{x})$.
(L8): $(\forall \bar{x}) f_{\{V, \bar{x}, \text{AVG}, Y\}}(\bar{x}) = f_{\{E_1, \bar{x}, \text{AVG}, Y\}}(\bar{x})$.
(L9): $(\forall \bar{x}) f_{\{V, \bar{x}, \text{COUNT}, Y\}}(\bar{x}) = f_{\{E_1, \bar{x}, \text{COUNT}, Y\}}(\bar{x}) \times Size(E_2)$.

where $Size(E_2)$ is the number of tuples in relation E_2. For example, the first rule says that the value of the minimum does not change as a result of cross product.

Union: Suppose $V(\bar{X}_1)$ is defined to be the union of $E_1(\bar{X}_1)$ and $E_2(\bar{X}_1)$. For each $\bar{X} \subset \bar{X}_1$ and $Y \in \bar{X}_1$, the following holds:

(L10): $(\forall \bar{x}) f_{\{V, \bar{x}, \text{MIN}, Y\}}(\bar{x}) \leq f_{\{E_1, \bar{x}, \text{MIN}, Y\}}(\bar{x})$.
(L11): $(\forall \bar{x}) f_{\{V, \bar{x}, \text{MAX}, Y\}}(\bar{x}) \geq f_{\{E_1, \bar{x}, \text{MAX}, Y\}}(\bar{x})$.
(L12): $(\forall \bar{x})(f_{\{V, \bar{x}, \text{MAX}, Y\}}(\bar{x}) = f_{\{E_1, \bar{x}, \text{MAX}, Y\}}(\bar{x})) \vee (f_{\{V, \bar{x}, \text{MAX}, Y\}}(\bar{x}) = f_{\{E_2, \bar{x}, \text{MAX}, Y\}}(\bar{x}))$.
(L13): $(\forall \bar{x})(f_{\{V, \bar{x}, \text{MIN}, Y\}}(\bar{x}) = f_{\{E_1, \bar{x}, \text{MIN}, Y\}}(\bar{x})) \vee (f_{\{V, \bar{x}, \text{MIN}, Y\}}(\bar{x}) = f_{\{E_2, \bar{x}, \text{MIN}, Y\}}(\bar{x}))$.
(L14): $(\forall \bar{x}) f_{\{V, \bar{x}, \text{COUNT}, Y\}}(\bar{x}) \geq f_{\{E_1, \bar{x}, \text{COUNT}, Y\}}(\bar{x})$.

For example, the first rule states that the minimum can only decrease as a result of a union.

Grouping and Aggregation: Suppose the view $V(\bar{X}_1, \bar{Z})$ is defined by grouping on a relation $E(\bar{X}_1, \bar{Y})$, where $\bar{X}_1$ is the grouping list, and $Z_i = A_i(Y_i)$ is the list of attributes obtained by applying aggregation function A_i on the attribute Y_i of relation E. Then, for each $Z_i \in \bar{Z}$, the following holds by definition:

(L15): $(\forall v \in V) v.Z_i = f_{\{E, \bar{x}_1, A_i, Y_i\}}(E.\bar{X})$.

Further, for each $\bar{X} \subseteq \bar{X}_1$, and $W \in \bar{X}_1$, and $A \in \{\text{MAX}, \text{MIN}\}$:

(L16): $(\forall v \in V) f_{\{V, \bar{x}, A, W\}}(v.\bar{x}) = f_{\{E, \bar{x}, A, W\}}(v.\bar{x})$.

while for COUNT we have:

(L17): $(\forall v \in V) f_{\{V, \bar{x}, \text{COUNT}, W\}}(v.\bar{x}) \leq f_{\{E, \bar{x}, \text{COUNT}, W\}}(v.\bar{x})$.

4.2 Intra-relation Inferences

Intra-relation inferences deduce relationships between functional terms concerning the *same* relation. For a given relation R, we need to consider functional terms that differ on (1) the aggregate function, (2) the groupby list, and (3) the aggregated attribute. In addition, we can deduce special relationships when the aggregated column is a member of the grouping list.

Changing the Aggregation function: Ross et al. [RSSS94] present a complete set of rules for the case that only the aggregation function changes. For example, the following two rules hold:

(L18): $(\forall \bar{x}) f_{\{R,\bar{x},\text{MAX},Y\}}(\bar{x}) \geq f_{\{R,\bar{x},\text{MIN},Y\}}(\bar{x})$.
(L19): $(\forall \bar{x}) f_{\{R,\bar{x},\text{MAX},Y\}}(\bar{x}) \geq f_{\{R,\bar{x},\text{AVG},Y\}}(\bar{x})$.

i.e., the maximum is greater than either the minimum or the average.

Changing the groupby list: We consider the case in which one groupby list is a subset of the other (note that a *groupby list* is actually a set, not a list). Given a relation $R(\bar{X})$, the following rules apply for changing the groupby list. For each $\bar{X}_1 \subset \bar{X}_2 \subset \bar{X}, Y \in \bar{X}$.

(L20): $(\forall \bar{x}_2) f_{\{R,\bar{x}_2,\text{MAX},Y\}}(\bar{x}_2) \leq f_{\{R,\bar{x}_1,\text{MAX},Y\}}(\bar{x}_1)$.
(L21): $(\forall \bar{x}_2) f_{\{R,\bar{x}_2,\text{MIN},Y\}}(\bar{x}_2) \geq f_{\{R,\bar{x}_1,\text{MIN},Y\}}(\bar{x}_1)$.
(L22): $(\forall \bar{x}_2) f_{\{R,\bar{x}_2,\text{COUNT},Y\}}(\bar{x}_2) \leq f_{\{R,\bar{x}_1,\text{COUNT},Y\}}(\bar{x}_1)$.

For example, the first rule states that aggregating on a subset of the columns can only increase the maximum.

Changing the Aggregated Attribute: When we change the aggregated attribute, then the count remains the same, as formalized by the following rule:

(L23): $(\forall \bar{x}) f_{\{R,\bar{x},\text{COUNT},Y_1\}}(\bar{x}) = f_{\{R,\bar{x},\text{COUNT},Y_2\}}(\bar{x})$.

All the inference rules we have stated up to now are axiom schemas, i.e., the conclusions can be inferred without any premises. The next few inference rules deduce a relationship between functional terms of different attributes given with premises that are ordinary predicates:

(L24): $(\forall t \in R)(t.Y_1 \leq t.Y_2) \longrightarrow (\forall \bar{x}) f_{\{R,\bar{x},\text{MIN},Y_1\}}(\bar{x}) \leq f_{\{R,\bar{x},\text{MIN},Y_2\}}(\bar{x})$.
(L25): $(\forall t \in R)(t.Y_1 \leq t.Y_2) \longrightarrow (\forall \bar{x}) f_{\{R,\bar{x},\text{MAX},Y_1\}}(\bar{x}) \leq f_{\{R,\bar{x},\text{MAX},Y_2\}}(\bar{x})$.
(L26): $(\forall t \in R)(t.Y_1 \leq t.Y_2) \longrightarrow (\forall \bar{x}) f_{\{R,\bar{x},\text{AVG},Y_1\}}(\bar{x}) \leq f_{\{R,\bar{x},\text{AVG},Y_2\}}(\bar{x})$.

Similar rules apply if $Y_1 < Y_2$, $Y_1 > Y_2$, or $Y_1 \geq Y_2$. Furthermore, if $Y_1 \leq k$, where k is a constant, the above rules can be simplified to:

(L27): $(\forall t \in R)(t.Y_1 \leq k) \longrightarrow (\forall \bar{x}) f_{\{R,\bar{x},\text{MIN},Y_1\}}(\bar{x}) \leq k$.
(L28): $(\forall t \in R)(t.Y_1 \leq k) \longrightarrow (\forall \bar{x}) f_{\{R,\bar{x},\text{MAX},Y_1\}}(\bar{x}) \leq k$.

(L29): $(\forall t \in R)(t.Y_1 \leq k) \longrightarrow (\forall \bar{x}) f_{\{R,\bar{x},\text{AVG},Y_1\}}(\bar{x}) \leq k$.

and similarly for $Y_1 < a$, $Y_1 > k$, and $Y_1 \geq k$.

Aggregating on a grouping column: When the aggregated column is one of the columns in the grouping list, the result of the aggregation function can often be statically determined. Given a relation $R(\bar{X})$, for each $\{X_1, \ldots, X_m\} \subset \bar{X}$, and for each X_i:

(L30): $(\forall \bar{x}) f_{\{R,\{X_1,\ldots,X_m\},\text{MAX},X_i\}}(\bar{x}) = x_i.$
(L31): $(\forall \bar{x}) f_{\{R,\{X_1,\ldots,X_m\},\text{MIN},X_i\}}(\bar{x}) = x_i.$
(L32): $(\forall \bar{x}) f_{\{R,\{X_1,\ldots,X_m\},\text{AVG},X_i\}}(\bar{x}) = x_i.$

For example, the first rule states that the maximum value of an attribute X_i in the grouping list $\{X_1, \ldots, X_m\}$ for the group defined by $\{X_1, \ldots, X_m\} = \{x_1, \ldots, x_m\}$ is x_i.

4.3 View-to-relation Inference

Suppose a view V is defined from the relations $E_1, \ldots, E_m$. As we saw in the example, it is often the case that if we know that some predicates are applicable to the tuples of V without changing the result of the query, then we can infer predicates on $E_1, \ldots, E_n$, that can be *safely* applied in the computation of V (i.e., they can be applied without changing the result of the query). This section describes conditions under which such predicates can be pushed down the query graph.

We assume the view V has the arguments $\bar{X} = X_1, \ldots, X_m$, and $\bar{Z} = Z_1, \ldots, Z_l$, where $\bar{X}$ is the set of grouped variables in the view definition, and $\bar{Z}$ is the set of attributes resulting from aggregation. The attribute Z_i is of the form $A(Y_i)$ where A is some aggregate function (one of MIN, MAX, AVG, SUM, COUNT) and Y_i is an attribute of one of the E_i's.

We assume we have a conjunctive predicate $\phi = c_1 \wedge \ldots \wedge c_n$, such that if ϕ is applied to the tuples of V, the result of the query will not change. Each of the c_i's is an ordinary atomic predicate of the form $\tau_1 \theta \tau_2$, where τ_1 and τ_2 are either constants or attributes of V (i.e., one of $\bar{X} \cup \bar{Z}$).

In our description below, we assume that ϕ is closed under logical deduction, except for the following condition:

> ϕ does not contain trivial redundancies, that is, if $\tau \leq k$ and $\tau \leq k_1$ are in the deductive closure of ϕ and $k < k_1$, then ϕ does not include $\tau \leq k_1$ (and the analogous rule for $\geq$).

We illustrate the intuition behind the pushing of predicates with the following example.

Example 1. Suppose the view V contains the attributes X_1, X_2, Z_1, Z_2, where $Z_1 = \text{MAX}(Y_1)$ and $Z_2 = \text{MIN}(Y_2)$, and suppose that we have the predicate $\phi =$

$(X_1 \leq X_2) \wedge (Z_1 \geq 5) \wedge (Z_2 \leq 2)$. The predicate $(X_1 \leq X_2)$ can be pushed down to the computation of V because it applies to *whole* groups resulting from the grouping operation, and therefore it can be applied before the grouping. Furthermore, only tuples for which $(Y_1 \geq 5)$ are relevant to the computation of Z_1, and similarly, only tuples for which $(Y_2 \leq 2)$ are relevant to the computation of Z_2. However, we cannot apply the conjunction of these two predicates, because a tuple with $(Y_2 > 2)$ may actually be the one containing the maximum of Y_1. However, the *disjunction* of these predicates can still be applied, i.e., we can apply the predicate $(X_1 \leq X_2) \wedge (Y_2 \leq 2 \vee Y_1 \geq 5)$. $\square$

Formally, the predicates that can be inferred are computed as follows:

1. Let $\phi_{\bar{X}}$ be the subset of ϕ that does not include variables in $\bar{Z}$.
2. For every Z_i compute a predicate ψ_i as follows:
   - If Z_i is of the form MAX(Y_i), then let $\bar{d} = d_1, \ldots, d_{m_i}$ be the set of predicates in ϕ of the form $Z_i \geq x$ or $Z_i > x$, where x is a constant or a variable in $\bar{X}$. $\psi_i = d_1' \wedge \ldots \wedge d_{m_i}'$, where d_j' substitutes Y_i for Z_i in d_j. If $\bar{d}$ is empty, then $\psi_i = True$.
   - If Z_i is of the form MIN(Y_i), ψ_i is computed analogously.
   - If Z_i involves AVG, SUM, or COUNT, then $\psi_i = True$.
3. The predicate that can be pushed into the view definition is: $\phi_{\bar{X}} \wedge (\psi_1 \vee \ldots \vee \psi_l)$.

In our example above, $\phi_{\bar{X}}$ would be $X_1 \leq X_2$. For Z_1 we would have $\psi_1 = Y_1 \geq 5$, and for Z_2 we would have $\psi_2 = Y_2 \leq 2$. Note that if we would have an additional attribute in the view, $Z_3 = $ MIN(Y_3), we would get $\phi_3 = True$, and therefore, we would only be able to push the predicate $X_1 \leq X_2$ to the definition of the view.

5 Aggregation Reasoning in Query Optimization

The aggregation constraint language and the inference rules for aggregation can be used to formalize the informal reasoning we outlined in Section 2 for optimizing queries. Algorithmically, the functional terms and the inference rules can be made a part of the constraint language and inference mechanism that an optimizer uses for predicate analysis. To do so in an effective manner, we first need to identify the functional terms *relevant* to a query on which the inference rules need apply, and then need to show how the inference rules can be applied to optimize the query. The inference rules infer ordinary predicates as well as aggregation predicates. After the inference process ends, the derived ordinary predicates can be used for more efficient query evaluation. However, the axiomatic aggregation predicates are not useful for query evaluation. Other aggregation predicates (such as $f_{\{R,\{X\},\text{MAX},Y\}}$) may be useful, but these are typically expensive to evaluate. Thus the optimizer's hope is that the inference process would have used aggregation predicates as intermediate predicates to

528

derive ordinary predicates that can be used in the optimized query to restrict computation.

To describe the use of aggregation reasoning in optimization, we will represent an SQL query using a query graph [MFPR90, PHH92, MP94, LMS94]. A query graph is a pictorial representation of the query. For example, the marketing query Q from Section 2 is represented by the query graph of Figure 1. The graph has

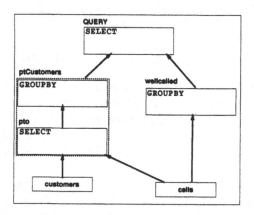

Fig. 1. The query graph for the marketing query of Section 2.

six nodes. The nodes labeled customers and calls represent base relations; all other nodes represent computed relations. The node labeled pt0 represents the result of the join between calls and customers that is grouped upon in the node labeled ptCustomers to generate the ptCustomers view. The node labeled wellCalled represents the grouping operation on the calls relation to generate the view wellCalled. Finally, the query node, labeled Q, takes a join between the two views to derive the answer.

5.1 Identifying the Functional Terms

The functional symbols that can be used in the aggregation reasoning are of the form:

$$f_{\{R,GL,A,Y\}}$$

where R can be any of the base or view relations labeling a node in the query graph of the query, the grouping list GL is a subset of the attributes of relation R, A is one of the aggregation functions (MIN, MAX, SUM, AVG, COUNT) applied to a single attribute Y of relation R.

If we were to introduce every one of these function symbols in the constraint language, we would have a large number of functional terms. Therefore, it important to restrict the functional terms we consider. Recall that in the end, we remove all of the predicates involving functional terms, and leave only the ordinary predicates (predicates that do not involve functional terms) that were derived using the functional terms. Therefore, we need only consider functional terms that are useful in deriving ordinary predicates. Below we show how to identify the functional terms that are relevant to deriving ordinary predicates. A functional term involving a relation R is useful only if the query does an aggregation on R or on a view derived from R. The grouping lists and the aggregated attributes can be restricted in a similar fashion:

- Let $\mathcal{R}$ be the set of base and view relation names derived as follows:
  - If R is the name of a base relation or the label of a node in the query graph that feeds into a groupby node, then it is in $\mathcal{R}$.
  - If $R1 \in \mathcal{R}$, $R1$ is the label of a node in the query graph, and $R2$ is the name of a base relation or the label of a node in the query graph that feeds into the node labeled $R1$, then $R2$ is in set $\mathcal{R}$.
- For every relation $R \in \mathcal{R}$, derive a set GL_R of pairs (grouping lists, aggregated column) as follows:
  - If R feeds into a groupby node, and GL is the groupby list used in the groupby node, then for each column Y aggregated in the groupby node, place (GL, Y) into GL_R.
  - If $(GL, Y) \in GL_R$, and relation S feeds into the node labeled R, and relation S provides the attribute Y into R, then include $(\pi_S(GL), Y)$ into GL_S. $\pi_S(GL)$ is the projection of the groupby list GL onto the attributes that appear in relation S.

The only functional terms that are relevant to query optimization are those with a relation name $R \in \mathcal{R}$, and with a grouping list and aggregation column in the set GL_R. Thus, the grouping lists and aggregation columns to be considered by the inference algorithm is restricted to the lists and columns actually used in the query, or derived from the query. In fact the number of resulting functional terms is linear in the size of the query.

Example 2. For the marketing query Q of Section 2:
$\mathcal{R} = \{\text{pt0}, \text{calls}, \text{customers}\}$
$GL_{\text{pt0}} = \{(\{\text{AC}, \text{Tel}, \text{ToAC}\}, \text{Length}), (\{\text{AC}, \text{Tel}, \text{ToAC}\}, \text{Date})\}$
$GL_{\text{calls}} = \{(\{\text{FromAC}, \text{FromTel}, \text{ToAC}\}, \text{Length}),$
$\qquad\qquad (\{\text{FromAC}, \text{FromTel}, \text{ToAC}\}, \text{Date}), (\{\text{ToAC}\}, \text{Length})\}$
$GL_{\text{customers}} = \{\}$

The following functional terms, one for each possible aggregation function A, are thus the only ones needed for query optimization:
$f_{\{\text{pt0}, \{\text{AC, Tel, ToAC}\}, A, \text{Length}\}}$
$f_{\{\text{pt0}, \{\text{AC, Tel, ToAC}\}, A, \text{Date}\}}$
$f_{\{\text{calls}, \{\text{FromAC, FromTel, ToAC}\}, A, \text{Length}\}}$
$f_{\{\text{calls}, \{\text{FromAC, FromTel, ToAC}\}, A, \text{Date}\}}$
$f_{\{\text{calls}, \{\text{ToAC}\}, A, \text{Length}\}}$

5.2 Inferring predicates during optimization

We illustrate the use of the inference rules of Section 4 for optimization through the marketing query Q of Section 2. The functional terms of interest were listed in Example 2.

Using inference rules $L3$, $L4$, $L7$, and $L8$ in Section 4.1, we derive:

$$(c1): \quad (\forall X, Y, Z) f_{\{\text{pt0},\{AC,Tel,ToAC\},\text{MAX},Length\}}(X, Y, Z)$$
$$\leq f_{\{\text{calls},\{FromAC,FromTel,ToAC\},\text{MAX},Length\}}(X, Y, Z).$$

$$(c2): \quad (\forall X, Y, Z) f_{\{\text{pt0},\{AC,Tel,ToAC\},\text{MIN},Date\}}(X, Y, Z)$$
$$\geq f_{\{\text{calls},\{FromAC,FromTel,ToAC\},\text{MIN},Date\}}(X, Y, Z).$$

Using inference rules $L22$ and $L23$ in Section 4.2, we derive:

$$(c3): \quad (\forall X, Y, Z) f_{\{\text{calls},\{ToAC\},\text{MAX},Length\}}(Z)$$
$$\geq f_{\{\text{calls},\{FromAC,FromTel,ToAC\},\text{MAX},Length\}}(X, Y, Z).$$

$$(c4): \quad (\forall X, Y, Z) f_{\{\text{calls},\{ToAC\},\text{MIN},Date\}}(Z)$$
$$\leq f_{\{\text{calls},\{FromAC,FromTel,ToAC\},\text{MIN},Date\}}(X, Y, Z).$$

Using inference rule $L17$ in Section 4.1, we derive:

$$(c5): \quad (\forall p \in \text{ptCustomers})$$
$$(p.MaxLen = f_{\{\text{pt0},\{AC,Tel,ToAC\},\text{MAX},Length\}}(p.AC, p.Tel, p.ToAC)).$$

$$(c6): \quad (\forall p \in \text{ptCustomers})$$
$$(p.MinDate = f_{\{\text{pt0},\{AC,Tel,ToAC\},\text{MIN},Date\}}(p.AC, p.Tel, p.ToAC)).$$

$$(c7): \quad (\forall w \in \text{wellcalled})(w.MaxLen = f_{\{\text{calls},\{ToAC\},\text{MAX},Length\}}(w.ToAC)).$$

From inferences $c1$ and $c3$, it follows that

$$(c8): \quad (\forall X, Y, Z)(f_{\{\text{calls},\{ToAC\},\text{MAX},Length\}}(Z)$$
$$\geq f_{\{\text{pt0},\{AC,Tel,ToAC\},\text{MAX},Length\}}(X, Y, Z).$$

From inferences $c5$, $c7$, and $c8$ it follows that

$$(c9): \quad (\forall p \in \text{ptCustomers}, w \in \text{wellcalled})$$
$$((w.ToAC = p.ToAC) \Rightarrow (w.MaxLen \geq p.MaxLen)).$$

Since it is known that $w.ToAC = p.ToAC$, the predicate $w.MaxLen \geq p.MaxLen$ can be inferred in the query. This then derives the predicate

$$(c10): \quad (\forall w \in \text{wellcalled}) \ w.MaxLen > 10.$$

We are also given the predicates

($c11$): ($\forall p \in$ ptCustomers) $p.MaxLen > 10$.
($c12$): ($\forall p \in$ ptCustomers) $p.MinDate < 1\_Apr\_1994$.

Now by applying the pushdown inference algorithm in Section 4.3, to the predicates $c10 - c12$ above, we derive the predicate

($c13$): ($\forall t \in$ calls) $t.Length > 10$.

in the view wellcalled, and the predicate

($c14$): ($\forall p0 \in$ pt0) ($p0.Length > 10$ OR $p0.Date < 1\_Apr\_1994$).

on the node ptCustomers, which further derives

($c15$): ($\forall t \in$ calls) ($t.Length > 10$ OR $t.Date < 1\_Apr\_1994$).

in the view pt0.

The exact place where the above inferences are made depends on the optimization framework within which the aggregation reasoning is incorporated. As an example, the predicate movearound [LMS94] technique works in four phases, and would make the following inferences in each:

- (*Initialization Phase*): Initialize predicates into each box. Infer $c1 - c4$, $c8$, and $c11 - c12$.
- (*Pull-up phase*): Infer predicates in each box and pull them up into the parent box. Infer $c5 - c7$.
- (*Push-down phase*): Infer predicates in each box and push them down into each child box. Infer $c9 - c10$, $c13 - c15$.
- (*Cleanup phase*): Remove predicates involving functional terms and predicates that are guaranteed to be true.

6 Related Work

The types of inferences we describe in this paper can be incorporated into several existing query rewrite techniques (e.g., predicate pushdown [Ull89], predicate move-around [LMS94]) and into rule based query optimizers [PHH92] and optimizer generators [GM93] fairly easily and modularly.

The predicate move-around algorithm [LMS94] provides a framework in which predicates are moved in a query graph, and we showed, in Section 5.2 how various aggregation inferences can be made within this framework. Some simple versions of the inferences described in Sections 4.2 and 4.3 were mentioned in [LMS94] as a way of showing the generality of the predicate move-around framework. Functional terms of a different type than the ones in this paper were also used in [LMS94] to reason with functional dependencies.

Ross et al. [RSSS94] considered a subset of our problem, namely a subset of the intra-relation inferences, when different aggregation functions are performed on the *same* relation, attribute and grouping columns (Section 4.2). For the case of a single groupby operation in a view, they studied predicates that can contain arbitrary linear constraints, and gave a complete inference procedure. They considered view-to-relation inferences (Section 4.3), but only when there is a single aggregation function in a grouping operation. The constraint language and the reasoning framework in [RSSS94] was not expressive enough to represent the types of predicates needed for the query optimization shown in Sections 2 and 5.

Gupta et al. [GHQ95] use a generalized projection operator to show that aggregation is similar to duplicate elimination in SQL, and that optimizations for the SQL distinct operator can be applied to aggregations. They do not give any rules to infer aggregation predicates between different types of aggregations or between views and relations.

There has been a lot of work on optimizing queries with aggregation in correlated subqueries by way of decorrelation (converting the subqueries into views) [Kim82, GW87, Day87, Mur92], with perhaps a magic-sets transformation to follow [MFPR90, MP94]. A different type of optimization involving aggregation was described by Chaudhuri and Shim [CS94] and Yan and Larson [YL95]. The main observation in that work is that often it is possible to perform a grouping operation *before* a join or selection operation in the same query block. Doing so may result in more efficient query plans. Our approach is orthogonal to that of decorrelation and commuting groupings with joins since the goal there is to change the structure of the query graph given a set of predicates, while ours is to infer predicates in the query graph without changing the graph. The problem of optimizing queries with aggregation by exploiting materialized views is considered in [DJLS95, GHQ95].

7   Conclusions

We have developed a framework in which a system can do reasoning with aggregation constraints. We identified a constraint language that lets us reason with aggregation. The key feature of the language is introduction of functional symbols of the form $f_{\{R,GL,A,Y\}}$ that are identified by the relation, the grouping list, the aggregation function, and the aggregated column. Use of such function symbols lets us relate aggregations done in different parts of the query. We then identified three types of inferencing that needs to be done: (1) intra-relation Inference: Inferencing predicates on functional terms with the same relation, (2) relation-to-view Inference: Inferencing predicates on functional terms on a relation and a view derived from the relation, and (3) view-to-relation Inference: Inferencing ordinary predicates on relations that define an aggregation view from predicates on the view. We presented a set of sound inference rules for each type of inference, and detailed an inference procedure that works in time linear in the number of rules and functional terms. We have several more rules that are similar or a special case of the rules presented here. However, even with all these rules, the inference procedure is not complete. In fact, it follows from [vdM92, MS95] that the satisfiability problem for queries with aggregation is undecidable. Thus, there cannot exist a complete inference procedure for aggregation constraints.

533

Aggregation constraints are very important in large database applications, where complex decision-support queries rely on reducing data by several different types of aggregation on several combinations of a small number of base tables, and then apply a large number of predicates on the aggregation views to study different fragments of the data and to test different hypotheses. Such queries can greatly benefit from optimization using the type of reasoning outlined above. In this paper we show how the aggregation reasoning framework can be incorporated into a database optimizer. A crucial observation is that the functional terms over which we need to reason is linear in the size of the query.

Beside query optimization, their are several other domains where reasoning with aggregation can be used – logic programming, constraint programming, constraint databases [KKR90, BK95], and global information systems [LSK95].

As future work, we would like to permit an aggregation function to be applied to more than one aggregated column, e.g. $\texttt{MAX}(Y_1 + Y_2)$. Though the general inference procedure on aggregation constraints is undecidable, it may be possible to identify fragments that are decidable, as done in [RSSS94] for the subcase considered there. Finally, this paper focussed mostly on the logic behind the inference rules. We plan to further explore the problem of controlling the application of the inference rules (as in Section 5).

References

[BK95]   A. Brodsky and Y. Kornatzky. The lyric language: Querying constraint objects. In *Proceedings of ACM SIGMOD 1995 International Conference on Management of Data*, San Jose, CA, May 23-25 1995.

[CS94]   Surajit Chaudhuri and Kyuseok Shim. Including groupby in query optimization. In Proceedings of VLDB–94, pages 354–366.

[DJLS95]   Shaul Dar, H. V. Jagadish, Alon Y. Levy and Divesh Srivastava. *Answering SQL Queries with Aggregation Using Materialized Views*. Working notes of the Post-ILPS95 Workshop on Constraints, Databases and Logic Programming.

[Day87]   Umeshwar Dayal. Of nests and trees: A unified approach to processing queries that contain nested subqueries, aggregates, and quantifiers. In *Proceedings of the Thirteenth International Conference on Very Large Databases (VLDB)*, pages 197–208, Brighton, England, September 1-4 1987.

[GM93]   Goetz Graefe and William J. McKenna. The volcano optimizer generator: Extensibility and efficient search. In *Proceedings of the Ninth IEEE International Conference on Data Engineering*, Vienna, Austria, April 1993.

[GW87]   Richard A. Ganski and Harry K. T. Wong. Optimization of nested SQL queries revisited. In *Proceedings of ACM SIGMOD 1987 International Conference on Management of Data*, pages 23–33, San Francisco, CA, May 1987.

[GHQ95]   A. Gupta, V. Harinarayan and D. Quass. *Generalized Projections: A Powerful Approach to Aggregation*. In Proceedings of VLDB–95.

[Hel94]   Joseph M. Hellerstein. Practical predicate placement. In Proceedings of SIGMOD–94.

[HS93]   Joseph M. Hellerstein and Michael Stonebraker. Predicate migration: Optimizing queries with expensive predicates. In *Proceedings of ACM SIG-*

MOD 1993 International Conference on Management of Data, pages 267–276, Washington, DC, May 26-28 1993.

[Kim82]   Won Kim. On optimizing an SQL-like nested query. ACM Transactions on Database Systems, 7(3), September 1982.

[KKR90]   Paris C. Kanellakis, Gabriel M. Kuper, and Peter Z. Revesz. Constraint query languages. In Proceedings of the Ninth Symposium on Principles of Database Systems (PODS), pages 299–313, Nashville, TN, April 2-4 1990.

[LMS94]   Alon Levy, Inderpal Singh Mumick, and Yehoshua Sagiv. Query optimization by predicate movearound. In Proceedings of VLDB-94, pages 96–107.

[LS92]   Alon Levy and Yehoshua Sagiv. Constraints and redundancy in datalog. In Proceedings of the Eleventh Symposium on Principles of Database Systems (PODS), pages 67–80, San Diego, CA, June 2-4 1992.

[LSK95]   Alon Y. Levy, Divesh Srivastava, and Thomas Kirk. Data model and query evaluation in global information systems. Journal of Intelligent Information Systems, 5(2), September, 1995.

[MFPR90] Inderpal Singh Mumick, Sheldon J. Finkelstein, Hamid Pirahesh, and Raghu Ramakrishnan. Magic is relevant. In Proceedings of ACM SIGMOD 1990 International Conference on Management of Data, pages 247–258, Atlantic City, NJ, May 23-25 1990.

[MP94]   Inderpal Singh Mumick and Hamid Pirahesh. Implementation of magic in starburst. In Proceedings of SIGMOD-94.

[MS95]   Inderpal Singh Mumick and Oded Shmueli. How expressive is stratified aggregation. To Appear in Annals of Mathematics and Artificial Intelligence, 1995.

[Mur92]   M. Muralikrishna. Improved unnesting algorithms for join aggregate SQL queries. In Proceedings of the Eighteenth International Conference on Very Large Databases (VLDB), pages 91–102, Vancouver, Canada, August 23-27 1992.

[PHH92]   Hamid Pirahesh, Joseph M. Hellerstein, and Waqar Hasan. Extensible/rule based query rewrite optimization in Starburst. In Proceedings of ACM SIGMOD 1992 International Conference on Management of Data, pages 39–48, San Diego, CA, June 2-5 1992.

[RSSS94] Kenneth Ross, Divesh Srivastava, Peter Stuckey, and S. Sudarshan. Foundations of aggregation constraints. In Alan Borning, editor, Principles and Practice of Constraint Programming, 1994. LNCS 874.

[Ull89]   Jeffrey D. Ullman. Principles of Database and Knowledge-Base Systems, Volumes 1 and 2. Computer Science Press, 1989.

[vdM92]   Ronald van der Meyden. The Complexity of Querying Indefinite Information: Defined Relations, Recursion, and Linear Order. PhD thesis, Rutgers, The State University of New Jersey, New Brunswick, NJ, October 1992.

[YL95]   Weipeng P. Yan and Per-Åke Larson. Eager Aggregation and Lazy Aggregation. In Proceedings of VLDB-95.

How to Tackle Schema Validation by View Updating

Hendrik Decker[*], Ernest Teniente[**], Toni Urpi[**]

Universitat Politècnica de Catalunya

LSI, Facultat d'Informàtica

carrer Pau Gargallo 5

E - 08028 Barcelona, Catalonia

hendrik@zfe.siemens.de, {teniente | urpi}@lsi.upc.es

[*]address: Siemens ZFE T SE 4, D - 81730 München, Germany

[*]supported by the DGICYT, ref. SAB94-0331

[**]supported by the PRONTIC program project TIC94-0512

ABSTRACT

Schema validation and view updating are database engineering problems which seem to differ significantly. Hence, for solving them, significantly different approaches are taken, usually. However, one of the contributions of this paper is: We show that any sound method for view updating can effectively be used also for validating schema specifications. We consider typical schema validation tasks such as checking schema satisfiability, liveliness of a predicate, reachability of partially specified states and redundancy of integrity constraint specifications, and we show how, with any sound method for view updating, these tasks can be tackled in a uniform way. For illustrating our point, we shortly recapitulate a concrete method for view updating and apply it to tackle these tasks. We emphasize that our general approach is independent of any particular method for view updating. Other contributions consists in refined concepts of schema satisfiability and integrity redundance. Both can be expressed in related terms of liveliness and reachability, and yield results that compare advantageously to what has been proposed so far, in the literature.

Introduction

This paper describes a uniform technique for the validation of a database schema. By validation we mean the process of checking whether a database schema correctly and adequately describes intended needs and requirements [ABC82]. This is an increasingly important problem in database engineering, particularly since database schema design is becoming more advanced. Indeed, detecting and removing possible flaws during schema design time will prevent those flaws from materializing as run time errors or other inconveniences during operation time. Validation has been widely investigated in the field of information systems engineering, in particular wrt conceptual models of information systems (see, e.g., [VF85, Bub86, CO92, OS95]).

In the field of databases, validation has been investigated in theory (e.g., [Kun84, BM86, BDM88, IKH92, CDM93, LMSS93, GSUW94]). However, in practice, different schema validation tasks are usually handled by different techniques. As opposed to that, we propose in this paper to handle several validation tasks such as schema satisfiability, liveliness of a predicate, reachability of partially specified states, and redundancy of integrity constraints specifications in a uniform way, viz. by using view updating.

Roughly, the main idea of this paper is to define, for each particular validation task, a distinguished view predicate which describes the accomplishment of the task. An attempt to execute a task t can then be made by attempting to satisfy the request of inserting the predicate corresponding to t. For instance, a successful attempt to insert the 0-ary predicate satisfiable shows that the database schema on which the insert request has been executed is satisfiable (in the sense defined in section 1); a finitely failed attempt to insert satisfiable shows the unsatisfiability of the schema. We should like to point out that this idea is independent of and applicable to any particular view updating method.

Our approach contributes to database schema validation by allowing the database designer to ask questions about the accomplishment of certain properties of the schema. Answers to these questions provide him/her information on whether the database schema correctly and adequately describes the users' intended needs and requirements.

In section 1, we set up the framework by using the terminology and formalisms of deductive databases, as known from, e.g., [GMN84, Ull88]. In section 2, we describe the general approach to using any given method for view updating also for database validation. For illustrating our approach, we describe its application to a known method for view updating, the Events Method [TO92, TO95], in section 3. We give reference and compare to related work ([Kun84, BM86, BDM88, IKH92, CDM93, LMSS93, GSUW94]) along the way. We conclude with an outlook on the further use of view updating methods for knowledge assimilation tasks such as schema updating, transaction design and belief revision.

1 Framework of View Updating and Schema Validation

In this section, we first briefly review the terminology and formalisms of deductive databases. Then, we give a declarative definition of view updating. Finally, we give definitions of the schema validation tasks considered in this paper. In the next section, we will show how these tasks can be uniformly handled by view updating.

1.1 Preliminary Definitions

For convenience, we assume that there is a sufficiently large language with which each database and each database schema considered in this paper is formulated, and that the set of predicates in that language is partitioned into a set of *intensional* (*view*) and a set of *extensional* (*base*) predicates. Function symbols are permitted. Among others, we may use (possibly subscripted) constant symbols a, b, c and variable symbols x, y, z.

A *database schema* (shortly, *schema*) is a tuple (IDB, IC) where IDB is a stratifiable finite set of deductive rules, each of which is about an intensional predicate, and IC is a finite set of sentences (i.e., closed well-formed formulae) called *integrity constraints* (shortly, *constraints*).

Constraints usually express negative information that restricts the admissibility of database information. Hence, we suppose that constraints are always represented as *denials*, i.e. negative clauses of the form ← B, which reads "for all variables in B, it must not be that B holds", where B is a conjunction of literals. Representation by denials entails no loss of generality, since each sentence F can be represented as ← ¬F and then be transformed into an equivalent set of clauses to be added to the schema, as described in [Llo87] [Dec89]. Another convenient representation of a constraint ← B is violated ← B, where violated is a distinguished predicate that is not used for other purposes.

For a schema (IDB, IC), a *database state* (shortly, *state*) D is a triple (IDB, IC, EDB) where EDB is a finite set of ground base facts. IDB is called the *intensional*, EDB the *extensional* part of D. A state may be identified with EDB if the schema is understood.

If, for a sentence F and a database state D = (IDB, IC, EDB), we say that F *is true* (resp., *false*) *in* D, we mean that F is true (resp., false) according to the semantic interpretation given to D (such as any of the common model- or proof-theoretic semantics). As usual, we identify a (Herbrand) model of a set of clauses with the ground facts that are true in that model.

In a database state D = (IDB, IC, EDB), *integrity is satisfied* if each constraint in IC is true (*satisfied*) in D; *integrity is violated* if there is a constraint which is false (*violated*) in D. A state in which integrity is satisfied is called *sound*.

For a database state D = (IDB, IC, EDB), an *update* is a bipartite set U = Ins ∪ Del of ground facts about extensional predicates which defines a successor state U(D) = (IDB, IC, EDB') such that EDB' = (EDB − Del) ∪ Ins. We call D "the *old* state" and U(D) "the *new* state".

Intuitively, a database is a dynamic system which changes over time, while the schema is invariant. Changes are effected by updates. Hence, for a fixed scheme S = (IDB, IC), a *database* can be defined as a sequence D_0, D_1, ... of states of S and updates U_1, U_2, ... such that, for i≥1, $D_i = U_i(D_{i-1})$.

1.2 View Updating

For a database state D, an *update request* is represented by a sentence R, which is required to be true in a state U(D) obtained by some update U. In terms of the definition above, *view updating* can be stated as the problem of finding an adequate update for some update request such that the request is true in the new state. Adequacy of an update U is usually defined by requiring that U is minimal, in some sense. Minimality may be defined in terms of the changes to EDB or to the model associated to IDB ∪ EDB. Independent of any particular definition of minimality, we can define:

For a database state D and an update request R, a *view update* is a minimal update U such that R is true in U(D). We then also say that U *satisfies* R.

Besides minimality and *basicness* (i.e., update requests should be satisfied by changing only the extensional part of the database, not the schema), other filter criteria can be expressed by integrity constraints, i.e., only updates which maintain integrity are considered adequate. We point out that view updating as considered in section 2 is not required to consider minimality.

1.3 Schema Validation Tasks

1.3.1 Satisfiability

Intuitively, a database schema is satisfiable if there is a state of the schema in which all of its integrity constraints are satisfied. Satisfiability checking is different from integrity checking, since the former is independent of any state and any update, while the latter is not. The next two properties are crucial for checking, at schema design time, whether the specification of a schema is satisfiable at all.

A database schema S = (IDB, IC) is *state-satisfiable* if there is a sound state of S. S is *model-satisfiable* if there is a model M of the set IDB ∪ IC of first-order sentences.

There are three essential differences between state-satisfiability (or simply, satisfiability) and model-satisfiability. First, the model M required for model-satisfiability may be infinite, while EDB as required for state-satisfiability must be finite. Second, state-satisfiability associates a possibly non-monotonic database semantics to IDB, while model-satisfiability interprets IDB "classically", as a set of first-order formulas. Third, M may contain facts about intensional predicates, while EDB may not. In fact, model-satisfiability does not entail state-satisfiability, as shown by the following example. Consider the schema

$$
\begin{array}{ll}
\text{IDB} \;=\; & p(x) \leftarrow q(x) \\
& q(x) \leftarrow r(x,x) \land \neg s(x) \\
& s(x) \leftarrow r(x,y)
\end{array}
\qquad
\begin{array}{ll}
\text{IC} \;=\; & \leftarrow t(x) \land \neg p(x) \\
& \leftarrow \neg\, t(a)
\end{array}
$$

It is easy to see that this schema is not satisfiable by any state. However, $\{p(a),\ t(a)\}$ is a model of IDB ∪ IC. An easier, though more contrived, example would be IDB = p ← q ∧ ¬q, IC = ← ¬ p, which is not satisfiable by any state, while p is a model of IDB ∪ IC.

It can be argued that state-satisfiability is a more interesting property than model-satisfiability when validating a database schema, since it is usually assumed that the database may not contain ground facts of intensional predicates. However, in other contexts such as in theorem proving, model-satisfiability is also an interesting property. As we will see in section 2.1, the approach proposed in this paper is able to check both of them.

It can be shown that state-satisfiability entails model-satisfiability, 'since each sound state determines a model. However, the converse is not true as we have just seen. Related work in this field is mainly concerned with checking model-satisfiability, e.g. [BDM88], [IKH92]. The methods proposed in the previous references would find the models given for the examples above, and hence conclude that both are model-satisfiable. However, none of these methods is able to conclude that these examples are not state-satisfiable. On the other hand, Kung [Kun84] proposes a method for checking schema satisfiability in the absence of deductive rules. Note that state and model-satisfiability coincide in the absence of rules.

It is well-known that satisfiability and other validation tasks are only semi-decidable and not tractable in general. However, if database restrictions such as range-restrictedness, absence of function symbols or acyclicity of evaluation are imposed, a reasonable behaviour of our approach to tackle these tasks can be achieved.

1.3.2 Liveliness and Reachability

Even if a schema is state-satisfiable, it may not be very useful: It may turn out that certain desirable extensions of some predicates, or certain intended properties, or some conceivable states, may never be reached at any point in the lifetime of the database. Mechanisms for checking the properties defined in this section help to avoid such ill-defined specifications at schema validation time.

Let S be a database schema.

a) A predicate p is *lively in* S if there is a sound state of S in which at least one fact about p is true.

b) A sentence F is *reachable* in S if there is a sound state of S in which F is true.

Predicates which are not lively correspond to relations that are empty in each sound state. Such predicates are clearly not useful and possibly ill-specified. As an example, consider the following schema:

$$\text{IDB} \; = \; q(x) \leftarrow r(x,y) \wedge s(x) \qquad\qquad \text{IC} \; = \; \leftarrow s(x)$$

Clearly, q is not lively since the integrity constraint impedes any fact about q to be true.

However, even if a predicate is lively, then it might still be that only a few (or even only a single) sound states with a non-empty extension of that predicate exist. But the database designer may have envisaged that other states are reachable as well. Hence, schema validation should also be interested in the reachability of any state which would soundly satisfy some specified property F (e.g., any set of facts, expressed as a conjunction, or any other requirement expressed by some arbitrary sentence; F can be seen as a partial specification of a state, or as a class of states).

Liveliness of an n-ary predicate p (n≥0) is equivalent to reachability of the existential closure of $p(x_1, ..., x_n)$. Yet, state-satisfiability *can* be expressed in terms of liveliness: If each integrity constraint in a schema is represented with violated in its head and satisfiable ← ¬violated is included in IDB as a definition of satisfiable, then state-satisfiability of that schema is equivalent to the liveliness of satisfiable.

Liveliness has been studied as "non-trivial consistency" in [CDM93]. Moreover, the definitions of "lively" in this paper and "satisfiable" in [LMSS93] essentially coincide, except that integrity constraints are not taken into account in [LMSS93]. Therefore, it could happen that a predicate is satisfiable in the sense of [LMSS93], but it is not lively due to some integrity constraints (like, for instance, predicate q of the previous example). A more recent definition of "satisfiable" given in [LM95] coincides with our definition of "lively", but stronger restrictions than ours are imposed on the considered deductive rules and integrity constraints. We do not speak of "satisfiable" here, for preventing confusion with the "classical" primary use of the word in this paper.

1.3.3 Redundancy

Intuitively, a constraint (or a subset of constraints) is redundant if integrity does not depend on it. For instance, a constraint of form $\leftarrow p \wedge \neg p$ must certainly be considered redundant since it can never be violated, i.e., integrity is independent of it. Clearly, such a redundancy should be detected by schema validation and then be eliminated. In general, however, we are interested in situations of redundancy that are possibly more subtle than the simple constraint above. They are captured by the following definitions.

Let S = (IDB, IC) be a schema and I an integrity constraint in IC.

a) I is *absolutely redundant* if I is true in each state of S.

b) I is *relatively redundant* if I is true in each sound state of (IDB, IC − {I}).

The following simple example illustrates both properties:

$$IDB \quad = \quad p \leftarrow r \wedge s \qquad\qquad IC = \quad \leftarrow q \wedge \neg p$$
$$p \leftarrow q \qquad\qquad\qquad \leftarrow t \wedge s$$
$$\leftarrow t$$

The first integrity constraint is absolutely redundant since q implies p and therefore it is not possible to violate this constraint. Moreover, the second integrity constraint is relatively redundant, since it is entailed by the third one. Therefore, the database schema consisting of IDB and only the third integrity constraint would admit the same sound states as the original one.

Both absolute and relative redundancy depend on IDB, in general (while the tautology $\leftarrow p \wedge \neg p$ from above is redundant in any scheme). On the other hand, absolute redundancy of a constraint does not depend on the satisfaction of other constraints, while relative redundancy does. Therefore, at schema validation time, all absolutely redundant constraints can be eliminated at once, while several relatively redundant constraints should not be discarded at a time.

Relative redundancy of I is similar to subsumption of I by IC − {I}, as defined in [GSUW94]. The essential difference is that redundancy of I is defined by satisfaction, while subsumption of I by violation of I (see also 2.5). Beside subsumption, other forms of redundancy that take updates into account (and hence can not be readily used at schema validation time) are studied in [GSUW94], but absolute redundancy is not considered. The following example illustrates the differences and similarities between both approaches.

Example: Consider the following database schema where IDB = {1, 2, 3, 4} and IC = {5 — 12}, where the numbers identify the following clauses.

1      $super(x) \leftarrow superior(x, y)$

2      $boss(x) \leftarrow super(x) \land salary(x, y) \land high\text{-}salary(y)$

3      $manager(x) \leftarrow salary(x, y) \land high\text{-}salary(y)$

4      $high\text{-}salary(y) \leftarrow y \geq 10.000.000$

5      $\leftarrow boss(x) \land \neg super(x)$

6      $\leftarrow super(x) \land \neg boss(x)$

7      $\leftarrow super(x) \land manager(x) \land \neg boss(x)$

8      $\leftarrow manager(x) \land \neg super(x)$

9      $\leftarrow super(x) \land \neg manager(x)$

10     $\leftarrow manager(x) \land \neg boss(x)$

11     $\leftarrow salary(x, y) \land y > 15.000.000 \land \neg boss(x)$

12     $\leftarrow salary(x, y) \land y > 12.000.000 \land \neg super(x)$

Base predicates are superior and salary. The intended meaning of $superior(x, y)$ is that x is a superior of y, of $salary(x, y)$ that the salary of x is y. Further, every individual with high salary is a manager and every superior with high salary is a boss. The constraints (which we have tossed into the schema, just to see what's happening) are self-explaining.

It is easy to see that 7 is relatively redundant, since it is entailed by 6, and also by 10. Besides that, we found out with an implementation of the method in section 3 that 7 is even absolutely redundant, and also 5 is, while, e.g., 6 is not. (Absolute redundancy of 5 can be seen as follows: The complete definition of boss is given by 2. Hence, each boss must be a superior. Hence, 5 can never be violated. Absolute redundancy of 7 can be seen similarly.) However, none of 5 and 7 remains absolutely redundant if, e.g., the IDB is modified by deleting 2 and making a base relation out of boss. Then, there are states (also found by our implementation) which violate 5 and 7; however, 7 remains relatively redundant. Moreover, we found that both 6 and 9 are relatively redundant, but if any one of them is dropped, then the other is no longer redundant. Thus, several relatively redundant constraints must not be discarded at a time. Similarly, each of 8 and 10 is relatively redundant. Also, 11 is relatively redundant, but no longer if both 8 and 10 are dropped. Yet, 11 remains relatively redundant if any subset of $IC - \{8, 10\}$ is discarded. Similarly, 12 is relatively redundant, but it remains so even if 8 and 10 are dropped, as long as 11 is in the schema.

After all, the schema above, with IDB fixed, is free of redundant constraints and admits exactly the same sound states as before if $\{5, 7, 11, 12\}$ and either one of the sets $\{6, 8\}, \{6, 10\}, \{8, 9\}, \{9, 10\}$ but nothing more is taken out. Hence, somewhat surprisingly perhaps, one of the optimized non-redundant sets of constraints is $\{8, 9\}$ (obtained by dropping $\{6, 10\}$). Indeed, $EDB_1 = salary(fred, 11.000.000)$ violates 8 but not 9, $EDB_2 = superior(mary, fred)$ violates 9 but not 8, which shows that there is no redundance in the schema (IDB, $\{8, 9\}$).

In terms of [GSUW94], 6 subsumes 9; 9 subsumes 6; each of 6 and 10 subsumes 7; 8 subsumes 10; 10 subsumes 8; each of 8 and 10 subsumes both 11 and 12; 12

subsumes 11. This entitles us to drop $\{7, 11, 12\}$ and either $\{6, 8\}$ or $\{9, 10\}$; the only other alternative legitimated by subsumption is to drop $\{6, 9, 11, 12\}$. Clearly, the optimizations obtained by differentiating between absolute and relative redundancy are somewhat better than that. In general, our notions of redundancy yield optimizations which are never worse than what subsumption alone allows us to do, and often better, since, beyond subsumption, we have the stronger notion of absolute redundancy, by which several constraints may be eliminated at a time, which is not possible if constraints are just known to be relatively redundant or subsumed.

Strictly speaking, $\varnothing$ subsumes both 5 and 7, by the definition in [GSUW94] which, however, recurs on query containment [Ull88] and hence does not really capture the border case of constraint subsumption by $\varnothing$ (since a query is always contained by some other query, not by nothing). Moreover, there is no indication how that case should be checked by applying any of the standard approaches for checking query containment. Yet, it follows from the discussion in 1.3.2 that subsumption of a constraint I by $\varnothing$ could be checked by applying any method for checking the liveliness (or, as well, reachability, or, in terms of [LMSS93], "satisfiability") of the distinguished head violated of I. In 2.3, we shall see how all cases of redundancy and subsumption as characterized above can be checked by any method for satisfying view update requests.

Generally, it is easy to show: For a schema $S = (IDB, IC)$ and a constraint $I \in IC$ of form violated ← B (where violated does not occur elsewhere), I is not relatively redundant in S if and only if violated is reachable in $(IDB \cup \{I\}, IC - \{I\})$. Moreover, I is not absolutely redundant iff violated is reachable in $(IDB \cup \{I\}, \varnothing)$. (The technicality of shifting I to IDB, such that the integrity component of the schema becomes empty, is needed since reachability is defined only for *sound* states. This technicality will reappear in similar ways throughout section 2.)

2 Schema Validation by View Updating

Below, we present the general approach of how to use view updating for schema validation, which is independent of any particular view updating method. For convenience, let us assume that there is a distinguished unary predicate insert and that, for an insert request F, the operational semantics of executing the goal ← insert(F) on some database state D is that an update U_F is computed which satisfies the request, if it is satisfiable at all by an update of the extensional database. The procedure for computing U_F can be considered a black box, at this stage.

Further, let us assume the following conventions. For a schema $S = (IDB, IC)$ with constraints $I_1, ..., I_n$ $(n \geq 0)$ in IC, let the predicate in the head of I_i $(1 \leq i \leq n)$ be violated_i, let violated be defined by the n clauses violated ← violated_i $(1 \leq i \leq n)$, and let satisfied be defined by satisfied ← ¬violated. Further, let IDB^* stand for what is obtained by adding all constraints and the definitions of violated and satisfied to IDB. Last, let S^* stand for the empty database state $(IDB^*, \varnothing, \varnothing)$.

As an example, consider again the database schema of section 1.3.1. In this case, IDB^* would be the following:

$p(x) \leftarrow q(x)$ violated_1 $\leftarrow t(x) \wedge \neg p(x)$

$q(x) \leftarrow r(x,x) \wedge \neg s(x)$ violated_2 $\leftarrow \neg t(a)$

$s(x) \leftarrow r(x,y)$ violated $\leftarrow$ violated_i % one rule for each i, i=1, 2

                                      satisfied $\leftarrow \neg$ violated

2.1 Satisfiability

With the conventions above and the definition in 1.3.1, it is easy to see that state-satisfiability of a schema S = (IDB, IC) can be checked by executing the request $\leftarrow$ insert(satisfied) in the database state S*. Hence, S is state-satisfiable iff the request is satisfiable in S*. In the example above, no translation that satisfies the request $\leftarrow$ insert(satisfied) exists since a translation would require r(a, a) to be true and false at the same time. Therefore, the database schema of section 1.3.1 is not state-satisfiable.

The model-satisfiability of a schema S = (IDB, IC) can be checked as follows: For each $n \geq 0$ and each n-ary view predicate p, let $\underline{p}$ be a distinguished n-ary base predicate which does not occur in S. Further, let S' = (IDB', IC) be obtained by adding, for each such p, the clause $p(x_1, ..., x_n) \leftarrow \underline{p}(x_1, ..., x_n)$ to IDB. Then, S is model-satisfiable iff S' is state-satisfiable. (Proof of *if*: Each sound state of S' determines a model of IDB' $\cup$ IC and hence also of IDB $\cup$ IC. *Only-if*: For each model M of IDB $\cup$ IC, M' = M $\cup$ {$\underline{p}(a_1, ..., a_n)$ | $p(a_1, ..., a_n)$ is ground fact about view p in M} is a model of IDB' $\cup$ IC. The base facts of M' define a sound state of S'.) Thus, model-satisfiability of S can be checked by checking state-satisfiability of S'. (For different purpose, similar transformations to the way S' is obtained from S are used in [Min82] [BR86]). An example will be given in section 3.

2.2 Liveliness and Reachability

It follows from the definition and discussion in 1.3.1 that liveliness of a predicate p with arity n, $n \geq 0$, can be defined on the schema level by lively_p $\leftarrow p(x_1, ..., x_n) \wedge$ satisfied. The condition satisfied is necessary because liveliness is restricted to sound states. Then, liveliness of p can be checked by including that clause in IDB* and executing the request $\leftarrow$ insert(lively_p) in the state S*. Hence, p is lively in S iff the request is satisfiable in S*.

A transformation is needed for checking the reachability of a partially specified state F of a schema S = (IDB, IC) if F is more general than a conjunction of literals: According to [Llo87] [Dec89], the "extended clause" reachable $\leftarrow$ F $\wedge$ satisfied can be transformed into an equivalent set of normal database clauses. Reachability of F can then be checked by including that set in IDB* and requesting $\leftarrow$ insert(reachable) in S*. Hence, F is reachable in S iff the request is satisfiable in S*.

2.3 Redundancy

Satisfiability, liveliness and reachability can be checked by showing the existence of some state. As opposed to that, the definition of absolute (and also relative) redundancy of a constraint requires something for *each* state. Hence, redundancy of a constraint is best checked by verifying or falsifying the lack of redundancy, which can be done by attempting to construct *one* state which would show that the constraint under investigation can be violated and hence cannot be discarded. Thus, absolute redundancy of a constraint I with violated in the head, in a schema with intensional database IDB, is checked by requesting ← insert(violated) in $S' = (IDB \cup \{I\}, \emptyset, \emptyset)$.

Similarly, relative redundancy of a constraint I_0 with, say, violated_0 in the head, in a schema of the form $S = (IDB, \{I_0, I_1, ..., I_n\})$ $(n \geq 0)$ is checked by requesting ← insert(not_redundant) in S'^*, where $S' = (IDB', \{I_1, ..., I_n\})$, and IDB' be defined by adding I_0 as well as the definition not_redundant ← violated_0 $\wedge$ satisfied to IDB, for checking if there is a state in which I_0 is violated while the other constraints are satisfied. Note that, by our construction, satisfied is defined for the constraints (second component) in S', which do not involve I_0. Hence, I_0 is relatively redundant in S iff the request of inserting not_redundant is not satisfiable in S'^*.

Similarly, subsumption of I_0 wrt $\{I_1, ..., I_n\}$ as defined in [GSUW94] can be checked by requesting ← insert(not_subsumed) in S'^*, with I_0 and not_subsumed ←violated_0 $\wedge$ ¬violated included in IDB'. Clearly, this formalization of checking subsumption effectively coincides with the formalization of checking redundancy of constraints, above (since satisfied is defined by ¬violated).

3 Using a Concrete Method for View Updating

In this section we illustrate our approach to tackle schema validation by using a concrete method for view updating. Given a method able to handle view updates in a certain class of deductive databases, it should satisfy two requirements to tackle the schema validation tasks described in previous sections. First, the class of deductive databases considered by the method must allow, at least, to express the declarative definitions of the tasks, given in section 2. Second, if there exists some solution that satisfies a given request, the method obtains one such solution (but not necessarily several or even all of them).

We have considered the Events Method [TO92, TO95] which fulfils the two requirements stated above for the class of stratified databases since the declarative definition of the schema validation tasks may be defined in this class of databases and because it was proved in [TO95] that the Events Method is sound and complete for stratified and allowed databases.

3.1 The Events Method [TO92, TO95]

The Events Method is based on a set of rules that define the difference between two consecutive database states. For each database predicate p in the underlying language of a given database D, a distinguished *insertion event predicate* ιp and a distinguished *deletion event predicate* δp are used to define the precise difference of deducible facts of consecutive database states. More precisely, the clauses about ιp and δp define exactly the facts about p that are effectively inserted or deleted in the extension of p by some transaction T. The definition of ιp and δp depends on the definition of p in D, but is independent of any transaction T and of any extensional database EDB.

A more formal declarative characterization of the meaning of ιp and δp and a description and discussion of the implementation of these event rules by database clause definitions of ιp and δp can be found in [Oli91, UO92, TO95].

For example, if **works(employee, unit)** is a derived predicate, ιworks(john, marketing) denotes an insertion event corresponding to predicate works: **works(john, marketing)** is true after the application of the transaction and it was false before. On the other hand δworks(mary, sales) denotes a deletion event: works(mary, sales) is false after the application of the transaction and it was true before.

Given a view update request, the Events Method is able to obtain all minimal translations that satisfy it. A translation is *minimal* when there is no subset of it which is also a translation. In general, several minimal translations may exist. Moreover, the Events Method, as most of the methods dealing with view updating, considers only translations that involve solely updates of the extensional part of the database, that is, insertions and deletions of ground facts of base predicates.

In the Events Method, a request for inserting a derived predicate p corresponds to an event ιp(a), where a is a vector of constants. A translation T of an insertion ιp(a) defines a set of base fact updates such that p(a) is a logical consequence of the completion of the deductive database updated according to T. In a similar way, a request for deleting a derived predicate p corresponds to an event δp(a). In this case, a translation T of a deletion δp(a) defines a set of base fact updates such that p(a) is not a logical consequence of the updated database.

Formally, let D be a deductive database, A(D) the augmented database of D (which consists of D and its associated event rules), U a view update request which consists of a conjunction of events of derived facts and T a translation consisting of a set of events of base facts. In the Events Method, a translation T satisfies the request U if, using SLDNF resolution, the goal {←U} succeeds from input set A(D) ∪ T. The translation set T is obtained by having some failed SLDNF derivation of A(D) ∪ {← U} succeed. Possible ways in which a failed derivation may succeed correspond to the different translations T_i that satisfy the request. If no translation T is obtained, then the view update cannot be satisfied by changing only the extensional part of the deductive database.

In order to facilitate the understandability of the ideas proposed in this paper, in the rest of the section we will try to explain the behaviour of the Events Method in an intuitive way, instead of providing a formal description of the examples. We refer the reader to [TO95] for a formal description of the Events Method.

In Sections 3.2 and 3.3, we show how the Events Method can be used for checking state-satisfiability and model-satisfiability. In a similar way, by considering the specifications of the database validation tasks in terms of view updating as defined in Section 2, it could also be shown that the Events Method can also be used for checking liveliness, reachability, absolute redundancy and relative redundancy.

3.2 Checking State-Satisfiability

Given a deductive database schema S=(IDB,IC), checking that S is state-satisfiable refers to the problem of checking whether there exists at least a sound state of S. As we said in section 2, our general approach for dealing with this problem consists in reformulating it in terms of view updating. Thus, state satisfiability can be checked by executing the request:

← insert(satisfied)

in the empty database state S*=(IDB*,∅,∅), where IDB* is obtained by adding all constraints and the definitions of violated and satisfied to IDB.

Given a deductive database schema S=(IDB,IC), checking state-satisfiability with the Events Method may be performed by considering the following two steps. First, we have to check whether satisfied is true in the empty database state S*=(IDB*,∅,∅) by simply querying this state of the database. If satisfied is true in S*, then all the integrity constraints are already satisfied in the empty database state and, therefore, S is state-satisfiable.

If satisfied is false in S*, then we have to consider the augmented database state A(S*) corresponding to S* and we have to request in it the view update ← ιsatisfied. If there exists some translation that satisfies this request, then there exists at least a sound state of S. On the other hand, if the Events Method fails to obtain a translation, S is not state-satisfiable.

The Events Method needs to consider the above two steps since in this method an insertion request ιsatisfied (and in general any insertion request) must be effective in the sense that it requires that satisfied does not hold in the state where it is requested. Therefore, before requesting the view update ←ιsatisfied, it must be checked that satisfied is not true in the empty database state. The following example illustrates our approach.

Consider the following deductive database schema:

```
some_cand   ←   cand(x)
violated_1  ←   ¬some_cand
violated_2  ←   cand(x) ∧ ¬app(x)
violated_3  ←   app(x)
violated    ←   violated_i     % one rule for each i, i = 1, 2, 3.
satisfied   ←   ¬violated
```

where cand stands for candidate, some_cand for some candidate and app for applicant.

It can be easily seen that satisfied is false in the initial state of the database since violated_1 is true because some_cand is false and, therefore, violated is also true.

Then, we try to satisfy satisfied by requesting the view update ιsatisfied which entails the request δviolated. The Events Method tries to satisfy it by deleting violated_1 and guaranteeing that violated_2 and violated_3 do not hold in the new state of the database. Deletion of violated_1 is performed by proposing the insertion of cand(a) for some value a of the domain of x. However, insertion of cand(a) violates violated_2, which is repaired by proposing the insertion of app(a). Now, this latter insertion violates violated_3 but there is no possible way to repair this violation. Thus, the Events Method does not obtain any translation that satisfies ιsatisfied, which shows that the integrity constraints of the example are unsatisfiable.

Satisfiability could be achieved, for instance, by removing integrity constraint violated_3. In this case, the Events Method would obtain the translation T={ιcand(a), ιapp(a)} that satisfies the request ιsatisfied. This translation corresponds to the extensional database state {cand(a), app(a)}.

In general, integrity constraints satisfiability considers that initially the extensional database is empty. However, we would like to note that the Events Method can also be applied with a non empty extensional database in the same way as explained above.

3.3 Checking Model-Satisfiability

Consider again the same deductive database schema as in previous section, which as we have seen is not state-satisfiable. We are going to show that, by applying the transformation described in Section 2.1, the Events Method may also be used for checking that this database schema is model-satisfiable. In this case, the transformed database schema is:

$$
\begin{array}{lll}
\text{some\_cand} & \leftarrow & \text{cand(x)} \\
\text{some\_cand} & \leftarrow & \text{base\_some\_cand} \\
\text{violated\_1} & \leftarrow & \neg\text{some\_cand} \\
\text{violated\_2} & \leftarrow & \text{cand(x)} \wedge \neg\text{app(x)} \\
\text{violated\_3} & \leftarrow & \text{app(x)} \\
\text{violated} & \leftarrow & \text{violated\_}i \quad \text{\% one rule for each } i, i = 1, 2, 3. \\
\text{satisfied} & \leftarrow & \neg\text{violated}
\end{array}
$$

It can be easily seen that satisfied does not hold in the initial state of the database since violated_1 is still true because some_cand does not hold.

Then, we try to satisfy satisfied by requesting the view update ιsatisfied which in turn entails the request δviolated. As before, the Events Method tries to satisfy it by deleting violated_1 and guaranteeing that violated_2 and violated_3 do not hold in the new state of the database. In this example, deletion of violated_1 may be performed by proposing the insertion of cand(a) for some value a of the domain of x or by proposing the insertion of base_some_cand. As we have seen in example 3.1, the first alternative does not lead to any valid solution. However, the insertion of base_some_cand repairs violated_1 and does not violate violated_2 (since cand(x) is not true) nor violated_3 (since app(x) is not true). Then, the Events Method would obtain one valid translation T = {ιbase_some_cand}, which means that the original database schema of example 3.1 is model-satisfiable. Note that the obtained translation would correspond to the model {some_cand} of the original database schema.

Conclusion

We have defined and discussed several kinds of schema satisfiability and integrity redundance that are more refined than the usual notions in the literature. We have shown that satisfiability, liveliness and reachability, on one hand, and reachability, integrity redundance and constraint subsumption, on the other, are closely related to each other. In particular, we have shown how these properties can be detected at schema validation time. Moreover, we have shown that, for checking satisfiability, liveliness, reachability and also redundancy of a schema, any method for view updating can be employed (which can be seen as a practical example of the successful re-use of software). This has been illustrated by using a known method for view updating for tackling the schema validation tasks discussed before. A broader perspective of applying the basic technology of view updating also for other knowledge assimilation tasks is given in [TU95].

Future work in this area is concerned with extended notions of schema specifications that comprise, besides intensional database and constraints, also concepts for knowledge assimilation and transaction design, such as schema updates (i.e., of rules and constraints), parametrizable schemes of frequently occurring updates and queries, etc. For such extensions, our definitions of reachability, redundancy etc. can be generalized and then used for extended forms of schema validation. For example, a natural analogy of our definition of relative redundancy would be to define that, for a schema (IDB, IC), a clause C in IDB is *schema-redundant* if C is true in each sound state of (IDB − {C}, IC). Clearly, this form of redundancy of clauses is closely related to the concept of query containment [Ull88]. However, schema redundancy is stronger, in the sense that it is interested only in sound states, while query containment does not address the soundness of states.

Acknowledgements

We would like to thank Juan Carlos Casamayor, Dolors Costal, Enric Mayol, Antoni Olivé, Joan Antoni Pastor, Fèlix Saltor and Maria Ribera Sancho for their helpful comments and suggestions.

References

[ABC82] W.R.Adrion, M.A.Branstad, J.C.Cherniavsky: Validation, Verification and Testing of Computer Software, *ACM Computing Surveys*, Vol. 14, No. 2, 159-192, 1982.

[BDM88] F. Bry, H. Decker, R. Manthey: A uniform approach to constraint satisfaction and constraint satisfiability in deductive databases, in J. Schmidt et al (eds): *Proc. 1st EDBT*, 488-505, Springer LNCS 303, 1988.

[BM86] F. Bry, R. Manthey: Checking consistency of database constraints: a logical basis. *Proc. Int. Conf. on Very Large Data Bases '86*, 13-20, Kyoto, 1986.

[BR86] F. Bancilhon, R. Ramakrishnan: An amateur's introduction to recursive query processing strategies, *Proc. SIGMOD '86*, 16-152, ACM Press, 1986.

[Bub86] J.A. Bubenko: Information system methodologies − A research review, in T.W. Olle et al (eds), *Information System Design Methodologies: Improving the Practice*, 289-235, North-Holland, 1986.

[CDM93] J.C. Casamayor, H. Decker, F. Marqués: A mechanism for verification of knowledge base schema specifications, in P. Meseguer (ed), *Proc. European Sympos. Validation and Verification of Knowledge-based Systems*, 103-115, 1993.

[CO92] D. Costal, A. Olivé: A Method for Reasoning about Deductive Conceptual Models of Information Systems, *Proc. Int. Conf. on Advanced Information Systems Engineering (CAiSE'92)*, 612-631, 1992.

[Dec89]   H. Decker: The range form of databases and queries, or: How to avoid floundering, in J. Retti, K. Leidlmair (eds), *Proc. 5th ÖGAI*, 114-123, Springer Informatik-Fachberichte 208, 1989.

[GMN84]   H. Gallaire, J. Minker, J.M. Nicolas: Logic and databases: A deductive approach, *Computing Surveys* 16, 153-185, 1984.

[GSUW94] A. Gupta, Y. Sagiv, J.D. Ullman, J. Widom: Constraint checking with partial information, *Proc. 13th PoDS*, 45-55, ACM Press, 1994.

[IKH92]   K. Inoue, M. Koshimura, R. Hasegawa: Embedding negation as failure into a model generation theorem prover, *Proc. 11th CADE*, 1992.

[Kun84]   C.H. Kung: *A Temporal Framework for Information Systems Specifications and Verification*, PhD Thesis, Univ. of Trondheim, Norway, 1984.

[LMSS93] A. Levy, I.S. Mumick, Y. Sagiv, O. Shmueli: Equivalence, query-reachability, and satisfiability in Datalog extensions, *Proc. 12th PoDS*, 1993.

[LS95]   A. Levy, Y. Sagiv: Semantic Query Optimization in Datalog Programs, *Proc. 14th PoDS*, 163-173, 1995.

[Llo87]   J.W. Lloyd: *Foundations of Logic Programming*, Springer, 1987.

[Min82]   J. Minker: On indefinite databases and the closed world assumption, *Proc. 6th Int'l Conf. Automated Deduction, CADE '82*, 292-308, Springer LNCS 138, 1982.

[Oli91]   Olivé, A.: Integrity Checking in Deductive Databases, *Proc. 17th VLDB Conference*, 513-523, 1991.

[OS95]   A.Olivé, M.R. Sancho: A Method for Explaining the Behaviour of Conceptual Models. *Proc. Int. Conf. on Advanced Information Systems Engineering (CAiSE'95)*, 12-25, 1995.

[TO92]   E. Teniente, A. Olivé: The Events Method for View Updating in Deductive Databases, *Proc. Int. Conf. on Extending Database Technology (EDBT'92)*, 245-260, 1992.

[TO95]   E. Teniente, A. Olivé: Updating Knowledge Bases while Maintaining their Consistency, *The VLDB Journal*, Vol. 4, No. 2, 193-241, 1995.

[TU95]   E. Teniente, T. Urpi: A Common Framework for Classifying and Specifying Deductive Database Updating Problems, *Proc. 11th International Conference on Data Engineering (ICDE'95)*, 173-183, 1995.

[Ull88]   J.D. Ullman: *Principles of Database and Knowledge-Base Systems*, volumes 1, 2, Computer Science Press, 1988, 1989.

[UO92]   T. Urpí, A. Olivé: A Method for Change Computation in Deductive Databases, *Proc. 18th VLDB Conference*, 225-237, 1992.

[VF85]   P.A.S. Veloso, A.L. Furtado: Towards simpler and yet more complete formal specifications, *Proc. IFIP Working Conf. Theoretical and Formal Aspects of Information Systems*, 175-189, 1985.

Parallel Databases

LoT: Dynamic Declustering of TSB-Tree Nodes for Parallel Access to Temporal Data

Peter Muth, Achim Kraiß, Gerhard Weikum

University of the Saarland
Department of Computer Science
P.O. Box 151150
D–66041 Saarbrücken, Germany
e–mail: {muth, kraiss, weikum}@cs.uni–sb.de

Abstract. In this paper, we consider the problem of exploiting I/O parallelism for efficient access to transaction-time temporal databases. As temporal databases maintain historical versions of records in addition to current ones, we consider range queries in both time dimension and key dimension. Multiple disks can be used to read sets of disk blocks in parallel, thereby improving the performance of such queries substantially.

The problem is to find an optimal declustering algorithm for spreading record versions across disks. The solution depends on the index structure used. We have adopted the time split B-tree, as it provides efficient support for time range and key range queries. Our declustering method coined *LoT* (**L**ocal Balancing for **T**SB-trees) aims to decluster runs of logically consecutive leaf nodes of a TSB-tree onto separate disks. The method is dynamic in the sense that it computes the disk address of a new node at its creation time, based on the disk addresses of the nodes in its neighborhood.

LoT is an extension of the local balancing algorithm presented in [SL91]. It considers different sets of disks for historical and current nodes, and uses a two-dimensional distance metric between TSB-tree leaf nodes. As historical nodes of TSB-trees are no longer subject to splits, the coordinates of new nodes in the time-key space are restricted. This is exploited in LoT for achieving good declustering for both time range and key range queries. We derive performance guarantees for LoT in terms of the speedup for range queries. Simulation results show the response time speedup of LoT compared to a scheme that assigns nodes to disks in a random manner.

1 Introduction

For many applications maintaining only current information is not sufficient; rather historical data must be kept to answer all relevant queries. Such applications include, for example, stock market information systems, risk assessment in banking, and scientific databases. Temporal database systems aim to support this kind of applications. In this paper, we consider a special type of temporal databases, namely, *transaction-time databases*, where multiple versions of a record are kept. Updating a record is implemented by inserting a new record version. Each record version is timestamped with the commit-time of the transaction that updated the record. The timestamp is considered to be the start time for a record version. The end time is implicitly given by the start time of the next version of the same record, if existing. Records are never physically deleted; a logical deletion is implemented by creating a special record version that marks the end of the record's lifetime.

Fig. 1 depicts an example with versions of bank account records. The owner of a bank account is shown on the vertical axis as a time-invariant record key, and the horizontal axis captures all points of time when the balance of an account was updated. The figure shows the corresponding account balance values for the indicated key and time coordinates. For example, at time t_7, Bill's account was updated to $10, and this remained the balance until time t_{10} when the balance was set to $5. The deletion marker for an account is illustrated by a balance value of 0 in Fig. 1 (i.e., Eva's account was closed at time t_9).

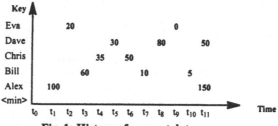

Fig. 1: History of account data

In this paper, we address the problem of improving the efficiency of index-supported access to transaction-time temporal data by means of disk I/O parallelism. We aim to support two basic query types: 1) *key range queries* which retrieve all record versions that were valid at a given point of time and which have a key value (e.g., account number) within a given value range, and 2) *time range queries* which track the history of a record with a given key over a time range. Note that key-based access to current data is a special case of the first query type. Thus, we are essentially dealing with a two-dimensional time-key search space, and, in principle, multidimensional indexing methods would be applicable here. However, due to the special nature of the temporal dimension (where, for example, updates are made only in the present), more specific indexing methods for temporal data have been proposed in the literature [LS89, LS93, EWK93, Kol93, ST94]. Here we have adopted the time split B-tree (TSB-tree) [LS89, LS 90, LS93] as the basis of our work. In contrast to most other proposals, the TSB-tree provides efficient support of both time range and key range queries while also ensuring good worst-case bounds with respect to space efficiency.

Even with an efficient index structure, the I/O bandwidth of the storage system might become a bottleneck. Assume that the complete history of a record with thousands of versions needs to be retrieved in a time range query. If only a single disk is used, all versions have to be read sequentially. However, if the blocks on which these record versions reside are spread across multiple disks, I/O parallelism can be exploited to improve the performance substantially. The main problem in this approach is to come up with a suitable *declustering* scheme for distributing the data across disks. Declustering methods for a single key dimension have been intensively studied in the literature and are state of the art in commercial parallel database systems [DG92, Mo94]. Declustering for multi-dimensional data is less well understood (despite some promising results; see e.g. [SNH94] and the references given there), and, furthermore, has been investigated only for static data. In our setting, however, we are dealing with an evolving database that grows continuously. So, unless we were willing to resort to occasional reorganizations of the declustering scheme [HLY93], we have to make *dynamic* and *incremental* decisions about where to allocate or re-allocate which data portion.

Such considerations on dynamic, incremental declustering have been published for block-structured files [SWZ94], for the leaf nodes of a standard B$^+$-tree [SL91], for R-tree leaf nodes [KF92], and for the Monotonic B$^+$-tree [KEC94]. In this paper, we develop a dynamic declustering method for the nodes of a TSB-tree. Among the prior related work, only [KF92] considers a two-dimensional index structure, but there the declustering aims to support spatial window queries whereas we are dealing with an index structure that is specifically geared for time range and key range queries on transaction-time databases. The work by

[KEC94] which is also concerned with declustering of temporal data is based on a hierarchy of one-dimensional index structures.

In deriving a dynamic declustering method for TSB-tree nodes, we proceed as follows. Since the TSB-tree distinguishes explicitly between current and historical nodes, we distribute the two sets of nodes separately across two different sets of disks. This simplifies the declustering method as explained later, and may also be desirable in order to have full control over the performance on the current data alone. The disk set for the historical data may, in fact, be based on a cheaper and possibly slower technology such as optical disks, but the specifics of optical disks (e.g., WORMs) are not considered here. For each of the two disk sets, we apply a generalized version of the *local balancing* algorithm that was proposed in [SL91] for declustering the leaf nodes of a standard B$^+$-tree. Local balancing assigns leaf nodes onto disks such that runs of logically consecutive leafs are spread across as many disks as possible. This is similar to block striping in disk arrays [Ch94], but the trick is to do this on a dynamic basis as new leafs are created by splits. The major problem in generalizing the local balancing method lies in reconciling the two dimensions of temporal data so that both time range and key range queries benefit from I/O parallelism as much as possible. We develop an appropriate declustering method that we coin *LoT* (Local Balancing for TSB-trees), and we derive worst-case guarantees for the degree of I/O parallelism that can be exploited in both query types. Our simulation results show that in the average case, LoT performs much better than guaranteed by our worst case analysis. In addition, LoT is up to about 50% better than a random assignment of nodes to disks.

The paper is organized as follows. Section 2 reviews the basic concepts of the TSB-tree (readers that are well familiar with the TSB-tree may choose to skip this section). In Section 3, we discuss the problems of a dynamic and incremental declustering approach in more detail, and derive the principles of our approach. Sections 4 and 5 present the specific heuristics that we apply in our declustering algorithm for current and historical TSB-tree nodes, respectively. Worst-case performance guarantees are derived in Section 6. Performance results are given in Section 7. Finally, Section 8 concludes the paper with more ideas on how to generalize our approach.

2 Review of the TSB-Tree

The TSB-tree is a B$^+$-tree like index structure for transaction-time databases [LS89, LS93]. It indexes record versions in two dimensions; one dimension is given by the conventional record key, the other by the timestamp of the record version. Its goal is to provide good support for exact match queries as well as range queries in both time dimension and key dimension. Most other approaches in the literature perform poorly in either the time dimension or the key dimension. This property makes the TSB-tree an intriguing candidate for exploiting I/O parallelism. Nodes of TSB-trees can be distinguished into leaf nodes and index nodes.

2.1 Leaf Nodes

Basically, each leaf node covers an open rectangle in the data space. A leaf node contains all record versions that have a (key, timestamp) coordinate covered by the corresponding rectangle. A node is represented by a pair of key and timestamp, defining the lower left corner of the rectangle it covers. The rectangle is open in the time-ascending and key-ascending directions. However, the space covered by a rectangle becomes bounded if there exists another rectangle defined by a higher key or time value. New rectangles are created when old ones become full. Like for B$^+$-tree this process is denoted splitting. In general, record versions are moved to the newly created node if their (key, timestamp) coordinate is in the corresponding new rectangle.

Two types of nodes are distinguished: current nodes and historical nodes. Current nodes store current data, i.e. data that is valid at current time, and have no neighbor node in the direction of future time. All other nodes are denoted historical.

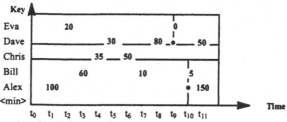

Fig. 2: Rectangles representing leaf nodes

Fig. 2 shows the rectangles representing leaf nodes with account data as given in Fig. 1. The key value *<min>* denotes the lower end of the key space. The lower left leaf node is identified by (*<min>*, t_0), i.e. it contains record versions with key ≥ *<min>* and timestamp ≥ t_0. It is bounded in the key and time dimension by the adjacent nodes (*Chris*, t_0) and (*<min>*, t_{10}), respectively, meaning that it does not contain record versions with key ≥ *'Chris'* or with a timestamp ≥ t_{10}. Leaf nodes (*Dave*, t_9), (*Chris*, t_0) and (*<min>*, t_{10}) are current nodes since they contain record versions being valid at current time. All other nodes are historical nodes. Note that the two dots at (*Dave*, t_9) and (*Alex*, t_{10}) represent redundant entries due to splits of current nodes. The entry (*Dave*, t_9, 80) has to be copied to the current node since it is valid at both times being covered by historical node (*Dave*, t_0) as well as current node (*Dave*, t_9). We will discuss details of splitting below.

2.2 Index Nodes

Index nodes store a set of index terms. An index term is a triple of a key, a timestamp and a pointer to another index node or a leaf node. Like the open rectangle defined for each leaf node, an index term also covers an open rectangle, defined by key and timestamp as the lower left corner. Other index terms with higher key or timestamp bound this area. The open rectangle defined by an index term x covers all rectangles defined by index terms in the index node x is pointing to. Index terms pointing to leaf nodes define the open rectangle of this leaf node.

Fig. 3 shows an example TSB-tree indexing the account data of Fig. 1. The tree contains three index nodes (including the root) and five leaf nodes. Throughout this and all subsequent examples we assume the capacity of all nodes being three entries, i.e. each index node and leaf node has at most 3 index terms or record versions, respectively. The root node points to index nodes (*<min>*, t_0) and (*Dave*, t_0), which contain entries for nodes that are covered by the corresponding time and key range. Index node (*<min>*, t_0) contains entries for leaf nodes (*<min>*, t_0), (*<min>*, t_{10}) and (*Chris*, t_0) since they contain record versions with a key value ≥ *<min>* and with timestamp ≥ t_0. All other leaf nodes are referenced by index node (*Dave*, t_0) as the keys of all record versions stored in the leaf nodes are greater than or equal to *'Dave'*.

2.3 Searching in TSB-Trees

Searching in TSB-trees can be viewed as an extension to the search procedure for B+-trees. Assume we are searching for a record version (k, t) with key k and timestamp t. At each level of the tree, the algorithm first discards all index terms with a timestamp greater than t. Within the remaining terms it follows the index term with the maximum key value being smaller than or

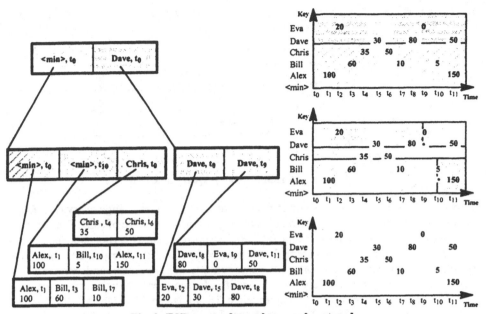

Fig. 3: TSB-tree nodes and covered rectangles

equal to key k. This process recursively descends in the tree and terminates when a leaf node is found. In the example of Fig. 3, looking for the balance of Eva's account as of time t_6 is done as follows. Starting at the root node the two index terms ($<min>$, t_0) and ($Dave$, t_0) have to be examined. As '$Dave$' is the maximum key value less than 'Eva', the algorithm follows the pointer of index term ($Dave$, t_0). At the index node, the term ($Dave$, t_9) is discarded because its timestamp is greater than t_6 and thus it does not contain relevant data. So the algorithm follows entry ($Dave$, t_0) and finally returns (Eva, t_2, 20), indicating that the account of Eva was updated to \$20 at time t_2 and was not changed until t_6.

2.4 Range Queries

Exact match queries require following a single pointer at each level in the tree, but the algorithm for range queries has to follow a set of pointers. The reason is that at each level we have to search for those rectangles that intersect with the query range. Thus, range queries use an extended algorithm as follows. For each index node traversed, starting with the root, we maintain two sets. The set with index terms containing pointers to be followed is denoted *ToBeFollowed*. It is initially empty. The set of index terms to be examined is denoted *ToBeExamined*. It initially contains all index terms of a considered index node. Let us consider a key range query defined by its two endpoints (min_k, t) and (max_k, t). At first, we determine the index term to be followed when searching for the single record version (min_k, t). After inserting the qualified index term into *ToBeFollowed*, it will be removed from *ToBeExamined*. Now we look for all index terms in *TobeExamined* with key between min_k and max_k (including max_k), and timestamp smaller than or equal to t. If existing, delete them from *TobeExamined*, and among terms with the same key value, select the one with the largest timestamp. Include the selected terms in *ToBeFollowed*. Now having found all index terms to follow, set *ToBeExamined* to all index terms of nodes being referenced by index terms in *ToBeFollowed* and repeat the search recursively until only leaf nodes are left. Locate all qualifying record versions there. For time range queries, we can use a symmetric version of this algorithm.

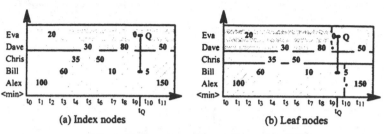

<table>
<tr><td>(a) Index nodes</td><td>(b) Leaf nodes</td></tr>
</table>

Fig. 4: Performing a Range Query in a TSB-tree

Using the TSB-tree of Fig. 3, we illustrate the execution of the key range query Q in Fig. 4. Query Q selects all record versions valid at time t_Q within a key range of (*Bill, Eva*). Initially the set *ToBeFollowed* is empty and the set *ToBeExamined* contains the root node index terms (*<min>, t_0*) and (*Dave, t_0*). Searching for the (*min_k, t*) point of the query returns index term (*<min>, t_0*). So the term (*<min>, t_0*) is inserted into *ToBeFollowed* and removed from *ToBeExamined*. Index term (*Dave, t_0*) also qualifies for the query since the upper part of the query intersects with the corresponding rectangle. Thus, it is also moved from *ToBeExamined* to *ToBeFollowed*. In the second iteration the set *ToBeExamined* is set to all leaf nodes. The reason is that in this example, all leaf nodes are referenced by the qualified index terms. At this level the leaf nodes (*<min>, t_0*), (*Chris, t_0*) and (*Dave, t_9*) qualify and finally the search algorithm returns (*Bill, t_7, 10*), (*Chris, t_6, 50*), (*Dave, t_8, 80*) and (*Eva, t_9, 0*).

2.5 Node Splitting

Only current nodes can be split, as inserts and updates of records are timestamped with current time. Hence, new record versions have to be stored in current nodes. As splitting of leaf nodes differs from splitting of index nodes, we have to consider them separately. If a leaf node becomes full, it is split. In general, a new open rectangle inside the old open rectangle is defined, and record versions are distributed over the new and old node according to their key and timestamp. Two different kinds of splits are considered: time splits and key splits.

A *time split* creates a new node having the same key range as the old one, i.e., the key-values of the new and the old rectangle are the same. In the example of Fig. 5a, the account of Bill is updated to $50 at time t_{12}. Since the leaf node (*<min>, t_{10}*) overflows, a split has to be performed. We choose a split time of t_{12}, leading to the historical node (*<min>, t_{10}*), and the new current node (*<min>, t_{12}*). Record versions with a timestamp smaller than the split-time and still being valid at the split-time have to be present in both the old and the new node. Considering the search procedure as defined above, the record version will be searched in the old node if the search time is lower than the split time, and in the new node if it is higher than or equal to the split time. This redundancy is inevitable to avoid degradation of the search performance. In the example of Fig. 5a, the balance of account 'Alex' is subject to this rule since it is valid at time t_{11} as well as at time t_{12}. We illustrate this form of redundancy by using a dot meaning that the version being valid at the split-time is replicated in the old and the new node.

A *key split* creates a new node having the same time range as the old one, i.e., the timestamps of the new and the old rectangle are the same. No redundancy is introduced by key splits. An example for a key split is illustrated in Fig. 5b. Here, the overflown leaf node is key split at key '*Bill*', leading to two new current nodes, (*<min>, t_{10}*) and (*Bill, t_{10}*).

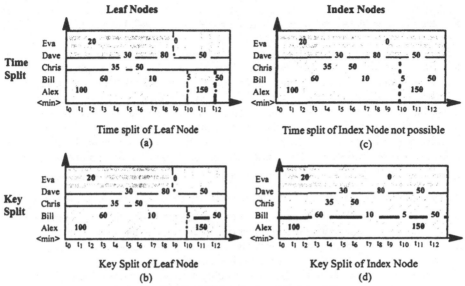

Fig. 5: Splitting leaf and index nodes

Splits of index nodes are performed similarly to splits of leaf nodes, but, in contrast to B+-trees, may convert a TSB-tree into a DAG. Consider the example of an index node shown in Fig. 5d, caused by the leaf node split shown in Fig. 5b. If the index node is split at key *'Bill'*, leaf node ($<min>$, t_0) must be referenced by both the old and the new index node as it contains data that is covered by the rectangles of both index nodes. The same argument holds for time splits of index nodes.

A restriction for choosing time split values is necessary if all historical data is stored on WORM disks as proposed in [LS89]. By time splitting an index node, the old node becomes historical and is transferred to a WORM disk making it read-only. This strategy is only applicable if the historical index node is guaranteed not to be split any more, meaning that all its leaf nodes have to be historical. In Fig. 5c, we illustrate a situation where the index node ($<min>$, t_0) cannot be time split as any time split would lead to a historical index node referencing the current leaf node (*Chris*, t_0). As the problem of choosing the right split time has an impact on our declustering algorithm, we reconsider it in Section 6. For a detailed discussion of splitting TSB-tree nodes see [LS89, LS90, LS93].

3 Exploiting I/O Parallelism in TSB-Trees

We assume a computer system with d disks, such that all disks can be independently accessed and data can be transferred from and to multiple disks in parallel. In order to exploit this potential for I/O parallelism to enhance the performance of range queries, a range query must utilize as many disks as possible. In addition, the total access load that is incurred by a query must be distributed across the disks as evenly as possible. This is our ultimate goal. Ideally each of the involved disks transfers the same amount of data.

For small queries (i.e., short query ranges or exact-match queries), however, it is preferable to utilize only a single disk, such that other independent queries can be served in parallel. For this reason, we exclude from further consideration approaches where a single TSB-tree node is partitioned and spread across multiple disks. Such approaches have been considered for large B$^+$-tree leafs (e.g., of size 32 KBytes) [PK90, MS94], but this incurs a significant degradation of the achievable throughput for small queries. We have chosen not to partition TSB–tree nodes, but nodes that contain logically consecutive record versions, with respect to the time or key dimension, shall be stored on different disks whenever possible.

The search algorithm for range queries given in Section 2 can benefit from a distribution of TSB–tree nodes over multiple disks as follows. After the set *ToBeFollowed* is constructed, the pointers contained in its index terms can be followed in parallel. This process continues recursively until all relevant leaf nodes are determined. They can be read from their disks in parallel. Suppose that n leaf nodes have to be read on behalf of a query, and that reading a node from a disk takes 1 millisecond (assuming sequential access). If these n nodes reside on d different disks such that each disk holds no more than $\lceil \frac{n}{d} \rceil$ nodes, then the response time of the query can ideally be improved from n milliseconds in the sequential case down to $\lceil \frac{n}{d} \rceil$ milliseconds in the parallel case (i.e., by a factor of approximately d). Obviously, the major leverage comes from declustering the leaf nodes of a TSB-tree, and gains due to a declustering of index nodes are rather marginal in most cases. Therefore, we do not consider index nodes in this paper, and concentrate on the declustering of leaf nodes.

Index structures like the TSB-tree are highly dynamic because of splits. As we do not want to resort to periodic reorganizations of the data placement [HLY93], we have to devise a dynamic and incremental declustering scheme, where newly created nodes are assigned to a disk in the best possible manner. The driving intuition for such a scheme is that a good declustering is achieved if a new node a is stored on a disk that does not yet hold any of the nodes in the logical proximity of a. For a more precise characterization, we introduce the notion of *distance* between tree nodes. We first consider one-dimensional B$^+$-trees, following [SL91]. For B$^+$-trees the distance of leaf nodes a and b is defined to be the number of nodes between a and b (in the key ordering) plus one:

(1)   *distance (a,b)* = *'number of nodes between a and b' + 1*

Using this metric, two successive nodes (i.e., nodes with no other node between them) have distance one. As the TSB-tree is a two-dimensional structure, we need to generalize this definition to a two-dimensional distance metric. However, we postpone this issue until Section 5, and proceed under the assumption that such a distance metric is already specified. The following heuristics for choosing the disk where a new node should be allocated can indeed be stated independently of the specific distance metric. Given the distance of nodes, we define the distance between a node a and a disk x:

(2) $distance(a, x) = \min\{distance(a, i) \mid node\ i\ resides\ on\ disk\ x\}$

Then, for allocating a new node, we choose the disk with the largest distance to it. In general, this selection may lead to more than one disk; the set of eligible disks is defined as follows:

(3) $best\_disks(a) = \{x \mid distance(a, x) = max!\}$

If the set *best_disks* contains more than one disk, we choose the disk with the lowest number of nodes stored on it. If still more than a single disk remain, we arbitrarily select the one with the lowest disk number as a tie-breaker.

(4) $choose\_disk(a) = \min\{x \in best\_disks(a) \mid number\ of\ nodes\ on\ x = min!\}$

For the allocation of B+-tree leaf nodes, a simple method for implementing *choose_disk* is the following heuristics that was coined *local balancing* in [SL91]. Assume that there are d disks.

Then, starting from the new node, we consider its $\lceil \frac{d}{2} - 1 \rceil$ successor and $\lceil \frac{d}{2} - 1 \rceil$ predecessor nodes with respect to the key order. Initially all disks are eligible. We exclude those disks that hold at least one of the considered nodes in the neighborhood of the new node. Finally, among the remaining disks, the one with the smallest number of nodes is chosen. Thus, as successor and predecessor nodes are considered symmetrically, the new node is assigned to a disk that does not hold any of the $\lceil \frac{d}{2} - 1 \rceil$ nodes around the new node in both directions. Consequently, in the absence of node deletions, every key range query that accesses at most $\lceil \frac{d}{2} \rceil$ successive leaf nodes is guaranteed to be served by $\lceil \frac{d}{2} \rceil$ different disks each of which returns one node. For large queries accessing s leaf nodes, the number of leaf nodes to be fetched from the same disk is bounded by $\lceil \frac{s}{\lceil \frac{d}{2} \rceil} \rceil$. (see [SL91] for the full proof of this theorem).

Now consider the two-dimensional TSB-tree. Good declustering for both time range and key range queries are potentially conflicting goals. Consider the disk assignment of TSB-tree leaf nodes shown in the example of Fig. 6a. The nodes are assigned to four different disks. Assume that the current node that resides on disk *3* is time split; this results in a new historical node that is indicated by a question mark in Fig. 6b. The problem then is to assign a disk number to the new node. Choosing disk number *4* or *1* would be suitable for optimizing time range queries. But at the same time this is a poor choice with respect to some key range queries since nodes with successive keys would be located on the same disk. Using analogous arguments, choosing disk number *2* or *3* leads to an optimization for key range queries at the expense of poor performance for time range queries. The problem of multidimensional declustering has been intensively studied for static data [DS82, FM91, FB93, GD94, HS94,KP88, ZSC94], but is more or less unexplored for the dynamic case considered here.

Thus, generalizing the local balancing method of [SL91] to the TSB-tree is not at all straightforward. We simplify this problem by breaking it up into two independent tasks. Namely, we handle current and historical nodes separately, by assigning them to two disjoint sets of disks. Note that such a partitioning of the available disks into two sets is quite natural, since we can thus control the disk load for the current database in a better way, e.g., by increasing the number of disks for current nodes if the load on these disks gets higher. After all, even in a temporal database system, the larger fraction of queries will probably access only current data. Moreover, if different disk types are available, for example, magnetic and optical disks, we may want to use the cheaper and possibly slower disks for the historical data anyway. Then, under this assumption, declustering the current nodes is an easy problem, as we will see in Section 4. The hard part is the declustering of the historical nodes, which we will address in Section 5. As we will discuss there, the key point is to come up with an appropriate distance metric between historical nodes.

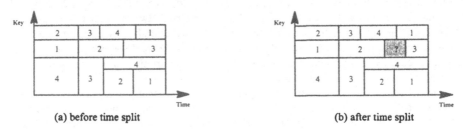

(a) before time split   (b) after time split

Fig. 6: Disk assignment of TSB-tree leaf nodes

4 Declustering Current Nodes

A new current node is created only if a current node is key split. If a current node is time split, this is not the case. Instead, a new historical node is created, and this historical node will be stored on a separate set of disks as discussed above. The time range of the current node becomes bounded by the new historical node in time-backward direction, its key range remains the same. Hence, the new current node should simply stay on the same disk (and at the same block address) where the old node resided. The placement of the newly created historical node is discussed in Section 5. In the remainder of this section, we discuss the placement of a new current node due to a key split.

We need to define the distance between current nodes in order to apply the *choose_disk* function introduced in Section 3. Because there is only a single current node for each key, a current node does not have an adjacent node in the time dimension which is also a current node. Thus, we are dealing with a one-dimensional structure of current nodes. So we can simply apply the distance metric given in equation (1): The distance of current leaf nodes a and b is defined to be the number of current nodes (in the key ordering) between a and b plus one. Fig. 7 illustrates a possible disk assignment of current nodes under this method (with $d=5$ disks). In Fig. 7a, a new current node is created. A disk address has to be assigned to it, indicated by the question mark. Disk I has the largest distance to the new node, as all other disks store a node which is closer to the new one than the closest node stored on disk I. Fig. 7b shows the result.

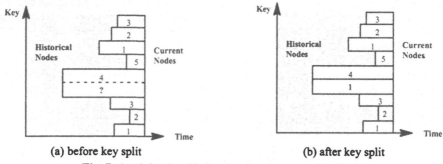

(a) before key split   (b) after key split

Fig. 7: Applying local balancing for current nodes (d=5)

5 Declustering Historical Nodes

In contrast to the declustering of current nodes, the declustering of historical nodes is a two-dimensional problem, since historical nodes may have adjacent nodes in both the key and the time dimension. Thus, we need to define a distance metric between historical nodes that considers both the key dimension and the time dimension. Recall, however, that we restrict ourselves in this paper to time range and key range queries; so we disregard time-key rectangle queries (i.e., truly two-dimensional range queries). This restriction simplifies the definition of the distance metric for historical nodes.

In the following, we denote two historical nodes to be *time-overlapping* or *key-overlapping*, respectively, if their time intervals or key intervals overlap. Consider, for example, the TSB-tree leaf nodes that correspond to the division of the time-key space shown in Fig. 8. In this tree, node Q is time-overlapping with nodes S, U, N, J, K, E, and key-overlapping with R, P, O, L. We denote two nodes to be *overlapping* if they are time- or key-overlapping. Note that two nodes cannot be time- and key-overlapping at the same time, due to the splitting rules of the TSB-tree. We denote two nodes *time-adjacent*, if they are adjacent in the time-key space and key-overlapping. Two nodes are *key-adjacent* if they are adjacent in the time-key space and time-overlapping. Two nodes are *adjacent* if they are time-adjacent or key-adjacent

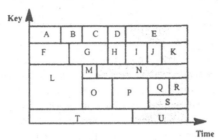

Fig. 8: Current and historical leaf nodes to be declustered

We now consider the creation of a new historical node. The only way to create a historical node is to time split a current node. In the time-forward direction, the only key-overlapping node of the new node is a current node, which is stored on a different set of disks anyway. In the time-backward direction, the new historical node may have an unbounded number of key-overlapping nodes. But avoiding that the new historical node is assigned to any disk that holds key-overlapping nodes in its neighborhood is still a one-dimensional problem, since each historical node has at most one time-adjacent node in the time-backward direction. This is because the only way to create two time-adjacent nodes in time-backward direction would be to key-split a historical node, but splits of historical nodes are disallowed in the TSB-tree. Thus, for two nodes a and b which are key-overlapping, we can use the same distance metric that we used for current nodes: the number of nodes between a and b, in time ordering, plus one. We denote this distance *time- distance*, as a different metric for time-overlapping nodes will be necessary.

$$(5) \quad \textit{time--distance } (a,b) = \begin{cases} 1 & \textit{if a and b are time--adjacent} \\ 1 + \textit{time--distance}(a',b) & \textit{if a' is time--adjacent to a} \end{cases}$$

For time-overlapping nodes, the distance metric needs to be more complex, as a historical node may have more than one adjacent node in both key-ascending and key-descending direction. For example, in Fig. 8 the node N has the time-overlapping adjacent nodes G, H, I, J, K, O, P, Q and R. Now assume that node N is to be time split. In this case, the resulting new historical node may have up to 9 key-adjacent nodes depending on the chosen split time, and one time-adjacent node in the time-backward direction. So in order to discriminate the relevance of these adjacent nodes in the disk assignment of the new historical node, we need a suitable distance metric between time-overlapping nodes.

Two time-overlapping nodes a and b have *key distance* e if there is a sequence of $e+1$ time-overlapping adjacent nodes, each of them also time-overlapping a and b, beginning with a and ending with b. If more than one such sequence exists, the length of the shortest one is chosen. For an example, consider again Fig. 8. In order to determine the key distance between nodes G and T, we have to consider three sequences: $G;L;T$, $G; M; O; T$, and $G; N; O; T$. The key distance between G and T equals 2, the length of the shortest sequence $G;L;T$. Note that current nodes may also be part of such a sequence. For determining the key distance between time-overlapping nodes a and b, they are treated just like historical nodes. We capture this intuition in the following definition in a recursive manner. As we have to make sure that all considered nodes between a and b time-overlap a and b, we introduce the set TO of all nodes that time-overlap a and b.

$$TO = \{c \mid c \text{ time–overlaps } a \text{ and } b\}$$

(6)

$$key\text{–}distance\ (a,b) = \begin{cases} 1 & \text{if } a \text{ and } b \text{ are key–adjacent} \\ 1 + min(key\text{–}distance\ (a',b)) & \text{if } a' \in TO \text{ is key–adjacent to } a \end{cases}$$

To further discriminate nodes with the same distance to a given node, we take into consideration the length of the time-overlap between nodes, i.e., the intersection of the corresponding time intervals denoted by t_int. Function $len(t\_int)$ returns the length of time interval t_int. To this end, we redefine the distance between two time-overlapping nodes a and b such that it is decreased by the ratio of the overlapping time period to the sum of the time intervals of nodes a and b. This introduces a "fine-tuning" correction between 0 and 1. Finally, for nodes which are neither key-overlapping nor time-overlapping we define the distance to be ∞.

In summary, the distance metric between historical nodes of a TSB-tree is specified as follows:

(7)

$$distance\ (a,b) = \begin{cases} time\text{–}distance\ (a,b) & \text{if } a \text{ and } b \text{ are key–overlapping} \\ key\text{–}distance\ (a,b) + 1 - \dfrac{2 * len\ (t\_int(a) \cap t\_int(b))}{len\ (t\_int(a)) + len\ (t\_int\ (b))} & \text{if } a \text{ and } b \text{ are time–overlapping} \\ \infty & \text{if } a \text{ and } b \text{ are non–overlapping} \end{cases}$$

We are now ready to present the complete LoT algorithm. The algorithm can be used for both current and historical leaf nodes. For current nodes, there will be at most two current nodes for a given key distance. For historical nodes, we have to consider potentially larger sets of nodes with the same key distance.

LoT algorithm for assigning a disk to a new TSB-tree leaf node:

```
FUNCTION LoT(Node a): {1..d}
BEGIN
        CS := {1..d}   // CS denotes the set of candidate disks
        N := List of leaf nodes nᵢ with 1 ≤ distance(a, nᵢ) < 2, sorted by distance
        j := 2          // j denotes the (key) distance counter
        WHILE |CS| > 1 AND |N| > 0 DO      // |CS| denotes the cardinality of CS
                CS := CS \ disk(firstOf(N))      // firstOf(N) is the first element of N,
                                                 // i.e., has the smallest distance to a
                REMOVE firstOf(N) FROM N    // remove first element from list
                IF N = ∅ THEN
                        N := List of nodes nᵢ with j ≤ distance(a, nᵢ) < j+1, sorted by distance
                        j := j +1
                END
        END
        IF |CS| > 1 THEN
                CS := {d ∈ CS | number of nodes stored on d = min!}
        END
        RETURN min(CS) // choose disk with smallest number
END
```

6 Analysis of Performance Guarantees

Our goal is to show that the LoT algorithm provides good worst-case guarantees for the degree of I/O parallelism in serving time range or key range queries and for the resulting speedup, similar to the guarantees of local balancing for B^+-trees (see [SL91]). Depending on the number of disks available, we want to derive a lower bound for the speedup queries are experiencing. The approach is to give the following guarantee: All nodes in all consecutive sequences of less than s nodes in either time dimension or key dimension are stored on different disks. In this case, the speedup of each range query accessing more than s nodes is at least s. For current data stored on magnetic disks, LoT and local balancing both guarantee a minimum sequence of $\lceil \frac{d}{2} \rceil$ nodes stored on different disks. The example of assigning a disk address to the node with the question mark in Fig. 7 discusses the worst case for both local balancing and LoT. Local balancing considers a sequence of $\lceil \frac{d}{2} - 1 \rceil$ adjacent nodes in each direction, removing their disk address from the set of candidate disks. Only disk 1 remains and is chosen. LoT removes disk addresses $4, 3, 5$ and 2 from CS in this order. Again, disk 1 remains and is chosen.

In the remainder of this section, we consider the declustering of historical nodes. It is generally hard to give a worst-case performance guarantee for LoT in the presence of time splits. Consider all nodes that time-overlap with a new node. For a given key distance i, the number of time-overlapping nodes at key distance i is unbounded. In the worst case, this means that a new node might have more key-adjacent nodes than there are disks available. In this case, two adjacent nodes have to be stored on the same disk. For B^+-trees, and for current nodes of TSB-trees, this problem does not exist, as each node has at most two adjacent nodes in one dimension. Now the idea is to enforce a limit on the number of key-adjacent nodes by imposing a restriction on the time chosen for time splits. It is easy to see that the number of time-overlapping nodes to consider decreases if earlier split-times are chosen. Consider all time-overlapping nodes having a timestamp later than the timestamp of the node to be split. If the split-time is the earliest timestamp of these nodes there is only a single node that time-overlaps the new historical node for each key distance i in any key direction.

In Fig. 8, for node N this results in a split time earlier than the split time between nodes G and H. As a drawback, restricting the split time may lead to a poorer storage utilization of nodes, as historical nodes will contain less record versions. Because of a poorer storage utilization, also the total number of nodes together with the number of disk accesses for a given query increases. We can not offer an analytical model for the tradeoff between better/worse declustering and a worse/better storage utilization. These considerations will be subject to simulations in Section 7.

In general, a declustering scheme should impose as few restrictions as possible on the original indexing method, to avoid that other aspects of performance are adversely affected. Therefore, we propose to impose the following restriction on the split-time that is chosen for a time split, thereby limiting the number of time-overlapping nodes for each key distance i:

Definition 1: (Split-time restriction for creating at most n time-overlapping nodes)

For a given number k, the latest possible split time is such that the new historical node has at most $2n$ time-overlapping nodes at each key distance i $(0 < i \leq k)$.

The value of k defines the maximum key distance for which the number of time-overlapping nodes has to be limited to $2n$ in order to give a guarantee for the shortest sequence of adjacent nodes in key dimension stored on different disks. We will see later that the guaranteed minimal length is $\lfloor \frac{d}{1+2n} \rfloor + 1$. As this sequence includes the new node, in the following we assume

$k = \left\lfloor \frac{d}{1+2n} \right\rfloor$. In practice, however, k might be smaller if the greater freedom in choosing time split values outweighs the loss in worst-case performance.

For $n=1$, there are at most 2 time-overlapping nodes at each key distance i. This is the conventional case like in B⁺-trees. By choosing different numbers for n, the time split algorithm can be tuned to different needs.

We are now able to define the worst case for the degree of parallelism for time range and key range queries achieved by LoT. The following theorem is a generalized version of the corresponding theorem in [SL91]. Note that LoT does not need to consider deletion of nodes, as no record versions will be deleted from the TSB-tree. By a contiguous sequence of nodes we denote a sequence of adjacent nodes with a non-empty intersection of their time or key ranges, respectively.

Theorem 1

If historical leaf nodes of a TSB-tree have been assigned to d disks by using LoT, and each node has at most $2n$ time-overlapping nodes at each key distance i $(0 < i \le \left\lfloor \frac{d}{1+2n} \right\rfloor)$, no two nodes of a contiguous sequence of $\left\lfloor \frac{d}{1+2n} \right\rfloor$ $+1$ or fewer nodes in time dimension and key dimension will be stored on the same disk.

Proof (Theorem 1)

The proof is by induction on the number of nodes. If there are at most d historical leaf nodes in the TSB-tree, it is easy to see that they will be assigned to different disks. Now assume that there are more than d historical leaf nodes, declustered such that the premise of the theorem is fulfilled and assume that a new historical leaf node is created. For the new historical node, there is no other historical key-overlapping node with a more recent timestamp. Hence, there is no key-overlapping node in time-forward direction to consider. The split-rules of TSB-trees preclude having more than a single key-overlapping node in time-backward direction for any given time distance i. The time split rule given by Def. 1 ensures that there are no more than $2n$ time-overlapping nodes for each given key distance $i \le \left\lfloor \frac{d}{1+2n} \right\rfloor$. In summary, at most $1 + 2n$ overlapping nodes have to be considered for each time distance or key distance i.

Even in the worst case, all nodes within a time distance and key distance of $\left\lfloor \frac{d}{1+2n} \right\rfloor$ are stored on different disks. LoT chooses the disk with the largest distance to the new node. This distance is at least $\left\lfloor \frac{d}{1+2n} \right\rfloor$.

For each contiguous sequence not including the new node the premise of the theorem is still true because their disk assignment remains unchanged. Now consider all contiguous sequences of nodes including the new node, in both time dimension and key dimension. Assume, one of these sequences with a length less than $\left\lfloor \frac{d}{1+2n} \right\rfloor$ $+1$ contains two nodes stored on the same disk. As for all nodes other than the new node, the condition of the theorem holds, one of the nodes that are stored on the same disk must be the new node. But this is impossible, as the new node has a distance of at least $\left\lfloor \frac{d}{1+2n} \right\rfloor$ to all disks. Hence, in both time dimension and key dimension, there is no contiguous sequence of less than $\left\lfloor \frac{d}{1+2n} \right\rfloor + 1$ nodes, with two nodes of the sequence stored on the same disk. This completes the induction step. ◆

For time range or key range queries accessing s nodes, by Theorem 1 , no disk will have to deliver more than $\left\lceil \frac{s}{\left\lfloor \frac{d}{1+2n} \right\rfloor + 1} \right\rceil$ nodes. This establishes a lower bound on the speedup of range queries.

In general, time range and key range queries will not be equally frequent. The declustering algorithms should be tailorable to a better declustering in either time dimension or key dimension. This can be achieved by using a weighted distance function. For example, if a good declustering in key dimension is preferred over a good declustering in time dimension, all distances in time dimension could be multiplied with a constant factor greater than one. Such an extension of the distance metric leads to an optimization problem taking the access probability of different queries into account. A general treatment of this problem is outside the scope of this paper.

7 Performance Results

In this section, we compare the performance of LoT with a random assignment of TSB-tree nodes onto disks (subsequently denoted Random). While the performance guarantees derived in the previous section provide only worst case results, the simulation results in this section show that the average case results are much better.

We have implemented a skeleton TSB-tree consisting of leaf nodes only. A tree is built by executing a fixed number of insert, update and delete operations, as discussed in Subsection 7.1. For each resulting tree, we have executed key range and time range queries of different length. For key range queries, we have distinguished between queries with a timestamp of *now*, which access current nodes only, and queries with older timestamps, which access also historical nodes.

7.1 Parameters Considered for Creating TSB-trees

In order to construct differently structured trees, i.e. reflect different insert/update workloads, we considered the following parameters:

- probability that an operation is insert, update or delete
- probability that an insert operation inserts a long lived version record, i.e. a record that is less frequently updated than other records
- the probability of updating a long lived version record in order to determine the lifetime of long lived versions.

Different parameter settings result in different ratios for the number of current versus historical nodes in the tree. We assumed a uniform distribution of keys over the keyspace and an exponential distribution of the length of the time intervals between two successive operations. Thus, the ratio between current and historical nodes determines the structure of the TSB-tree. In addition, we have chosen different values for the number of available disks. The splitting policies have been chosen according to the policies given in [LS 90]. For deciding whether a node is to be time-split or key-split, we have adopted the *Isolated-Key-Split (IKS)* policy, i.e., a key split is performed whenever two third or more of the splitting node consists of current data. Otherwise a time split is performed. The time value chosen for the time split is the time of the last update of all records in the splitting node. Table 1 lists all parameters for the building of TSB trees with the values we have taken for our performance evaluations.

In the worst case analysis of Section 6 we imposed an additional restriction on the split time. As this restriction is needed only for deriving worst case guarantees, we decided not to enforce it in the simulations. Instead, we measured the percentage of time splits where enforcing our restriction would have led to a split time different from the time of last update. In all cases, the percentage was less than one percent. Thus, the impact of such a split restriction was extremely low.

Parameter	Value(s)
Tree Node Size	4 KB
Record Version Size	100 Bytes
Total Number of Operations	$3*10^6$
Initial Insert Operations	4000
Probability of Insert Operations	80%, 40%, 10%
Probability of Update Operations	10%, 50%, 80%
Probability of Delete Operations	10%
Probability of Inserting Long–Lived Versions	0%
Probability of Updating a Long–Lived Version	–
Number of Disks for Historical/Current Nodes	10/10, 50/50

Table 1: Parameters for the TSB tree build phase

We also found that varying the percentage of long lived version records has very little impact on the structure of the TSB-tree and the declustering performance of LoT. Therefore, we restrict our discussions to the case of inserting no long lived version records as the only difference we found was the quantity of nodes because of the imposed redundancy at time splits. In the following we consider only three important cases of TSB trees, which are distinguished by their insert versus update probabilities. Furthermore, we declustered historical nodes and current nodes over 10 disks versus 50 disks.

Table 2 lists the important properties of the three trees resulting from the building parameters of Table 1. For each time split, we have measured the key-distance between the newly created historical node and the next time-overlapping node that is stored on the same disk. Table 2 lists the minimal and average values of this key-distance (*Min Distance* and *Avg Distance*) over all time-splits that occurred while building the tree. The average length is very high, as usually many nodes that time-overlap the newly created historical node are current nodes, and are therefore stored on a different disk anyway. Fig. 9 shows the frequency distribution for the key-distances of historical nodes to the nearest time-overlapping node on the same disk, for both LoT and Random. The curve for Random corresponds to a geometric distribution, as the probability that a node has no time-overlapping node with key-distance less than k on the same disk and at least one such node with key-distance k is $P[x=k] = ((d-1)/d)^{k-1} * (1/d)$ where d denotes the number of disks. In contrast, LoT exhibits a better frequency distribution, as small key-distances are extremely infrequent.

Parameters		Values		
		80% Insert Prob. 10% Upd. Prob.	40% Insert Prob. 50% Upd. Prob.	10% Insert Prob. 80% Upd. Prob
Number of Current Nodes		99627	45475	930
Number of Historical Nodes		5687	77312	91630
10 Disks	Min Distance	54	5	2
	Avg Distance	246.29	19.54	15.61
50 Disks	Min Distance	580	46	11
	Avg Distance	1270.04	133.8	86.84
Total Size of Nodes		411 MB	479 MB	361 MB

Table 2: Properties of the TSB trees resulting from the build phase

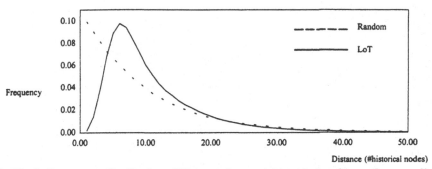

Fig. 9: Frequency distribution of distances between historical nodes on the same disk (10% insert probability, 80% update probability)

7.2 Query Performance

We have run extensive series of both key range and time range queries against each TSB-tree. We have systematically varied the length of the query interval, measured in the number of historical nodes or current nodes, depending on the query type. For key–range queries we have considered queries with a timestamp of *now*, accessing current nodes only, as well as queries with older timestamps, which access also historical nodes. As in section 6, the query response time is defined by the maximum over the number of nodes that are retrieved from a each single disk.

Fig. 10 shows the response time ratio between LoT and Random for key range queries with a timestamp of *now*, i.e., Random always corresponds to 1.0. We ran simulations for both 10 and 50 disks. Fig. 10 shows the results for one tree only, as the curves for all trees are nearly identical. This is because the declustering of LoT on current nodes implements local balancing and is independent of the ratio between current and historical nodes. Fig. 11 shows the response time ratio for key range queries with timestamps older than *now*. LoT consistently outperformed Random, and we observed response time benefits of up to a factor of 2 (i.e. performance ratio 0.5). For small queries that access only a single node, LoT and Random have the same response time. For larger queries, LoT performs better than Random, as LoT avoids storing time-overlapping nodes with small key-distances on the same disk. This is not true for Random as one can conclude from Fig. 9. Therefore, for a query range up to about half of the number of disks, the improvement by LoT constantly increases.

Beyond this point, the curve becomes highly non-monotonic. The reason is that the response time of a query is determined by the *maximum* number of nodes fetched from the same disk, and thus the response time does not necessarily increase with increasing query size. This holds for both LoT and Random. However, LoT does generally do a better job on minimizing the variance of the number of accessed nodes per disk, as we can infer from the key-distance distribution given in Fig. 9. It is due to the local balancing property that LoT keeps an implicit advantage over Random also for larger queries. However, at the points where the maximum number of nodes fetched from one disk increases for LoT, Random may happen to stay at the same, usually worse, level. This is the reason for the 'second order bumps' in the performance ratio curve.

For small queries, the performance ratio of LoT with 10 disk is better than with 50 disks. In both cases, LoT creates an almost optimal declustering, whereas Random benefits from an increased number of disks. For larger queries, LoT employs all 50 disks and achieves a better ratio.

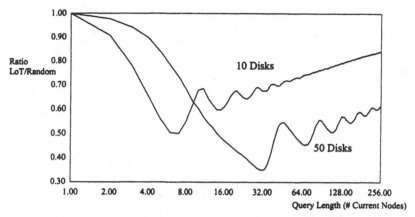

**Fig. 10: Performance ratio LoT/Random for key range queries on current nodes
(80% insert probability, 10% update probability)**

The performance ratio also depends on the structure of the TSB-tree. As shown in Table 2, the average key-distance (*Avg Distance*) of a newly created historical node to the next time-overlapping node on the same disk becomes lower if the fraction of updates is increased. As expected, Fig. 11 shows that the performance ratio for queries of the same length is increasing for trees with a higher update probability, because the declustering becomes poorer with decreasing average distance.

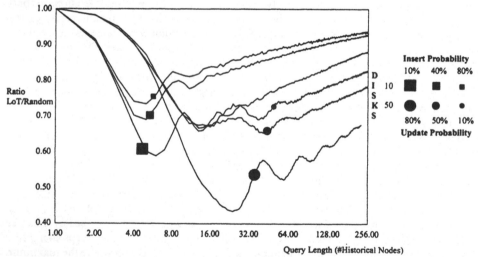

Fig. 11: Performance ratio LoT/Random for key range queries on historical nodes

Fig. 12 shows the performance ratio for time range queries. It is based on the tree with insert probability of 10% which is the tree with the highest number of historical nodes and, therefore, the most interesting one for time range queries. Since LoT treats key distance and time distance between historical nodes in the same way, the overall performance trends of time range queries are the same as for key range queries.

In all cases, LoT is superior to Random, with gains up to a factor of 2.

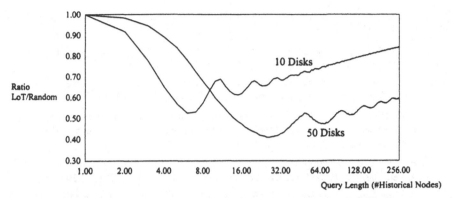

Fig. 12: Performance ratio LoT/Random for time range queries on historical nodes
(10% insert probability, 80% update probability)

8 Conclusion

We have presented a declustering scheme for leaf nodes of TSB-trees in order to exploit I/O parallelism for time range and key range queries. Declustering of data is an important challenge for the implementation of temporal database systems, as (time) range queries are very important here. Our approach, coined LoT, adopts a key idea from the local balancing method of [SL91]. It dynamically assigns disk addresses to newly created TSB-tree nodes. Unlike local balancing, LoT considers the neighborhood of a new node in *both* the time dimension and key dimension for determining its disk address. Furthermore, for good declustering, LoT takes specific properties of TSB-trees into account.

We have derived analytical worst-case guarantees for the performance of LoT. To obtain insight into the average case performance, we simulated LoT and compared it to a scheme that assigns nodes onto disks in a random way. The simulations have shown that, for some cases, LoT performs 50% better than the random scheme and *never* performs worse. As LoT does not incur any noticeable overhead, LoT is always preferable over random placement.

At this point, LoT does not take into account specific probability distributions of different query types. We believe that this is particularly important for temporal databases as queries that access current data are expected to be more likely than those on historical data. In addition, time intervals containing frequent updates may be of interest to a higher fraction of queries. We plan to extend our notion of node distance accordingly. Our future work will also include the evaluation of different types of storage devices for historical data. As inexpensive, high-capacity tape farms are advancing, it is important to consider their applicability for storing historical data.

9 References

[AE93]   Abdel-Ghaffar, K., El Abbadi, A.: Optimal disk allocation for partial match queries, ACM TODS, Vol. 18 No. 1, 1993

[Ch94]   Chen, P.M., Lee, E.K., Gibson, G.A., Katz, R.H., Patterson, D.A., RAID: High-Performance, Reliable Secondary Storage, ACM Computing Surveys Vol.26 No.2, 1994

[DG92]   DeWitt, D.J., Gray, J.: Parallel Database Systems: The Future of High Performance Database Systems, Communications of the ACM Vol.35 No.6, 1992, pp. 85-98

[DS82]   Du, H.C., Sobolewski, J.S., Disk Allocation for Cartesian Product Files on Multiple Disk Systems, ACM Transactions on Database Systems Vol. 7 No.1, 1982, pp. 82-101

[EWK93] Elmasri, R., Wuu, G.T.J., Kouramajian, V.: The Time Index and the Monotonic B⁺-tree, in: [Tan93]

[FB93] Faloutsos, C., Bhagwat, P., Declustering Using Fractals, 2nd International Conference on Parallel and Distributed Information Systems, San Diego, 1993

[FM91] Faloutsos, C., Metaxas, D., Disk Allocation Methods Using Error Correcting Codes, IEEE Transactions on Computers Vol.40 No.8, 1991, pp. 907-914

[GD94] Ghandeharizadeh, S., DeWitt, D.J.: MAGIC: A Multiattribute Declustering Mechanism for Multiprocessor Database Machines, IEEE Transactions on Parallel and Distributed Systems Vol.5 No.5, 1994, pp. 509-524

[HLY93] Hua, K., Lee, C., Young, H.C.: Data Partitioning for Multicomputer Database Systems: A Cell-Based Approach, Information Systems Vol.18 No.5, 1993, pp. 329-342

[HS94] Himatsingka, B., Srivastava, J.: Performance Evaluation of Grid Based Multi-Attribute Record Declustering Methods, 10th IEEE International Conference on Data Engineering, Houston, 1994

[KEC94] Kouramajian, V., Elmasri, R., Chaudry, A.: Declustering Techniques for Parallelizing Temporal Access Structures, Proc. Data Engineering, 1994

[KF92] Kamel, I., Faloutsos, C.: Parallel R-trees, Proc. SIGMOD, 1992

[KP88] Kim, M.H., Pramanik, S., Optimal File Distribution for Partial Match Queries, ACM SIGMOD International Conference on Management of Data, Chicago, 1988

[Kol93] Kolovson, C.P.: Indexing Techniques for Historical Databases, in [Tan93]

[LS89] Lomet, D., Salzberg, B.: Access Methods for Multiversion Data, Proc. SIGMOD, 1989

[LS90] Lomet, D., Salzberg, B.: The Performance of a Multiversion Access Method, Proc. SIGMOD, 1990

[LS93] Lomet, D., Salzberg, B.: Transaction-Time Databases, in: [Tan93]

[LSR92] Li, J., Srivastava, J., Rotem, D.: CMD: A multidimensional declustering method for parallel database systems. Proc. VLDB, 1992

[MS94] Matsliach, G., Shmueli, O.: A Combined Method for Maintaining Large Indices in Multiprocessor Multidisk Environments, IEEE Transactions on Knowledge and Data Engineering Vol.6 No.3, 1994, pp. 479-496

[Mo94] Mohan, C., Pirahesh, H., Tang, W.G., Wang, Y.: Parallelism in Relational Database Management Systems, IBM Systems Journal Vol.33 No.2, 1994, pp. 349-371

[PK90] Pramanik, S., Kim, M.H.: Parallel Precessing of Large Node B-trees, IEEE Transactions on Computers, Vol. 39, No. 9, 1990

[SL91] Seeger, B., Larson, P.A.: Multi-Disk B-trees, Proc. SIGMOD, 1991

[SNH94] Srivastava, J., Niccum, T.M., Himatsingka, B., Data Declustering in PADMA: A PArallel Database MAnager, Bulletin of the IEEE TC on Data Engineering Vol.17 No.3, September 1994

[ST94] B. Salzberg, V.J. Tsotras, A Comparison of Access Methods for Time Evolving Data, Technical Report NU-CCS-94-21, Northeastern University, Boston, 1994

[SWZ94] Scheuermann, P., Weikum, G., Zabback, P., "Disk Cooling" in Parallel Disk Systems, Bulletin of the IEEE TC on Data Engineering Vol.17 No.3, September 1994

[Tan93] Tansel et al.: Temporal Databases, Benjamin Cummings Publishing, 1993

[ZSC94] Zhou, Y., Shekhar, S., Coyle, M.: Disk Allocation Methods for Parallelizing Grid Files, 10th IEEE International Conference on Data Engineering, Houston, 1994

LH*LH: A Scalable High Performance Data Structure for Switched Multicomputers

Jonas S Karlsson[1], Witold Litwin[2] and Tore Risch[1]

[1] EDSLAB - Engineering Databases and Systems Laboratory,
Department of Computer and Information Science, Linköping University,
Sweden, Email: {jonka,torri}@ida.liu.se
[2] Universite Paris 9 Dauphine, Place du Marechal de Lattre de Tassigny
75775 Paris Cedex 16, France, Email: litwin@cidmac.dauphine.fr

Abstract. LH*LH is a new data structure for scalable high-performance hash files on the increasingly popular switched multicomputers, i.e., MIMD multiprocessor machines with distributed RAM memory and without shared memory. An LH*LH file scales up gracefully over available processors and the distributed memory, easily reaching Gbytes. Address calculus does not require any centralized component that could lead to a hot-spot. Access times to the file can be under a millisecond and the file can be used in parallel by several client processors. We show the LH*LH design, and report on the performance analysis. This includes experiments on the Parsytec GC/PowerPlus multicomputer with up to 128 Power PCs divided into 64 nodes with 32 MB of RAM per node. We prove the efficiency of the method and justify various algorithmic choices that were made. LH*LH opens a new perspective for high-performance applications, especially for the database management of new types of data and in real-time environments.

1 Introduction

New applications of databases require increased performance. One way is to use parallel and distributed architectures [17][2]. The *multicomputers*, i.e., networks of multiple CPUs with local storage become a popular hardware platform for this purpose[17][2][21]. In particular, multicomputer files need to be able to scale to large sizes over the distributed storage, especially the RAM. The *Scalable Distributed Data Structures* (SDDSs)[15] is an approach towards this goal. An SDDS file can gracefully expand with the inserts from a single storage site to as many as needed, e.g., thousands, appended dynamically to the file. The data sites termed *servers* can be used from any number of autonomous sites termed *clients*. To avoid a hot-spot, there is no central directory for the addressing accross the current structure of the file. Each client has its own *image* of this structure. An image can become outdated when the file expands. The client may then send a request to an incorrect server. The servers forward such requests, possible in several steps, towards the correct address. The correct server appends to the reply a special message to the client, called *Image Adjustment Message* (IAM). The client adjusts its image, avoiding to repeat the error. A well designed SDDS should make addressing errors occasional and forwards few, and should provide for the scalability of the access performance when the file grows.

Up to now, the design of SDDSs was aimed at *network* multicomputers constituted of autonomous PCs and WSs linked through a local network. A promising type of multicomputer is also *shared-nothing multiprocessor multicomputers*, also called *switched multicomputers* (SM) [21]. Both types of multicomputers share the idea of cooperating autonomous CPUs communicating through message passing. This suggests that an SDDS could be useful for an SM as well. We have developed and implemented a variant of LH*, which we call LH*LH, designed specifically for this purpose. Performance analysis showed that LH*LH should be an attractive data structure for CPU and RAM intensive multiprocessor applications.

LH*LH allows for scalable RAM files spanning over several CPUs of an SM and its RAMs. On our testbed machine, a Parsytec GC/PowerPlus with 64 nodes of 32 MB RAM each, a RAM file can scale up to almost 2 GB with an average load factor of 70%. A file may be created and searched by several (client) CPUs concurrently. The access times may be about as fast as the communication network allows it to be. On our testbed, the average time per insert is as low as 1.2 ms per client. Eight clients building a file concurrently reach a throughput of 2500 inserts/second i.e., 400 μs/insert. These access times are more than an order of magnitude better than the best ones with the current disk file technology and will probably never be reached by mechanical devices.

Below we present the LH*LH design and performance. With respect to LH* [15], LH*LH is characterized by several original features. Its overall architecture is geared towards an SM while that of LH* was designed for a network multicomputer. Then, the design of LH*LH involves local bucket management while in [15] this aspect of LH* design was left for further study. In LH*LH one uses for this purpose a modified version of main-memory Linear Hashing defined in [19] on the basis of [11]. An interesting interaction between LH and LH* appears, allowing for much more efficient LH* bucket splitting. The reason is that LH*LH allows the splitting of LH*-buckets without visiting individual keys.

The average access time is of primary importance for any SDDS on a network computer or SM. Minimizing the worst case is, however, probably more important for an SM where processors work more tightly connected than in a network computer. The worst case for LH* occurs when a client accesses a bucket undergoing a split. LH* splits should be infrequent in practice since buckets should be rather large. In the basic LH* schema, a client's request simply waits at the server till the split ends. In the Parsytec context, performance measurements show that this approach may easily lead to several seconds per split, e.g. three to seven seconds in our experiences (as compared to $1 - 2$ msec per request on the average). Such a variance would be detrimental to many SM applications.

LH*LH is therefore provided with an enhanced splitting schema, termed *concurrent splitting*. It is based on ideas sketched in [14] allowing for the client's request to be dealt with while the split is in progress. Several concurrent splitting schemes were designed and experimented with. Our performance studies

575

shows superiority of one of these schemes, termed concurrent splitting with bulk
shipping. The maximal response time of an insert while a split occurs decreases
by a factor of three hundred to a thousand times. As we report in what follows,
it becomes about 7 msec for one active client in our experiences and 25 msec for
a file in use by eight clients. The latter value is due to interference among clients
requesting simultaneous access to the server splitting.

Given the space limitations, in what follows we assume basic knowledge of
LH* as in [15], and of LH as defined in [13]. Section 2 discusses related work.
Section 3 presents the Parsytec machine. Section 4 describes LH*LH. Section 5
shows performance study. Section 6 concludes the paper.

2   Related Work

In traditional distributed files systems, in implementations like NFS or AFS, a
file resides entirely at one specific site. This gives obvious limitations not only
on the size of the file but also on the access performance scalability. To overcome
these limitations distributions over multiple sites have been used. One example of
such a scheme is *round-robin* [1] where records of a file are evenly distributed by
rotating through the nodes when records are inserted. The *hash-declustering* [8]
assigns records to nodes on basis of a hashing function. The *range-partitioning* [4]
divides key values into ranges and different ranges are assigned to different nodes.
All these schemes are *static* which means that the declustering criterion does not
change over time. Hence, updating a directory or declustering function is not
required. The price to pay is that the file cannot expand over more sites than
initially allocated.

To overcome this limitation of static schemes, the dynamic partitioning started appearing. The first such scheme is DLH [20]. This scheme was designed for a
shared memory system. In DLH, the file is in RAM and the file parameters are
cached in the local memory of each processor. The caches are refreshed selectively when addressing errors occur and through atomic updates to all the local
memories at some points. DLH shows impressively efficient for high insert rates.

SDDSs were proposed for distributing files in the network multicomputer
environment, hence without a shared memory. The first scheme was LH* [15].
Distributed Dynamic Hashing (DDH) [3] is another SDDS, it is based on Dynamic Hashing [10]. The idea with respect to LH* is that DDH allows greater
splitting autonomy by immediately splitting overflowing buckets. One drawback
is that while LH* limits the number of forwardings to two[3] when the client
makes an addressing error, DDH may use $O(\log_2 N)$ forwardings, where N is
the number of buckets in the DDH file.

Another SDDS has been defined in [22]. It extends LH* and DDH to more
efficiently control the load of a file. The main idea is to manage several buckets
of a file per server while LH* and DDH have basically only one bucket per server.
One also controls the server load as opposed to bucket load for LH*.

---

[3] In theory, communication delays could trigger more forwarding [22].

Finally, in [9] and in [16] SDDSs for (primary key) ordered files are proposed. In [9] the access computations on the clients and servers use a distributed binary search tree. The SDDSs in [16], collectively termed RP*, use broadcast or distributed n-ary trees. It is shown that both kinds of SDDSs allow for much larger and faster files than the traditional ones.

3 The Parsytec Multicomputer

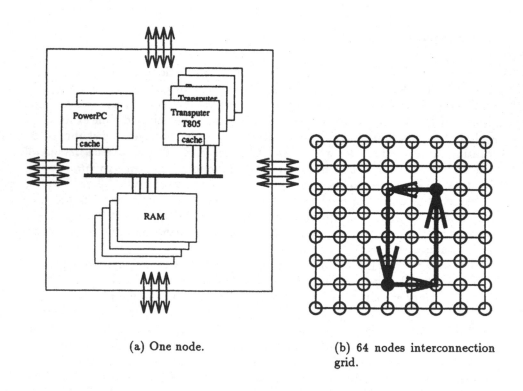

(a) One node.

(b) 64 nodes interconnection grid.

Fig. 1. The Parsytec architecture.

The Parsytec GC/PowerPlus architecture (Figure 1) is massively parallel with distributed memory, also know as MIMD (Multiple Instruction Multiple Data). The machine used for the LH*LH implementation has 128 PowerPC-601 RISC-processors, constituting 64 nodes. One node is shown in Figure 1a. Each node has 32 MB of memory shared between two PowerPC processors and four T805 Transputer processors. The latter are used for communication. Each Transputer has four bidirectional communication links. The nodes are connected through a bidirectional fat (multiple) grid network with packet message routing.

The communication is point-to-point. The software libraries [18] support both synchronous and asynchronous communication and some other types of communication, e.g. mailboxes.

The response time of a communication depends on the actual machine topology. The closer the communicating nodes are the faster is the response. Routing is done statically by the hardware as in Figure 1b with the packages first routed in the horizontal direction.

4   LH*LH Overview

4.1   Overall Architecture

An LH*LH-*client* is a process that accesses an LH*LH file on the behalf of the application. An LH*LH-*server* at a node stores data of LH*LH files. An application can use several clients to explore a file. This way of processing increases the throughput, as will be shown in Section 5. Both clients and servers are created dynamically. In the current implementation, the allocation of clients start from the higher numbered nodes. The servers are allocated from the lower nodes, as in Figure 2a.

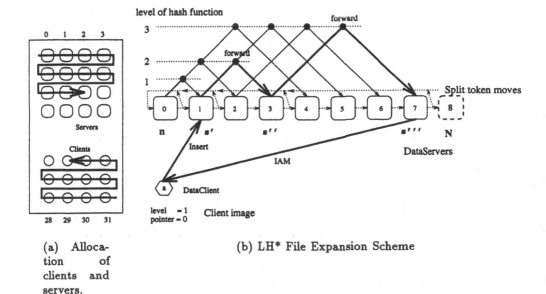

(a) Allocation of clients and servers.

(b) LH* File Expansion Scheme

Fig. 2. Clients and Servers.

At a server, one *bucket* per LH* file contains the stored data. The bucket management is described in Section 4.5. The file starts at one server and expands to others when it overloads the buckets already used.

4.2 LH* Addressing Scheme

The global addressing rule in LH*LH file is that every key C is inserted to the server s_C whose address $s = 0, 1, ...N-1$ is given by the following LH addressing algorithm [13]:

$$s_C := h_i(C)$$

$$\text{if } s_C < \text{ then } s_C := h_{i+1}(C),$$

where i (LH* file level) and n (split pointer address) are file parameters evolving with splits. The h_i functions are basically:

$$h_i(C) = C \bmod (2^i \times K), K = 1, 2, ..$$

and $K = 1$ in what follows. No client of an LH* file knows the current i and n of the file. Every client has its own *image* of these values, let it be i' and n'; typically $i' \leq i$ [15]. The client sends the query, e.g. the insert of key C, to the address $s'_C(i', n')$.

The server s'_C verifies upon query reception whether its own address s'_C is $s'_C = s_C$ using a short algorithm stated in [15]. If so the server processes the query. Otherwise, it calculates a forwarding address s''_C using the forwarding algorithm in [15] and sends the query to server s''_C. Server s''_C acts as s'_C and perhaps resends the query to server s'''_C as shown for Server 1 in Figure 2b. It is proven in [15] that then s'''_C must be the correct server. In every case, of forwarding, the correct server sends to the client an Image Adjustment Message (IAM) containing the level i of the correct server. Knowing the i and the s_C address, the client adjusts its i' and n' (see [15]) and from now on will send C directly to s_C.

4.3 LH* File Expansion

LH* file expands through bucket splits as in Figure 2. The bucket next to split is generally noted bucket n, $n = 0$ in the figure. Each bucket keeps the value of i used (called LH*-bucket level) in its header starting from $i = 0$ for bucket 0 when the file is created. Bucket n splits through the replacement of h_i with h_{i+1} for every C it contains. As result, typically half of its records move to a new bucket N, appended to the file with address $n+2^i$. In Figure 2, one has $N = 8$. After the split, n is set to $(n + 1) \bmod 2^i$. The successive values of n can thus be seen as a linear move of a *split token* through the addresses $0, 0, 1, 0, 1, 2, 3, 0, ..., 2^i-1, 0, ...$ The arrows of Figure 2 show both the token moves and a new bucket address for every split, as resulting from this scheme.

There are many strategies, called *split control* strategies, that one can use to decide when a bucket should split [14] [13] [22]. The overall goal is to avoid the file to overload. As no LH* bucket can know the global load, one way to proceed is to fix some threshold S on a bucket load [14]. Bucket n splits when it gets an insert and the actual number of objects it stores is at least S. S can be fixed as a file parameter. A potentially more performant strategy for an SM environment is to calculate S for bucket n dynamically through the following formula:

$$S = M \times V \times \frac{2^i + n}{2^i},$$

where i is the n-th LH*-bucket level, M is a file parameter, and V is the bucket capacity in number of objects. Typically one sets M to some value between 0.7 and 0.9.

The performance analysis in Section 5.1 shows indeed that the dynamic strategy should be preferred in our context. This is the strategy adopted for LH*LH.

4.4   Communication Mode

In the LH*LH implementation on the Parsytec machine a server receiving a request must have issued the *receive* call before the client can do any further processing. This well known *rendezvous* technique enforces entry flow control on the servers, preventing the clients from working much faster than the server could accept requests[4]. Insert operations do not give any specific acknowledge messages by the LH* manager since communication is "safe" on the Parsytec machine (if send returns ok the message is guaranteed to be received). IAMs, split messages with the split token, and general service messages use the asynchronous type of communication.

4.5   Server Architecture

The server consists of two layers, as shown in Figure 3a. The LH*-Manager handles communications and concurrent splits. The LH-Manager manages the objects in the bucket. It uses the Linear Hashing algorithm [12].

The LH Manager LH creates files able to grow and shrink gracefully on a site. In our implementation, the LH-manager stores all data in the main memory. The LH variant used is a modified implementation of Main Memory Linear Hashing [19].

The LH file in an LH*-bucket (Figure 3b) essentially contains (i) a header with the *LH-level*, an *LH-splitting pointer*, and the count x of objects stored, and (ii) a dynamic array of pointers to LH-buckets, and (iii) LH-buckets with records. An LH-bucket is implemented as a linked list of the records. Each record contains the calculated hash value, called a *pseudo-key*. Both the pointer to the

---

[4] The overloaded server could run out of memory space and could send outdated IAMs [6].

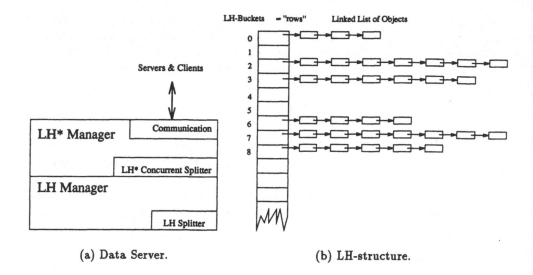

(a) Data Server.   (b) LH-structure.

Fig. 3. The Data Server and the LH-structure.

actual key, and the pointer to the object are stored as bitstrings. Pseudo-keys make the rehashing faster. An LH-bucket split occurs when $L = 1$, with:

$$L = \frac{x}{b \times m},$$

where b is the number of buckets in the LH file, and m is a file parameter being the required mean number of objects in the LH-buckets (linked list). Linear search is most efficient up to an m about 10.

LH* Partitioning of an LH File The use of LH allows the LH* splitting in a particularly efficient way. The reason is that individual keys are not visited for rehashing. Figure 4 and Figure 5 illustrate the ideas.

LH and LH* share the pseudo-key. The pseudo-key has J bits, in Figure 4; $J = 32$ at every bucket. LH* uses the lower l bits $(b_{l-1}, b_{l-2}, ...b_0)$. LH uses j bits $(b_{j+l-2}, b_{j+l-3}, ...b_l)$, where $j + l \leq J$. During an LH*-split l increases by one whereas j decreases by one. The value of the new lth bit determines whether an LH-bucket is to be shipped. Only the odd LH-buckets i.e. with $b_l = 1$ are shipped to the new LH*-bucket N. The array of the remaining LH-buckets is compacted, the count of objects is adjusted, the LH-bucket level is decreased by one (LH uses one bit less), and the split pointer is halved. Figure 5 illustrates this process.

Further inserts to the bucket may lead to any number of new LH splits, increasing j in Figure 4 to some j'. Next LH* split of the bucket will then decrease j' to $j' := j' - 1$, and set $l := l + 1$ again.

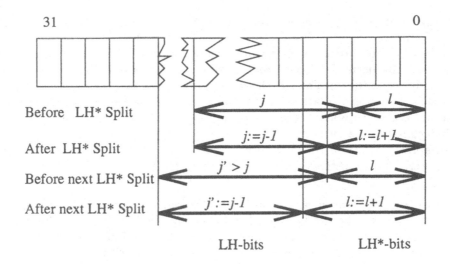

Fig. 4. Pseudo-key usage by LH and LH*.

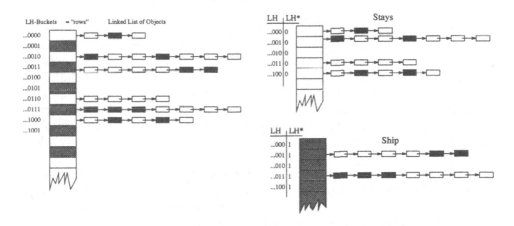

Fig. 5. Partitioning of an LH-file by LH* splitting.

Concurrent Request Processing and Splitting A split is a much longer operation than a search or an insert. The split should also be atomic for the clients. Basic LH* [15] simply requires the client to wait till the split finishes. For the high-performance applications on an SM multicomputer it is fundamental that the server processes a split concurrently with searches and inserts. This is achieved as follows in LH*LH.

Requests received by the server undergoing a split are processed as if the server had not started splitting, with one exception: a request that concerns parts of the local LH structure processed by the Splitter is queued to be processed by the Splitter.

The Splitter processes the queue of requests since these requests concern LH-buckets of objects that have been or are being shipped. If the request concerns an LH-bucket that has already been shipped the request is forwarded, since the data is guaranteed to arrive at the destination. If the request, concerns an LH-bucket not yet shipped it is processed in the local LH table as usual. The requests that concerns the current LH-bucket being shipped is first searched among the remaining objects in that LH-bucket. If not found there it is forwarded by the Splitter. All forwardings are serialized within the Splitter task.

Shipping *Shipping* means transferring the objects selected during the LH*-bucket split to the newly appended bucket N. In LH* [14] the shipping was assumed basically to be of the *bulk* type with all the objects packed into a single message. After shipping has been completed, bucket N sends back a *commit message*. In LH*LH there is no need for the commit message. The communication is safe, and the sender's data cannot be updated before the shipping is entirely received. In particular, no client can directly access bucket N before the split is complete.

In the LH*LH environment there are several reasons for not shipping too many objects in a message, especially all the objects in a single message. Packing and unpacking objects into a message requires CPU time and memory transfers, as objects are not stored contiguously in the memory. One also needs buffers of sizes at least proportional to the message size, and a longer occupation of the communication subsystem. Sending objects individually simplifies these aspects but generates more messages and more overhead time in the dialog with the communication subsystem. It does not seem that one can decide easily which strategy is finally more effective in practice.

The performance analysis in Section 5.2 motivated the corresponding design choice for LH*LH. The approach is that of bulk shipping but with a limited message size. At least one object is shipped per message and at most one LH-bucket. The message size is a parameter allowing for an application dependent packing factor. For the test data using bulks of a dozen of records per shipment showed to be much more effective than the individual shipping.

5 Performance Evaluation

The access performance of our implementation was studied experimentally. The measurements below show elapsed times of various operations and their scalability. Each experiment consists of a series of inserts creating an LH* file. The number of clients, the file parameters M and m, and the size of the objects are LH*LH parameters.

At the time when the tests were performed only 32 nodes were available at our site. The clients are allocated downwards from node 31 and downwards and servers from node 0 and upwards. The clients read the test data (a random list of words) from the file system in advance to avoid that the I/O disturbs the measurements. Then the clients start inserting their data, creating the example LH*LH-file. When a client sends a request to the server it continues with the next item only when the request has been accepted by the server (rendezvous). Each time before the LH* file is split measures are collected by the splitting server. Some measurements are also collected at some client, especially timing values for each of that client's requests.

5.1 Scalability

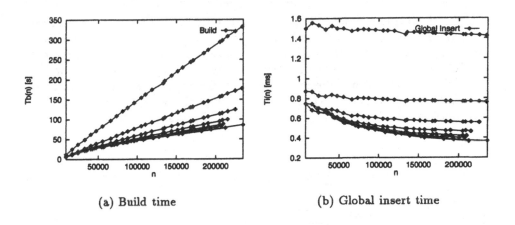

(a) Build time   (b) Global insert time

Fig. 6. Build and insert time for LH*LH for different number of clients (1-8).

Figure 6a plots the elapsed time to constitute the example LH*LH file through n inserts; $n = 1, 2..N$ and $N = 235.000$; performed simultaneously by k clients $k = 1, 2..8$. This time is called *build time* and is noted $Tb(n)$, or $Tb^k(N)$ with k as a parameter. In Figure 6a, $Tb(N)$ is measured in seconds. Each point in a curve corresponds to a split. The splits were performed using the concurrent splitting with the dynamic control and the bulk shipping. The upper curve is $Tb^1(n)$. Next lower curve is $Tb^2(n)$, etc., until $Tb^8(n)$.

The curves show that each $Tb^k(n)$ scales-up about linearly with the file size n. This is close to the ideal result. Also, using more clients to build the file, uniformly decreases Tb^k, i.e., $k' > k'' - > Tb^{k'}(n) \leq Tb\ k''(n)$ for every n. Using two clients almost halves Tb, especially $Tb(N)$, from $Tb^1(N) = 330$ sec to $Tb^2(N) = 170$ sec. Building the file through eight clients decreases Tb further, by a factor of four. $Tb(N)$ becomes only $Tb^8(N) = 80$ sec. While this is in practice an excellent performance, the ideal scale-up could reach k times, i.e., the build time $Tb^8(N) = 40$ sec only. The difference results from various communication and processing delays at a server shared by several clients, discussed in the previous sections and in what follows.

Figure 6b plots the curves of the global insert time $Ti^k(n) = Tb^k(n)/n$ [msec]. Ti measures the average time of an insert from the perspective of the application building the file on the multicomputer. The internal mechanics of LH*LH file is transparent at this level including the distribution of the inserts among the k clients and several servers, the corresponding parallelism of some inserts, the splits etc. The values of n, N and k are those from Figure 6a. To increase k improves Ti in the same way as for Tb. The curves are also about as linear, constant in fact, as they should be. Higly interestingly, and perhaps unexpectedly, each $Tb^k(n)$ even decreases when n grows, the gradient increasing with k. One reason is the increasing number of servers of a growing file, leading to fewer requests per server. Also, our allocation schema decreases the mean distance through the net between the servers and the clients of the file.

The overall result is that Ti always is under 1.6 msec. Increasing k uniformly decreases Ti, until $Ti^8(n) < 0.8$ msec, and $Ti^8(N) < 0.4$ msec. These values are about ten to twenty times smaller than access times to a disk file, typically over 10 msec per insert or search. They are likely to remain forever beyond the reach of any storage on a mechanical device. On the other hand, a faster net and more efficient communication subsystem than the one used should allow for even much smaller Ti's, in the order of dozens of μsecs [14] [16].

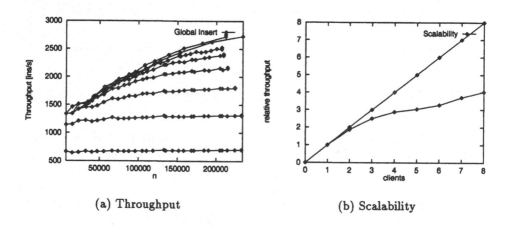

(a) Throughput   (b) Scalability

Fig. 7. Throughput scale-up for different number of clients.

Figure 7a plots the global throughput $T^k(n)$ defined as $T^k(n) = 1/Ti(n)[i/sec]$ (inserts per second). The curves express again an almost linear scalability with n. For the reasons above discussed, T^k even increases for larger files, up to 2700 i/sec. An increase of k also uniformly increases T for every n. To see the throughput scalability more clearly, Figure 7b plots the relative throughput $Tr(k) = T^k(n)/T^1(n)$ for a large n; $n = N$. One compares Tr to the plot of the ideal scale-up that is simply $T'r(k) = k$. The communication and service delays we spoke about clearly play an increasing role when k increases. Although Tr monotonically increases with k, it diverges more and more from $T'r$. For $k = 8$, one has $Tr = 4$ which is only the half of the ideal scale-up. It means that the actual throughput per client, $Tc^k(n) = T^k(n)/k$, comparatively also decreases until the half of the throughput T^1 of a single client.

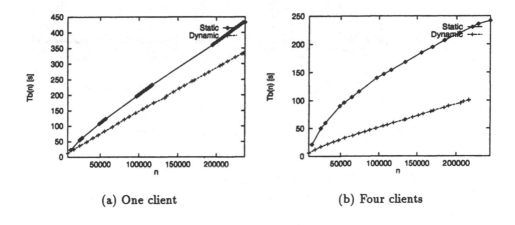

(a) One client   (b) Four clients

Fig. 8. Static and dynamic split control.

Figure 8 shows the comparative study of the dynamic and the static split control strategies. The plots show build times, let it be $Tb'(n)$ for the static control and $Tb(n)$ for the dynamic one. The curves correspond to the constitution of our example file, with $k = 1$ in Figure 8a and $k = 4$ in Figure 8b. The plots Tb are the same as in Figure 6a. Figure 8 clearly justifies our choice of the dynamic control strategy. Static control uniformly leads to the longer build time, i.e., for every n and k one has $Tb'(n) > Tb(n)$. The relative difference $(Tb' - Tb)/Tb$ reaches 30% for $k = 1$, e.g. $Tb'(N) = 440$ and $Tb(N) = 340$. For $k = 4$ the dynamic strategy more than halves the build time, e.g from 230 to 100 sec.

Note that the dynamic strategy also generates splits generally more uniformly over the inserts, particularly for $k = 1$. The static strategy leads to short periods when a few inserts generate splits of about every bucket. This creates a heavier load on the communication system and increases the insert and search times during that period.

5.2 Efficiency of Concurrent Splitting

Figure 9 shows the study of comparative efficiency of individual and bulk shipping for LH* atomic splitting (non-concurrent), as described earlier. The curves plot the insert time $Ti^1(t)$ measured at t seconds during the constitution of the example file by a single client. A bulk message contains at most all the records

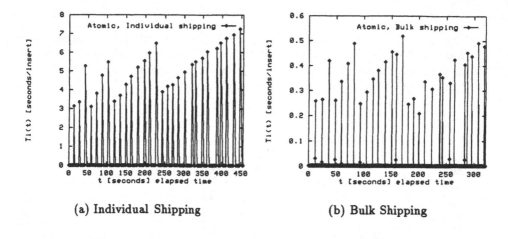

(a) Individual Shipping   (b) Bulk Shipping

Fig. 9. Efficiency of (a) individual and (b) bulk shipping.

constituting an LH-bucket to ship. In this experiment there are 14 records per bulk on the average. A peak corresponds to a split in progress, when an insert gets blocked till the split ends.

The average insert time beyond the peaks is 1.3 msec. The corresponding Ti's are barely visible at the bottom of the plots. The individual shipping, Figure 9a, leads to a peak of $Ti = 7.3$ sec. The bulk shipping plot, Figure 9b, shows the highest peak of $Ti = 0.52$ sec, i.e., 14 times smaller. The overall build time $Tb(N)$ decreases also by about 1/3, from 450 sec in Figure 9a, to 320 sec in Figure 9b. The figures clearly prove the utility of the bulk shipping.

Observe that the maximal peak size got reduced accordingly to the bulk size. It means that larger bulks improve the access performance. However, such bulks require also more storage for themselves as well as for the intermediate communication buffers and more CPU for the bulk assembly and disassembly. To choose the best bulk size in practice, one has to weight all these factors depending on the application and the hardware used.

Figure 10 shows the results of the study where the bulk shipping from Figure 9 is finally combined with the concurrent splitting. Each plot $Ti(t)$ shows the evolution of the insert time at one selected client among k clients; $k = 1..4, 8$; concurrently building the example file with the same insert rate per client. The peaks at the figures correspond again to the splits in progress but they are much lower. For $k = 1$, they are under 7 msec, and for $k = 8$ they reach 25 msec. The worst insert time with respect to Figure 9 improves thus by a factor of 70 for $k = 1$ and of 20 for $k = 4$. This result clearly justifies the utility of the concurrent splitting and our overall design of the splitting algorithm of LH*LH.

The plots in Figures 10a to 10e show the tendency towards higher peaks of Ti, as well as towards higher global average and variances of Ti over $Ti(t)$, when more clients build the file. The plot in Figure 10f confirms this tendency for the

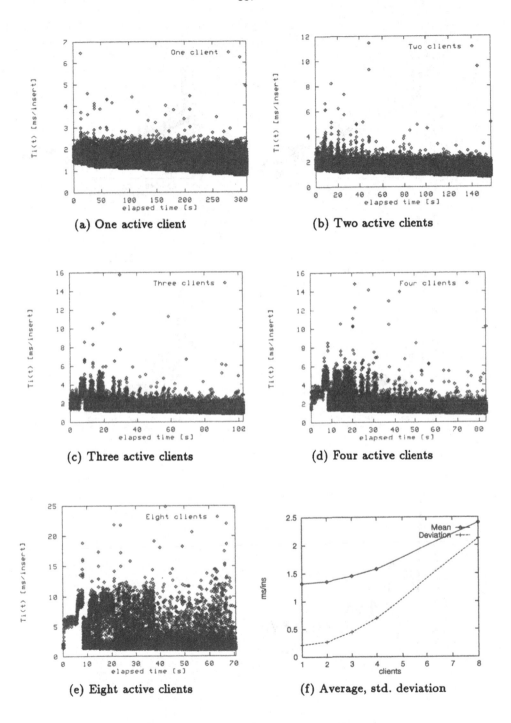

Fig. 10. Efficiency of the concurrent splitting.

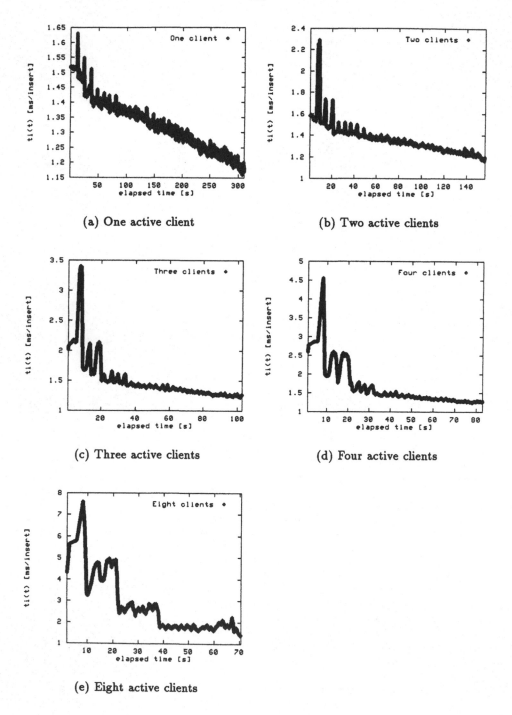

(a) One active client

(b) Two active clients

(c) Three active clients

(d) Four active clients

(e) Eight active clients

Fig. 11. LH*LH client insert time scalability.

average and the variance. Figures 10d and 10e show also that the insert times become especially affected when the file is still small, as one can see for $t < 10$ in these figures. All these phenomena are due to more clients per server for a larger k. A client has then to wait more for the service. A greater k is nevertheless advantageous for the global throughput as it was shown earlier.

Figure 10 hardly allows to see the tendency of the insert time when the file scales up, as non-peak values are buried in the black areas. Figure 11 plots therefore the evolution of the corresponding *marginal client insert time* Tm^k. Tm^k is computed as an average over a sliding window of 500 inserts plotted in Figure 10. The averaging smoothes the variability of successive values giving the black areas in Figure 10. The plots $Tm^k(t)$ show that the insert times not only do not deteriorate when the file grows, but even improve. Tm^1 decreases from 1.65 msec to under 1.2 msec, and Tm^8 from 8 msec to 1.5 msec. This nice behavior is due again to the increase in the number of servers and to the decreasing distance between the clients and the servers.

The plots show also that $Tm^k(t)$ uniformly increases with k, i.e. $k'' > k' \rightarrow Tm^{k''}(t) > Tm^{k'}(t)$, for every t. This phenomena is due to the increased load of each server. Also interestingly, the shape of Tm^k becomes stepwise, for greater k's, with insert times about halving at each new step. A step corresponds to a split token trip at some level i. The drop occurs when the last bucket of level i splits and the split token comes back to bucket 0. This tendency seems to show that the serialization of inserts contributing most to a Tm^k value occurs mainly at the buckets that are not yet split.

The overall conclusion from Figure 11 is that the insert times at a client of a file equally shared among k clients, is basically either always under 2 msec, for $k = 1$, or tends to be under this time when the file enlarges. Again this performance shows excellent scale-up behavior of LH*LH. The performance is in particular largely superior to the one of a typical disk file used in a similar way. For $k = 8$ clients, for example, the speed-up factor could reach 40 times, i.e., 2 msec versus $8 * 10$ msec.

6 Conclusions

Switched multicomputers such as the Parsytec GC/PowerPlus are powerful tools for high-performance applications. LH*LH was shown an efficient new data structure for such multicomputers. Performance analysis showed that access times may be in general of the order of a milisecond, reaching 0.4 msec per insert in our experiences, and that the throughput may reach thousands of operations per second, over 2700 in our study, regardless of the file scale-up. An LH*LH file can scale-up over as much of distributed RAM as available, e.g., 2 Gbytes on the Parsytec, without any access performance deterioration. The access times are in particular an order of magnitude faster than one could attain using disk files.

Performance analysis confirmed also various design choices made for LH*LH. In particular, the use of LH for the bucket management, as well as of the concurrent splitting with the dynamic split control and the bulk shipping, effectively reduced the peaks of response time. The improvement reached a thousand times in our experiences, from over 7sec that would characterize LH*, to under 7 msec for LH*LH. Without this reduction, LH*LH would likely to be inadequate for many high-performance applications.

Future work should concern a deeper performance analysis of LH*LH under various conditions. More experiments with actual data should be performed. A formal performance model is also needed. In general such models yet lack for the SDDSs. The task seems of even greater complexity than for more traditional data structures. If the algorithm is to be used for more than one file a different physical mapping (e.g. randomization) to the nodes should be used for each file to distribute the load.

The ideas put into the LH*LH design should apply also to other known SDDSs. They should allow for the corresponding variants for switched multi-computers. One benefit would be scalable high performance ordered files. SDDSs in [16], or [9] should be a promising basis towards this goal.

A particularly promising direction should be the integration of LH*LH as a component of a DBMS. One may expect important performance gain, opening to DBMSs new application perspectives. Video servers seem one promising axis, as it is well known that major DBMS manufacturers look already upon switched multicomputers for this purpose. The complex real-time switching data management in telephone networks seems another interesting domain.

To approach these goals, we plan to make use of the implementation of LH*LH for high-performance databases. We will interface it with our research platform AMOS [5], which is an extensible object-relational database management system with a complete query language [7]. AMOS would then reside on an ordinary workstation, whereas some datatypes/relations/functions would be stored and searched by the MIMD machine. AMOS will then act as a front-end system to the parallel stored data. The query optimization of AMOS will have to be extended to also take into account the communication time and possible speed-up gained by using distributed parallel processing. Other SDDSs than LH* are also of interest for evaluation, a new candidate is the RP* [16] that handles ordered data sets.

Acknowledgment

This project was supported by NUTEK (The Swedish National Board for Industrial and Technical Development), and CENIIT (The Center for Industrial Information Technology).

References

1. Teradata Corporation. DBC/1012 data base computer concepts and facilities. Technical Report Teradata Document C02-001-05, Teradata Corporation, 1988.
2. D. Culler. NOW: Towards Everyday Supercomputing on a Network of Workstations. Technical report, EECS Tech. Rep. UC Berkeley, 1994.

3. R. Devine. Design and implementation of DDH: A distributed dynamic hashing algorithm. In *Proc. of the 4th Intl. Conf. on Foundations of Data Organization and Algorithms (FODO)*, 1993.
4. D. DeWitt, R. Gerber, G. Graefe, M. Heytens, K. Kumar, and M. Muralikrishna. GAMMA: A high performance dataflow database machine. In *Proc of VLDB*, August 1986.
5. G. Fahl, T. Risch, and M. Sköld. AMOS - An Architecture for Active Mediators. In *IEEE Transactions on Knowledge and Data Engineering*, Haifa, Israel, June 1993.
6. J. S. Karlsson. LH*LH: Architecture and Implementation. Technical report, IDA, Linkping University, Sweden, 1995.
7. J. S. Karlsson, S. Larsson, T. Risch, M. Sköld, and M. Werner. *AMOS User's Guide*. CAELAB, IDA, IDA, Dept. of Computer Science and Information Science, Linköping University, Sweden, memo 94-01 edition, Mars 1994. URL: http://www.ida.liu.se/labs/edslab/amos/amosdoc.html.
8. M. Kitsuregawa, H. Tanaka, and T. Moto-Oka. Architecture and performance of relational algebra machine GRACE. In *Proc. of the Intl. Conf. on Parallel Processing*, Chicago, 1984.
9. B. Kroll and P. Widmayer. Distributing a Search Tree Among a Growing Number of Processors. In *ACM-SIGMOD Int. Conf. On Management of Data*, 1994.
10. P.Å. Larson. Dynamic hashing. *BIT*, 18(2):184–201, 1978.
11. P.Å. Larson. Dynamic hash tables. In *Communications of the ACM*, volume 31(4), pages 446–57. April 1988.
12. W. Litwin. Linear Hashing: A new tool for file and table addressing. Montreal, Canada, 1980. Proc. of VLDB.
13. W. Litwin. Linear Hashing: A new tool for file and table addressing. In Michael Stonebraker, editor, *Readings in DATABASE SYSTEMS, 2nd edition*, pages 96–107. 1994.
14. W. Litwin, M-A. Neimat, and D. Schneider. LH*: A Scalable Distributed Data Structure. submitted for journal publication, Nov 1993.
15. W. Litwin, M-A Neimat, and D. Schneider. LH*: Linear hashing for distributed files. ACM SIGMOD International Conference on Management of Data, May 1993.
16. W. Litwin, M-A Neimat, and D. Schneider. RP*: A Family of Order Preserving Scalable Distributed Data Structures. VLDB Conference, 1994.
17. M. Tamer Özsu and Patrick Valduriez. *Principles of Distributed Database Systems*. Number ISBN 0-13-715681-2. Prentice Hall, 1991.
18. Parsytec Computer GmbH. *Programmers Guide, Parix 1.2-PowerPC*, 1994.
19. M. Pettersson. Main-Memory Linear Hashing - Some Enhancements of Larson's Algorithm. Technical Report LiTH-IDA-R-93-04, ISSN-0281-4250, IDA, 1993.
20. C. Severance, S. Pramanik, and P. Wolberg. Distributed linear hashing and parallel projection in main memory databases. In *Proceedings of the 16th International Conference on VLDB*, Brisbane, Australia, 1990.
21. Andrew S. Tanenbaum. *Distributed Operating Systems*. 1995.
22. R. Wingralek, Y. Breitbart, and G. Weikum. Distributed file organisation with scalable cost/performance. In *Proc of ACM-SIGMOD*, May 1994.

Declustering Spatial Databases on a Multi-Computer Architecture

Nikos Koudas[1] and *Christos Faloutsos*[2]* and *Ibrahim Kamel*[3]

[1] Computer Systems Research Institute
University of Toronto
[2] AT&T Bell Laboratories
Murray Hill, NJ
[3] Matsushita Information
Technology Laboratory

Abstract. We present a technique to decluster a spatial access method on a shared-nothing multi-computer architecture [DGS+90]. We propose a software architecture with the R-tree as the underlying spatial access method, with its non-leaf levels on the 'master-server' and its leaf nodes distributed across the servers. The major contribution of our work is the study of the optimal capacity of leaf nodes, or 'chunk size' (or 'striping unit'): we express the response time on range queries as a function of the 'chunk size', and we show how to optimize it.

We implemented our method on a network of workstations, using a real dataset, and we compared the experimental and the theoretical results. The conclusion is that our formula for the response time is *very* accurate (the maximum relative error was 29%; the typical error was in the vicinity of 10-15%). We illustrate one of the possible ways to exploit such an accurate formula, by examining several 'what-if' scenarios. One major, practical conclusion is that a chunk size of 1 page gives either optimal or close to optimal results, for a wide range of the parameters.

Keywords: Parallel data bases, spatial access methods, shared nothing architecture.

1 Introduction

One of the requirements for the database management systems (DBMSs) of the future is the ability to handle spatial data. Spatial data arise in many applications, including: Cartography [Whi81], Computer-Aided Design (CAD) [OHM+84], [Gut84a], computer vision and robotics [BB82], traditional databases, where a record with k attributes corresponds to a point in a k-d space, rule indexing in

---

* On leave from the University of Maryland, College Park. His research was partially funded by the Institute for Systems Research (ISR), and by the National Science Foundation under Grants IRI-9205273 and IRI-8958546 (PYI), with matching funds from EMPRESS Software Inc. and Thinking Machines Inc.

expert database systems [SSH86], temporal databases [SS88], where time can be treated as one more dimension [KS91], scientific databases, with spatial-temporal data, etc.

In several of these applications the volume of data is huge, necessitating the use of multiple units. For example, NASA expects 1 Terabyte $(=10^{12})$ of data per day; this corresponds to 10^{16} bytes per year of satellite data. Geographic databases can be large, for example, the TIGER database of the U.S. Bureau of Census is 19 Gigabytes. Historic and temporal databases tend to archive all the changes and grow quickly in size.

In the above applications, one of the most typical queries is the *range query*: Given a rectangle, retrieve all the elements that intersect it. A special case of the range query is the *point query* or *stabbing query*, where the query rectangle degenerates to a point.

We study the use of parallelism in order to improve the response time of spatial queries. We plan to use R-trees [Gut84b] as our underlying data structure, because they guarantee good space utilization, they treat geometric objects as a whole and they give good response time.

We envision a shared-nothing architecture, with several workstations connected to a LAN. The challenge is to organize the data on the available units, in order to minimize the response time for range queries.

The paper is organized as follows. Section 2 briefly describes the R-tree and its variants. Also, it surveys previous efforts to parallelize other file structures. Section 3 proposes our architecture and describes its parameters and components. Section 4 presents the analysis for computing the optimal chunk size. Section 5 presents experimental results and validates the formulas derived from our analysis. Section 6 lists the conclusions and highlights directions for future work.

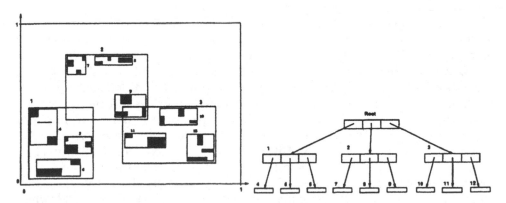

Fig. 1. (a) Data (dark rectangles) organized in an R-tree with fanout=3 (b) the resulting R-tree, on disk.

2 Survey

Several spatial access methods have been proposed. A recent survey and classification can be found in [Sam90]. This classification includes (a) methods that transform rectangles into points in a higher dimensionality space [HN83], subsequently using a *point access method*, like a grid file [NHS84] (b) methods that use linear quadtrees [Gar82] or, equivalently, the z-ordering [Ore86] or other space filling curves [FR89] [Jag90], and finally, (c) methods based on trees (k-d-trees [Ben75], k-d-B-trees [Rob81], cell-trees [Gun86], the BANG file [Fre87], hB-trees [LS90], n-d generalizations of B-trees [Fre95] e.t.c.)

Among the above three approaches, we focus on the R-tree family, for the following reasons:

- the R-trees do not cut data rectangles into pieces (unlike the linear-quadtree approach). Cutting data into pieces results in an artificially increased database size (linear on the number of *pieces*); moreover, it requires a duplicate-elimination step, because a query may retrieve the same object-id several times (once for each piece of the qualifying object)
- the R-trees operate on the native address space, which is of lower dimensionality; in contrast, transforming rectangles into points in a higher-dimensionality space invites the 'dimensionality curse' problems early on.
- R-trees seem more robust for higher dimensionalities [FBF$^+$94]. Scientific, medical and statistical databases may involve several dimensions, eg., (x, y, z, time, pressure, wind velocity, temperature), or (gender, age, cholesterol-level, blood-pressure, etc.).

Thus, we mainly focus on the R-tree [Gut84b] and its variants. The R-tree is an extension of the B-tree for multidimensional objects. A geometric object is represented by its minimum bounding rectangle (MBR). Non-leaf nodes contain entries of the form (ptr, R), where ptr is a pointer to a child node in the R-tree; R is the MBR that covers all rectangles in the child node. Leaf nodes contain entries of the form ($obj - id$, R) where $obj - id$ is a pointer to the object description, and R is the MBR of the object. The main innovation in the R-tree is that parent nodes are allowed to overlap. This way, the R-tree can guarantee good space utilization and remain balanced. Figure 2 illustrates data rectangles, (in black), organized in an R-tree with fanout 3 (a), while (b) shows the file structure for the same R-tree, where nodes correspond to disk pages.

The R-tree inspired much subsequent work, whose main focus was to improve the search time. A packing technique is proposed in [RL85] to minimize the overlap between different nodes in the R-tree for static data. An improved packing technique based on the Hilbert Curve is proposed in [KF93]; it is extended for dynamic environments in [KF94]. The R^+-tree [SRF87] avoids the overlap between non-leaf nodes of the tree, by clipping data rectangles that cross node boundaries. Beckmann et. al. proposed the R^*-tree [BKSS90], which seems to have very good performance. The main idea is the concept of *forced re-insert*, which tries to defer the splits, to achieve better utilization: When a node overflows, some of its children are carefully chosen and they are deleted and re-inserted, usually resulting in a better structured R-tree.

There is also much work on how to organize spatial access methods on multi-disk or multi-processor machines. The majority of them examine the parallelization of grid-based structures. Typical representatives include the 'disk modulo allocation' method and its variants [DS82], [WYD87], methods using minimum spanning trees [FLC86], the field-wise exclusive-OR ('FX') method [KP88], methods using error correcting codes [FM89], methods based on the Hilbert curve [FB93], and methods using lattices [CR93]. The objective in all these methods is to maximize the parallelism for partial match or range queries. An adaptive algorithm to achieve dynamic re-declustering, to 'cool-off' hot spots is presented in [WZS91].

However, the above methods try to do the best possible declustering without taking into account the communication cost. One of the exceptions is the work by Ghandeharizadeh et. al. [GDQ92], which considers a grid file with a certain profile of range queries against it; a major contribution of this work is a formula to estimate the optimal number of activated processors for a given query.

Here, we focus on the parallelization of R-trees. The difference between the R-tree and the grid file is that the latter will suffer if the attributes are correlated. Moreover, the grid file is mainly designed for point data; if the data are rectangles, the R-tree is better equipped to handle them. Little work has been done on the parallelization of R-trees: In [KF92] we studied the multi-disk architecture, with no communication cost, and we proposed the so-called 'proximity index' to measure the dis-similarity of two rectangles, in order to decide which unit to assign each rectangle to. DeWitt et al. [DKL+94] discuss a client-server architecture for Geographical Information Systems, with a rich data model and a storage manager that uses a variation of R-trees.

In this paper, we present a software design to achieve efficient parallelization of R-trees on a multi-computer ('shared-nothing') architecture, using commodity hardware and interconnect, as well as fast processors. Unlike previous work, our major focus is to optimize the *unit of declustering* itself, which will implicitly optimize the number of activated processors. We derive closed-form formulas and we validate our results experimentally, on a network of SUN workstations, operating on real data.

3 Proposed Method and System Architecture

An overview of the hardware architecture is in figure 2. It consists of a number of workstations connected together with a LAN (e.g., Ethernet) that does not support *multi-casting* (ability to send a message at all or a subset of nodes at the cost of one message). The problem is defined as follows:

Given a set of n-dimensional rectangles

Organize them on the available machines

to minimize the response time for range queries.

Target applications are, for example, GIS applications (*'retrieve the elevation data for a given region'*); statistical queries (eg., *'find the average salary in the*

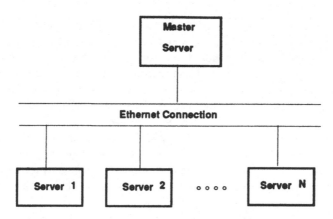

Fig. 2.

The proposed architecture

state of Michigan, for a census database '); 'data mining' applications [AS94] and decision support systems (eg., *'find correlations/rules among demographic data and symptoms, for a collection of patient records'*).

Given a spatial database, our first reaction would be to do declustering over the available machines. Thus, similar (=nearby) data rectangles should not be stored on the same machine. This approach is only partially correct, because it neglects the communication cost. In this case, it is not optimal to decluster at the data-rectangle level. The reason is the following: a small query, who retrieves, say, 5 data rectangles, will have to engage 5 machines (sending at least 5 messages on the network). For such a small query, it would be best if those 5 data rectangles were stored on the same machine, which hopefully could be identified easily and could get activated with 1 only message.

Thus, we still want to do declustering, but not on the rectangle level. Therefore we propose (a) to group similar data rectangles in 'chunks' (also termed *'striping units'*, eg., in the RAID literature) and (b) to decluster the *chunks*. We have the following three design decisions:

1. what is the optimal *chunk* size, i.e., the unit of the amount of data that we should place in every server such that the search time is minimized.
2. data placement: Once the chunk size has been determined, what is the best algorithm to distribute the chunks among several servers, to optimize the response time and the parallelism.
3. How to do the book-keeping, to record the server-id for each chunk.

We discuss briefly the last two issues in the next two subsections. The first issue, the optimal chunk size selection, is the main focus of this work, and is discussed in detail in section 4.

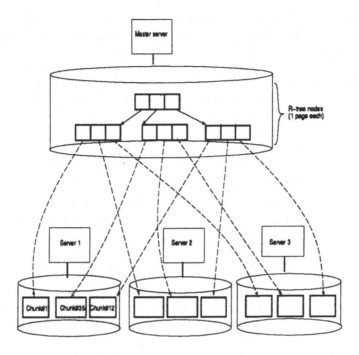

Fig. 3.

Parallel Decomposition for 3 servers

3.1 Book-keeping

As mentioned before, we have to do some book-keeping, to record which chunks reside on which machine. This is necessary, because we need to know which machine should be activated, as well as where to put new data rectangles, if insertions (and, eventually, splits) are allowed.

We propose to dedicate one of the machines to the book-keeping. This machine will be referred to as the '*master server*' (≡ 'host', in the terminology of database machines). The rest of the machines are plain *servers*: they receive a (range) query and some chunk requests from the master server, they retrieve the appropriate chunks from their local disks and ship the (qualifying) data rectangles to the master server.

A natural way for the master server to do the book-keeping is through a spatial access method. For the reasons explained in section 2, we propose to use an R-tree (any R-tree variant would work). Figure 3 gives an example of an R-tree, distributed across the master server and $N=3$ servers. Chunks are stored on the servers and they are represented by their MBRs. Chunks correspond to the leaves of the R-tree. We have decided to store *all* the non-leaf nodes in the master server, for the following reasons:

- the non-leaf portion of the R-tree in the master server will be small (for an R-tree with a fanout of f=100, the non-leaf nodes will take roughly 1/100 of the total space of the SAM). Thus, the non-leaf portion of the R-tree might even fit in the main memory of the master server, and definitely on its disk.
- It does not pay off to decluster the non-leaf levels of the R-tree across the servers, because this will introduce inter-server pointers, higher communication cost, and longer delays, as each node access may have to go through a potentially slow/congested network.

The proposed method has only the following structural differences from a traditional, centralized R-tree;

- the leaf nodes (=chunks) span C pages, where C is not necessarily 1 page.
- the pointers from the master server to the chunks (denoted by dashed lines in Figure 3) consist of a chunk-identifier and a machine-identifier.

The query-resolution algorithm for the proposed system is as follows:

- A query starts at the master server, who examines the (locally stored) non-leaf nodes of the R-tree. Note that this search is done in the normal way that R-trees are searched, by comparing MBR's. This search will result in some chunk-ids and the corresponding machine-ids
- The master server activates the servers identified in the previous step, by sending a message. The message contains the MBR of the query and the chunk id's to be retrieved from the specific server. Notice that the activation can be done either by broadcasting, or by 'selective activation'. Both our implementation and our analysis can handle either case, with small modifications; however, we focus on the 'selective activation', because it scales-up better. This is the typical approach that commercial parallel DBMSs follow (eg., the parallel version of IBM's DB2 [BFG+95]).
- Each activated server fetches the relevant chunks from its local disk, processes them (to discard data rectangles that do not intersect the query rectangle), and ships the qualifying data back to the master server.

3.2   Data placement

The goal is that 'similar' chunks should be declustered: that is, if two chunks have MBR's that are nearby in space and therefore likely to qualify under the same range query, these chunks should not be stored on the same server. We distinguish two cases: (a) a static database (no insertions/deletions/updates) and (b) a dynamic one.

For a static database, following [FB93], we propose to use Hilbert Curves to achieve good declustering. A Hilbert curve is a type of space filling curve that visits all points in a k-dimensional grid exactly once and never crosses itself. Thus, it can be used to linearize the points of a grid. In [FR89], it was shown experimentally that the Hilbert curve achieves better clustering than several other

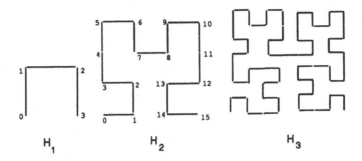

Fig. 4.

Hilbert Curves of order 1,2 and 3

space-filling curves. We can achieve good declustering by using a variation of the Hilbert-based declustering method [FB93], as applied in the so-called 'Hilbert-packed R-trees' [KF93]). For a static collection of data rectangles, the method works briefly as follows: we sort the data rectangles on the Hilbert values of their centers and pack them into R-tree leaf-nodes ($\equiv$ chunks, each of size C pages); we scan the resulting list of chunks, assigning chunks to servers in a round-robin fashion. Thanks to the good clustering properties of the Hilbert curve, successive chunks will be similar; thanks to the round-robin assignment, they will be assigned to different servers. Thus, similar chunks will be de-clustered.

For a dynamic database, the quality of declustering depends on the insertion and deletion routines. Insertions and deletions in our proposed structure can be handled by modifying the corresponding R-tree routines. The only thing that needs to be added is that, during a split, we have to decide where to put the newly created chunk. There are several criteria, ranging from a random assignment, to elaborate methods such as the so-called *proximity index* [KF92]: This method tries to put a new chunk on a server that has the most un-similar chunks.

To keep the discussion simple and the emphasis on the optimal chunk-size selection, we restrict ourselves to the *static case*, ignoring insertions and splits.

4 Optimal chunk-size selection

In this section we describe our approach to optimize the chunk size. Figure 5 illustrates the problems of a poor choice for the chunk size: a tiny chunk size will result in activating several servers even for small queries (see Q_small in Figure 5(b)), resulting in high message traffic; a huge chunk size will limit parallelism unnecessarily, even for large queries (see Q_large in Figure 5(c)).

The goal of this whole section is to find the optimal chunk-size C_{opt}, so that to minimize the response time for a range query. Thus, the major part of the effort is to express the response time as a function of C and apply some optimization technique (something like setting the first derivative to zero).

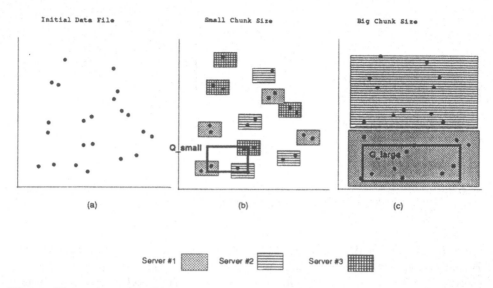

Fig. 5. *Illustration of problems with too small and too large chunk sizes: A small chunk size will force small queries (Q_small) to execute on many servers, resulting in high message traffic. A large chunk size will force large queries (Q_large) to execute in one only server, resulting in little parallelism.*

Symbols	Explanation	Values
N	Number of servers in the architecture	2-9
PS	Average packet size (in pages)	1 page
CC_{idle}	Time to send a message on an idle Network	10ms
CC	Time to send a message and wake up cost under load	-
q_x, q_y	query sides	-
D	Total #of records in the data base	39717
P_{rec}	Records per page	50 rec
$T_{local-per-page}$	Disk plus CPU time to fetch and process 1 page	10 ms
Q	Average #of qualifying pages for query q_x, q_x	-
C	chunk size in Pages	-
C_{opt}	optimal chunk size in Pages	-

Table 1. Symbols, definitions and typical values

As a first step, we shall express the response time as a function of the number K of servers that get activated (also called 'promising servers' from now on). Then, we express K as a function of C (and the volume of qualifying data Q), and finally we optimize the resulting (piece-wise continuous) function. Each subsection is devoted to each of the three above steps.

4.1 Response time as a function of number of activated servers K

Recall that, as soon as a range query arrives to the master server, it consults the R-tree index and determines which K servers to activate; it sends a message to each of them, and it waits for results from all of the K servers.

The method can be applied to any n-dimensional address space. Without loss of generality, we use examples from 2-d space, to simplify the presentation and the drawing of the examples. For further clarity, we assume that the address space has been normalized to the unit square. Let Q be the expected number of data pages that a query of size $q_x \times q_y$ will retrieve. There are various ways to estimate Q, with varying degrees of accuracy: Using the uniformity assumption [KF93], we have $Q = \frac{q_x \times q_y \times D}{P_{rec}}$ where D is the total number of records in the database and P_{rec} is the number of records per page. More accurate estimates require formulas that use the fractal dimension of the specific dataset [FK94]. However, as the experiments section shows, even the uniformity assumption gives satisfactory results because the fractal dimension of the specific data set was ≈ 1.7 [FK94], rather close to the value of 2, that corresponds to the uniformity assumption.

Let $T_{local-per-page}$ be the time that each server takes to process one disk page locally, including the disk access time and the CPU processing time.

The response time or round trip time $RT(q_x, q_y)$ for a query of size $q_x \times q_y$ can be expressed as a sum of (at most) three terms. The first is the local processing time in each server. This time includes CPU time and disk access time and is referred as T_{LOCAL}. The second is the time required to send the query to each server that is involved in the execution, $T_{COMMUNICATION}$. The last is the time required to ship all the qualifying data to the master server, T_{RESULT}. Notice that the time to traverse the R-tree on the master server is ignored because it is constant, regardless of the chunk size, and thus does not participate in the optimization. Moreover, the R-tree of the master server will most probably be small, typically fitting in core, and thus requiring only some small CPU time to be traversed.

Thus the response time can be expressed as:

$$RT(q_x \times q_y) = T_{COMMUNICATION} + T_{LOCAL} + T_{RESULT} \qquad (1)$$

To keep the analysis simple (but still accurate, as the experiments show), we make the optimistic assumption of *perfect load balance*: Thus, we assume that all the servers will have the same local processing cost, and will ship back the same amount of qualifying data. In figures 6(a,b) we show how each server spends its time: Gray, black and striped boxes indicate the time receive a message, to do local processing and to ship back the results, respectively. Lack of a box indicates an idle period for this server.

Notice that messages on the network *may not* overlap. The dashed lines in Figure 6 help illustrate exactly this fact. Also, for the moment, we assume that there are no other users on the network; we shall see shortly how to take them into account. Figure 6 illustrates the two possible scenarios, depending on which is the dominating delay (communication time vs. local processing).

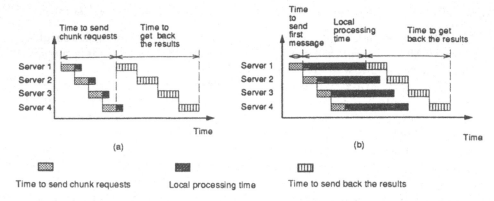

Fig. 6. *Timings when the dominating factor is (a) the communication and (b) the local processing.*

Domination of communication time: Figure 6(a) illustrates this situation. The first server receives the message, collects its results, and has to wait, because the network is still busy with the messages from the master server to the rest of the K servers. In this case, T_{LOCAL} will not appear in the expression for $RT(q_x, q_y)$ because this term is completely overlapped by the communication time. Therefore, we have:

$$T_{COMMUNICATION} = K \times CC \qquad (2)$$

where K is the number of activated (ie., 'promising') servers and CC is the time to send a message (of size PS) from the master server to one of the servers;

$$T_{RESULT} = CC \times \frac{Q}{PS} \qquad (3)$$

which is the total time to ship the results back to the master site (in packets of size PS). Thus, $RT(q_x, q_y)$ becomes:

$$\boxed{RT(q_x, q_y) = K \times CC + CC \times \frac{Q}{PS}, \quad \text{when } (K-1) \times CC \geq Q \times \frac{T_{local-per-page}}{K}}$$
$$(4)$$

Domination of local processing time: Figure 6(b) illustrates this setting. Since the local processing time is long, the first server is still retrieving data, even after all K servers have been activated. Thus, the response time $RT(q_x, q_y)$ can be estimated as the time to send the first message, the time for the first server to finish its local processing, and the time to ship all the results back. Thus,

$$T_{COMMUNICATION} = CC \qquad (5)$$

(for the first message only);

$$T_{LOCAL} = \frac{Q \times T_{local-per-page}}{K} \tag{6}$$

which is the local processing time for the first (as well as every other) server activated, and

$$T_{RESULT} = CC \times \frac{Q}{PS} \tag{7}$$

as before. Thus, we finally have:

$$RT(q_x, q_y) = CC + \frac{Q \times T_{local-per-page}}{K} + \frac{Q \times CC}{PS}, \text{ when } (K-1) \times CC \leq Q \times \frac{T_{local-per-page}}{K} \tag{8}$$

where $\frac{Q \times T_{local-per-page}}{K}$ represents the local processing time in each node: Recall that it includes the disk access time (to fetch the page), plus the CPU time, to check whether the data rectangles indeed intersect the query rectangle.

It is important to highlight how overhead from other users using the network can be represented in the formulas above. As analyzed in [BMK88], the time to send a packet grows linearly with the number α of active nodes transmitting, that is:

$$CC = \alpha \times CC_{idle} \tag{9}$$

where α is the number of active (transmitting) nodes simultaneously with the node in question and CC_{idle} is the time to transmit a message on an idle network. Thus, α expresses the overhead due to other use of the network. Ideally, the time to send a small message on an Ethernet under very light load is on the average $CC_{idle}=10$ms.

4.2 K as a function of C

The next step is to find the connection between the number of activated servers (K) and the chunk size (C). For a given chunk size C, the average number K of servers that will be activated can be estimated by the formula:

$$K = (1 - (1 - \frac{1}{N})^{\frac{Q}{C}}) \times N \tag{10}$$

This formula assumes that the qualifying chunks are randomly and independently distributed among the servers (eg., through good hashing function). The justification of the formula is as follows:

- Q/C estimates the number of chunks that the query will retrieve.
- $1/N$ is the probability that a given server will contain a specific chunk of interest.
- $1 - 1/N$ is the probability that a given server will not contain a specific chunk.

604

- $(1 - 1/N)^{Q/C}$ is the probability that a given server will not contain any of the Q/C qualifying chunks.
- $1 - (1 - 1/N)^{Q/C}$ is the probability that a given server will contain at least one of the requested chunks.

4.3   Final optimization

Combining the results of the previous steps, we can express the response time as a function of C. From equations (4,8) (repeated here for convenience), we have:

$$RT(q_x, q_y) = K \times CC + CC \times \tfrac{Q}{PS}, \text{when} \quad (K-1) \times CC \geq Q \times \tfrac{T_{local-per-page}}{K} \quad (4)$$

$$RT(q_x, q_y) = CC + \tfrac{Q \times T_{local-per-page}}{K} + \tfrac{Q \times CC}{PS}, \quad \text{when} \quad (K-1) \times CC \leq Q \times \tfrac{T_{local-per-page}}{K} \quad (8)$$

Our goal is to find the optimal value K_{opt} of K (and, eventually, C_{opt}) that minimizes $RT(q_x, q_y)$. Notice that Eq. 4 increases with K (being linear on K), while Eq. 8 decreases with K (since K is in the denominator). Moreover, the combination of Eq.(4,8) forms a piece-wise continuous function, whose minimum is achieved at the point of discontinuity, that is, when

$$(K-1) \times CC = Q \times \frac{T_{local-per-page}}{K} \quad (11)$$

Solving for K, we have

$$K^2 - K - \frac{Q \times T_{local-per-page}}{CC} = 0 \quad (12)$$

and, after discarding the negative root (which has no physical meaning):

$$K_{opt} = \frac{1 + \sqrt{1 + 4 \times \frac{Q \times T_{local-per-page}}{CC}}}{2} \quad (13)$$

The above can be solved for C_{opt} using (10), giving

$$C_{opt} = \frac{-Q}{N \times \log(1 - K_{opt}/N)} \quad \text{when} \quad K_{opt} \leq N \quad (14)$$

In the formula above the computation for the chunk size holds as long as, $K_{opt} \leq N$. When the number of servers available (N) is less than K_{opt} then the optimal value of chunk size tends to become 0, from equation 14. Intuitively this is expected, since in this case the best we can hope is that all units participate in the query execution, and this is guaranteed by making the chunk size as small as possible. However, choosing the chunk size to be less than 1 page will increase the I/O cost: several pages will be retrieved in order to access only a tiny portion of their contents. This observation is confirmed in our experiments (see figure 7). Thus:

$$\boxed{C_{opt} = 1 \text{ page} \quad \text{when} \quad K_{opt} \geq N} \tag{15}$$

Summarizing, the goal of this section was to provide a formula for the optimal value of the chunk size C_{opt}; this is achieved with Eqs. (14, 15), where K_{opt} is given by Eq. 13. Notice that Eqs. (13,14,15) hold for *any* dimensionality of the address space.

5 Experimental Results

In this section we present experimental results with the proposed architecture. All the experiments were conducted on a set of rectangles, representing the MBRs (minimum bounding rectangles) of road-segments from the Montgomery County, MD. The data set consisted of 39,717 line segments; the address space was normalized to the unit square. In all cases we built a Hilbert-packed R-tree and declustered it as explained in subsection 3.2. The above R-tree package stored the tree in main-memory; thus, we had to simulate each disk access with a 10msec delay. A disk page was taken to be 1Kbyte. The CPU time to process a page was timed and found two orders of magnitude smaller than the disk access time; thus, we ignored it in our formulas ($T_{local-per-page}=$ disk-access-time = 10msec).

The implementation of the communication software was done in the 'C' language under UNIX, using TCP sockets. For the experiments, we used several Sun SPARC 4/50 (IPX) workstations, with 16MB of main memory and sparc processors at 40MHz, connected via Ethernet at 10Mbits/sec. To avoid variations in the message traffic due to other users, we ran the experiments at night, where the load was light and the communication cost CC per message was fairly stable.

The queries were squares ($q_x = q_y$) of varying side q; they were randomly distributed in the address space. For each query side q, we report the averages over 100 queries.

We performed the following 3 sets of experiments:

- In the first set we illustrate the accuracy of the formula for the response time.
- In the second set, we experimented with various chunk sizes to show that indeed our choice of chunk size minimizes the response time.
- The third set of graphs uses the formulas to plot analytical results in 'what-if' scenarios.

Each set of experiments is discussed in the corresponding subsection next.

5.1 Accuracy of the formula

Our very first step was to estimate the communication cost CC (ie., startup costs and transmission of a message) in our environment. Since our network was not isolated, random overhead was imposed to our system, from other users of the network.

We performed several measurements, to obtain estimates at different times during the night, when the network traffic was low. All our experiments were also done at night. To obtain one measurement, we set up the communication interface between two processes and exchanged 100 messages of size $PS=1$ page, at random times. The averages times are presented in table 2. The estimate of $CC=30$ms was very consistent and is the one we use from now on.

Measurement	CC (msec)
Measurement 1	32.502194
Measurement 2	25.664210
Measurement 3	29.409790
Measurement 4	22.373228
Measurement 5	35.966356
Measurement 6	33.273418
Average:	29.86486

Table 2. Experiments to measure the communication cost CC for a single message

$CC/T_{local-per-page}=3$, $N=3$	Response Time (msec)		
Query Side	Experimental	Theoretical	error %
0.1	232	192	17
0.2	806	569	29
0.3	1577	1230	22

Table 3. Theoretical and Experimental values for response time (in ms) for $N=3$ servers

Given an accurate estimate for CC, we can use it in Eq's (4) and (8) to make predictions about the response time. Tables 3, 4 and 5 compare theoretical

$CC/T_{local-per-page}=3$, $N=5$	Response Time (msec)		
Query Side	Experimental	Theoretical	error %
0.1	228	208	9
0.2	786	625	20
0.3	1461	1229	16

Table 4. Theoretical and experimental values for response time, for $N=5$ servers

$CC/T_{local-per-page}$ =3, N=7	Response Time (msec)		
Query Side	Experimental	Theoretical	error %
0.1	290	288	1
0.2	730	672	20
0.3	1289	1289	1

Table 5. *Theoretical and Experimental values for response time (in ms) for N=7 servers*

and experimental values for the response time (in milli-seconds), for $N = 3$, 5, 7 servers, respectively, and for chunk size C=1 page. We also present the percentage of error of each experiment performed, rounded up to the nearest integer.

The main observation is that our formula for the response time is accurate within 29% or better for all the experiments we performed.

5.2 Optimal chunk-size selection

In this set of experiments we vary the chunk size, and we plot the response time for a given setting (number of servers N, query side q). The goal is to find the chunk size that minimizes the response time.

Figures 7(a,b) present our results for N=3 and 5 servers, respectively. The various lines correspond to different query sides q. In all these plots, the response time is minimized when the chunk size is one page (C_{opt}=1).

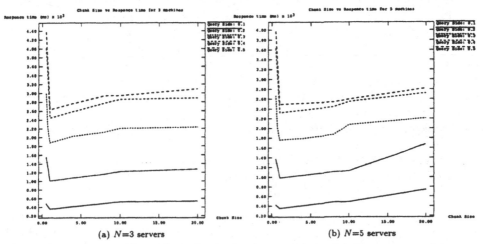

(a) N=3 servers   (b) N=5 servers

Fig. 7. Response time (in ms) vs chunk size (in pages) for (a) N=3 servers (b) N=5 servers. Notice the spike for $C < 1$ page.

This result agrees with the outcome of our formula for the estimation of the optimal chunk size (Eq. 14, 15): Substituting the parameter values of the experiment of Figure 7a into (Eq. 14), for query sides $q_x = q_y = 0.1$, we obtain $C_{opt} = 0.94$; using the parameter values of figure 7b, we obtain $C_{opt} = 1.3$. For the other values of query sides, the optimal value of processors K_{opt} returned by (Eq. 13) is greater than the number of servers $(K_{opt} > N)$; thus, (Eq. 15) gives $C_{opt} = 1$ page, in agreement with the experiments.

Also, notice that $C < 1$ gives poor results, justifying (Eq. 15). The reasons have been explained in section 4: With a smaller-than-page chunk size, each server will have to retrieve several disk pages, only to discard most of their contents (since it will only need a small 'chunk' from each page); thus, the I/O subsystems will be unnecessarily overloaded, doing useless work.

5.3 Extrapolation for other scenarios

Having obtained confidence in our analysis, in this subsection we study its behavior through arithmetic examples. We choose some realistic settings, and do extrapolations and 'what-if' scenarios. Our goals are to study

1. large databases
.2. networks of different speeds, in anticipation of fast networks (eg., fiber optics), as well as slower networks (eg., heavily loaded ones).

For the database size, we use two sizes:

 – a 'medium db', with $D = 1$Mb
 – a 'large db', with $D = 1$GigaByte

From our analysis (eq. 13, 14), it follows that $CC/T_{local-per-page}$ affects the choice of chunk size. Intuitively, this is expected: When $CC/T_{local-per-page} \ll 1$, the local processing time will be the bottleneck; thus, increasing the use of the network and decreasing the local processing per server is the proper action. As a consequence, more servers should participate in query execution, and therefore a small chunk size is preferable. In the reverse situation, when $CC/T_{local-per-page} \gg 1$, the communication is the bottleneck. The network should be off-loaded, which can be achieved by engaging fewer servers; thus, a larger chunk size is favorable now.

We experiment with three settings:

 – 'current network', where $CC/T_{local-per-page} = 30$msec$/10$msec $= 3$
 – 'fast network', where $CC/T_{local-per-page} = 0.1$
 – 'slow network', with $CC/T_{local-per-page} = 10$

We present the results in Figures (8, 9, 10). For each combination of network speed and database size, we plot the response time as a function of the chunk size, for the following query sides $q = q_x = q_y = 0.01, 0.02, 0.03, 0.1, 0.2$ and 0.3.

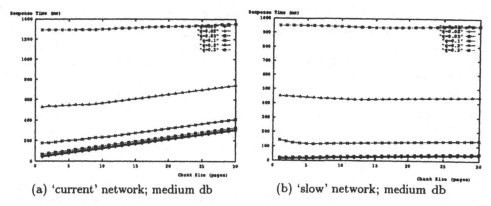

(a) 'current' network; medium db   (b) 'slow' network; medium db

Fig. 8. Analytical results for a $D=1$Mb ('medium') database. Response time (in ms) vs chunk size (in pages) for: $N = 5$ servers and query sides $q=$ 0.01, 0.02 ,0.03, 0.1,0.2,0.3 (bottom to top). (a) current network ($CC/T_{local-per-page} = 3$) (b) slow network ($CC/T_{local-per-page} = 10$)

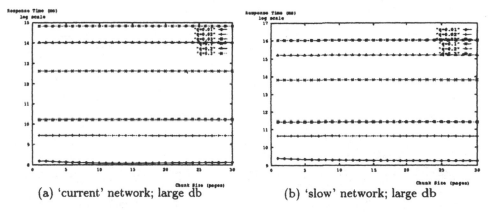

(a) 'current' network; large db   (b) 'slow' network; large db

Fig. 9. Analytical results for a 'large' database ($D=1$Gb). Logarithm of response time (in ms) vs chunk size (in pages); $N = 20$ servers, query sides $q=0.01$, 0.02, 0.03, 0.1,0.2,0.3 (bottom to top). (a) current network ($CC/T_{local-per-page} = 3$) (b) slow network ($CC/T_{local-per-page} = 10$)

Figure 8 shows the results for a database of size 1MB, for the 'current' network ($CC/T_{local-per-page} = 3$) and for a 'slow' network ($CC/T_{local-per-page} = 10$). For the first case, the response time is minimized for $C_{opt} = 1$ page: all the curves increase with C, because messages are relatively cheap, and therefore it pays off to distribute the work among many servers (ie., small chunk size).

For the 'slow' network (Figure 8(b)), messages are more expensive and therefore larger chunk sizes are more favorable. However, even then, $C = 1$ gives a response time that is close to the minimum. The largest deviation from the minimum response time is 19.4%, which occurs for $q=0.1$ for the query sizes in the Figure. Notice that this performance penalty diminishes for larger queries (top two curves, $q=0.2, 0.3$). The reason is that, for larger queries, the response time becomes insensitive to the chunk size. The explanation is the following: Unless the chunk size has a huge value, a large query will activate all the N servers anyway, each of which will do roughly $1/N$ of the total local processing, which will be the bottleneck.

Notice also that, for small queries, the optimal chunk size is $C=1$. The reason is that small queries retrieve a small amount of data; a large chunk size will be an over-kill, because all the qualifying data will fit in a chunk, with room to spare (ie., wasted I/O time to fetch extraneous data from the disk)

Figures 9a,b show the same plots for a 1GB database, for the 'current' network ($CC/T_{local-per-page} = 3$) and for the 'slow' network ($CC/T_{local-per-page} = 10$), respectively. Notice that the vertical axis is in logarithmic scale, because a linear scale would visually collapse the curves of the small queries. The response time is rather insensitive to the chunk size: the plots are almost straight lines, indicating that $C_{opt} = 1$ is a good choice (as good as anything else). Only for very small queries (eg., $q=0.01$) the curves bend a little; even then, the choice of $C=1$ page gives response time that is within 13% of the minimum.

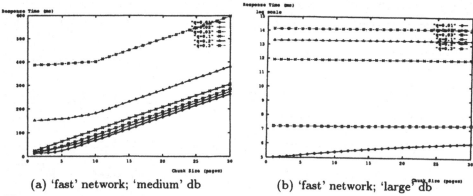

(a) 'fast' network; 'medium' db
(b) 'fast' network; 'large' db

Fig. 10. Analytical results for a 'fast' network ($CC/T_{local-per-page} = 0.1$). Response time (in ms) vs chunk size(in pages); $N=20$ servers, query sides $q=0.01, 0.02, 0.03, 0.1, 0.2, 0.3$ (bottom to top). (a) 'medium' db ($D=1$MB) (b) 'large' db ($D=1$GB) - notice the logarithmic y-axis.

Figure 10 gives the plots for the 'fast' network ($CC/T_{local-per-page} = 0.1$), plotting the response time RT as a function of the chunk size C for several values of the query sides q. If the network is fast, we want to maximize parallelism. This is achieved with the smallest allowable chunk size ($C_{opt}=1$). This is very pronounced for the 'medium' database (Figure 10(a)), where the response time increases with the chunk size, for all the query sizes. For the 'large' database (notice the logarithmic y-axis in Figure 10(b)), we see again that $C=1$ gives the minimum for small queries; for large queries, the response time is insensitive to the chunk size, as discussed before. Thus, the overall conclusion is that $C = 1$ is a 'safe' choice for a wide range of parameters: it will either give the optimal response time, or very close to it.

6   Conclusions

In this paper we have studied a method to decluster a spatial access method (and specifically an R-tree) on a shared-nothing multi-computer architecture. The nodes are connected through an off-the-shelf LAN. The major contributions of this work are

1. The derivation of formulas for the optimal chunk size C_{opt} ($\equiv$ striping unit), for a given query size (Eqs 14, 15).
2. The observation that $C_{opt} = 1$ page is a 'safe' choice, for a wide range of the problem parameters (query size, network/disk speed, database size etc). This choice either gives the minimum response time, or close to the (rather flat) minimum of the response time.

Additional, smaller, contributions include

1. the software architecture, with the R-tree at the master-server, and the leaf nodes ('chunks') at the rest of the servers. We made and justified several design decisions (eg., 'selective activation' vs. broadcasting; no pointers of the R-tree across servers, etc)
2. the derivation of simple, but accurate formulas that estimate the response time for a given query size (Eq 4,8).

We implemented the proposed method and we ran several experiments on a network of SUN workstations, operating on real data (road segments from the Montgomery county of Maryland, U.S.A). The experiments showed that

- the formulas (Eq 4,8) for the response time are accurate within 29% or better
- the formulas (Eq 14, 15) for the optimal chunk size agree very well with the experimental results

Having an accurate formula for the response time is a strong tool. One of its uses is for extrapolation and 'what-if' scenarios: We can obtain estimates about the performance of our system when the network is faster or slower (= loaded), when the disks (or, in general, the I/O units) are slower (e.g., juke-boxes of optical disks), or when the disks are faster (e.g., thanks to large buffer pools at each server, and high buffer-hit ratios), etc. All we have to do to simulate these cases is to adjust the appropriate values for the parameters (CC for the communication cost, $T_{local-per-page}$ for the I/O and CPU cost per page, etc.). A second use of the formula could be the analytical study of the throughput in case of multiple, concurrent queries: We believe that the effects of the additional queries can be modeled by appropriately 'inflating' the service time (CC) of the network, as well as of the disks and CPUs of the servers ($T_{local-per-page}$).

Using our formulas, we studied several 'what-if' scenarios. A useful, practical conclusion from this exercise is that using 1-page 'chunks' typically leads to optimal performance, or very close to it. This is especially true for fast networks, as well as for large queries. This conclusion is important from a practical point of view, because it provides a simple, intuitive rule for the optimal choice of the chunk size.

Future work includes the design of parallel R-tree algorithms for other types of queries, such as spatial joins [BKS93], and experimentation with other types of interconnects, such as ATM switches.

References

[AS94]   Rakesh Agrawal and Ramakrishnan Srikant. Fast algorithms for mining association rules in large databases. *Proc. of VLDB Conf.*, pages 487–499, September 1994.

[BB82]   D. Ballard and C. Brown. *Computer Vision.* Prentice Hall, 1982.

[Ben75]   J.L. Bentley. Multidimensional binary search trees used for associative searching. *CACM*, 18(9):509–517, September 1975.

[BFG+95]   C. K. Baru, G. Fecteau, A. Goyal, H. Hsiao, A. Jhingran, S. Padmanabhan, G. P. Copeland, and W. G. Wilson. DB2 Parallel Edition. *IBM Systems Journal*, 32(2):292–322, 1995.

[BKS93]   Thomas Brinkhoff, Hans-Peter Kriegel, and Bernhard Seeger. Efficient processing of spatial joins using r-trees. *Proc. of ACM SIGMOD*, pages 237–246, May 1993.

[BKSS90]   N. Beckmann, H.-P. Kriegel, R. Schneider, and B. Seeger. The r*-tree: an efficient and robust access method for points and rectangles. *ACM SIGMOD*, pages 322–331, May 1990.

[BMK88]   David Boggs, Jeffrey C. Mogul, and Christopher A. Kent. Measured capacity of an ethernet: Myths and reality. *WRL Research Report 88/4*, 1988.

[CR93]   Ling Tony Chen and Doron Rotem. Declustering objects for visualization. *Proc. VLDB Conf.*, August 1993. to appear.

[DGS+90]   D. DeWitt, S. Ghandeharizadeh, D. A. Schneider, A. Bricker, H. Hsiao, and R. Rasmussen. The gamma database machine project. *IEEE Transactions on Knowledge and Data Engineering*, 2(1), March 1990.

[DKL+94]   David. J DeWitt, Navin Kabra, Jun Luo, Jignesh Patel, and Jie-Bing Yu. The client/server paradise. *Proceedings of the VLDB, 1994 Santiago, Chile*, September 1994.

[DS82]   H.C. Du and J.S. Sobolewski. Disk allocation for cartesian product files on multiple disk systems. *ACM Trans. Database Systems (TODS)*, 7(1):82–101, March 1982.

[FB93]   Christos Faloutsos and Pravin Bhagwat. Declustering using fractals. In *2nd Int. Conference on Parallel and Distributed Information Systems (PDIS)*, pages 18–25, San Diego, CA, January 1993.

[FBF+94]   Christos Faloutsos, Ron Barber, Myron Flickner, J. Hafner, Wayne Niblack, Dragutin Petkovic, and William Equitz. Efficient and effective querying by image content. *J. of Intelligent Information Systems*, 3(3/4):231–262, July 1994.

[FK94]   Christos Faloutsos and Ibrahim Kamel. Beyond uniformity and independence: Analysis of r-trees using the concept of fractal dimension. *Proc. ACM SIGACT-SIGMOD-SIGART PODS*, pages 4–13, May 1994. Also available as CS-TR-3198, UMIACS-TR-93-130.

[FLC86]   M.F. Fang, R.C.T. Lee, and C.C. Chang. The idea of de-clustering and its applications. In *Proc. 12th International Conference on VLDB*, pages 181–188, Kyoto, Japan, August 1986.

[FM89]   C. Faloutsos and D. Metaxas. Declustering using error correcting codes. *Eighth ACM SIGACT-SIGMOD-SIGART Symposium on Principles of Database Systems (PODS)*, pages 253–258, March 1989. Also available as UMIACS-TR-88-91 and CS-TR-2157.

[FR89]   C. Faloutsos and S. Roseman. Fractals for secondary key retrieval. *Eighth ACM SIGACT-SIGMOD-SIGART Symposium on Principles of Database Systems (PODS)*, pages 247–252, March 1989. also available as UMIACS-TR-89-47 and CS-TR-2242.

[Fre87]   Michael Freeston. The bang file: a new kind of grid file. *Proc. of ACM SIGMOD*, pages 260–269, May 1987.

[Fre95]   Michael Freeston. A general solution of the n-dimensional b-tree problem. *Proc. of ACM-SIGMOD*, pages 80–91, May 1995.

[Gar82]   I. Gargantini. An effective way to represent quadtrees. *Comm. of ACM (CACM)*, 25(12):905–910, December 1982.

[GDQ92]   Shahram Ghandeharizadeh, David J. DeWitt, and W. Qureshi. A performance analysis of alternative multi-attribute declustering strategies. *SIGMOD Conf.*, June 1992.

[Gun86]   O. Gunther. The cell tree: an index for geometric data. Memorandum No. UCB/ERL M86/89, Univ. of California, Berkeley, December 1986.

[Gut84a]   A. Guttman. *New Features for Relational Database Systems to Support CAD Applications.* PhD thesis, University of California, Berkeley, June 1984.

[Gut84b]   A. Guttman. R-trees: a dynamic index structure for spatial searching. *Proc. ACM SIGMOD*, pages 47–57, June 1984.

[HN83]   K. Hinrichs and J. Nievergelt. The grid file: a data structure to support proximity queries on spatial objects. *Proc. of the WG'83 (Intern. Workshop on Graph Theoretic Concepts in Computer Science)*, pages 100–113, 1983.

[Jag90]   H.V. Jagadish. Linear clustering of objects with multiple attributes. *ACM SIGMOD Conf.*, pages 332–342, May 1990.

[KF92]   Ibrahim Kamel and Christos Faloutsos. Parallel r-trees. *Proc. of ACM SIGMOD Conf.*, pages 195–204, June 1992. Also available as Tech. Report UMIACS TR 92-1, CS-TR-2820.

[KF93]   Ibrahim Kamel and Christos Faloutsos. On packing r-trees. *Second Int. Conf. on Information and Knowledge Management (CIKM)*, November 1993.

[KF94]   Ibrahim Kamel and Christos Faloutsos. Hilbert r-tree: an improved r-tree using fractals. In *Proc. of VLDB Conference,*, pages 500–509, Santiago, Chile, September 1994.

[KP88]   M.H. Kim and S. Pramanik. Optimal file distribution for partial match retrieval. *Proc. ACM SIGMOD Conf.*, pages 173–182, June 1988.

[KS91]   Curtis P. Kolovson and Michael Stonebraker. Segment indexes: Dynamic indexing techniques for multi-dimensional interval data. *Proc. ACM SIGMOD*, pages 138–147, May 1991.

[LS90]   David B. Lomet and Betty Salzberg. The hb-tree: a multiattribute indexing method with good guaranteed performance. *ACM TODS*, 15(4):625–658, December 1990.

[NHS84]   J. Nievergelt, H. Hinterberger, and K.C. Sevcik. The grid file: an adaptable, symmetric multikey file structure. *ACM TODS*, 9(1):38–71, March 1984.

[OHM⁺84]   J. K. Ousterhout, G. T. Hamachi, R. N. Mayo, W. S. Scott, and G. S. Taylor. Magic: a vlsi layout system. In *21st Design Automation Conference*, pages 152 – 159, Alburquerque, NM, June 1984.

[Ore86]   J. Orenstein. Spatial query processing in an object-oriented database system. *Proc. ACM SIGMOD*, pages 326–336, May 1986.

[RL85]   N. Roussopoulos and D. Leifker. Direct spatial search on pictorial databases using packed r-trees. *Proc. ACM SIGMOD*, May 1985.

[Rob81]   J.T. Robinson. The k-d-b-tree: a search structure for large multidimensional dynamic indexes. *Proc. ACM SIGMOD*, pages 10–18, 1981.

[Sam90]   H. Samet. *The Design and Analysis of Spatial Data Structures*. Addison-Wesley, 1990.

[SRF87]   T. Sellis, N. Roussopoulos, and C. Faloutsos. The r+ tree: a dynamic index for multi-dimensional objects. In *Proc. 13th International Conference on VLDB*, pages 507–518, England,, September 1987. also available as SRC-TR-87-32, UMIACS-TR-87-3, CS-TR-1795.

[SS88]   R. Stam and Richard Snodgrass. A bibliography on temporal databases. *IEEE Bulletin on Data Engineering*, 11(4), December 1988.

[SSH86]   M. Stonebraker, T. Sellis, and E. Hanson. Rule indexing implementations in database systems. In *Proceedings of the First International Conference on Expert Database Systems*, Charleston, SC, April 1986.

[Whi81]   M. White. *N-Trees: Large Ordered Indexes for Multi-Dimensional Space*. Application Mathematics Research Staff, Statistical Research Division, U.S. Bureau of the Census, December 1981.

[WYD87]   J.-H. Wang, T.-S. Yuen, and D.H.-C. Du. On multiple random accesses and physical data placement in dynamic files. *IEEE Trans. on Software Engineering*, SE-13(8):977–987, August 1987.

[WZS91]   Gerhard Weikum, Peter Zabback, and Peter Scheuermann. Dynamic file allocation in disk arrays. *Proc. ACM SIGMOD*, pages 406–415, May 1991.

Advanced Applications

Object Framework for Business Applications

Marco Emrich, Ph.D.

Senior Director, Advanced Technology Group, Cincom Systems, Inc.

TOTAL FrameWork provides an environment for assembling cross-functional business applications, which are critical for businesses anxious to build and/or maintain customer focus and market leadership. TOTAL FrameWork tightly couples several core technologies that are key to such applications, enabling customers to avoid the complexity of assembling them on their own.

Because technology is so important in operationally excellent companies, one usually has to look inside the companies' computer systems to understand their core business processes. The systems -- and related databases and applications -- are so highly automated that they don't just track the process, they contain and perform it.

The information contained in integrated computer systems is useful not just in core operating processes. Operationally efficient companies are passionate about measuring and monitoring to ensure rigorous quality and cost controls. Most advanced systems generate detailed data with which to make strategic and tactical management decisions.

Technological innovations have continually provided incremental advantages for organizations seeking to become more agile and responsive to the ever-changing needs of customers. But today and for the future, small incremental advantages are insufficient. In order to capture a competitive advantage, visionary organizations are making radical changes in the way they operate and greatly enhancing their ability to adapt to new opportunities.

Cincom's TOTAL FrameWork ™ is a breakthrough, component-based application assembly environment that enables organizations to redefine their business by rapidly assembling and executing customized business solutions.

TOTAL FrameWork provides an information environment in which strategic cross-functional business applications enable a seamless integration between functional groups, customers, and suppliers. It supports an enterprise in which business information flows quickly and easily, allowing important tactical and strategic management decisions to be made rapidly and intelligently.

An object framework has been described as a set of software building blocks that is used, extended or customized for specific computing solutions. In today's business environment, no one, stand-alone software product can enable an organization to redefine its business. Rather, an environment is needed which facilitates a drastic improvement in business process management.

These building blocks of TOTAL FrameWork are also frameworks that are used, extended and customized for specific computing solutions. By harnessing the power of all three components -- the WorkFlow, Assembly and Persistence FrameWorks -- organizations can create a customized information environment that will allow them to redefine their business.

The WorkFlow FrameWork ™

Leading-edge companies are focusing on improving processes to enhance products and services. Most processes involve actions from multiple people in different functional departments, often touching numerous divisions and even other organizations. These processes are called cross-functional.

The critical components of the WorkFlow FrameWork -- the Process Modeling Tool, WorkFlow Automation System, Document Management System, and Image Management System -- align information technology to core business processes and drives those processes to completion. The WorkFlow FrameWork gives internal performers a direct line of sight to external customers, allowing the goals of the customer to become the goals of each internal performer. This component automates the intelligent flow of information, prods appropriate participants to act, and enforces quality initiatives such as TQM and ISO9000.

As customer-focused organizations continue to optimize business processes as a means to differentiate themselves, the WorkFlow FrameWork enables organizations to stop measuring their business processes with a calendar, and start using a stopwatch.

The Assembly FrameWork ™

With the pace of business change accelerating, flexibility has become a requirement for information systems. But for too long, application development has been a time consuming exercise in futility. By the time the application is running, the business needs shift. But with the emergence of business objects, application development is being redefined.

Business objects are a combination of data and programs that represent some real-world business entity. These objects can be nested to create even more compound software building blocks or components that greatly reduce the time and complexity of application development.

With TOTAL FrameWork, business objects and components can be used to *assemble* applications rather than rewriting vast amounts of code, bringing information technology up to pace with the dynamic environment of business.

The Assembly FrameWork components -- Business Object Modeling Tool, Object Repository Mapping Tool, and the Smalltalk, Visual C++, and Visual Basic environments -- facilitates the assembly of highly flexible cross-functional business applications, enabling a quick response to market opportunities. By exploiting the power of component-based technology, developers can quickly assemble customized applications that model the real-world business. With the Assembly FrameWork, application development time is slashed, and IT is strategically positioned to respond to customer requests like never before. And once these applications are in place, they can be modified quickly to allow instant pursuit of new business opportunities.

In short, the Assembly FrameWork provides the components necessary to assemble critical, yet flexible cross-functional applications that accurately reflect the real-world business.

The Persistence FrameWork ™

In order to become more customer-focused, organizations need information. Having the right information about customers, products, services, and processes allows decisions to be made quickly and effectively. One of the chief barriers organizations face as they focus on customer satisfaction through business processes is integrating the information within the enterprise.

In order to solve cross-functional business problems, widespread information from disparate systems must be accessible. The Persistence FrameWork's object-relational database management technology allows efficient management and sharing of business objects enables the organization to come together. This component provides a single, global view to an organization's disparate information, thereby leveraging existing systems and minimizing the disruption caused by adopting new technology.

In short, the Persistence FrameWork enables information managers to integrate existing diverse database systems with new technology, thereby breaking down the technology barriers that exist within and among organizations.

Integration

The TOTAL FrameWork architecture integrates all of these components through a distributed object computing backplane, such as an Object Request Broker (ORB), that hides the details of networking and protocols, allowing your entire organization to communicate seamlessly.

TOTAL FrameWork is integrated around de facto and de jure industry standard software, including Microsoft's Object Linking and Embedding/Component Object Model (OLE/COM), and the Object Management Group's Common Object Request Broker Architecture (CORBA). Through these standards, Cincom has created an open extendible architecture for business solutions.

Figure 1: TOTAL FrameWork components -- the WorkFlow, Assembly, and Persistence FrameWorks -- are integrated to provide a complete environment for the assembly of cross-functional business applications.

Conclusion

TOTAL FrameWork represents an entirely new way to develop and maintain applications that support the real business issues. By promoting *boundaryless* behavior, TOTAL FrameWork allows people to work together for optimal customer satisfaction by breaking down the technological barriers between organizations, departments, divisions and people. It also helps *delinearize* processes, reducing the amount of time that passes over the life of a process by handling multiple tasks simultaneously.

Many traditional applications have historically been fulfilled through one-size-fits-all packages. But with the dramatic shift to a customer-focused business environment, flexibility and customization are critical to success. Visionary organizations are not satisfied buying an outsider's "solution" to their business processes; they are building their own solutions, the *real solutions,* with the power of TOTAL FrameWork.

TOTAL FrameWork enables organizations to focus on business processes by providing a system that supports, and, in fact, drives them. Applications are also easy to change, allowing organizations to seize market opportunities.

Commit Scope Control in Nested Transactions

Qiming Chen and Umesh Dayal

HP Laboratories
Palo Alto, California 94034

Abstract. A common limitation of all the existing nested transaction models is that they only allow subtransactions to commit either to parent transactions or to databases. In order to adequately balance atomicity and concurrency *at selected levels* of a transaction hierarchy, the notion of *scoped commitment* is proposed, that allows a subtransaction to commit to a selected ancestor independently of its parent, making its results visible to that ancestor and thus improving the concurrency in the transaction subtree beneath that ancestor. A corresponding *scoped undo* approach is also developed that allows a transaction hierarchy with subtransactions having mixed commit scopes to partially and consistently roll back upon failure, then restart and roll forward.

1 Introduction

A flat transaction can only commit to database. A *closed nested* transaction commits to its parent upon termination [4], making its effects visible to its parent's scope. Transactions in a transaction group, as described in Cooperative Transaction Hierarchy and Transaction Tool Kit, are under flexible control semantics but still required to commit to their parent. An *open nested* transaction is allowed to commit to database independently of its parent, making its effects accessible to public and thus improving the concurrency of transactions requiring these results [4] [3]. However, for the ancestors of that subtransaction, including the top-level transaction, their atomicity and protection are sacrificed. In general, all the existing transaction models only support committing to parent or to database, and as a result, they only offer two extremes between maintaining *atomicity* and gaining *concurrency*. For example, In the transaction hierarchy "project" shown in Figure 1, if "function_design" is treated as a closed transaction, upon termination its effects are only visible to "function_development", but inaccessible to "interface_development" until "function_development" further commits to "software_development", and that would take a long time if "coding" is a long duration transaction. On the other hand, if "function_design" is treated as an open transaction, it can commit to database directly, making its results accessible to "interface_development" soon after it is terminated. This improves concurrency but sacrifices top-level atomicity.

In order to adequately balance atomicity and concurrency and to control visibility and protection at selected levels of a transaction hierarchy, in this paper we extend the notion of in-process open transaction described in [1] by introducing a more generalized notion: *scoped transactions*. A scoped transaction

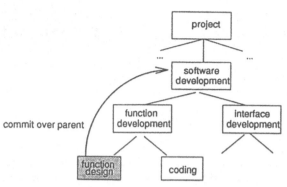

Fig. 1. Commit Scoping

can commit to a selected ancestor independently of its parent, making its results visible to that ancestor and thus improving the concurrency in the transaction subtree beneath that ancestor. Accordingly, such commitment is referred to as *scoped commitment*.

Introducing scoped-commitment imposes new requirements on transaction recovery. This is because some effects of a nested transaction, T, with *scoped* subtransactions may be externalized beyond its scope before it is terminated, so when T fails those effects need to be compensated for in the scope that matches T's commit scope. The *scoped undo* algorithm is developed that allows a transaction hierarchy with subtransactions having mixed commit scopes to partially and consistently roll back upon failure, then restart and roll forward.

2 Scoped Commitment

A transaction T can acquire objects from databases or inherit objects from its parent or ancestors which form the *access set* of T, denoted by D_T^{acs} [2]. Transaction T commits to P means $T \prec P$ (T is a sub-transaction of P) and T delegates to P the commit/abort responsibility of its operations on certain data objects, which form a *delegate set* denoted by $D_{T \to P}^{dlg}$, then P is called the *commit scope* of T. A transaction *commits to database* means making its effects permanent and visible to public, with the database as its commit scope, which is denoted by $D_{T \to db}^{dlg}$. To simplify our discussion, in this report we only allow a transaction to have a single commit scope. A nested transaction can be provided with controlled granularity of delegation at its subtransaction levels. Thus for a *closed transaction* T with parent P, $D_{T \to db}^{dlg} = \emptyset$ and $D_{T \to P}^{dlg} = D_T^{asc}$; for an *open transaction* T, $D_{T \to db}^{dlg} = D_T^{asc}$ and $D_{T \to P}^{dlg} = \emptyset$.

While the atomicity property of closed nesting is too rigid and the data protection of open nesting is too weak, the notion of *scoped transaction* provides a compromise between the two. A *scoped transaction* T can directly commit to an ancestor, say A, by delegating to A all the operations it is responsible for, as $D_{T \to db}^{dlg} = \emptyset, \quad D_{T \to A}^{dlg} = D_T^{asc}, \quad A \neq P \to D_{T \to P}^{dlg} = \emptyset.$

In the example shown in Figure 1, if "function_design" is treated as a scoped transaction

- it can commit to its ancestor "software_development" independently of its parent, making its results visible to "interface_development" immediately without being blocked by its long-duration sibling "coding";
- however, before the whole process "project" commits the results of "function_design" is not made persistent thus still inaccessible to other top-level transactions.

3 Scoped Undo

Transaction nesting provides failure protection in two general situations. First, when a failed transaction is *non-vital* to its parent, the failure can be ignored, and the parent transaction can continue. Second, when a failed transaction can be replaced by a contingency transaction acting as its exception handler, the process can continue by retrying the contingency transaction. Therefore, when a transaction T fails, the "abort-up" chain terminates at the closest ancestor of T that is non-vital, associated with a contingency transaction, or *without a parent*(e.g. the top-level transaction of a process, a contingency transaction, or a compensation transaction). We call such a transaction the *Undo Root* (UR) of T. Potentially, every transaction in a transaction hierarchy has a corresponding UR . Failure recovery consists in

(a) bottom-up searching for the UR of the originally failed transaction, and
(b) top-down logically rolling back the transaction subtree under that UR in terms of *compensate* and *abort* operations.

For the purpose of failure handling a transaction at any level may be paired with a contingency transaction $\tilde{T}$. A certain transaction T may also be paired with a compensation transaction $\bar{T}$ that can logically eliminate its effects. When T is open or scoped, $\bar{T}$ should also be open or scoped, and the *commit scope* of $\bar{T}$ should match that of T; for example, when a seminar announcement is made accessible in a department, the seminar cancellation notification should be made accessible in the same department, rather than in a smaller or a larger scope.

In top-down undoing, transactions with effects internal to the subtree under UR should be aborted and transactions with effects externalized over it should be compensated for. However, a scoped transaction may or may not necessarily be compensated for directly since its effects may be logically eliminated by a compensation applied at a higher level. For a transaction T that needs to be compensated for, if T is associated with a compensation transaction $\bar{T}$, then T and the whole transaction hierarchy beneath T can be directly compensated for by executing $\bar{T}$ with *same commit scope* as T; otherwise the children of T are processed, and such iteration may spread down along the transaction hierarchy, each branch ends up with a direct compensation or abortion. This process is described by the following *scoped undo* algorithm.

Applying *scoped-undo* to a transaction hierarchy T is based on its instance execution history. To express *scoped-undo* abstractly, we first introduce the following *scoped-undo$_{sub}$* operation

[Algorithm of scoped-undo$_{sub}(T)$]

$T:<T_1, ..., T_n> \rightarrow <scoped\text{-}undo(T_n), ..., scoped\text{-}undo(T_1)>;$
$T:\{T_1, ..., T_n\} \rightarrow \{scoped\text{-}undo(T_1), ..., scoped\text{-}undo(T_n)\}.$

where $T:< T_1, ..., T_n >$ expresses that T has a list of child transactions $T_1, ..., T_n$ executed sequentially, and $T:\{T_1, ..., T_n\}$ expresses that T has a set of child transactions $T_1, ..., T_n$ executed concurrently. Sequential subtransactions are *scoped-undone* in the inverse order. In the definition of function *scoped-undo*, *nested(T)* implies that T has subtransactions; $T_{\rightarrow db}$ and $T_{\rightarrow A}$ represent committing to database and ancestor A respectively; $\xi(T)$ denotes the *execution status* of T; $\sigma(T)$ denotes the *commit scope* of T, e.g. *db* or an ancestor. The remaining notations are self-explanatory.

[Algorithm of scoped-undo(T)]

$\xi(T) ==idle \rightarrow nil;$
$\xi(T) ==executing \rightarrow (nested(T) \rightarrow scoped\text{-}undo_{sub}(T); abort(T));$
$\xi(T) ==aborted \rightarrow (executed(\tilde{T}) \rightarrow scoped\text{-}undo(\tilde{T}); nil);$
$\xi(T) ==committed \rightarrow ($
$\quad \sigma(T) == db \rightarrow (compensate\text{-}defined(T) \rightarrow exec(T_{\rightarrow db}); nested(T) \rightarrow scoped\text{-}undo_{sub}(T); nil);$
$\quad \sigma(T) == A \wedge ur(T) \prec A \wedge A \neq ur(T) \rightarrow (compensate\text{-}defined(T) \rightarrow exec(\tilde{T}_{\rightarrow A}); nested(T) \rightarrow scoped\text{-}undo_{sub}(T); nil);$
$\quad nested(T) \rightarrow scoped\text{-}undo_{sub}(T);$
$\quad abort(T)).$

4 Conclusions

We have introduced *scoped transactions* and provided a pair of semantically consistent mechanisms: *scoped commitment* and *scoped undo*. The proposed approach extends the ATM model [3] and offers a unique solution for adequately balancing atomicity and concurrency *at selected levels* of a transaction hierarchy. A prototype system implemented at HP Labs has demonstrated the significance and feasibility of this approach.

References

1. Q. Chen and U. Dayal. A transactional nested process management system. *Proc. of 12th International Conference on Data Engineering (ICDE'96)*, 1996.
2. P. K. Chrysanthis and K. Ramamritham. Acta: The saga continues. *in A. Elmagarmid (ed) Transaction Models for Advanced Database Applications, Morgan-Kaufmann*, 1992.
3. U. Dayal, M. Hsu, and R. Ladin. A transactional model for long running activities. In *Proc. VLDB'91*, 1991.
4. J. Gray and A. Reuter. Transaction processing: Concepts and techniques. *Morgan Kaufmann Publishers*, 1993.

Fundamental Techniques for Order Optimization

David Simmen *   Eugene Shekita[†]   Timothy Malkemus[‡]

Abstract

This paper briefly describes some of the novel techniques used by the query optimizer of IBM's DB2 to process and optimize the way order requirements are satisfied.

1 Introduction

Decision support applications typically include complex SQL queries that can test the capabilities of an optimizer. One area that gets tested by these applications is an optimizer's ability to process order requirements. In a single complex query, an optimizer can be confronted with multiple order requirements arising from merge-joins, an ORDER BY, a GROUP BY, DISTINCT, and so on.

Sorting is one of the most expensive operations in a relational database system. Consequently, an optimizer must be capable of determining when sorting can be avoided, the minimal number of sorting columns, and whether two or more order requirements can be satisfied by a single sort.

Although hash-based set operations can eliminate the need for sorting, an index may already provide the required order for some operation, making the hash-based alternative more expensive. This is particularly true in warehousing environments, where indexes are pervasive. As a result, an optimizer should always consider both hash- and order-based operations and pick the least costly alternative [3].

This paper describes some of the novel techniques used by the query optimizer of IBM's DB2/CS to process and optimize the way order requirements are satisfied. DB2/CS is the client-server version of DB2 that runs on OS/2, Windows NT, and various flavors of UNIX.

---
*IBM Santa Teresa Lab, San Jose, CA 95120
[†]IBM Almaden Research Center, San Jose, CA 95120
[‡]IBM Austin, Austin, TX 78758

2 Overview

The DB2 optimizer is a direct descendent of the Starburst optimizer described in [5]. This section provides a brief overview of the DB2 optimizer to establish some background and terminology.

During optimization, a graphical representation of an input query is traversed and a *query execution plan* (QEP) is generated. A QEP can be viewed as a dataflow graph of *operators*, where each node in the graph corresponds to a relational operation. Each operator takes one or more more input record *streams* and produces an output record stream.

Each record stream in a QEP has an associated set of *properties* [4, 5]. Examples of properties include the columns that make up each record in the stream, the set of predicates that have been applied to the stream, the order of the stream, etc.

A QEP is built bottom-up, operator-by-operator. At each step, different alternatives are tried and more costly subplans with comparable properties are pruned [5]. As a QEP is built, *order requirements* are tested. The optimizer looks at the order property of the input stream and sees if it satisfies the order requirement. If not, a sort is added to the QEP. Order requirements arise from joins, ORDER BY, GROUP BY, and DISTINCT. Here, both order properties and order requirements will be denoted as a simple list of columns in major to minor order, i.e., $(c_1, c_2, ..., c_n)$.

3 Fundamental Algorithms

3.1 Reduce Order

The most fundamental algorithm for processing orders is something referred to as *reduction*. Reduction is the process of rewriting an order specification (i.e., an order property or order requirement) so that all redundant columns in the specification are removed. This is essential for testing whether an order property satisfies an order requirement.

As a motivating example, consider an arbitrary order requirement $OR = (x, y)$, and suppose an input stream has the order property $OP = (y)$. A naive test would conclude that OR is not satisfied by OP, and a sort would be added to the QEP. Suppose, however, that the predicate $x = 10$ has been applied to the input stream. Then the column x in OR is redundant since it has the value 10 for all records. Hence, OR can be rewritten as $OR = (y)$. After being rewritten, it is easy to determine that OP satisfies OR, so no sort is necessary.

In addition to predicates of the form $col = constant$, reduction also needs to take column equivalence classes into account. These are generated by predicates of the form $col = col$. For example, suppose $OR = (x, z)$ and $OP = (y, z)$.

Further suppose that the predicate $x = y$ has been applied. The equivalence class generated by $x = y$ allows OP to be rewritten as $OP = (x, z)$. After being rewritten, it is easy to determine that OP satisfies OR.

Reduction also needs to take keys into account. For example, suppose $OR = (x, y)$ and $OP = (x, z)$. If x is a key, then these can be rewritten as $OR = (x)$ and $OP = (x)$. Here, y and z are redundant since x alone is sufficient to determine the order of any two records.

Keys are really just a special case of functional dependencies (FDs) [2]. So rather than keys, FDs are actually used by reduction, since they are more powerful. In fact, all of the above examples really boil down to just testing FDs. As a result, the algorithm for Reduce Order is as follows:

<u>Reduce Order</u>
input: a list of FDs, applied preds., and order specification $O = (c_1, c_2, ..., c_n)$
output: the reduced version of O
    rewrite O in terms of each column's equivalence class head
    scan O backwards
    for (each column c_i scanned)
        let $P = \{c_1, c_2, ..., c_{i-i}\}$, i.e., the columns of O preceding c_i
        if ($P \rightarrow \{c_i\}$) then
            remove c_i from O
        endif
    endfor

3.2 Test Order

As it generates a QEP, the optimizer has to test whether a stream's order property OP satisfies an order requirement OR. If not, a sort is added to the QEP. The algorithm for Test Order is as follows:

<u>Test Order</u>
input: an order requirement OR and an order property OP
output: true if OP satisfies OR, otherwise false
    reduce OR and OP
    if (OR is empty or the cols. in OR are a prefix of the cols. in OP) then
        return true
    else
        return false
    endif

3.3 Cover Order

The DB2 optimizer tries to combine order requirements whenever possible. This often allows one sort to satisfy multiple order requirements. When two order requirements are combined, a *cover* is generated. The cover of two order requirements OR_1 and OR_2 is a new order requirement C such that any order property which satisfies C also satisfies both OR_1 and OR_2. The algorithm for Cover Order is as follows:

Cover Order
input: order requirements OR_1 and OR_2
output: the cover of OR_1 and OR_2 or the empty order if no cover is possible
    reduce OR_1 and OR_2
    w.l.o.g., assume OR_1 is the shorter order requirement
    if (OR_1 is a prefix of OR_2) then
        return OR_2
    else
        return the empty order
    endif

4 Conclusion

This paper briefly described some of the novel techniques used by the query optimizer of IBM's DB2 to process and optimize the way order requirements are satisfied. Algorithms were provided for testing whether an order requirement is satisfied and for combining two order requirements. Both of these hinge on a core algorithm called *reduction*, which uses functional dependencies to remove redundant columns from an order requirement.

References

[1] C. Beeri and P. Bernstein. Computational problems related to the design of normal form relational schemas. In *ACM Transactions on Database Systems*, March 1979.

[2] H. Darwen and C. Date. The role of functional dependencies in query decomposition. In *Relational Database Writings 1989-1991*. Addison Wesley, 1992.

[3] G. Graefe. Query evaluation techniques for large databases. In *ACM Computing Surveys*, June 1993.

[4] G. Graefe and D. DeWitt. The exodus optimizer generator. In *Proc. of the 1987 SIGMOD Conf.*, June 1987.

[5] G. Lohman. Grammar-like functional rules for representing query optimization alternatives. In *Proc. of the 1988 SIGMOD Conf.*, June 1988.

Technology Transfer and Cooperation

Dealing with Asynchrony in Technology Transfer

Gio Wiederhold

Stanford University

A major problem discussed throughout industry and government is Technology Transition (TT). New computing concepts originate in industrial, governmental, and academic laboratories must to be disseminated and, if found effective, adopted. The receptors are industrial development, organizations devoted to improvement of existing, and enterprises doing systems integration. The use of computing is broad, an most of the receptors are not primarily focused on computing but have a broader palette. There are many problems that hinder technology transfer, this note focuses on the problem of temporal and terminological gaps. We believe that these gaps encompass a large and critical fraction of TT problems. We will deal here with innovations and developments that are beneficial and should be marketable at some point, and not with the issues of irrelevant research, nor with the filtering needed to determine relevancy.

The Problem

Industry is rarely ready to accept an innovation when it first presented. There are many reasons for lack of acceptance: the two major ones are:
1. The innovation is not understood by industry because, as a byproduct of the innovation new terms have been defined.
2. The innovation is understood or at least understandable, but there are no resources at that time to try to develop and market the innovation

These conditions are so common that it appears that direct TT from academic or industrial laboratories to industry must be the unusual case. To address these problems we will define a third party, namely a 'transition agent' (TTA) interposed between researchers and industry. The role of a TTA is to be a holder and developer for research results in preparation for industrial requirements.

Sources for Innovation

In an academic research setting most innovation is associated with a student and a thesis When the thesis is complete the student leaves, but publication and dissemination often takes years. Even if new electronic services for rapid review and self-publishing speed up this phase, time still elapses before new concepts are appreciated and industrial interest ensues. If a thesis produces an isolatable result the student may become an entrepreneur, but to be successful many new concepts have to be integrated into larger settings. It is generally wise to plan academic thesis research so that it is not competitive with industry. Targeting one's research with an precise trajectory for industrial implementation is also risky. First of all, focusing on a specific recognized industrial need is likely to compete with convenient narrow specific solutions and reduces the intellectual and educational content of the thesis. Secondly, especially if a broader topic is addressed it is easy to fall short of the goal either in scope or in time and be bypassed before the thesis work is completed. In industrial laboratories less research is performed than in earlier days, and there is much stress on development. It would be good if industrial researchers would have good access to all types of innovative research results, but even though nearly all results are published and available on on-line networks they are very hard to find. Reasons are both the volume and the marginal refereeing with respect to industrial value of what is being published, and the use of new and often excessively innovative terms to distinguish one's work from that of predecessors. Most initial contacts leading to TT are in fact personal, made at workshops and meetings, typically during informal discussions. Many meetings that do not have TT as their objective serve as TT venues, for instance review meetings where academic and industrial participants assess new proposals, and in the process learn from each other about what is needed and what is already available. Much of the success that MITI can claim in TT is due to their frequent and lengthy meetings to evaluate proposals that will anyhow be funded. It to industry's credit that in Japan industrial line managers participate in these discussions [Ref JTEC study 1991]. Today the pressures and time schedules many government labs are similar to the pressures found in industry. However, the remoteness from industrial delivery pressures makes performing in a product role difficult. In addition, there is much oversight and a great deal of time is spent in writing reports to justify ones' existence. Needs for innovation. The industrial need for innovation is controlled primarily by schedules and market forces which are unrelated to research schedules. When the need for innovation in development becomes clear, the sources are hard to access. The student and the advisor are already involved in other enterprises, and the industrial researcher has been pulled off to another project, or else left in frustration. Although we can assume that relevant information will be available on some digital library somewhere, it is unlikely that the terms used to express a need will be the same as the terms used to identify the research result, for instance research results supporting 'multi-attribute search for information' was published as 'partial match retrieval' and ignored for some time. Especially in fast-moving fields these terminological gaps are prevalent. Without people able to span those gaps adoption of the innovation, even if recognized, will be awkward.

Transition Agents

There is hence a need for intermediate organizations to be the initial receptors, normalizers, and maintainers of research results. Vic Reis, when director at ARPA, recognized that many research results will not be of immediate use and will rest on shelves until needed However, no overt provision was being made in Vic Reis' model to establish the shelves, making delayed use unlikely.

Not only passive shelves are needed, a potential adopter needs people to talk to, get explanations, assess the status, and feedback on transition potential. Most research results also warrant some level of maintenance. For instance, demonstrations age rapidly as equipment changes. As standards become established the utility of many prototypes can be enhanced by adaptation to standard interfaces, often simplifying the product in that process. As the terminology of a field normalizes, descriptions and keywords used for search may be updated to enhance access.

Within the ARPA setting for instance, the Intelligent Integration of information (I3) program funds a base level TTA effort at ISX Corp., a small ARPA-oriented contractor. The role assigned to ISX is to help assemble research results from the various participants in the program, adapt them to the interoperation conventions being developed, support interactions with emerging standards efforts, demonstrate capabilities to potential user organizations, and prepare business plans for technology insertion if requested. The expense, at about 1 person-year/ year is well worth it in terms of reduced confusion and rapid availability of resources. A major benefit is, of course, having someone to talk to when I3 related problems arise.

A person who is involved both with researchers and industry can bridge the terminological gaps better than individuals on either side of the fence. All other program participants are (or should be) aware of the role that ISX plays. The ISX company, of course, also benefits by having an early handle on opportunities for further work, including tasks outside of DoD. An increasing fraction of informative interactions leading to TT can take place on the Internet, although initial resolution of terminological differences will require human mediation. The people at the TTA are to be quite capable, willing to gain insight into the prototypes and products they are supporting, maintain awareness of the changing infrastructure of computing platforms, networks, services, and interface standards, and at the same time be able to understand the needs of the recipients and honestly point out which of their wishes and expectations will be satisfied and which are best deferred into yet another timeframe.

Helping in Setting Research Directions

The structure established for TTAs should also support TT in the opposite direction. If the TTA personnel can abstract the needs voiced by industry into terms and concepts that are understandable by researchers, they can help focus research on topics of eventual interest. When industry rejects research results because they duplicate products already available or in advanced stages of development the TTA gains high-value knowledge, that normally would never be transmitted to researchers. The TTA will also, in time, understand the end-users needs in depth. Without deep understanding their is a danger to solve problems by applying instant 'hack' solutions, leading to worse problems later. Without guidance from industry many researchers are left to wallow in problem spaces of their own imagination. This direction is not meant to disparage 'curiosity-driven research'=17if a researcher is truly driven curious to gain some new insight, that is marvelous. But many researchers would just as soon work on foundational research on which substantial industrial structures can eventually be built.

Who are Candidates to be Transition Agents (TTAs)?

There are quite a number of industrial research groups, both profit and non-profit, who seem well able to take on the role of a TTA. Many government labs, as NIST, the requirements of the task outlined for TTAs. A governmental organization is by its very nature more stable than either academia or modern industry. Investment in advancing broad industry needs is justified, and the tasks of integration, requiring establishing and validating standards are part of NIST's perceived mission. Being a transition agent is also unlikely to be viewed by industry as undue interference, and the aspects of industrial policy are minor. The change in manpower supply in computing (much greater) makes the implementation of such a role for NIST's computing laboratories more feasible than it would have been, say, 5 years ago. Today many graduates would enjoy having the chance to come to a post-doc position at NIST where they could demonstrate, enhance, and package their work. Such an effort will benefit with interaction of NIST permanent staff who can convey industrial insights often lacking in academia. At the same time an influx of young rotators can enhance the staff awareness of the changing world and technology outside of the government. They are likely to put pressure on the environment that would discourage going along with old, comfortable systems. Those postdocs that eventually obtain academic positions will also bring valuable experience and awareness of terminology used from their industrial contacts to their future students.

No matter if the TTA is in industry or government, is profit or non-profit, it will be crucial that management defines the role and the criteria for success. The TTA model presented above can only work if the reward system is appropriate. If promotions and status depends on counting papers published, or on transitioning ones own research to industry, then the required functions for aiding TT will be abrogated. We believe that the need for the TTA role is sufficiently crucial that it behooves laboratories that can perform in this role to assess how to implement these functions.

Barriers.

The change that is required to go the model of technology transfer I am proposing here can be a wrenching change to methods that have been established elsewhere. A discussion that analyzes both Japaneses efforts, spearheaded by MITI, and European efforts, led by Esprit, could clarify these issues further. In the meantime, we have to consider the community that may provide barriers in our own environment:
1. academics, since they fear losing money (and power), and many actually believe they know how to do Technology Transfer.
2. industry, who would like to get `useful', i.e., saleable stuff directly and cheaply from universities.
3. NSF managers, who are pressured to show results from their funding of universities, and do not have the funds to support transfer agents in addition to researchers.
4. current managers at NIST, who want to upgrade the computer lab to do `better' research.

Conclusion:

The issue of Technology Transfer in our work is crucial, and absorbs much of our research resources, likely more than 50%. Given its importance it is useful to devote some rational discussion and analysis to this topic, since its metrics are today mainly guesses and hopes. If it were science, we would insist on hypotheses and proofs before devoting so many millions to its development and achievement. Let's at least bring the alternatives on a scientific table beyond committee meetings and coffee breaks.

Index of Authors

Springer-Verlag
and the Environment

We at Springer-Verlag firmly believe that an international science publisher has a special obligation to the environment, and our corporate policies consistently reflect this conviction.

We also expect our business partners – paper mills, printers, packaging manufacturers, etc. – to commit themselves to using environmentally friendly materials and production processes.

The paper in this book is made from low- or no-chlorine pulp and is acid free, in conformance with international standards for paper permanency.

Lecture Notes in Computer Science

For information about Vols. 1–987

please contact your bookseller or Springer-Verlag

Vol. 1023: K. Kanchanasut, J.-J. Lévy (Eds.), Algorithms, Concurrency and Knowlwdge. Proceedings, 1995. X, 410 pages. 1995.

Vol. 1024: R.T. Chin, H.H.S. Ip, A.C. Naiman, T.-C. Pong (Eds.), Image Analysis Applications and Computer Graphics. Proceedings, 1995. XVI, 533 pages. 1995.

Vol. 1025: C. Boyd (Ed.), Cryptography and Coding. Proceedings, 1995. IX, 291 pages. 1995.

Vol. 1026: P.S. Thiagarajan (Ed.), Foundations of Software Technology and Theoretical Computer Science. Proceedings, 1995. XII, 515 pages. 1995.

Vol. 1027: F.J. Brandenburg (Ed.), Graph Drawing. Proceedings, 1995. XII, 526 pages. 1996.

Vol. 1028: N.R. Adam, Y. Yesha (Eds.), Electronic Commerce. X, 155 pages. 1996.

Vol. 1029: E. Dawson, J. Golić (Eds.), Cryptography: Policy and Algorithms. Proceedings, 1995. XI, 327 pages. 1996.

Vol. 1030: F. Pichler, R. Moreno-Díaz, R. Albrecht (Eds.), Computer Aided Systems Theory - EUROCAST '95. Proceedings, 1995. XII, 539 pages. 1996.

Vol. 1031: M. Toussaint (Ed.), Ada in Europe. Proceedings, 1995. XI, 455 pages. 1996.

Vol. 1032: P. Godefroid, Partial-Order Methods for the Verification of Concurrent Systems. IV, 143 pages. 1996.

Vol. 1033: C.-H. Huang, P. Sadayappan, U. Banerjee, D. Gelernter, A. Nicolau, D. Padua (Eds.), Languages and Compilers for Parallel Computing. Proceedings, 1995. XIII, 597 pages. 1996.

Vol. 1034: G. Kuper, M. Wallace (Eds.), Constraint Databases and Applications. Proceedings, 1995. VII, 185 pages. 1996.

Vol. 1035: S.Z. Li, D.P. Mital, E.K. Teoh, H. Wang (Eds.), Recent Developments in Computer Vision. Proceedings, 1995. XI, 604 pages. 1996.

Vol. 1036: G. Adorni, M. Zock (Eds.), Trends in Natural Language Generation - An Artificial Intelligence Perspective. Proceedings, 1993. IX, 382 pages. 1996. (Subseries LNAI).

Vol. 1037: M. Wooldridge, J.P. Müller, M. Tambe (Eds.), Intelligent Agents II. Proceedings, 1995. XVI, 437 pages. 1996. (Subseries LNAI).

Vol. 1038: W: Van de Velde, J.W. Perram (Eds.), Agents Breaking Away. Proceedings, 1996. XIV, 232 pages. 1996. (Subseries LNAI).

Vol. 1039: D. Gollmann (Ed.), Fast Software Encryption. Proceedings, 1996. X, 219 pages. 1996.

Vol. 1040: S. Wermter, E. Riloff, G. Scheler (Eds.), Connectionist, Statistical, and Symbolic Approaches to Learning for Natural Language Processing. IX, 468 pages. 1996. (Subseries LNAI).

Vol. 1041: J. Dongarra, K. Madsen, J. Waśniewski (Eds.), Applied Parallel Computing. Proceedings, 1995. XII, 562 pages. 1996.

Vol. 1042: G. Weiß, S. Sen (Eds.), Adaption and Learning in Multi-Agent Systems. Proceedings, 1995. X, 238 pages. 1996. (Subseries LNAI).

Vol. 1043: F. Moller, G. Birtwistle (Eds.), Logics for Concurrency. XI, 266 pages. 1996.

Vol. 1044: B. Plattner (Ed.), Broadband Communications. Proceedings, 1996. XIV, 359 pages. 1996.

Vol. 1045: B. Butscher, E. Moeller, H. Pusch (Eds.), Interactive Distributed Multimedia Systems and Services. Proceedings, 1996. XI, 333 pages. 1996.

Vol. 1046: C. Puech, R. Reischuk (Eds.), STACS 96. Proceedings, 1996. XII, 690 pages. 1996.

Vol. 1047: E. Hajnicz, Time Structures. IX, 244 pages. 1996. (Subseries LNAI).

Vol. 1048: M. Proietti (Ed.), Logic Program Syynthesis and Transformation. Proceedings, 1995. X, 267 pages. 1996.

Vol. 1049: K. Futatsugi, S. Matsuoka (Eds.), Object Technologies for Advanced Software. Proceedings, 1996. X, 309 pages. 1996.

Vol. 1050: R. Dyckhoff, H. Herre, P. Schroeder-Heister (Eds.), Extensions of Logic Programming. Proceedings, 1996. VII, 318 pages. 1996. (Subseries LNAI).

Vol. 1051: M.-C. Gaudel, J. Woodcock (Eds.), FME'96: Industrial Benefit and Advances in Formal Methods. Proceedings, 1996. XII, 704 pages. 1996.

Vol. 1052: D. Hutchison, H. Christiansen, G. Coulson, A. Danthine (Eds.), Teleservices and Multimedia Communications. Proceedings, 1995. XII, 277 pages. 1996.

Vol. 1053: P. Graf, Term Indexing. XVI, 284 pages. 1996. (Subseries LNAI).

Vol. 1054: A. Ferreira, P. Pardalos (Eds.), Solving Combinatorial Optimization Problems in Parallel. VII, 274 pages. 1996.

Vol. 1055: T. Margaria, B. Steffen (Eds.), Tools and Algorithms for the Construction and Analysis of Systems. Proceedings, 1996. XI, 435 pages. 1996.

Vol. 1056: A. Haddadi, Communication and Cooperation in Agent Systems. XIII, 148 pages. 1996. (Subseries LNAI).

Vol. 1057: P. Apers, M. Bouzeghoub, G. Gardarin (Eds.), Advances in Database Technology — EDBT '96. Proceedings, 1996. XII, 636 pages. 1996.

Vol. 1058: H. R. Nielson (Ed.), Programming Languages and Systems - ESOP '96. Proceedings, 1996. X, 405 pages. 1996.

Vol. 1059: H. Kirchner (Ed.), Trees in Algebra and Programming - CAAP '96. Proceedings, 1996. VIII, 331 pages. 1996.

Vol. 1060: T. Gyimóthy (Ed.), Compiler Construction. Proceedings, 1996. X, 355 pages. 1996.

Vol. 1061: P. Ciancarini, C. Hankin (Eds.), Coordination Languages and Models. Proceedings, 1996. XI, 443 pages. 1996.

Vol. 1062: E. Sanchez, M. Tomassini (Eds.), Towards Evolvable Hardware. IX, 249 pages. 1996.

Vol. 1063: J.-M. Alliot, E. Lutton, E. Ronald, M. Schoenauer, D. Snyers (Eds.), Artificial Evolution. Proceedings, 1995. XIII, 396 pages. 1996.